Task Force 58

Also by Rod Macdonald

Dive Scapa Flow
Dive Scotland's Greatest Wrecks
Dive England's Greatest Wrecks
Great British Shipwrecks – A Personal Adventure
Force Z Shipwrecks of the South China Sea – HMS Prince of Wales *and*
  HMS Repulse
Dive Truk Lagoon – The Japanese WWII Pacific Shipwrecks
Dive Palau – The Shipwrecks
Shipwrecks of Truk Lagoon

The Diving Trilogy

Vol. I, Into the Abyss – Diving to Adventure in the Liquid World
Vol. II, The Darkness Below
Vol. III, Deeper into the Darkness

Task Force 58

The US Navy's Fast Carrier Strike Force that Won the War in the Pacific

ROD MACDONALD

Naval Institute Press
Annapolis, Maryland

TASK FORCE 58

First published in Great Britain in 2021 by

Frontline Books
An imprint of
Pen & Sword Books Ltd
Yorkshire – Philadelphia

Published and distributed in the United States of America and Canada by
the Naval Institute Press, 291 Wood Road, Annapolis, Maryland 21402-5043
www.nip.org

Library of Congress Cataloging Number: 2021947311

ISBN 978 1 68247 738 0

Typeset in 10.5/13 pt Palatino
by SJmagic DESIGN SERVICES, India.

Printed and bound by CPI Group (UK) Ltd, Croydon, CR0 4YY

Pen & Sword Books Ltd incorporates the Imprints of Aviation, Atlas,
Family History, Fiction, Maritime, Military, Discovery, Politics, History,
Archaeology, Select, Wharncliffe Local History, Wharncliffe True Crime,
Military Classics, Wharncliffe Transport, Leo Cooper, The Praetorian Press,
Remember When, Seaforth Publishing and Frontline Publishing.

For a complete list of Pen & Sword titles please contact

PEN & SWORD BOOKS LTD
47 Church Street, Barnsley, South Yorkshire, S70 2AS, England
E-mail: enquiries@pen-and-sword.co.uk
Website: www.pen-and-sword.co.uk

Or

PEN AND SWORD BOOKS
1950 Lawrence Rd, Havertown, PA 19083, USA
E-mail: Uspen-and-sword@casematepublishers.com
Website: www.penandswordbooks.com

Contents

Explanatory Notes

US Plane General Abbreviations

Prefix

'V' = heavier than air
'B' = Bomber/Dive-bomber
'F' = Fighter
'T' = Torpedo plane
'SB' = Scout-bomber
'TB' = Torpedo-bomber

Designation ending:
'C' = aircraft manufactured by Curtiss Aeroplane & Motor Co.
'D' = aircraft manufactured by Douglas Aircraft Co.
'F' = Grumman Aircraft Engineering Corp.
'M' = aircraft manufactured by General Motors

US Plane Designations

B-17   US Army Air Force (USAAF) four-engine bomber, the Boeing
        Flying Fortress
B-24   USAAF four-engine bomber, Consolidated or Ford Liberator
B-25   USAAF two-engine bomber, the North American Mitchell
B-29   USAAF four-engine bomber, the Boeing Super-Fortress
F4U   Navy single-engine fighter, the Chance-Vought Corsair
F6F   Navy single-engine fighter, the Grumman Hellcat
PBY   Navy two-engine long-range maritime reconnaissance flying
        boat – the Consolidated Catalina
PB4Y   Navy-Marine four-engine bomber – the Consolidated or Ford
        Liberator

SBD	Navy single-engine Scout Bomber Douglas – the Douglas Dauntless
SB2C	Navy single-engine scout dive-bomber – the Curtiss Helldiver
TBD	Navy single-engine torpedo-bomber – the Douglas Devastator
TBF	Navy single-engine torpedo-bomber – the Grumman Avenger
TBM	Navy single-engine torpedo-bomber – the General Motors Avenger

Allied Japanese Aircraft Reporting Code Names – Designations

Betty	Mitsubishi G4M/G4M3 Navy Type 1 Attack Bomber
Dave	Nakajima E8N Navy Type 95 Reconnaissance Seaplane
Emily	Kawanishi H8K Navy Type 2 Flying Boat
Hamp	Mitsubishi A6M3 Navy Type O (Zero variant) Carrier Fighter
Jake	Aichi E13A Navy Type O Reconnaissance Seaplane
Jill	Nakajima B6N Navy Carrier Attack Bomber
Judy	Yokosuka D4Y Navy Carrier Bomber Suisei
Kate	Nakajima B5N Torpedo-Bomber
Mavis	Kawanishi H6K Navy Type 97 Flying Boat
Nate	Nakajima Ki-27 Army Type 97 Fighter
Nell	Mitsubishi G3M Navy Type 96 Medium Attack Bomber
Pete	Mitsubishi F1M Navy Type O Observation Seaplane
Rufe	Nakajima A6M2 Navy Type 2 Fighter Seaplane
Sam	Mitsubishi A7M *Reppū* Navy fighter
Tojo	Nakajima Ki-44 Army Type 2 Single-seat fighter
Tony	Kawasaki Ki-61 Army Type 3 Fighter
Val	Aichi D3A Navy Type 99 Carrier Bomber
Zeke	Mitsubishi A6M Navy Type O Carrier Fighter Reisen (Zero)

US Naval Squadron/Unit Designations

BatDiv	Battleship Division
CarDiv	Carrier Division
CruDiv	Cruiser Division
DesDiv	Destroyer Division
DesRon	Destroyer Squadron
ServRon	Service Squadron
TF	Task Force
TG	Task Group: a subunit of a Task Force
TU	Task Unit: a subunit of a Task Group

xi

VB	Dive-bomber
VF	Fighter
VB(F)	Fighter-bomber
VF(N)	Night-fighter
VSB	Scout Dive-bomber
VT	Torpedo Plane
VTB	Torpedo-bomber

The number following the initials VB, VF, VB(F), VF(N), VT and VTB refers to the air group. Initially these were linked to the carrier's number, such as CV-6, CV-7 etc. but later in the war squadron numbers were assigned randomly to prevent the enemy working out a specific carrier's deployment from the squadron numbers of its air group.

US Ship Type Designations and Acronyms List

AGC	Amphibious Command Ship
AK	Cargo Ship
AM	Minesweeper
AP	Transport
AO	Fuel Oil Tanker
BB	Battleship
CA	Heavy Cruiser
CC	Battlecruiser
CH	Submarine Chaser
Cha	Auxiliary Submarine Chaser
CL	Light Cruiser
CV	Aircraft Carrier (heavier than air)
CVE	Aircraft Carrier Escort
CVL	Light Aircraft Carrier
DD	Destroyer
DUKW	Amphibious trucks (*Ducks*)
LCT	Landing Craft, Tank
LCVP	Landing Craft, Vehicle, Personnel
LST	Landing Ship, Tank
LVT	Landing Vehicle Tracked
SS	Submarine

The number following the initials BB, CA, CL, CVL, DD and SS refers to the assigned vessel number and class.

Miscellaneous

AA	Anti-Aircraft
AAF	Army Air Force
AP	Armour Piercing
ASDIC	Anti-Submarine Detection Investigation Committee
ASP	Anti-Submarine Patrol
ASW	Anti-Submarine Warfare
CAP	Combat Air Patrol
CIC	Combat Information Centre – the nerve centre of the ship where information from radars and sounding was plotted, evaluated and sent to the bridge
CINC	Commander-in-Chief
CINCLANTFLT	Commander-in-Chief US Atlantic Fleet
CINCPAC	Commander-in-Chief Pacific
CINCPACFLT	Commander-in-Chief US Pacific Fleet
CINCPOA	Commander-in-Chief Pacific Ocean Areas
COMINCH	Commander-in-Chief, US Fleet
CNO	Chief of Naval Operations
GP	General Purpose
IJA	Imperial Japanese Army
IJN	Imperial Japanese Navy
JCS	US Joint Chiefs of Staff
LCVP	Higgins boat
RDF	Radio Direction Finder
SAP	Semi-Armour Piercing
TBS	High-frequency short-range radio used for tactical manoeuvring in a naval formation
UDT	Underwater Demolition Team

Introduction

The reign of the battleship as the supreme naval striking weapon ended in December 1941 when the brand new British battleship HMS *Prince of Wales* was sent to the bottom of the South China Sea by waves of Japanese aircraft. It was the first time a modern battleship had been sunk in open sea by aircraft. The era of air power projected at sea had arrived.

The great carrier battles in 1942 at the Coral Sea and at Midway revealed the new way wars would be fought at sea – where no ship directly sighted the opposing fleet. Opposing fleets could be hundreds of miles away from each other, the fight being taken to the enemy ships by fast fighters, dive-bombers and torpedo-bombers. The new fast carriers became the fleet's main striking weapon – and they led the thrust west and north across the Pacific as the Allies seized, or neutralised and bypassed, Japanese-held islands and territories, until the eventual capitulation of Japan itself.

The final evolution of carrier warfare during the Second World War was Task Force 58, created on 6 January 1944. TF 58 comprised a core of fast modern aircraft carriers, split into a number of task groups, each with three to four carriers. The carriers were protected by Combat Air Patrols, anti-submarine patrols and by a screen of battleships, cruisers, destroyers and submarines. At times there were more than 100 ships in the task force, carrying more than 100,000 men afloat. When the fast-carrier task force was part of Admiral Raymond Spruance's Fifth Fleet, it carried the designation Task Force 58 – and when command of the task force rotated (as it did on a regular basis) to Admiral William Halsey's Third Fleet, its designation became Task Force 38. The composition remained the same under either fleet commander – a ruse that for a while fooled the Japanese into thinking there were two carrier task forces.

The immense striking power of Task Force 58 is legendary – by 1945, some 1,000 combat aircraft could be launched in under an hour. These aircraft carried out many famous operations as TF 58 swept north west from the Solomon Islands, through the Gilbert Islands, the Marshall Islands, neutralising the fortress of Truk in Micronesia and then hitting Palau in the Western Caroline Islands. The fast carriers supported the Mariana Islands operations such as at Saipan and Guam, fighting legendary air battles in the Philippine Sea as Japan rolled the dice for an all-out decisive naval engagement that would turn the war. Task Force 58 aircraft supported the invasion of the Philippines and corked the Luzon bottleneck – before moving northwards to attack Iwo Jima and Okinawa. Finally, strikes began against the Japanese home islands themselves – as, unknown to most, the Pacific War drew towards its nuclear finale in late 1945. Such was the secrecy surrounding the Manhattan Project, the development of the atomic bomb, that only the highest navy commanders knew about it – as they, meanwhile, planned for a bloody final invasion of the Japanese home islands, an invasion that was expected to take hundreds of thousands of Allied lives.

For the last thirty years or so I have dived on the sunken relics of Task Force 58 operations around the Pacific. I have been staggered by what I have seen – by the obvious power and brutality of Task Force 58 aircraft. I have dived on shipwrecks where, literally in a flash, 1,000 lives or more were ended. At Truk alone, some forty ships were sent to the bottom in the two-day Operation HAILSTONE fast-carrier raid on 17/18 February 1944. The shipwrecks that today lie silently on the bottom of the lagoon are the graves of thousands of Japanese soldiers and seamen killed during the raid. The scale of what I have seen is humbling and awe-inspiring.

As I dived these wrecks, sunken relics frozen in a brutal moment of time, I began to notice similarities in some shipwrecks. Nearly all wrecks of Japanese tankers and oilers had bomb or torpedo holes in the engine-room areas at the stern. Tankers were so strongly built and internally compartmentalised with sealed oil tanks that it was known that two to three hits in their tanks might not sink the ship. The engine rooms of tankers and oilers are vast cathedral like spaces that run from the bottom of the ship up through multiple deck levels to the top of the superstructure. A hit in this area disabled the propulsion system and stopped the ship dead in the water – a hull breach also allowed this huge space to flood. The ship would settle by the stern and drag the rest of the ship down with it. It is common in archive combat photos of Japanese anchorages to see a tanker down by the stern, its stern resting on the seabed whilst the buoyancy of its forward compartments kept the bow out of the water. These hits in the stern were not random chance, this was precise US bombing by the seasoned aircrew of Task Force 58/38.

I dived several Japanese shipwrecks where only half of the ship was left on the seabed. These ships had been carrying munitions – and when hit by a US bomb or torpedo, a massive secondary munitions explosion, similar to the tragic explosion in August 2020 of some 2,750 tonnes of ammonium nitrate stored in a warehouse at the Beirut docks, had almost vapourised the half of the ship that was hit. The wrecks of these ships seem cleaved straight across from one side of the ship to the other by a huge force – and where the rest of the ship had once been, filled with the weapons of war and unfortunate crew, there was now only a depression in the seabed excavated by the force of the blast.

As I continued to dive the sunken legacy of Task Force 58 around the Pacific, and as I researched the momentous events for books such as *Dive Truk Lagoon – The Japanese WWII Pacific shipwrecks* and *Dive Palau – The Shipwrecks*, I began to realise with some surprise that although there had been much written in the years immediately following the war, there has been little coverage of this huge story in recent times.

The tale of Task Force 58/38 is a moving and powerful story of great men and great deeds – deeds that shaped the world we live in today. It is a story that needs to be told, and retold.

So, here is my take on what happened during those fateful years in the Pacific War.

Fair winds and following seas
Rod Macdonald

Chapter 1

Naval Aviation – Genesis

With the first flight of a heavier than air powered aircraft by Wilbur and Orville Wright in 1903, the following years of the early part of the twentieth century were a time of great experimentation and innovation as the possibilities of using aircraft at sea for military purposes were explored. Naval aviation had been born.

As naval aviation developed, a number of important firsts took place in rapid succession. The *first powered seaplane* appeared in 1910 – the *Hydravion* designed by the Frenchman Henri Fabre, which took off from water and flew about half a kilometre on 28 March 1910. Seaplanes are powered fixed wing aircraft fitted with wing and/or fuselage floats that allow them to take off from and land on water. The fuselage itself is held up out of the water by the floats, unlike a 'flying boat' where the fuselage sits on the water when stationary.

As no flight deck was required for seaplanes, the early seaplane tender vessels could remain relatively small and inconspicuous, simply requiring space for the aircraft themselves and cranes to launch and recover them. The first seaplane tender appeared late in 1911, with the modified 389ft-long, 6,000-ton French torpedo boat tender *La Foudre*, whose original role in 1896 when she had been built was to carry torpedo boats to the high seas for launch and attack. Work began late in 1911 to convert her to a *seaplane tender*, with hangars installed on the main deck. Initially her cranes were used to lift seaplanes (or floatplanes) onto the water – and to hoist them aboard on their return. Seaplanes however required large pontoons to enable them to float, and these made them suffer aerodynamically and thus be unsuitable for air combat roles. The trick would be to work out how to fly bespoke combat aircraft directly to and from ships.

The *first launch of a fixed wing aircraft from a stationary ship* took place on 14 November 1910. A Curtiss Model D (the Curtiss Pusher), piloted by

1

Eugene B. Ely, roared off a temporary inclined wooden platform fitted to the stationary US cruiser USS *Birmingham* near Hampton Roads, Virginia. Almost incredibly it was still just seven years after the Wright brothers' first successful flight.

The evolutionary pace of naval aviation was accelerating. The *first deck landing*, again using a temporary wooden platform, took place just two months later on 18 January 1911, when the same pilot, Eugene B. Ely, landed his Curtiss Pusher on the afterdeck of the 13,680-ton armoured cruiser *Pennsylvania*, anchored in San Francisco Bay. This landing was also the first use of a tailhook-arrested landing that had been designed and built by circus performer and aviator Hugh Robinson. The new era of the aircraft carrier had now arrived – but with military aviation still in its infancy, even as these tentative steps towards fixed wing aircraft launching and landing on ships progressed, the full potential was not fully apparent. The development of the role of the seaplane still progressed in tandem.

Several navies experimented with using aircraft on different types of ships. The *first powered fixed wing launch from a stationary British ship* took place on 10 January 1912 – when S.38, piloted by Commander Charles Samson, lifted into the air from a flying off platform fixed to the fore part of the 15,885-ton pre-dreadnought British battleship HMS *Africa*. This platform ran from her bridge to her bow above her forward 12in main battery gun turret.

Africa then transferred her flying off platform and equipment to the King Edward VII-class pre-dreadnought battleship HMS *Hibernia*, on which further development of the concept took place resulting in the *first recorded flight from a moving ship* taking place at the Royal Fleet Review in Weymouth Bay, England in early May 1912. Commander Samson, again flying the modified biplane S.38, launched from the flying off platform on the forepart of *Hibernia* whilst she was under way at 10.5 knots. In late 1912, at the Grand Naval Review in Yokohama, Japan, a seaplane landed near the imperial flagship carrying the Japanese emperor and other high-ranking officials. A second floatplane and a non-rigid airship flew over the Japanese Fleet.[1] The possibilities were obvious to everyone.

The British protected cruiser HMS *Hermes* was temporarily converted as an experimental seaplane carrier, for two months in April–May 1913, to allow the Royal Navy to evaluate how aircraft could operate with the fleet. Her forward 6in gun was removed, and a tracked launching platform constructed over the fo'c'sle with a canvas hangar installed to shelter her aircraft at the end of the tracks and a derrick on the foremast to lift the seaplane from the water on its return. *Hermes* is thus often seen as the first true *seaplane carrier* – in preference to seaplane tender *La Foudre*, which had a 10m flying off platform added seven months later in November 1913.

As a result of their experimental flights, the Royal Navy came to the view that shipborne aircraft were important for reconnaissance, spotting and other purposes. The aircraft available at the time however were slow and vulnerable and there were no weapons they could carry that could pose a serious threat to a warship – naval aircraft were not yet ship-killers. But even though the possibilities for spotting ahead of the fleet were recognised, their presence, and the flying off platforms, interfered with the firing of the big guns, then of paramount importance in sea warfare. The Royal Navy also had concerns that even if successfully lowered down to the water, seaplanes sometimes could not take off, if water conditions were too rough. In addition, there were practicalities and dangers involved in recovering seaplanes from the water after flight in anything other than calm conditions. These reasonable fears negated the desirability of having aircraft launching from capital ships. Some other way of solving the problem of carrying aircraft at sea would have to be found.

The answer came in 1914 with the *first ship designed and built as a seaplane carrier*, HMS *Ark Royal*. She had originally been laid down as a 366ft-long civilian freighter with a beam of 50ft in November 1913 by the Blyth Shipbuilding Company. The Royal Navy purchased the ship in May 1914, whilst she was still under construction, in frames with her keel laid. The hull was launched in September 1914 for fitting out and extensive changes were made to her original civilian design to convert her for her role as a seaplane carrier. Her planned superstructure, smokestack and machinery were moved aft, like a tanker – and the forward section of the ship was outfitted as a working deck, not for flying off aircraft, but for recovering aircraft from the sea and for running up seaplane engines. A large aircraft hold was created that was 150ft long by 45ft wide and 15ft high and which had extensive workshops. Two steam-driven cranes on the sides of the fo'c'sle lifted aircraft through the sliding hatch of the hangar onto the flight deck or lowered them into the water.

Ark Royal was commissioned on 10 December 1914 and carried five floatplanes and two to four wheeled aircraft. The seaplanes were craned into the water alongside the seaplane carrier for take-off and on return, were craned back aboard. Although her wheeled aircraft could launch, they could not land back on the seaplane carrier and had to land ashore.

The early *aircraft carrier* concept of launching wheeled aircraft directly from a flying off deck as opposed to craning seaplanes over the side of the ship to the water to launch had now arrived.

In the Battle of Tsingtao, from 5 September 1914, the Imperial Japanese Navy (IJN) seaplane carrier *Wakamiya* carried out the world's first naval launched air raids from Kiaochow Bay during the Siege of Tsingtao. The *Wakamiya* was fitted with a couple of derricks for hoisting the seemingly fragile Maurice Farman MF.11 seaplanes in and out of the water. Her seaplanes bombarded German communications and command centres, unsuccessfully attacked the German protected cruiser SMS *Kaiserin Elisabeth* with bombs and damaged a German minelayer in the Tsingtao peninsula.

On 6 August 1914, German Army Zeppelin airships bombed the Belgian city of Liège, and after other night raids on Antwerp and Warsaw, Britain would deploy *seaplanes in action for the first time* – in an effort to prevent Zeppelin bombing raids on British ports and cities.

German Zeppelins were known to be housed in vast sheds at Cuxhaven, on Germany's small section of North Sea coastline on the German Bight. From there they could threaten British ports and cities – but the Zeppelin sheds were out of range of British aircraft based in the UK.

On Christmas Day 1914, British seaplanes were carried into action by the three seaplane tenders, *Engadine, Riviera* and *Empress*, supported by the cruisers, destroyers and submarines of the Harwich Force commanded by Commodore Reginald Yorke Tyrwhitt. The powerful British naval force moved to within range of the German Zeppelin sheds and then launched three seaplanes from each seaplane tender near Heligoland Island, some 40 nautical miles distant from Cuxhaven. Although two of the seaplanes were unable to start their engines, the remaining seven successfully got airborne and set off to locate and destroy the sheds. Several sites were attacked, although low cloud, fog and AA fire largely thwarted the raid. Nevertheless, the strategic offensive importance of naval aviation was now clear.

Germany experimented with *submarine aircraft carriers* – by carrying a seaplane on the decks of a submarine close to the British coast, where it could partially submerge and allow the seaplane to float off. In January 1915, *U-12* left Zeebruge with a lightweight two-seat FF-29 seaplane carried on its deck in a take-off position – carrying a single bomb.

The British also experimented with the concept of submarines carrying aircraft, with HMS *E22* being commissioned on 8 November 1915 and designed to carry two Sopwith Schneider seaplane scouts on her casing. She would submerge and the planes would float off for a water take-off. The planes could not be recovered to the submarine and would return to the east coast of England once their mission was complete.

Naval aviation weapons and deployment techniques were also developing in tandem. On 11 August 1915, the first *attack* using an *air-launched aerial torpedo*, from a British Short Admiralty Type 184 seaplane deployed from the seaplane carrier HMS *Ben-my-Chree*, took place on a Turkish vessel that had already been crippled by the British submarine *E14*, in the Sea of Marmora.

The *Ben-my-Chree* was a 390ft-long, 2,651grt packet steamer, launched in 1908 and chartered by the Royal Navy on 1 January 1915. Part of her superstructure abaft her aftmost smokestack was removed and replaced by a large hangar that could house four to six seaplanes – the seaplanes being lifted in and out of the water onto her deck by derricks. A removable 18m-long flying off platform was fitted forward of her superstructure that was equipped with a trolley and rails to allow a seaplane to take off from the foredeck.

The Short Admiralty Type 184 launched by *Ben-my-Chree* was a two-seat reconnaissance, bombing and torpedo-carrying seaplane with folding wings. It attacked the Turkish vessel, dropping its torpedo from a height of just 15ft at a range of 800yd. It transpired that its target had in fact beached, after the damage by *E14*.

Five days later, another Short Type 184 was the first aircraft to actually *sink* a ship using an aerial torpedo, the victim being a Turkish transport vessel a few miles north of the Dardanelles on 17 August 1915.

The first use of a seaplane for *reconnaissance in an action at sea* took place on 31 May 1916 during the Battle of Jutland, fought between British and German fleets in the North Sea when, at 1445 hours, Admiral Beatty ordered his seaplane tender HMS *Engadine*, of the 3rd Light Cruiser Squadron in the battlecruiser screen, to launch an aircraft to investigate a sighting of smoke reported by the light cruiser *Galatea*, which was scouting ahead of the British battlecruiser squadron. *Engadine* was carrying two Short Type 184 floatplanes fitted with low-power wireless – and two Sopwith Baby floatplanes designed to shoot down Zeppelins.

A Short Type 184 floatplane was launched – and after about 10 minutes of flight, at 1530, its crew of two sighted German naval units – whilst flying at about 1,000ft, due to low clouds. The Type 184 closed to within a mile and a half to see what the ships actually were – before turning to head back to *Engadine*, reporting the presence of three enemy battlecruisers and ten destroyers turning to the south. As it headed back towards *Engadine*, the British battlecruiser *Lion* passed by below steaming into action at flank speed as it led the fifty-two warships of Beatty's battlecruiser force, six battlecruisers, four battleships and a screen of cruisers and destroyers, into the initial clash with the German battlecruiser squadron. The greatest clash of steel warships the world had ever seen, the Battle of Jutland, had begun.

The frailties of the big gun battlecruiser concept, which sacrificed armour for speed, were subsequently brutally demonstrated as the Battle of Jutland developed, with the catastrophic losses of three British battlecruisers, *Indefatigable*, *Queen Mary* and *Invincible*. Despite these losses, with naval aviation still in its infancy, most naval officers, educated in the late nineteenth century, still held firmly to the traditional belief that the dreadnought was the undisputed super weapon of the maritime battlefield. Every nation that had the industrial might to build them, did so – and put them on display as a lavish statement of national power.

But despite the well-entrenched belief in the supremacy of the big guns of a capital ship, the pace of the development of naval aviation quickened. The *first landing on a moving ship*, the flying off deck of the modified Courageous-class battlecruiser HMS *Furious*, took place at Scapa Flow in the Orkney Islands off northern Scotland on 2 August 1917 – when Squadron Commander Edwin Dunning landed a Sopwith Pup biplane in relatively benign conditions. The forward main battery turret of *Furious* had been removed whilst she was under construction and a flight deck added in its place, such that aircraft had to manoeuvre around the superstructure and crab in sideways above the deck to land. (Later in the war her single aft main battery turret was removed, and a second flight deck installed.) Such were the dangers of the developing techniques that Squadron Commander Dunning would sadly die just a few days later on 7 August, when his plane went over the side as he attempted a third landing.

As the war progressed, the Royal Navy began to develop naval aviation further with two purpose-designed *aircraft carriers*, that could launch both wheeled aircraft and seaplanes. Being designed in 1916 and laid down towards the end of the war, they would be too late to see action. An Italian ocean liner under construction on the Clyde was purchased and modified to become HMS *Argus*, the first example of the standard pattern of aircraft carrier with a full-length flat-top flush flight deck that allowed wheeled aircraft to take off and land. HMS *Hermes* (Pennant Number 95) was ordered in 1917 and was the world's first ship to be purpose designed as an aircraft carrier and the first to feature an *island superstructure*. The IJN's *Hōshō*, launched in 1921, was however the first aircraft carrier to be commissioned – in 1922. For although *Hermes* was launched in September 1919, some two years before *Hōshō*, as a result of delays caused by multiple changes in her design as construction progressed, she was only finally commissioned (after the *Hōshō*) in 1924.

When *Hermes* (95) was designed in 1916, she was to be fitted with a stern seaplane slipway, comprising three sections. Seaplanes would taxi onto the rigid submerged aft section of the slip and dock with a trolley that would carry the aircraft to the hangar, via a submerged middle portion that was flexible to counteract the roll of the ship – and finally a rigid forward portion of the slip. The entire slipway could ingeniously be retracted into the ship – but by mid-June 1918, the idea of the retractable slipway had already been superseded.

Unsure for the moment how best to develop the carrier concept, the Admiralty delayed any work above the hangar deck whilst they waited for results of trials that would determine what the best configuration would be. All this led to further modifications in 1920 with an island superstructure and funnel to starboard being added – apparently as pilots generally preferred to turn to port when recovering from an aborted landing. Further design modifications were implemented in 1921. Three further experimental carriers were completed by the Royal Navy during the coming decade, but Britain did little more to develop or strengthen her naval air capability. In the USA, in October 1919, Air Detachment, Pacific Fleet was formed – and quickly morphed into three divisions: Fighting, Spotting and Seaplane Patrol Squadrons. Naval aviation was now formally part of the US Pacific Fleet.

In the early 1920s, Britain and Japan were allies – and Britain, leading the development of carriers and naval aviation, played a major role in the growth of Japanese carrier aviation, sending advisors to Japan to instruct. At the Washington Naval Conference, held in Washington DC, from 12 November 1921 to 6 February 1922, a ten-year agreement was achieved to halt a runaway naval arms race in battleship construction. The deal fixed the maximum displacement of battleships at 35,000 tons and set the ratio of battleships between the USA, Britain and Japan at 5:5:3: 525,000 tons for the USA, 525,000 tons for Britain and 315,000 tons for Japan with smaller limits for France and Italy. The Treaty essentially allowed Britain and the USA a tonnage equivalent to fifteen capital ships; the Japanese were allowed nine capital ships; and France and Italy five capital ships apiece. Crippled by the huge costs of the First World War, Britain feared that it could not match Japanese and US shipbuilding programmes – and so accepted the terms of the Washington Naval Treaty. At a stroke, Britain had abandoned her cherished nineteenth-century *two-power policy* — that the Royal Navy must be equal in size to the next two largest navies in the world.

The Japanese were pointedly displeased that they had not been granted parity with Britain and the USA – however they were partly placated by a deal whereby Britain would not develop naval bases east of Singapore and the USA would not develop bases west of Hawaii. Japan had effectively been granted control of a huge slice of the North-West Pacific.

An effective end to an arms race of building new battleship fleets had however been achieved. Any new battleships built under the agreement would comply with limits on size and armament – displacement was capped at 35,000 tons and the maximum gun barrel size pegged at 16in. Many older capital ships would now be scrapped to comply with the agreement tonnages – but the Treaty however allowed for the conversion of two battleships or battlecruiser hulls to aircraft carriers of up to 33,000 long tons displacement. Britain, still the leading maritime power, suggested to both its allies, Japan and the USA, that each should convert two of its battlecruisers, then under construction, into fast carriers.[2]

Both countries bought into the idea. The USA converted two of its large 888ft-long Lexington-class battlecruisers, *Lexington* (CC-1) and *Saratoga* (CC-3), into 36,000-ton, 33-knot, seventy-five-plane carriers. Converting a battlecruiser into a carrier would give the carrier better anti-torpedo protection and offer larger magazines for aircraft bombs – but it would be slightly slower and have less hangar space and a narrower flight deck than a new bespoke carrier.

The two converted battlecruisers were reclassified as carriers in July 1922 – *Lexington* being assigned the hull number CV-2 and *Saratoga* the hull number CV-3. 'V' is the US Navy symbol for heavier than air craft, 'C' in this case stood for carrier. The two new carriers augmented the US Navy's first aircraft carrier, the much smaller 542ft-long converted collier *Langley* (CV-1) which had been commissioned on 20 March 1922. *Saratoga* was launched on 7 April 1925 whilst *Lexington* was launched on 3 October 1925.

Until this point, Japan had only had the small purpose-built 7,470-ton, 25-knot carrier *Hōshō*, launched on 13 November 1921 and completed as an experimental vessel in 1922. Embracing Britain's suggestion about converting battlecruiser hulls to aircraft carriers, in late 1923, Japan began conversions of the 817ft-long, Amagi-class battlecruiser *Akagi* and the 772ft-long Tosa-class battleship *Kaga*.

Akagi was commissioned on 25 March 1927 as a fast carrier capable of 32.5 knots and able to carry sixty aircraft. *Kaga* was commissioned in late 1929 as a 28-knot fast carrier that could carry seventy aircraft. Once completed, *Kaga* and *Akagi* each had a beam of more than 100ft and a deep-load displacement of around 34,000 tons (deep-load displacement is when the vessel is loaded with fuel, aircraft, munitions, crew, etc. as for combat). Both new carriers had three superimposed flight decks, the only carriers ever to use this design – intended to improve the launch and recovery cycle by allowing simultaneous launch and recovery of aircraft. These carriers would be modernised in the 1930s as newer naval aircraft required longer flight decks for launch and recovery. The lower flight decks were converted into hangars and the main flight deck was extended to the bow, raising aircraft capacity for *Akagi* to eighty-six and for *Kaga* to ninety.

The race for air supremacy at sea was hotting up. The role of aircraft at sea, and of the aircraft carrier itself, was still evolving, and it was common for cruisers and battleships to be equipped with their own catapult-launched reconnaissance seaplanes.

As the possibilities for naval aviation were explored in the 1920s, Britain adjusted an order for four large K-class steam-driven submarines to an order for four M-class submarines. HMS *M2* was completed in 1927 as a submarine aircraft carrier that had a watertight aircraft hangar integral to the hull, set just in front of the conning tower. This hangar housed a small Parnall Peto seaplane that was specifically designed for the *M2* – it was the smallest seaplane in the world at the time. In 1928, a steam-driven hydraulic aircraft catapult was fitted on *M2*'s foredeck to enable the seaplane to take off directly from the deck instead of being hoisted by a crane onto the water alongside. On its return the seaplane was craned back aboard and stowed in its hangar. The experimental submarine *M2* would, however, tragically sink on exercise on 26 January 1932 in West Bay, Dorset, in the English Channel with the loss of her entire crew of sixty. The disaster was believed to be due to water entering the submarine through the hangar door, which had been opened to launch the aircraft shortly after surfacing. The concept of a submarine cruiser was pursued with *X1* but was not a success and the British abandoned the idea.

Despite being ostensible allies, US strategists in the early part of the twentieth century regarded Japan as the next potential enemy. As a result, US naval strength began to migrate from the Atlantic to the Pacific in late 1922. The US Navy began to carry out *Fleet Problem* exercises in the Pacific and Caribbean – beginning in 1923. By 1927, these had demonstrated the need for aircraft carrier mobility and flexibility in the face of changing weather and enemy fleet movements. Carriers should be free to operate independently from the traditional battle line of battleships. These conclusions led to the recommendation that the carrier admiral should be given 'complete freedom of action in employing carrier aircraft . . .'.[3] The subsequent operations of *Lexington* (CV-2) and *Saratoga* (CV-3), which entered service in late 1927, would confirm the findings of the Fleet Problem exercises.[4]

In 1925, the outspoken US naval commander Admiral William S. Sims despite, like most, being initially sceptical of the potential of naval aviation, told Congress that: 'A small, high speed carrier alone can destroy or disable a battleship, . . . a fleet whose carriers give it command of the air over the enemy fleet can defeat the latter'.[5]

Sims defined the high-speed or fast carrier, as 'an airplane carrier of thirty-five knots and carrying one hundred planes . . . in reality a capital ship of much greater offensive power than any battleship'.[6] Although he concluded that 'the fast carrier is the capital ship of the future', little would be done to advance this concept until the rise of Japanese expansionism and of Nazi Germany in the mid-1930s made the world wake up to the threat posed.

In Fleet Problem IX in 1929, Admiral William V. Pratt, Commander Battleships Divisions, Battle Fleet, allowed Rear Admiral Reeves to take *Saratoga* in a high-speed run and surprise air attack on the Panama Canal, which was defended by an opposing fleet with carriers. *Saratoga* achieved devastating success – however it was found that as soon as the carriers came within range of the big guns of the enemy battleships, they became extremely vulnerable and were quickly sunk. Many admirals, ingrained in the belief of the invincibility of the battleship, seized on this vulnerability. Admiral Henry V. Wiley, Commander-in-Chief of the Fleet (CINC) stated that there was 'no analysis of Fleet Problem IX fairly made which fails to point to the battleship as the final arbiter of Naval destiny'.[7]

The older non-aviator admirals viewed the new fast carriers as the eyes of the fleet – their aircraft being primarily suited for scouting and reconnaissance. But evidence was mounting that showed the offensive capability of carriers – of a role that would come to define its future position in naval warfare.

Admiral Pratt went on to become Commander-in-Chief (CINC) of the US Fleet and then Chief of Naval Operations (CNO) in September

1930. Having seen the results of the Fleet Problem exercises, he championed deploying carriers in offensive roles in war games – and his recommendations were adopted by commanding admirals in every fleet exercise thereafter.[8]

At dawn on the morning of Sunday, 7 February 1932, there would be a chilling portent of the surprise Japanese carrier raid on Pearl Harbor ten years later on 7 December 1941. To demonstrate that Hawaii was vulnerable to naval air power, during Grand Joint Exercise No. 4, Rear Admiral Harry E. Yarnell launched a surprise war games air attack with 152 planes from *Lexington* and *Saratoga* on Pearl Harbor, without having been detected on approach to the holding position to the north. Such was the success of the raid, that Yarnell thereafter recommended that six to eight carriers be used to confront Japan in the Pacific.[9] Japanese writers reported on the exercise and its outcome did not go unnoticed.

Although naval doctrine by the early 1930s now held that fast carriers should be highly mobile and operate independently of the traditional battle line, the position was complicated by the fact that all of the USA's battleships, being pre-1922 vintage, could only make fleet speed of 21 knots. They could not keep up with the fast carriers that could make up to 33 knots. There were concerns that if the fast carriers were allowed to operate beyond the battle line, they would be vulnerable to a battleship action. Conversely, without carrier air support, the battleships in the battle line would be vulnerable if enemy aircraft were to threaten. A detached fast-carrier force would be particularly at risk in an amphibious operation, which demanded command of air and sea, and the presence of heavy fleet units.

The apparent vulnerability of the carriers and the battle line, if acting independently, was explored with Fleet Problem XVIII in May 1937 in Alaskan waters and in the vicinity of Hawaii and Midway. Whilst practising tactics for seizing advanced base sites, the carrier commander and the fleet commander disagreed as to whether the carriers should be left mobile and allowed to depart from the main force as a landing was practised. In the end, the fleet commander prevailed and elected to restrict the carriers to flying air patrols over the battleships and supporting the landing forces. In the exercise, the carrier *Langley* was subsequently sunk by air attack and *Saratoga* and *Lexington* were heavily bombed in addition to being seriously damaged by an enemy submarine.

Although the landing itself was ultimately successful, with the loss and damage to the three carriers, the fleet had lost its air capability. The naval airmen came away from the exercise believing that the situation had come about because of the restriction of the mobility of the carriers.

Fleet Problem XIX in 1938 again tested the defences of Hawaii – with aircraft from *Saratoga* and *Lexington* successfully attacking Pearl Harbor at dawn on 29 March. In the same exercise the two carriers subsequently attacked San Francisco without being spotted by the defending fleet. Further Fleet Problem exercises took place in 1939 and 1940 as war in Europe raged and Japan's leaders made their preparations for war.

Of the four US carriers deployed to the Pacific, *Lexington* (CV-2), *Saratoga* (CV-3), *Enterprise* (CV-6) and the old converted collier *Langley* (CV-1), none would be present at Pearl Harbor when the Japanese surprise carrier raid took place on 7 December 1941. Task Force 8 with *Enterprise* departed Pearl Harbor on 28 November 1941 to deliver Marine Fighter Squadron 211 aircraft to Wake Island, some 2,500 miles west. On 5 December 1941, Task Force 12, consisting of *Lexington*, three heavy cruisers and five destroyers, was despatched from Pearl Harbor with Marine Corps dive-bombers destined to reinforce Midway Island.

On 6 January 1941, *Saratoga* had begun a long-deferred modernisation and refit at the Bremerton Navy Yard on the West Coast. Her flight deck was widened at the bow and modern radar and additional anti-aircraft (AA) guns installed. Refit would be completed late in November 1941 – but she would not be at Pearl by 7 December. *Langley* (CV-1) was off Cavite in the Philippines when the Japanese carriers struck.

The US Navy had six heavy carriers in all at this time. *Lexington*, *Saratoga* and *Enterprise* were deployed in the Pacific. The other three, *Yorktown* (CV-5), *Wasp* (CV-7) and the newly commissioned *Hornet* (CV-8), were deployed in the Atlantic. The smaller *Ranger* (CV-4) was the first US vessel to be designed and built from the keel up as a carrier within the limits of the Washington Naval Treaty. She was returning to Norfolk, Virginia, from an ocean patrol to Trinidad and Tobago.

As a result, none of the US carriers would be present at Pearl Harbor on 7 December 1941 when six Japanese carriers launched their brutal surprise dawn raid and triggered the USA's entry into the war.

Chapter 2

Prelude to War in the Pacific – A Little Bit of Background

At the dawn of the twentieth century, Japan, a small island country with limited natural resources of its own, was determined to become a modern, industrial nation. She wanted to avoid what happened to China where, by the middle of the nineteenth century, European powers had forced the weakened Chinese Empire to open its doors to trade. The Chinese coast had become dominated by European trading posts such as Hong Kong and Shanghai.

Japan admired and envied the naval power and dominance of Great Britain and Japanese naval reform was largely based on the Royal Navy template. Over time, Japan grew in power and influence – but she was an industrial nation with little natural resources of her own to feed her growing industry and therefore became heavily dependent on imported raw materials.

During the First World War, the 1902 Anglo-Japanese alliance encouraged Japan to enter the war against Germany – seeing the opportunity to further expand its power and influence in the Pacific region. The alliance suited British interests as it allowed the Royal Navy to maintain only a small squadron in the Pacific to deal with the small German naval presence.

Thus emboldened, Japan declared war on Germany on 23 August 1914. Publicly, Japan maintained that she was honouring her commitments under the 1902 Anglo-Japanese alliance. But in reality, Japan was moving to protect her Pacific freight and passenger shipping routes – whilst the IJN saw the war as an opportunity to acquire advanced naval bases in the South Pacific. Japan joined Britain in attacking the German held colony of Tsingtao on the coast of China.

On the declaration of war, the IJN moved to eliminate German naval power in the Pacific by pursuing and destroying the Imperial German East Asiatic Squadron, which consisted of six major warships under the command of Vice Admiral Maximilian Reichsgraf von Spee: the Scharnhorst-class armoured cruisers SMS *Scharnhorst* and *Gneisenau*, the Dresden-class light cruisers *Dresden* and *Emden*, the Bremen-class light cruiser *Leipzig* and the Königsberg-class light cruiser *Nürnberg*.

The German East Asiatic Squadron ships were already dispersed at various colonies in the Pacific on routine peacetime missions. The outbreak of war left them outnumbered and outgunned by the Allies in the Pacific – with no secure harbour and unable to safely reach Germany. Resigned to his Squadron's fate, von Spee determined to plough the seas of the world inflicting as much damage as he could until his ammunition was exhausted or until he was caught by the superior firepower of the Allies. He took the Squadron around Cape Horn into the Atlantic, intent on forcing a way north towards home. The Squadron was caught and decimated by a British battlecruiser force on 8 December 1914 at the Battle of the Falkland Islands – in which von Spee himself would lose his life.

By October 1914, with the German East Asiatic Squadron making itself scarce in the Pacific, the IJN had seized German possessions in the Mariana, Caroline, Marshall and Palau Islands groups. Intent on expansion, gaining territories and securing access to raw materials, as Germany became vulnerable, Japan also seized German possessions in China and elsewhere in the Pacific.

After the First World War ended, the victorious Allies established the League of Nations under the Treaty of Versailles of 28 June 1919 – and the ex-German colonies in the Pacific were divided amongst the victors under the League's South Pacific Mandate. Japan was granted a South Pacific Class C Mandate to administrate the former German Pacific Islands north of the equator. She retained the conquered German colony of Tsingtao – and China was forced to relinquish other land in the area to her.

Under her South Pacific Mandate, Japan was awarded hundreds of island territories, comprising the extensive Caroline Islands archipelago, situated to the north of New Guinea which has the Federated States of Micronesia (such as Truk) at its eastern end and Palau and Yap to its west. The Marshall Islands, at the north east of the Carolines, such as Kwajalein, Bikini and Majuro all fell under Japanese dominion as did the Northern Mariana Islands. The USA retained control of Guam at the southern end of the Marianas. All the territories mandated to Japan would be administered under the laws of the Mandatory (i.e. Japan) as its own territory. It was a fine return for the loan of a battalion of infantry and a few naval escort vessels to Britain.

Japan established a new unified command – the *Provisional South Seas Defence Force* under the command of the IJN. Naval districts were set up at Palau, Yap, Saipan, Truk, Ponape and Jaluit under a command based at Truk and the Governors appointed were mostly admirals or vice admirals. The IJN took on immediate administration of the islands, issuing laws, promoting Japanese enterprises, instigating public works programmes and beginning a policy of educating the indigenous population in the Japanese way of life. Japanese cultural institutions such as schools, shrines and temples were constructed. Economically, the Japanese were particularly interested in sugar cane whilst a thriving fishing industry was created on Saipan.

There were provisions built into the Mandate that prohibited Japan from establishing military or naval bases and from erecting fortifications. No open door trade policy was provided for, however – and Japan established a trade monopoly that allowed her to effectively seal off the islands from the outside world. Japan would not allow any foreign ships to enter the waters of its newly occupied territories – the ban extending to the ships of her erstwhile allies in the First World War.

The USA was deeply alarmed at the League of Nations policy on Japan and strongly opposed Japanese administration of the islands – insisting on military neutralisation. President Woodrow Wilson, who had been a driving force behind the creation of the League of Nations, refused to recognise the Japanese Mandate over the islands – and Congress refused to ratify the Treaty of Versailles. The USA would not be part of the League of Nations – and US isolationism began.

Japanese bureaucrats began to replace military officers in the post-war years and in 1920, the military Provisional South Seas Defence Force relinquished all authority to the Civil Affairs Bureau, which relocated its HQ to Palau. Over the next two decades the Bureau was responsible for the expansion of Japanese influence in the islands by controlling infrastructure such as schools, courts, hospitals, building, agriculture and mining. Palau became the chief centre for Japanese commerce, shipping and air transport in the South Seas.

The Nippon Yusen Kaisha shipping line (NYK) was given a government contract to provide a steamship service between the Japanese home islands and the main ports in the South Seas. This service would enable the importing to the Japanese home islands of vast quantities of natural resources that were vital to Japan's aims to expand in the Pacific.

Two main shipping routes were established – one western and one eastern. Ships would carry cargoes of building materials, machinery, coal and foodstuffs out to the South Seas islands from Japan for use in developing their island infrastructures. On the return leg, the same ships would carry natural resources back to Japan such as the aluminium ore known as bauxite, which was the world's main source of aluminium, vital for aircraft manufacture. Vast quantities of lignite were carried back – a combustible brown sedimentary rock known as the lowest form of coal. Mined phosphate minerals were also carried back to Japan for use in agriculture and industry along with other local products such as shell products, fish, copra (the dried meat or kernel of the coconut used to extract coconut oil), coconut oil, starch and pineapple.

(i) The Political Situation in 1930s Japan – Manchuria

The Great Depression from 1929 onwards, and the subsequent collapse in world trade, hit Japan's export-orientated economy hard. The depressed Western economies placed barriers on Japanese trade to protect their own colonial markets. Many Japanese believed that the international peace established by the League of Nations favoured the Western nations that controlled the world's resources. The economic crisis led the Japanese military to become increasingly convinced that Japan needed guaranteed access to new markets, and raw materials, on the Asian mainland. Japan's population had more than doubled and demand was high for food, coal and materials. The idea began to emerge in Japan of an East Asian federation, or cooperative body, based on traditional pan-Asian ideals of universal brotherhood. An 'Asia for Asians' sentiment began to emerge.

During the negotiations towards the London Naval Conference Treaty in 1930, the Prime Minister of Japan, Osachi Hamaguchi, had tried – but failed – to secure a better ratio of battleships for Japan viz a viz Great Britain and the USA. His failure, and subsequent settlement of the Treaty, led to the Japanese public feeling that he had sold out Japanese national security – prompting a surge of Japanese nationalism. On 14 November 1930, Hamaguchi was shot by a member of an ultra-Nationalist group in Tokyo Station. He was hospitalised for several months until he returned to office on 10 March 1931. He resigned a month later.

With Hamaguchi's firm rule no longer at the helm, a growing militarism took hold in Japanese politics. Coincidentally, just six months after Hamaguchi's resignation, the local warlord in the Manchuria area of north-east China formally recognised the Chinese Nationalist government in Nanking. Japan had won control of the southern half of this area, and of Korea, from Russia in the 1905 Russo-Japan War – they now found their presence there being obstructed.

By the early 1930s, after years of development, three-quarters of the Manchurian economy was under Japanese control and it was a major source of coal and iron ore for Japan, as well as being an important export market. With Japan's vital economic position in Manchuria at risk to the Chinese, on 18 September 1931, officers of the Kwantung Army (the Japanese forces in Manchuria) took matters into their own hands. Without advising their Commander-in-Chief, or the Tokyo civilian government, the Japanese officers staged a bombing incident on a railway they were guarding near the town of Mukden.

The Kwantung Army claimed that local Chinese forces were responsible and launched a military campaign, shelling the local Chinese garrison and destroying the small Chinese air force. In addition, 500 Japanese troops assaulted the garrison of some 7,000 Chinese troops, who were mostly irregulars or conscripts. The fighting was over by the evening and the Japanese occupied Mukden at the cost of 500 Chinese dead to 2 Japanese dead. The Japanese then went on to occupy the major Manchurian cities of Changchun and Antung, as well as the surrounding areas. The military established a puppet state, which the Tokyo civilian government was forced to rubber stamp after the event.

Aggrieved Chinese leaders appealed to the League of Nations – of which China was a member – for a peaceful solution. Whilst a League of Nations investigation into the war in Manchuria was ongoing, Inukai Tsuyoshi was appointed prime minister on 13 December 1931. He tried to place fiscal restraints on the military but failed – and he was also unable to control the military's designs on China. Early in 1932 a Japanese expeditionary force deployed to Shanghai to counter anti-Japanese riots. The fighting lasted for weeks.

A *coup d'état* was staged in Japan by reactionary elements of the IJN on 15 May 1932. Eleven young naval officers assassinated Prime Minister Tsuyoshi and brought the civilian government to its knees. The military had now gained control of the country and unchecked by a civilian administration, massive increases in Japanese military spending began.

At the League of Nations Assembly in Geneva on 24 February 1933, the League called upon Japan to withdraw her troops and restore Manchuria to Chinese sovereignty. The Japanese delegation, in defiance of world opinion and unwilling to accept the Assembly's report, dramatically withdrew from the League of Nations. Grandstanding, their officials walked out of the Assembly hall. Japan's isolation from the community of nations had begun – and suspicion and mistrust of Japan's intentions intensified.

In 1933, with Japan no longer part of the League of Nations and thus not effectively bound by the Mandate prohibitions against the establishment of military bases, Japanese militarism grew stronger, and the IJN began preliminary surveys of their mandated South Seas islands for potential naval and air bases. In 1936, more detailed surveys followed on from those preliminary surveys to establish locations for airfields, anchorages, communications, fuel and ammunition storage facilities and defensive emplacements. The Caroline Islands were identified as the first line of defence in the event of war with the USA in the Pacific.

It seemed that the world was once again descending into chaos. In Italy, the Fascists had seized control in the 1920s whilst the Great Depression soon overwhelmed the USA. In Germany, the Nazi Party came to power – with Hitler being appointed Chancellor in 1933. Nazi Germany left the League of Nations that year and repudiated the military clauses of the 1919 Treaty of Versailles. In 1935, Italy invaded Abyssinia (now Ethiopia) and in 1936, the Spanish Civil War broke out.

In 1937, the IJN undertook a clandestine programme of militarisation of many of their island holdings, builing fortifications, establishing naval ports and constructing airfields. Japan viewed her scattered island aerodromes as unsinkable aircraft carriers that provided a network of mutual air support. A major airfield construction programme started in Palau in 1939 to allow long-range offensive air missions against US and British holdings in the Pacific.

Kwajalein atoll, in the Marshall Islands, lies more than 2,200 nautical miles out into the Pacific east of Palau. It was developed into an air base, which supported the attack on Pearl Harbor, which lay some 2,500 nautical miles further north east towards the USA. Palau would be used to support the campaign to take the Philippines whilst Truk, in Micronesia, more than 1,100 nautical miles out into the Central Pacific to the east of Palau, would be used as a forward base for the amphibious landings on Tarawa, Makin and Rabaul.

Japan adopted a pre-war philosophical policy of expansion called the *Greater East Asia Co-Prosperity Sphere*. Central to that policy was the creation of a bloc of Asian nations comprising Japan, Manchuko, China and parts of South-East Asia that would be led by Japan and be free of the influence of Western colonial powers.

Whilst Japanese policy theorists, and the Japanese population at large, envisaged pan-Asian ideals of freedom and independence from Western colonial oppression, the vision was corrupted by Japanese militarists and Nationalists who in 1940 formally announced the concept, seeing it as a way to gain resources as raw materials for war and to strengthen Japan's position in Asia.

Many of the nations within the boundaries of the Sphere were under European colonial rule and, tired of foreign exploitation, elements of local populations such as Indonesia were already sympathetic to Japan – and this made Japanese development of the *Greater East Asia Co-Prosperity Sphere* attractive. Using phrases such as 'Asia for the Asiatics', Japanese propaganda would use the concept of the Sphere to advance Japanese domination in Asia. Whilst in some cases Japanese troops were welcomed by the local populace who were ruled by puppet governments, the subsequent brutality to civilians shown by the Japanese military, particularly in China, led to the indigenous populations of the occupied areas coming to view the Japanese as much worse than the Western imperialists.

Japan lacked her own natural resources – in particular, her absence of oil resources was a critical vulnerability. Japan had an industrial economy and a large navy and merchant marine but yet imported 90 per cent of her oil, and much of her iron primarily from the USA. Ironically, it was US trade and exports throughout the 1930s that had largely underpinned Japan's war industries and expansionism. With the USA as the likely main foe, this critical vulnerability led Japan to eye the oil-rich Dutch East Indies (now Indonesia) and French Indochina (now Vietnam, Laos and Cambodia) with special interest. These territories were part of Japan's vital supply route for men and materials to and from the Chinese mainland. The Japanese government directed that local economies within the Sphere be managed strictly for the production of raw war materials, a Cabinet member declaring: 'There are no restrictions. They are enemy possessions. We can take them, do anything we want.'[1]

But US tolerance of Japanese aggression was wearing thin. The Japanese invasion of China in 1937 and the subsequent brutal treatment of Chinese civilians by Japanese troops quickly led to a souring of relations between Japan and the USA, which had substantial commercial interests in China. US public opinion turned sharply against Japan when, on 12 December 1937, Japanese aircraft attacked a US oil tanker convoy as it was being escorted up the Chinese Yangtze River by the US gunboat *Panay*. The *Panay* was sunk – and Japanese aircraft then fired on survivors. Two months later the US consul in Nanking was attacked and US property looted.

Contrary to what she sought to achieve by securing her own resources in Manchuria and China, Japan's China Policy, far from making her self-sufficient by securing raw materials, was in fact making her more dependent than ever on imports from the West. The US and British lack of response to Japan's war in China however did much to make Japanese leaders believe that Western democracies were weak and lacked resolve. All the time, as the war in China dragged on, Japanese troops were becoming battle-hardened and ruthless.

On 26 July 1939, after continued attacks by the Japanese military on US citizens and the encroachment on US interests in China, the USA withdrew from the US-Japan Treaty of Commerce and Navigation – which regulated trade between the two countries.

In Europe the year before, events began to spiral further out of control. On 12 March 1938, the *Anschluss* of Austria, the occupation by Nazi Germany, took place, followed on 1 October 1938 by the annexation of the Sudetenland German speaking area of Czechoslovakia. On 15 March 1939, Germany then moved to occupy the rest of Czechoslovakia – before on 1 September 1939, invading Poland and finally triggering the Second World War.

In November 1939, as war in Europe erupted and Japan made ready for her Pacific war, the IJN 4th Fleet was organised to protect her Pacific island territories and those that she intended to seize to create the *Greater East Asia Co-prosperity Sphere* – or empire. Rear Admiral Isoroku Yamamoto was now Commander-in-Chief of the Combined Fleet and Oikawa Navy Minister in the Cabinet of Prime Minister Konoe Fumimaro. Japanese naval aviation was now represented at the highest operational and political levels and Yamamoto was promoted to Admiral on 15 November 1940. The belligerent General Hideki Tōjō was however appointed Minster of War in July 1940 and succeeded Konoe as prime minster on 18 October 1941. With Tōjō now in charge of Japan's highest political office, it became clear that the Army would lead the Navy into a war.

During 1940, as Japan's political leaders deliberated a Pacific war, her strategic planners schemed to determine the means of winning such a war. The Imperial Japanese Army (IJA) wanted to push into South-East Asia and the Dutch East Indies, seizing the Philippines whilst supported by the Combined Fleet, including the four carriers under the command of Admiral Chūichi Nagumo, and by Admiral Nishizō

Tsukahara's 11th Air Fleet, which was based on Formosa. Yamamoto, who had spent much time in the USA, and appreciated its industrial might, had serious reservations about the likely outcome.

(ii) Palau

A major airfield construction programme began on the ex-German mandated territory of Palau in 1939 when it was realised that airfields here could be used for long-range offensive missions against US- and British-held islands and territories in the Pacific.

In 1940, the IJN 4th Fleet was given responsibility for protecting the Inner South Seas area by developing the military land, sea and air facilities required to sustain a large mobile naval fleet and establish forward air power. The 4th Fleet's HQ was established at Truk and the Inner South Seas area was divided into four sectors, each with a Base Force HQ. Koror in Palau became the HQ for the Third Base Force – which covered the whole Palau sector.

The Japanese had identified Palau as having the most extensive anchorages in the western Carolines and with the arrival in the South Seas of the main bulk of the IJN in 1940, pre-existing plans were initiated to develop it into a major naval base which would serve as a strategically important forward shipping centre and fuelling station. Storage facilities were built for fuel, ammunition and supplies, and wharves were built to handle merchant ships. IJN destroyers and submarines could use dockside facilities whilst lighters would victual larger heavy naval vessels anchored offshore. Docking facilities and workshops were developed to allow repair work on the full range of merchant and naval vessels that would soon throng her waters.

The 4th Fleet improved Palau's air base facilities to handle land-based aircraft and seaplanes. A major airfield was installed at the southern Palauan island of Peleliu and a seaplane base at Arakabesan. Plans were developed for further airstrips on the largest Palauan island, Babelthuap.

Work commenced on barracks, command posts, ammo depots, coastal defence gun batteries and AA emplacements. The build-up of Palau as a military base progressed so well that Palau along with Truk and Ponape in the Caroline Islands, Kwajalein, Wotje, Jaluit and Maloelap in the Marshall Islands and Saipan in the Mariana Islands were sufficiently developed to enable them to be designated on 5 November 1941, just one month before war, as supply bases for Admiral Yamamoto's Combined Fleet for the initial offensive phase of the planned Pacific war.

Admiral Ibō Takahashi's 3rd Fleet, an amphibious fleet unit of carriers, cruisers and destroyers, with the battleships and heavy cruisers of the 2nd Fleet providing cover, would stage from Palau for the invasion of the Philippines and Netherlands East Indies, which would begin at the same time as the Pearl Harbor raid in December 1941. Palau assumed a vital role as a base for scouting and reconnaissance missions and for staging amphibious forces.

Admiral C. Nagumo's 1st Air Fleet was based in Palau – and its four carriers would sortie from Palau to make a massive strike against Port Darwin in the Northern Territory of Australia on 19 February 1942, again supported by the battleships and heavy cruisers of the 2nd Fleet.

As the war progressed, Palau would become an increasingly important linking port for movements of ships, aircraft and supplies between Japan and the operational areas of the South-West Pacific. It served as a fuelling station and port of assembly for transport vessels and convoys moving from Japan to New Guinea and Rabaul with supplies.

Palau also became a major strategic port for the New Guinea front as a base for three naval Escort Squadrons. The First Escort Squadron, consisting initially of 10 destroyers, 8 coastal defence ships, 3 minesweepers and several Submarine Chasers and gunboats, was responsible for convoy protection over the long distances between Japan and the Philippines, East Indies and Palau. In 1943, the 9th Fleet was established at Wewak and Medang and assisted with convoys from Palau to Wewak.

(iii) Truk

The lagoon at Chuuk, as Truk has been known since 1990, is a great natural harbour ringed by a protective reef some 140 miles in circumference and 40–50 miles in diameter. The atoll rises up from the deep-blue oceanic depths of the Western Pacific just north of the equator to the north east of New Guinea. It is some 1,165 nautical miles almost directly east out into the Pacific from Palau.

Truk was initially the IJN's 4th Fleet Base and became the Combined Fleet's forward base from 1942 until 1944. The Japanese Combined Fleet had been formed during the 1904–5 Russo-Japanese War and comprised a unified command for the three separate fleets of the IJN. The 1st Fleet had been the main battleship fleet, the 2nd Fleet was a fast, mobile cruiser fleet and the 3rd Fleet a reserve fleet of obsolete vessels. By the Second World War the Combined Fleet had become synonymous with the IJN and consisted of battleships, aircraft carriers, cruisers and all the ancillary craft that made up the main fighting strength.

Truk served as a safe, sheltered and well-protected forward base for the IJN fleet. The two new 27.5-knot fast battleships, the 71,659-ton *Yamato* (commissioned on 16 December 1941) and *Musashi* (commissioned on 5 August 1942), would each spend time there. Each massive battleship (built outwith the Washington Naval Treaty limits) carried three triple 46cm Type 94 naval guns (18.1in) that were the largest guns used on battleships during the Second World War. In addition to these new battleships, strategically vital aircraft carriers, cruisers, destroyers, tankers and submarines, along with countless minor vessels such as tugs, gunboats, minesweepers and landing craft, all thronged Truk's waters. A large number of naval auxiliary transport ships worked as tenders for the fleet and its submarines, carrying shells, propellant, ammunition, torpedoes, stores, spares and everything needed to keep a battle fleet operational. Truk's land defences were fortified and airfields constructed for land-based aircraft as well as seaplane bases.

The Allies had long suspected that Truk was a fortified anchorage but as Truk had been closed to foreigners for decades, as the Pacific War loomed, little was known about the scale of the operation.

Chapter 3

The Fast Carriers
Begin to Appear

(i) USA

As the world spiralled towards war, a slow naval re-armament began in the USA during the mid-1930s – under the eye of President Franklin D. Roosevelt, himself a naval minded Chief Executive. The Vinson-Trammell Act of 1934 included appropriations for two new carriers and many new naval aircraft. With the small *Langley* (CV-1) and the two converted battlecruisers *Lexington* (CV-2) and *Saratoga* (CV-3) currently in commission, the fourth US carrier, *Ranger* (CV-4) was commissioned on 4 June 1934. Laid down in September 1931, she was the first US Navy aircraft carrier to be purpose-built from the keel up. At 730ft long and displacing 14,576 tons (standard), she could make 29 knots. Originally designed with a flush deck, an island superstructure was added after completion – but she was deemed too slow for use with the Pacific Fleet and would spend most of her war in the Atlantic facing the Nazi threat.

    Ranger would be followed by the two larger 824ft 9in, 19,800-ton Yorktown-class 32.5-knot fast carriers *Yorktown* (CV-5), commissioned on 30 September 1937, and *Enterprise* (CV-6), commissioned on 12 May 1938. The reduced size version of the Yorktown-class *Wasp* (CV-7) was commissioned on 25 April 1940 and was followed by the third Yorktown-class fast carrier *Hornet* (CV-8), commissioned on 20 October 1941, just months before the surprise Japanese raid on Pearl Harbor on 7 December 1941. The three Yorktown-class carriers *Yorktown*, *Enterprise* and *Hornet* would bear the brunt of the fighting during the early months of the Pacific War in 1942, such as at the Battle of the Coral Sea, the Battle of Midway and the Guadalcanal campaign. The lead

24

ship of the subsequent new twenty-four-ship Essex-class, *Essex* (CV-9), would only launch for fitting out on 31 July 1942 and be commissioned on 31 December 1942. The Essex-class carriers however would go on to become the backbone of the US fast-carrier force during the Pacific War.

(ii) Japan

The Japanese carrier concept continued to evolve during the 1930s. IJN *Kaga* had originally launched on 17 November 1921 as one of two Tosa-class battleships – but on 5 February 1922, both Tosa-class ships were cancelled and scheduled to be scrapped under the Washington Naval Treaty. The Treaty did however allow for the conversion of two battleships or battlecruiser hulls to aircraft carriers of up to 33,000 long tons displacement. *Kaga* was selected for conversion in December 1923 – along with the Amagi-class battlecruiser *Akagi*. Once the conversion works were completed, *Kaga* was commissioned on 31 March 1928. She had a superimposed three-level flight deck with the main upper flight deck being completely flat and 562ft long by 100ft wide. Her middle flight deck was only 50ft long and started in front of the bridge: her lower flight deck was 180ft long. She had two main hangar decks and a third auxiliary hangar, the hangars opening onto the middle and lower flight decks to allow aircraft to take off directly from the hangars whilst landing operations were in progress on the flight deck above.

As the new generations of aircraft increased in performance, size and weight the bottom flight deck on *Kaga* became unable to accommodate the take-off roll needed. Thus, when she was modernised at Sasebo Dockyard during 1934 and 1935, it was plated over and a much longer 812.5ft flight deck that was 100ft wide with a starboard-side superstructure island was completed. These works increased her displacement to 38,200 tons standard and 42,541 tons deep load.

Work began to construct the battlecruiser *Akagi* as an aircraft carrier on 19 November 1923 and although she was launched more than four years after *Kaga*, on 22 April 1925, she was commissioned into the IJN a year before *Kaga*, on 25 March 1927. She also initially had a superimposed three-level flight-deck system. The main flight deck was completely flat, 624ft long and almost 100ft wide. Her middle deck was 49ft long whilst her lower deck was 180ft long.

Akagi was modernised between 1935 and 1938, being reconstructed with a much longer full-length flight deck that was 817.5ft long and 100ft wide with a superstructure island on her port side. Her middle and lower decks were eliminated to give two enclosed hangar decks that extended almost the full length of the ship. She now displaced 36,500 tons standard load and 41,300 tons deep load.

Design and construction of new Japanese naval aircraft was given much attention. Aware that the USA was developing aircraft carriers for operations in the Pacific, Japan now accelerated her own production of carriers. Set on expansionism, she was strengthening and gearing up towards war. The advances in US carrier aviation had led her to conclude that the odds would 'weigh heavily in favour of an attack force' of enemy carriers approaching Japan.[1]

In the early 1930s Japan strove to eliminate the threat of enemy carriers by diplomacy. British naval analyst Hector C. Bywater observed in 1934 that Japan wanted 'the total abolition of aircraft carriers on the grounds of their essentially aggressive character'. He believed that Japan feared carriers 'more than any other naval craft. She dreads the possibility of large enemy carriers steaming across the Pacific to send off swarms of bombing planes against Tokyo and other populous centres' constructed of light, inflammable materials.[2] Japan's efforts to curb enemy carrier production by diplomacy however failed.

Yamamoto had argued as far back as 1933, when he was Commander Carrier Division 1, that the best defence against possible US carrier attacks on Japanese territory was Japan's *own* carrier force. He pressed political leaders to allocate resources for more carriers to be built – and initiated the design and construction of a new breed of modern naval aircraft. Such was the strength of his personality and strategic thinking that towards the end of the 1930s he had succeeded in both causes. The new Mitsubishi A5M fighter, the world's first monoplane naval fighter, entered service in 1936 whilst new carriers began to join the IJN in tandem with the modernisation of older carriers such as *Kaga* and *Akagi*.

The smaller 590ft-long, 7,900-ton (standard), forty-eight-plane light carrier *Ryūjō* had been laid down in November 1929, to complete the Combined Fleet's aerial reconnaissance, patrol and torpedo-bombing capability. Japan was exploiting a loophole in the Washington Naval Treaty that provided that carriers under 10,000 long tons standard displacement were not regarded as 'aircraft carriers'. This loophole was closed under the London Naval Treaty in 1930 and hence once she was commissioned on 9 May 1933, she would be the only such light carrier completed by Japan.

Between 1937 and 1939, the two new 34-knot, 746.5ft-long, 15,900-ton (standard load) fast carriers *Sōryū* and *Hiryū*, each able to carry sixty-three planes, were completed. By October 1941, a new Fifth Carrier Division had been formed, from the newly completed 25,675-ton

IJN *Kaga*, starboard bow, *c.* 1930. (Maritime History & Science Centre, Kure)

IJN *Kaga* following her 1934–6 modernisation. (NH 73060 courtesy of the U.S. Naval History & Heritage Command)

IJN *Hiryū*. (Maritime History & Science Centre, Kure)

USS *Yorktown* (CV-5) anchored in Hampton Roads, Virginia, 30 October 1937. (NH 50330 courtesy of the U.S. Naval History & Heritage Command)

standard load, 34.5-knot, seventy-two-plane Shōkaku-class fast carriers *Shōkaku* and *Zuikaku* – all in time for a possible raid on Pearl Harbor.

Carrier aircraft supported IJA operations in China in 1937 – and in 1939, carrier aircraft successfully bombed a mock-up of the US carrier *Saratoga* at the Kashima Bombing Range. As in the USA, older traditional non-air admirals however kept their faith in the invincibility of the battleship – and supported the construction of the 71,659-ton (F) Yamato-class super battleships.[3]

(iii) US Preparations

The new fast carriers *Yorktown* (CV-5) and *Enterprise* (CV-6) joined the older carriers *Langley* (CV-1), *Lexington* (CV-2), *Saratoga* (CV-3) and *Ranger* (CV-4) in the fleet in the mid to late 1930s. *Wasp* (CV-7) was laid down in April 1936 and was still building – she would be commissioned into the fleet on 25 April 1940. *Hornet* (CV-8) was also under construction, having been laid down in September 1939. She would be commissioned on 20 October 1941.

The growing number of fast carriers took part in fleet battle-line manoeuvres that included amphibious landing operations. They also conducted independent carrier operations exercises and practised a new and vital operation, at-sea replenishment. In June 1939, *Saratoga* refuelled from a fleet tanker off California – and thus began the logistical procedures necessary to support fast carriers operating in the vast expanses of the Pacific. No US battleship refuelled at sea until July 1940.

As the number of US carriers increased during the 1930s, so the need for pilots grew correspondingly. A series of Congressional bills were passed, beginning in 1935, calling for 6,000 Naval Reserve pilots.[4] These new pilots were given twelve to fifteen months of pre-flight and flight training, after which they were commissioned and ordered to active duty. This would provide a solid core for a large wartime naval air force.

In the Pacific, the billet of Commander Aircraft Battle Force came to be known as the 'Carrier Command'. The then Vice Admiral, Ernest J. King, who had commanded destroyers in the First World War and submarines in the inter-war period, occupied the post in 1938. He would subsequently ascend to become Commander in Chief, US Fleet (COMINCH) and Chief of Naval Operations (CNO) during the war.

Twelve years previously, in 1926, the US Congress had passed a law requiring all commanders of aircraft carriers, seaplane tenders and aviation shore establishments to be qualified naval aviators or naval aviation observers. To comply with these requirements, King had taken aviator training at the Naval Air Station Pensacola, Florida, receiving his wings on 26 May 1927. He was then appointed captain of *Lexington* (CV-2) on 20 June 1930. He was promoted to Vice Admiral on 29 January 1938.

In 1940, the billet of Commander Aircraft Battle Force, previously occupied by King, went to Vice Admiral William F. Halsey Jr, a tough uncompromising leader who had earned the nickname 'Bull' Halsey. He had come to naval aviation in 1934 after a long career in destroyers, when he was offered command of the *Saratoga* (CV-3). He received his naval aviation wings on 15 May 1935 at the age of 52, the oldest person to do so in the history of US naval aviation. The Navy would subsequently enter the war in December 1941 using the tactical doctrine for carrier operations that would be developed by Halsey in March 1941.[5]

After the last Fleet Problem XXI in 1940, officers with a background in naval aviation, naval airmen, arrived at a belief that was to continue through the war – that only naval aviators could understand the intricacies of carrier operations. Those admirals who had been schooled in the more traditional battle line of big-gun battleships couldn't see or fully understand the potential of the carriers – the naval airmen felt that only they were qualified to command the movements of a carrier fleet.[6] At that time in 1940, the naval aviators wanted freedom to allow the carriers to operate independently of the battle line of battleships. In the coming war, this belief would evolve and develop until eventually the carriers in the Pacific would exercise control over the entire fleet – and battleships would be relegated to a carrier support role.

Existing US naval aircraft were vastly inferior to the Japanese equivalent in the immediate run up to war. The new fast and nimble 330mph Mitsubishi A6M Zero fighter entered service in 1940 and by the outbreak of the Pacific War was far more advanced than any US fighter. The glaring shortcomings of US naval fighters led to the Navy getting priority over the Army in new aircraft production contracts. But the die was already cast, and the hour was late – the new aircraft under development would ultimately not be ready by the time war broke out in December 1941.

With *Lexington* (CV-2), *Saratoga* (CV-3), *Yorktown* (CV-5) and *Enterprise* (CV-6) already operating with the fleet, by October 1941, with *Wasp* (CV-7) and *Hornet* (CV-8) now commissioned, the US Navy had six fast heavy carriers (excluding the smaller *Ranger* (CV-4) and the aging and slow *Langley* (CV-1)). In addition, there were also two new 36,600-ton North Carolina-class fast battleships, *North Carolina* (BB-55), commissioned on 9 April 1941, and *Washington* (BB-56), commissioned on 15 May 1941 – both of which carried nine 16in/45 calibre Mark 6 main battery guns in three triple turrets. Two triple turrets were placed in a super firing pair forward and the third set aft. These heavily armoured and powerful battleships could make 28 knots and thus keep up with the carriers.

Four 35,000-ton South Dakota-class, 28-knot fast battleships, *South Dakota* (BB-57), *Indiana* (BB-58), *Massachusetts* (BB-59) and *Alabama* (BB-60), were also under construction. They would also carry nine 16in/45 calibre Mark 6 guns set in three triple main battery turrets. Commissioned during 1942, they were the first US battleships to be designed after the breakdown of the Washington Treaty system.

Although carrier doctrine was flexible at this time, immediately before the Pacific War began, the fast carriers were still in principle subordinated to the battle line of battleships. The six fast carriers could

USS *Wasp* (CV-7) en route to sea, 1940. (NH 43464 courtesy of the U.S. Naval History & Heritage Command)

have operated in one single tactical formation – but with both Germany and Japan threatening to bring the USA into the war, they were of necessity split between the Atlantic and Pacific theatres. As the end of 1941 neared, the Navy waited for more ships and better aircraft – and prayed for more time before war came.

Meanwhile, in Britain, as command and control of carriers developed, naval aviation also finally in 1937 began to get the attention it deserved. Previously, when the full potential of naval air had been underestimated, a captain had been in charge of the small Naval Air Section of the Royal Air Force (RAF). The Fleet Air Arm was now however transferred from the RAF back to the Royal Navy – and a Rear Admiral was appointed to sit on the board of the Admiralty, in place of the previous RAF captain. This position was upgraded the following year to Fifth Sea Lord and Chief of Naval Air Services with the rank of Vice Admiral.

In December 1938, Britain commissioned the 22,000-ton (standard) HMS *Ark Royal* (Pennant Number 91) into the fleet – its first modern triple-screw 31-knot fast carrier. *Ark Royal* had been designed in 1934 to comply with the anticipated 22,000-ton maximum displacement restriction for aircraft carriers in a new treaty that would replace the Washington and London Naval Treaties, which were due to expire at the end of 1936. Built by Cammell Laird at Birkenhead in England, *Ark Royal* was the first aircraft carrier on which two aircraft hangars and the flight deck were an integral part of the hull, the strength deck, rather than an add-on or part of the superstructure.

Ark Royal was designed to carry a large number of aircraft – the number being successfully increased to seventy-two by shortening the landing and take-off distances of aircraft by using arrestor gear and compressed steam catapults. The flight deck was strongly built with 0.75in (19mm) thick Ducol steel plating. Three lifts moved aircraft between the hangars and the flight deck, which was 800ft long – some 118ft longer than the keel. Installation of an armoured flight deck was not possible – as it would have put her above the Washington and London Naval Treaties limits that Britain was still observing.

Ark Royal was protected by a 4.5in-thick vertical waterline armour belt over the engine rooms and magazines – and a side protection system, often called the *liquid sandwich*. This three-layer anti-torpedo system was similar to that fitted on the new King George V-class battleships such as *Prince of Wales*. The side protection system comprised air spaces immediately inboard of the shell plating of the hull into which an explosion could dissipate. Inboard of these air spaces was a water or oil-filled partition that was designed to bend or buckle and absorb any remaining explosive force. Inboard of this partition were further spaces to dissipate any residual explosive force that penetrated the partition. Then came the 1½in-thick anti-splinter torpedo bulkhead of the ship proper itself. These side protection systems had been designed to withstand torpedoes with up to a 750lb (340kg) warhead.

In 1937, Britain also laid down four 23,000-ton 30-knot Illustrious-class, 740ft-long fast carriers: *Illustrious* (87), *Formidable* (67), *Victorious* (38) and *Indomitable* (92). Commissioned in 1940/1, they were the nearest contemporaries to the US Essex-class carrier, able to carry, after wartime modifications, up to fifty-seven aircraft. These carriers, plus two modified versions, the larger and faster 32.5-knot Implacable-class carriers, *Implacable* (R86) and *Indefatigable* R10), formed Britain's wartime fast-carrier force. The 32,110-ton Implacable-class carriers were 766ft long, could carry about eighty planes but were begun later and would complete in 1944.

Charged with protecting sea lanes between Britain, Gibraltar, Malta, Alexandria and Singapore, and operating in relatively confined waters where attack from land-based enemy aircraft was likely, the new Illustrious-class fast carriers were equipped with armoured flight decks to withstand anticipated heavy bombing. The British carriers could however often rely on friendly land-based air cover to keep enemy bombers away – something that US carriers later in the Pacific War could not.

Unlike the British Illustrious-class fast carriers, US fast carriers were not fitted with armoured decks – and this made them vulnerable and susceptible to damage and consequent fires. During the Second World War, British carriers could withstand hits more easily than US carriers. The drawback however was that the heavy deck armour took space from fuel tanks and aircraft storage areas and reduced the carrier radius and carrier squadron sizes.[7] Each British carrier was fitted with sixteen 4.5in dual purpose (DP) guns along with multiple 40mm and 20mm anti-aircraft batteries.

The British fast carriers played a prominent part in many Second World War battles, including service with the British Pacific Fleet. But even with the new carriers, after two decades of virtual neglect, in the first years of the Second World War, until better naval aircraft were developed, the British carriers only carried antiquated slow Fairey Swordfish biplane torpedo-bombers, poor Blackburn Skua monoplane fighter/dive-bombers and modified land aircraft.

The required role of the British carriers in Europe would be very different to that of the US fast carriers in the wide expanses of the Pacific.

Unlike the US fast carriers, British carriers did not operate as a combined force – their primary mission up to 1944 being to keep British sea lanes open. British fast carriers thus usually operated singly, with a screen of escorts. With a large number of carriers required to combat the U-boat threat, the Royal Navy relied on smaller, slower escort carriers that could be built quickly and cheaply in comparison with fleet carriers.

The Royal Navy based *Force H*, a task force of one fast carrier, one battleship or battlecruiser along with several cruisers and destroyers, at Gibraltar, from where the force could operate speedily as required both in the Atlantic and in the Mediterranean.

On 26 May 1941, Swordfish biplane torpedo-bombers from *Ark Royal* played an important role in sinking the German battleship *Bismarck* in the Atlantic following the Battle of the Denmark Strait on 24 May 1941 – when shells from the new British battleship *Prince of Wales* struck *Bismarck* and forced her to abandon her Atlantic commerce raid. Down by the head and trailing a slick of oil, she turned to head back to St Nazaire in France for repair.

On the return passage, the damaged German battleship was spotted by Catalina flying boats searching from Northern Ireland – and Force H, centred on *Ark Royal*, was sent north from Gibraltar to intercept. An aerial torpedo from one of her Swordfishs subsequently hit *Bismarck* on the port side aft, jamming her rudder and steering gear at 12° to port. The great battleship lost the ability to navigate – and could only initially steer in a large circle. British capital ships closed with her – and eventually sent *Bismarck* to the bottom of the Atlantic.

Although it was the British battleships that delivered the *coup de grâce* with their big guns and torpedoes, the vulnerability of a modern super battleship to an aerial torpedo delivered by an antiquated British biplane torpedo-bomber had been exposed. The Swordfish had a slow top speed of just 139mph and required a long straight approach to ideally a range of 1,000–1,500yd before it could release its torpedo at a height of just 18ft.

But even though the power and striking possibilities of the fast carrier had been championed for a long time, and now demonstrated, on the eve of the USA's entry into the war in December 1941, many people both within and outside the US Navy, and in other navies around the world, doubted the hailed revolutionary change that would be brought to naval warfare by the introduction of the fast carriers. Many non-naval aviators still clung to the traditional invincibility and striking power of the battleship. The naval analyst Bernard Brodie wrote in 1941: 'The carrier . . . is not likely to replace the battleship . . . The carrier can strike over a vast range and at the most swiftly moving targets, but she cannot strike with the accuracy and forcefulness that is characteristic of the large naval gun within the limits of its range'.[8]

When, subsequently, on 7 December 1941, five US battleships were put out of action at Pearl Harbor by aircraft flying from six Japanese fast carriers, this outdated analysis and belief was itself sunk.

(iv) The US Pacific Fleet Moves to Hawaii

Up until May 1940, the US Battle Force had its HQ at Los Angeles Harbor, where its battleships, heavy cruisers and carriers were stationed. Light cruisers, destroyers and submarines were stationed at San Diego.

In early 1940, Japan began to fortify her Marshall Island territories, which lie between Hawaii and the Philippines. This move threatened US communications between Hawaii and the Philippines to such an extent that in June 1940, President Franklin D. Roosevelt ordered the US Pacific Fleet to move its main base from the west coast of California to Pearl Harbor in the Hawaiian Islands. This deployment was intended as a demonstration of US naval power in the Pacific and it was hoped that it would act as a deterrent to Japanese aggression against US, British and Dutch colonial possessions in East Asia. It was a risky move – as it placed the US Pacific Fleet within striking distance of Japan's navy.

The great US naval building programme of the late 1930s and early 1940s was viewed with deep suspicion by Japan, who understood that the US Navy would eventually replace her own Imperial Navy as the most powerful navy in the Pacific region. A powerful US naval presence in the Pacific, with a base in Pearl Harbor, would jeopardise Japan's plans to seize British, US and Dutch colonial possessions in South-East Asia. Japanese strategists felt that they must seize the territories it wanted – before the USA could rebuild its navy.

The Philippines had been ceded to the USA after the Spanish-American War of 1898 and after decades of US rule had been granted Commonwealth status in 1935. Yamamoto, Commander in Chief of the Combined Fleet, feared that if Japan seized the Philippines, the US Fleet would cross the Pacific and attack his left flank, relieving the Philippines and interrupting the IJA's lines of communication to the south. He therefore approved the reorganisation of Japanese carrier forces into the 1st Air Fleet, a consolidated striking force that massed Japan's six largest carriers into one unit.

The book *The Influence of Sea Power upon History, 1660–1783* by US naval historian Alfred Thayer Mahan was published in 1890. It made him world famous and perhaps the most influential US author of the nineteenth century. Mahan emphasised that naval operations were chiefly to be won by decisive battles and blockades, and his thinking on British sea power as being the most important reason for Britain's rise to world power was adopted worldwide. Kaiser Wilhelm II in Germany insisted that all German naval recruits must read the book as part of their training. Mahan's ideas were adopted by France, USA – and Japan.

By 1940, Japan now had the third largest navy in the world, after Great Britain and the USA. As a result of the Washington Naval Treaty of 1922, the numbers of new capital ships were limited in the ratio of 5:5:3 for Britain, USA and Japan. Japan was allowed 60 per cent of the numbers of capital ships that either Britain or the USA could have. Even though Japan had renounced the Second London Naval Treaty years earlier in 1936, she still had only ten battleships to the USA's fifteen.

The Treaty however dealt with secondary smaller vessels, such as cruisers and destroyers, in a different way to 'capital ships', which are the largest or most important ships in a navy, at this time principally battleships, battlecruisers and heavy aircraft carriers. The actual numbers of secondary ships were not limited – instead a 10,000-ton maximum displacement and a maximum of 8in-calibre guns were imposed. Utilising this to her advantage, by 1940, although Japan had fewer capital ships, she had a greater number of carriers, cruisers and destroyers. The IJN bristled with well-designed and well-armed modern ships – and well-drilled and exercised crews.

Between 1921 and 1941, the combat tonnage of the IJN had doubled whilst that of the British and US navies had only increased modestly.[9] The number of carriers and battleships had increased after Japan withdrew in 1936 – twenty new vessels were constructed in 1937 with more in succeeding years. The last additions were the super battleships *Yamato*, launched on 8 August 1940 for fitting out (and commissioned on 16 December 1941), and *Musashi*, launched on 29 March 1940 for fitting out (and commissioned on 5 August 1942). Each displaced 71,659 tons (F) and carried massive 18.1in main guns, the largest ever installed on a battleship.

By 1941, with US and British fleets split between the Atlantic and the Pacific, Japan's fleet was more powerful than the combined US and British fleet units present in the Pacific.[10] In the Pacific theatre, Japan had 10 battleships to the USA's 9, 7 aircraft carriers to 3 US carriers, 18 heavy cruisers to 12 US heavy cruisers, 17 light cruisers to 9 US light cruisers, 100 destroyers to 67 US destroyers and 68 submarines to 27 US submarines. Japan's naval power was superior in every category.[11]

Japan knew that she would never have the industrial capacity to create a navy that was equal in size to the entire US Navy – but her strategists felt they that if Japan could achieve just 70 per cent of US strength, they should be victorious in the Pacific. This belief was based on two pillars of thought that became fundamental to Japanese naval construction, tactical development and training between the wars:

1. Japan should have the weapons and tactics to inflict severe attrition on the US Pacific Fleet and bring the two sides to an approximate parity in strength before the *decisive battle*.
2. Once a rough parity had been achieved, Japanese naval units, with superior speed, and capable of hitting at ranges beyond the US ranges, would triumph.

Therefore, as a result of the previous ratio of capital ships imposed by the Washington Naval Treaty, Japanese strategic planning for a war with the USA had, for the last two decades, since the Treaty, been based on the concept that Japanese light surface forces, such as her destroyers and cruisers, along with submarines and land-based air units would sink or disable as many US naval units as possible as the US Fleet crossed the Pacific to relieve the Philippines. Japan had gone to great lengths to develop new torpedoes that could be launched from submarines, ships and torpedo-bombers that were a quantum leap ahead in technology from the conventional Allied equivalents. Once the US Fleet had crossed the Pacific and been suitably degraded, the Combined Fleet would then seek out Mahan's *decisive battle*.

Japan developed the Type 91 aerial torpedo in the early 1930s – which was designed to be launched from Japanese aircraft and was specially adapted for attacks on ships in shallow harbours, such as Pearl Harbor. It used a softwood breakaway nose cone and wooden aerodynamic stabilisers attached to the tail fins, which made sure the torpedo was in the correct attitude before entry into the water, when they were shed. A clever advanced angular acceleration control system controlled rolling movements. The Type 91 could be released by an aircraft at a cruising speed of 180 knots, and also in a power glide torpedo-bombing run at the maximum speed of the Nakajima B5N Kate torpedo-bomber of 204 knots. Compare this with the British Swordfish torpedo-bombers of the time, which made their attack runs at just 80 knots. Whereas the early versions of the Type 91 torpedo carried a 213.5kg (470lb) warhead, later versions carried by larger twin-engine bombers had a 526kg (1,169lb) warhead.

In addition to the Type 91 aerial torpedo, the Japanese developed the Type 93 *Long Lance* oxygen torpedo, which was designed to be ship-launched from light Japanese naval units such as destroyers and cruisers. The Type 93 had a long effective firing range of 22,000m (13.5 miles approx.) at a speed of 48–50 knots and carried a 490kg (1,080lb) warhead. The maximum firing range was approximately 25 miles at 38 knots. Its long-range, high-speed and heavy warhead marked it as a quantum leap forward in torpedo development – and it was far ahead of any Allied torpedo of the time. The US Navy's standard surface-launched torpedo of the Second World War, the Mark 15, had a maximum range of just 7.4 nautical miles at 26 knots or just 3 nautical miles at 45 knots and it carried a smaller 827lb warhead. The first Type 93 torpedoes were fitted in two triple-deck-mounted swivel launchers aboard the IJN Mutsuki-1st class destroyers in 1935/6.

The Type 95 submarine-launched torpedo, developed in tandem with the Type 93, was the fastest torpedo in common use by any navy at the time – it had a range of 9,000m (5.5 miles approx.) at 50 knots and 12,000m (7.5 miles approx.) at 45 knots, about three times the range of the US Type 14 at the same speed. The first versions had a 405kg (893lb) warhead but this was increased in subsequent versions to 550kg (1,210lb).

US torpedo defence systems in the South Dakota and Iowa-class battleships were designed to absorb torpedo hits with warheads up to 317kg (700lb) of TNT, the Navy's guesstimate of Japanese torpedoes. British anti-torpedo side protection systems on capital ships were designed to withstand torpedoes with a warhead of up to 340kg (750lb).[12] The new Japanese torpedoes had the potential to penetrate Allied side protection systems and sink or cripple heavy Allied units such as battleships.

Japan formed the 1st Air Fleet as a major component of the Combined Fleet on 10 April 1941. When the new aircraft carrier *Zuikaku* was commissioned on 25 September 1941, the 1st Air Fleet included six fleet carriers that along with light carriers could deploy 474 aircraft. *Kidō Butai*, the Mobile Force, was the Combined Fleet's tactical designation for its combined carrier battle group of Japan's six large fleet carriers – the concentration of the fleet carriers *Akagi*, *Kaga*, *Sōryū*, *Hiryū*, *Shōkaku* and *Zuikaku* into a single tactical formation was something that no Western power had yet done. This revolutionary move laid the basis for the true carrier task force, a battle group that could range over vast distances and bring overwhelming air power to bear.

The 1st Air Fleet was subdivided into five *kōkū sentai*, or carrier divisions, with each *kōkū sentai* of the 1st Air Fleet usually having a pair of aircraft carriers. Each individual *kōkū sentai* was a tactical unit that could be deployed separately or combined with other *kōkū sentai* as required. The larger fleet carriers carried some eighty planes of three types: fighters, level/torpedo-bombers and dive-bombers. The smaller carriers usually carried only two types of aircraft, fighters and torpedo-bombers.

Kidō Butai was created for the attack on Pearl Harbor under Vice-Admiral Chuichi Nagumo and carried some 414 planes with 2 battleships, 3 cruisers, 9 destroyers, 23 submarines and 4 midget submarines with 8 replenishment oilers.

Emboldened with new weapons, new carriers and new aircraft, led by Tōjō and the Army, Japan made the fateful decision to go to war. Japan's senior seagoing admiral, Isoroku Yamamoto, Commander-in-Chief of the Combined Fleet, unlike the confident army and naval planners, had few illusions about the way a war against the USA would go and in private queried whether the politicians had confidence as to the final outcome and would be prepared to make the necessary sacrifices. But once Japan had made the fateful decision to invade the resource-rich lands of South-East Asia, Yamamoto threw out the established old inter-war strategy that the IJN had been planning and training for. Instead of first seizing the Philippines, and then waiting for a US naval advance across the Pacific and attempting to degrade the fleet before engaging in the decisive battle, Yamamoto proposed to first reduce US naval forces with a pre-emptive strike on the US Fleet.[13] The recent move of the US Pacific Fleet base from the West Coast of the USA to Pearl Harbor in Hawaii in May 1940 had suddenly made such a pre-emptive strike a real possibility.

Meantime, President Franklin D. Roosevelt had ordered a military build-up in the Philippines, hoping that the fleet move to Pearl Harbor and the fortification of the Philippines would discourage Japanese aggression. On 14 February 1941, the president issued an Executive Order to create naval defence areas in Central Pacific territories. The US began construction of a military base on Wake Island, on which an airfield had already been constructed in 1935.

Midway Island lies halfway between Japan and the USA – and there had been a navy radio station there since 1903. Lying between Hawaii and Wake Island, Midway was an important seaplane stop in the 1930s for Pan American Airways Clipper flying boats island hopping between San Francisco and China. As war loomed in 1940, Midway became militarily important, deemed second to Pearl Harbor in significance for the protection of the West Coast of the USA. A navy presence began building up with three airstrips in a triangular pattern, batteries of gun

Admiral Isoroku Yamamoto, Commander in Chief, IJN Combined Fleet.

emplacements and a seaplane base. As war neared, supplemental dive-bombers were sent.

Japanese high command believed that any attack on British South-East Asia territories such as Singapore, Malaya or Hong Kong would bring the USA into the war. Thus, the idea of a devastating pre-emptive strike on the US Fleet seemed the only way to prevent US interference with Japan's militaristic expansionist goals. The Japanese emperor Hirohito adopted Yamamoto's view.

With the shallow water Type 91 aerial torpedo, it was felt that if an attack on the US naval base at Pearl Harbor could successfully knock out the battleships and carriers of the US battle fleet, the (by now) eleven IJN battleships, carriers, cruisers, destroyers and submarines should be more than a match for any remaining Allied naval forces in the Pacific. The Japanese battleships and aircraft carriers could then be relied upon to shield the Army's invasion convoys as they sailed for South-East Asia. Any such pre-emptive strike would be followed by the Combined Fleet seeking out Mahan's *decisive battle* with the remainder of the US Fleet in the northern Philippine Sea at an opportune time – where traditional battle lines of battleships would face off.

Yamamoto first discussed the idea of such a pre-emptive strike on Pearl Harbor as soon as the main elements of the US Fleet moved there in May 1940, directing that a feasibility study of such an attack should be prepared under the greatest secrecy. By December 1940, he had decided to implement the Pearl Harbor operation, convinced that war with the USA was inevitable once Japan began any hostilities – and that a traditional victory against the might of the USA was not possible. He felt he had to shatter US morale and force a negotiated peace.

Yamamoto had a background in naval aviation and the recent success of British carrier launched biplanes against the Italian Fleet at Taranto on 11 November 1940 had not gone unnoticed by him. Twenty-one antiquated Swordfish torpedo-bombers from the carrier *Illustrious* attacked six of Italy's *Regia Marina* battleships in the harbour at Taranto and torpedoed three of them, putting all three out of action, one permanently, and forcing the Italian Fleet to abandon Taranto as a base.

The success of this attack at Taranto was yet another herald of the end of the era of the battleship – and the ascendency of naval aviation over big guns. The British force commander, Admiral Andrew Cunningham, stated: 'Taranto, and the night of 11–12 November 1940, should be remembered for ever as having shown once and for all that in the Fleet Air Arm the Navy has its most devastating weapon.'

Yamamoto had had two tours of duty in the USA before the war and had come to appreciate the USA's enormous industrial strength. But he felt that successive US governments had starved the defence forces of adequate funding and that the USA had neglected to maintain its fleet in top fighting condition. He realised that it would take the USA at least a year to gather its full military strength after two decades of neglect of its armed forces. This understanding largely determined his strategic planning and influenced his two major aims: 1. the destruction of the US Pacific Fleet at Pearl Harbor; and 2. the creation of 2,400 miles of unbroken ocean between the location of the USA's likely naval strength in 1943 on the West Coast of the USA and Japan's eastern defensive perimeter anchored in Hawaii. Yamamoto however was under no illusions as to the final outcome: he wrote to Prime Minister Konoye before the launch of the Pearl Harbor raid: 'In the first six to twelve months of a war with the United States and Great Britain, I will run wild and win victory upon victory. But then, if the war continues after that, I have no expectation of success.'

Yamamoto knew Japan only had a limited chance of winning a prolonged war with the USA, but with the move of the US Fleet forward to Hawaii, Japan had the opportunity to destroy the main US offensive weapon, its Pacific Fleet, in one blow. This might buy enough time for Japan to forge a viable Pacific Empire. Despite his forebodings, Operation AI, the *Kidō Butai* six-carrier surprise attack on Pearl Harbor to destroy the US Pacific Fleet, had become a reality.

Chapter 4

Let Loose the Dogs of War

Japan had long coveted South-East Asia, viewing it as the *Southern Resource Area* – if it was added to the planned *Greater East Asia Co-Prosperity Sphere*, Japanese control would encompass the eastern regions of China, Vietnam, Cambodia, Laos, the resource-rich Philippines (then a US protectorate), Malaya (under British administration), Singapore and the Dutch East Indies (present-day Indonesia). Japan sought to be self-sufficient in resources of oil, petroleum, iron, rubber, nickel, tin, bauxite, rice and much more.

France had controlled modern day Vietnam, Cambodia, Laos and parts of Thailand, as French Indochina, since the latter part of the nineteenth century – but with the fall of France to Nazi Germany earlier in 1940, the French hold on Indochina was now weak. With Great Britain fighting against Nazi Germany in Europe, her ability to defend her colonial possessions such as Singapore and Hong Kong was weakened. Dutch troops in Holland surrendered to German forces on 14 May 1940 – Holland would not be able to put up much of a fight to protect her Asian territories such as the Netherlands East Indies which had abundant resources such as rubber and oil. The developments in Europe were of great interest to Japan.

Japan disliked US support for China, with whom it had been at war since 1937 – and was anxious to block US aid from reaching China as well as asserting her interest in direct dominance of the region. On 19 June 1940, just a month after the Fall of France to Germany, Japan (an ally of Germany since 1935) demanded the closure of all supply routes through French Indochina to China and the admission of a forty-man Japanese inspection team. Although initially reluctant to agree, when French intelligence reported that the Japanese army and navy were moving into threatening positions, and unwilling and unprepared to defend the colony, the French governor complied the next day, 20 June.

On 22 June, the Japanese issued a second ultimatum – demanding naval basing rights at the small south China port of Guangzhouwan, which harboured shipping and coal-mining industries and was leased by France as part of Indochina. Japan also demanded the total closure of the Chinese border by 7 July 1940.

On 3 July, a third demand was issued – the granting of air bases and the right to transit combat troops through Indochina. These demands were referred to the government in France and negotiations began.

On 6 September, an infantry battalion of the 22nd Army based in Nanning and part of the Japanese Southern China Area Army violated the Indochinese border near the French fort at Đồng Đăng. Echoing the Mukden Incident of 1931, the 22nd Army officers were trying to force their superiors to adopt a more aggressive policy. On 18 September, Japan sent an ultimatum to the French governor of Indochina warning that Japanese troops would enter Indochina, regardless of any French agreement on 22 September. Just 7½ hours before the ultimatum expired at 2200 hours, the two sides signed an agreement authorising the stationing of 6,000 Japanese troops in Tonkin, an area of French Indochina in modern day northern Vietnam, that lay on the southern border of China. The use of four airfields in Tonkin was also granted, along with the right to transit 25,000 troops through Tonkin to the southern Chinese province of Yunnan and the right to transit one division of the 22nd Army through Tonkin via Haiphong for use elsewhere in China.

The agreement was communicated to all relevant commands an hour before the ultimatum was set to expire, the French believing that the first troops would subsequently arrive by ship. The 22nd Army however did not wait for the accord to come into effect and immediately at 2200 hours, when the ultimatum expired, columns of the 5th (Infantry) Division crossed the border at Đồng Đăng, triggering an intense exchange of fire with French border troops. The French position at Lạng Son was surrounded by Japanese armour and forced to surrender on 25 September.

On 24 September, Japanese aircraft flying from aircraft carriers in the Gulf of Tonkin attacked French positions on the coast. On 26 September, Japanese forces came ashore at Dong Tac, south of Haiphong, and moved to the port. A second landing put tanks ashore and Japanese carrier aircraft bombed Haiphong itself. By the afternoon, Japan had 4,500 troops ashore and a dozen tanks outside Haiphong. Japan also seized Gia Lam Airbase outside Hanoi, the rail marshalling yard on the Yunnan border at Lao Cai, and Phu Lang Thuong on the railway from Hanoi to Lạng Sơn. There were 900 troops stationed in the port of Haiphong and 600 in Hanoi.

The Vichy government subsequently agreed that a further 40,000 Japanese troops could be stationed in southern French Indochina. Japan however did not immediately move troops there – believing that such a move would inflame relations with the USA and Great Britain, whose colonies of Malaya, Singapore and Borneo lay to the south, and Burma to the west.

Japan's move into Vichy-controlled Indochina, coupled with its war with China, its alliance with Germany and Italy, and an ominous and obvious increasing militarism, led the USA to begin a series of legislative measures and sanctions intended to restrain Japan economically. In the late 1930s Japan depended on the USA for one-third of its general imports from cotton to oil – and more than 70 per cent of its scrap iron, which was used to make munitions and ships. Japan relied on the USA for almost 80 per cent of its fuel oil and more than 90 per cent of its copper – used to make detonators and shell casings.

As tensions heightened between Japan and the USA and its allies, moves began to try and stop the Japanese war machine. The US government passed the Export Control Act on 26 July 1940, which authorised the licensing or prohibition of the export of essential defence materials including iron, steel, oil, aircraft, parts, chemicals, minerals and munitions. Beefing this up, on 16 October 1940, in a move clearly aimed at Japan, a US embargo was placed on all exports of aircraft, parts, machine tools, scrap iron and steel to destinations other than Britain and the nations of the western hemisphere: the Panama Canal was closed to Japanese shipping. The USA did not however cut off Japan's oil at this stage – knowing that an oil embargo would likely lead to war and an oil-starved Japan moving to seize the oil fields of the Netherlands East Indies. These export controls caused Japan to eye more closely the resource-rich French, British, Dutch and US possessions – and finally free herself from her dependency on the West.

On 13 April 1941, Japan signed a non-aggression Neutrality Pact with the Soviet Union. With the Russian threat in the north removed, she could now shift her focus south. The same month, under German and Japanese pressure, the Vichy government in France allowed Japan the use of air and naval bases in south Indochina. Japan was now directly threatening British interests in Malaya, Burma, North Borneo and Brunei.

On 22 June 1941, Germany invaded the Soviet Union and with Russia (with whom, despite the recently signed Neutrality Pact, Japan had a long history of conflict) now concentrated on fighting off the Nazis, Japan was free to consider a more aggressive policy in South-East Asia.

At the Imperial Conference in Tokyo on 2 July 1941, Japan determined to 'construct the *Greater East Asia Co-prosperity Sphere* regardless of the changes in the world situation'. She resolved to continue the war in China, to await developments with Russia and to prepare for an expansion into South-East Asia.

On 14 July 1941, the French authorities in Indochina were given a set of Japanese demands. With little room to manoeuvre, the demands were accepted on 23 July and on 24 July 1941, the first of some 140,000 Japanese troops destined for the invasion of the Dutch East Indies moved into southern French Indochina. French troops and the civilian administration were allowed to remain – under Japanese supervision. Japanese warships were stationed at coastal ports and Air Force units were stationed at key airfields around Saigon.

Once the Japanese had established themselves in southern Indochina, they were closer than ever to Singapore, the Philippines and the Dutch East Indies. Without firing a shot, the Japanese had secured bases only 450 miles from Malaya and 700 miles (less than the length of Britain) from Singapore. These British possessions were now well within range of Japanese bombers and Japan soon had over 400 land-based aircraft stationed in Indochina and 280 carrier-based aircraft available in addition.

Responding to the Japanese occupation, the US froze or seized all Japanese assets on 26 July 1941 – only a special licence from the US government could release Japanese assets to pay for US exports, including, most critically, oil. By early August the previous year's export controls had thus been increased to a full embargo – preventing the export to Japan of the oil and other materials that had been fuelling the Japanese war machine for years. Japan lost 93 per cent of its oil supply. Fearing such a move, Japan had already stockpiled 54 million barrels of oil – but that was estimated to last just 18 months.

Commercial relations between the USA and Japan were now at an end. Britain and Holland followed the US lead by imposing their own trade embargoes on Japan from their colonies in South-East Asia – cutting off the South-East Asian sources of raw materials vital to Japan. Japan was now isolated from the West and desperately in need of raw materials. Japan had either to give up its war in China or secure its own supplies.

The oil embargo was particularly damaging to Japan – oil was Japan's most crucial import. From the Army's perspective, a secure fuel supply was essential for its warplanes, tanks and trucks and the Navy also needed vast amounts of oil for its warships and planes. The complete oil embargo had effectively reduced Japan's options to either seizing South-East Asia before her own eighteen-month stockpile was depleted – or giving in to the US demand that, before it would supply Japan with oil, she must withdraw her forces from the Asian mainland of China, Korea and Manchuria.

Japan had essentially boxed herself into a corner – and her leaders determined that she must gain control of the badly needed supplies of oil, coal, iron, bauxite, tin and rubber in the colonies and territories of South-East Asia. She had to free herself from her dependency on Western imports – and the pressure the Western powers were applying with their economic sanctions. The solution was to send the Navy south and seize the oil fields in the Netherlands East Indies and seize the Philippines and British possessions.

Japan had been building closer relations with Germany throughout the 1930s. With Germany at the peak of its power, and faced with crippling 1940 export controls by the USA and Britain, and with France, Britain and Holland all weakened by the war in Europe, the moment seemed ideal for Japan to form an alliance with Germany. Japan entered the Axis Pact with Germany and Italy on 27 September 1940, in which the three nations agreed to aid each other if one of their number was attacked by a power not involved in a current conflict. Membership of the Axis Pact for Japan ensured that Germany recognised that East Asia was a Japanese sphere of influence. Germany and Italy intended to establish a New Order in Europe – Japan would do likewise in Greater East Asia.

Germany, for her part, hoped that Japan would restrain the USA, whilst she dealt a final knockout blow to Britain. The Axis Pact enabled Japan's leaders to consider the possibility of simultaneous war with the USA and Britain more seriously. Japan's entry into the Axis Pact led the USA and Britain to increasingly view Germany and Japan as a joint threat.

At the Imperial Japanese Conference of 6 September 1941, in the presence of the emperor, it was decided to complete war preparations by the end of October. In the meantime, Japan would continue negotiations with the USA in an attempt to end the trade embargo. If Japan did nothing, the slow strangulation of the trade embargoes would cause the country to collapse in a few years for lack of raw materials. If the embargoes could not be lifted, Japan would go to war – her leaders believing she had a 70–80 per cent chance of initial victory.

During the closing months of 1941, the USA and Japan entered into fruitless negotiations to find an agreement that could end the trade embargo. But on 14 October, Army Minister General Hideki Tōjō, an advocate of war with the USA, and a name that would become infamous during the war to come, told the Japanese Cabinet that widespread troop withdrawals in China were not acceptable to the military. On 16 October the Cabinet resigned, unwilling to launch another war.

On 18 October, soon after the government resigned, Army Minister General Tōjō became Prime Minister of Japan – he would also continue as War Minister. Essentially the Army had become dictator to Japan – and Tōjō, the Army representative, was now prime minister.

Both the IJA and IJN wanted war for their own reasons. The IJN was concerned about the diminishing oil reserves – and the IJA believed that US aid to China would increase and undermine its position there. Japan would pursue the diplomatic negotiations to end the embargo – but only until midnight on 30 November.

At a Japanese Imperial Conference on 1 December 1941, with no end to the embargo agreed, General Tōjō advised that war was necessary to preserve the Japanese Empire – and war was finally sanctioned against the 'United States, England and Holland'.[1] Orders were sent out to military commanders that hostilities would commence on 8 December (7 December east of the International Date Line).

By striking powerfully and expanding rapidly, Japan's war planners hoped to quickly build an empire so large that the Western powers would not be able to countenance the cost of retaking it. She also hoped that in Europe her Axis partners, Germany and Italy, would prevail over the Soviets and Britain and that thereafter Japan might negotiate peace with an isolated USA. Anti-war rhetoric and political divisions very apparent in the USA encouraged the Japanese in this view. The Japanese plan however depended to a large degree upon Germany winning in Europe. It was a gamble, and they didn't hold all the cards.

Japanese military planners had formulated five separate simultaneous operations to take place at the outbreak of war on 7 December 1941 (8 December in Asia/West Pacific time zones), against key strategic targets vital to her campaign:

1. Six fast Japanese carriers under the command of Admiral Nagumo would sail eastwards to strike Pearl Harbor, refuelling en route from oilers.
2. Strikes would launch against the US Clark and Iba airfields in the Philippines, a precursor to a full amphibious invasion of the Philippines.

3. The strategically important islands of Guam (at the south of the Mariana chain of islands) and Wake, 1,501 miles east of Guam in Micronesia, would be seized along with Tarawa and Makin in the Gilbert Islands. Midway atoll, between Hawaii and Japan, and second in importance to Pearl Harbor for the protection of the US West Coast, would be attacked. These operations would allow the establishment of airfields and a defensive perimeter through the Marshalls and Gilberts to New Guinea and the Solomons.
4. Hong Kong would be assaulted along with attacks on British and US warships at Shanghai. Operations against British positions in Burma and Borneo would soon begin.
5. Landings in Siam (Thailand) and Malaya would be followed by a thrust toward the great British naval base of Singapore. From Singapore, the Combined Fleet could operate to meet any threat to the perimeter – allied to the Japanese bases already established at Rabaul in the Bismarck archipelago or Truk in the eastern Carolines.

The plan was breathtaking in its audacity.

In advance of the deadline for operations to commence, Japanese troop transports left ports in modern day Vietnam bound for selected Thai and northern Malayan invasion beaches. There were 26,640 soldiers crammed into the 19 troop transports of the first wave of ships deployed from Hainan Island, off China – destined for the invasion of Malaya. These troop transports would sail close to the coast of Indochina to avoid detection for their four-day journey south towards Singora. The Japanese were relying on the bad weather of the breaking monsoon to shield the convoys from British reconnaissance aircraft. They knew that if the vulnerable heavily packed troop transports were spotted and intercepted, they would be sitting ducks and the invasion would be in trouble from the start.

Other Japanese naval units moved out across the Pacific in total secrecy towards the other targets: Pearl Harbor, the US airfields at Luzon in the Philippines, Guam, Wake and the Gilbert Islands, and British Hong Kong.

(i) 7 December 1941 – Japan's Surprise Attack on Pearl Harbor

Early on Sunday, 7 December 1941, without (for complicated and controversial reasons) formally declaring war, Japan initiated her Pacific offensive with the surprise attack on Pearl Harbor, intended to destroy the ability of the US Pacific Fleet to impede her operations.

The six Japanese carriers of the *Kidō Butai* Striking Force, *Akagi*, *Kaga*, *Sōryū*, *Hiryū*, *Shōkaku* and *Zuikaku*, departed Hittokapu Bay on Kasatka (now Iterup) in the Kuril Islands, north of Japan on 26 November 1941. The Striking Force carried a total of some 360 strike aircraft for 2 waves of the planned attack – and a further 48 aircraft for Combat Air Patrol (CAP) to protect the Striking Force itself. The first wave of 183 planes would carry most of the weapons designed to attack capital ships – such as the Type 91 aerial torpedo. First-wave dive-bombers were to attack ground targets whilst fighters were to strafe and destroy as many parked aircraft as possible to ensure they could not get airborne to attack the slower bombers.

The six carriers of the *Kidō Butai* successfully crossed the Pacific and arrived undetected at their holding positions north of Hawaii where 183 Japanese aircraft launched for the first wave of the now infamous raid. Just after 0700 (Hawaiian time), a US radar operator in Hawaii spotted a large flight of aircraft to the north on his screen. Alerting his superior, he was told that the planes were six scheduled B-17 Flying Fortress bombers en route from California. There was no coordinated system of US aerial reconnaissance in place at this time.

Just before 0800, the first wave of 183 torpedo-bombers, dive-bombers and fighters swept across Pearl Harbor – taking everyone on the ground by complete surprise. Of the Nakajima B5N Kate bombers, 49 were armed with 1,760lb armour piercing bombs, whilst 40 others were armed with Type 91 aerial torpedoes. There were 51 Aichi D3A Val dive-bombers armed with 550lb general-purpose bombs, whilst 43 Mitsubishi A6M Zero fighters would provide air control and strafing and destroy as many parked-up US aircraft on the ground as possible to maintain air superiority. As Japanese aircraft headed for the US military airfields, hundreds of largely unprotected US planes were neatly lined up in rows.

The largest Japanese air group attacked US Pacific Fleet warships lined up in pairs in Battleship Row. The battleship *Arizona* (BB-39) exploded from a bomb hit at the forward magazine, killing 1,177 officers and men. There were 429 men trapped inside the battleship *Oklahoma* (BB-37) as it capsized after flooding caused by aerial torpedo strikes. The battleship *West Virginia* (BB-48) was engulfed in flames whilst the battleship *California* (BB-44) was hit by a pair of torpedoes and a bomb. She flooded slowly and settled on the bottom in shallow water. The other four battleships in the port were all damaged, with the crippled *Nevada* (BB-36) being successfully beached.

A second wave of 170 Japanese level bombers, dive-bombers and fighter aircraft swept over Pearl Harbor at 0845, the B5N Kate torpedo-bombers and D3A Val dive-bombers targeting warships and fighter and bomber airfields across Hawaii with 550lb and 132lb GP bombs, whilst 36 A6M Zeros provided air defence and carried out strafing.[2]

By the time the assault was over, 8 battleships, 3 light cruisers, 3 destroyers and a training ship and other smaller vessels had been sunk or damaged, a total of some 21 naval units. Of the US aircraft, 188 been destroyed and 159 damaged. US personnel losses totalled 2,403 killed and 1,143 wounded.

Although an apparently stunning success for Japan that resonated around the world, strategically the attack was less significant. The vast fuel storage facilities for the Pacific Fleet had surprisingly not been damaged and none of the US carriers deployed in the Pacific had been present or damaged. The US carriers had escaped destruction and would soon play a pivotal role in halting Japanese expansion at the Battle of the Coral Sea and at Midway.

Instead of launching a third wave to destroy the US fuel dumps and vital shore facilities for torpedo storage, repair, maintenance and dry dock facilities, which would have rendered the whole base at Hawaii useless, Admiral Nagumo withdrew his fleet. Hawaii would remain a powerful naval base; a submarine and intelligence base that was later instrumental in Japan's defeat. Rather than crippling US naval power in the Pacific for long enough to allow Japan to secure her position, the raid had left Hawaii – and US naval power in the Pacific – to fight another day. Japan declared war on the USA later in the day and a few days later, on 11 December, Germany and Italy also both declared war on the USA.

All eight US battleships present had been damaged, with four sunk. All but the *Arizona* were later raised, although the *Oklahoma* was so badly damaged that it was never fully repaired and returned to service. The other six battleships would be repaired, modernised and returned to the war. Their big guns would wreak a terrible revenge as they carried out pre-invasion bombardments of shore positions across the Pacific, tangled with Japanese warships at Leyte and provided task-force AA cover, their armour supplying crucial protection during the latter stages of the war as attacks by kamikazes intensified.

Meanwhile, again without declaring war on Britain, Japanese forces gathered for an assault on Hong Kong, which only had a garrison of six British, Indian and Canadian battalions, artillery and some volunteer units. As the siege of Hong Kong Island began, the small garrison was not expected to hold out long.

USS *Arizona* (BB-39) sunk at her moorings at Pearl Harbor on 10 December 1941. (NH 84004 courtesy of the U.S. Naval History & Heritage Command)

In the Philippines, 10 hours after the Pearl Harbor raid, despite having received intelligence about the attack on Pearl, the US Army Air Force was still caught by surprise as Japanese aircraft swooped in from the sea to find US bombers and fighters parked wing to wing in neat rows at their air bases; many were destroyed on the ground in the opening attacks. The initial bombardment was followed by troop landings at several points along the Philippine coastline. Lacking air cover, the US Asiatic Fleet in the Philippines withdrew to Java on 12 December.

Off southern Thailand, at about 0220 on 8 December, the main Japanese invasion troop convoy anchored off Singora, just north of the Malaya–Thailand border. Japanese assault troops went ashore by landing craft and the light resistance encountered ended after just a few hours. The Japanese advance down the Malayan peninsula was dramatic and speedy and the British fortress of Singapore would fall on 14 February 1942.

The surprise Japanese six-carrier raid on Pearl Harbor on 7 December 1941 began the Pacific theatre of the Second World War as a fast-carrier war. If the British carrier attack at Taranto on the night of 11/12 November 1940, which crippled 3 Italian battleships, had failed to convince US naval leaders of the sea change in naval warfare, from the big guns of capital ships to naval aircraft from carriers, the 360-plane Japanese attack at Pearl Harbor left no doubt. All eight US battleships had been damaged by air attack – with four sunk. Most of the US battle line had been eliminated – and the few surviving older battleships retreated to safer bases in California whilst the carriers and submarines were left to hold the line in the Pacific. The role of the US carriers for the time being would now be to defend Allied bases and lines of communication and to escort convoys to forward bases.

The Pacific War would be the greatest naval war in history with mastery of the vast expanses of the Pacific the prize – but it was a time of great change in naval warfare. On 10 December 1941, just three days after the Pearl raid, the end of the era of the battleship, heralded by the battleship sinkings at Taranto and Pearl, was brutally concluded with the sinking, in one action, of the brand new British battleship *Prince of Wales* and the battlecruiser *Repulse* with great loss of life, almost 200 miles north of Singapore in a massed attack by eighty-five Japanese long-range Mitsubishi G3M Nell and Mitsubishi G4M Betty bombers, some carrying aerial torpedoes, others 1,100lb bombs. This was the first time a modern battleship had been sunk in action in open water by air attack.

The Pacific War would be a very different naval contest from the decisive battles of the past – it would be an air war at sea. No longer was the primary weapon the big-gun hitting power of the battleship – it would be aircraft, brought to the battle by the fast carriers.

Reeling from the loss of her battle line, all US naval operations during the period immediately following Pearl were on an emergency basis – doing only what was necessary to avoid defeat. The carriers *Ranger* and *Wasp* remained in the Atlantic – whilst all other carriers, *Lexington, Saratoga, Yorktown, Enterprise* and *Hornet,* would be based at Hawaii. The carriers operated separately in task formations – the fear of having too many carriers exposed at any one time pervaded US command.

To make the US position even worse, there would be early losses that quickly reduced the number of available US carriers. *Saratoga* was torpedoed by the Japanese submarine *I-6* on 11 January 1942 – some 420 nautical miles south west of Pearl Harbor. The explosion killed six of her crew, flooded three of her boiler rooms and reduced her speed to 16 knots. After temporary repairs at Pearl, she was withdrawn to Bremerton Navy Yard in Puget Sound, Washington on the Pacific North-West Coast of the USA.

Lexington would be sunk at the Battle of the Coral Sea in May 1942 in the first of the new style of actions, a battle fought entirely between aircraft carriers, in which no ship sighted the enemy. *Yorktown* would be sunk at the Battle of Midway the following month, in June 1942.

(ii) Japan's Second Offensive

Central to the *Greater East Asia Co-Prosperity Sphere* was the extension of Japanese power and the acquisition of an empire similar to those of the European powers.

The first strikes of the Japanese offensive on 7 December 1941 and the days that followed had been stunningly successful – and yet had cost the Japanese only relatively light casualties. The apparent weakness of US and British military power had in Japanese eyes been demonstrated. Japan had achieved its initial strategic goals – and as a result, began planning for a second expansion, commencing in January 1942.

Initially, Japan would seize Tulagi, in the Solomon Islands, which had a fine natural harbour, and Port Moresby, on the southern tip of Papua New Guinea. Success in these operations would give Japan control of the seas and once airfields were dotted throughout the area, they would have mastery of the air above the vital Coral Sea – which lies between north-east Australia and the bounding island groups of New Caledonia and Vanuatu to the east, and the Solomon Islands and Papua New Guinea to the north. Gaining control of these strategically important bases would prevent an Allied build-up of forces in Australia and would secure Japan's southern flank. It would also allow Japanese aircraft to disrupt Allied shipping between Australia and the USA. Japan could even threaten an invasion of Australia, albeit that unknown to the Allies the IJA was firmly against such an idea. They were already heavily committed in the long-running and bitter war against China and also had large numbers of troops stationed to the north to prevent an attack by their old enemy, Russia. Stretched so far, they could not entertain the thought of opening another front on a massive continent like Australia.

If those assaults on Tulagi and Port Moresby were successful, then in a second phase to this operation the Combined Fleet would cross the Pacific to annihilate the remains of the US Pacific Fleet at Pearl Harbor – and capture Midway Island and the western Aleutian Islands. A ribbon defence anchored at Attu, Midway, Wake, the Marshall Islands and the Gilbert Islands would be set up – followed by the invasion of New Caledonia, Fiji and Samoa to isolate Australia.

Japanese military commanders felt that with the US Fleet crippled at Pearl Harbor, these new Japanese conquests could be made impregnable. From Midway, Japanese air power could threaten Pearl Harbor and the West Coast cities of the USA. It was hoped that, tiring of a futile war in the Pacific, and war against Germany and Italy to the east, the USA would negotiate a peace that would leave Japan as masters of the Pacific.

But Japanese commanders failed to understand that their plans to carve out a Pacific empire depended on having an adequate sea supply system to support the distant perimeter – and on having the naval and air power required to protect long lines of communication and shipping supply. Japan's merchant tonnage was in fact insufficient and too inefficiently organised to meet these sea supply requirements. She did not have the industrial capacity or manpower necessary to build the large numbers of additional merchant ships that would be required to service and supply the distant perimeter. It was a fatal flaw – the obsessive aggressive focus on winning Mahan's *decisive battle* had blinded Japan to the need to supply her distant holdings and to protect her sea routes. This failing would cost her the war.

Chapter 5

1942 – The US Navy Goes to War – The Coral Sea and Midway

(i) Command Appointments

The Pearl Harbor raid and the USA's entry into the Second World War raised the issue of who should command the theatres to which fast carriers were assigned, the fleets in which the carriers operated and the individual task forces they comprised. Denuded of battleships, and reliant on carriers, there would be a preference for admirals who understood naval aviation and fast-carrier operations – but in 1941, very few carrier admirals existed.

The initial choices for command assignments were made by President Roosevelt, Admiral Harold Rainsford Stark, Chief of Naval Operations (CNO) and William Franklin 'Frank' Knox, the Secretary of the Navy.

Admiral Ernest J. King, Commander-in-Chief of the Atlantic Fleet, was appointed Commander-in-Chief, US Fleet (COMINCH) on 30 December 1941. Rear Admiral Chester W. Nimitz was appointed Commander-in-Chief US Pacific Fleet (CINCPACFLT) and promoted to full admiral on 31 December 1941. He immediately left Washington for Pearl Harbor to take command. Both King and Nimitz would remain in these positions for the duration of the war, whilst in March 1942, King took on the additional role of Chief of Naval Operations (CNO).

Ernest J. King graduated from the US Naval Academy in 1901 (USNA '01). In later command, he was a tough, quick-witted and quick-tempered task master who had a cold streak of hardness in him. He demanded the best of every subordinate, punishing those who failed him – and rewarding those who succeeded. His ability to coordinate the many fronts – and the ships and men assigned to those fronts, as well as developing Allied strategy at the highest levels, equipped him admirably for his dual role as COMINCH-CNO. King was an experienced leader not only in the air, but also in battleships, destroyers, submarines and with staff. The carrier men regarded him as a pilot, albeit a latecomer to naval air.

Chester W. Nimitz (USNA '05) was a stickler for detail and form with a gift for delegating authority. He was a commander who interfered with his delegated subordinates only in serious circumstances or if he lacked information – attributes that won him a tremendously loyal following throughout the war. He had served in submarines and surface ships – but never in the air. His bureaucratic experience as a Rear Admiral in personnel before his appointment served him well in the Pacific War – where air was but one problem of many. As well as dealing with carriers and naval air, he had to deal with submarines, auxiliaries, battleships, amphibious operations, logistics, the Marine Corps – and the Army land forces under the charge of the colourful General Douglas MacArthur.

The leader of the carrier men in the Pacific held the billet of Commander Aircraft Battle Force – known as the 'Carrier Command'. This was the inspiring leader and tough slugger Vice Admiral William F. Halsey, Jr, who had been in this position for several months after a long career in destroyers. He had been slated for relief when the war started with the attack on Pearl – but a tough and charismatic leader, he was just the sort of commander needed in wartime. With him at Pearl were two other prominent air admirals, Rear Admiral Patrick N.L. Bellinger (USNA '07) who commanded the land-based and amphibian patrol aircraft and Rear Admiral Aubrey W. 'Jake' Fitch (USNA '06), the local carrier division commander.

The new Yorktown-class carrier *Hornet* (CV-8) had been fitted out at Newport News, Virginia, and commissioned in October 1941. She was still in Virginia getting crew and ship ready for combat when the Pearl Harbor raid took place. Her Captain was Marc A. 'Pete' Mitscher (USNA '10) who, despite being small in stature and softly spoken, would become a colossus of naval aviation in the war. He had been known since his entry into the US Naval Academy in July 1904 as 'Pete' Mitscher – originally hailing from Oklahoma, he had quickly been nicknamed 'Oklahoma Pete' after a fellow Oklahoman flunked out of the Academy the previous year.

Pete Mitscher had been closely associated with the top echelons of naval aviation since the early days. He was an intelligent and effective leader who knew his people, his equipment – and the enemy. He was simple and direct – a born leader. Such was his command and the loyalty he garnered that he would become a legendary figure of the Pacific War.

Admiral Chester Nimitz, Commander-in-Chief Pacific and Pacific Ocean Areas (left), confers with Admiral William F. Halsey, Commander, South Pacific Area and South Pacific Force, aboard USS *Curtiss* (AV-4) at Espiritu Santo, New Hebrides on 20 January 1943. (National Archives 80-G-34822)

Although the right people were now being put in place in the right positions, the US naval aircraft they would command at the beginning of the war were a sad testament to just how unprepared the USA was for a war with Japan. The basic fighter was the Grumman F4F Wildcat, a good aircraft but no match for the newer Japanese A6M 'Type O', the Zero. The fleet dive-bomber was the Douglas SBD Dauntless, a tough, dependable, effective aircraft that was versatile enough to serve in three roles as fighter, scout and bomber. Its replacement, the Curtiss SB2C Helldiver, would be introduced in December 1942.

The Navy torpedo plane was the Douglas TBD Devastator – antiquated, slow and un-manoeuvrable, it had acquired the nickname 'torpecker'. The Navy had already contracted for its replacement – the Grumman TBF Avenger, but that was not yet in service. The Devastator would fair disastrously at the Battle of Midway on 4 June 1942 when forty-one were launched to attack the Japanese Fleet. Only four returned safely – and none had scored a successful torpedo hit on Japanese naval units. The remaining Devastators were immediately withdrawn from service thereafter.

(ii) Early US Fast-Carrier Operations, 1942

Within months of the Pearl Harbor raid, by early 1942, the Japanese held much of South-East Asia, Singapore, Malaya, the Dutch East Indies, the Philippines and the Central Pacific islands. The US Navy initially had the four carriers *Lexington* (CV-2), *Saratoga* (CV-3), *Yorktown* (CV-5) and *Enterprise* (CV-6) available in the Pacific to counter the Japanese expansion – they were spread out over West-Coast harbours and at Pearl Harbor. *Hornet* (CV-8) was still in training at Norfolk – she would sail for the West Coast on 4 March 1942, via the Panama Canal. *Ranger* (CV-4) had been absent from Pearl when the Japanese attacked, returning to Norfolk Navy Yard from an ocean patrol in the Caribbean. She sailed for patrol in the South Atlantic a fortnight after the Pearl raid on 21 December 1941 before entering Norfolk Navy Yard for repairs on 21 March 1942. She would then serve as flagship for the Commander, Carriers in the Atlantic Fleet.

With her battleships sunk or damaged at Pearl, in January, the fast carriers were required to cover a US convoy to Samoa. But heading south, *Saratoga* was torpedoed and seriously damaged on 11 January and had to retire for repair to Pearl and then to the West Coast. She was out of the war for months.

Keen to strike back against the Japanese, after the Samoa operation, Nimitz ordered his carrier commander, Vice Admiral Halsey, to carry out carrier raids on the Japanese-controlled Marshall and Gilbert Islands. In the first four months of 1942 these raids would be carried out by two separate carrier task forces, Task Force 8 (TF 8), centred on Halsey's *Enterprise*, and Task Force 17 (TF 17), centred on the *Yorktown* and commanded by Rear Admiral Frank Jack Fletcher. *Lexington* was far away supporting an operation to strike at the powerful Japanese base at Rabaul on New Britain.

The two carriers split into their separate task groups on 29 January 1942 and Task Force 17 moved to attack Japanese naval installations and aircraft on Jaluit, Mili and Makin islands in the Gilbert Islands before retiring towards Pearl on 1 February. Simultaneously, Halsey's

The forward flight deck of USS *Enterprise* (CV-6) is packed with Douglas SBD Dauntless scout-bombers and Grumman F4F Wildcat fighters, April 1942. (National Archives 80-G-10150)

Task Force 8 planes struck enemy positions in the Marshall Islands of Kwajalein, Wotje and Taroa. When the two task groups arrived back at Pearl on 5 and 6 February, they received a rapturous welcome – the fast carriers had struck the first real blows back against Japan.

The *Enterprise* task force left Pearl on 14 February to strike Wake Island on 24 February before moving to hit Marcus Island on 4 March. Marcus lay just 1,000 nautical miles from Tokyo, to the west of Wake. After the strike on Marcus, Halsey took *Enterprise* back to Pearl, arriving there on 9 March as *Yorktown* and *Lexington* busied themselves with strikes launched in waters off Port Moresby against Japanese positions at Lae and Salamaua on New Guinea. On conclusion of these raids, *Lexington* returned to Pearl whilst *Yorktown* stayed in the South Pacific to cover the vital shipping lanes between the USA and Australia.

Halsey proved to be an aggressive and inspiring commander whose slogan 'Hit hard, hit fast, hit often' soon permeated the Navy. In April 1942, he led the famous Doolittle Raid on Tokyo, delivering Lieutenant Colonel James (Jimmy) Doolittle's sixteen Army medium sized B-25B Mitchell bombers from the decks of the Yorktown-class carrier *Hornet* for a bombing strike on Tokyo on 18 April. USS *Enterprise* and her escort of cruisers and destroyers provided protection for the entire task force against a Japanese air attack, as *Hornet*'s own fighters were stored in the hangar below deck to allow the bombers use of the flight deck. The daring raid served notice to both the Japanese military and the civilian population that the Japanese mainland was vulnerable to US air attack. The fast carriers had gained valuable operational combat experience that would allow them to fight successfully in the Coral Sea and at Midway in just a few months' time.

During this early period of the war, each of the fast carriers formed a separate task force with its own screen of cruisers and destroyers. In multi-carrier operations, in the main, the individual carrier task forces steamed together – but separated before the attack into their individual task forces of single fast carrier screened by their own defensive vessels. The aircraft from the various task forces would rendezvous in the air at designated points on the approach to the assigned target.

Each carrier, at the beginning of the war, carried an air group comprising 72 aircraft; 18 fighters (VF), 36 scout dive-bombers (VSB) and 18 torpedo planes (VT). As with carrier (CV) nomenclature, 'V' simply stood for 'heavier than air'. 'F' denoted fighter, SB scout-bomber and 'T', a torpedo plane.

The Naval Expansion Act of Congress, passed on 17 May 1938 after Japan had abrogated disarmament treaties in 1936, had authorised an

A view aft from the rear of the island of USS *Hornet* (CV-8). USAAF B-25B bombers are tied down on the flight deck en route to the mission launching point for the Doolittle Raid on Tokyo on 18 April 1942. (NH 53426 courtesy of the Naval History & Heritage Command)

increase of 40,000 tons in aircraft carriers. This had originally permitted the building of the third Yorktown-class, *Hornet* (CV-8) (commissioned on 20 October 1941), and a new class of carrier, *Essex* (CV-9), the lead ship of twenty-four Essex-class carriers that would ultimately be built. *Essex* would be laid down in April 1941 and commissioned on 31 December 1942.

On 3 July 1940, as the trade-war tensions in the Pacific escalated, the Navy had ordered the first three of the new design, *Essex* (CV-9), *Yorktown* (CV-10) and *Intrepid* (CV-11). Under the Two-Ocean Navy Act, ten more of these carriers were programmed, with eight being ordered on 9 September 1940, CV-12 to CV-15 from Newport News and CV-16 to CV-19 from Bethlehem Steel's Fore River Shipyard in Braintree and Quincy, Massachusetts. The last two, CV-20 and CV-21, were ordered

An Army Air Force B-25B bomber takes off from USS *Hornet* (CV-8) at the start of the Doolittle Raid on Japan, 18 April 1942. (National Archives 80-G-41196)

eight days after the Pearl Harbor raid from the Brooklyn Navy Yard and Newport News. But these new fast carriers would take time to build.

In January 1942, with *Essex* (CV-9) still under construction, in desperation, the Cleveland-class light cruiser *Amsterdam* was converted into an 11,000-ton light carrier renamed as *Independence* (CVL-22). Two more conversions were authorised in February, followed by three more in March. These converted light carriers carried only half the aircraft of an Essex-class heavy carrier – but could still make over 31 knots.

On 14 March 1942, the General Board called for 'tougher carriers . . . which can engage in offensive operations without being easily placed out of action by a few light bombs, one or two torpedoes or medium sized projectiles'.[1] The General Board recommended the design of a 45,000-ton carrier with an armoured deck that could make 33 knots and carry 6 squadrons of planes (36 fighters (VF), 48 dive-bombers (VB) and 36 torpedo-bombers (VT)). Three such carriers would eventually be built – and be named the Midway-class.

The US Fleet at the beginning of the Pacific War in December 1941 comprised three fleets: the Atlantic Fleet, the Pacific Fleet and the Asiatic Fleet (reorganised in 1942) and each operated by way of a flag officer having the title commander-in-chief (CINC). Each fleet was subdivided into area or task commands that were usually assigned a number designation.

There were six heavy fast carriers in the fleet as war began in late 1941 – excluding the smaller *Ranger* – and two new fast battleships able to accompany them. But the carriers were split between the Atlantic and Pacific. After Pearl, whilst *Ranger* and *Wasp* remained in the Atlantic, all the other carriers, *Lexington*, *Saratoga*, *Yorktown*, *Enterprise* and *Hornet*, were based in Hawaii. But *Saratoga* was torpedoed by a Japanese submarine and taken out of the war temporarily in January 1942. *Lexington* would be sunk after receiving heavy battle damage at the Battle of the Coral Sea in May 1942. *Yorktown* would be sunk at the Battle of Midway in June 1942. As 1942 wore on, US carrier numbers would get thin.

On 24 March 1942, the British and US Combined Chiefs of Staff designated the Pacific Ocean as an area of US strategic responsibility. On 30 March, the US Joint Chiefs of Staff (JCS) divided the Pacific theatre into three large areas – the Pacific Ocean Areas (POA), the Southwest Pacific Area (SWPA) and the Southeast Pacific Area (SEPA).

On 8 May 1942, Nimitz (Commander-in-Chief, US Pacific Fleet, CINCPACFLT) assumed the role of Commander-in-Chief Pacific Ocean Areas (CINCPOA) with operational control over all air, land and sea units in that area. The theatre included most of the Pacific Ocean, but mainland Asia was excluded as were the Philippines, Australia, the Netherlands East Indies, New Guinea and the western part of the Solomon Islands, including part of Guadalcanal Island. General Douglas MacArthur was appointed Supreme Commander of Allied forces in the Southwest Pacific Area (CINCSOWESPAC). Both Nimitz CINCPOA and MacArthur CINCSOWESPAC were overseen by the US Joint Chiefs of Staff and the Western Allies Combined Chiefs of Staff.

Nimitz's Pacific Ocean Areas were subdivided into North, Central and South Pacific Areas. Nimitz designated subordinate commanders for the North and South Pacific Areas and retained the Central Pacific Area under his direct command. The South Pacific Area was bounded to the west by the Southwest Pacific Area and to the north by the equator.

Nimitz, as CINCPAC, was tasked to 'win the 85 million square miles of the Pacific back from the Japanese'.[2] CINCPAC would protect essential sea and air communications and prepare for major amphibious offensives against Japanese positions initially to be launched from the South Pacific and Southwest Pacific Areas. CINCPAC would cooperate with General Douglas MacArthur, CINCSWPA, in a two-prong advance against the Japanese Empire. MacArthur was to check the enemy advance towards Australia and degrade its essential lines of communication by destroying enemy assets in the New Guinea–Bismarck Solomon Island region.

At the very core of this advance was the strategy of island hopping from one island to the next using coordinated air, sea and land attacks to cut off heavily defended Japanese bases. Once cut off and isolated, the Japanese garrisons could then be bombed into submission at will.

One prong would move from the south through New Guinea to the Philippines and would be coordinated by General MacArthur, supported by the US Seventh Fleet. The second prong would move through the Central Pacific and would comprise the Third and Fifth Fleets.

To support the island-hopping strategy, the USA and its Allies assembled the most powerful armada in naval history to complement overwhelming air power. Carrier task-force groupings would provide the naval air power for offensive and defensive operations. The fast-carrier task forces proved pivotal in turning the tide of war against the Japanese.

(iii) Halting the Japanese Expansion

(a) Battle of the Coral Sea, 4–8 May 1942

The Battle of the Coral Sea is particularly significant in naval history as it was the first action in which aircraft carriers engaged each other directly. It was also the first battle in which the ships of the two opposing sides neither sighted each other directly, nor fired on each other.

The Coral Sea lies off north-east Australia and is bounded to the north west by New Guinea, by the Solomon Islands chain to the north and by the islands of Vanuatu and New Caledonia to the east.

Control of the Coral Sea was vital to Japan's strategic aims. It would strengthen her defensive position in the Pacific and allow strikes against the coastal cities of Coen, Cooktown and Townsville in Queensland, north-east Australia, which were vital Allied terminal points in the supply line between the USA, Australia and New Zealand.

In April 1942, Japan initiated her attempt to win control of the Coral Sea by implementing the four-prong Operation MO, which involved the invasion and occupation on 7 May of Port Moresby, the last Allied stronghold in New Guinea, the world's second largest island. The south coast of New Guinea is separated from the north of Australia by the shallow Torres Strait and Port Moresby is situated on the south-western coast of the Papuan peninsula of New Guinea. Operation MO was a typically complicated operation that involved the coordination of a number of widely separated naval forces.

The actual landings on 7 May would be carried out by more than 5,000 troops of the Port Moresby Invasion Force, who would be carried in 11 transport vessels which sortied from Rabaul, some 840 nautical miles distant, on 4 May. This force was escorted by the Port Moresby Attack Force of one light cruiser and six destroyers.

A separate Carrier Striking Force sortied from Truk on 1 May to support the operation and included the two fleet carriers *Shōkaku* and *Zuikaku*, two heavy cruisers and six destroyers. The Carrier Striking Force was to proceed down the eastern side of the Solomons chain of islands and enter the Coral Sea south of Guadalcanal where the carriers would provide air cover for the invasion forces, soften up Allied forces at Port Moresby and deal with any Allied naval forces which entered the Coral Sea in response to the operation. The carriers were to deliver nine Zero fighters to Rabaul on the way, but bad weather thwarted these attempts and delayed the Carrier Striking Force by two days.

To cover the flank and provide reconnaissance support for the Port Moresby assault, on 3 May, a few days before the Port Moresby invasion was to take place, the small island of Tulagi and other nearby islands in the British Solomon Islands Protectorate, to the east of New Guinea, would be seized. Tulagi is situated directly north of Guadalcanal Island, across a stretch of water just over 20 miles wide that would come to be known as Ironbottom Sound. Guadalcanal and Tulagi lie at the south-east end of the two roughly parallel lines of the Solomon Islands chain, which runs broadly north west to south east. Tulagi has a fine natural anchorage – such that during the First World War the British Admiral John Jellicoe had proposed it as the base for Royal Navy operations. Control of Tulagi would give Japan a naval anchorage and a seaplane base and provide greater defensive depth for the major Japanese base at Rabaul.

The Tulagi Invasion Force comprised a transport ship carrying about 400 troops along with minesweepers, minelayers, 2 destroyers and 2 subchasers. This invasion force would be supported by the Tulagi Covering Group, which comprised the light carrier *Shōhō* with 30 aircraft, 4 heavy cruisers and 1 destroyer. A separate Support Group of 2 light cruisers, 1 seaplane tender and 3 gunboats would provide distant protection for the Tulagi invasion.

As Japan initiated her complicated Operation MO, they were however crucially unaware of the extent and success of US efforts to break Japanese military and diplomatic codes, codenamed Operation MAGIC, which had been ongoing since the 1920s. During the 1930s an extensive network of listening stations had been set up in the Pacific – and by March 1942, the US Office of Naval Communications was able to decipher about 15 per cent of the IJN Naval Codebook D code, which was used for roughly 50 per cent of Japanese transmissions. A US radio monitoring station on Hawaii picked up the Japanese harbour master at Truk routinely transmitting in this code and was able to establish the identities of vessels coming and going from the great harbour.

In March 1942, the first mention of Operation MO flagged up in intercepted messages. On 13 April, the British intercepted and deciphered an IJN transmission to the 4th Fleet in the Southwest Pacific Area, signalling that the Fifth Carrier Division, with *Shōkaku* and *Zuikaku*, was en route to the South Pacific from Formosa via Truk. The British passed the intelligence to the US along with their assessment that Port Moresby was the likely target of Operation MO. By monitoring the Truk harbour master's coded transmissions, US analysts were able to establish the names of the Japanese aircraft carriers involved in the operation and the times they left Truk. (Even after the battle, the Truk harbour master continued a strict regime of radioing arrival and departures of ships.)

After discussions with Admiral Ernest King, Commander-in-Chief of the US Fleet, and armed with the decoded Japanese signal intelligence, Nimitz decided to contest the Japanese operation with all four available carriers. However, Task Force 16, commanded by Vice Admiral Halsey, and including the two carriers *Enterprise* and *Hornet*, had just returned to Pearl Harbor after the Doolittle Raid. Task Force 16 was immediately despatched for the Coral Sea – but the two-carrier task force would not reach the South Pacific in time to participate in the forthcoming battle.

The Allied forces would be under the overall command of Rear Admiral Frank Jack Fletcher, sailing with Task Force 17. Task Force 17, comprising *Yorktown*, the 3 cruisers *Astoria*, *Portland* and *Chester*, and 4 destroyers and a replenishment group of 2 oilers and 2 destroyers, was already in the South Pacific, returning to the Coral Sea after 7 days of upkeep and provisioning in Tonga.

Contact was established with Task Force 11, commanded by Rear Admiral Aubrey W. Fitch and comprising *Lexington* (under the command of Rear Admiral Frederick Carl 'Ted' Sherman), the two cruisers *Minneapolis* and *New Orleans* and five destroyers. TF 11 was already deployed between Fiji and New Caledonia – and received orders to rendezvous with Task Force 17 on 4 May.

Task Force 44, a joint Australian-US Support Force comprising the cruisers HMAS *Australia*, HMAS *Hobart* and USS *Chicago* and several destroyers, under the command of Rear Admiral Sir John Gregory Crace, RN, was en route from Sydney and Nouméa. TF 44 was despatched to the same rendezvous with TF 11 and TF 17.

On the evening of 2 May, Allied Coastwatchers on Bougainville reported that five to six enemy vessels had been spotted at the southern end of Santa Isabel Island in the Solomons, possibly headed for Tulagi. This intelligence allowed the small Allied garrisons to evacuate safely and destroy their base and facilities on Tulagi and Gavutu–Tanambogo.

The same intelligence of enemy ship movements from the Coastwatchers on Bougainville reached Rear Admiral Fletcher in Task Force 17 at 1900 on 3 May. Preparing for a strike, he arranged a new rendezvous for his Task Forces for daylight on 5 May. Task Force 17 (*Yorktown*) then headed north towards Guadalcanal, throttling up to 24 knots and then to 27 knots as the fast-carrier task force raced towards the Solomons. Meanwhile, as *Yorktown* raced north, the Japanese successfully landed on Tulagi and neighbouring islands in New Georgia Sound on 3 May, with air support provided by the light carrier *Shōhō*. She then turned north west to rendezvous with and support the Port Moresby invasion forces.

4–6 May 1942

At 0700 on 4 May, Task Force 17 (*Yorktown*) was about 100 nautical miles south of Guadalcanal – close enough to the Japanese beachhead at Tulagi to launch a CAP of 18 F4F-3 Wildcat fighters and a first strike patrol of 12 TBD Devastator torpedo-bombers and 28 SBD Dauntless dive-bombers. A second strike patrol by the same aircraft launched at midday and a final third patrol during the afternoon. There was little air opposition encountered over New Georgia Sound and several Japanese ships had been attacked and damaged or sunk by 1330 when *Yorktown* turned southwards to depart the area and rendezvous with Task Force 11 (*Lexington*) the next day. The planes of *Yorktown*'s last patrol had been landed aboard by 1702, and returning pilots had reported sinking in total, throughout the 3 raids, 1 destroyer, 1 cargo ship and 3 minesweepers – with 1 light cruiser forced to beach. In addition, 4 enemy seaplanes were reported destroyed and a number of other vessels damaged. TF 17 had lost 1 torpedo plane – and 2 fighters that had become lost and run out of fuel. The pilots were later picked up by a destroyer and landed on Guadalcanal. Early on the morning of

5 May, TF 17 (*Yorktown*) rendezvoused with TF 11 (*Lexington*) and TF 44 (cruisers/destroyers) some 320 nautical miles south of Guadalcanal.

With the attacks on Japanese shipping by US naval aircraft on 4 May having now alerted the Japanese to the presence of at least one US carrier, the Japanese Carrier Striking Force, which was refuelling some 350 nautical miles north of Tulagi, terminated refuelling and headed south east down the north east of the Solomons, sending out scout planes to search east of the Solomons to locate and then destroy the Allied naval forces. But no Allied ships were in that area and no ships were found.

At the foot of the Solomons chain, the Japanese carriers turned west and entered the Coral Sea and on 6 May commenced refuelling 180 nautical miles west of Tulagi, in preparation for the battle which looked likely the next day. Throughout 5 and 6 May, Allied intelligence reported a large number of enemy ships of all types in the area between New Guinea, New Britain and the Solomon Islands. The Japanese Carrier Striking Force moved south throughout 6 May – and the two sides unknowingly closed each other that evening.

7 May 1942

On the first day of the battle, 7 May 1942, scout planes from *Lexington* and *Yorktown* were sent out on a regular planned visual search to about 175 nautical miles looking for the two Japanese carriers, *Zuikaku* and *Shōkaku*, as well as the Port Moresby Invasion Group, which according to intelligence was coming round the eastern tip of New Guinea Island.[3]

Zuikaku and *Shōkaku*, to the north, had the advantage of poor weather cover and were not discovered – but at 0828, a *Yorktown* SBD Dauntless scout-bomber sighted the screen of the Japanese Port Moresby Invasion Force coming round the coast of New Guinea, north of Misima Island. As a result of a miscode, the sighting was inaccurately reported as confirming the presence of two carriers and four heavy cruisers. Rear Admiral Fletcher was thus led to believe that this was the main Japanese carrier force, with the two large 845ft-long fleet carriers *Shōkaku* and *Zuikaku* – each capable of carrying seventy-two planes.

Based on this (faulty) intelligence, at 1013, Fletcher launched a full strike of 93 aircraft to move up the east end of New Guinea. From *Lexington* and *Yorktown*, 53 SBD Dauntless dive-bombers and 22 TBD Devastator torpedo-bombers, escorted by 18 F4F Wildcat fighters, were launched. But after the SBD that had made the contact report was landed, it was learned that a reporting error had been made – and that in fact no carriers had been sighted, it had been two cruisers and four destroyers that had been sighted. But at about the same time, an Army

B-17 also reported an enemy force close to Misima, comprising 1 carrier, 10 transports and some 16 warships about 30 nautical miles south of the SBD's reported position. Believing that the B-17's sighting was the main Japanese carrier force, Fletcher diverted the airborne attack planes towards this target – and contact was made with the enemy. It was in fact the same Port Moresby Invasion Force spotted by the SBD, screened by the light carrier *Shōhō* and cruisers. After half an hour's flying, at 1040, the 93 strike aircraft sighted *Shōhō*, with 4 cruisers and escorts. *Shōhō*, at 674ft long, was much smaller than the fleet carriers, displacing some 11,260 tons and carrying 30 aircraft for Combat Air Patrol (CAP) protection of the invasion convoy.

At 1110, the US strike aircraft arrived over the enemy ships – the two Japanese Fleet carriers of the Carrier Striking Force were not present. As the SBD Dauntlesses began their attack, pushing over for their dive towards the light carrier *Shōhō*, they were pounced upon by three of *Shōhō*'s A5M CAP fighters. One Dauntless was shot down – and no bomb hits were scored.

The second wave of *Lexington* SBD Dauntlesses had more success. Beginning their attack at 1118, they hit *Shōhō* twice with 1,000lb bombs which penetrated her unarmoured flight deck and exploded in her hangars, setting fuelled and armed aircraft on fire. This attack was followed up minutes later by a torpedo attack from the TBM Devastator torpedo-bombers towards both sides of the ship. They scored five hits and flooded both engine and boiler rooms and disabled the light carrier's steering.

At 1125, *Yorktown*'s aircraft now took over the attack on the virtually immobilised light carrier. The SBD dive-bombers hit *Shōhō* with eleven 1,000lb bombs. Then, at 1129, TBM Devastator torpedo-bombers followed – claiming multiple hits. The F4F Wildcat fighter escorts engaged the Japanese CAP fighters in an attempt to protect the torpedo-bombers, which were vulnerable as they made their low, slow attack runs. Despite losing three SBD Dauntlesses, after the attack, Lieutenant Robert E. Dixon, commander of *Lexington*'s dive-bombers, sent his famous radio message: 'Scratch one flattop.'

Shōhō had by now been hit by some thirteen bombs and seven torpedoes in just over 10 minutes of attack. She settled quickly, forcing the order to abandon ship to be given at 1131. Just 4 minutes later she was gone – with the loss of 834 officers and men. She was the first Japanese carrier sunk during the war.

Meanwhile, earlier that morning, Japanese search planes had spotted a section of the US replenishment group. It was the fleet oiler *Neosho* (AO-23) which had refuelled the *Yorktown* and the heavy cruiser *Astoria*

IJN *Shōhō* is torpedoed by US Navy aircraft late on the morning of 7 May 1942 during the Battle of the Coral Sea. This photograph was taken from a *Lexington* (CV-2) plane. (National Archives 80-G-17026)

(CA-34) the day before retiring south from the task force with a single escort, the destroyer USS *Sims* (DD-409). The *Neosho* and *Sims* were misidentified by the Japanese reconnaissance aircraft crew as a carrier and her escort.

When this was reported, Admiral Takeo Takagi, in command of the Japanese Carrier Striking Force, ordered a full attack – and more than seventy aircraft from *Shōkaku* and *Zuikaku* were despatched. After searching in vain for the 'carrier', at 1115, almost simultaneously with the US attack on *Shōhō*, thirty-six Aichi D3A Val dive-bombers attacked the destroyer *Sims* from all directions. Although the destroyer had skilfully evaded two earlier attacks, there was no escape from this starfish formation attack and she was hit by three 550lb bombs, two exploding in the engine room. She had been fatally wounded and sank stern first, going under with a loud explosion.

Neosho took seven bomb hits and a suicide dive from one of the Vals and was left ablaze and in danger of breaking her back. Damage-control parties however managed to keep her afloat for the next four days. The destroyer USS *Monaghan* (DD-354) was detached during the night of 7/8 May to search for survivors the next morning – leaving seven destroyers and five cruisers with the carriers *Yorktown* and *Lexington*.

It would take four days however until *Neosho* was spotted by a RAAF aircraft – and then by a US Consolidated PBY Catalina flying boat. The destroyer USS *Henley* (DD-391) was sent to her aid and recovered 123 survivors – before scuttling the stricken ship by gunfire.

Late on 7 May, US ship radar showed a group of planes south eastward on a westerly course and fighters were vectored to attack. The US fighters broke up the enemy formation, downing a reported fifteen to twenty enemy carrier aircraft for the loss of three US fighters. As the US planes were landing after dark, lights from more returning planes flying in formation were seen coming over the horizon towards the task force – but the red shade with a bluish tint on the port running lights was a different shade from US planes. These were in fact returning Japanese dive-bombers who had come across the US carriers in the darkness. Confused as to their identity, the Japanese planes now began to circle *Yorktown* and *Lexington* with their lights on as they got into landing formation. Everyone began firing at them – the Japanese planes broke formation, turned out their lights and promptly disappeared.[4] It was obvious to everyone that the two carrier forces were quite close.

As nightfall ended aircraft operations on 7 May, the first day of the battle, with radio intelligence indicating that the enemy fleet carriers might be either to the east or to the west, Fletcher ordered Task Force 17 to head west and prepare to launch a full 360° search at first light the next day. The Japanese carriers went north during the night opening the range between the combatants – as both sides readied their air groups for the battle they knew would come the following day.[5] The contacts of 7 May had essentially been the preliminary skirmishes – before the main battle on 8 May.

8 May 1942

At dawn the following day, at 0616, seven Japanese scout planes launched from their carriers up north, to search out to 250 nautical miles. Meanwhile, eighteen US SBD scout planes launched at 0635 to search out to all points of the compass.

At 0828, a *Lexington* SBD scout plane spotted *Shōkaku* and *Zuikaku*. This was amplified at 0835 as being two carriers, four heavy cruisers and many destroyers, distance 120 nautical miles, bearing 006°, roughly to the north. *Lexington* signalled that the true bearing of the enemy was 028°, 175 miles distant from its own force. Just a few minutes later, a *Shōkaku* scout plane spotted Task Force 17.

The two opposing carrier forces were by now about 220 nautical miles apart. The Japanese carriers had come about and were now heading south, to close the distance for the torpedo aircraft, which carrying their heavy torpedoes had a reduced range. As the two opposing air armadas closed on each other's ships, scout planes continued to shadow the enemy, reporting back on movement.

At 0900, both US carriers began launching their attack planes for separate strikes, as their escort warships formed a circular screen around them, axis 305. Commander Air (Rear Admiral Fitch) was given tactical command at 0907 to reduce signalling between carriers and allow him complete freedom of action for his carriers and air groups. *Yorktown's* planes (6 VF, 24 VB, 9 VT) were away by 0915 and *Lexington's* (9 VF, 15 VB, 12 VT) by 0925. At 0915, the Japanese carriers launched their own strike of 18 fighters, 33 dive-bombers and 18 torpedo planes.

The first US strike planes reached the Japanese carriers about 20 minutes before Japanese aircraft attacked the US carriers, encountering some sixteen Japanese CAP fighters above the two carriers. *Yorktown* dive-bombers arrived just after 1030, holding position to allow the slower torpedo-bombers to approach and enable a textbook simultaneous coordinated attack to split Japanese AA fire against the low attack torpedo planes and the high-altitude dive-bombers. *Zuikaku* was hidden by low clouds and a rain squall.

Yorktown dive-bombers began their attack at about 1057, hitting *Shōkaku* with two 1,000lb bombs that blasted open her fo'c'sle and damaged her flight and hangar decks so badly that she was rendered unable to launch or recover her aircraft. This attack was followed up at 1130 by *Lexington* dive-bombers – who hit the wounded carrier with another 1,000lb bomb. With her flight deck out of action and more than 220 crew dead or wounded, *Shōkaku* was out of the battle and had to retire, accompanied by 2 destroyers. None of the torpedo planes scored a hit and two *Yorktown* SBDs and three Wildcat fighters had been shot down.

US shipboard radar picked up indications of enemy aircraft approaching at 1055 – and the Japanese retaliatory strike came shortly after 1100. Rear Admiral Fitch had employed Sherman's tactic (only recently trialled in New Guinea), of keeping the two carriers together in the same destroyer screen. American CAP F4F Wildcat fighters successfully shot down seventeen of the approaching Japanese aircraft – but under intense Japanese air attack, the two carriers performing radical manoeuvres at high speeds moved apart. The ships nearest each carrier formed a screen around each and threw up effective AA fire.

Yorktown was initially attacked at about 1113, without success, by four Nakajima B5N Kate torpedo-bombers. At 1120, fourteen Kate

IJN *Shōkaku* under attack by *Yorktown* (CV-5) planes on the morning of 8 May 1942 during the Battle of the Coral Sea. Flames are visible from a bomb hit on her fo'c'sle to left of shot. (National Archives 80-G-17031)

torpedo-bombers then attacked *Lexington*. Although the US CAP shot down four, ten managed to launch torpedoes in an anvil attack from both sides, scoring two hits on the port side. The first torpedo strike at the bow jammed both elevators in the up position and started leaks of aviation fuel vapours. The second hit was near the bridge and ruptured the port primary water main and allowed water to flood into three port fire rooms forcing the boilers to be shut down. *Lexington* took on a list to port, but despite losing some propulsion, she was still able to make 24 knots.

The Japanese dive-bombers began their attack from 14,000ft a few minutes after the torpedo planes with nineteen Aichi D3A Val dive-bombers from *Shōkaku* targeting *Lexington*. They scored two bomb hits and several near misses. The explosions started fires below decks whilst fragments pierced the hull flooding two compartments.

Lexington damage-control parties were able to extinguish the fires and pump fuel from the port tanks to the starboard side to correct the list. Flight operations were able to continue and *Lexington* began recovering damaged aircraft. Within an hour, the carrier was back on an even keel – but down by the bow and only able to make 24 knots.

View on the flight deck of USS *Lexington* (CV-2), at about 1500, 8 May 1942, during the Battle of the Coral Sea. The ship's air group is spotted aft, with Grumman F4F-3 fighters nearest the camera. SBD scout-bombers and TBD-1 torpedo planes are parked further aft. Smoke is rising around the after aircraft elevator from fires burning in the hangar. (National Archives 80-G-16802)

A group of fourteen Val dive-bombers attacked *Yorktown* – and at 1127, she was hit in the centre of her flight deck by a single 550lb semi-armour-piercing bomb that penetrated through several decks before exploding deep within the ship, killing sixty-six crew and causing severe structural damage. The compression of some twelve near misses damaged some of her plating below the waterline.

The air battle ended at about noon, as the Japanese aircraft began to withdraw, no doubt believing that they had done serious damage to both US carriers.

Despite the fine work that *Lexington* damage-control parties had done, at 1247, sparks from electric motors ignited gasoline vapour that had been emanating from the port aviation gasoline tanks fractured in the initial torpedo attack. An explosion suddenly ripped through her innards, killing twenty-five men and starting a large fire. But although the refuelling system had to be shut down, flight-deck operations were able to continue with fuelled SBD Dauntlesses being launched and aircraft landed.

At 1442, a second explosion followed starting further fires in the hangar which damaged the forward elevator. Then at 1525, a third explosion followed. The fires now raged out of control and at 1710, the crew began to abandon ship. At 1800, a series of further explosions started.[6]

Once the crew had been safely recovered, commencing at 1915, the destroyer USS *Phelps* (DD-360) fired eight torpedoes into the burning carrier (only four of which exploded), before she finally sank into abyssal depths just before 2000, with a tremendous underwater explosion

A destroyer alongside USS *Lexington* (CV-2) as the carrier is abandoned during the afternoon of 8 May 1942. Note crewmen sliding down lines on *Lexington*'s starboard quarter. (National Archives 80-G-7398)

occurring as she went down. Of *Lexington*'s crew of 2,735 officers and men, 216 had perished.

The first carrier versus carrier dual had been a brutal confrontation. The venerable *Lexington* (CV-2) and the light carrier *Shōhō* had both been sunk, *Shōkaku* had been heavily damaged, as was *Yorktown* (CV-5).

There were heavy losses of Japanese aircraft. On *Zuikaku*, which had escaped significant damage, many of her air group's planes had to be pushed overboard to clear the flight deck for emergency landings of *Shōkaku*'s aircraft – when her flight deck became a mangled wreckage. *Zuikaku* lost more than half of her aircraft, with only 24 Zekes, 9 Vals and 6 Kates remaining operational, barely a quarter of the original total of bombers aboard both carriers prior to the battle.[7] The US had sixty-nine aircraft destroyed.

With both sides having lost many aircraft, with their carriers damaged or sunk, along with many other ships sunk on both sides, the two forces disengaged. Each returned to safe waters to lick their wounds – each claiming victory. The Japanese had indeed won a tactical victory by sinking a US Fleet carrier, an oiler and a destroyer – for the loss of a light carrier, a destroyer and some smaller ships. With only four operational fleet carriers deployed in the Pacific, the US had just lost 25 per cent of its carrier strength.

The battle was however a strategic Allied victory – as a result of the heavy loss of Japanese carrier aircraft, the Japanese invasion fleet bound for Port Moresby was recalled and the amphibious invasion did not proceed. Both damaged Japanese Fleet carriers *Shōkaku* and *Zuikaku* would be kept out of the Japanese battle order for the attack on the US base at Midway – scheduled for just a few weeks later in early June 1942. This turned out to be a decisive disadvantage.

Vice Admiral Halsey had missed the Battle of the Coral Sea. Whilst returning from the lengthy Doolittle Raid on Tokyo, he had contracted a skin infection that took him out of operations for the next few months. As his replacement, he selected his cruiser commander Rear Admiral Raymond Spruance (USNA '07), a quiet man, meticulous and brilliant, with a reputation as a fine strategist. His handling of his orders and staff would be key to the subsequent victory at the Battle of Midway. Spruance, although not a naval aviator, had served for several months with Halsey's carriers and inherited the carrier orientated staff.

As Halsey was turning over the carriers to Spruance at Pearl, Rear Admiral Fitch went to San Diego to pick up the *Saratoga*, now ready to return to combat after repairs to her torpedo damage – but she would arrive too late for the Battle of Midway, leaving three non-aviators to command the carriers – Nimitz, Spruance and the Commander Cruisers, Rear Admiral Frank Jack Fletcher.

In the early air battles, Japanese carrier pilots had had the edge in training and experience over the average US carrier pilot. Japanese pilots had logged 700 hours of flight time during training whereas their US counterparts had only 305 hours before being assigned to a squadron. The light and swift Mitsubishi A6M Zero fighter, introduced to the IJN in July 1940, was better in almost every respect than the US F4F Wildcat. US aerial tactics and pilot skill kept fighter losses down – but it was clear that more fighters were needed to escort dive- and torpedo-bombers, as well as to provide cover for the fleet itself.

As a result, after the Battle of the Coral Sea, several more fighters were added to each carrier air group. The Americans rotated pilots from combat to training duties – where they could pass on their knowledge to new trainees.

With a lack of protected fuel tanks, when a Japanese aircraft was hit, it had a tendency to burst into flames with the loss of both the aircraft and the crew The Japanese maintained their carrier pilot elite, which meant that when losses in combat of the top-flight pilots occurred, their replacements were usually greener, more poorly trained recruits. The quality of Japanese pilots began to drop.

The IJN General Staff were so flushed with the success of the first attacks of the early phase of Japanese expansion, following Pearl, that the losses at the Battle of the Coral Sea were viewed as a minor setback and did little to restrain their ambition. Overall, Japan had lost much fewer warships than the Allies whilst achieving her initial strategic goals with the seizure of the Philippines, Malaya, Singapore, Hong Kong – and the Dutch East Indies (modern day Indonesia), which was of particular strategic importance due to its oil resources.

Admiral Yamamoto had studied at Harvard University from 1919–21 and had twice been posted as a naval attaché to Washington DC, where he learned to speak fluent English. He travelled extensively in the USA, studying US business and industry. As a result, he was very aware of the power and capability of the sleeping giant of US industrial might. He feared the speed at which the USA would recover from the initial shock and damage inflicted by the first phase of the Japanese offensive.

Yamamoto was very aware that whilst the raid on Pearl Harbor had successfully sunk or disabled the USA's battleships, the US carriers had not been eliminated and were still a huge threat that he wanted eradicated. His fears had been compounded by the Doolittle Raid on Tokyo on 18 April 1942, which had shocked Japan out of the belief that the home islands were immune from direct attack. A group of sixteen US Army Air Force B-25B Mitchell bombers had launched from the carrier *Hornet* and bombed Tokyo and several other Japanese cities. This raid, and several other hit-and-run carrier raids, although militarily of little significance in terms of damage done, had revealed a gap in Japan's defences around her home islands and demonstrated to the Japanese public that Japanese cities were vulnerable to US bombers.

With *Lexington* sunk at the Battle of the Coral Sea, Yamamoto argued that another air attack on Pearl Harbor would trigger the US Fleet, including the three remaining fleet carriers, to come out and fight. In his assessment, *Yorktown* had been so badly damaged in the Coral Sea that it perhaps would not be battle ready, it may even have sunk – he didn't know. But if that was the case, then the only carriers available to the Americans would be the *Enterprise* and *Hornet*. Either way, in addition to a superiority in battleships, Japan also had a superiority in numbers of carriers. Now was the time for the decisive battle that would buy time to allow consolidation of an advanced defence perimeter that would be a barrier to any further attacks on Japan itself and her most important possessions.

Yamamoto assessed that Pearl Harbor itself was by now too well protected by land-based aircraft that had deployed there following the initial surprise raid of 7 December 1941. Therefore, he selected Midway as the bait to draw out the remaining US carriers. Midway is a tiny atoll at the extreme north-west end of the Hawaiian Island chain, and already had a US airfield on Eastern Island. Crucially, Midway lay some 1,300 miles from Oahu and was thus outwith the effective range of the US land-based planes stationed on the Hawaiian Islands. Simultaneously, in a single concerted mass sweep, the Aleutian Islands of Attu and Kiska would also be seized.

The two-island atoll of Midway itself was not of any great significance to the overall Japanese Pacific aim, but Yamamoto felt that the Americans would view Midway as a vital outpost of Pearl Harbor and would defend it strenuously. Japanese commanders believed that the USA, with her battleships sunk or disabled at Pearl, would commit her remaining and now vulnerable carriers to defend Midway. With the US battleships out of action at Pearl, Yamamoto had a much more powerful battleship fleet at his disposal. The chance was there for Yamamoto to draw out the US carriers from Pearl into a trap where his own carriers and battleships would be ready to spring upon the US carriers and extinguish their threat once and for all. Then, with her battleships *and* carriers sunk, US naval power in the Pacific would be decimated. With Japan in control of

Aerial view of Midway Atoll, 24 November 1941. (National Archives 80-G-451086)

Midway and the Aleutian Islands to the north, it would be game over for Pearl Harbor as a US forward base. Following a successful landing on Midway, the existing US airfield would be converted into a base for Vice Admiral Nishizō Tsukahara's 11th Air Fleet, which would then begin bombing Hawaii.

Japan would have mastery of the Pacific and be able to threaten the West Coast of the USA itself. Midway would become part of a 'barrier' strategy that would extend Japan's defensive perimeter, preparatory to further attacks on Fiji, Samoa and Hawaii itself. There would be no impediment to Japan establishing its *Greater East Asia Co-Prosperity Sphere*.

Just some four weeks after the Coral Sea, the two sides would clash once again in the Battle of Midway, one of the most decisive battles in naval history – a complicated battle in which the IJN suffered crippling losses of aircraft carriers.

(b) Battle of Midway, 3–7 June 1942

Yamamoto's battle plan for the invasion of Midway, codenamed Operation MI, would pitch the 4 carriers *Akagi, Kaga, Sōryū* and *Hiryū* of the 1st Carrier Striking Force, carrying some 248 strike aircraft, against the 3 remaining US Pacific Fleet carriers, *Enterprise, Hornet* and *Yorktown*. Whilst the Japanese would be able to field several battleships in support, in contrast, the US naval force would have no battleships – they remained damaged or sunk at Pearl.

Midway would be a decisive naval battle that would inflict devastating damage on the Japanese Fleet, damage from which it would never recover. The four Japanese carriers *Akagi, Kaga, Sōryū* and *Hiryū* (all part of the six-carrier *Kidō Butai* force that had attacked Pearl Harbor six months earlier) and the heavy cruiser *Mikuma* would be sunk. On the US side, the battle-scarred *Yorktown* (CV-5) would be sunk – as well as the destroyer *Hammann* (DD-412), as it tried to assist the stricken carrier.

The Battle of Midway would be a devastating blow for Japan's aims in the Pacific. It took place just a month after the Battle of the Coral Sea, in which the light carrier *Shōhō* was sunk, and the fleet carrier *Shōkaku* so badly damaged that she had had to be dry-docked for months of repair and was unable to participate. Although the fleet carrier *Zuikaku* had escaped the Coral Sea undamaged, she had lost almost half of her air group and also would not participate in the Midway operation. After the Coral Sea, she had headed back to Kure in Japan and was still languishing there as she awaited replacement planes and pilots. Experienced Japanese pilots were becoming thin on the ground as a result of failings in the IJN crew-training programme, which was unable to replace losses quickly enough. *Zuikaku* would also not be ready for the forthcoming battle.

As a result of this combination of events, Carrier Division 5, with the two most advanced fleet carriers of the *Kidō Butai, Shōkaku* and *Zuikaku*, would not be available for Operation MI at Midway. Instead, Vice Admiral Nagumo, in command of the 1st Carrier Striking Force, would have *Kaga* and *Akagi* of Carrier Division 1 and *Hiryū* and *Sōryū* of Carrier Division 2 available. His Striking Force would be escorted by the 36,000-ton Kongō-class battleships *Haruna* and *Kirishima* of the 3rd Battleship Division, deploying along with the 8th Cruiser Division

81

11,000-ton heavy cruisers *Tone* and *Chikuma*, the light cruiser *Nagara* and eleven destroyers.

Yamamoto's intelligence reports suggested that *Enterprise* and *Hornet*, which formed Task Force 16, were the only carriers available to the USA – and that they were in Pearl Harbor. *Lexington* (CV-2) had been sunk one month earlier at the Battle of the Coral Sea – and *Yorktown* (CV-5) had suffered so much damage that the Japanese believed she was out of action and might even have been lost. IJN Rear Admiral Chūichi Hara, Commander of the 5th Carrier Division (*Shōkaku* and *Zuikaku*) at the Coral Sea, had stated in his official combat report on the battle: 'The Yorktown-type aircraft carrier received hits by more than eight bombs and more than three torpedoes, and was left burning. Listing heavily to port, she is believed to have sunk, although we

USS *Yorktown* (CV-5) in dry dock at the Pearl Harbor Navy Yard, 29 May 1942, receiving urgent repairs for damage received at the Battle of the Coral Sea. She left Pearl Harbor the next day to participate in the Battle of Midway. (National Archives 80-G-13065)

have not as yet confirmed the destruction of the vessel.'[8] But in reality, following hasty repairs at Pearl, *Yorktown* sortied, with welders still working aboard – and would go on to play a vital role in the sinking of the Japanese carriers at Midway.

Four months earlier, *Saratoga* had been torpedoed 420 nautical miles south west of Pearl on 11 January 1942. Since then, she had been undergoing repairs at the Bremerton Navy Yard on the north-west coast of the USA. Repairs completed, she arrived at San Diego on 25 May to begin embarking aircraft and supplies and to wait for her commander, Admiral Fitch, to arrive from the South Pacific. She sailed from San Diego on 1 June and arrived at Pearl Harbor on 6 June – the final day of the Battle of Midway. She would not participate in the battle.

In typical Japanese style, Yamamoto's battle plan, Operation MI, to trap the US carriers was complicated. He felt that deception would be required to lure the US Fleet into a strategically weak position – a trap in which the US carriers could be sunk. Virtually the entire Combined Fleet would be involved both to escort the invasion Occupation Force to Midway Island and also to mount a simultaneous invasion of the Aleutian Islands chain to the north. The Aleutians are a volcanic chain of islands that stretch across the North Pacific between the Alaskan peninsula and the Russian Kamchatka peninsula – they are mostly part of Alaska, USA.

In all, for Operation MI, Yamamoto would field some 350 warships of all types, more than 1,000 aircraft would participate along with more than 100,000 officers and men. But the complicated plan required that he disperse his numerically superior forces into four separate, individually weaker, task groups – so that the full extent of the Japanese sortie, particularly of his powerful battleships, would be hidden from the Americans before the battle began. Multiple battle groups would need to be coordinated over hundreds of miles of open ocean. None of his dispersed formations would be able to support the others. It would be a fatal error.

Vice-Admiral Chūichi Nagumo in *Akagi* would command the 1st Carrier Striking Force of the four carriers *Akagi*, *Kaga*, *Hiryū* and *Sōryū*. They would carry out initial strikes against Midway with their 248 available aircraft and strike at any US naval units encountered. They would also bear the brunt of any US counter-attack. This 1st Carrier Striking Force was supported by the two Kongō-class fast battleships *Haruna* and *Kirishima*, the heavy cruisers *Tone* and *Chikuma*, the light cruiser *Nagara* and eleven destroyers.

Yamamoto himself would command the 1st Fleet (Main Force) from the 71,659-ton super battleship *Yamato*, deploying with the battleships *Mutsu* and *Nagato*, the light escort carrier *Hōshō*, the light carrier *Chiyoda*, the seaplane tender *Nisshin* and an escort of light cruisers, destroyers and minesweepers. Vice Admiral Nobutake Kondō would command the 2nd Fleet (Midway Invasion Force), which comprised the fast battleships *Kongō* and *Hiei*, the heavy cruisers *Atago, Chōkai, Myōkō* and *Haguro*, a light cruiser and eight destroyers – with air support provided by the light carrier *Zuihō*.

Thus, in addition to the 4 carriers, 2 battleships, 2 heavy cruisers and escort vessels in Nagumo's 1st Carrier Striking Force, Yamamoto had in reserve 5 battleships, 4 heavy cruisers, 2 light cruisers and 2 light carriers in his 1st Fleet (Main Force) and the 2nd Fleet (Midway Invasion Force), a combined force vastly superior to any surface force the Americans could field.

Yamamoto and Kondō's two big-gun forces would trail Vice Admiral Nagumo's 1st Carrier Striking Force by several hundred miles with the intention that these big gun forces would remain undetected and be ready to come up and destroy whatever elements of the US Fleet might come to defend Midway, once Nagumo's 1st Carrier Striking Force aircraft had weakened Midway's defences and any US naval units sufficiently for a decisive daylight gun battle to take place.[9] But being so heavily dispersed and so far to the rear, none of these powerful warships would see action in the battle to come at Midway. In addition, trailing so far to the rear, the invaluable reconnaissance ability of the scout planes carried by the cruisers and light carriers, as well as the additional AA capability of the battleships, cruisers and destroyers, would not be available to the carriers of Nagumo's 1st Carrier Striking Force once the battle began.

The transport vessels of the Midway Occupation Force itself would carry some 5,000 IJA invasion troops. This Occupation Force would be screened by an Escort Force, commanded by Rear Admiral Raizo Tanaka, of light cruisers, destroyers and aircraft of the light carrier *Chitose* and the seaplane tender *Kamikawa Maru*. Additional support would be provided by the Occupation Support Force, under Vice Admiral Takeo Kurita, of four heavy cruisers, destroyers, a minesweeper group and a large number of submarines.

Yamamoto believed that Nagumo's vanguard of four carriers and its screen of the two fast battleships *Haruna* and *Kirishima*, the heavy cruisers *Tone* and *Chikuma* and attendant light cruiser and destroyers was a far superior surface force than the remaining US surface fleet at Pearl, which had no battleships following the Pearl Harbor raid. Nagumo's carrier planes would soften up Midway's defences beginning on 4 June. The invasion troops carried by the Transport Group would go ashore on 7 June.

For the landings by the IJA far to the north, on the Aleutian Islands of Attu and Kiska, Yamamoto would provide a powerful Northern Area Force of battleships, cruisers and destroyers to screen the IJA landing forces.

Once the IJA had seized Kiska and Attu, this would prevent or break up any potential Allied offensives moving across the Northern Pacific against Japan and put the Japanese home islands out of range of US land-based bombers across Alaska. The distance from Attu to the Alaskan mainland was around 1,100 miles and the distance from Attu to the north of Japan some 1,500 miles. The USA feared that if the Aleutian Islands were occupied by Japan they could be used as bases from which to bomb US West-Coast cities such as Anchorage, Seattle or Portland.

Japan already had long-range bombers such as the Mitsubishi G4M Betty bomber with a long range, dependent on payload, of over 2,000 nautical miles.[10] However, in 1942 Japan began Project Z, the development of the Nakajima G10N *Fugaku* – an ultra-long-range intercontinental bomber with a design range of more than 11,000 miles. The G10N *Fugaku* could take off from the Kuril Islands chain to the immediate north east of Japan and bomb continental US cities and industrial centres along the West Coast, such as San Francisco as well as Detroit and Chicago in the Midwest and even hit the north-east cities of New York and Norfolk. (As the war went against Japan, Project Z would eventually be cancelled in 1944.)

Yamamoto hoped that with Pearl Harbor under constant Japanese bombing from Midway, and the US West Coast threatened from the Aleutian Islands, the USA would realise the futility of opposing Japan in the Pacific – and negotiate a settlement. It was a bold and complicated plan designed to knock the USA quickly out of the war – before the might of her industrial power could move to a war footing in the construction of ships, weapons and armaments.

However, unknown to Japan, US cryptographers had already broken the main Japanese naval code and deciphered some details of the plan concerning a target designated 'AF', although it was not known exactly which target had been designated 'AF'. To find out, an elaborate intelligence ruse was set up deliberately to broadcast an uncoded radio message to the effect that Midway's water purification system had broken down (when in fact it had not). When subsequent intercepted Japanese transmissions were picked up reporting that 'AF' was short on water, the Americans knew that Midway was the target. They also established the date of the attack as either 4 or 5 June.

Now forewarned of the operation, the US Navy was able to plan its own ambush – with a good understanding that four enemy carriers were being deployed with supports and escorts – but although Midway was known as the target, it was unclear how the enemy naval assets would be deployed. Nimitz believed that the Japanese would operate their carriers in two separate groups and was aware that the support force would hold the rest of the heavy ships and be some distance behind the carriers. He judged that Yamamoto had squandered his numerical advantage in heavy ships and carriers by dividing their units into separate task groups that would be too widely separated to support each other. The splitting up of the Japanese battleships and escorts meant that the AA firepower available to protect the carriers was also divided.

Nimitz may have had only three carriers against Yamamoto's four carriers – but he calculated that his own fast carriers carried larger air groups that would be augmented by land-based aircraft on Midway. If he positioned his carriers carefully near Midway, in advance of the Japanese operation beginning, his forces would be at least on parity with Nagumo's four carriers. Far from languishing in Pearl Harbor and having to sortie once the Japanese landings at Midway were under way, the US carriers would be ready and waiting in proximity to the north east of Midway, as the Japanese carriers approached for the initial carrier air strikes. The hunter had unknowingly become the hunted.

With this critical intelligence to hand, Admiral Nimitz began to plan the defence of Midway. He recalled Vice Admiral Halsey's Task Force 16, comprising *Enterprise* and *Hornet*, to Pearl Harbor for a quick replenishment. Halsey himself was stricken with severe dermatitis and had to be replaced by Rear Admiral Raymond A. Spruance, Halsey's escort commander.

Nimitz hurriedly recalled Rear Admiral Frank Jack Fletcher's Task Force 17, centred on the carrier *Yorktown*, from the Southwest Pacific Area. Carrying considerable damage from the Battle of the Coral Sea, she arrived at Pearl Harbor on 27 May and entered dry dock the following day. Navy Yard inspectors assessed that it would take two weeks for repairs to be completed – but Nimitz ordered that she be made ready immediately so that she could sail with *Enterprise* and *Hornet*. Further close inspection revealed that her flight elevators had not been damaged and that the damage to her flight deck and hull could be speedily repaired – and with Navy Yard labourers working around the clock, she was ready to put to sea again in 48 hours. One vital repair to her power plant could not however be made in time – and this limited her top speed. Her air group was augmented by planes and crew from *Saratoga* (CV-3), which was then heading westwards for Pearl – after her refit on the West Coast of the USA.

Task Force 16, *Enterprise* and *Hornet*, under the command of Rear Admiral Raymond Spruance departed Pearl Harbor on 28 May 1942, bound for Point Luck, a position nearly 1,500 nautical miles distant that was roughly 325 nautical miles to the north east of Midway. Here they would be in a flank position to ambush Japan's mobile carrier striking force, which was expected to approach Midway from the north west. *Yorktown* was able to sail on 30 May as the core of TF 17, flying Rear Admiral Frank Jack Fletcher's flag as Officer in Tactical Command of the combined force. TF 17 would rendezvous with TF 16 and take up a position 10 miles to its north.

On 1 June, the newly appointed Rear Admiral 'Pete' Mitscher, in command of *Hornet*, had a message read over the bull horn to his crew: 'The enemy are approaching for an attempt to seize Midway. This attack will probably be accompanied by a feint at western Alaska. We are going to prevent them taking Midway, if possible. Be ready and keep alert. Let's get a few more yellowtails.'[11] On 2 June, Task Force 16, *Enterprise* and *Hornet*, rendezvoused with TF 17 *Yorktown* north east of Midway.

Notwithstanding that her battleships had been sunk or disabled at Pearl, the US Navy was still able to field 3 carriers carrying 233 aircraft along with 7 heavy cruisers, 1 light cruiser and 15 destroyers. Opposing this force, the Japanese 1st Carrier Striking Force had 4 fleet carriers carrying 248 aircraft along with 2 battleships, 2 heavy cruisers, 1 light cruiser, 12 destroyers and some 16 floatplanes. Yamamoto's heaviest battleships were trailing behind in the support group, several hundred miles to the rear.

The Japanese 1st Carrier Striking Force would keep its four carriers in a concentrated box until the US three-carrier group was detected and a fleet engagement brought on. Ignorant of the sortie of the US carriers, Nagumo maintained this four-carrier box formation – and meanwhile had his torpedo-bombers of the first wave armed with bombs for the initial softening up attacks on Midway's land defences.

Japanese carrier AA guns and fire-control systems had a number of design and configuration deficiencies. The standard IJN medium AA weapon was the 25mm Type 96 auto cannon – it was one of Japan's most effective AA guns with a rate of fire of between 200 and 260 rounds per minute. But it was most effective only at close ranges of fewer than 1,000m with fire at aircraft at a height of 1,000m, and beyond a range of 2,000m, being completely ineffective.

The Japanese 25mm Type 96 was in fact a mediocre weapon hampered by slow training and slow elevation speeds, excessive vibration and muzzle flash. The sights were found to be ineffective against high-speed targets – a critical problem that would be badly exposed when new fast breeds of US aircraft subsequently appeared. Worse, ammunition was fed from a fifteen-round fixed magazine so that the gun had to cease firing every time the magazine had to be changed. The Type 96 was vastly inferior to the 40mm Bofors used by US vessels which could put out a sustained rate of fire with a constant-fire top-fed ammunition-clip design.

The IJN's Fleet Combat Air Patrol had too few aircraft and an inadequate early warning system, including, crucially, a lack of radar. Poor radio communications with the fighter aircraft hindered effective command and control of the Combat Air Patrol. The escort warships were deployed as visual scouts at long range, not held close to the carriers where their coordinated AA fire could be brought to bear in force. A picket line of Japanese submarines was late in getting into position partly due to the haste in which the operation was put together – and this let the three US carriers and their escorts reach their assembly point, Point Luck, 325 nautical miles north east of Midway, without being detected.

At Point Luck, Fletcher, in command of Task Force 17, and Spruance, in command of Task Force 16, marked time, conducting light flight operations whilst they waited for word of the approach of the Japanese invasion fleet. A second Japanese attempt at reconnaissance, using long-range four-engine Kawanishi H8K flying boats (Allied reporting name Emily), to scout Pearl Harbor prior to the battle and establish if carriers were present was thwarted when Japanese submarines assigned to refuel the Emilys discovered that the intended replenishment RV point, a deserted bay off French Frigate Shoals, was now home to US warships alerted by an identical first search mission in March.[12] Yamamoto and his commanders were therefore unaware of the movements of US carriers before the battle. Were they at Pearl – or were they at sea? The Japanese did not know.

3 June

As TF 16 and TF 17 held station at Point Luck, some 10 miles apart, air patrols from both Midway and from the carriers were flown regularly – as the anticipated battle drew near. At about 0900, a US Consolidated PBY Catalina flying boat from Midway spotted the Japanese Occupation Force approximately 500 nautical miles to the west south west of Midway – mistakenly reporting this group as the Main Force and the alarm was broadcast for US forces defending the atoll. Rear

Admiral Frank Jack Fletcher, in overall tactical command of the two Task Forces aboard TF 17 *Yorktown*, ordered Spruance's TF 16 to move to locate and strike the enemy carrier force. Spruance (CTF 16) split his forces into two parts, allowing 'Pete' Mitscher, the skipper of *Hornet*, to operate independently from the flagship *Enterprise*. Fletcher (CTF 17), in *Yorktown*, would send his scout planes to the north to search for the as yet undetected Japanese carriers. *Yorktown* would arrive just as the battle began the following day, 4 June.

Nine Boeing B-17 Flying Fortress four-engine bombers took off from Midway at 1230 for the first air attack. At about 1700, they found Rear Admiral Raizō Tanaka's Transport Group carrying the 5,000 IJA landing troops and escorted by the light cruiser *Jintsu* and 10 destroyers 570 nautical miles to the west. As the Japanese destroyers opened up with their AA guns, the B-17 Flying Fortresses released their payloads – but no serious damage was done, although two transport ships received near misses. It is extremely difficult to hit a moving ship from altitude.

4 June

In the small hours of the next morning, at about 0100, four long-range US Consolidated PBY Catalina flying boats carrying torpedoes attacked the Transport Group convoy. The tanker *Akebono Maru* was hit on her bow by a Mark 13 Mod 1 aerial torpedo, which detonated the tanker's defensive gun magazine and tore a 10m-long gash in her side.

By 0430 (local time), Nagumo's carriers had closed Midway sufficiently to launch his initial air attack on Midway itself, designed to take out any US land-based aircraft present and degrade the atoll's defences to allow the amphibious troops to make their landings. A first wave of 108 aircraft armed with high-explosive bombs launched from the four carriers *Kaga*, *Akagi*, *Hiryū* and *Sōryū*. Of the 108 planes of the first wave, there were 36 Aichi D3A Val dive-bombers (each carrying a 550lb bomb under the fuselage and 2 130lb wing-mounted bombs), 36 Nakajima B5N Kate torpedo-bombers armed with bombs – and an escort of 36 Mitsubishi A6M Zero fighters.[13] Eight search aircraft were also launched.

Nagumo had held about half of his planes in reserve – and had them armed with anti-ship torpedoes. The sea was flat and still with about 4 knots of wind – but that belied the gravity of the situation. The Japanese still had no idea that three US fast carriers lurked to the north east of Midway, attempting to remain undetected by Japanese scout planes.

Almost simultaneously with Nagumo's launch, eleven long-range US PBY Catalina flying boats were leaving Midway to patrol in designated search patterns. At 0534, one PBY reported sighting two Japanese carriers – leaving two Japanese carriers unaccounted for. Another PBY spotted the first inbound Midway airstrike from the Japanese carriers 10 minutes later and radioed 'Many planes heading Midway.' The inbound bombing strike was also picked up on radar on Midway – and a group of Marine, Navy and Army land-based fighters were scrambled and lifted off from Midway. Instead of finding and surprising US fighters neatly lined up in rows on the tarmac, US fighters would be in the air.

Torpedo-bombers and dive-bombers then lifted into the air from Midway– along with a dozen US Army B-17 Flying Fortress bombers that were vectored to attack the Japanese carriers from 20,000ft. They would have no fighter cover as the fighters would be used to protect Midway itself. But as seen the day before, hitting a moving ship from high altitude was extremely difficult – even without having to deal with enemy AA fire and CAP attention.

The subsequent initial attacks on Japanese shipping by these disparate groups of land-based planes from Midway would begin about 0710 when six TBF Avenger torpedo-bombers and four twin-engine Martin B-26 Marauder medium bombers attacked, the latter engaging *Akagi* and forcing her to make evasive manoeuvres to evade two torpedoes and for the CAP to engage. Little damage was however initially inflicted on the Japanese ships. Two Marauders were shot down by Japanese CAP and AA fire for the loss of one Zeke.

Three-quarters of an hour later at 0755, Japanese lookouts spotted the inbound raid by a dozen USAAF B-17 Flying Fortress bombers from Midway. The carriers were able to evade all the bombs released from high altitude. The US attacks began a series of running engagements by land-based planes from Midway. The attacks would be repelled at a total loss to the US of 5 TBF torpedo-bombers, 2 old Vought SB2U Vindicator dive-bombers, 8 SBD scout dive-bombers and 2 Martin B-26 Marauder medium bombers. Amongst the casualties was Major Lofton R. Henderson, commander of Marine Scout Bombing Squadron 241 (VMSB-241), who led sixteen Marine Corps SBD Dauntless dive-bombers in a glide-bombing attack on the carrier *Hiryū*. His left wing was hit by AA fire and burst into flames as he began his final approach. He continued the attack and was killed as his plane dived towards the enemy carrier, leading his squadron off into action. (The main airfield at Guadalcanal captured from the Japanese in August that year would subsequently be renamed Henderson Field in his honour and is now the site of Honiara International Airport).

Earlier, whilst the first land-based planes from Midway were still en route to make the initial attacks on Japanese ships, 20 American Brewster F2A Buffalo fighters and 7 Grumman F4F Wildcat fighters attacked the inbound 108-strong Japanese formation of planes some 30 miles out from Midway, starting a running fight that lasted all the way to Midway. As a result, 2 American F4F Wildcat fighters and 13 out-dated Brewster F2A Buffalo fighters were destroyed for the loss of 5 Japanese bombers and fighters.

At 0620, the first Japanese carrier aircraft arrived over Midway – bombing and heavily damaging the US base. Three Japanese aircraft were destroyed by ground AA fire whilst three more were forced to ditch. The Japanese attack however failed to destroy fully the US airfield and facilities at Midway – such that returning US planes were still able to use the airbase to refuel and mount their further attacks on the Japanese invasion force. Japanese pilots reported to Nagumo that a second air attack on Midway would be required before the invasion troops being carried by the Transport Group could go ashore as planned on 7 June.

Aboard *Yorktown*, after receiving the PBY sighting reports of two enemy carriers at 0534, Rear Admiral Fletcher had tasked the three US carriers of the two Task Forces 16 and 17 to sail south west to close the distance on the unsuspecting Japanese force. Task Force 16 (Spruance – *Enterprise* and *Hornet*) was to proceed towards the enemy and attack as soon as possible, whilst TF 17 (Fletcher – *Yorktown*) would follow as soon as her scout planes searching to the north for the two, as yet undetected, Japanese carriers were recovered. She would then also launch strikes against the two carriers that had already been reported. The two task groups had now been separated and *Yorktown* rendered vulnerable.

Spruance delegated Halsey's Chief of Staff, Captain Miles Browning, to finalise the attack and oversee the launch. Browning guessed that if the US aircraft launched 2 hours ahead of schedule, they would catch the first wave of Japanese planes after they returned from the Midway strike. Instead of being aloft, the decks of the Japanese carriers would be crowded with planes in transition, refuelling and vulnerable to fire. Spruance judged that although the range was extreme, a strike could succeed and gave the order to launch – he felt he had to attack the Japanese carriers and protect his own carriers from a counter-strike.

Rather than waiting to assemble at a rendezvous point to launch a well-coordinated attack involving fighters, torpedo-bombers and dive-bombers, the launches would take place in piecemeal fashion with US aircraft proceeding to the target in several different groups. The usual practice would be a combined strike with both dive-bombers and torpedo-bombers. Torpedo-bombers had to attack low and slow to deliver their torpedoes – and would be escorted by fighters to suppress AA fire. The dive-bombers attacked from altitude – and this form of combined attack from both low and high altitudes split the enemy AA fire and rendered it less dense and effective.

Following Browning's advice, Spruance launched his attack. Shortly after 0700, fighter pilots were called to deck from their ready rooms – then the scout-bombers were manned and finally the torpedo planes. Aboard *Hornet*, Mitscher addressed his crew via the bridge microphone: 'We intend to launch planes to attack the enemy while their planes are still returning from Midway. We will close to about a hundred miles from the enemy's position.'[14] Starting cartridges popped and echoed across the flight deck as engines roared into life – the launching took almost an hour, and the departing planes kept strict radio silence. Latest intelligence reporting placed the enemy as 155 miles distant, to the south west.

Enterprise and *Hornet* had completed launching by 0755. The last planes roared off the flight deck, the fighters climbing to 19,000ft and heading towards the enemy at 110 knots, whilst the slower torpedo-bombers made 100 knots at low altitude below the cloud cover.

As instructed by Yamamoto, Nagumo had kept half of his carrier aircraft aboard in reserve whilst his first-wave strikes went in against Midway – two squadrons each of dive-bombers and torpedo-bombers remained on each of his four carriers. The dive-bombers were as yet unarmed – whilst the torpedo-bombers were already armed with torpedoes, ready for immediate use should any US warships be located.

At 0715, following pilot reports from the first wave that a second strike against Midway's defences would be required before the invasion could proceed, Nagumo ordered that his reserve aircraft be re-armed with contact-fuzed general purpose (GP) bombs for use against land installations and defences. This was a direct contravention of Yamamoto's orders to keep the reserve force armed for anti-ship operations. Re-arming began immediately and had been underway for about 30 minutes when, at 0740, a report was received from a scout plane from the cruiser *Tone* that a US naval force had been detected to the east of Midway, although the report did not specify what ships were present.

Nagumo belayed his order to re-arm the reserve planes with GP bombs whilst he sought further intelligence on the composition of the enemy force – armour-piercing bombs and aerial torpedoes might be required for use against US warships. About half an hour later, Nagumo received a report clarifying that at least one carrier had been sighted.

Nagumo now had a dilemma – the report had changed everything; it was the pivotal moment of the battle. One of his carrier division commanders pressed for Nagumo to launch a strike immediately against the US ships with the forces he presently had on his carriers. However, Nagumo's Midway strike aircraft and CAP fighters were on their way back to the carriers and, by now running low on fuel, would need to land quickly or face ditching in the sea.

As a result of the constant flight-deck activity over the last hours however the Japanese had not had the opportunity to spot (position) their reserve squadrons and CAP fighters on the carrier flight decks for launch. It would take 30–60 minutes to complete re-arming his reserve aircraft below decks, spot them on the flight deck and launch for a coordinated attack on the US carrier and warships. If Nagumo made that move, his returning first-strike bombers and CAP fighters would have to wait for the reserve squadrons to launch before they could land. In the event, Nagumo decided to belay launching his reserve aircraft for a second strike, to allow the incoming aircraft to land. The returning fighters and bombers would be refuelled and rearmed – and launch with the aircraft held in reserve, armed with torpedoes, for a coordinated strike on the US units. Nagumo believed he had time to do so – but he was wrong.

Meanwhile, some 150 miles away, the *Hornet* air group had assigned all ten of its Fighting 8 (VF-8) Wildcat fighters to escort the SBD dive-bombers of Bombing Squadron 8 (VB-8) and Scouting Squadron 8 (VS-8). The US fighters and dive-bombers headed towards the enemy at 125mph at 19,000ft – whilst the fifteen slower torpedo-bombers of Torpedo Squadron 8 (VT-8) were making 110mph, much lower down at 1,500ft. (Each carrier's Fighting, Scouting, Bombing or Torpedo Squadron took the identifying number of their carrier, e.g., *Hornet* was CV-8, thus at this point of the war, her Air Group 8 squadrons were referred to as Fighting 8, Scouting 8, Bombing 8, Torpedo 8 and so on for the other carriers. *Yorktown* (CV-5) however had had her air group augmented by planes and crew from *Saratoga* (CV-3), which was east of Pearl and not involved in the battle itself, hence reference to Fighting 3, etc.) (Later in the war, squadron numbers were assigned randomly rather than taking the number of the assigned carrier, to prevent the enemy working out a carrier deployment from its squadron numbers.)

The *Enterprise* (CV-6) Air Group assigned its Fighting 6 (VF-6) Wildcats to cover Bombing 6 (VB-6) and Scouting 6 (VS-6) at altitude. The slower torpedo-bombers of Torpedo Six (VT-6), flying much lower, could call down support from the Wildcats if required.

On *Yorktown*, as the last of her search group aircraft returned at 0830, the deck was hastily respotted for launch of her attack group – 17 Dauntless SBDs from VB-3, 12 Devastator TBDs from VT-3 and 6 Wildcats from Fighting 3 rose into the air. All three carriers kept a reserve of fighters to protect the two task forces if attacked. An apparent shortage of fighters was forcing commanders to choose between protecting their ships or supporting the air strikes.

The *Enterprise* and *Hornet* strike aircraft initially had difficulty in locating the Japanese carrier force. The thirty-seven dive-bombers and torpedo-bombers of *Hornet*'s Air Group 8, escorted by ten Wildcat fighters flew west, not south west, for hours – passing well to the north of the Japanese carriers and missing them completely. Gradually the shorter range Wildcats began to run low on fuel and first in pairs, then in divisions, they were forced to turn back, leaving the dive-bombers and TBD Devastators to go on alone. None of the returning VF-8 Wildcats managed to find *Hornet* – all ten ran out of fuel and ditched. Eight pilots were picked up by patrols in the following days but two were never seen again.

The dive-bombers of *Hornet*'s Bombing 8 (VB-8), loaded with 1,000lb bombs, turned back soon afterwards, their poor fuel situation forcing them to fly to Midway rather than to their carrier and jettison their bombs just outside the reef before landing.

The fifteen TBD Devastator torpedo-bombers of *Hornet*'s Torpedo Squadron 8 (VT-8) pressed on, on a different but correct bearing. And finally, the enemy was sighted – all four carriers, *Akagi, Kaga, Hiryū* and *Sōryū*, appearing in the distance.

At 0920, the VT-8 Devastators commenced their attack – but ominously, with the Wildcats gone, they had no fighter cover. The Douglas TBD Devastator torpedo-bomber had first flown for the Navy in 1935 when it had been the first widely used carrier-based monoplane – and the most advanced naval aircraft flying. However, the fast pace of aircraft development had meant that by the time of the Pearl Harbor raid in December 1941, it was already out-dated. It carried the Mark 13 aerial torpedo, which was prone to faults – such as hitting a target but failing to explode or running deeper than the depth set. The Devastators had a long, slow, straight-line glide-bombing approach at a speed of just 200mph – making them relatively easy prey on attack for both CAP fighters and ship-borne AA guns. As a result of the low, slow attack run, they were usually flanked by fighters to suppress AA fire. Torpedo-bombers would usually split up for an 'anvil attack' – where planes would come in against a carrier from various points around at least

94

180 degrees of the compass. If the quarry turned to the right, it presented a broadside shot for several torpedoes – likewise if it turned to the left.

Without their Wildcat fighter escort, all fifteen TBD Devastator's from *Hornet*'s VT-8 were extremely vulnerable as they attacked, low and slow. Initially they targeted *Akagi*, but heavy AA fire and the arrival of an estimated thirty Mitsubishi A6M CAP Zeros led them to break off that attack and target another flattop, most likely *Sōryū*. Without being able to inflict any damage, one by one the fifteen vulnerable VT-8 Devastators were shot down by AA fire and by swarms of Zeros with the loss of twenty-nine US aircrew.

The fourteen Devastators of VT-6 from *Enterprise* attacked shortly afterwards – losing nine aircraft (one later ditched).

The twelve Devastators of VT-3 from *Yorktown* attacked *Hiryū* at 1010, about 50 minutes after the attacks began. They were escorted by six VF-3 Wildcats and had seventeen SBD dive-bombers of VB-3 high

Douglas TBD-1 Devastator torpedo plane of *Enterprise* (CV-6) Torpedo Squadron Six (VT-6) drops a Mark XIII torpedo during exercises, October 1941. (National Archives 80-G-19230)

above. This later attack drew the majority of the Japanese CAP fighters towards *Hiryū* in the south-east quadrant of the fleet. Ten of the twelve VT-3 Devastators were shot down.

Fierce Japanese shipborne AA fire and the Japanese Combat Air Patrol, flying the much faster and more manoeuvrable Mitsubishi A6M2 Zero fighter, had decimated the slow unescorted, under-armed TBD Devastators, which only had a defensive .30in (7.62mm) Browning machine gun for the rear gunner and a .30in or .50in (12.7mm) M2 Browning machine gun fitted in its cowling. But as costly and apparently futile as the TBD Devastator attacks had been, they did prevent the Japanese from preparing to launch their own counter-strike against the US carriers.

The TBD Devastators however had been virtually annihilated. Of the forty-one Devastators launched from the three US carriers, only six were able to return to their own carriers. Some TBDs did get close enough to the Japanese carriers to drop their torpedoes and strafe the enemy ships, forcing the carriers to make sharp evasive turns – but all of their torpedoes either missed or failed to explode on contact. There were no successful torpedo hits. (The attack by the forty-one Devastators was such a costly slaughter that Midway would be the last time the TBD Devastator was used in combat.)

Poor control of Japanese CAP fighters however meant that most were now down at lower altitudes chasing the vulnerable TBD Devastator torpedo-bombers, which had now released their weapons. The Japanese CAP was out of position for the next US attack – and its aircraft were also now beginning to run low on fuel and ammunition.

At the same time as Japanese observers spotted the torpedo attack by *Yorktown*'s VT-3 and the Japanese CAP was vectored to intercept, three squadrons of dive-bombers, flying from *Enterprise* and *Yorktown* (VB-6, VS-6 and VB-3), were by chance approaching independently from the south west and north east – undetected by Japanese aircraft. The Japanese ships had no radar.

The two squadrons from *Enterprise* (VB-6 and VS-6) were running low on fuel due to the time spent searching for the seemingly elusive enemy – but they had spotted the wake of the Japanese destroyer *Arashi* steaming at full speed to re-join Nagumo's carriers after unsuccessfully depth-charging the US submarine *Nautilus* (which had unsuccessfully attacked the battleship *Kirishima*). The two squadrons turned to follow the *Arashi*'s heading – hoping to be led to the Japanese Fleet. Some dive-bombers however ran out of fuel and had to ditch – but finally, the great prize appeared below them in the distance. The Japanese carriers.

All three dive-bomber squadrons, VB-6, VS-6 and VB-3, arrived over the Japanese carrier force almost simultaneously in the optimum position and altitude to attack – from either side of the Japanese carriers. With none of the Japanese ships having radar they were unaware of the approach of the US dive-bomber squadrons until they were physically eyeballed by lookouts aloft. The dive-bombers found that most of the Japanese CAP fighters were off station, glory hunting and attacking the VT-3 torpedo planes from *Yorktown* at low altitude in the south-east quadrant.

As the Americans had earlier suspected, after Japanese carrier aircraft had bombed Midway, Nagumo had ordered his returning torpedo-bombers regassed and re-armed with torpedoes for attacking US shipping. In the hangar decks, armed aircraft were crowded together – fuel hoses criss-crossed the decks to aircraft. Bombs, torpedoes and munitions were stacked around the hangars ready for fitting, rather than being protected in the magazines below the strength deck. For Nagumo, this period of transition was precisely the worst moment that his carriers could be attacked.

At this vulnerable moment, the three squadrons of US dive-bombers had also caught Nagumo's low-flying CAP fighters completely by surprise. After the war, Jiro Horikoshi, who designed the Zero, and Masatake Okumiya, who led many Zero squadrons during the war, wrote in *Zero!*: 'It was the beginning of the end, for our fleet, having no radar to warn them of the approach, was caught completely unaware by this sudden assault. Almost unopposed, the enemy bombers plunged in vertical dives from above the clouds. Our carriers were helpless.'[15] It was another pivotal moment in the battle – a moment that would have seismic ramifications for the war in the Pacific. Nagumo's ships had survived attacks by some ninety US planes so far throughout the morning. He was apparently readying to complete his mission, to destroy Midway's land and air defences and pave the way for successful amphibious landings. But the tide of the battle was about to turn, from apparent success for Nagumo – to crushing defeat.

The two *Enterprise* squadrons VB-6 and VS-6 pushed over for their dives on *Kaga* at 1022 – scoring four or five direct hits, which caused heavy damage, the flight deck was ripped open exposing a large section of the hangar below. The flight deck was rippled and curled back in all directions. One bomb hit right beside the carrier's island, killing Captain Jisaku Okada and most of the ship's senior officers. Another bomb exploded amongst parked planes forward. Several fierce fires were started and began to spread.

Yorktown's VB-3 simultaneously attacked *Sōryū*, scoring at least three hits with 1,000lb bombs that ignited gasoline, creating an inferno that in turn set off stacked bombs and ammunition. Within 6 minutes of the attacks beginning, *Sōryū* and *Kaga* were ablaze from stem to stern, and as the fires intensified, the sides of the *Kaga* blew out.

On *Akagi*, one bomb struck the edge of the mid-ship deck elevator and penetrated to the hangar deck, exploding amongst the armed and fully fuelled aircraft. Some damaged planes stood tail up belching flame and jet-black smoke in fires that were impossible to control. Another bomb was a near miss at the stern, causing critical rudder damage. The fires on *Akagi* spread uncontrollably – and she was soon enveloped in flames.

As none of the Japanese carriers had suffered damage below the waterline, other than the rudder damage to *Akagi*, all three carriers *Sōryū*, *Kaga* and *Akagi* remained afloat but with wooden flight decks and stocked with flammable gasoline and munitions they were consumed by fierce fires. The three carriers were each a couple of miles apart, and within 5–10 minutes of the dive-bombers beginning their attack, each was on fire with a tall column of black smoke rising upwards. It was an astonishing sight.

As firefighting efforts began on Nagumo's flagship *Akagi*, it was initially hoped that she could be saved and towed back to Japan for repair. But as with the other two carriers, the fires grew in intensity, flames licking the glass of the bridge windows. Thousands of gallons of burning fuel found its way into the lower decks and torpedoes began to detonate, the blasts blowing though the sides of the ship. Eventually, all three carriers had to be abandoned and scuttled by torpedoes.

With three Japanese Fleet carriers consumed by fires, the one surviving operational Japanese carrier, *Hiryū*, launched her own aircraft to counter-attack. Once aloft, her first wave of eighteen Aichi D3A Val dive-bombers and six fighter escorts was able to follow US aircraft as they headed for home – they were led to the *Yorktown*. Unlike the Japanese carriers however *Yorktown* had detected the approaching enemy aircraft on onboard radar and had been able to take steps to prevent the type of catastrophic fires that had beset the Japanese carriers. US CAP fighters were aloft, waiting. Shipboard AA guns were manned, gunners at action stations. Flammable gasoline drums on deck were pushed over the side and non-flammable carbon dioxide pumped into fuel hoses. These precautions might not stop her being hit – but they may stop a hit becoming life critical for the carrier.

Between 1400 and 1430, the first wave of Japanese aircraft arrived over *Yorktown* and the nimble Zero fighters engaged the US CAP fighters, allowing the dive-bombers to begin their dives with 550lb and 130lb bombs. *Yorktown* was quickly hit by three bombs that blew a hole in her deck, extinguishing some of her boilers and damaging some AA guns. A column of black smoke rose high into the air and no doubt the Japanese pilots thought that the *Yorktown* was going the same way as their carriers. Rear Admiral Fletcher, in tactical command aboard *Yorktown*, was forced to move his command staff to the heavy cruiser *Astoria* and Spruance meanwhile assumed local tactical command.

However, unlike on the Japanese carriers, as damage-control parties sprang into action, they were able to stop the fires spiralling out of control and setting off catastrophic secondary explosions of flammable materials and munitions. They temporarily patched the hole in *Yorktown's* flight deck and restored power to her boilers sufficient to give her a speed of 19 knots. With these running repairs, she was able to resume air operations.

The cost of this attack had been high for the first wave of strike planes from *Hiryū*. Of the 18 Japanese dive-bombers 13 were shot down as well as 3 of the 6 escort fighters, 2 being damaged by the tough *Enterprise* SBD Dauntlesses returning from their own attack on the Japanese carriers.

About an hour later, the range between the *Hiryū* and the US carriers had closed to less than 100 miles. With one of the three US carriers, the *Yorktown*, badly damaged, the Japanese were determined to strike back and disable a second US carrier and even the score at one carrier left apiece. The fight was still on.

A second wave of ten Nakajima B5N Kate torpedo-bombers escorted by six Zekes launched from the *Hiryū* and some 2 hours after the first wave had attacked *Yorktown*, the second wave spotted and attacked another seemingly operational US carrier with torpedoes. If they could disable or sink this carrier then each side would have one carrier left.

Ironically however the damage-control parties on the *Yorktown* had done such a good job in repairing the flight deck in the lull since the first dive-bombing attack, that although the Japanese believed the carrier below them was a different undamaged carrier, it was in fact the *Yorktown*.[16] The Japanese planes attacked, and despite 5 torpedo-bombers and 2 Zekes being shot down in this attack, 2 aerial torpedoes hit and crippled *Yorktown* – to the extent that she lost all power and developed a 23° list to port.

The Japanese now believed they had crippled a second US carrier – bolstering morale after the serious blows they had received. As the returning aircraft were recovered aboard *Hiryū*, the Japanese prepared for a further strike against what they believed to be the one remaining

US carrier. At 1630, the captain of the *Hiryū* radioed Nagumo with his intention to launch a third strike against the US carriers, timed to attack around dusk. But instead of authorising the attack, Nagumo ordered a withdrawal to the west, no doubt in an attempt to save his one remaining carrier.

Sinking the one remaining Japanese carrier, *Hiryū*, was now the priority for the Americans – and late in the afternoon, a *Yorktown* scout aircraft relocated her. As the contact report reached *Enterprise*, a strike of twenty-four SBD dive-bombers was launched, which included fourteen SBDs of the crippled *Yorktown*'s VB-3. *Hornet* launched sixteen more SBDs at 1600. The US planes closed the *Hiryū* just before 1700, the *Hornet* SBDs circling at 20,000ft as nine B-17s from Midway attempted to bomb *Hiryū*'s escort battleships without success.

At about 1700, the *Hornet* SBDs pushed over into their dives – successfully hitting *Hiryū* with four 1,000lb bombs, possibly five. 'The rain of bombs crippled the flagship in short order and, like her sister ships, the *Hiryū* soon became a helpless hulk, wracked with flaming explosions and abandoned by her crew.'[17]

USS *Yorktown* (CV-5) burning and listing during the Battle of Midway, June 1942. Crew abandon her after she was hit by two Japanese Type 91 aerial torpedoes, 4 June 1942. USS *Balch* (DD-363) is standing by at right of shot. A large oil slick surrounds the damaged carrier, and an inflatable life raft is being deployed off her stern. (National Archives 80-G-17061)

With *Hiryū* ablaze and unable to operate aircraft, the SBDs targeted other ships – scoring hits on a battleship and a heavy cruiser. The US strike planes then withdrew to return to their own carriers – by the time they found them it was getting dark.

The fires on *Hiryū* proved uncontrollable – forcing the evacuation of the crew as the remainder of the Japanese warships steamed away. The Japanese attempted to scuttle *Hiryū* that evening by a torpedo from one of their own destroyers – but *Hiryū* remained afloat for several hours, before finally sinking the next morning.

As darkness fell, seeking to avoid a possible night encounter with heavy Japanese surface units, and believing Yamamoto still planned to invade Midway, Spruance changed course and withdrew to the east. At midnight, he turned back westwards towards the enemy.

The burning Japanese carrier *Hiryū* shortly after sunrise, 5 June 1942 – it would sink a few hours later. Note the collapsed flight deck over the forward hangar. (NH 73065 courtesy of the U.S. Naval History & Heritage Command)

Yamamoto meantime had sent his powerful surface ships, including the super battleship *Yamato*, eastwards to search for the US carriers. He simultaneously detached a cruiser raiding force to bombard Midway. They may have lost their carriers, but the Japanese Fleet still bristled with powerful heavy warships whose guns could inflict huge damage on the US carriers if they could get in range in the darkness.

But, with Spruance having withdrawn to the east, the Japanese search vessels failed to locate the US task forces – and Yamamoto eventually ordered a general withdrawal to the west. This was a piece of good fortune for the US naval forces – as in a night action, the powerful Japanese heavy ships, battleships and cruisers could have overwhelmed Spruance's cruisers and potentially sunk his vulnerable carriers. The next day, despite extensive searches as Spruance headed west again, there was no contact with Yamamoto's forces, which were now retiring to the west.

Over the coming days, several strikes were launched at damaged Japanese stragglers. The Mogami-class heavy cruiser *Mikuma* was spotted on 5 June by a PBY Catalina flying boat from Midway leading a group of vessels including the heavy cruiser *Mogami*. Six SBDs and six Vought SB2U-3 Vindicator dive-bombers from Midway attacked the group – but only near misses were scored, with little damage. The group was then attacked around 1000 the next day as it headed for Wake Island by twenty-six *Hornet* SBDs and then later by thirty-one *Enterprise* SBDs. *Mikuma* was sunk whilst *Mogami* was damaged and had to head to Truk for repair. The destroyer *Arashi* was hit by one bomb that killed thirty-seven of her crew – whilst the destroyer *Asashio* took a bomb hit that killed twenty-two crew.

The fleet tug *Vireo* had taken the crippled *Yorktown* in tow for safety and repair. But late in the afternoon of 6 June, the Japanese submarine *I-168* spotted *Yorktown* and successfully hit her with two torpedoes. A third torpedo struck the destroyer *Hammann*, which had been secured alongside *Yorktown* to assist salvage parties correct her trim and repair battle damage. *Hammann* was mortally wounded – she broke in two and sank alongside the towering carrier – and as she sank, her depth charges went off. The shock waves from the detonations travelling through the incompressible water killed any unfortunate crew who had abandoned ship and were swimming for their lives. In all, eighty of her crew were killed.

With this additional damage to *Yorktown*, and an enemy submarine lurking, the salvage parties aboard *Yorktown* abandoned their attempts and boarded *Vireo*. *Yorktown* sank the following morning just after first light – at 0500 on 7 June.

Japanese heavy cruiser IJN *Mikuma*, photographed from an *Enterprise* (CV-6) SBD on the afternoon of 6 June 1942, after she had been bombed by planes from *Enterprise* and *Hornet* (CV-8). Her midships structure is shattered, a torpedo is dangling from the after port side tubes and there is wreckage atop her No. 4 8in gun turret. (National Archives 80-G-414422)

In all, four Japanese carriers, *Akagi*, *Kaga*, *Sōryū* and *Hiryū* (all part of the *Kidō Butai* six-carrier force that had attacked Pearl Harbor six months earlier), and the heavy cruiser *Mikuma* were sunk at Midway – for the loss of the one US carrier, *Yorktown*, and the destroyer *Hammann*. More than 3,000 Japanese and more than 300 US personnel had perished.

> The loss of the four aircraft carriers *Akagi*, *Kaga*, *Hiryū* and *Sōryū*, shocked the Japanese people. We could not under-estimate the gravity of our defeat, for these four carriers had played the major role in the Navy's smashing victories across the breadth of the entire Pacific. An even greater blow however was the loss of the irreplaceable veteran aircrews and the skilled maintenance crews which went down with their ships.[18]

Mitscher had always believed that carriers should operate as a single unit or group – instead of individually, believing that the CAP could protect the entire force whilst each ship in the group could give supporting AA fire to the others. 'Maybe the *Yorktown* will convince them,' he remarked to one of his staff.[19]

At Midway, Japan learned the hard way that the carrier, the new backbone of any fleet, required maximum concentrated anti-aircraft and anti-submarine protection with all available battleships, cruisers and destroyers. The four Japanese carriers would have been sufficient to defeat the US carrier force at Midway – provided the IJN warships of the Combined Fleet had been concentrated and used to protect Nagumo's flattops, instead of the massively powerful striking force being split up into a number of smaller units.

The light carrier *Zuihō* was trailing the battle providing air support for the powerful warships of Kondō's 2nd Fleet. Of the other Japanese light carriers, the newly completed *Jun'yō* along with the *Ryūjō* were absent from the battle, providing air support for the landings in the Aleutians far to the north, landings that were in fact an unnecessary complication of the multi-prong plan. The *Hiyō*, converted from the ocean liner *Izumo Maru*, was nearing completion at the Kawasaki Dockyard in Kobe and would not enter service until a few weeks later on 31 July 1942.

Had the available seven or eight Japanese carriers been concentrated under Yamamoto's command at Midway, and protected by his many battleships and heavy cruisers, the Japanese would have almost certainly defeated the inferior US naval forces present. Command of air and sea could and should have initially been decisively achieved, allowing the powerful IJN Combined Fleet warships and carriers to then support the landings at Midway. As it transpired however as a result of Nagumo's defeat and the loss of the 4 fleet carriers, the planned landing of 5,000 IJA troops on Midway was cancelled and the Occupation Force was turned back.

On 14 July 1942, after the bitter lessons learnt, the IJN finally reorganised the Combined Fleet around the carriers and land-based air forces. The main fighting fleet was organised as an aircraft carrier task force centred on the fleet carriers *Shōkaku* and *Zuikaku* and designated the 3rd Fleet. Admiral Chūichi Nagumo, whose carrier force had been so comprehensively trounced at Midway, was appointed commander-in-chief of the 3rd Fleet, which would be based at Truk and comprise two carrier divisions of three carriers each, with defensive screens of battleships, cruisers and destroyers. Japan had lost more than 250 planes at Midway – but most of the highly trained pilots had been rescued by destroyers.

Despite her crushing loss of four carriers, Japan could however still field a six-carrier force. *Shōkaku*, *Zuikaku* and the light carrier *Zuihō* now formed CarDiv 1. The light carriers *Jun'yō* and *Ryūjō* formed CarDiv 2, which would be augmented by the converted fifty-three-plane flattop *Hiyō*, shortly after Midway. Only the two fleet carriers *Shōkaku* and *Zuikaku* carried as many as seventy-five planes each.

After Midway, almost overnight, the Japanese emphasis on construction of naval shipping moved from building battleships to the construction of carriers, including conversions and new builds. But working at full capacity, Japanese industry would take until late 1944 to float another carrier armada. The race of industry between Japan and the USA had in itself become a major battleground.

It is impossible to over emphasise how great a turning point Midway was in the Pacific War. The cumulative effect of the Battles of the Coral Sea and Midway had seriously degraded Japan's ability to undertake major offensives and paved the way for the Operation WATCHTOWER landings on Guadalcanal from 7 August 1942 to 9 February 1943 – and for the bitter Solomon Islands campaign, which would later converge with the New Guinea campaign. WATCHTOWER marked the turning point of the war, when the Allies, on the back foot since the Pearl Harbor raid on 7 December 1941, were finally able to begin to move from defending against the Japanese onslaught to an offensive campaign.

With the loss of the four Japanese fast carriers at Midway, from then on, the balance of sea power had swung firmly in favour of the Allies. Japan's expansionist aims were at an end – and in reality, Japan had by now already lost the ability to win the war. Japan did not have the resource base, the population or the industrial might to win a war of attrition against the Allies once her cutting edge of naval power had been smashed. Japan did continue to try to secure more strategic territory in the Pacific – but the cumulative effect of the Battles of the Coral Sea and Midway had reduced her ability to prosecute major offensives successfully. Japan would now concentrate on holding on to the vast territories she had seized as she waited for the inevitable Allied counter-attack. The geography of the Pacific, the difficult terrain of jungle-clad mountainous islands, would take a heavy toll of any Allied invaders that attempted to retake them. Perhaps the Allied populations would tire of a long drawn-out and costly war and seek a negotiated peace – Japan would still have achieved her war aims.

After the battle, Midway would serve as a US seaplane base and as a forward staging point for bombing raids on Wake Island. A US submarine base was subsequently established on Midway, which allowed submarines from Pearl Harbor to refuel and re-provision, extending their radius of operations by 1,200 miles.

Chapter 6

From Defence to Offence –
The Guadalcanal Campaign,
7 August 1942–9 February 1943

By May 1942, the Japanese expansion had reached Guadalcanal, where they had quickly established a seaplane base. At some 90 miles in length and 30 miles wide, Guadalcanal is the largest island, and capital, of the Solomon Islands archipelago, a chain of two roughly parallel north-west to south-east lines of islands, almost 900 miles long, that sit to the north east of the Solomon Sea, east of Papua New Guinea, and to the north east of Australia and the Coral Sea. The Solomons comprise 6 major islands and some 900 minor islands and were at the time a British Protectorate. Guadalcanal sits amidst the southernmost chain of the Solomons, and the channel between it and the island chain to the north is called New Georgia Sound.

But now that the US fast carriers had successfully stopped the Japanese advance following the Battle of Midway, the course of the war had changed. The Allies were no longer on the defensive and were able to consider a limited offensive. Admiral Ernest King (COMINCH-CNO) proposed invasion of the southern Solomon Islands, from where enemy aircraft and naval units presently threatened Allied supply routes from the USA to Australia.

On 2 July 1942, the Joint Chiefs of Staff determined that the first major target to allow a Solomons operation would be the large Japanese base of Rabaul, a township and fine anchorage on the island of New Britain in the Bismarck archipelago group of islands, situated off the north-east coast of New Guinea. Rabaul lies some 370 miles to the north east of New Guinea and had been seized by the Japanese in January 1942, following the Pearl Harbor raid. Since then, it had been developed into the main Japanese base for military and naval activity in the South Pacific.

To attack Rabaul, General Douglas MacArthur, Supreme Commander of the Southwest Pacific Area proposed to advance in a series of rapid operations up the Solomon Islands and New Guinea. Because his land-based Army Air Force bombers could not reach that far without building airfields, MacArthur lobbied for Nimitz's carriers to cover his flanks.[1] MacArthur proposed using his own land-based Army Air Force (AAF) as his main air arm – with the Navy fast carriers assisting and neutralising Japanese airfields and fleet units in the Central Pacific.[2]

Admirals King and Nimitz were horrified. They had already recently lost two fleet carriers, *Lexington* (CV-2) at the Coral Sea and *Yorktown* (CV-5) at Midway, and had suffered heavy losses of the more inferior naval aircraft, such as the TBD Devastator. They did not want to expose their few remaining fast carriers to the confined waters of the Solomon Sea, where they would be easy targets for swarms of Japanese land-based aircraft and deadly submarines.

MacArthur's proposal forced the Navy to reflect on its own strategy. They were clear that fast carriers needed a lot of sea room and could not in any circumstance be dangerously exposed to attack by land-based enemy aircraft. They also reflected on whether their remaining carriers should be placed at the disposal of someone who did not understand their uses as highly mobile, long-range strategic capital ships.

The Navy therefore initially refused to place the fast carriers under MacArthur's direct tactical command.[3] But in the end a compromise strategy was agreed in which the operation would be carried out by both Nimitz's (CINCPOA) South Pacific Area forces, under the direct command of Vice Admiral R.L. Ghormley (COMSOPAC), and by MacArthur's Southwest Pacific Area forces. The previous boundary between the two Areas, which had bisected Guadalcanal, was moved to accommodate the arrangement.

Both Army and Navy would therefore undertake a limited offensive towards Rabaul. The Navy would use its carriers to cover landings by the Marine Corps around Tulagi and Guadalcanal in the southern Solomons in August 1942. MacArthur would meanwhile use the Army Air Force and the small Seventh Fleet to work up the Papuan peninsula of New Guinea.

The Florida Islands (known locally as the Nggela Islands) sit between the two lines of Solomon Islands, towards the south of New Georgia Sound. They comprise two main islands – Nggela Sule to the north and Nggela Pile to the south – along with a number of other smaller islands such as Tulagi, Gavutu and Tanambogo. The IJN had landed on Guadalcanal and occupied Tulagi in May 1942, setting up a seaplane base on Tulagi.

The situation however became critical when, in early July 1942, US reconnaissance revealed that the Japanese had begun construction of a strategic airfield on Guadalcanal. This Japanese air base lay only 555 miles from the large island of Espiritu Santo, in Vanuatu, which the Allies had occupied a few months before in March, and which was being developed into a major Allied supply and support base. An airbase on Guadalcanal would give Japan air superiority over the proposed Allied invasion beaches. The enemy air base also threatened the sea lines of communication from the west coast of the USA to the east coast of Australia. Admiral King announced an accelerated timetable for the first Allied land offensive of the Pacific War, Operation WATCHTOWER, the Guadalcanal campaign. It would begin in just three weeks' time at the beginning of August.

Driven by King, this was an impressively ambitious target. But if the Allies could seize the enemy airfield under construction on Guadalcanal, and also take control of the strategic Florida Islands, which had a fine anchorage at Tulagi Harbour, this would allow Allied naval and air support for the proposed campaign to capture or destroy the Japanese base at Rabaul, far to the north west. The natural harbour at the small island of Tulagi was well placed and well protected – such that the British First World War naval Commander-in-Chief Admiral Jellicoe had visited the area during the First World War and was so impressed by its naval potential that he had proposed it then as a base for British Pacific naval forces.

Whilst Vice Admiral Robert L. Ghormley (COMSOPAC) was in overall command of the operation, Vice Admiral Frank Jack Fletcher, who had commanded the carrier task forces at the Coral Sea and at Midway, would command the Allied expeditionary force, Task Force 61. Fletcher's TF 61 comprised seventy-five US and Australian warships and transports, and he flew his flag in *Saratoga*, one of the three fast carriers taking part. Rear Admiral Thomas C. Kinkaid, who had commanded the Task Group 16.2 screen at Midway, was in *Enterprise* (CV-6), with Rear Admiral Leigh Noyes in *Wasp* (CV-7).

The Guadalcanal campaign began on 7 August 1942, when the 1st US Marine Division, under the command of Rear Admiral Richmond Kelly Turner, carried out amphibious landings on Guadalcanal and the three Florida Islands of Tulagi, Gavutu and Tanambogo. South Pacific Force warships carried out a pre-invasion softening up naval bombardment of the landing beaches, whilst carrier aircraft bombed Japanese positions.

A detachment of 11,000 US Marines landed on Guadalcanal and faced little resistance as they advanced and seized the airfield, which had been abandoned by the construction workers and Japanese troops during the naval bombardment. A total of 3,000 US Marines landed on Tulagi, Gavutu and Tanambogo – they faced stiffer resistance but soon overwhelmed the numerically inferior Japanese garrisons. By the afternoon of the second day, a defensive perimeter encircled the beachhead and airfield on Guadalcanal. But Japanese forces still surrounded the fragile perimeter.

Work began immediately on completing the runway using captured Japanese construction hardware, and the airfield became the focus of all future operations in the area. On 12 August, the airfield was named Henderson Field in honour of the US Marine Corps aviator Major Lofton Henderson, who had been killed during the Battle of Midway on 4 June 1942 as he led sixteen SBD Dauntless dive-bombers in a glide-bombing attack on the carrier *Hiryū*.

Japanese naval aircraft from Rabaul attacked the US amphibious forces several times, sinking the transport *George F. Elliott* (AP-13) and heavily damaging the destroyer *Jarvis* (DD-393). Vice Admiral Fletcher (CTF 61) had begun the operation with ninety-nine carrier aircraft, but losses in combat and to accidents reduced the total to seventy-eight.

Fletcher, the Commander of Task Force 61 (CTF 61), was concerned about the large number of Japanese planes in theatre, and the losses of his own carrier aircraft and the potential for further attacks on his carriers. Fuel for the carriers was also beginning to run low. Getting Ghormley's approval, he advised Rear Admiral Kelly Turner, the commander of the amphibious forces, that with the beachhead established, he was pulling his carriers out a day early. The few remaining fast carriers could not be risked in these dangerous confined waters where they could be targeted by Japanese land-based torpedo- and dive-bombers in an inevitable counter-attack. He also feared the appearance of the Japanese Fleet carriers *Shōkaku* and *Zuikaku* and the three light carriers *Zuihō*, *Jun'yō* and *Ryūjō*, now believed to be at Rabaul. The three US fast carriers *Enterprise*, *Wasp* and *Saratoga* moved out of the combat area and out of range of enemy search planes. *Enterprise* and *Saratoga* loitered to the south of the Solomons, guarding sea lines of communication whilst they waited for the Japanese carriers that were now reported as being en route to be spotted. *Wasp* was ordered south to refuel.

Japanese reaction to the US landings on Guadalcanal was quick and powerful. On 8 August, at about 1600 and just a few hours before darkness, a powerful Japanese force of cruisers and destroyers in a single column that was almost 2 miles long entered New Georgia Sound from the north to begin a run south east towards Guadalcanal. In the darkness of the early hours of 9 August, in the area of sea between the two chains of the Solomon Islands nicknamed 'The Slot' by US forces, undetected by radar, the Japanese naval force achieved complete surprise. Increasing speed to 26 knots and then 30 knots as they approached, at 0138 they began launching Type 93 Long Lance torpedoes at the Allied warships that were providing cover for the landings on Guadalcanal and the Florida Islands. The Long Lance torpedoes had a maximum speed of some 50 knots, carried a warhead of some 490kg of explosive and had an effective range of more than 13 miles.

Shortly afterwards, as they closed, the Japanese ships opened up with their main batteries. The Battle of Savo Island had begun – it would be one of the worst defeats suffered by the US Navy during the war.

In under 2 hours of battle, three US heavy cruisers and an Australian heavy cruiser were sunk, with another heavy cruiser and two destroyers being damaged. More than 1,000 Allied service personnel were dead. A third destroyer was also damaged – and was subsequently sunk after a follow-up Japanese air raid later the same day. The loss of the battle allowed Japanese units to bombard Allied positions ashore – and to reinforce and resupply its own troops, whilst restricting Allied support to a trickle. From the battle onwards, Allied troops received barely enough ammunition and provisions to resist several Japanese operations to retake the islands.

(i) Battle of the Eastern Solomons, 24–5 August 1942

Some two weeks after the initial landings, on 23 August, long-range US patrol planes from Guadalcanal spotted four troop transports escorted by destroyers, elements of an apparent occupation force, 250 miles to the north – on a southerly course. The Japanese intended to land troops on Guadalcanal on 24 August, covered by air support from the fleet carriers *Shōkaku* and *Zuikaku*, the light carrier *Ryūjō* and the seaplane tender *Chitose*.

A strong Japanese naval force was also spotted 100 miles to the east – and reported as consisting of 8 battleships, 6 cruisers and 21 destroyers.[4] Although *Wasp* had withdrawn to the south and would not be involved, the third great carrier versus carrier battle of the Pacific campaign was about to begin.

At 0415 on 24 August, search planes were sent out from the Japanese carriers – and at 1250, a search plane reported sighting *Saratoga* and *Enterprise*. Although the plane was shot down before it could give the

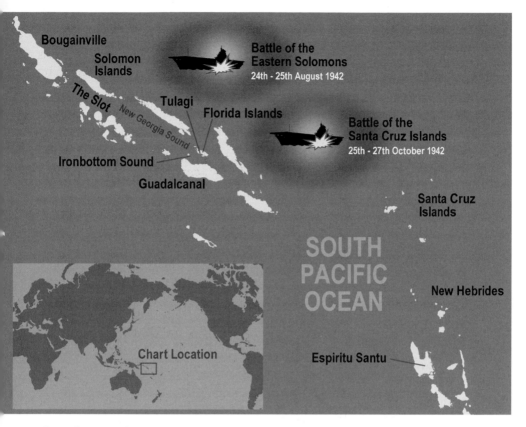

Chart showing the location of the battles of the Eastern Solomons and the Santa Cruz Islands.

exact position, *Shōkaku* and *Zuikaku* launched a first strike of 27 Aichi D3A2 Val dive-bombers and 15 Zeros. About an hour later, a second wave of 27 Vals and nine Zeros lifted off from the carriers – heading south towards *Enterprise* and *Saratoga*. Meanwhile, the light carrier *Ryūjō* launched her aircraft for 2 strikes on Henderson Field.

As Japanese aircraft were inbound to strike the 2 US fast carriers, at about 1400, *Saratoga* aircraft located *Ryūjō*. Consequently, 30 US dive-bombers and 8 torpedo-bombers attacked the light carrier, scoring 4 bomb hits, 1 torpedo hit and numerous near misses. Such was the damage, that at 1755, the stricken light carrier capsized on the surface and sank stern first.

The Val dive-bombers and Zero fighter escorts from *Shōkaku* and *Zuikaku* closed *Saratoga* and *Enterprise* and began their own attacks at 1440. The *Enterprise* became the focus of attention, taking 3 direct bomb

111

hits and 4 near misses that started fires, killed 74 and wounded 95. Despite being badly damaged, with a 10ft-wide hole in her flight deck, after effective damage-control repair work, she was able to withdraw and begin a long limp back to Pearl under her own steam for repair. *Enterprise* was however out of the war for the time being and would remain at Pearl from 10 September until 16 October 1942. That evening aircraft from *Saratoga* damaged the seaplane tender *Chitose* whilst Japanese destroyers were able to shell Henderson Field before turning to run north to join the Occupation Force convoy.

The US warships then retired to the south – to get out of range of any approaching Japanese warships. It was a prudent decision as the Japanese battleship group was in fact steaming south to try and engage the US carriers in a surface battle. But in darkness, at midnight, when no contact had been established with US units, they gave up the chase and turned around.

The battle continued into the following morning of 25 August. Suspecting that the two US carriers engaged the previous day had been taken out of the battle by heavy damage, the Japanese group of troop transports moved towards Guadalcanal – and by 0600, the occupation convoy was just 150 miles to the north.

Just after 0600 however eighteen US aircraft flying from Henderson Field attacked the Japanese convoy – hitting the 9,310-ton armed merchant cruiser *Kinryu Maru*, which was carrying troops, with a 1,000lb bomb amidships in her aftship that started fires and caused ammunition to cook off in a large explosion. The 475ft-long ship began to sink, forcing her embarked troops to be evacuated to destroyers and patrol boats before she was scuttled at 0835 by a torpedo from the destroyer IJN *Mutsuki*. The 5,477-ton transport *Boston Maru* was damaged by a near miss whilst a 1,000lb bomb hit the light cruiser IJN *Jintsu* at her fo'c'sle, killing twenty-four crew. Fires were started, that led to her forward magazines being flooded to avoid her munitions cooking off.

By now, the Japanese had lost dozens of valuable aircraft, with their experienced aircrew, from *Shōkaku* and *Zuikaku*. With those losses, allied to the loss of the light carrier *Ryūjō*, the troop transports and naval units, the landing of reinforcement troops was cancelled at 0730 – and both sides withdrew to lick their wounds. Land-based B-17 Flying Fortress bombers from Espiritu Santo however then appeared and at 0944 hit and sunk the stationary destroyer *Mutsuki* as she was embarking troops from the *Kinryu Maru*.

Although *Saratoga* had survived the battle, seven days later she was sighted and torpedoed by a Japanese submarine. Such was the damage that she had to withdraw from her area of operations for repair for three months. Both *Enterprise* and *Saratoga* were now out of action, albeit temporarily.

From their advance bases, both the Americans and Japanese attempted to build up their strength on Guadalcanal, and a number of grim struggles on land, sea and in the air followed, which lasted six months. The Japanese made several attempts to retake Henderson Field between August and November 1942, ushering in three major land battles, seven major naval battles and daily aerial contacts that would eventually culminate in the four-day-long decisive Naval Battle of Guadalcanal from 12–15 November 1942.

On 15 September, *Wasp* (CV-7), *Hornet* (CV-8), the battleship *North Carolina* (BB-55) and ten other warships were escorting troop transports carrying the 7th Marine Regiment to Guadalcanal. Whilst some 150 nautical miles south east of San Cristobal Island in an area nicknamed 'Torpedo Junction', *Wasp* was suddenly struck by three torpedoes in quick succession, from a spread of six fired by the Japanese submarine *I-19*. There was a rapid series of explosions and within half an hour of the strikes, nearly 200 crew had been killed and the position was so dire that the carrier had to be abandoned. She was eventually scuttled by torpedoes fired from destroyers.

Rear Admiral Leigh Noyes, in command of the task force aboard his flagship *Wasp*, suffered burns during the attack, and was criticised for crossing the same track twelve times in three days.[5] He was ordered to Pearl Harbor for temporary duty as ComAirPAc. With *Wasp* sunk and *Enterprise* and *Saratoga* undergoing repair, *Hornet* was now left as the only operational US carrier in the South Pacific Area – responsible for providing air cover in the Solomons. The Japanese determined that her destruction was the primary objective of the Imperial Fleet.

Whilst the Allies maintained air superiority over the Solomons during the day from Henderson Field, at night, when Allied aircraft could not operate effectively, the Japanese were able to operate their ships around Guadalcanal without fear of significant interruption – delivering troops and supplies by fast warships in an operation that became known as the Tokyo Express. By mid-October the two sides had roughly the same number of troops on the 90-mile-long island of Guadalcanal.

These were precarious days for the US Navy – and tough for the troops on Guadalcanal. Enemy planes pounded the beachhead – whilst on 13 and 14 October the battleships *Kongō* and *Haruna* carried out a naval bombardment with an estimated 1,000 rounds of main battery 14in shells. The troops ashore knew the air and naval bombardment was a preliminary to an all-out enemy assault, which was massing at Rabaul, Bougainville and Truk. Morale had cratered, the beleaguered and exposed troops ashore knew their predicament was critical.

The Japanese were determined to win back control of Guadalcanal and to recapture Henderson Field, which they intended to use as a staging point for carrier planes to harass and destroy the beleaguered Allied troops. Japanese bombers could then use the airfield to support an assault on Allied naval forces – cutting off and isolating Allied forces in the South Pacific. Guadalcanal was the key to the whole campaign – and almost nightly the enemy poured in men and materiel and sent submarines, planes and light fast surface units to harass Allied supply lines, whilst continuing to build up their own naval force to the north.

With Vice Admiral William Halsey now recovered from his severe bout of dermatitis, on 18 October Admirals King and Nimitz ordered him to relieve Vice Admiral Robert Lee Ghormley in command of the entire Solomons operation. Both Nimitz and King had become concerned at the state of the campaign under Ghormley's command. A sealed despatch from CINCPAC marked 'SECRET' was handed to Halsey on 18 October 1942 – and read bluntly: 'YOU WILL TAKE COMMAND OF THE SOUTH PACIFIC AREA AND SOUTH PACIFIC FORCES IMMEDIATELY.'[6]

After the war, in his book *Admiral Halsey's Story*, Halsey summarised the strategic situation at this point:

> As early as January (1942) the Japanese had occupied Rabaul and Bougainville, both under Australian mandate, and had started their march down the steppingstones of the Solomons, with the obvious intention of jumping to the New Hebrides and New Caledonia, from which they could easily hack through our thin lifeline to New Zealand and Australia. . . . Too many advantages lay with the enemy. . . . he had the initiative and was on the offensive. . . . . three of his major bases – Rabaul, Truk and Kwajalein – were within 1,200 miles, whereas our own nearest base – Pearl Harbor – was 3,000 miles away.[7]

Morale in the South Pacific soared when 'Bull' Halsey arrived in theatre as Commander South Pacific (COMSOPAC) and took over the reins. He was briefed by local commanders and was visible to the troops ashore as he toured the area, visiting the front line to assess the situation.

In addition to Halsey, the new COMSOPAC, two new fast battleships also arrived – under the command of Rear Admiral Willis Augustus

'Ching' Lee. These added to the nine cruisers, twenty-four destroyers and the carriers *Hornet* (CV-8) and *Enterprise* (CV-6), the latter now back in theatre after her repairs at Pearl.

Eight days after Halsey assumed command, Admiral Yamamoto committed nearly all of Nagumo's carrier strength in another attempt to drive the Americans out of Guadalcanal deploying *Shōkaku*, *Zuikaku*, *Jun'yō* and *Zuihō* in what would become the Battle of the Santa Cruz Islands on 26 October 1942. It was another naval battle in which there would be no contact between the surface ships of the two opposing forces.

(ii) Battle of the Santa Cruz Islands, 26 October 1942

By late October, the Japanese had gathered substantial naval and air forces at Truk and New Guinea as they prepared to attempt to regain control of Guadalcanal. The exact composition of the Japanese forces wasn't known to the Allies at this time but in fact consisted of 5 battleships, 4 carriers, 8 heavy and 4 light cruisers, 27 destroyers, 12 submarines supported by 220 land-based aircraft at Rabaul.[8] With the IJA planning to launch a major offensive on Guadalcanal on 20 October, Yamamoto's warships began to move towards the southern Solomons in support of that operation and to engage any Allied carriers or warships that closed on Guadalcanal to oppose it.

Opposing Yamamoto's powerful naval forces, with the sinking of *Wasp* and torpedoing of *Saratoga*, the US Third Fleet had at first consisted of 2 small task forces: 1 commanded by Rear Admiral Norman Scott and comprising the battleship *Washington* (BB-56), 1 heavy cruiser, 1 light cruiser and 3 destroyers. The other was commanded by Rear Admiral George D. Murray and comprised the sole remaining carrier, *Hornet* (CV-8), with 2 heavy cruisers, 2 light cruisers and 6 destroyers. Once the newly repaired *Enterprise* arrived back in the South Pacific from Pearl, a third task force under the command of Rear Admiral Thomas C. Kinkaid was formed that included the battleship *South Dakota* (BB-57), 1 heavy cruiser, 1 light cruiser and attendant destroyers. The *Enterprise* task force rendezvoused with the *Hornet* group on 24 October, some 273 nautical miles north east of Espiritu Santo, where the combined forces were reorganised.

On that morning of 24 October, a Japanese heavy cruiser and four destroyers landed troops and supplies on Guadalcanal, then stood off and bombarded Allied shore positions. Two other large enemy naval forces were then reported as steaming south. It was clear a major operation was in hand and Halsey ordered his own naval forces to search for the enemy and destroy it, issuing a final despatch to all his combat commands: 'ATTACK REPEAT ATTACK.'[9]

On the night of 25 October 1942, Rear Admiral Kinkaid's TF 16 (*Enterprise*, 2 heavy cruisers and 8 destroyers) and Rear Admiral Murray's TF 17 (*Hornet*, 4 heavy cruisers and 6 destroyers) were operating together and about 10 miles apart as they conducted a counter-clockwise sweep north of the Santa Cruz Islands, some 200 miles east of Guadalcanal. Task Force 64, under command of Rear Admiral 'Ching' Lee in the battleship *Washington*, and operating with three heavy cruisers and six destroyers, was deployed closer to Guadalcanal in a supporting position. Some sixty combat aircraft were now based at Henderson Field on Guadalcanal with more at Espiritu Santo, 400 miles to the south east.

At about 0300 on 26 October, Japanese naval forces were initially located some 300 miles north west of the US carrier groups by PBY Catalina reconnaissance flying boats – but the reports were unclear and delayed, reaching Kinkaid just after 0500. As a result of the delay, and the likely change in position of the enemy forces, no immediate strike was launched pending confirmation of the enemy position.

The Japanese had divided their forces into three groups, a Vanguard, an Advanced force and the Main Body, the latter containing the carriers *Shōkaku*, *Zuikaku* and *Zuihō* with one heavy cruiser and eight destroyers under Nagumo's command. At 0645, SBD scout planes launched at first light from *Enterprise* located the enemy Main Body, by which time the range had closed to under 200 miles. Almost simultaneously a scouting Japanese seaplane spotted the *Hornet* Task Force 17 and reported back. The Japanese were first to launch – and by about 0740, a first strike of sixty-four Japanese dive-bombers, torpedo-bombers and fighters had roared down their flight decks into the wind and were on their way to hit the US carriers.

About 20 minutes later, at about 0800, the US carriers began launching their air groups for an immediate attack. By 0815 there were seventy-four US planes aloft and heading towards the enemy whilst thirty-eight CAP fighters patrolled above the US carriers.

As the air battle began to develop, the Vanguard force of 2 battleships, 3 heavy cruisers, 1 light cruiser and escort destroyers, under the command of Rear Admiral Hiroaki Abe, was sent forward to attempt to engage the US forces. The Advanced force, consisting of the 48-plane carrier *Jun'yō*, 2 more battleships, 4 heavy cruisers, 1 light cruiser and 10 destroyers, was also brought forward at flank speed so that *Jun'yō*'s planes could join the attack. Meanwhile, two *Enterprise* SBD scout dive-bombers, responding to the earlier contact reports, pushed over and

116

dived on the carrier *Zuihō* in the Main Body, damaging its flight decks with 500lb bombs and preventing aircraft operations.

At 0810, *Shōkaku* in the Main Body launched a second wave of twenty-four strike aircraft to follow in after the sixty-four planes of the first wave that were now closing the US carriers. Half an hour later, *Zuikaku* launched 16 torpedo-bombers and 4 Zeros – there were now a combined 110 Japanese aircraft on their way to hit the US carriers. The two opposing strike forces passed each other in the air, there was some contact – but largely each group proceeded with their own individual primary mission.

As the Japanese first-strike planes arrived over the US carriers, *Enterprise* was temporarily shrouded by a rain shower – and the Japanese planes initially concentrated on the more exposed *Hornet*. Meanwhile, by 0850, the first US planes had passed by Abe's Vanguard force and contacted the Main Body. As they arrived over the Japanese carriers, *Hornet* SBD's began to pound *Shōkaku* for the second trial she had faced in six months. The Japanese CAP responded, shooting down two SBDs and causing two more to abort. Several US bombs however hit *Shōkaku* and wrecked her flight deck.

Just after 0900, sixteen Aichi D3A Val dive-bombers and twenty Nakajima B5N Kate torpedo-bombers made a coordinated attack on *Hornet*'s port side. In just 15 minutes, *Hornet* was hit by a semi-armour-piercing 551lb bomb on her flight deck aft, which penetrated three decks down before exploding and killing more than fifty men. A second bomb hit the flight deck, detonating on impact and killing thirty men. The third bomb penetrated three decks before exploding.

An Aichi D3A Val dive-bomber, on fire and badly damaged by AA, fire crashed into *Hornet*'s island and stack, killing seven crew and spreading burning aviation gasoline over the deck.

Simultaneously, twenty Nakajima B5N Kate torpedo-bombers were approaching *Hornet* from two directions. Twelve Kates, in line abreast, each some 100ft apart, scored two torpedo hits amidships, seriously damaging electrical systems and engines. A third torpedo detonated on hitting the carrier's wake during a hard-right turn – jamming her rudders at full right. *Hornet* began to flood and take on a list, and as her engines stopped, the great carrier slewed to a halt. Another damaged Val crashed into her port side near the bow, starting fires.

Hornet was now dead in the water, on fire and listing. With no power available, she was unable to launch or recover her aircraft, which had to land on *Enterprise* or ditch. The heavy cruiser *Northampton* (CA-26) established a tow to *Hornet* and with the remaining Japanese aircraft now attacking *Enterprise*, *Northampton* began to tow *Hornet* away from the contact, managing to make about 5 knots. Below decks on *Hornet*, repair crews attempted to contain the flooding and restore power.

The Japanese first-strike aircraft began to return to their carriers – and *Enterprise* was spotted emerging from the rain squall that had cloaked her – and the carrier's position was reported back. Believing that *Hornet* was sinking, *Enterprise* now became the focus of attention for the second wave of Japanese strike planes – from about 1000 onwards. Twenty-four Aichi D3A dive-bombers initially attacked her, the US CAP shooting down two of them.

Enterprise took two 551lb bomb hits and one near miss, which killed forty-four crew and wounded seventy-five. One bomb jammed her forward elevator whilst another hit the forward end of her flight deck, penetrating her fo'c'sle and bursting in the water. Another bomb was a near miss, the shock tossing a parked plane overboard and rupturing a seam in one of her fuel tanks and triggering her to leave a trail of oil.

Sixteen *Zuikaku* torpedo planes arrived 20 minutes later and attacked *Enterprise*. The CAP pounced them on, shooting down three and damaging a fourth. None were able to hit *Enterprise*, and the contact had ended by 1100.

The *Enterprise* and *Hornet* CAP fighters, allied to shipborne AA fire, had successfully downed more than half of the Japanese dive-bombers.

USS *Hornet* (CV-8) dead in the water with a destroyer alongside at the Battle of the Santa Cruz Islands, 26 October 1942. (National Archives 80-G-304514)

It was a tale that was repeated wherever the Japanese planes attacked – the rate of attrition of their aircraft was simply staggering.

Damage control suppressed the fires on *Enterprise*, such that at 1115, *Enterprise* was able to reopen her flight deck and begin landing her own aircraft that were now returning from hitting the Japanese carriers. But some 10 minutes later, *Jun'yō* aircraft arrived and attacked *Enterprise*, damaging her further.

Between 1130 and 1400, the two undamaged Japanese carriers that were still able to land aircraft, recovered the few aircraft that were returning from the first strikes and prepared a second strike. The obvious scale of the loss in aircraft was shocking to Japanese eyes. Whereas the skies had been full of planes as the first strike departed, now there were only a few planes in the air, staggering back to the carriers, each one bullet-holed by AA fire, pilots and crew shaken by what they had just been through.

At 1520, a second strike of nine Kate torpedo-bomber planes from *Jun'yō* attacked *Hornet*. One scored a crucial torpedo hit on *Hornet*'s starboard side, which destroyed the repairs to her electrical system. The carrier took on a 15° list and with no electrical power for the pumps, she was now in sinking condition. With *Hornet* crippled, and *Enterprise* badly damaged, believing that the Japanese had two undamaged carriers in the combat area, Kinkaid decided to withdraw *Enterprise* and her screen from the battle to the south east, leaving *Hornet* behind.

A couple of hours later, at 1727, Halsey was advised that a Japanese surface force was now approaching, which would overhaul any towing attempt – he promptly ordered *Hornet* abandoned and sunk.

Once *Hornet*'s crew had been picked up by escort destroyers, US warships then began to scuttle the stricken carrier, firing nine torpedoes into her, some of which did not explode. The destroyers *Mustin* (DD-413) and *Anderson* (DD-411) also fired more than 400 5in rounds into her – before having to leave the area when the Japanese surface force began to approach.

The Japanese surface force closed on the abandoned and badly listing *Hornet*, and the destroyers *Makigumo* and *Akigumo* administered the *coup de grâce* with four 24in Long Lance torpedoes. *Hornet* finally slipped under the surface at 0135 early the next morning, 27 October. Of her crew of 2,200, 140 had lost their lives. (Less than a year later her name would be allocated to the new Essex-class carrier *Kearsarge*, which would be commissioned as *Hornet* (CV-12).)

The Japanese naval units then withdrew from the contact area, refuelled near the Solomons and were back at Truk by 30 October. The US forces retired to Espiritu Santo and New Caledonia where the sole surviving US carrier in theatre, the battered *Enterprise*, underwent temporary repairs before returning to the Solomons just two weeks later to support Allied forces during the Naval Battle of Guadalcanal.

Despite the attacks on *Hornet* and *Enterprise*, the new fast battleship *South Dakota*, with her fine array of modern AA weaponry, had claimed dozens of attacking Japanese aircraft. The battle convinced Halsey of the folly of operating fast carriers in the confined waters of the Solomons. In the meantime, he awaited the return to service of the damaged *Saratoga*.

On the Japanese side, *Shōkaku* and *Zuihō* had both been badly damaged and had to return to Japan for repair. *Zuihō* would return to Truk three months later in late January 1943. *Shōkaku* would be unable to return to duty until July 1943.

The number of Japanese airmen killed was devastating. They had lost almost 100 planes and 148 pilots and aircrew, with a high ratio of experienced pilots, group leaders and squadron leaders being lost. By now, after the great carrier battles of the Coral Sea, Midway, the Eastern Solomons and the Santa Cruz Islands, almost half of the more than 750 elite carrier aviators who had taken part in the Pearl Harbor raid just a year previously in December 1941 were now dead. Although *Zuikaku* had largely escaped physical damage, with so few aircrew left and no quick way to replace them, she had to return to Japan for training of new crew and aircraft ferrying duties and would not return to the South Pacific until February 1943. The four air groups on the Japanese carriers had been decimated – Japan was left with only one active carrier in the area, *Jun'yō*. As a result of being so weakened, there would be little effective carrier air support in the Battle of Guadalcanal a few weeks later.

By contrast, although seventy-four US aircraft had been lost at the Santa Cruz Islands, only twenty had been combat losses.[10] With a higher survivability of aircraft, only twenty-six pilots and aircrew had been killed.

(iii) Naval Battle of Guadalcanal, 12–15 November 1942

The final Japanese attempt to reinforce her forces on the 90-mile-long island of Guadalcanal developed into the Naval Battle of Guadalcanal fought between 12 and 15 November 1942. It was a decisive engagement in a series of combined air and sea engagements over four days, mostly near Guadalcanal.

US intelligence analysts detected the beginning of yet another enemy offensive. Halsey was briefed on 9 November that it was expected that planes would bomb Guadalcanal on the 11th and that enemy naval units would bombard Henderson Field on the night of the 12th to destroy Allied aircraft that might attack a subsequent invasion convoy. After a day-long carrier attack on the 13th, troops would land and attempt to retake Henderson Field.[11]

A heavily protected Japanese convoy of 11 transports carrying 7,000 troops, with 13 destroyer escorts, was detected on 12 November running down New Georgia Sound (The Slot), closing on Guadalcanal. A powerful battleship force was present to provide big-gun support.

As Allied surface forces contacted the inbound Japanese force, Halsey sent the *Enterprise* task force 100 miles west of the Solomons axis, with Rear Admiral 'Ching' Lee's fast battleships force taking a parallel course inboard, midway between *Enterprise* and the Solomons chain. *Enterprise* planes would strike across the screening battleships.

Although not a fast-carrier action, *Enterprise* aircraft shuttling out of Henderson Field helped sink the battleship *Hiei*, the first enemy battleship lost during the war, along with a heavy cruiser, two destroyers and seven transports – although most of the credit goes to 'Ching' Lee, whose two fast battleships fought a successful night battleship versus battleship engagement with the Japanese on 14/15 November.

The four surviving damaged Japanese troop transports managed to run down to Guadalcanal and beach themselves near Tassafaronga early on the morning of 15 November, where they were shelled, bombed and strafed. Only an estimated 2–3,000 IJA troops successfully landed, but most of their ammunition had been lost. The Japanese invasion attempt had been thwarted.

Both sides subsequently withdrew their carriers and battleships from major operations for a full year, Halsey taking his two remaining carriers beyond the range of land-based Japanese aircraft.

Both sides had lost many ships during the Guadalcanal operations – so many that Savo Sound, the stretch of water between Guadalcanal and the Florida Islands came to be known as Ironbottom Sound by the Allies during the campaign. But despite the losses, US naval forces had successfully fought off the Japanese naval force, thwarted the naval bombardment and sunk many of the Japanese troop transports, preventing the planned invasion. The three-day Naval Battle of Guadalcanal ended Japan's attempts to retake Guadalcanal and won Halsey his fourth star. The battle was Japan's last attempt to oust US forces from Guadalcanal and was a decisive strategic victory – pivotal in the outcome of the conflict in the area.

But victory in the Guadalcanal campaign had come at a high cost to Allied naval forces. During the campaign, between 7 August 1942 and 8 February 1943, the carriers *Hornet* (CV-8) and *Wasp* (CV-7) had been sunk along with the heavy cruisers *Astoria*, *Chicago*, *Northampton*,

Quincy, *Vincennes*, RAN *Canberra* (Royal Australian Navy), the light cruisers *Atlanta* and *Juneau*, the destroyers *Barton*, *Benham*, *Blue*, *Cushing*, *De Haven*, *Duncan*, *Jarvis*, *Laffey*, *Meredith*, *Monssen*, *O'Brien*, *Porter*, *Preston* and *Walke*. The Motor Torpedo Boats *PT-37*, *PT-43*, *PT-44*, *PT-111*, *PT-112* and *PT-113* were lost along with the transports *Colhoun*, *George F. Elliott*, *Gregory* and *Little*, and the fleet tug *Seminole*.

The list of Allied naval vessels badly damaged during the campaign was even longer, and included the battleships *North Carolina* and *South Dakota*, the carriers *Enterprise* and *Saratoga*, and countless heavy and light cruisers, destroyers, minesweepers and transports.

In return, the INJ had lost 2 battleships, 1 light carrier, 3 heavy cruisers, 1 light cruiser, 11 destroyers, 6 submarines, 13 transports and 5 cargo ships. It was little wonder that Ironbottom Sound acquired its nickname.

Following the battle, with US forces now in undisputed command of Henderson Field and having secured air superiority, the Japanese were forced to resort to daring high-speed supply runs by IJN warships, mainly destroyers but later submarines, down The Slot, to bring personnel, supplies and equipment to their beleaguered isolated garrisons, under cover of darkness. The Japanese supply campaign came to be known by the Allies as the Tokyo Express.

With command of Guadalcanal now secured, the pre-dominantly US Allied forces could now threaten, as planned, the strategically important Japanese base of Rabaul, situated at the north-east-most end of the 323-mile-long crescent-shaped island of New Britain, itself located off north-east Papua New Guinea at the north-western end of the Solomon chain of islands. Rabaul was strategically important to the Japanese due to its proximity to the Japanese-held Caroline Islands, where the major base at Truk was situated.

Victory at Guadalcanal, together with the successful halting and repulse of the Japanese advance in south-eastern New Guinea, marked the turning point of the Pacific War. From this point onwards, following the earlier crucial Battle of the Coral Sea in May 1942 and the Battle of Midway in June 1942, Japan had lost the ability to win the war, and was forced into a defensive posture to try and slow the Allied advance and hold on to seized territory. The Japanese eventually evacuated Guadalcanal in February 1943.

Saratoga completed her repairs at Pearl and on 12 November sailed with Task Force 11 for the US South Pacific HQ at Nouméa, New Caledonia, just as the Naval Battle of Guadalcanal began. Task Force 11 arrived at Nouméa on 1 December 1943. In late January 1943, *Saratoga* launched strike aircraft for Henderson Field, from where they attacked a Japanese airfield at Vila in the Solomons.

(iv) US Fleet Reorganisation Post Guadalcanal, March 1943

In March 1943, a standardised system of numbering the components of the US Atlantic and Pacific Fleets was introduced with even numbers assigned to the Atlantic Fleet and odd numbers to the Pacific Fleet. In anticipation of new ships and new aircraft arriving in the Pacific, the Pacific Fleet was reorganised into three separate fleets, the Third, Fifth and Seventh, the two primary components for CINCPAC in the Pacific being the Third Fleet (formerly the Southwest Pacific Force) and the Fifth Fleet (formerly the Central Pacific Force). The (odd numbered) First and Ninth Fleets were also assigned to the Pacific theatre but were administrative groupings used to facilitate organisation and communications to the task-force system. The Seventh Fleet (which included US and Australian naval forces) was subordinated to the Commander-in-Chief Southwest Pacific Area, General MacArthur.

The Third Fleet would be officially established on 5 August 1943 and included aircraft carriers, battleships, cruisers, destroyers, land-based aircraft and an amphibious force that would be under the command of Admiral 'Bull' Halsey with its onshore HQ at Pearl Harbor. The Third Fleet units would eventually form the basis of the Fifth Fleet when it was established on 26 April 1944 under the command of Admiral Raymond A. Spruance – it became known as the 'Big Blue Fleet'. Spruance and Halsey would in the future alternate command of the Third Fleet, one admiral being in operational command whilst the other admiral and his staff at Pearl would be free to plan future operations. When the fleet was under the command of Spruance it was designated the Fifth Fleet, when under the command of Halsey, it was designated the Third Fleet. (By June 1944, the Fifth Fleet was the largest combat fleet in the world with some 535 warships.)

The carrier situation however in early 1943 remained critical. *Enterprise* needed an overhaul – potentially leaving the venerable *Saratoga* alone. Admiral King called on the British to help – and despite the Admiralty being reluctant to spare a much-needed carrier from the bitter fighting in Europe, the fast carrier HMS *Victorious* was despatched to Pearl Harbor, arriving there on 4 March 1943 to begin familiarisation with US Pacific Fleet units. (*Victorious* would deploy to the South Pacific on 17 May and the two Allied fast carriers would operate together for the next two months.)

On 28 March 1943, the US Joint Chiefs of Staff set forth the course of future operations in the South Pacific. MacArthur's Southwest Pacific Area forces would establish air bases on Woodlark and Kiriwina Islands and seize the Huon peninsula and Madang, all in Papua New Guinea. His forces would also occupy the western end of the 323-mile-long crescent-shaped island of New Britain, situated off north-east Papua New Guinea at the north-western end of the Solomon chain of islands. The powerful Japanese base of Rabaul lay at the north-east-most end.

In a second prong, Allied naval forces under Nimitz were to move up through the Solomon Islands toward Bougainville Island at the north of the Solomons and just to the east of New Britain. This phase of the operation would begin with the New Georgia Islands, north west of Guadalcanal. The net was closing on Rabaul where, in addition to its fine harbour, the Japanese had built five airfields, fortified the surrounding mountains and poured in troops and supplies. It was now a bastion second in strength to Truk, 700 miles northward.

In May 1943, with HMS *Victorious* now operational in the South Pacific, *Enterprise* withdrew for overhaul. *Saratoga* was now the only operational US fast carrier in theatre.

Following the successful conclusion of the Guadalcanal campaign, Halsey began moving north up the Solomons as planned towards Rabaul. The US Navy was rebuilding and strengthening – waiting for the new fast carriers under construction to begin to arrive at Pearl Harbor, ready to open a second Pacific front. It was a time of preparation, planning, recruitment of crew, training – and shipbuilding. The scale of US industry that was brought to bear in the ship-building programme is staggering.

On 14 April 1943, the US naval intelligence effort, code-name MAGIC, intercepted and decrypted a message revealing that Admiral Isoroku Yamamoto, Commander-in-Chief of the IJN Combined Fleet, would be flying from Rabaul to an island near Bougainville in the Solomon Islands. On 18 April 1943, sixteen long-range USAAF Lockheed P-38 Lightning fighters were sent to intercept – and after a dogfight with six escort A6M Zekes, they were able to shoot down the two Mitsubishi G4M Betty bombers being escorted by the Zekes, one of which was carrying Yamamoto.

Following Yamamoto's death, Admiral Mineichi Koga, who had commanded naval operations at the Battle of Hong Kong from 9 December 1941, was appointed Commander-in-Chief of the IJN Combined Fleet.

Chapter 7

Summer of 1943 – The Allies Begin to Move West Across the Pacific

The war in 1943 had bogged down in the Southwest Pacific Area, particularly in New Guinea, where MacArthur's forces battled the Japanese on land. In the South Pacific Area under Nimitz's overall command as CINCPOA, 'Bull' Halsey was finalising preparations for a drive north from Guadalcanal towards Rabaul. In one of the first steps along the Solomons towards Rabaul, he ordered the occupation of the Russell Islands, which are located 25 miles west north west of Guadalcanal. These islands had been briefly occupied by the Japanese in January 1943 but had since been evacuated. If the Japanese reoccupied them, they could establish airfields from where they could launch attacks on Guadalcanal. In US hands, they could be developed into a base that could be used in the upcoming invasion of New Georgia in June 1943. The islands were seized unopposed on 21 February 1943.

It was by now fully appreciated that the fast carriers were not suited to the confined waters of New Guinea and the Solomons – and Navy strategists wanted to avoid the scale of losses by air attack that had blighted the Guadalcanal campaign. Therefore, land-based air would fight in the South Pacific skies whilst the carriers withdrew, retiring to the safety of Hawaii.

The great carrier battles of 1942 provided valuable experience for the US naval aviators – and all fast-carrier captains were promoted to rear admiral. This meant that all fast-carrier task forces would now progressively be commanded by experienced pilots who had handled carriers in battle. By August 1942, Nimitz's carrier task-force commanders included Vice Admirals Frank Jack Fletcher and William 'Bull' Halsey, and Rear Admirals Marc Mitscher, George D. Murray, Frederick C. Sherman, Leigh Noyes and Thomas C. Kinkaid, although Fletcher and Kinkaid were non-air. Halsey was promoted to admiral on 18 November 1942.

With the promotions to admiral, a new set of carrier captains had appeared, all seasoned pilots who had spent their entire careers in aviation. Captain DeWitt C. 'Duke' Ramsey (USNA '12) took *Saratoga* (CV-3). Captain Charles P. Mason (USNA '12) took over the new *Hornet* (CV-12). Captain Arthur C. Davis (USNA '15) took *Enterprise* (CV-6) whilst Captain Forrest P. Sherman (USNA '18) had commanded *Wasp* (CV-7) and brought her to the Pacific after delivering aircraft to the beleaguered Malta in the Mediterranean, before she was sunk a few weeks after the Battle of the Eastern Solomons on 14 September 1942.

The TBD Devastator had proved wholly inadequate in fast-carrier battles of 1942 and was hastily retired after Midway as the new rugged Grumman TBF Avenger torpedo-bomber, overdue in joining the fleet, finally took its place.

The Battle of Midway had also provided additional stimulus to the carrier construction programme. In July 1942, Congress authorised funds for fourteen more carriers. Although one was cancelled six months later, keels were laid for ten more Essex-class heavy or medium carriers (CV) and three of what became known as the Midway-class battle or large carrier (CVB) of 45,000 tons.

Essex (CV-9), the new 34,000-ton (full load) lead ship of the Essex-class of twenty-four such aircraft carriers planned, had joined the fleet on 31 December 1942. The Essex-class were bigger than the preceding Yorktown-class and carried more aircraft, were better armoured and had better AA firepower. They would become the core of the fast-carrier task force – and four more would be launched during 1943: *Yorktown* (CV-10) (ex-*Bon Homme Richard*) in January, *Intrepid* (CV-11) in April 1943 and *Franklin* (CV-13) in October. *Hornet* (CV-12), originally slated to be named *Kearsarge*, was launched for fitting out on 30 August 1943, taking the famous name of the previous *Hornet* (CV-8), which had been bombed, torpedoed and sunk at the Battle of the Santa Cruz Islands on 26 October 1942. In addition, three more converted Independence-class light carriers (CVL) were called for, making a total of nine carriers of this class. The Bureau of Aeronautics (BuAer) therefore expected to have thirty-five to forty fast carriers in commission or building before final victory. To meet the demands of anti-submarine warfare in the Atlantic, the Navy also had planned a minimum of thirty-two small, slow escort carriers (CVE) plus many more being built for the Royal Navy. BuAer had plans to produce 27,500 aircraft by June 1945, such had been the impact of carrier warfare.

By mid-August 1942, only six new battleships had been commissioned since early 1941, the first new battleships since 1923. These were the two North Carolina-class and four South Dakota-class, each displacing 35,000 tons with nine 16in guns. But these new battlewagons could only make 27 knots – compared with 33-knot carriers.

Six new 45,000-ton fast battleships of the Iowa-class, carrying nine 16in guns and able to make 33 knots, had been ordered in 1939 and 1940 – and the hulls of the first two had been launched in late 1942 for fitting out. Five 63,000-ton super battleships of the Montana-class, boasting twelve 16in guns in four triple turrets, had been ordered in July 1940. But the evidence from the battleship sinkings at Pearl and the loss of *Bismarck*, *Prince of Wales* and others had sealed the future of the battleship and by mid-1943, as the new fast carriers began arriving in the Pacific, only two of the Iowas had been commissioned. (On 21 July 1943, the authorised construction of the five Montanas, none of which had yet been laid down, was suspended indefinitely, the funds could be better used building more Essex-class carriers. Eventually only four of the six Iowas were completed.[1])

(i) Allied Timetable of Operations – *Rainbow 5*

During the 1920s and 1930s, the US Joint Army and Navy Board had developed a number of colour-coded strategic war plans to meet perceived hypothetical war scenarios. *War Plan Orange* was a series of many contingency plans for fighting a war with Japan alone, whilst *War Plan Red* was a plan for a hypothetical war against Britain and Canada. Following the events in Europe in 1938 and 1939, US war planners realised that the USA faced the possibility of war on a number of fronts against multiple enemies and thus developed a new series of war plans, the *Rainbow* plans, a wordplay on the multiplicity of the previous colour-coded plans.

Rainbow 5 formed the basis for US strategy in the Second World War and assumed that USA was allied with Britain and France and provided for US offensive operations. *Rainbow 5* was based on a US government document, the *Plan Dog* memorandum, prepared by the Chief of Naval Operations Harold Rainsford Stark in 1940. This set out the main options for dealing with a war on two fronts: against Germany and Italy in Europe – and Japan in the Pacific. *Rainbow 5* was approved

127

at the close of the Trident meeting between the US President Roosevelt and the British Prime Minister Winston Churchill on 25 May 1943.[2] It covered the following points relevant to the Pacific:

1. Conduct of air operations against the Japanese home islands from China.
2. The ejection of Japanese forces from the US mainland.
3. Seizure of the Marshall and Caroline Islands.
4. Seizure of the Solomon Islands, the Bismarck archipelago and New Guinea.
5. Intensification of operations against enemy lines of communications.

The imminent arrival of so many new carriers and battleships in the Pacific theatre began to shape Allied strategy during the summer of 1943. The first two 45,000-ton Iowa-class fast battleships joined the Pacific Fleet: *Iowa* (BB-61) was commissioned on 22 February 1943 and *New Jersey* (BB-62) commissioned on 23 May 1943. These modern battleships carried nine 16in Mark 7 guns and bristled with AA weaponry. Twenty 5in/38-calibre Dual Purpose Mark 12 guns were fitted that could fire fifteen rounds per minute with a Variable Time (VT) proximity fuzed shell. Eighty 40mm Bofors AA guns and forty-nine 20mm Oerlikon AA guns completed her AA firepower.

The four other Iowa-class battleships ordered were laid down – although the war would be over before the last two, *Illinois* (BB-65) and *Kentucky* (BB-66), could be completed. These battleships would have a long life, going on later to fight in the Korean War and the Vietnam War. All four were reactivated and modernised in 1981 and armed with missiles during the 1980s. During Operation DESERT STORM in 1991, *Missouri* (BB-63) and *Wisconsin* (BB-64) fired missiles and their 16in guns at Iraqi targets.

President Franklin D. Roosevelt directed the Maritime Commission to produce 24 million tons of merchant cargo shipping during 1943, whilst more than 500 new destroyers and destroyer escorts were launched in the second half of 1943 alone. The scale of the shipbuilding was staggering – and it was this industrial might that allowed the Navy's long-planned-for drive through the Central Pacific to finally happen. The number of aircraft authorised was increased from 27,500 to 31,000 planes.

The Central Pacific was the obvious choice for the next Allied offensive. Here, as a result of pre-war mock battles, US naval strategists believed the Pacific Fleet could draw the Japanese into battle – and that victory would allow a swift offensive culminating in an attack against the Japanese home islands themselves.

Commander-in-Chief of the US Fleet, Admiral Ernest King, COMINCH-CNO, had, since 1933, favoured a route through the Mariana Islands, which he considered the 'key to the Western Pacific'. Following the end of the Guadalcanal campaign in February 1943, King had been urging the Joint Chiefs to approve an invasion of the Marianas, which lay within Japan's inner defensive perimeter. They were heavily fortified and would be bitterly contested by the Japanese. Conquest of the large islands of the Marianas would be a quantum leap in scale compared with the operations to date.

The Joint Chiefs of Staff finally determined that the most feasible approach to achieving strategic positions in Formosa, Luzon and China that would allow direct bombing of the Japanese homeland as per *Rainbow 5* was by way of the Mariana Islands, the Caroline Islands, Palau and Mindanao. The JCS recognised however that the large, easily defendable and rugged southern Mariana Islands would take a heavy toll on any amphibious assault forces. There was not yet any support available from Allied land-based aircraft – as no airfields were held in range. Any operations in the Mariana Islands would be open to attack by Japanese medium bombers protected by fighters flying from Japanese airfields on Iwo Jima. A successful conquest of the Palauan islands would provide a naval base and airfields from where Japan's most important holdings, the Philippines, just over 500 nautical miles away to the west, could be threatened.

Allied strategists formulated the timetable for these operations as being:

1. 1 January 1944 – the Marshall Islands would be seized.
2. 1 June 1944 – Ponape atoll (called Pohnpei today), in Micronesia to the west of the Marshalls, would be seized. It was the last Japanese position to protect Truk from any westward advance (it was eventually bypassed).
3. 1 September 1944 – Truk in Micronesia to the west of the Marshalls would be seized (it was eventually neutralised by air strikes and bypassed much earlier in February and April 1944.
4. 31 December 1944 – the Palau island chain, west of Micronesia in the western Carolines, would be seized (only Peleliu and Angaur would eventually be invaded, earlier than originally planned in September 1944).

The most vulnerable Japanese-held islands and atolls in these island groups would be assaulted, taken and used for airstrips and anchorages. Better defended islands or atolls, or those where heavy casualties had to be expected, would not be invaded; they would be neutralised by air strikes and rendered useless to the Japanese.

In June 1943, the Joint Strategic Survey Committee recommended that Allied strategy in the Pacific be switched from MacArthur's Southwest Area to Nimitz's Central area.[3] MacArthur and many of his officers protested against the Army being subordinated to the Navy, believing the carriers vulnerable to land-based air attack – but General George Marshall, Army Chief of Staff, agreed that the massive new carrier armada should be put to use. On 15 June 1943, the Joint Chiefs of Staff informed MacArthur that Central Pacific Forces would attack the Marshall Islands and possibly the Gilbert Islands beginning in mid-November 1943. This would be an operation led by the Navy and orientated around two new experimental weapon concepts, the fast-carrier task force and the Navy-Marine Corps amphibious assault team.[4]

(ii) Two-prong Advance Across the Pacific

The summer of 1943 marked the end of the period in which the Allies had been strategically on the defensive in the Pacific War. In the Aleutian Islands, where the two US sovereign islands Attu and Kiska had been seized by Japan in June 1942, US forces invaded and regained control of Attu on 29 May 1943. The island of Kiska fell to US forces on 15 August 1943. The US position in the Aleutian Islands to the north was now secure and vital supply lines from the USA to the South and South-West Pacific were no longer threatened from the Aleutians in the north. Supply lines in the South Pacific were protected by air and naval bases in the Solomon Islands and New Guinea.

Japan had invaded the Australian mandated Territory of New Guinea in January 1942, followed by the Australian Territory of Papua in July 1942 and western New Guinea, then part of the Netherlands East Indies. From late 1942 however Japanese forces were being slowly driven back. Japan lost important forward naval and air bases and suffered attrition of her navy, and carrier and land-based air forces to such an extent that she was unable to build up her forces for further offensive operations. Conversely, Allied forces were now building and strengthening rapidly, towards a level that would permit a major offensive – although crucially they still lacked advanced positions from which essential Japanese supply lines could be attacked.

By early August 1943, the Joint Chiefs of Staff accepted that a landing and siege of 'Fortress Rabaul' would be too costly in human lives and that the Allies ultimate strategic goals could be achieved by simply neutralising and bypassing it. On 6 August 1943, the JCS issued a five-phase directive calling for a two-prong advance across the Pacific. Nimitz, in overall charge, *in the first prong*, would first seize the Gilbert Islands, which would be reconnoitred in advance by US land-based aircraft, that would also be able to support landings, which would now begin on 15 November 1943. By taking the Gilberts, advance bases would be secured for initial photo-intelligence of the Marshalls before a subsequent attack – with landings there to take place around New Year's Day, 1944. Halsey, moving through the central and northern Solomons, would neutralise or capture Rabaul by 1 February 1944.

Simultaneously with the first prong, *in the second prong*, MacArthur, leading the Southwest Pacific Area offensive, would cross northern New Guinea moving towards the port of Hollandia, on the north coast, which had been held by the Japanese since 1942. Today, Hollandia sits almost midway along the north coast of New Guinea and is known as Jayapura. New Guinea is the second largest island in the world and stretches over 1,500 miles from west to east – Hollandia was the only anchorage between the ports of Wewak to the east and Geelvink Bay far to the west.

Hollandia would be attacked from the sea in the spring of 1944 and once secure would be developed into a staging post for the Allied advance along the north coast of New Guinea into the Dutch East Indies and then to the Philippines – the invasion of the southern Philippine Island of Mindanao would take place in mid-November 1944.

With the Gilbert and Marshall Islands secured and Ponape neutralised, the Central Pacific Forces could then, in September 1944, assault the great Japanese fortress of Truk, the IJN Combined Fleet Anchorage and powerful air base situated in the eastern Carolines. The Carolines controlled the Central Pacific – and Truk controlled the Carolines. In order to take Truk, other Japanese strongholds to the south east of the Carolines would require to be seized and Japanese bases as far as Woleai, Yap and Palau neutralised. After landing at Truk, Nimitz would continue on to the Palau islands in the western Carolines, beginning on 31 December 1944.[5]

With Truk neutralised, Central Pacific forces would move to occupy Saipan, Tinian and Guam in the Marianas, to the north west, and then in November 1944, would support the second phase, MacArthur's invasion of the Philippines.

131

A subsequent third phase would see troops going ashore on the Chinese coast. In the fourth phase, Hong Kong would be recaptured – and the fifth phase would see a strategic bombing campaign launched against the Japanese home islands. A subsequent sixth phase was later added – the invasion of the Japanese home islands.

The ultimate objective of the two-prong drive was the Luzon 'bottleneck', the strait between the Chinese mainland running from Hong Kong to Amoy, the island of Formosa and the northern tip of Luzon in the Philippines. By landing on the Chinese coast, and on Formosa and Luzon in 1945, Allied forces could cut the flow of Japanese ships carrying vital raw materials such as oil and rubber back from the East Indies to the home islands. After the bottleneck had been corked, Allied forces could seize Malaya to the west and the Ryukyu Islands in the north during 1945–6. Final operations against the four Japanese home islands, including a naval blockade and final invasion, could be carried out in 1947–8. Such were the initial plans for the counter-offensive against Japan that would be spearheaded by the new fast carriers.[6]

Allied forces would now attack in strength with the two-prong advance, capturing a succession of Japanese positions from which attacks could be launched against Japanese strongpoints such as Truk and the Marianas – and also against essential Japanese lines of communication.

At the very heart of this two-prong advance was the strategy of island hopping, leapfrog hops from one island to another made by coordinated air, sea and land attacks. Once cut off on an island, the Japanese fortresses could be bombed into submission at will or left to starve and wither on the vine.

To support this island-hopping strategy, the Allies assembled the most powerful and diverse naval armada in history, which would operate with overwhelming air power, both land and carrier based. Mobile carrier-based aircraft provided an offensive capability that could move in great force to attack Japanese holdings – as well as providing defensive control of the skies above the fleets and positions held by the Allies. Carrier-based aircraft were integral in turning the tide against the Japanese.

(iii) The Japanese Position Deteriorates, Reorganisation and New Carriers

The Japanese were well aware that there would be an eventual US attack on the Gilbert and Marshall Islands Area and in May 1943, to defend this outer line, had prepared the 'Z' plan for using the Imperial

Fleet based at Truk to assist land-based aircraft and garrison troops in the islands.

During the summer of 1943 however the Japanese position in the Solomon Islands deteriorated to such an extent that the 'Z' plan was modified by removing the Bismarck, Gilbert and Marshall Islands from the vital areas that the fleet would defend. Notwithstanding that the fleet would not assist the defence of the Gilberts and Marshalls, the troop garrisons in these areas would be reinforced. Plans were developed to redeploy land-based aircraft from flank areas to meet any attack as it developed.

Japan also had to consider the possibility that the Allies would accelerate their attacks in the Solomon Islands or New Guinea, where Japanese forces were already losing ground slowly. The Allies held the initiative – they had a choice of several widely separated objectives in a theatre of war whose geography allowed full use of superior naval and air power.

In August 1943, the IJN 3rd Fleet Striking Force – Japan's fast-carrier force – consisted of six carriers, four of them being converted carriers. CarDiv 1 included the fleet carriers *Zuikaku* and *Shōkaku* and the light carrier *Zuihō*. CarDiv 2 comprised the 24,140-ton *Hiyō* and *Jun'yō*, each of which carried fifty-four aircraft – and the new 13,360-ton converted light carrier *Ryūhō*. Due to a shortage of aviation fuel to reorganise and train its air groups it had to remain in the Singapore area before being deployed to Truk in December.[7] This left only one other carrier, the old and inactive *Hōshō*, commissioned in 1922. Supporting the carriers was a powerful force that included the two 65,000-ton Yamato-class super battleships, *Musashi* and *Yamato*, five modernised older battleships and ten heavy cruisers.

With the loss of four carriers at the Battle of Midway, emergency conversions were implemented to provide additional carriers by mid-1944. Two 11,190-ton sister light carriers, *Chitose* and *Chiyoda*, would be completed in late 1944. Two older First-World-War-era battleships, *Ise* and *Hyūga*, were undergoing conversion to hybrid carriers. This involved the removal of the rear pair of main battery turrets and the installation of an aft aircraft hangar that was surmounted by a short flight deck equipped with two rotating catapults to launch floatplanes. They became half-battleship – with big guns – and half-carrier.

New carriers to be built from the keel up were also scheduled to join the Imperial Fleet. The Modified Fleet Replenishment Programme of 1942 had provided for 15 modified 17,300-ton Hiryū-class carriers, each capable of carrying 64 planes, and 5 larger 75-plane Taihōs. The

29,300-ton 75-plane lead ship of the class, *Taihō*, was nearing completion and would be the first. She would be fitted with an armoured flight deck, as on British carriers, and had been laid down in July 1941. Her hull was launched for fitting out on 7 April 1943 and she would be commissioned in March 1944.

Japan's planned carrier building programme was in fact comparable to the parallel US construction of Essex-class carriers. Although several of the Hiryūs were laid down, Japan's already weakened industrial strength however would struggle to accommodate the building plans. A 'battle' carrier similar to the US Midway-class, the huge 64,800-ton *Shinano*, had been converted from a Yamato-class super battleship hull laid down in May 1940 to a heavily armed and armoured ferry and supply ship to carry aircraft, fuel and ordnance for the other carriers. It would launch for fitting out in October 1944.

Both with the quality of her aircraft and of her pilots, Japan was already suffering greatly. The Mitsubishi A6M Zero fighter had been modified, but the US .50-calibre incendiary shells could still set the fuel tanks on fire. As the months went by experienced Japanese pilots watched the qualitative superiority of the Zero fade before the increased performance of new US fighters, which by now not only outfought but also outnumbered the Zero.[8]

Japanese land-based aircraft operated in an interlocking grid-like system between island air bases, which the Japanese considered to be unsinkable aircraft carriers – indeed Eten Island in Truk lagoon had been artificially constructed with forced labour to resemble an aircraft carrier. But Japanese insistence on a trained elite cadre of pilots led to her failing to rotate veterans to training duties to pass on their skills and knowledge. As the best pilots were lost in action, the replacement pilots were much poorer. By mid-1943, the average Japanese pilot was now training 500 hours in the air – compared with the 700 hours of airtime at the beginning of the Pacific War in December 1941. In contrast, US pilots were now getting more training, up from 305 to 500 hours in the same period.[9]

The Japanese had learned their lesson from the Midway disaster previously in June 1942. Yamamoto's unwieldy system of dividing up the fleet during major operations was abandoned and the carrier was now made the nucleus of the fleet, with a screen of battleships, cruisers and destroyers to provide AA protection. Three carriers per task group was established, beginning with the Guadalcanal battles in late 1942.

Vice Admiral Nagumo's defeat at Midway and the failure to stop the US Guadalcanal offensive had led to him being replaced in November

1942 as Commander-in-Chief 3rd Fleet by Vice Admiral Jisaburō Ozawa, who had previously commanded a cruiser, then a battleship, been Chief of Staff to the Combined Fleet and then commander of Carrier Division 1 (ComCarDiv 1) in 1939–40.

Based at Truk, Ozawa's 3rd Fleet comprised the six carriers and supporting battleships, cruisers, destroyers and submarines. It was supported by land-based air strength from her unsinkable carriers – the interlocking system of island airfields. The 3rd Fleet was still a potent force that could inflict great damage on Allied forces.

But attrition of her land- and carrier-based pilots weighed heavily against Japan – with many being lost defending Rabaul and the Solomons. By the end of 1943 Japan had lost more than 7,000 aircraft and a similar number of pilots and aircrew.[10] Time was needed to train replacement pilots and aircrew and strengthen her carrier forces. But it was time that the Japanese did not have – by autumn 1943 the Japanese Fleet was not ready to fight a major battle.

By September 1943, Japanese High Command had completely abandoned its offensive strategy and was consolidating its positions into a defensive perimeter known as the 'Absolute National Defence Sphere'. This perimeter extended from Timor to Western New Guinea to Truk to the Marianas. As part of this Defence Sphere, the Japanese Army would be deployed in numbers to build up, fortify and strengthen all key islands in the Caroline and Marshall Islands.

Approximately 40 battalions of 2,000 men each were reorganised from various units in Japan, Manchuria and the Philippines into South Sea Detachments and amphibious brigades were moved to the islands. Each island base was tasked to resist the Allies independently until reinforcements arrived – making it possible to free up most of the Imperial Fleet for the decisive battle advocated by Admiral Mineichi Koga, the Commander-in-Chief of the IJN. He wanted to engage and annihilate the US Fleet in one massive confrontation, Mahan's Decisive Battle – and his attempts to do so were based on the belief that the Allies would attack the Inner South Seas first.

Chapter 8

US Fast Carriers and Naval Aircraft

(i) The Fast Carriers

Long-range, fast-carrier striking task forces would be crucial to US plans to implement the Trident Conference aims for the Pacific War.

The newly created US fast carrier of 1943 was a modern war machine. The 27,100-ton (standard) Essex-class carrier surpassed every other US flattop that had preceded it, such as the Yorktown-class, which had been designed when arms-control treaty limitations were still in effect. USS *Essex* (CV-9), the lead ship of the new Essex-class, had been commissioned on 31 December 1942 – and under the terms of the Two-Ocean Navy Act of 1940, ten more of the Essex-class had been programmed. But after the US declaration of war in December 1941, Congress appropriated funds for nineteen more Essex-class carriers.

Learning the lessons of the preceding 15 years of naval aviation, the new Essex-class vessels were designed to carry a larger air group of 90–100 aircraft, and now free of the naval treaty limits, the basic Essex-class design was over 60ft longer and nearly 10ft wider in the beam than the Yorktowns. A longer, wider flight deck and the addition of an innovative portside deck-edge elevator, in addition to the two standard inboard deck elevators, to lift aircraft from the hangar to the flight deck, facilitated more efficient air operations. Travelling vertically on the port side of the ship, this meant that there would be no large section of deck missing, the elevator pit, when the elevator was in the 'down' position. When the elevator was in the 'up' position it also provided additional deck space for parking outside the standard flight deck.

To deliver an attack, known as the carrier's 'Sunday Punch', each Essex-class ship would carry an air group of 3 squadrons – 36 VF fighters,

USS *Essex* (CV-9) underway in May 1943 with 24 SBD scout-bombers parked aft, 11 F6F fighters parked in the after part of midships area and 18 TBF/TBM torpedo planes parked amidships. (National Archives 80-G-68097)

36 VB scout/dive-bombers and 18 VT torpedo planes. The basic design would be repeatedly modified. In comparison, the smaller Independence-class light carriers had roughly a third of this strength, 24 VF fighters and 9 VT torpedo-bombers.

The arrangement of machinery, AA weaponry and armour in the Essex-class were also greatly improved from the previous classes – and increased the ship's survivability. The new carriers had better armour protection and better ammunition handling facilities than their predecessors. Safer and greater fuelling capacity extended their range. Survivability was also increased by more effective damage-control equipment. These ships were so good that some would serve in the US Navy until after the end of the Vietnam War.

The new Essex-class carriers could make 33 knots and had a range of 20,000 nautical miles at 15 knots. The older 37,000-ton (standard) *Saratoga* (CV-3) had originally been designed as a battlecruiser and was launched almost twenty years before, in 1925. Although she was bigger than the Essex-class, and could also make 33 knots, she carried fewer aircraft at seventy-eight. *Saratoga* was less manoeuvrable – and had a much shorter operating range of 10,000 nautical miles which resulted in logistical re-fuelling issues.

The Yorktown-class carrier *Enterprise* (CV-6), the 'Big E', had been designed and built later, in 1936. She was purpose-built as a fast carrier and was more like the new breed of Essex-class fast carrier – but by 1943, she was also an older vessel that required modernisation, which she got in mid-1943. She could make 32.5 knots, carry ninety aircraft and had a range of 12,500 miles. The 45,000-ton Midway-class 'battle' carrier was still at the design stage in mid-1943.

The new Essex-class carriers had a design displacement of 33,000 long tons at full load. They carried a crew of some 215 officers and 2,171 men along with 175 officers and 130 enlisted men of an air group. The smaller Independence-class light carrier displaced 11,000 tons and carried a crew and air group of 159 officers and 1,410 enlisted personnel and, typically, 34 aircraft.

On the Essex-class, the captain's bridge, located forward on the 'island' superstructure, on the starboard side of the flight deck, was the command post of the ship. Beneath it was the signal and flag bridge, from which the air officers directed flight operations and from where the admiral, if onboard, directed the task force. Next to the signal bridge were gunnery control and the photographic laboratory, which developed and analysed aerial reconnaissance images. The radio air plot, which relayed all relevant information to pilots and aircrew in their ready rooms or to their planes when aloft, was also close by. The flag plot, also located off the signal bridge, housed the radar equipment that monitored the position of all aircraft aloft in the vicinity – and the ship's own position. The captain, flag plot and air plot received their information from the Combat Information Centre (CIC) which was situated below the flight deck on the gallery deck.

The Essex-class were 820ft long, post to post – with length overall on the short-bow units of 872ft and 888ft on the long-bow units. This allowed a 862ft-long flight deck on the short-bow units and a 844ft flight deck on the long-bow units.

The strength (armour) deck was at hangar deck level, reducing the weight located high in the ship – and this produced smaller supporting structures and more aircraft capacity for the desired displacement. The position of the strength or armour deck on carriers had both advantages and disadvantages – and there was a choice between open or closed hangar. Where the strongest deck was placed affected the strength of the hull, the further apart the deck and keel, the stronger the design. If the flight deck was placed above the strength deck, then it had to be built to allow for structural movement with expansion sections. A closed hangar design was the strongest structurally and made for a lighter hull.

Anticipating bombing from land-based aircraft in the confined waters of the Mediterranean, the Royal Navy had designed the armoured flight deck on their carriers to also act as the strength deck without any underlying plating. This achieved an armoured flight deck with the lowest possible displacement that protected the hangar deck below, and aircraft stored there, from most enemy bombs. The US open hangar design, placing their armour one deck lower at hangar deck level, essentially treated the hangar spaces and flight deck above it as superstructure. US carrier doctrine favoured the launch as rapidly as possible of as many aircraft as could be spotted on the flight deck before hand – a 'deck-load strike'. The open hangar design allowed large numbers of aircraft to be warmed up whilst inside, theoretically reducing the time required to range and launch a strike.

The US flight deck was usually wooden decking over thin mild steel, which was easy to repair. But stowed fuelled and armed aircraft below in an unarmoured hangar was an extremely hazardous arrangement and made these areas very vulnerable to the effects of bomb hits. An enemy bomb would likely penetrate the flight deck and explode in the hangar deck – where the armour deck would protect the ship's vital parts such as engine machinery and fuel spaces. The Royal Navy approach of armoured flight decks was in principle a passive form of defence from bombs – and was subsequently invaluable when the kamikaze attacks began. US carriers essentially relied on fighters to prevent the carriers being hit. The Navy would move the strength deck to the flight deck in later classes of carriers.

The debate about whether fast carriers should operate in single- or multi-carrier task forces was brought into focus by the British invention of radar (**ra**dio **d**etection **a**nd **r**anging). This allowed tracking of ships and aircraft and enabled a multi-carrier force to maintain a high-speed formation at night or in foul weather. All vessels could provide continuous mutual anti-aircraft protection fire – performed by the Plan Position Indicator (PPI) radar display, which every new carrier and screening vessel was equipped with. In addition, the Dead Reckoning Tracer (DRT) handled general navigation and the tracking of surface ships.

All Essex-class units were commissioned with SK air-search and SC and SG surface-search radars and several received SM fighter-direction radar. Aircraft detection was essential for the fighter director in air plot to direct his combat aircraft air patrols, and for the gunnery officer to direct his AA batteries. Each Essex-class carrier was equipped with air search radars to determine the composition and vertical formation of incoming flights. At this time in 1943 however the horizontal sweep of the Mark 4 radar could not detect low-flying aircraft between the horizon and 10 degrees above it. A new Mark 12 radar was due when the carriers went into combat that would fill the one gap in the Mark 4 radar performance – but production delays kept it out of the fleet until 1944.[1]

As clever as it was, radar could not however tell the identity of incoming aircraft. The US Navy adopted another British invention, by fitting during the second half of 1943, the IFF (Identification, Friend-or-Foe) device on all warships and aircraft. With the IFF turned on inside a friendly aircraft, the identity of an incoming aircraft was clear to surface vessels. If an incoming aircraft did not respond to an IFF signal, the ship assumed it was a hostile, and there were many casualties of US aircraft when crew had forgotten to switch it on.

Until mid-1943, a ship could talk to pilots at long range, but this could be eavesdropped by the enemy and the single channels of the time restricted the amount of radio traffic. For the new fast carriers, the USA developed a four-channel very-high-frequency (VHF) radio that permitted four separate conversations from one ship, all short-ranged so the enemy could not listen in. With four channels, combat intelligence officers could simultaneously communicate to their counterparts in another ship, whilst the fighter director officer could direct his pilots from air plot on another channel – and the ship could maintain contact with its defensive Combat Air Patrol (CAP) and anti-submarine aircraft patrolling above the task force. One channel would still be free.

Radar and radio were essential to coordinated AA fire, which was the carrier's sole means of defence against air attack other than its own aircraft. By summer 1943 the standard AA weapons fitted were 65 Oerlikon 20mm rapid fire cannon in single mounts, 17 quadruple Bofors 40mm cannon (offering 68 barrels) and 12 5in/38-calibre dual-purpose (DP) guns mounted in 4 twin turrets located near the island on the starboard side and 4 single mounts located on the port side forward and port side aft. These 5in guns had a maximum effective range of 7 miles, a ceiling of 6 miles and could fire 15 rounds per minute – firing 'variable time' (VT) or proximity fuzed shells. These were the same guns fitted as the standard main battery on many US destroyers.

Until 1943, all US AA shells had been *contact* shells, which detonated on impact – an unreliable defence against the fast and nimble Japanese fighter. After two years of research, US scientists developed the *proximity fuze*, which had a radio transmitter and receiver built into the head of the shell that would gauge its own distance from the target, before detonating. When the shell was 70ft from an enemy plane, a strong ripple pattern of radio waves set off a chain of reaction triggers that culminated in detonation of the warhead, a near miss usually taking down the enemy craft. The effectiveness of the 5in DP gun was thus increased hugely from the simple contact shell. Although a few VT-fuzed shells had been used towards the end of the Guadalcanal campaign, the new device was first tested on a large scale on the fast carriers. Two Mark 37 fire control directors fitted with FD Mark 4 tracking radar for the 5in battery were installed.

The free-swinging Oerlikon 20mm cannon was fitted in a flexible mount, being manually aimed by a gunner. The Oerlikon was designed in 1939 and began to be installed aboard US Navy ships from 1942 onwards to replace the Browning M2 machine gun, fitted on previous carriers, which had limited range and stopping power. The Oerlikon became an iconic sight aboard naval vessels during the Second World War, and in its role as an anti-aircraft (AA) gun it provided effective dense fire at around 300 rounds per minute (rpm) at short ranges of up to 1.5km, at which range heavier guns had difficulty tracking targets. Many versions of it are still in use by navies around the world today.

As the war progressed, as ranges to attacking aircraft increased and the Japanese turned to night attacks, it was found that the Oerlikon performed poorly in comparison with the 40mm Bofors autocannon. The powerful and effective 40mm Bofors autocannon were controlled by Mark 51 optical directors with integrated gyro gun-sight lead-angle indicators. The Bofors could knock down an enemy aircraft at long range, before it could release its weapon, whereas the Oerlikon could only knock down an aircraft when it was a lot closer and had possibly released its weapon. There was a saying in the US Navy at the time that when the 20mm Oerlikons opened fire, it was time to hit the deck. The Oerlikon was largely abandoned later in the war due its lack of stopping power against heavy Japanese aircraft and Japanese kamikaze attacks.

With these developments the US Navy developed a circular formation for carrier task-group operations with carriers in the centre and then a concentric ring of alternating battleships and cruisers that

A couple of 40mm Bofors guns in action aboard USS *Hornet*. (National Archives 80-G-520746)

provided tremendous anti-aircraft fire. Outside that would be a circular screen of destroyers, usually a squadron to provide AA and submarine protection. 'Then we came to not only handling just one task group built around two or three carriers, we had 2, 3 and 4 task groups. That became quite a potent organization and became the fast carrier force.'[2]

The striking capability of the new fast carriers, its 'Sunday Punch', was its air group – and US industry had designed and geared up to supply the new breeds of aircraft needed for the new fast carriers. New fighters, new scout/dive-bombers and new torpedo-bombers were either in commission or undergoing trials by the summer of 1943.

(ii) US Navy Aircraft

(a) Fighters

The new fast carriers needed a new fighter plane to match the Japanese Mitsubishi A6M Zero, king of the skies at the beginning of the war. The F4F Wildcat had held its own against the Zero but was not sufficiently good to maintain command of the air with certainty. Following the Battle of Midway, three of the Navy's leading fighter pilots, Lieutenants Butch O'Hare, Jimmy Thach and Jimmy Flatley, told President Roosevelt that the Navy needed 'something that will go upstairs faster', something 'with climb and speed'.[3] Two superb fighters would follow – the Vought F4U Corsair and the Grumman F6F Hellcat.

Vought F4U Corsair

Originally conceived before the war, the F4U Corsair entered the Navy Inventory after some design changes in 1942 – and entered combat as a land-based Marine Corps fighter-bomber in February 1943. The prefix

Vought F4U-1A Corsair over Bougainville, March 1944. (National Archives 80-G-217819)

143

'F' denotes it as a fighter, whilst the suffix 'U' denotes it as manufactured by United Aircraft Corp of which Vought was part.

The Corsair was a very distinctive aircraft as a result of its large three-blade propeller and its inverted gull wings that allowed the length of the landing gear struts to be shortened. The Corsair is also famous for its very distinctive sound at high speeds, which earned it the nickname amongst the Japanese as the 'Whistling Death'. The sound came about as a result of air running through intake slots in the inboard leading edges of the wings for the turbo-supercharger and oil cooler.

The Vought F4U Corsair was a single-seat fighter-bomber that had been designed as a carrier-based aircraft. However, the long cowling, low cockpit and weak undercarriage initially gave the Corsair a difficult carrier landing performance that made it unsuitable for navy use – until the British Fleet Air Arm later overcame the issues.

After the carrier landing issues had been tackled, in late 1944 it quickly became the most capable carrier-based fighter-bomber of the Second World War and would go on to serve throughout the subsequent Korean War in the 1950s. The Corsair was in service with several air forces until the 1960s.

The F4U was 33ft 8in long with a wingspan of 41ft with 150lb of armour plate fitted to the cockpit and a bullet-resistant glass screen installed behind the curved windscreen. Flush riveting and a new technique called *spot welding* along with a slick design that had nothing protruding into the air stream made the Corsair as aerodynamically clean as possible. The F4U incorporated the largest aircraft engine available at the time, the 2,000hp Pratt & Whitney R-2800, coupled with a large three-bladed propeller. This gave the first variants a maximum speed of 405mph, becoming the first production aircraft to exceed 400mph in level flight. Later F4U variants could make 446mph. This was faster than the 380mph of the Grumman F6F Hellcat and much faster than the 328mph of the early Zero models and still faster than the A6M3 Type O Model 22 introduced in December 1942, which had a top speed of 341mph. The F4U Corsair had a combat range of about 900–1,000 miles and a service ceiling of 41,000ft – comparable to the 39,800ft of the later Zero-32 variant introduced in December 1944.

The Corsair was armed with six 0.50 calibre (12.7mm) Browning machine guns with 400 rounds per gun, three in each of the outer wing panels. She also could carry four High Velocity 5in rockets under each wing or two 1,600lb bombs on wing pylons. The F4U-4 could be equipped with four 20mm cannon. It was an awesome fighter-bomber.

A new threat that arose during the Guadalcanal campaign was Japanese night air-bombing operations that pounded US ground forces with 100lb bombs. With no night-fighters available, the raids simply had to be endured by the troops below, crushing morale. A team of Marine Corps aviators returned from Britain in June 1943 with the information that the British 'have found out very definitely that (the) twin-engine night-fighter is a necessity'.[4] The Bureaus of Ordnance and Aeronautics turned to Grumman who had been developing a heavily armed radar-equipped twin-engine night-fighter, the XF7F Tigercat. The first production model of this aeroplane would fly in December 1943.

In the interim, with Japanese night air attacks increasing in the Solomons and likely being a herald of what might transpire throughout the Central Pacific, the Navy badly needed a night-fighter. It adopted the land-based F4U Corsair.

A detachment of five radar-equipped Navy night corsairs was trained during the summer of 1943 and taken to the Solomon Islands for combat testing with an eye to possibly placing them aboard the fast carriers. Admiral Nimitz suggested to the Commander, Air Force Pacific Fleet, Vice Admiral John Henry Towers, that four-plane night-fighter detachments be placed aboard each new carrier. Towers however wanted to wait for the results of the combat testing trial in the Solomons. Thus, the new fast carriers would initially go to war without a night defensive capability.

By the end of the war, the Corsair had proved itself as one of the most capable carrier-based fighter-bombers of the Second World War. Corsairs flew more than 64,000 Navy and Marine Corps sorties, scoring more than 2,000 victories in air combat with less than 200 losses. It had a kill ratio against the Zero of approximately 12:1.

Grumman F6F Hellcat
Bogged down with the initial difficulties in carrier operations besetting the F4U Corsair, and looking to replace its F4F Wildcat, the US Navy adopted the new F6F Hellcat, as its carrier fighter. Although it didn't have the performance of the F4U Corsair, it had nevertheless been developed to counter the Zero's strengths and win air superiority in the Pacific. The prefix 'F' denotes it as a fighter, whilst the suffix 'F' denotes it as being manufactured by Grumman Aircraft Engineering Corporation.

Grumman had been working on a successor to the F4F Wildcat since 1938. The 318mph Wildcat had been found to be outperformed by the faster 328mph Mitsubishi A6M Zero, which was also more

Grumman F6F-3 Hellcat fighters landing on USS *Enterprise* (CV-6) after strikes on Truk, 17–18 February 1944. Flight-deck crew are folding the plane's wings and guiding them towards the parking area. (National Archives 80-G-59314)

manoeuvrable and had a longer range. The leap forward came during the Midway campaign in June 1942 – when an A6M Zero from the carrier *Ryūjō*, one of the two Japanese light carriers involved in the Japanese operation against the Aleutian Islands, crash-landed on an isolated island. The remains of the downed Zero were recovered by US forces and shipped to the USA for analysis.[5]

BuAer flyers and engineers were stunned to find that the Zero's outstanding superior performance was achieved by a small 1,000hp engine – and that to lighten the aircraft and gain speed, Japanese designers incorporated every possible weight-saving measure into the design. There was no armour protection for the pilot, engine and critical parts of the plane – and no self-sealing fuel tanks were fitted. High-altitude capability had also been sacrificed.

Now forearmed with this knowledge, Grumman engineers began an intensive effort to produce a fighter that could counter the Zero's strengths and help gain command of the air in the Pacific. Such are the pressures of war, that an experimental aircraft was produced in

A Grumman F6F Hellcat fighter preparing for take-off from USS *Lexington* (CV-16) for a raid on Formosa, October 1944. (National Archives 80-G-285037)

three months, the XF6F Hellcat. Although the final version of the F6F Hellcat would resemble the F4F Wildcat, it was a completely new design.

The F6F Hellcat was 33ft 10in long with a wingspan of 42ft 10in. The wings could be hydraulically or manually folded for use on carriers – with a folded stowage position parallel to the fuselage with the leading edges pointing down.

A new 2,000hp Pratt & Whitney R-2800 Double Wasp radial engine that had been powering Vought's Corsair design since its beginnings in 1940 was installed with a combat range of about 945 miles and a ferry range of around 1,500 miles. Grumman redesigned and strengthened the F6F airframe to accommodate the new engine, which drove a three-bladed Hamilton Standard propeller that gave later versions, such as the F6F-5 introduced in November 1944, a maximum speed of 380mph at 23,400ft, 30mph faster than the 341mph Mitsubishi A6M Type O Model 22 Zero introduced in December 1942.[6] The F6F Hellcat was faster at all altitudes and marginally outclimbed the Zero above 14,000ft and rolled faster than the Zero above 235mph. The Zero however could outturn the Hellcat with ease at low speed and had a better rate of climb below 14,000ft. The Zero was poorer than the Hellcat in dives and had manoeuvrability limitations at speeds above 180mph.

The first production F6F-3 powered by the R-2800-10 flew on 3 October 1942. The first squadrons, untried in combat, arrived in Hawaii with the new carriers and the class reached operational readiness on *Essex* in February 1943. The new plane was faster and could, with a service ceiling of 37,300ft, operate several thousand feet higher than the 33,000ft ceiling of the A6M Zero. The Hellcat could outdive and outclimb the Zero, whilst its heavier engine allowed for heavier guns.

The Hellcat was designed to take damage and get the pilot safely back home, the new engine allowed for a bullet-resistant windshield and 212lb of cockpit armour protected the pilot, the fuel tanks and the oil cooler. A 250 US gallon self-sealing fuel tank fitted in the fuselage was made of rubber encased in a canvas hammock to nullify the effect of bullet punctures.[7] A centre-section hardpoint under the fuselage could carry a single 150 US gallon disposable drop tank.

The heavy cockpit armour and fuel tank protection is in stark contrast to the almost complete lack of pilot and fuel protection in most Japanese combat aircraft. Just a few rounds striking a Japanese aircraft could be enough to set it on fire. The lack of pilot armour and fuel protection was a crucial flaw in the Zero and led to the early loss of a large percentage of their experienced front-line pilots.

Six 0.50-calibre M2 Browning air-cooled machine guns with 400 rounds per gun were fitted on the Hellcat, three on each wing. It was a much more powerful punch than the Zero's two 20mm and two 12.7mm guns. The .50 M2 fired more than 1,000 rounds per minute and could pierce aircraft armour. With suspended containers, it could also carry more ammunition than its predecessor, the Wildcat. Later variations were equipped to carry bombs – with single bomb racks installed under each wing, inboard of the undercarriage bays. With these and the centre-section hardpoint rack, late model F6F-3s could carry a total bomb load of more than 2,000lb. The Bureaus of Ordnance and Aeronautics were ordered in June 1943 to begin the development of a forward-firing High Velocity 3.5in wing-mounted rocket for fighters.[8] Six High Velocity Aircraft Rockets (HVARs) would eventually be carried, three under each wing.

The Hellcat could be used in a variety of combat roles – as fighter, night-fighter, fighter-bomber and rocket platform. In all, more than 12,000 Hellcats would go on to be produced in 2 major variants. F6F Hellcats were credited with destroying 5,223 aircraft whilst in service with the US Navy, US Marine Corps and the British Royal Navy – more than shot down by all the other combat aircraft combined. They are the iconic US Navy fighters of the Pacific War.

With the Grumman F6F Hellcat proving to be a resoundingly successful carrier-based aircraft, the Navy initially released the Corsair to the US Marine Corps. With no requirement for carrier landings, the Marine Corps deployed the Corsair to heavy and devastating success from land bases supporting US Marine Corps operations.

The Adversary – Mitsubishi A6M Zero
The predominant Japanese fighter to be faced in 1943 was the Mitsubishi A6M Reisen, a long-range fighter developed as a greatly improved successor to the Mitsubishi A5M fighter, which had entered service in 1937. Based on their immediate combat experiences of the A5M in China, in May 1937, the IJN sent out their requirements to Nakajima and Mitsubishi for a new fast-carrier-based fighter that could climb to 9,840ft in 3.5 minutes. The fighter was to have drop tanks and 6–8 hours flight at an economical cruising speed. The prefix 'A' denotes a 'Carrier Fighter', '6' that it was the sixth to be designed by 'M' Mitsubishi. The final figure indicates the version.[9]

The first prototype A6M1 fighter was completed in March 1939. Fifteen were built and before testing had been concluded, they were shipped to the war zone in China. They arrived in Manchuria in July 1940 and first saw combat in August. They proved to be almost

A Japanese A6M Mitsubishi 'Zero' fighter – Allied reporting name Zeke.

untouchable for the Chinese fighters, the Polikarpov I-16s and I-153s, that had been such a problem for the A5Ms. In one clash, thirteen A6Ms shot down twenty-seven I-16s and I-153s in under 3 minutes – for no loss. After the delivery of only sixty-five A6M1 aircraft by November 1940, a variant was developed, the 328mph A6M2 Type O Model 21, which had folding wing tips to allow them to deploy to aircraft carriers.

Carrier-based A6M2 Type O fighters spearheaded the surprise attacks on Pearl Harbor and the Philippines on 7 December 1941 and were involved in the attacks on Wake Island, Darwin and Ceylon. The A6M2 was virtually untouchable during the first six months of the war emerging victorious over all Allied carrier- and land-based aircraft it encountered.

The A6M2 Type O was usually referred to by its pilots as the 'Zero-sen', zero being the last digit of the Imperial year 2600 (1940) when it entered service with the Navy. The Allied reporting name during the Second World War for the A6M was Zeke, although the use of Zero was commonly adopted by the Allies later in the war.

The A6M2b Model 21 Zero, or Zeke, was almost 30ft long with a wingspan of just over 39ft. It was fitted with two 12.7mm machine guns in the upper fuselage decking with 500 rounds per gun and two wing-mounted 20mm Type 99-1 cannon with 60 rounds per gun. The Zero could also carry two 132lb bombs.

The Zeke had a cruising speed of 230mph, and the most common A6M2b Model 21 version had a top speed of 328mph at 15,000ft. Later variants such as the Model 52 could achieve 348mph, and then with the Model 54 up to 382mph with a ceiling of 39,800ft. The A6M2 Type 21 had a range of over 1,580 miles on its internal fuel tanks and this increased to 1,930 miles with drop tanks.[10] The seaplane version was A6M2-N, Allied reporting name Rufe.

This plane's exceptional manoeuvrability and extraordinary range meant it become the backbone of Japanese air power and it participated in the majority of naval actions – outmatching all Allied aircraft early in the Pacific War. It has become the iconic Japanese Second World War fighter.

In Malaya, the RAF had set up a handful of new fighter squadrons – but with a shortage of fighters due to the European war, these were equipped with US-built Brewster F2A Buffalo fighter aircraft, which had a top speed of 323mph. These had been rejected for service in Britain because of fuel starvation issues above 15,000ft but, desperate for fighters for the Pacific and Asia, Britain had ordered a number from the USA. The Buffalo would be shown to be no match for the Zeke in combat. The RAF in Malaya was almost wiped out during the first days of the Pacific War in December 1941.

With the introduction, from 1942 onwards, of modern Allied fighters in the Pacific theatre such as the Vought F4U Corsair, Grumman F6F Hellcat, the twin-engine Lockheed P-38 Lightning and the Supermarine Spitfire, the A6M Zero, once king of the skies, was unable to match their speed, armament and protection and began to take heavy losses in combat. The Zero could still hold its own in low-altitude engagements but it was outclassed at higher altitudes and was no match for the new Allied fighters.

Heavy losses of aircraft and carriers at the great carrier battles in 1942, such as Midway, halted the Japanese offensive. Japan was pushed on to the back foot and the Zero was then relegated to operating in a more defensive role for the rest of the war – where lack of armour and fuel-tank protection made it very vulnerable, the Zero commonly catching fire when hit.

After further developments with the A6M3 and A6M4, in September 1943, the A6M5 was deployed – it is considered the most effective variant and carried heavier gauge skin, redesigned wings and thrust augmentation exhaust stacks – although the same engine was retained. The A6M5 could match the F6F Hellcat for performance but in fact fared poorly in combat with the Hellcat, which was more strongly built, better protected and had a higher top speed.

By March 1944, other Zero variants were introduced to improve on previous weaknesses with improved armament, armour glass for the cockpit and automatic fire extinguishers for fuel tanks. Even these later models were however outdated in comparison with the new US fighters and they suffered heavy losses to US Navy Hellcats during the Great Marianas Turkey Shoot.

Late in the war, the need to have as many fighters as possible to stave off the inexorable Allied advance towards Japan kept the by now almost obsolete A6M in production. From October 1944, when the Philippines came under assault by US forces, many Zekes were fitted with bombs and used in kamikaze attacks against US ships.

(b) Dive-bombers

The main striking weapon of the fast carriers, its 'Sunday Punch', was the dive-bomber and torpedo-bomber. The dive-bombers in use during 1943 are described below.

Douglas SBD Dauntless

The Douglas Dauntless SBD (Scout Bomber Douglas) was the US Navy's main carrier-borne scout plane and dive-bomber from 1940 to mid-1944. The SBD, nicknamed Slow But Deadly, was a long-range

Douglas SBD-2 Dauntless scout-bombers of Scouting Squadron Six (VS-6) above USS *Enterprise* (CV-6). Note the perforated air brakes on the aft edge of wings. (National Archives 80-G-6678)

aircraft that was manoeuvrable and handled well with good diving characteristics from its perforated dive breaks on the trailing edges of its wings. The SBD was a low-wing cantilever configuration of all-metal construction except for fabric covered flight controls. Its range of just over 1,100 nautical miles could be extended with droppable tanks. It was well armed and rugged and could carry a potent bomb load – it could survive heavy battle damage and was much loved by its crews.

The roles of light bombers such as the SBD were still not well defined by 1943. Originally during the 1920s, they had been designed as scout planes – with the VS scout type being adapted for dive bombing as the VSB scout-bomber after 1927. 'V' denotes heavier than air, 'S' denotes 'scout'. With the advent of extensive bulky radio gear and airborne radar in 1942–3, the relatively compact VSB could not fully perform both bombing roles and scouting missions – and after November 1943 it became a full-time dive-bomber, VB. In early 1944, fighters could be equipped with a lightweight airborne radar set for reconnaissance missions.

The SBD was some 33ft in length with a wingspan of 41ft 6in. It carried a crew of two, pilot and a radio operator/gunner, in a two-man tandem cockpit that was fitted with dual flight controls. It was more lightly armed than its successor the SB2C Helldiver, the SBD-1 carrying two 0.50in (12.7mm) forward-firing synchronised Browning M2 fixed machine guns in the engine cowling and twin 0.30in (7.62mm) flexible Browning machine guns mounted in the rear of the cockpit. The SBD-2 went to the Navy in early 1941 and by the time the SBD-5 variant entered production, the armament had been altered to a single forward-firing 0.50in machine gun in the cowling and two rearward firing 0.30in machine guns. It lacked the more powerful 20mm wing-mounted cannon of the SB2C Helldiver.

Compressibility had proved to be a major problem in the early development of dive-bombers. During a dive, as the aeroplane approaches the sound barrier, shock waves can form on flight control surfaces causing tail buffeting. Excessive air loads on flight control surfaces can make them unusable and speed can build up very quickly. The aeroplane can go into an unrecoverable dive, be unable to pull up and impact the ground. Many pilots were lost in this way in the early days before compressibility was understood. The SBD had hydraulically actuated perforated split dive brakes, air brakes to control speed in the dive and reduce air frame stress.

The SBD had a maximum speed of 255mph at 14,000ft – slow compared with the top speed of its 1944 successor the Helldiver at 295mph and much slower than the 341mph of the Model 22 A6M Zero fighter. The SBD-2s were retrofitted with self-sealing tanks, whilst the SBD-3 was the first fully combat ready version with a total production of 585 planes. Flotation gear was removed, and armour and a bullet-proof windscreen were added. The SBD could carry 2,250lb of bombs with one 1,000lb fuselage bomb and two wing bombs.

The Dauntless was the first US Navy plane to sink an enemy vessel in the Second World War, the Japanese submarine I-70 being sent to the bottom just three days after Pearl Harbor. The first real blooding of the SBD came on 7 May 1942 at the Battle of the Coral Sea where the SBD Dauntless and TBD Devastators sank the light carrier *Shōhō*, damaged the *Shōkaku* and badly depleted *Zuikaku*'s air group. At the Battle of Midway shortly afterwards, US naval aircraft attacked and sunk the four Japanese Fleet carriers *Akagi*, *Kaga*, *Sōryū* and *Hiryū*. The SBDs were in the thick of the action.

The SBD Dauntless would go on to be deployed during the Allied landings in North Africa and in the Battle of the Atlantic – and had the lowest rate of attrition amongst US carrier aircraft due to its ability to absorb battle damage. The SBD Dauntless would finish its wartime career as an anti-submarine bomber carrying depth charges and rockets.

In late 1944, the SBD Dauntless was superseded by the Curtiss SBC2 Helldiver.

Curtiss SB2C Helldiver

The Curtiss Wright Company had designed a new dive-bomber, the carrier-launched two-person dive-bomber SB2C Helldiver in 1938, but initial development and production of the SB2C Helldiver was plagued by delay. Meanwhile, the rugged SBD Dauntless, which had entered service in 1940, by 1943 no longer had the range or speed of the new breeds of US fighter. When in spring 1943, the first Helldivers began to join the carriers for trials, the results were poor. Wing fold and arresting

A Curtiss SB2C-4 Helldiver bomber, 1944. (Naval History & Heritage Command NH 95054-KN)

gear failed, fuselage and wing skin wrinkled, tail wheels collapsed and hydraulic systems leaked. The Royal Navy and the Royal Australian Air Force cancelled substantial orders as a result.

The SB2Cs were returned by the carrier commanders to the factory for remedial work – allowing the carriers to continue to rely on the old Dauntless for dive-bombing. Modified SB2Cs were finally deployed in limited numbers in November 1943 from *Bunker Hill* in an attack on the Japanese stronghold of Rabaul on New Britain. It was still the rugged, old Dauntlesses that would be instrumental in the great raid against the Truk fortress in February 1944 and then against Palau in March 1944, six weeks later.

Early opinions of the Helldiver in combat were very negative – due to its size, weight, electrical problems, poor stability, lack of power and reduced range compared with the Douglass SBD Dauntless. In the Battle of the Philippine Sea, forty-five Helldivers were lost due to running out of fuel as they returned to their carriers. The lack of power was finally corrected in 1944 with a change of engine.

The Helldiver was a much larger aircraft than the Douglas Dauntless it replaced, 36ft 8in long with a wingspan of 49ft 9in. It was able to operate from the latest aircraft carriers and carry a considerable array of firepower in addition to having an internal bomb bay that reduced drag.

The aircraft had folding wings for storage and carried a crew of two, the pilot and radio operator/gunner. It had a top speed of 295mph (the SBD Dauntless was 255mph), and early variants had a range of 1,165 miles and a service ceiling of 29,100ft, the range increasing to 1,420 miles with the SB2C-4 in November 1944.

The SB2C-4 carried two 20mm wing-mounted cannon and two 0.30-calibre 7.62mm Browning machine guns in the rear cockpit. It could carry two 1,000lb bombs in its internal bomb bay or one aerial torpedo – in addition to 500lb of bombs on each underwing hardpoint.

The SB2C Helldiver in the end proved to be a very formidable aircraft and was flown during the last two years of the Pacific War, participating in battles over the Marianas, the Philippines (where it was partly responsible for sinking the Japanese battleship *Musashi*), Taiwan, Iwo Jima and Okinawa. They saw service in 1945 against the Ryukyu Islands and the Japanese home island of Honshu in tactical attacks on airfields, communications and shipping as well as combat patrols at the time of the nuclear bombs being dropped. The advent of air to ground rockets ensured that the SB2C was the last purpose-built dive-bomber produced. Rockets allowed precision attacks against surface naval and land targets whilst avoiding the airframe stresses and aircraft vulnerability of near vertical dives close to the target.

(c) Torpedo-Bombers
Grumman TBF Avenger and General Motors TBM Avenger
The Grumman TBF Avenger was a US Navy torpedo-bomber that had its inaugural flight in August 1941 and entered service in 1942 and first saw action during the Battle of Midway. The suffix 'F' denotes a Grumman aircraft. The aircraft was designated TBM when manufactured by General Motors. The Avenger was the successor to the Douglas TBD Devastator which had been the Navy's main torpedo-bomber since 1935 but which by 1939 had become relatively obsolete and which would be decimated at the Battle of Midway in 1942. The Avenger was the heaviest single-engined aircraft of the Second World War.

The Avenger was 40ft 11½in in length and had a wingspan of 54ft 2in and carried a crew of three: pilot, rear-turret gunner and radio operator, who doubled as the ventral gunner and bombardier.

A Grumman TBF-1 Avenger torpedo-bomber dropping a Mark XIII torpedo, October 1942. The torpedo is fitted with a plywood tail shroud to improve aerodynamic performance. (National Archives 80-G-19189)

The early TBFs had a maximum speed of almost 270mph, a service ceiling of 22,400ft and a range of just over 1,100 miles. In early models the Avenger was fitted with one forward-firing 0.30in (7.62mm) nose-mounted M1919 Browning machine gun along with one 0.50in (12.7mm) M2 Browning machine gun in a rear-facing electrically powered dorsal turret for a dedicated rear turret machine-gunner, and a 0.30in (7.62mm) hand-fired M1919 Browning machine gun mounted under the tail in a rear-facing ventral position for the bombardier, used to defend against fighters attacking from below and to the rear. Later models dispensed with the nose-mounted gun in favour of a 0.50in wing-mounted M2 Browning machine gun in each wing for better strafing ability. Latterly, up to eight Forward-Firing or High Velocity aircraft rockets were carried.

The Avenger had a large bomb bay that could carry a Mark 13 aerial torpedo, depth charges and mines or a single 2,000lb bomb (or alternatively, up to four 500lb bombs). This was a rugged and stable aircraft, well equipped, with good handling and a long range. The same folding wings as used on the Hellcat were fitted for use on carriers.

The Avenger's traditional role was to torpedo surface ships – and Avengers played an important role in several naval battles, such as in the Solomon Islands in August 1942, when they sank a Japanese light carrier, and at Guadalcanal in November 1942, when they helped sink the crippled battleship *Hiei*. In addition to surface shipping kills, Avengers claimed about thirty submarine kills and were the most effective submarine killers in the Pacific theatre.

In June 1943, future US President George H.W. Bush was commissioned as one of the youngest naval aviators of the time, flying a TBF Avenger in the Pacific from the *San Jacinto* (CVL-30). On 2 September 1944, his Avenger was hit over the Pacific island of Chichi Jima and both his crewmates killed. Bush managed to release his payload over the target before having to bail out. He was subsequently picked up by the submarine *Finback* (SS-230), but several other fellow aviators who were shot down in the attack were captured and executed. He was later awarded the Distinguished Flying Cross. The Hollywood actor Paul Newman flew as a rear-seat radioman and gunner in an Avenger during the Second World War. The post-war disappearance of a flight of Avengers, known as Flight 19, added to the mystery of the Bermuda triangle.

Rugged and versatile, the TBFs acquired the nickname 'turkey'.

From 1943 until the end of the war, with new carriers and new planes, the fast-carrier task force would be trialling several new pieces of equipment in battle – the Essex-class heavy carrier, the Independence-class light carrier, the F6F Hellcat fighter, the Curtiss SB2C dive-bomber, the Vought F4U Corsair, multi-channel VHF radios, and the Plan Position Indicator radar (PPI) and Dead Reckoning Tracer (DRT).

Supporting these ships would be the new proximity fuzed 5in/38 shell, and a multiplicity of 40mm and 20mm AA guns. New fast battleships joined the fleet along with modernised older battleships, cruisers and destroyers.

It was time to begin the great push westwards and northwards towards Japan.

Chapter 9

Late 1943 – The Isolation of Rabaul – The Central Pacific Drive Begins

(i) The Isolation of Rabaul – Operation CARTWHEEL, 13 June 1943–20 March 1944

As plans were finalised by Central Pacific Force commanders for the invasion of the Gilberts and the Marshall Islands in late November 1943, Operation CARTWHEEL, begun in June that year, was approaching its finale – the isolation and neutralisation of the major Japanese forward base at Rabaul, on the island of New Britain in Papua New Guinea.

Such was Rabaul's strategic position, that its fine harbour had seen a number of colonial overseers. The German New Guinea administration had controlled the area from 1884 until during the First World War, when Australian British Empire troops defeated the German garrison and occupied the territory. Following the defeat of Germany in the First World War, the occupied territory was delegated to Australia as a League of Nations Mandate. Rabaul became the capital of the Territory of New Guinea. Just over twenty years later, shortly after the Pearl Harbor raid unleashed war in the Pacific, the Battle of Rabaul began on 23 January 1942. Rabaul was quickly captured by thousands of Japanese naval landing forces – the local population had acquired another colonial overseer.

The Japanese Army constructed army barracks, fortified the area and dug many kilometres of tunnels and the harbour became a major Japanese Fleet base. By 1943, an estimated 110,000 Japanese troops were stationed there and Rabaul had become the most heavily defended Japanese position in the South Pacific. It had a strategically important location as Japan's major forward base, with several airfields and a large natural

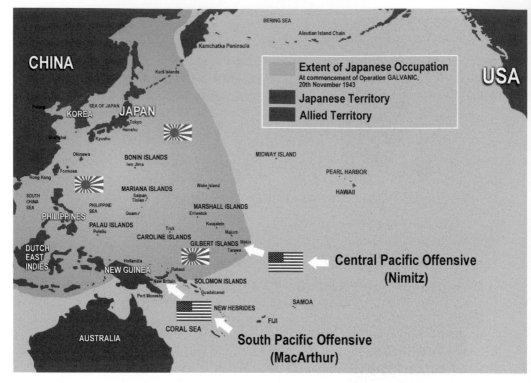

Chart of the Pacific showing extent of Japanese occupation by November 1943.

harbour from where ships, aircraft, troops and supplies had staged during the New Guinea and Guadalcanal campaigns. It lay in relatively close proximity to Japan's major base at Truk, 700 miles northward.

Operation CARTWHEEL was directed by the Supreme Allied Commander in the Southwest Pacific Area, General Douglas MacArthur and comprised thirteen separate subordinate operations, beginning after the successful conclusion of the Guadalcanal campaign. Beginning in June 1943, MacArthur's forces would advance along the north-east coast of New Guinea and western New Britain and occupy nearby islands. Admiral Halsey, then in command of the South Pacific Area, would attack the central Solomons.

CARTWHEEL originally envisaged an Allied invasion of Rabaul, but given the strength of the Japanese defensive position, it was realised how difficult and costly in lives this would be. A full invasion was determined to be unnecessary – and of the original thirteen planned subordinate operations, Rabaul, Kavieng and Kolombangara were eliminated and

A Douglas SBD-5 on the flight deck of USS *Yorktown* (CV-10) awaits the take-off signal, September 1943. Note flight-deck officer holding chequered flag and crewman (left) holding sign with last-minute instructions for the pilot. (National Archives 80-G-43861)

only ten actually proceeded. Rabaul would be neutralised by bombing and then bypassed, cut off from the rest of the Japanese Empire and left to wither on the vine.

The invasion of New Georgia began on 30 June 1943 with the capture of Rendova Island. The Battle for Munda, on New Georgia Island, lasted until 5 August 1943. The Japanese were forced off Arundel Island by 20 September and Vella Lavella by 6 October. The isolated base of Kolombangara was evacuated by 2–3 October, ending the New Georgia campaign.

(ii) The Battle of Empress Augusta Bay – Operation CHERRYBLOSSOM, 1–2 November 1943

Admiral Halsey, had meanwhile used the Third Fleet to attack the central Solomon Islands, moving north west along the two parallel chains of islands towards the largest island in the Solomons archipelago, Bougainville Island, in Papua New Guinea (also known as part of the Northern Solomon Islands). Bougainville Island is some 125 miles long by 38 miles across at its widest and lies more than 200 miles south east of New Britain, on which Rabaul was situated. Halsey wrote later: 'Bougainville was blocking our path to Rabaul, and Rabaul was the keystone of the whole Japanese structure in the southern Pacific.'[1]

After a number of preparatory subordinate operations, the next move in Operation CARTWHEEL would be to establish a beachhead at Empress Augusta Bay, around Cape Torokina, halfway up the west coast of Bougainville Island, designated Operation CHERRYBLOSSOM. There, an airfield could be built that would allow land-based aircraft to strike anywhere on Bougainville and at Rabaul itself, which only lay some 215 miles distant, a range that US fighters could easily cover. Empress Augusta Bay was isolated from the main Japanese concentrations of troops around the north and south of Bougainville Island, and offered a fine anchorage for Allied shipping.

Several groups of US and Australian forces were inserted around Bougainville in the months preceding the operation by small boat, submarine or seaplane to carry out patrols, gather local intelligence and study the terrain. Meanwhile, aerial reconnaissance built up a good picture of Japanese defences. Allied estimates assessed 35,000 Japanese ground forces on Bougainville.[2]

Halsey assigned Rear Admiral Theodore S. Wilkinson as Commander Third Fleet Amphibious Forces to direct the landings at Cape Torokina, situated at the north end of the wide expanse of Empress Augusta Bay. Here, Wilkinson's ships would disembark the I Marine Amphibious Corps of more than 14,000 men comprising the 3rd Marine Division and the US Army 37th Infantry Division, the Marines being trained to assault and capture a position but not heavily enough equipped to hold it, as the Army is.

To disguise Allied intentions, the assault troops would be carried to battle by three transport divisions of Task Force 31, that would form up at different locations throughout October. The transport divisions comprised eight transport ships and four attack cargo transports and would be escorted by a screen of eleven destroyers, fleet tugs, minesweepers and minelayers. Direct air support for the landings would be provided by aircraft from the Army Air Force, the US Navy, the Marine Corps and the Royal New Zealand Air Force.

The 3rd Marines would land first, with the Army 37th Infantry Division forming the second wave of the invasion. H-Hour for the first wave of the invasion was set as 0710 on L Day, 1 November to allow the transport ships to navigate the waters of Empress Augusta Bay in daylight. The pre-war charts of the area were inaccurate and missing details of underwater obstructions.

In the early hours of 1 November, a naval bombardment by the light cruisers and destroyers of Task Force 39 began on two airfields, one at Buka at the southern end of Bougainville Island, and the other situated near the Bonis peninsula on the northern tip of the island. Proceeding south, a fire mission on the Shortlands then began at 0631, as part of a diversion to move Japanese attention away from Cape Torokina.

The amphibious landings began at 0710 with the first wave of 7,500 men disembarking their transports and going ashore in a large number of LCVP (Landing Craft, Vehicle, Personnel) using eleven pre-designated beaches in Empress Augusta Bay and one on nearby Puruata Island, where there was a small Japanese garrison. As the Marines came ashore, USMC aircraft attacked Japanese positions on the landing beaches, with high-altitude cover provided by forty USAAF and RNZAF fighter aircraft. Naval gunfire was also brought down ahead of the landing forces.

Halsey sent the air groups from the Task Force 38 carriers *Saratoga* (CV-3) and *Princeton* (CVL-23), under the command of Ted Sherman, to support the 3rd Marine Division landings at Cape Torokina, the first time the fast carriers had seen action in that theatre since the Guadalcanal campaign in late 1942. Operating in open water well to the west, the two carriers launched two strikes against the battered Buka and Bonis airfields. Most of the landing beaches were undefended but troops landing close to Cape Torokina at the south of the landing area encountered stiff resistance – the area had however been cleared by 1100.

A Japanese air attack by forty-four fighters and nine dive-bombers on the landings took place at 0735 but RNZAF and USMC fighters intercepted the incoming Japanese fighters and twenty-six Japanese

USS *Yorktown*, November 1943. The motion of its props causes an aura to form around this F6F. Rotating with blades, the halo moves aft. (National Archives 80-G-204747A)

aircraft were shot down by the fighters and by AA fire from the screen of destroyers. A second wave of Japanese fighters and bombers was then seen off by Marine fighters. No Allied ships were sunk, although the attacks did delay the landings as unloading was halted whilst the transports began defensive manoeuvres for some 2 hours.

A further Japanese air attack of around 70–100 aircraft arrived at about 1300 – this was once again intercepted by Allied aircraft. However, twelve enemy aircraft managed to penetrate the fighter screen and arrived over the transport area but their attack did little damage – with only a near miss on the Fletcher-class destroyer *Wadsworth* (DD-516). The Japanese air attack however forced the landing transports to withdraw for a second time. Despite the attacks and delays, eight of the twelve transports had completed unloading by 1730.

The next day, 2 November, a strike by TF 38 carrier aircraft on Japanese airfields knocked out some twenty aircraft that could have targeted the

US landing troops. Task Force 38 then withdrew 100 miles to the south of Guadalcanal to refuel, safe from air attack.

The audacious landings triggered an immediate Japanese response. Admiral Mineichi Koga, Commander-in-Chief of the Combined Fleet, despatched carrier planes from *Zuikaku*, *Shōkaku* and the light carrier *Zuihō* of CarDiv 1, then harbouring in Truk, to Rabaul. On 1 November, 173 aircraft from these 3 carriers landed at Rabaul – bringing its air strength to some 375 planes.

In addition, Koga also despatched Vice Admiral Takeo Kurita with 8 heavy cruisers, 2 light cruiser and 8 destroyers from Truk to Rabaul. This powerful naval force was to run south to destroy Halsey's vulnerable transport shipping and its light surface screen of eleven destroyers. Halsey had no intelligence about the Japanese naval and air deployments at the time that Sherman's Task Force 38 carriers withdrew for Guadalcanal on 2 November.

In the early hours of 2 November, four US light cruisers and eight destroyers of Task Force 39, under the command of Rear Admiral Aaron S. Merrill, alerted by reconnaissance aircraft, engaged a local Japanese force that had been hastily put together from those ships that had been in the area when the US landings began. The Japanese force comprised 2 heavy cruisers, 2 light cruisers and several destroyers tasked with bombarding the landed troops and escorting 5 destroyer transports carrying 1,000 Japanese troops for a counter-landing.

As the Japanese naval force sortied towards Cape Torokina, Merrill's Task Force 39, which had been shelling Japanese positions around Buka the day before, broke off and began steaming to intercept the Japanese ships. The naval battle was a victory for the US force, which with no sinkings of its own managed to sink a Japanese light cruiser and a destroyer – and damage 2 cruisers and 2 destroyers with up to 25 Japanese aircraft damaged or destroyed.

The remnants of the beleaguered Japanese naval force returned to Rabaul, where they were joined by Kurita's cruisers and destroyers, which had now arrived from Truk – in time for a second more powerful assault on the US landing forces. US scouts detected Kurita's force of heavy units on 4 November inbound to Rabaul, it was a desperate situation as Halsey believed that the combined force would run down to Torokina the following night and sink the transports and bombard the precarious beachhead.[3]

Lacking a comparable surface force of his own to counter the Japanese threat, Halsey ordered a dawn air attack on the Japanese cruisers and destroyers at Rabaul on 5 November by the air groups from *Saratoga* and *Princeton*. So far, he had avoided using his carrier air groups directly against heavily defended Rabaul – but the powerful Japanese naval force was a direct threat to the Empress Augusta Bay beachheads. It was an emergency – 'I sincerely expected both air groups to be cut to pieces and both carriers to be stricken, if not lost . . . but we could not let the men at Torokina be wiped out while we stood by and wrung our hands'.[4]

A force of 97 US aircraft, comprising TBF Avenger torpedo-bombers and SBD Dauntless dive-bombers escorted by 52 F6F Hellcats, attacked Kurita's warships in foul weather – running into intense AA fire and some 70 Zekes, ready to dogfight with the new Hellcat fighter. The US attack was a success – with 25 Japanese aircraft shot down and four Japanese heavy cruisers heavily damaged, *Mogami*, *Maya*, *Takao* and *Atago*, as well as 2 light cruisers and 2 destroyers damaged. The Japanese surface fleet had been temporarily crippled, and those Japanese ships that could, withdrew to Truk – leaving the heavy cruiser *Maya* and the light cruiser *Agano* behind, both of which were too heavily damaged to withdraw. The threat posed by the Japanese navy to the precarious Bougainville landings was at an end.

By 5 November, the US Marines had secured a beachhead that was 10,000yd long along the beaches and reached 5,000yd inland. Preliminary work began on the construction of an airfield at Cape Torokina.

That same day, to reinforce the South Pacific Force prior to the forthcoming Operation GALVANIC amphibious assaults on Tarawa and Makin (planned for late November), three more carriers arrived in the South Pacific with Task Group 50.3 under the command of Alfred Montgomery – *Essex* (CV-9), the new Essex-class *Bunker Hill* (CV-17), carrying the as yet untried SB2C Helldiver bomber, and the light carrier *Independence* (CVL-22).

There were now an unprecedented five carriers in theatre – and this allowed Halsey to have Sherman's two carriers hit Rabaul once again from the north, whilst Montgomery's three carriers would strike from the south. As Halsey wrote after the war: 'Five air groups, we figured, ought to change the name of Rabaul to Rubble.'[5] The combined strikes against Rabaul took place on 11 November and confirmed the striking power and mobility of the new carrier task forces. The light cruiser *Agano* was damaged, two destroyers sunk and thirty-five Japanese aircraft downed. The new carriers were attacked as they withdrew following the strikes, but no significant damage was inflicted.

The capture of Bougainville, the construction of an airfield on the west coast at Cape Torokina and the capture of the Buka airfield at the southern end of Bougainville, and Bonis airfield at the northern end, brought Rabaul within range of land-based US Navy and Marine Corps tactical bombers and allowed the pacification of Rabaul to begin.

Bombing attacks took place throughout December 1943 and into January 1944. The Japanese continued to sacrifice valuable carrier aircraft and pilots in the defence of Rabaul – and these were shot down in great numbers – with 266 Japanese fighters downed in January 1944 alone. The Japanese carriers at Truk became virtually planeless – whilst the Japanese battleships there now had no air cover and were thus vulnerable at sea. In February 1944, Japanese command would eventually pull all remaining aircraft and crews from Rabaul, some 100 aircraft flying to Truk on the morning of 19 February, the day after the 2-day Task Force 58 air strike on Truk, Operation HAILSTONE.

No further attempts to send Combined Fleet naval units to Rabaul would be made – the Rabaul garrison of approximately 90,000 Japanese military personnel would be left cut off and isolated until the end of the war.

With the successful neutralisation of Rabaul, major operations in Halsey's South Pacific Command came to an end. Ted Sherman's Task Force 38 received its new designation, Task Group 50.4 and along with Montgomery's TG 50.3 headed north to join the Central Pacific Force.

(iii) The Gilbert and Marshall Islands Campaign – the Central Pacific Drive Begins, Operation GALVANIC, 20–8 November 1943

General MacArthur's Southwest Pacific Force and Admiral Nimitz's Central Pacific Force would each continue driving westwards separately – towards a common objective: the area of Formosa-Luzon-China. Japan's raw materials passed by sea from the East Indies to Japan through this natural restriction, which would become known as the Luzon bottleneck. Once the Formosa-Luzon-China area was secure, the indirect blockade of Japan could begin.

If all went to plan, in about spring 1945, a major assault in this area would take place. The exact landing place would be determined later as the operation advanced – and could be northern Luzon, the island of Formosa or the coast of China itself. The blockade would include mining operations, air and submarine attacks on Japanese shipping both at sea and in harbours and intensive bombardment from progressively advanced bases by the new long-range B-29 strategic bombers, which could be based in China or in the Mariana Islands.[6]

To be able to establish forward land-based air bases that would be capable of supporting US operations across the Central Pacific, towards the Philippines and Japan, US strategists determined to take the Mariana Islands, landing on 1 October 1944 on Guam and other Mariana Islands, and thus enabling B-29 strikes on Japan to commence by the end of 1944.

The Marianas are a crescent-shaped archipelago comprising the summits of fifteen mostly dormant ancient volcanic mountains in the western North Pacific Ocean. They lie south south east of Japan, south west of Hawaii, north of New Guinea and east of the Philippines. The Marianas form the eastern limit of the Philippine Sea – the southernmost islands of the chain being the US territory of Guam – and Rota, Tinian and Saipan.

The nearest islands capable of supporting the seizure of the Marianas, by providing land-based airfields, were the Marshall Islands, situated well to the east of the Marianas, and north east of the Solomon Islands. The Marshalls comprise some 29 coral atolls with 1,156 individual islands and islets. They share maritime boundaries with the Federated States of Micronesia to the west (which includes Truk), Wake Island to the north, Kiribati to the south east and Nauru to the south.

The Marshall Islands host many names that became iconic of the Pacific War in the Second World War – such as Kwajalein, Bikini, Wotje and Majuro, the capital. The Marshalls are located approximately 220 miles north west of the Gilbert Islands and had been occupied by the Japanese as part of the South Pacific Mandate since the First World War.

The Marshall Islands however were cut off from direct communications with the US naval base at Pearl Harbor in Hawaii by a Japanese garrison and air base on the small island of Betio on the western side of Tarawa atoll in the Gilbert Islands. The Gilbert Islands, now known as the Republic of Kiribati, are a 500-mile-long chain of sixteen main atolls and hundreds of small coral islands, straddling the equator in an almost north–south line. They lie short of halfway between Papua New Guinea and Hawaii – and south east of the Marshall Islands. Thus, to be able to seize the strategically important Mariana Islands, the Allied advance westwards towards Japan had to begin far to the east with the seizure of the Gilbert Islands. The Gilberts had been a British Protectorate since 1892 but had been seized by Japan immediately following the Pearl Harbor raid.

On 20 July 1943, the Joint Chiefs directed Admiral Nimitz to prepare plans for the operation against Tarawa and Makin, which formed part of the outer perimeter of the Japan's eastern defences – they were to be taken by November 1943. Operations GALVANIC and KOURBASH were the code names for the Gilberts campaign, KOURBASH being the Army portion of the operation. The Marshall Islands would then be taken in a subsequent operation in early 1944, Operations FLINTLOCK and CATCHPOLE would see the invasion and capture of Japanese bases at Kwajalein, Eniwetok and Majuro.

In August 1943, with Halsey busy driving through the Solomons towards Rabaul, Vice Admiral Raymond Spruance assumed command of the Central Pacific Force for the occupation of the Gilberts. Spruance flew to New Zealand to meet with the new commander of the 2nd Marine Division, General Julian Smith, and begin planning the invasion of the Gilbert and Marshall Islands.

Makin is the northernmost atoll of the Gilberts chain – the southernmost is Arorae. The atoll of Tarawa, a name that is today synonymous with the first bloody US amphibious assault of the Pacific War, lies south of Makin, almost two-thirds of the way to the north of the chain. None of the islands of these atolls has land higher than 12ft above sea level. They are formed of a coral bedrock overlaid by sand and poor soil. The atolls all had a lagoon-side road and piers for seagoing vessels.

The Japanese 51st Guard Force had seized three of the strategic Gilbert Island atolls, Makin, Marakei and Abaiang on 8 and 9 December 1941 as part of plans to protect their south-eastern flank from Allied counter-attacks and to begin the isolation of Australia. The Japanese expelled the local occupants – whilst most Europeans had been evacuated before the Japanese South Seas Detachment troops landed, those few Europeans still present were interned.

The Gilberts were also intended to be a staging post for the planned invasion of the island of Tuvalu, north west of the Santa Cruz Islands to the north of Fiji. But the setbacks in 1942 at the Coral Sea, Midway and Guadalcanal had forced the Japanese to abandon that proposed operation.

The Japanese established a radio station and a seaplane base at Makin and on 10 December, a Japanese air raid went in against Tarawa atoll, the island group's administrative centre. A second raid followed on 24 December and Japanese forces landed the same day. Japanese troops were placed along the coastlines of the atolls to monitor Allied movements in the South Pacific.

Following a diversionary raid in August 1942 on the Japanese garrison on Makin by the US 2nd Marine Raider Battalion, known as 'Carlson's Raiders', in honour of their legendary leader Brigadier General Evans Carlson, Japanese command realised the strategic importance, and vulnerability, of the Gilbert Islands. Tarawa atoll and Abemama atoll, south of Tarawa, were quickly fortified in September. Garrisons were built up on the small flat Tarawa atoll island of Betio, situated at the south-west point of the atoll lagoon, and on Butaritari, to the south of Makin atoll, with only small deployments of Japanese troops to the other Gilberts.

The tiny island of Betio, at the south-west point of Tarawa atoll, was shaped like a long thin triangle on its side, pointing in towards the centre of the atoll. It was only 2 miles long and some 800m across at its widest point. A long pier had been constructed by the Japanese projecting out from the north shore into the sheltered lagoon where Japanese transport ships could offload cargo whilst anchored north of the shallow reef that extended 500m out from the shore around the whole island. The southern and western sides of the island opened to the deep oceanic waters of the Pacific, from where it was believed any Allied assault would come.

In February 1943, Betio was further reinforced by the 6th Yokosuka Special Naval Landing Force under the command of Rear Admiral Tomonari Saichiro, an experienced engineer who directed construction of intricate defensive structures. Some 500 pillboxes and stockades were constructed with interlocking fields of fire over the water and shore. A command post and a large number of bomb shelters were set up using forced Korean labourers in the interior of the island to allow the defenders to survive an anticipated pre-invasion bombardment.

Fourteen coastal defence guns, including four Vickers 8in guns purchased from Britain during the Russo-Japanese War of 1904–5, were installed in concrete bunkers, to guard and destroy any vessels attempting to navigate the open water approaches to the lagoon's sheltered anchorage. There were forty field artillery pieces deployed around the island, set into reinforced firing pits. An intricate trench system was constructed that would allow troops to move safely around the island under cover, where needed, and an airfield was constructed straight down the centre of the island.

Betio was soon the base for some 4,500 Japanese troops who were well supplied, well prepared and well dug in for an anticipated US assault. The defence was completed with fourteen Type 95 Ha-Go light tanks. As Rear Admiral Keiji Shibazaki, an experienced combat operations officer, took over command on 20 July 1943, he rallied his men by stating that it would take 1 million men 100 years to conquer Tarawa. The scene was set for the first great test of the US Marines amphibious assault capability.

In May 1943, Admiral Koga's Combined Fleet set up plans for a new outer defence line running from the Aleutian Islands, through the Marshall and Gilbert Island groups to the Bismarck Islands group. This new line would be a series of strongly defended islands intended to delay any US invasion force sufficiently to allow the IJN time to organise a counter-attack and destroy the US Fleet in a decisive battle.

Unsure of which of the Marshall and Gilbert Islands the Americans would strike at first, Admiral Koga dispersed his troops primarily to the outer islands of Maloelap, Wotje, Jaluit and Mili. Japanese defensive planning envisaged stopping the enemy in the water as the assault began or pinning them down on the beaches.

(a) Strike Force Composition

The subsequent plan for the invasion of the Gilbert Islands brought together the largest gathering of ships yet assembled by either side in the Pacific War. The bulk of the Pacific Fleet, the Central Pacific Force, was committed under Vice Admiral Raymond Spruance, the immediate subordinate of Admiral Nimitz. This large, powerful invasion force comprised some 17 aircraft carriers (CVs, CVLs and CVEs), 12 battleships, 8 heavy cruisers, 4 light cruisers, almost 70 destroyers and 36 transport ships. The actual landings of about 35,000 troops would be conducted by V Amphibious Force under Rear Admiral Richmond Kelly Turner, who had led the amphibious landings at Guadalcanal and Tulagi and directed a similar force at New Georgia.

The basic naval organisation for GALVANIC was issued on 25 October by Vice Admiral Spruance aboard his flagship, the Portland-class heavy cruiser *Indianapolis* (CA-35), which would later transport to Tinian parts of 'Little Boy', the first nuclear device to be dropped in combat on Hiroshima. The Carrier Force, Task Force 50, would be commanded by Rear Admiral Charles A. Pownall in *Yorktown*. The Assault Force, Task Force 54, its ships and troops, would be under the direct command of Rear Admiral Turner aboard the battleship *Pennsylvania* (BB-38).

Of the approximately 35,000 invasion troops of V Amphibious Corps, commanded by Major General Holland M. Smith USMC, the 27th Infantry Division (Army) under Major General Ralph C. Smith would assault Makin – whilst the 2nd Marine Division under Major General Julian C. Smith would hit Tarawa.

Kelly Turner's naval Assault Force was divided into two attack forces. The Northern Attack Force (Task Force 52), under Turner's command, would capture Makin. The Southern Attack Force (Task Force 53), commanded by Rear Admiral Harry H. Hill aboard the battleship *Maryland* (BB-46), would seize Tarawa and Apamama.

The fast carriers of Task Force 50 under Pownall were tasked with establishing and maintaining air superiority in the area, to aid the amphibious landing forces by neutralising Japanese defences and help spot the fall of supporting naval shell fire and fly observation missions over Makin, Tarawa and Apamama. TF 50 would also provide CAP fighter cover and search ahead of the invasion convoys and conduct Anti-Submarine Warfare patrols.

The Carrier Force (Task Force 50) comprised 6 fleet carriers and 6 light carriers with 6 battleships, 3 heavy cruisers, 3 AA light cruisers and 21 destroyers in the AA screen – and was subdivided into:

1. Task Group (TG) 50.1, the Carrier Interceptor Group – Rear Admiral Pownall:
   Yorktown (CV-10) (task-force flagship)
   Lexington (CV-16)
   Cowpens (CVL-25) (light carrier)
   Screen: the three fast battleships *Washington* (BB-56), *South Dakota* (BB-57) and *Alabama* (BB-60), each capable of making 28 knots. Six Fletcher-class destroyers.
2. Task Group 50.2, the Northern Carrier Group – Rear Admiral Arthur W. Radford:
   Enterprise (CV-6)
   Belleau Wood (CVL-24) (light carrier)
   Monterey (CVL-26) (light carrier)
   Screen: three fast battleships, *North Carolina* (BB-55), *Indiana* (BB-58) and *Massachusetts* (BB-59). Six Fletcher-class destroyers.
3. Task Group 50.3, the Southern Carrier Group – Rear Admiral Alfred E. Montgomery:
   Essex (CV-9)
   Bunker Hill (CV-17)
   Independence (CVL-22) (light carrier)
   Screen: three heavy cruisers *Pensacola* (CA-24), *Salt Lake City* (CA-25) and *Chester* (CA-27), the light cruiser *Oakland* (CL-95). Five Fletcher-class destroyers.
4. Task Group 50.4, the Relief Carrier Group – Rear Admiral Frederick C. Sherman:
   Saratoga (CV-3)

Princeton (CVL-23) (light carrier)
Screen: two light cruisers, *San Diego* (CL-53) and *San Juan* (CL-54).
Four destroyers.

The Northern Attack Force (Task Force 52), under Rear Admiral Richmond Kelly Turner in *Pennsylvania* (BB-38), tasked to seize Makin, the northernmost of the Gilberts, comprised 35 ships in total. The Transport Group (TG 52.1) would embark elements of the 27th Infantry Division (Army) in 4 attack transports, 1 attack cargo ship and 1 Landing Ship, Dock (LSD), which had a well deck that could transport and launch landing craft and amphibious vehicles (much easier than by using cranes or a stern ramp). TG 52.1 was escorted by 4 destroyers.

The Fire Support Group (TG 52.2), for naval bombardment and to handle any surface threats, comprised 4 battleships, 4 heavy cruisers and 6 destroyers, in 3 units. The Air Support Group (TG 52.3) comprised the 3 escort carriers *Liscome Bay* (CVE-56), *Coral Sea* (CVE-57) and *Corregidor* (CVE-58) carrying Wildcat fighters and Avenger torpedo-bombers with a screen of 4 destroyers. The Makin LST Group No. 1 (TG 54.4) held 3 Landing Ship, Tanks (LST) (landing ships that could carry tanks, vehicles and troops directly to the shore and release them by lowering its front ramp on the beach without the need for a dock or pier) and was screened by the destroyer *Dale* (DD-353).

Task Force 52 sailed for the Gilberts from Pearl Harbor on 10 November 1943, refuelling at sea en route.

The Southern Attack Force (Task Force 53), commanded by Rear Admiral Harry W. Hill in *Maryland* (BB-46), was tasked with seizing Tarawa – and was much larger than the Northern Attack Force (TF 52). The Transport Group (TG 53.1) would embark the 2nd Marine Division (less 1 regiment in corps reserve) in 12 attack transports, 3 attack cargo ships, 1 Landing Ship, Dock and 1 transport. It would have a screen of 7 destroyers.

In all, TF 53 comprised some 56 ships: the Fire Support Group (TG 53.4) was divided into 5 sections and held 3 battleships, 2 heavy cruisers, 2 light cruisers and 9 destroyers. The Air Support Group (TG 53.6) comprised 5 escort carriers and a screen of 5 destroyers. The Tarawa LST Group No. 1 (TG 54.5) comprised 3 Landing Ship Tanks and a destroyer escort. The Minesweeper Group (TG 53.2) had the 2 minesweepers *Pursuit* (AM-108) and *Requisite* (AM-109).

With Task Force 52 on its way from Pearl, Task Force 53 sailed for the Gilberts from New Zealand on 16 November 1943.

USS *Enterprise* (CV-6) en route to attack Makin Island. Crash landing of a F6F-3 of Fighting Squadron Two (VF-2) into the carrier's port-side 20mm gun gallery, 10 November 1943. Although the plane's belly fuel tank ruptured, the pilot, Ensign Bryon M. Johnson, escaped without significant injury. (National Archives 80-G-205473)

The subsequent amphibious assaults on Makin, and particularly on Tarawa, were the first time that US amphibious forces had faced determined enemy opposition in force. In particular, the 4,500 Japanese defenders on Tarawa were well dug in, well supplied and well prepared – and they would fight with fanatical determination almost to the last man.

(b) Battle of Tarawa, 20–8 November 1943
As the great armada approached the Gilberts from Hawaii and from New Zealand, Vice Admiral Spruance, in command of the Central Pacific Force, was aboard his flagship, the 9,950-ton Portland-class heavy cruiser *Indianapolis* (CA-35). But, exhibiting one of the many qualities that would endear him to his subordinates, he left his subordinate task-force commanders to deal with the actual mechanics of the operation.

Softening up the target landing beaches at Makin and Tarawa by land-based air began several days before the Central Pacific Force arrived. Then as the Carrier Force closed, carrier planes bombed Tarawa on 18 and 19 November. Carrier planes hit airfields on Mili and Jaluit in the southern Marshalls, bombed Makin and knocked out Japanese air capability at Nauru. The carriers of TGs 50.1, 50.2 and 50.3 then maintained their defensive sector stations whilst Sherman's Relief Carrier Group, TG 50.4, with *Saratoga* and the light carrier *Princeton*, turned east to escort garrison convoys towards the objective.

The plan was that 3 hours before the amphibious assault on 20 November 1943, a pre-invasion naval bombardment and counter-battery fire, designed to neutralise Japanese heavy coast defence guns, would be delivered by the Fire Support Group battleships, cruisers and destroyers at moderately long range.

But as the assembled might of the Southern Attack Force hove into view of Tarawa over the horizon in the pre-dawn hours, the four Japanese 8in coastal guns opened fire at 0507 and a long-range gunnery duel developed with the 16in main battery guns of the battleships *Colorado* and *Maryland*, which provided accurate counter-battery fire. Three of the Japanese coastal defence guns were quickly knocked out – leaving the approach to the lagoon open, although the one remaining Japanese 8in gun continued with intermittent and inaccurate fire.

At 0610, following the gunnery duel, the naval bombardment of Tarawa began with a sustained bombardment by cruisers and destroyers at close range of the landing beach areas, pausing for a short period to allow carrier aircraft to strafe and bomb. The two minesweepers *Pursuit* and *Requisite* of Minesweeper Group (TG 53.2), covered by two destroyers, entered the lagoon and cleared the shallows of mines. Once the carrier aircraft departed, the naval bombardment resumed and would continue, following a postponement of H-hour, for more than 2 hours until 0845.

Further strafing by carrier aircraft and air bombardment began at 0749, and when the strafing carrier aircraft departed, the gunfire support ships recommenced their neutralisation fire and continued to shoot until 0855 when the naval bombardment stopped and further strafing and bombing runs took place. The island was becoming increasingly shrouded in a pall of dust and smoke and it had become difficult to identify targets.

The air bombing was however disappointing, close-air support proved inefficient, enemy concealment was good and it was found that if bomb hits went in 10–15ft away from assigned targets, after a slight pause the Japanese guns were firing again – the bombs simply blasted a hole in the coral, raising a cloud of coral dust.

Meanwhile earlier, as the Fire Support Group ships prepared to commence their pre-invasion bombardment, the troop transports had halted in the Transport Area at 0355 and the tracked landing vehicles (LVTs) of the first waves at both Makin and Tarawa launched through the bow doors of the LSTs. Other Landing Craft, Vehicle, Personnel (LCVP or Higgins boat) were hoisted over the side of assault transports and in darkness Marines clambered down nets over the side to board. The troop-laden LCVPs and LVTs then moved to the Rendezvous Area to form up. Before the LVTs of the first three waves had reached the Rendezvous Area, the Japanese coastal defence batteries had opened up on the Expeditionary Force. The big assault transports retreated out of range.

Once all units were ready at the Rendezvous Area, at 0636, they moved in line astern towards the Line of Departure, which was 6,000–6,600yd from the assault beaches RED 1, RED 2 and RED 3. Shells from the fire-support ships continued to pound the beaches ahead of them. The assault waves of some 125 LVTs and LCVPs were however beset by a strong westerly current which carried the slow-moving heavy craft away from the Line of Departure and their planned speed-over-the-ground (SOG) could not be achieved. They arrived at the Line of Departure at 0825 – 39 minutes late.

When, finally abreast the beaches, the first three waves executed a simultaneous turn towards the beach, the first wave turning towards the beach at 0830, 44 minutes later than originally scheduled. The second and third waves followed across the Line of Departure at 33-minute intervals. With 3 miles to run to the beaches with an adjusted speed-over-the-ground now being less than 4 knots, the timetable, which allowed for a 40-minute run to the beaches, slipped even further. As the assault waves moved from the line of departure, shells began bursting over the exposed Marines, although the air bursts proved ineffectual.

The US battle planners had expected that the amphibious assault troops in their LCVPs and LVTs at Betio would meet a water depth of 5ft over the wide-fringing reef, which would allow their 4ft draft untracked LCVP Higgins boats to pass over. Unfortunately, it was the time of the weaker *neap tides* and the water depth failed to rise to the expected 5ft, leaving just 3ft to a few inches over the reef.

The Marines discovered that their Higgins boats could not get over the reef – and these were left stranded on the reef, 500m off the beach. The Marines had to disembark from the LCVPs and wade across the reef chest-deep under enemy fire.

The tracked LVTs however could get over the reef – but as the LVTs made their way over the reef and into the shallows, Japanese troops who had survived the naval shelling began to man their firing pits again and more troops were moved up the landing beaches from the southern beaches. Whilst the LVT cab had armour plates, the LVT cargo holds packed with Marines had no such protection. The LVTs began to face an increasing volume of incoming fire and eight of forty-two LVTs in the first wave were knocked out.

Touch down on RED 1 was at 0910 – and 0917 for RED 2 and RED 3. Those LVTs that crossed the reef and reached the beach then encountered a sea wall, which they couldn't clear. As troops disembarked from the LVTs, they were pinned down along the wall.

Behind the first three waves, came waves of LCVPs and LCM landing craft carrying infantrymen, tanks and artillery. With standard draughts of 4ft, they were also barred from crossing the reef by the shallow depth of water. Many LVTs went back out to the reef to pick up infantrymen and howitzer crews, whilst others, stranded out there in their Higgins boats, had to wade ashore with their equipment. Japanese riflemen and machine-gunners caught them as they struggled through the water heavily laden.[7]

By the end of the first day, one half of the LVTs had been knocked out, 5,000 Marines were ashore with 1,500 dead or wounded. As night fell and the Marines clung to their beachhead – many of the second wave were unable to land and spent the night floating out in the lagoon and trying to sleep in their Higgins boats.

Out at sea that evening, long-range Betty bombers from Kwajalein and Maloelap attacked Montgomery's Task Group 50.3 off Tarawa. Although nine were shot down by CAP and AA fire, one successfully torpedoed the light carrier *Independence*, which had to withdraw and would be out of the war for six months.

Meanwhile, Japanese marines were swimming out in darkness to some of the wrecked LVTs and to the wrecked Japanese steamship *Saida Maru*, which lay to the west of the main pier. Hiding themselves away, they awaited dawn when they would be able to fire on the landing troops from behind.

The next three days saw intense fighting on this small island before it was declared secure at 1330 D+3.

For the next several days, the 2nd Battalion, 6th Marines moved up through the remaining islands in the atoll, completing this sweep on 28 November.

The US 2nd Marine Division suffered more than 1,000 men killed in action on Tarawa alone with more than 2,000 wounded during the 76 hours of the battle. Only 1 Japanese officer and 16 men surrendered out of the entire force of 4,500. It was a chilling portent of what was to come.

(c) Battle of Makin, 20–3 November 1943

At 0830, simultaneous with the Tarawa landings, after the naval bombardment, assault troops of the Northern Attack Force began to go ashore on Makin, which had a much smaller Japanese garrison. Here, the landings on Red Beach went smoothly with the assault troops moving rapidly inland – despite the attentions of Japanese snipers.

With little opposition on Red Beach, as assault landing craft approached Yellow Beach from the lagoon they came under heavier Japanese small arms and machine-gun fire. As with Tarawa, as the troops in their Higgins boats approached the landing beach at high tide they ran into the same difficulty – there was insufficient water to let the boats clear the reef. The Marines were forced to walk the last 250m to the beach, waist deep in water.

It took two days of bitterly fought fighting before Makin atoll was cleared. An estimated 395 Japanese were killed in action with 66 US dead and 152 wounded.

Japanese air attacks from the Marshalls continued on 23 and 24 November, being dealt with by TG 50.1 planes. Then in the pre-dawn darkness of 24 November, the escort carrier *Liscome Bay* (CVE-56) was torpedoed and sunk by the Japanese submarine *I-175*. The Japanese torpedo detonated the aircraft bomb stockpile, causing an explosion which engulfed the entire ship and caused it to sink quickly with the loss of 644 officers and men.

Organised resistance on the target islands and enemy air attacks ended on 28 November. The heavy losses encountered at Tarawa and Makin were a terrible blow – and caused public protest back in the USA. US commanders were forced to reassess future amphibious assaults.

But however costly, seizure of Tarawa and Makin now allowed regular reconnaissance missions and continuous bombing of the Japanese-held Marshall Islands to be flown. Their seizure shortened the seaborne logistic support line to the Solomons and Australia by permitting a more direct route from Pearl Harbor and also opened the south-eastern door to carrier raids on Truk, the so-called Gibraltar of the Pacific. US forces also now had their own forward bases to combat the Japanese Fleet, which was at least as strong as the US Fleet at the time.

With Rabaul neutralised and Operation GALVANIC successfully concluded with the seizure of Tarawa and Makin, three US submarines were tasked to take station off Truk and report on any sortie by Japanese warships. It was not yet appreciated by the Americans just how crippled the IJN Combined Fleet was as a result of the losses of carrier-based

USS *Cowpens* (CVL-25). A pilot evacuates his burning F6F-3 fighter after making an emergency landing unaware it was on fire during the Gilberts operation, 24 November 1943. (National Archives 80-G-208140)

aircraft used during the defence of Rabaul. The loss to Japan of these carrier aircraft would be pivotal in the eventual US air strikes against Truk – when those aircraft were not available to repulse the US aerial assault.

Tarawa and Makin had cost a huge number of US dead and wounded – it was supposed to have been a minor operation. What losses would be suffered in taking fortress strongholds such as Truk? Whilst GALVANIC was the foundation of the future Marshall and Mariana Islands operations – it was also an ominous portent of what the future would hold for those troops assaulting heavily defended Japanese garrisons.

Japan knew that after the Gilbert Islands had been taken, the next target for the Allied war machine would be the Marshall Islands. With her heavy carrier aircraft losses severely weakening the Combined Fleet, Japanese command effectively wrote off the Marshall Islands – the island garrisons were ordered to fight a holding front to delay US progress as much as possible.

A Japanese Nakajima B6N Jill torpedo-bomber explodes in air after a direct hit from a 5in shell as it attempted an unsuccessful attack on USS *Yorktown* (CV-5) off Kwajalein, 4 December 1943. (National Archives 80-G-415001)

As resistance ended, Spruance sent *Saratoga* and *Princeton* back to Pearl and left two carriers under Ted Sherman, *Bunker Hill* and *Monterey*, north of the Gilberts in case any surprise enemy operation developed. He sent the other carriers around the Marshalls for a six-carrier strike on Kwajalein to neutralise enemy air and photograph the atoll for the landings there scheduled to begin in January 1944.

The carrier raid on Kwajalein took place on 4 December, destroying four Japanese merchant ships and an estimated fifty-five aircraft in the air and on the ground. But as the carrier planes withdrew, they spotted a number of Betty long-range torpedo-bombers parked on the airfield at Roi-Namur. Admiral Pownall however wanted his carriers out of the Marshalls as quickly as possible and chose not to launch a second strike to destroy them. He withdrew the carriers – opening up the possibility of the feared enemy night torpedo attack.

At about noon, Task Force 50 was attacked by Nakajima B5N Kate torpedo planes, but no damage was caused other than to one of the screen cruisers by *Yorktown*'s own AA friendly fire. Once darkness came, an estimated thirty to fifty Betty bombers from Roi-Namur began attacks on the task force that lasted several hours. *Lexington* (CV-16) was hit astern but the damage was minimal and she was able to continue. The last attack was fought off by AA fire in the early hours of 5 December.

With GALVANIC completed, Task Force 50 returned to Pearl Harbor. Although the Central Pacific Force was now largely away from the action, for some naval aviators there would be no rest. Far to the south west, Halsey was now encircling Rabaul and capturing airfields to its east and north. The experienced Ted Sherman reported to Halsey as Commander Task Group 37.2 with *Bunker Hill* and *Monterey*, his planes going on to hit Kavieng and New Ireland (north of Rabaul) until 4 January 1944.

Chapter 10

Task Force 58 is Formed –
The Gilbert and Marshall Islands
Campaign Continues

(i) Rear Admiral Marc 'Pete' Mitscher Takes Command, 23 December 1943

In late 1943, with the Operation GALVANIC landings at Tarawa and Makin under Vice Admiral Raymond Spruance (Commander Central Pacific Force) completed, Nimitz (CINCPAC CINCPOA) and Halsey (Commander Southwest Pacific Force) conferred with Admiral Ernest King, Commander in Chief, US Fleet (COMINCH-CNO), to decide on a new commander for the fast-carrier spearhead of the Fifth Fleet. They agreed that Rear Admiral Marc 'Pete' Mitscher was the best choice for the post. He had performed well at Guadalcanal and was kicking his heels back in San Diego, so was immediately available. He was advised of his new command on 23 December 1943.

Mitscher was a modest, quiet person – sometimes so quiet he could barely be heard. But he had a vast experience in naval air warfare that went back to the First World War. His skill at handling his command and the people under him, often simply using stern, severe expressions, inspired a devotion and confidence amongst junior officers that was greater than most other naval aviators. No one seemed dissatisfied with the choice of Mitscher as fast-carrier commander – although at this point he was largely unknown to Spruance. He would regard the next steps of the Gilbert and Marshall Islands campaign, the forthcoming Operation FLINTLOCK invasion of Kwajalein and the seizure of Majuro atoll in the Marshall Islands, as a trial for Mitscher. Majuro atoll lies between Maloelap and Mili and has a fine anchorage that would be suitable as a

182

forward naval base. A second phase to capture Eniwetok (today known as Enewetak) and other islands was codenamed Operation CATCHPOLE.

Spruance himself was a traditional non-aviator admiral, one who still believed that naval confrontations were settled by the surface-orientated battleship action – he placed his faith in the commander of the fast battleships, ComBatPac, Rear Admiral Willis Augustus 'Ching' Lee (Commander, Battleships, Pacific Fleet). But to Spruance's credit, he had immediately realised from GALVANIC that battleships were ideal as anti-aircraft weapons platforms – in addition to being big-gun platforms. Battleships would now be assigned to carrier task groups.

Spruance quickly learned to appreciate Pete Mitscher's strengths and as Admiral Halsey later observed: 'Putting Ching Lee and Pete Mitscher together was the smartest thing the Navy ever did. You had the best surface tactics and the best air tactics the world has ever known.'[1]

Mitscher had won his spurs in modern naval warfare by launching the sixteen Doolittle B-25 bombers from *Hornet* (CV-8) to bomb Tokyo on 18 April 1942 under Halsey's overall command. Mitscher commanded *Hornet* during the subsequent Battle of Midway and then as Commander Air, Solomon Islands, directed Army, Navy, Marine and New Zealand aircraft in the air war over Guadalcanal and up the Solomon chain. Halsey said: 'I knew we'd probably catch hell from the Japs in the air. That's why I sent Pete Mitscher up there. Pete was a fighting fool and I knew it.'[2] His officers knew he was a fighter – and trusted him implicitly.

Although Mitscher was absolute commander of the fast carriers in a carrier battle, if a surface engagement threatened, he gave way to Rear Admiral 'Ching' Lee who was afloat aboard the battleship *Washington* (BB-56) in Mitscher's screen. If a surface action developed, Lee assumed command of Task Force 54, and the fast battleships would form the battle line – although Spruance might assume overall tactical command.

Mitscher reported to Pearl Harbor on 5 January 1944 as Commander, Carrier Division 3 (ComCarDiv 3) – and the fast-carrier command was designated Task Force 58 the following day on 6 January 1944. Mitscher hoisted his flag aboard *Yorktown* (commanded by Joseph James 'Jocko' Clark) on 13 January 1944. Operation FLINTLOCK (Kwajalein and Majuro) would begin in just a few weeks' time – and Operation HAILSTONE, the great Task Force 58 fast-carrier strike at Truk, was just one month away. Mitscher's appointment was a popular choice amongst the old-time navy pilots.

January 1944 was a busy month in Pearl Harbor, where the Central Pacific Force was based, as planners prepared for Operation FLINTLOCK, which would begin on 31 January 1944 and continue until 4 February 1944.

Nimitz believed that air power would neutralise all the islands around Kwajalein and that task-force carrier aircraft would then be able to eliminate the threats from Truk, the Marianas or Japan. Such was the command of the air following the pacification of Rabaul and the success of Operation GALVANIC that Nimitz had the confidence to bypass all the Marshall Islands, except Kwajalein, Majuro and Eniwetok atolls, leapfrogging lesser islands to get at the larger ones.

(ii) Service Squadrons 4 and 10

Admiral Nimitz knew that to make the future fighting force he referred to as the 'Big Blue Fleet' effective at projecting its power across the vast distances of the Pacific, he would have to devise a way to keep it supplied and fully effective. The ongoing resupply of a large fleet across the expanse of the Pacific was something no navy had done before.

In autumn 1943 he ordered the creation of two Service Squadrons (ServRon) that would allow the Navy to operate freely at advanced positions across the Pacific, creating temporary forward bases that would allow the active naval fighting forces to spend less time in transit, and more time in the areas of conflict. Instead of having the fleet spend valuable time returning thousands of miles to port to replenish and rearm, he would bring the port to the fleet. One Service Squadron would operate near the front and serve as fleet base. The other Service Squadron would remain in the rear until more advanced positions were occupied when it would move to the front and act as fleet base.

Service Squadron 4 (ServRon 4) was commissioned on 1 November 1943 and initially comprised twenty-four vessels with its base at Funafuti atoll, 1,000 nautical miles east of the Solomon Islands and 1,200 nautical miles south of the Marshalls. ServRon 4 fuelled the fast carriers for GALVANIC.

ServRon 10 was formed at Pearl Harbor and commissioned on 15 January 1944 to service the fast carriers exclusively for Operation FLINTLOCK. US Marines landed in the Marshalls on 30 January 1944 and the islands that made up Majuro atoll, with its fine harbour being one of the largest in the Pacific, were secured without incident. As soon as Majuro atoll was taken, ServRon 10 based itself there.

ServRon 10 comprised provisions and stores ships, barrack ships, oilers, tankers, hospital ships, destroyer tenders, net cargo ships, net tenders, repair ships, submarine chasers, picket boats, rearming boats, buoy boats, harbour tugs, salvage tugs, self-propelled lighters, ammunition ships and barges, floating dry docks, floating cranes and piers.

Majuro became the first major forward base for the US Pacific Fleet and became the largest and most active port until the war moved far to the west, when its importance waned as it fell too far behind the front. Ulithi in the Caroline Islands in time superseded Majuro as the major forward base – Ulithi was as far forward from San Francisco as San Francisco was from Great Britain, such was the immense scale of the Pacific.

Whilst based at Majuro, and other advance bases, as the US Fleet moved westwards ServRon 10 repaired and serviced vessels at the anchorage and despatched fleet oilers to rendezvous with and replenish the fast-carrier forces at sea. Oilers are essentially tankers that are equipped for refuelling/replenishment at sea (RAS). During GALVANIC, thirteen oilers provided the entire Central Pacific Force with its fuel. Each oiler carried 80,000 barrels of oil, 18,000 barrels of aviation gasoline and 6,800 barrels of diesel oil.[3] The number of oilers would steadily increase throughout the war.

Early in 1944, escort carriers would be added to the ServRon for anti-aircraft and anti-submarine protection and also to ferry replacement aircraft and parts to the fast carriers to make up for those lost or damaged.

(iii) Task Force 58 is Formed, 6 January 1944

The new fast-carrier Task Force 58 comprised a core of fast carriers surrounded by a screen of battleships, cruisers and destroyers to provide direct air support to ground units and short- and long-range bombing and reconnaissance operations. Task Force 58 would become the main strike force of the US Navy from January 1944 through to the end of the war in August 1945 and was composed of a number of smaller task groups, each of which was typically focused around three or four carriers and their support screen vessels of destroyers, cruisers and modern fast battleships.

The once-mighty battleship was now seconded to the protection of the new capital ships, the carriers – a task it was eminently qualified to carry out with its heavy armour, armament and AA capability. Supporting the task force were fleet oilers, ammunition ships and refrigeration and dry stores ships. In all there were often more than 100 ships in the task force carrying more than 100,000 men afloat.

Using the same subterfuge as with the designation of the Third and Fifth Fleets, when the fast-carrier force was part of Admiral Spruance's Fifth Fleet, the carrier task force was designated Task Force 58. When, after rotation of command, it was subsequently led by Admiral Halsey as part of the Third Fleet, the carrier force was designated Task Force 38.

185

Onshore planning for upcoming operations was completed when each admiral and his staff rotated out of active command of the fast-carrier task force. By allowing significant periods of time for shore-based planning, this allowed the Navy to perform at a higher operational tempo, whilst initially fooling the Japanese into believing that there were in fact two fleets and that the US was able to deploy greater naval assets than were actually available.

The two Pacific commanders, Raymond A. Spruance and William Halsey Jr, were two very different types of admiral – each under the ultimate command of Admiral Chester Nimitz. Whilst Halsey was aggressive and a risk-taker – hence his nickname in the press as 'Bull' Halsey, Spruance, on the other hand, was more calculating and cautious. Each brought different skills to the fleet. Most higher ranking officers preferred to serve under Spruance whilst the ordinary sailor preferred to serve under Halsey.

Task Force 58, from inception on 6 January 1944, would eventually grow to a total of nine fleet carriers of 27,000–34,000-tons and eight light carriers of 11,000 tons by the time preparations were being made for the landings on Leyte in Philippines islands, in October 1944. The enlarged Fifth Fleet continued to push back the boundaries of the Japanese Empire with successful operations against the Volcano, Ryukyo and Bonin Islands and in support of the air campaign against the Japanese home islands. (During the later Okinawa campaign, the Third Fleet was reconstituted from Fifth Fleet units and both fleets continued on until the end of the war and into the occupation of Japan.)

Task Force 58 would go on to take part in all the US Navy's Pacific battles in the last two years of the war. The operational area of Task Force 58 and its components spanned the distance from the Palau Islands to the East China Sea, from the Japanese home island of Honshu to the coral atoll islands of Marcus and Wake.

Task Force 58 usually consisted of four task groups that could operate independently or combine for major operations as required. Each individual task group was commanded by a rear admiral and centred around two to four carriers. The task groups would remain distinct – but operate in close proximity to provide the task force with maximum striking power and protection. The captain of any carrier would remain in charge of his own ship – even if a task-group or task-force admiral was a guest on the flagship, he had nothing to say about the day-to-day operation of the ship, that was the sole domain of the captain. Each division of battleships and cruisers was also led by its own admiral and the destroyers were organised into squadrons each with its own officer in command, usually a commodore.

The overall command of Task Force 58 lay with Rear Admiral Mitscher, who deployed the task force, designated missions and gave instructions to the task-group commanders, who in turn passed on those orders to the ships' captains and in turn to the air-group commanders. Above Mitscher was the fleet commander, either Spruance or Halsey, who directed the fleet in accordance with the area strategy that came from Nimitz's HQ at Pearl. Only rarely did Spruance or Halsey assume tactical command – both accepting that Mitscher was supreme in operation of the fast-carrier task force. Similarly, Mitscher seldom interfered with his task-group commanders once he had given them their orders.

The operational tactics of the fast carriers were developed principally by Pete Mitscher – who determined early on that the best defence for a carrier was its own Combat Air Groups. He concluded that carriers were best defended if they operated together in groups, with supporting ships to provide concentrated AA fire and anti-submarine defence – and to rescue any downed airmen.

Admiral Raymond A. Spruance, Vice Admiral Marc A. Mitscher, Fleet Admiral Chester W. Nimitz and Vice Admiral Willis A. Lee Jr, left to right, photographed aboard USS *Indianapolis*, February 1945. (NH 49705 courtesy of the U.S. Naval History & Heritage Command)

In a memorandum dated 24 September 1945 to Secretary of the Navy at war's end, commenting on composition of the Navy after the war, Mitscher set out that the 'ideal composition of a fast-carrier task group is four carriers, six to eight support vessels and not less than 18 destroyers, preferably 24. More than four carriers in a task group cannot be advantageously used due to the amount of air room required. Less than four carriers requires an uneconomical use of support ships and screening vessels.'[4]

The ships of each task group sailed in a circle formation centred on the carriers – with another concentric ring of alternating battleships and cruisers that provided tremendous AA fire. Outside this ring would be a circular screen of destroyers, usually a squadron that would carry out Anti-Submarine Warfare (ASW) sweeps and provide AA cover. The support ships sailed in relatively close proximity so that their AA guns could be added to those aboard the carriers to provide a dense AA screen against enemy aircraft that tried to close the task group.

When under attack by Japanese torpedo-bombers, the task group would turn towards the attacking aircraft to limit attack angles and aid combing the tracks. Other than this, the carriers would not take evasive action from enemy planes – making the carriers a stable platform for AA fire, allowing a long run of firing that would allow corrections to be steadily applied. The primary defence for a task group against air attack was the fighters of the group's own Combat Air Patrol (CAP). US submarines patrolled the group and prowled for enemy targets still further out.

Often a task-group commander could be hundreds of miles away from other task groups, carrying out an independently assigned mission and preserving strict radio silence so that Japanese radio detection finders couldn't locate the group. Only once battle was joined was radio silence broken – when Mitscher's flag bridge would begin to receive radio information from the often widely spread out group commanders. If task groups were operating in the same area, information was transmitted to the flag ship by high-frequency short-range radio (TBS) or by visual signals for tactical manoeuvring. Aircraft were also used for message drops onto other vessels.

The fast-carrier task groups of Task Force 58 would become the major naval strike force in the Pacific, providing strategic air support for operations in the Gilbert, Marshall and Mariana Islands, whilst targeting areas of Japanese logistical and force build-up behind the front line of combat. More than 500 combat aircraft, flying from 9 Task Force 58 carriers, would neutralise the Japanese forward island fortress of Truk in a 2-day air raid on 17 and 18 February 1944 – when more than 40 major Japanese ships were sunk, and shore-based air facilities and naval infrastructure destroyed. Truk was denied to Japan as a meaningful naval and air operations base for the rest of the war. For Operation DESECRATE 1, the air assault on the major Japanese shipping and aircraft base of Palau, just 6 weeks later on 30 and 31 March 1944, a total of 11 Task Force 58 carriers launched more than 1,000 combat aircraft. Task Force 58 aircraft and surface vessels would defeat the Japanese Fleet in the First Battle of the Philippine Sea on 19–20 June 1944 and operating as Task Force 38 would participate in the Second Battle of the Philippine Sea, the Battle of Leyte Gulf on 23–6 October 1944 – considered to be the largest naval battle of the Second World War. The fast-carrier task force would continue to strike at Japan remorselessly until the last major naval operation of the Pacific War, the Battle of the East China Sea on 7 April 1945 – when the super battleship *Yamato* would be sunk.

Task Force 58 aircraft and support vessels supported General MacArthur's Hollandia operation in New Guinea and participated in the seizure of Iwo Jima and Okinawa. Detached sections of TF 58 were briefly subordinated to the British Eastern Fleet for air strikes in the Netherlands East Indies. Strategic air strikes were made against targets in the Caroline, Palau, Volcano, Bonin and Ryukyu Islands to draw off naval and air reinforcements.

Task Force 58 aircraft conducted the first large-scale carrier bombing operation against the Japanese home islands in support of the Iwo Jima campaign. Close air support and offshore bombardment operations were conducted in conjunction with the various amphibious operations.

Task Force 58.7 was unique in that it was composed primarily of ships-of-the-line, battleships, heavy cruisers and screening vessels. Designated the Battle Line Carrier Group, this task force engaged in offshore bombardment operations against Ponape (Caroline Islands), Saipan (Mariana Islands) and Okinawa (Ryukyu Islands).

With the armistice and final surrender, initial occupation and demilitarisation of Japan was carried out by three naval forces – the Fifth and Third Fleets, and the North Pacific Force. On 19 September 1945, the Fifth Fleet relieved the Third Fleet and North Pacific Force of their responsibilities and assumed command of all naval activities in the former Japanese Empire.

Admiral Raymond A. Spruance would turn over command of the Fifth Fleet to Admiral J.H. Towers on 8 November, thus ending the wartime commitment of the Fifth Fleet.

Chapter 11

Central Pacific Drive, 1944 – The Gilbert and Marshall Islands Campaign Continues

(i) The Invasion of Kwajalein and Majuro Atolls – Operation FLINTLOCK, 29 January 1944–7 February 1944

Having successfully seized Tarawa and Makin in the Gilberts, the Allies now had the land and naval territories necessary for the next stage of the overall plan to knock Japan out of the war – the invasion of 7 islands, in 9 phases, of the 29 coral atolls that make up the Marshall Islands. The other atolls and islands would be bypassed.

The most strategically important atolls for US planners were Kwajalein, which had a Japanese airfield, and Majuro, which had a large lagoon of some 114 square miles that was suitable as a sheltered fleet anchorage. Majuro is situated at the south east of the Marshalls and could also serve as an air base for conducting air operations against the rest of the Marshall Islands and in time the Marianas, where Guam lay – just over 1,600 miles distant. The operation to seize Kwajalein and Majuro was codenamed FLINTLOCK.

Kwajalein atoll, situated in the Ralik Chain of islands, is the largest atoll in the Marshalls. It is an irregularly shaped boomerang atoll that stretches approximately 66 miles in a straight line from north west to south east and is surrounded by a barrier reef. The islands of Roi-Namur sit at the north of the atoll whilst the island of Kwajalein itself is situated at the very south of the atoll. Kwajalein atoll lies some 1,100 nautical miles east of the Japanese fortress of Truk – whilst Truk itself is almost 1,200 nautical miles to the east of Palau.

Majuro atoll sits in the Ratak Chain of the Marshall Islands – and comprises sixty-four islands that have in total a land area of just 4 square miles. The islands ring around the 114 square miles of Majuro's fine lagoon. Majuro was claimed in 1884 by the German Empire with the rest of the Marshall Islands, at which point a trading post was established. It was captured by the Japanese in 1914 and subsequently had been mandated to Japan by the League of Nations in 1920.

The second phase of the operation, codenamed Operation CATCHPOLE, was the invasion of Eniwetok in the very north west of the Marshalls, along with other important islands – this would take place three months after FLINTLOCK. It was decided that Nauru, a small island of just 8 square miles to the south west of the Marshalls, seized by the Japanese in 1942 (on which a Japanese airfield had been constructed) would not be invaded. It was felt to be too close to Truk – which likely harboured the Japanese Combined Fleet. Whilst contingency plans were drawn up for a possible sortie of the Combined Fleet from Truk, Nauru itself would be neutralised and then bypassed and left to wither on the vine. Once the Marshall Islands had been taken, it was believed that Nauru would be rendered useless for the Japanese.

The Japanese 6th Base Force under the command of Rear Admiral Monzo Akiyama had been based on Kwajalein since August 1941 with some 4,000 troops, which had been widely spread out. IJN air bases had been established on the smaller Kwajalein atoll island of Roi-Namur with other air bases on the Marshall Island atolls of Mili, Maloelap, Eniwetok and Wotje.

Admiral Mineichi Koga, in command of the IJN Combined Fleet, knew the Marshalls would be next in line to be attacked – but he was unsure of which islands the Americans would strike at first. Vice Admiral Masami Kobayashi, in command of the IJN 4th Fleet, was responsible for the defence of the South Pacific and he dispersed his forces primarily to the outer islands of Maloelap, Wotje, Jaliuit and Mili. The 1st Amphibious Brigade arrived on 4 January 1944 and more than 2,500 of its troops were assigned to defend Eniwetok atoll. They began to fortify the atoll against a possible US assault using aviation personnel, civilian employees and forced labourers. The Japanese installed twin 5in (12.7cm) guns on each end of the islands with 80mm guns on the ocean and lagoon sides. The 22nd Air Flotilla, weakened after the Gilberts campaign, had about 150 operational aircraft in the Marshalls, with 10 on Kwajalein. Rear Admiral Monzo Akiyama, in

191

command of the 6th Naval Base Force was sent to Kwajalein after the fall of the Gilberts where he had 5,000 troops at his disposal with a further 3,000 on the islet of Roi-Namur. He created what fortifications he could and made plans for an aerial counter-strike against any US landing forces using the available aircraft. He knew however that there were no plans to send further reinforcements – as the Marshalls had been declared outside Japan's absolute defence zone by Imperial General HQ.

Allied intelligence however had broken Japanese codes and the Allies knew which of the islands were most heavily defended. They decided to invade the least protected but strategically important islands of Majuro, Kwajalein and Eniwetok.

Building on the lessons learned in practice from recent operations, US forces adopted a number of innovations. The assault would be preceded by several days, not hours, of naval bombardment and day and night air attacks, the Japanese would be given no rest day or night for at least a week prior to the landing. Immediately before the landing the selected beaches should be subjected to a devastating bombing and naval bombardment. The confused air support at the Gilberts disappeared with the formation of new specialised amphibious command ships (AGC) in which Commander Support Aircraft had twelve officers and thirty-eight men in each AGC. Two major islands at Kwajalein atoll would be assaulted, Roi-Namur and Kwajalein island – each assault would have its own AGC and support aircraft commander.[1]

The Air Support Control Unit ashore was strengthened and in the event of failure of ship-to-air communications, as had happened at Tarawa, the Air Support Control Unit would be able to act as liaison with landing force commanders ashore. Commander Support Aircraft in the AGC relieved the carriers of their control over Target Combat Air Patrol and assumed responsibility over local air target selection using these standby planes. To enhance strafing, one squadron of TBF Avengers was armed with rockets – which packed a far heavier punch than .50-calibre machine-gun rounds.[2]

The Americans were unaware just how high the attrition of Japanese carrier pilots had been at Rabaul and over the Gilberts. In fact, Japan had almost no carrier pilots left – an important factor in Admiral Koga's decision to relocate his main naval fleet units to Truk and Palau, leaving behind an estimated 150 aircraft to defend the Marshalls, many of them long-range Betty bombers that were no match for fighters.[3]

Rear Admiral Mitscher, (CTF 58) had operational control of twelve carriers (including the two new light carriers, *Langley* (CVL-27) and *Cabot* (CVL-28)). Commander Task Force 54 (ComBatPac), Rear Admiral W.A. 'Ching' Lee commanded six of the newest fast battleships along with heavy cruisers, light cruisers and twenty-seven destroyers and would provide the support screen for the carriers.

The 12 carriers of Task Force 58 carried 650 combat planes and were divided into 4 smaller task groups – each built around 3 aircraft carriers and their support vessels.

Task Force 58 Composition
1. Task Group 58.1 – Rear Admiral J.W. Reeves Jr (ComCarDiv 4):
   Enterprise (CV-6), Air Group 10
   Yorktown (CV-10), Air Group 5
   Belleau Wood (CVL-24), (light carrier) Air Group 24
2. Task Group 58.2 – Rear Admiral A.E. Montgomery (ComCarDiv 12):
   Essex (CV-9), Air Group 9
   Intrepid (CV-11), Air Group 6
   Cabot (CVL-28) (light carrier), Air Group 31
3. Task Group 58.3 – Rear Admiral F.C. Sherman (Com CarDiv 1):
   Bunker Hill (CV-17), Air Group 17
   Monterey (CVL-26) (light carrier), Air Group 30
   Cowpens (CVL-25) (light carrier), Air Group 25
4. Task Group 58.4 – Rear Admiral S.P. Ginder (ComCarDiv 11):
   Saratoga (CV-3), Air Group 12
   Princeton (CVL-23) (light carrier), Air Group 23
   Langley (CVL-27) (light carrier), Air Group 32

After a delay of about a month due to logistical problems, Spruance was able to deploy the fleet towards Kwajalein in late January 1944. When Task Force 58 sortied from Pearl Harbor, it was the last sortie of the fast carriers from Hawaii as on completion of the Marshall Islands campaign, Hawaii would be left far in the rear. The new forward base would be Majuro. On the long insertion passage, Mitscher's TF 58 aircraft exercised procedures and tactics.

On 29 January 1944, as Task Force 58 closed, Reeves' TG 58.1 planes from *Enterprise*, *Yorktown* and *Belleau Wood* hit Maloelap whilst Ginder's TG 58.4 planes from *Saratoga*, *Princeton* and *Langley* bombed Wotje, which had previously been hit in December 1943 by Seventh Air Force B-24 Liberator bombers, staging through Baker Island airfield, and by carrier aircraft.

The same day, Montgomery's TG 58.2 planes from *Essex*, *Intrepid* and *Cabot* attacked the airfield on the Kwajalein atoll islet of Roi-Namur, the Hellcats strafing parked aircraft on the airstrip before hitting Kwajalein Island itself. A total of ninety-two Japanese fighters and bombers were destroyed – and by mid-morning on 29 January, Mitscher's planes had full air superiority over their Marshall Islands targets. Their dominance would remain unchallenged throughout the operation. The battleships then closed on the beaches to commence a pre-invasion bombardment on 30 January.

To ensure the Japanese did not stage aircraft into the fight through Eniwetok, Sherman's Task Group 58.3 aircraft from *Bunker Hill*, *Monterey* and *Cowpens* hit Eniwetok for the next three days – whilst Ginder's TG 58.4 aircraft from *Saratoga*, *Princeton* and *Langley* hit Maloelap for two days before joining Sherman's TG 58.3 off Eniwetok. The next five days were spent pounding Roi-Namur in close support whilst Kwajalein island was also hit remorselessly, as were Mili and Jaluit, by land-based air. The US carriers lost 17 Hellcat fighters and 5 torpedo-bombers to enemy fire and 27 additional planes operationally.[4] Rear Admiral Monzo Akiyama now lacked the ability to effectively mount a counter-offensive.

Rear Admiral Richmond Kelly Turner's Fifth Fleet Amphibious Force carrying V Amphibious Corps, under the command of Major General Holland M. Smith, would execute the simultaneous landings on Majuro and Kwajalein atolls. The invasion force comprised the 4th Marine Division under the command of Major General Harry Schmidt (assigned to take Roi-Namur, which had an airfield), the Army's 7th Infantry Division under the command of Major General Charles H. Corlett ('Cowboy Pete'), along with the 22nd Marines and the Army's 106th and 111th Infantry regiments.

The 4th Marine Division and 7th Infantry Divisions were assigned to the initial landings at Kwajalein, whilst the 2nd Battalion of the 106th was assigned to the simultaneous capture of Majuro atoll. The remainder of the 106th and the 22nd Marines were held in reserve for deployment to Kwajalein as necessary.

(a) The Invasion of Majuro Atoll, 31 January 1944

On 31 January 1944, the Reconnaissance Company of V Amphibious Corps of the Marines and the Army's 2nd Battalion of the 106th Infantry landed on Majuro for the opening act of Operation FLINTLOCK. The landing troops discovered that the Japanese had evacuated their fortifications for Kwajalein and Eniwetok some time previously, leaving only a single Japanese officer as caretaker. The US force took control of the atoll in that one day without any casualties, giving the US Navy the use of one of the largest anchorages in the Pacific.

(b) The Invasion of Kwajalein Atoll

Kwajalein Island is only 2.5 miles long and 880yd wide – so the Japanese defenders had no alternative but to make plans to counter-attack the US landing beaches. But until the Battle of Tarawa, they had not appreciated that tracked US amphibious vehicles could cross coral reefs and land on the lagoon side of an atoll. They had concentrated their strongest defences on the other side of Kwajalein, facing the ocean.

On 31 January 1944, as softening up for the amphibious assault, the big naval guns of seven old First-World-War-era battleships, along with cruisers and destroyers, B-24 bombers from Apamama in the Gilberts, aircraft from eight escort carriers and artillery on Carlson Island, gave the low-lying Kwajalein atoll island a punishing pre-invasion bombardment – a softening up tactic that came to be known as a 'Spruance Haircut' – a word play on the 'Mitscher Shampoo' the carrier planes delivered. TF 58 aircraft took directions from air support commanders, striking enemy defensive positions as they flew more than 4,000 sorties over the target.

The pre-invasion air attacks and the heavy naval bombardment wreaked havoc on the beaches and airfield – such that resistance was much weaker than in the Gilberts. On Kwajalein the pre-invasion bombardment was so effective that of some 3,000 troops garrisoned on Kwajalein, only some 300 were left alive to oppose the US invaders as they landed. The concentrated pre-invasion bombardment had so reduced US infantry casualties that it established the template for future use of carrier aircraft in the Pacific.

The 7th Infantry Division seized a number of small islands designated Carlos, Carter, Cecil and Carlson, which could be used as artillery bases to support the next day's assault on Kwajalein Island itself. The 4th Marine Division seized the islets at the north of the atoll – designated Ivan, Jacob, Albert, Allen and Abraham.

1 February 1944
The amphibious assault on Kwajalein began at 0930 with landings on beaches Red 1 and Red 2, Major General Charles Corlett's 7th Infantry Division landing successfully despite Japanese pillboxes, bunkers and infantry offensives. The US experience of amphibious landings was

effective, the pre-landing naval bombardment had been devastating and the Japanese defences on the wrong side of the island assisted the position. The landing troops had reached halfway across the airfield runway by sunset. Although the Japanese counter-attacked every night, Kwajalein Island was nevertheless declared secure by the end of the fourth day.

The 4th Marines captured the airfield on the western half of the northernmost islet in the atoll, Roi – the eastern half, Namur, was captured the next day. The whole atoll had been secured after eight days, on 7 February.

Of the 8,000 Japanese troops guarding Majuro and Kwajalein, less than 100 were taken prisoner (discounting Korean labourers) to US losses of 372 killed in action, 1,462 wounded and 183 missing. The Japanese lost an estimated 155 planes with Mitscher's losses a total of 57 planes.[5]

The original date for the invasion of Eniwetok had been slated for 1 May 1944 – with Truk to be hit and neutralised by an air raid before late March 1944.[6] But after the success of Kwajalein and Majuro, this could now be accelerated. Spruance favoured leaping ahead to take the Japanese-held Eniwetok atoll, an important anchorage in the western Marshall Islands where the Japanese had built an airfield on Engebi Island for refuelling planes travelling between Truk and the islands to the east. If the proposed action came off, it would be the furthest US advance of the war. As soon as Kwajalein was secure, Nimitz, adopting Spruance's reasoning, radioed Spruance suggesting Eniwetok be taken with the fresh unused reserve troops still afloat. Nimitz also considered a carrier strike on Truk that might possibly bring on a fleet engagement.[7]

Spruance took Nimitz's proposal to his amphibious commanders, Rear Admiral Richmond Kelly Turner, in command of the Fifth Fleet Amphibious Force, and Major General Holland M. Smith, in command of V Amphibious Corps. Both endorsed the plan – having already drawn up an operation plan for just such an event.[8]

Spruance replied to Nimitz positively – and on 10 February 1944, got the go-ahead to strike at Eniwetok and Truk.[9] The next day, 11 February, Spruance assembled his commanders aboard his flagship, the battleship *New Jersey*, and briefed them on the planned operation. Spruance would lead the Truk raid from his flag battleship – with air operations being under the command of Pete Mitscher in *Yorktown*. If the Japanese Fleet sortied and offered battle, Spruance would assume command, using 'Ching' Lee's battle line of six fast battleships.

With Kwajalein and Majuro airfields now able to provide land-based air power, the fast carriers of Task Groups 58.1, 58.2 and 58.3 withdrew, heading for the new anchorage at Majuro to replenish – whilst Ginder's TG 58.4 was left behind to pound the next target, Eniwetok atoll.

(ii) The Invasion of Eniwetok Atoll – Operation CATCHPOLE, 17 February 1944

Enewetak atoll is a large almost circular coral atoll, 50 nautical miles in circumference and 23 miles in diameter that comprises some forty islands surrounding a deep lagoon. During the Second World War it was known as Eniwetok, its name changing to Enewetak in 1974. It is the second-westernmost atoll of the Ralik Chain in the Marshall Islands, situated to the northwest of Kwajalein atoll and approximately 190 nautical miles west of Bikini atoll. Eniwetok's narrow strips of coral have a total land area of just over 2 square miles, and none are more than 5m above sea level. Today some 600–700 islanders live on the atoll, which was the scene of US nuclear testing during the Cold War. In the late 1970s a concrete dome, the Runit Dome, was built on Runit Island to deposit radioactive soil and debris.

Japan had possessed the atoll since 1914 – and had constructed an airfield on Engebi Island in late 1942, and this was used for refuelling aircraft travelling between Truk, to its west, and other islands to the east. A seaplane base was also established at Parry Island.

The invasion of Eniwetok atoll would provide US forces with an airfield and a large lagoon harbour that could be used to support the forthcoming campaign to take the Mariana Islands, more than 1,000 nautical miles to the west towards the Philippines.

As the threat of US attack grew during 1943, the Japanese established light defences throughout Eniwetok atoll. Following the loss of the Gilbert Islands, in early January 1944, the atoll was reinforced by the battle-hardened 1st Amphibious Brigade, which had previously been stationed in Manchukuo. They began to construct heavier defences.

Major General Yoshimi Nishida had some 4,000 troops spread out around the atoll islands – but as with Kwajalein, the small flat coral islands of Eniwetok atoll did not allow inland defence in depth. This would be a fight in the open – and Nishida decided to try and stop the US invasion forces on the beaches. The heavy fortifications had not however been completed by the time of the US attack.

A company of nine light Type 95 Ha-Go three-man tanks, each mounting a 37mm (1.5in) main gun and two 7.77mm machine guns, had been landed. These light tanks were effective against lightly armed infantry such as the US amphibious troops – but they had thin armour, a light main gun and a number of weaknesses. These tanks were encountered in assaults on many Japanese island garrisons – they could be taken out by a bazooka, and were no match for the much bigger, more heavily armed and armoured US tanks.

There was however one major complication for any assault on Eniwetok – that would have to be dealt with first. Any Allied shipping in the vicinity of Eniwetok, and any troops on the beaches, would come within range of aircraft based at the greatest Japanese naval and air base in the Central Pacific – Truk, which lay almost 800 nautical miles west south west of Eniwetok.

By early 1944 it had become obvious to US strategists that Truk was a main staging area for Japanese supplies of men and machines into the Southern Pacific. Truk had supplied the powerful Japanese base of Rabaul on New Guinea, some 700 nautical miles to the south – before it had been pacified by Halsey. Conscious of Truk's threat, Spruance proposed a fast-carrier raid to hit Truk, simultaneous with the Eniwetok invasion. The Truk raid was codenamed Operation HAILSTONE.

Japanese aircraft losses by this point of the war were at a critically high level, following the ill-fated deployment of carrier aircraft to defend Rabaul. Although several Japanese carriers had been lost to enemy action, there were still Japanese Fleet carriers available – but heavy losses of experienced pilots and their planes had made them ineffective. Japanese commanders now considered the remaining air cover as inadequate for Combined Fleet operations at sea. There was no alternative but for the Combined Fleet to hole up in the perceived safety of the Truk fortress – virtually immobilised.

On 5 January 1944, the first of thousands of IJA troops arrived on Truk to consolidate its defences against a possible US land invasion – that Japanese intelligence believed would possibly be made on about 21 February 1944. Three of the five navigable passes into the 140-mile circumference barrier reef of the Truk lagoon were mined. The remaining two navigable passes, one to the north and one to the south, were left open but protected by coastal defence guns and *kaiten* suicide units.

As Truk now became vulnerable to attack, Admiral Mineichi Koga, Commander-in-Chief of the Combined Fleet, who had based himself in Truk, began dispersing units of the Combined Fleet westwards, away from the Allied advance to safety. 2nd Fleet naval units were sent west towards Palau, which was still at this point out of range of Allied land-based and carrier aircraft. Palau became the 2nd Fleet HQ.

The battleships *Nagato* and *Fūso* and escort destroyers left Truk west bound for Palau on 1 February 1944 – and the super battleship *Yamato* along with other battleships, cruisers and destroyers left on 3 February 1944. Admiral Koga remained at Truk aboard his flagship, the battleship *Musashi*.

On 11 and 13 February, aircraft from Sam Ginders' Task Group 58.4 carriers *Saratoga*, *Princeton* and *Langley* worked over the Eniwetok atoll islets – destroying most of the atoll's defences. The naval bombardment of Eniwetok began on 17 February 1944, the same day as the nine carriers of Task Groups 58.1, 58.2 and 58.3 began their two-day air attack on Truk to destroy the Japanese air capability and ensure that no Japanese aircraft interfered with the Eniwetok amphibious landings. As TG58.1, TG58.2 and TG58.3 assaulted Truk, TG 58.4 carriers *Saratoga*, *Princeton* and *Langley* provided air cover for the Eniwetok amphibious naval force, launching several strikes and Combat Air Patrols.

The following day, 18 February, with the air and naval ability of Truk already heavily degraded by the first day's air attacks of Operation HAILSTONE, the 22nd Marine Regiment landed on Engebi Island at Eniwetok, meeting resistance that cost 85 US dead and missing – and more than 160 wounded – before the island was declared secure. The Japanese lost almost 1,300 dead with only 16 taken prisoner.

US landings on Eniwetok atoll faced determined counter-attacks before the island was deemed secure on 21 February. The smaller Parry Island was secured on 22 February.

The US 110th Naval Construction Battalion arrived on Eniwetok between 21 and 27 February and began clearing the island to construct a bomber airfield, which required a 2,100m by 120m runway with taxiways and supporting infrastructure. The first US aircraft landed on the new strip on 11 March and the first operational bombing mission had taken place by 5 April.

Once Eniwetok atoll was secure, the lagoon would become a major forward anchorage and base for future operations. During the first half of 1944, almost 500 ships thronged the lagoon waters daily.

(iii) Task Force 58 Smashes Truk – Operation HAILSTONE, 17–18 February 1944

The lagoon at Chuuk, as Truk has been known since 1990, is a great natural harbour ringed by a protective barrier reef some 140 miles in circumference and 40–50 miles in diameter.

Rising up from the deep-blue oceanic depths of the Western Pacific, Chuuk State is one of the Federated States of Micronesia, an independent sovereign island nation formed in 1979 that consists of four states, Yap, Chuuk, Pohnpei and Kosrae. Together the four states comprise some 607 islands scattered over almost 1,700 miles just north of the equator, to the north east of New Guinea. Micronesia forms part of the larger archipelago of the Caroline Islands, which span a distance of more than 2,000 miles from the Palauan Islands in the west to Kosrae, far to the east of Chuuk.

Seized by Japan from Germany during the First World War, Truk was administered by the Japanese until their defeat in 1945 – when Truk became one of the six districts of the Trust Territory of the Pacific Islands administered by the USA under charter from the United Nations until 1986.

Truk, Japan's major forward naval and air base, lies just over 1,100 nautical miles east of Palau. During the early part of the Second World War, although aware of Truk's strategic location, the Allies knew very little about enemy operations there. But they were aware of its excellent natural defences – Truk became known as the 'Gibraltar of the Pacific'.

At the start of the Second World War in 1939, Truk became the IJN's 4th Fleet Base. On 5 November 1941, the island bases of Truk and Ponape in the Carolines, along with Kwajalein, Wotje, Jaluit and Maloelap in the Marshall Islands, and Saipan in the Mariana Islands, were well enough developed to be designated as supply bases for Admiral Isoroku Yamamoto's Combined Fleet – just in time for the initial offensive phase of the planned Pacific War the following month, December 1941. Truk became the Combined Fleet's main forward naval base from 1942–4.

The 140 miles of barrier coral reefs around the Truk lagoon protect some 245 islands and islets within it. Although there are a number of passes into the lagoon, in all 140 miles of barrier reef, only five were wide enough and deep enough for large vessels to safely navigate as they entered and left the lagoon. During the war, these five passes were heavily defended – flanked by coastal defence guns set on the islands either side of the pass. With the exception of North Pass and South Pass (used by the Japanese), the other passes were mined and closed off to shipping.

Coastal defence guns can be classified as either *close defence guns* or *counter-bombardment guns*. Counter-bombardment guns were usually large-calibre naval guns with a high elevation, designed to destroy any enemy capital ships that might stand off, 10 miles or more away, and bombard from a distance. The Japanese used 8in (20cm) counter-bombardment guns, often old naval guns set in their turrets, salvaged from decommissioned warships – these 8in guns formed the main battery of Japan's heavy cruisers in the inter-war years leading up to the Second World War. They had a range of 25,000–30,000yd – some 14–17 miles. Close defence guns were quick-firing guns of a much smaller calibre, 6in or less, with lower elevation mountings so the barrels could be depressed to target enemy vessels much closer.

The Japanese positioned their counter-bombardment guns on strategically important peaks, hillsides and promontories so that they could deal with any enemy warships attempting to penetrate through the navigable passes. On the main island of Moen (now Weno) with its wartime large airfield, a battery of four 8in guns mounted in heavy cruiser turrets were set in open pit emplacements near the lighthouse – covering North Pass. Three 6in (15cm) naval guns were set in tunnelled out cave complexes high on a hill overlooking the airfield.

On the southernmost large island in the lagoon, Uman Island, three 6in guns in turrets were set high on the mountain top on its south-east side. These guns covered the approach into the lagoon via South Pass. Similar gun emplacements, AA gun emplacements and other fortifications were dug in throughout the other islands in the lagoon – and possible beach landing sites were made into killing zones with mortar emplacements for short-range engagements, beach mines, pillboxes and fortified firing positions.

In addition to these defences the many islands of Truk harboured a number of airfields and seaplane bases that bristled with hundreds of fighters, dive-bombers, torpedo- and high-altitude bombers and reconnaissance float planes. The large island of Moen accommodated Moen No. 1 Airfield at its north-western tip – and Moen No. 2 Airfield and the Moen Seaplane Base at its south-western corner. The next largest island, Dublon (now Tonoas), to the south of Moen, held the Dublon Seaplane Base. There was another airfield on Param Island and an airfield under construction during 1944 on Mesegon Island.

The primary Japanese fighter airfield used for the defence of Truk was located on Eten Island to the south of Dublon Island – known to the Japanese as Takeshima Air Base and housing the 21st, 22nd, 25th, 26th and *Kōkū Sentai* carrier division. Eten Island was originally a small island with a higher central hill. During 1941, the Japanese used forced labour to begin the creation of an aircraft-carrier-shaped island, an unsinkable aircraft carrier. Rubble and stone were quarried from the central hill and used to create a carrier-shaped rubble stone seawall with a pier measuring 95ft by 30ft with a boom rigged crane. Once the carrier-shaped island had been formed, infilled and levelled, a single runway extended the length of the island, and measuring 3,440ft long by 270ft wide, was created and surfaced with 1.5in of concrete for all-weather use. The island HQ was situated to the south east of the runway along with repair facilities, living quarters for 1,200 personnel, power plant, radio and the air traffic control tower; 40 fighter and 7 larger bomber revetments were set alongside the runway, along the remaining hillside.

Truk served as a safe, sheltered and well-protected forward base for the IJN main battle fleet. Super battleships such as the *Yamato* and *Musashi*, along with aircraft carriers, cruisers, destroyers, tankers, tugs, gunboats, minesweepers, landing craft and submarines, all thronged her waters.

In addition to the front-line battle fleet, a large number of naval auxiliary transport ships, often converted former civilian passenger/cargo vessels, worked as tenders for the fleet and its submarines, carrying naval shells, ammunition, torpedoes, stores, spares – and everything else needed to keep a battle fleet in operation.

Other auxiliary transport vessels, usually freighters and cargo vessels, either requisitioned or purpose built under the mass standard shipbuilding programme, arrived continuously. The deep cargo holds of these large transport vessels held munitions, tanks, trucks, land artillery, beach mines and the like – all destined to be offloaded to fortify Truk's land defences and to resupply troops billeted there. Landing craft were heavily used to ferry the war cargoes from the auxiliaries to the shore. Convoys of escorted transport ships holding similar cargoes stopped over at Truk to refuel, replenish and regroup, before heading off in convoy for other outlying Japanese island garrisons.

The fortification of Truk before the war had been carried out in the utmost secrecy – with no foreigners allowed anywhere near the islands. Allied code breaking in the run up to the Battle of the Coral Sea in early 1942 had confirmed suspicions that Truk was a major fortified anchorage – but due to the strict shroud of military secrecy, they had no idea of the scale of the operation. It was believed that there was a large Japanese air base holding as many as 300 aircraft – but little else was known. In a later interview in December 1944, Mitscher commented: 'All I knew about Truk was what I'd read in the National Geographic, and the writer had been mistaken about some things.'[10]

An advance party of 300 officers and men of the IJA 52nd Division arrived in Truk in November 1943 to assess the position – and quickly concluded that Truk was poorly equipped to defend against an amphibious invasion. A first echelon of IJA troops then arrived on 4 January 1944, following the Allied amphibious assaults on the Gilbert and Marshall Islands. There were no permanent fortifications on Truk at this point and so, believing that Truk may be next in line to be assaulted, the Japanese began actively building up Truk's defences. Beach defences of reinforced concrete pillboxes and blockhouses were established at the shoreline, supplemented by mine fields. Numerous anti-aircraft gun positions were established and eventually there would be over eighty 25mm and 12cm AA guns in emplacements, along with many lighter AA weapons. In mid-February 1944, a second echelon of IJA troops arrived at Truk.

Meanwhile, *kaiten* manned suicide torpedo bases would be established on the outer islands and Daihatsu landing craft were converted into torpedo boats. More heavy naval coastal defence guns were set in caves on strategic island peaks and promontories. Anti-submarine netting was placed around docks and key anchorages.

By February 1944, Truk was heavily fortified with a military infrastructure of roads, trenches, bunkers, caves, five airstrips, seaplane bases, a torpedo-boat station, submarine repair centres, a communications centre and a radar station. The Japanese garrison now consisted of IJN personnel and almost 17,000 IJA personnel. A significant portion of the Japanese Fleet was based there – battleships, carriers, cruisers, destroyers, tankers, naval auxiliary transport ships, tugs, gunboats, minesweepers, subchasers and submarines.

As they were pushed back in the Gilberts and Marshalls, between November 1943 and early 1944, much of the Combined Fleet retreated and gathered in their perceived stronghold of Truk – amidst the intense work ashore to fortify Truk's defences. The scene was set for the showdown.

On the evening of 3 February 1944, two US Marine long-range Consolidated PB4Y-1 Liberator photo-reconnaissance planes rose into the air from their Stirling Island airfield in the Solomon Islands, for a 2,000-mile round trip to overfly Truk and photograph Japanese shipping and land fortifications. The PB4Y-1 reconnaissance aircraft had four Pratt & Whitney radial engines that gave them a top speed of 300mph – fast for such a big aircraft and almost as fast as the Japanese Zero fighter. In addition to speed, the Navy PB4Y-1 Liberator was well armed, bristling with six gun turrets, each accommodating twin M2 Browning 0.50-calibre machine guns. Armour plating protected the pilots and it had a service ceiling of 21,000ft.

After their long flight, the two navy PB4Ys arrived undetected over Truk early the next morning, 4 February 1944. Scattered cloud cover partially obscured some of the shipping below, but through gaps in the cloud they were still able to take a number of photographs from a height of 20,000ft. The US aircraft were spotted and the Japanese AA battery on Dublon Island opened up – and was soon followed by other shore batteries and some naval AA guns. The super battleship *Musashi*, at anchor below, opened up with her AA batteries.

Caught napping, with no patrolling fighters in the air, the Japanese scrambled two or three fast and agile land-based Mitsubishi A6M Zero fighters and a similar number of Nakajima A6M2-N Rufe (Zero variant) seaplane fighters. Japanese pilots rushed to their aircraft as ground crew prepared them for flight – but it would take time to get airborne and rise up to 20,000ft to attack the fast US aircraft. The Zeros had a ceiling of more than 30,000ft and a top speed, slightly faster than the PB4Ys, of 328mph.

After spending 20–30 unopposed minutes overflying and photographing shipping in the lagoon and land fortifications, the two US aircraft turned unscathed to head back to their distant Solomon Islands airbase at full speed – knowing that Japanese fighters would be coming after them. Although one fighter seaplane almost caught up, the Navy PB4Ys were able to outdistance the Japanese fighters and disappear to return the precious film for analysis.

The US reconnaissance overflight was enough to convince Admiral Koga that an attack by the Americans was now imminent and that his Combined Fleet battleships, aircraft carriers, cruisers, submarines and ancillary craft – the main fighting strength of the IJN – was in danger. Koga believed that the Americans, now converging on Truk from the Gilberts and Marshalls, would next attack the Philippines, Guam and Saipan, all well to the west of Truk. He knew that Nimitz could not bypass Truk without attacking – Nimitz could not leave Truk to his rear, able to mount air attacks from behind the Allied front, for its submarines to put to sea, for its warships to attack Allied shipping. Following the fall of Kwajalein, Vice Admiral Takeo Kurita's 2nd Fleet had begun to move more than 1,000 nautical miles west to the naval stronghold of Palau. On the day of the Truk overflight, a further group of battleships and cruisers departed for Palau.

On 10 February 1944, Admiral Koga left Truk bound for Japan aboard his flagship, the super battleship *Musashi*, with four carriers, escort cruisers and destroyers and several fleet supply ships. Admiral Ozawa's valuable Carrier Fleet was sent to the great harbour of Singapore, seized from the British in February 1942 – and much further

The Marine aviators who made the first reconnaissance mission over Truk on 4 February 1944 beside their PB4Y-1 patrol bombers soon after their 2,000-mile combat mission. (National Archives 80-G-208975)

to the west. The super battleship *Yamato* and a number of escort cruisers and destroyers left the lagoon soon after the carriers.

Admiral Koga also ordered part of the 4th Fleet underway, from its anchorage to the east of Dublon Island. But not all of the ships' captains had yet been given their sailing orders and many ships lingered in the 4th Fleet anchorage – such as the light cruisers *Naka*, *Agano* and *Katori*, the large auxiliary transports *Aikoku Maru* and *Kiyosumi Maru*, the submarine tenders *Rio de Janeiro Maru* and *Heian Maru*, the destroyers *Fumizuki*, *Tachikaze*, *Maikaze* and *Nowake* together with an assortment of tankers and other auxiliary vessels, all busily engaged in off-loading their war supplies. They could not leave with their badly needed cargoes still onboard. Other ships had been damaged by attacks elsewhere and were in Truk for repair – not fit to leave for the open sea.

There was a frantic rush to move fuel from tankers to the shore-based installations and to finish the general re-supplying of the Truk base – but the holds and decks of many auxiliary transports were still packed with tanks, trucks, tanker vehicles, beach mines, land artillery, vital aircraft and spare parts, huge cargoes of shells for the big land guns and for the warships, together with massed amounts of small arms ammunition – all earmarked to be offloaded to Truk in preparation for the anticipated US amphibious assault.

When the US aerial reconnaissance photographs were safely returned and analysed, they revealed the land fortifications of the Japanese stronghold in astounding detail and permitted the drawing up of a well-coordinated plan of attack. Suddenly, from not knowing what shipping was at Truk before the overflight, it now became instantly clear that nearly all of the Combined Fleet was there.

The *Musashi* was clearly identified along with 2 aircraft carriers, 20 destroyers, 10 cruisers, 12 submarines and more than 50 other surface vessels. US High Command immediately advanced plans to attack shipping in the anchorage – the original plan had been for an attack on 15 April 1944.

With Vice Admiral Spruance, Commander Central Pacific Force, in overall command afloat his flagship, TG 50.2 battleship *New Jersey* (BB-62), Mitscher as Commander of the Fast-Carrier Force had operational control of twelve Task Force 58 carriers.

Of the assembled might of Task Force 58, three task groups, Ginder's three TG 58.4 carriers *Saratoga*, *Princeton* and *Langley*, were away covering the Eniwetok landings. The remaining 9 carriers of 3 task groups carrying more than 500 combat aircraft would hit Truk – Reeves' TG 58.1 with *Enterprise*, *Yorktown* and *Belleau Wood*; Montgomery's TG 58.2 with *Essex*, *Intrepid* and *Cabot*; and Sherman's TG 58.3 with *Bunker Hill*, *Cowpens* and *Monterey*.

To protect the task groups destined for Truk, if the Japanese Fleet came out and offered battle, Task Group 50.9 under Vice Admiral 'Ching' Lee (ComBatPac) would form a battle line of the 6 fast battleships *Iowa*, *New Jersey*, *Massachusetts*, *Alabama*, *South Dakota* and *North Carolina* with 6 heavy cruisers, 4 light cruisers and 29 destroyers of the screen. Two other fast battleships remained with Ginder at Eniwetok.[11]

As the air attacks went in, Task Unit 50.9.1, attached to TG 58.3 and consisting of the two battleships *Iowa* and *New Jersey*, the cruisers *New Orleans* (CA-32) and *Minneapolis* (CA-36) and the Fletcher-class destroyers *Bradford* (DD-545), *Izard* (DD-589), *Charrette* (DD-581) and *Burns* (DD-588), would detach from TG 58.3 and under Spruance's direct command make a counter-clockwise sweep around the lagoon to catch and destroy any enemy vessels attempting to leave the lagoon.

Ten Task Force 17 lifeguard submarines were sent to patrol the waters outside Truk with orders to remain submerged until the attack – when the submarines would surface as required to rescue any US aviators downed outside the lagoon. The submarines *Tang*, *Sunfish* and *Skate* were tasked to operate south and south west of Truk whilst *Sea Raven* and *Darter* would be stationed to the north. *Aspro*, *Burrfish*, *Dace* and *Gato* would cover the remaining exits from the lagoon. US aviators downed inside the lagoon would be rescued by Kingfisher floatplanes and flown out to the submarines.

On 10 February 1944, the US submarine *Permit* reported that two Japanese heavy ships, believed to be the battleships *Nagato* and *Fusō*, had left Truk. The Americans were unaware however that, by now, the majority of the IJN warships had left the lagoon, leaving only a few lighter IJN warships along with almost fifty naval auxiliaries, tenders, cargo vessels, oilers and tankers. Most of the vessels at anchor in Truk were lightly armed merchantmen.

Task Force 58 sortied from Majuro on 12–13 February for the first independent carrier strike of that size of the war – a nine-carrier force bound for Truk that was much more powerful than the Japanese six-carrier force that had raided Pearl Harbor at the very beginning of the war. Commander Phil Torrey, skipper of Air Group 9 on *Essex*, said: 'They didn't tell us where we were going until we were well on the way. They announced our destination over the loudspeaker. It was Truk. My first instinct was to jump overboard.'[12]

On 14 February, the task force refuelled from ServRon 10 oilers, 640 miles north east of Truk. The ServRon 10 oilers then returned to Kwajalein to take on oil from tankers in readiness for the post-strike refuelling rendezvous, a procedure that would become standard.

Every day, unaware of the approach of the undetected US carrier force, more and more Japanese naval transport ships were arriving from Japan, some destined for, or returning from, other Japanese island strongholds. Such was the pace of the war that supply ships, setting off from Japan to reinforce outposts like the Solomon Islands, reached Truk en route – only to learn that the Allies had overrun their final destinations.

On the morning of 15 February, the Japanese Fleet Monitoring Unit intercepted a radio message from a US carrier pilot to the carrier *Essex*. The Japanese now knew for certain that at least one carrier was somewhere out there in the vast expanses of the Pacific. A US attack

Ships of the US Pacific Fleet anchored at Majuro Atoll in the Marshall Islands, 25 April 1944, shortly before leaving to attack Truk. (National Archives 80-G-225251)

was now suspected – and a number of Japanese aircraft were deployed in a search pattern around Truk. The Americans however already knew the Japanese search patterns, from previously intercepted radio transmissions, and took precautions to avoid known search areas.

Just after midday the same day, 15 February, during refuelling operations 40 miles due west of the task force, CAP Hellcats from the light carrier *Belleau Wood* shot down a single long-range Japanese twin-engine Mitsubishi G4M reconnaissance bomber (Allied reporting name Betty). It was one of four Bettys conducting routine search missions that day – and was splashed before it sighted the task force. The Betty was shot down so quickly that its crew didn't have time to transmit a warning radio message back to Truk.[13]

When the Betty bomber from the Japanese air patrol subsequently failed to return, at 0230 on 16 February, Vice Admiral Kobayashi, commander of the 4th Fleet, ordered the Truk defences to their highest state of alert. At 0500, five Japanese Betty bomber reconnaissance aircraft took off from Moen airfield for a special search. They did not spot any US forces during their patrol and so, at 0900, the alarm status was reduced to a regular alarm. After 12 hours, when no attack had come and there was still no sign of the enemy, the alarm was cancelled. Japanese forces were stood down and returned to a state of normal preparedness.

The ten US submarines took up their assigned positions as some fifty-three ships of the striking group, battleships, cruisers, destroyers and fast carriers, closed on Truk completely undetected. The surface units arrived on station in darkness 94 miles north east on the evening of 16 February 1944.

Each of the nine carriers supported an air group which comprised two sections of fighters, dive-bombers and torpedo-bombers that would alternate combat duties to minimise aircrew fatigue. By now, air group squadron numbers were randomly assigned to a carrier's fighter, dive and torpedo squadrons. Thus, *Enterprise* (CV-6) carried Air Group 10 and deployed its Hellcats as Fighting Squadron 10 (VF-10), its dive-bombers as Bombing Squadron 10 (VB-10) and torpedo-bombers as Torpedo Squadron 10 (VT-10), although the torpedo planes mostly carried bombs during the strikes and fighters also carried bombs. The dive-bombers were mostly SBD Dauntless except for those aboard *Bunker Hill*, which had the only squadron of SB2C Helldivers.[14]

Operation HAILSTONE was scheduled to commence before dawn the following day, 17 February 1944 – designated DOG-DAY-MINUS-ONE.

Over the two days of the planned raid, thirty waves of attacking aircraft would continuously bomb and strafe any shipping they encountered and destroy shore facilities.

(a) DOG-DAY-MINUS-ONE, 17 February 1944

US commanders knew that they had to gain air superiority before committing to a bombing and torpedo attack on the shipping and land installations. Mitscher came up with the idea of an initial all-fighter sweep designed to clear the air of Japanese fighters and give the bombers a clear approach to the target.[15] A sweep gave the fighters great latitude to attack targets of opportunity – as opposed to a strike, which was an attack against pre-briefed specific targets. It was a great improvement on the previous inflexible tactic of having the fighters escort the bombers all the way in.

The Hellcats from the four light carriers, *Belleau Wood, Cabot, Monterey* and *Cowpens*, would provide Combat Air Patrols above the task force, at the holding position 90 miles outside the lagoon – to deal with any Japanese attack that may materialise and to act as a reserve force should the need arise.

Just over an hour before dawn on 17 February 1944, between 0440 and 0454 (local time), the first twelve VF-10 Hellcat fighters of a planned combined force of seventy-two Hellcats started to take off from the Task Group 58.1 carrier *Enterprise*. Their launch was timed so that they would arrive over Truk at 0600 – sunrise was at 0609, sunset would come at 1804. Similar squadrons of Hellcats prepared to take off from the other carriers.

The twelve VF-5 Hellcats roaring off the flight deck of *Yorktown* in the pre-dawn half-light would join the twelve *Enterprise* Hellcats for the low attack sweep at an altitude of 6,000–8,000ft. The twelve VF-9 Hellcats lifting into the air from *Essex* would carry out an intermediate sweep at 10,000–15,000ft along with the twelve VF-6 Hellcats from *Intrepid*. The twenty-four VF-17 Hellcats from *Bunker Hill* would provide high-altitude cover at 25,000ft.

Once airborne, the groups of twelve strike fighters flew low and fast towards Truk from a northerly direction at about 1,000ft above sea level – to avoid Japanese radar. Once they were about 15 minutes flying time from Truk, the flights of Hellcats started to rise up to their designated patrol altitudes at designated rendezvous points. TG 58.1 – 15 miles north of North Pass, TG 58.2, 15 miles north east of North Pass and TG 58.3, 15 miles east of North Pass.

At 0520, Japanese radar based in Truk detected the approach of a large formation of aircraft and the Truk commander, Vice Admiral Masami Kobayashi, ordered the highest state of alarm. An initial Japanese analysis of the radar reflections however concluded that a large land-based bomber formation was approaching Truk – it wasn't believed that such a large force could be solely carrier-based fighter aircraft.

After about 46 minutes of flight, at about 0600, the first of the seventy-two Hellcats, swept into the skies above the lagoon at 8,000ft – above the two northerly sea passages into the lagoon, North Pass and North-East Pass. They made an unchallenged circular run around nearly the whole lagoon before encountering any enemy fighters. Once alerted however, Japanese fighters scrambled and made to rise into the air, striving to quickly gain enough altitude to attack the successive groups of Hellcats that were now arriving over Truk.

As well as dealing with enemy fighters, the Hellcats were tasked with strafing Japanese airfields to destroy enemy aircraft on the ground before they could get into the air – and to render the airstrips unserviceable. Japanese air strength had to be sufficiently degraded to allow the slower more vulnerable dive-bombers and torpedo-bombers that would soon follow on to do their job.

The large airfield at the north end of the largest and most northerly island, Moen (now Weno), was strafed. From there, Hellcats swept south to strafe the seaplane base at the southern end of Moen before moving on to Dublon (now Tonoas), the next largest island just to the south, to strafe the seaplane base. Other Hellcats vectored further south to strafe the airfields on the much smaller islands of Eten and Param.

Although Japanese radar had detected the approaching formation about half an hour before the first aircraft reached the coral barrier reef of the lagoon, there were problems with Japanese command and communications. As a result, the Takeshima Air Base on Eten Island only learned of the incoming US strike some 10 minutes before strafing fire swept the runway – and the mass of stationary, parked fighters. The first target, the larger Moen Island airfield, received no warning at all of the attack – the first they knew of the raid was when Hellcats swept over the runway destroying valuable Japanese aircraft parked up on the ground.

Having been stood down from highest alert the day before, when highest alert was initiated again at 0530, most Japanese pilots were in town or in bed – some on different islands from their planes. Japanese aircrew scrambled to get to their aircraft and get airborne as fast as possible – whilst all the time, Hellcats were strafing their parked-up Zeros and Nakajima Ki-44 Tojo fighters – as well as hitting Nakajima A6M2 Rufe seaplane fighters afloat at the seaplane bases.

Desperate to save as many aircraft as possible, Japanese officers ordered aircraft mechanics and technicians to take off and head north. On Eten Island airstrip, absent pilots arriving by boat from other islands were beaten by their 2nd Commanding Officer. As the local Trukese population on the islands realised the expected attack was now happening, many of them fled to caves in the hills.

On the aircraft-carrier-shaped Eten Island airfield, there was a congestion of planes that had been offloaded from supply ships – many of which had not yet been assembled. As the Hellcats swept overhead on their strafing runs, they found Zekes, Bettys and Nakajima Ki-44 Tojo fighters lined up wingtip-to-wingtip – easy prey. Many Japanese aircraft started their motors and attempted to take off – but they were

211

Operation HAILSTONE fast-carrier raid on Truk, 17/18 February 1944. The man-made carrier-shaped Eten Island airfield was photographed from a *Yorktown* (CV-10) plane, 17 February 1944. A large number of Japanese planes are parked up on the field which has numerous bomb craters. Dublon Island is in the background, to the north. (National Archives 80-G-216891)

shot up as they taxied along the runway or shot down as they laboured into the sky shortly after taking off.

Japanese land-based AA emplacements opened up on the attacking US aircraft, throwing up a thick hail of flak. Long, seemingly slowly moving trails of flak followed the fighters through the skies, Lieutenant John Sullivan from Fighting 9 Air Group on *Essex* recalling: 'Our first sight of Truk was a black curtain of A.A. They held it until we got over the target, but they weren't too sharp. We surprised them. Their ships were at anchor, dead in the water, and that made them duck soup. It was wonderful!'[16] Lieutenant Marvin Franger: 'Right over the center of Truk all hell broke loose. God Damn! That was the worst scared I ever was.'

The carrier planes strafed and destroyed some 150 Japanese aircraft in all, parked up on Truk's various air strips – leaving more than

100 undamaged. Despite these losses on the ground, some 80–100 Japanese fighters finally gained enough altitude to take on the Hellcats – and the sky was soon filled with swirling fighters as dogfights broke out in what would become one of the greatest all-fighter aerial battles of the Second World War. Some fifty Zeros were shot down for the loss of four Hellcats. Lieutenant Eugene A. Valencia shot down three Japanese planes: 'These Grummans are beautiful planes. If they could cook, I'd marry one.' Herb Houck said: 'It was our superior pilots and superior tactics that gave us victory over the Japs.'[17]

In the early days of the war, the Japanese Zero fighter had been untouchable by most other aircraft and superior to the early US fighters, being more manoeuvrable with a rate of climb three times more rapid than any US plane in theatre at the time. The Zero was by now however simply outclassed by the F6F Hellcat. 'The Hellcats performed well, and outclimbed, outturned and outdove the Japanese planes which only seemed to have an edge at slower speeds.'[18]

The twelve battle-hardened Hellcats from the *Enterprise* were covering the lowest altitude layer at 8,000ft where it was expected the heaviest enemy opposition would be. They encountered about forty-seven enemy aircraft airborne and shot down sixteen with the loss of a single Hellcat.[19] *Yorktown* planes in wild and turbulent dogfights shot down eleven planes. *Essex* Hellcats made five strafing runs on the Moen seaplane base where about twenty-five planes were parked on the ramp and in shallow water, claiming ten to twelve Rufes destroyed before they could take off. They then moved on to strafe Param airfield where some twelve Kates and Bettys were shot up. The division from *Essex* at higher altitude was attacked by Japanese fighters coming out of the sun from above and a 45-minute-long dogfight ensued. *Intrepid* Hellcats shot down seventeen Japanese aircraft aloft and claimed forty-three destroyed on the ground. At the highest altitude, 20–25,000ft, *Bunker Hill* Hellcats watched the cloud tops – looking for Japanese fighters that had run out of the combat zone at lower levels and were climbing out of sight of the dogfight until they reached high altitude – from where they would dive down out of the sun onto the Hellcats deployed at lower levels.

As a great fighter battle now took place in the skies above Truk, combat reports being fed back from the fighters and observer planes to their carriers revealed however that the Japanese warships the two PB4Y-1 Liberator reconnaissance aircraft had spotted twelve days before were nowhere to be seen. The main elements of the IJN, the battleships, battlecruisers and carriers and most of the other heavy warships, had escaped the trap and vanished. There were however still some fifty armed merchantmen as well as a number of IJN light cruisers and destroyers below.

With Truk now under heavy attack, the Operation CATCHPOLE assault on the islets of Eniwetok could take place simultaneously without fear of Japanese interference from Truk.

Immediately following the launch of Initial Fighter Sweep, successive carrier group strikes of Douglas SBD Dauntless and Curtiss SB2C dive-bombers, and Grumman TBF Avenger torpedo-bombers, protected by Hellcat fighter escorts, were spotted on the carrier flight decks. They were armed and fuelled, ready to take off to attack shipping and designated land targets once air supremacy had been achieved – each strike being assigned areas and targets identified by aerial reconnaissance aircraft.

In all, six waves of dive- and torpedo-bomber aircraft would lift off from each of the carriers – forming up in the air for six coordinated group strikes spread throughout the day, designated A, B, C, D, E and F. A prefix number was assigned according to their individual task groups. Thus, strikes by TG 58.1 carriers *Enterprise* and *Yorktown* were designated 1A, 1B, 1C–1F etc. Strikes by TG 58.2 carriers *Essex* and *Intrepid* were designated 2A, 2B, 2C–2F and for TG 58.3 *Bunker Hill* strikes were designated 3A–3F. Strike 1A, 2A and 3A aircraft launched to arrive over Truk between 0615 and 0700. Strike 2A, 2B and 2C aircraft launched to arrive over Truk between 0815 and 0900.

With the Hellcats now establishing air superiority, torpedo- and dive-bombers were soon attacking Japanese shipping in the anchorages east and west of Dublon, where some fifteen Japanese transport ships had been spotted – as well as attacking shipping in the Eten anchorage to the south, where another fifteen ships were seen. On the land, airfields, barracks, ammunition and fuel supplies were attacked. In these early raids, the US pilots were careful not to hit the large land-based fuel tanks – they would be left until later in the day to avoid black smoke obscuring the selection of targets.

Down at sea level, it was a scene of carnage on the Japanese ships – one they had only limited AA weaponry to defend against. One of the largest vessels below was *Aikoku Maru*, a fast and spacious 492ft-long, 10,437gross registered ton (grt), twin-screw passenger and cargo liner anchored in the 4th Fleet anchorage, east of Dublon Island. An elegant liner with a large, long and tall central superstructure that housed

Operation HAILSTONE, Truk, 17/18 February 1944. Japanese ships under attack in the Fourth Fleet anchorage south east of of Dublon Island (at left) in the Truk lagoon, photographed from a USS *Intrepid* aircraft on the first day of the air raids. Four ships are burning. Moen Island is in the background. (National Archives 80-G-215151)

the bridge, smokestack and a myriad of corridors with cabins off, the superstructure was flanked fore and aft by large cargo holds. She was launched on 25 April 1940 and requisitioned on 1 September 1941 by the IJN, just months before the war began. Japan had been making preparations for war for some time prior to her construction – and although she was ostensibly a luxury ocean liner, the military had had a say in the design of the ship with a view to using her as a troop transport.

Aikoku Maru was better able to defend herself than most of the naval auxiliaries. Up on the boat deck, abaft the navigation bridge, two dual mount Type 96 25mm AA autocannon positions were set, one dual mount either side of the searchlight platform and two further dual mount Type 96 25mm autocannon situated one deck higher, one twin pair either side of the bridge. She also carried eight 5.5in guns, one on an elevated circular platform on the fo'c'sle deck at the bow and another on a similar platform atop the stern superstructure. The remaining guns were set on either side of the foredeck Hold Nos 2 and 3 and either side of the aft holds.

Her forward holds were filled with a cargo of munitions – mines, bombs and other high explosives along with the magazines for her forward defensive gun. In addition to her crew, more than 700 troops were billeted in her cabins and third-class passenger rooms and in makeshift billets in her aft holds.

After the initial dawn Hellcat fighter sweep, *Aikoku Maru* was repeatedly attacked by SBD Dauntless dive-bombers and TBF Avenger torpedo-bombers. Her AA guns opened up but despite the AA fire she threw up, and AA fire from land-based emplacements on Dublon, she was struck by several 500lb bombs. At about 0825 a bomb struck her hull in the vicinity of Hold No. 1, which housed her cargo of munitions. Moments later, there was a catastrophic secondary explosion that

Operation HAILSTONE, Truk, 17/18 February 1944. On the first day of the fast-carrier raid, the cargo of munitions carried in the foredeck holds of the 10,437grt auxiliary transport ship *Aikoku Maru* explodes after a dive-bombing attack. (National Archives 80-G-215155)

scattered debris and parts of the ship all around the epicentre of the blast. The forward section of the ship, from just in front of the smokestack to the bow, was almost vapourised, its pieces being spread out all over the lagoon. Japanese sources report that 730 troops in her aft section, billeted in the superstructure cabins, temporary billets in the aft holds and in the stern accommodation, were all killed in an instant, along with her crew. The remaining aft section of the ship sank quickly taking almost 1,000 troops and crew to the bottom – there was only one survivor.

Just after 0700, Strike 1B Hellcats escorting SBD Dauntlesses and TBF Avengers were launched from *Enterprise* and *Yorktown* for the second combined group strike of the day – tasked with targeting enemy warships with priority to battleships, then carriers, heavy cruisers and light cruisers. As they sped towards the lagoon, two Japanese cruisers were spotted and attacked 20–30 miles north west of North Pass. They were left damaged and smoking. Another group of warships was spotted about 10 miles north west of North Pass and attacked.

The 7,624grt *Amagisan Maru* had been constructed as a passenger cargo liner in 1933 but was now requisitioned and serving as an auxiliary transport vessel. A large vessel, she was 454ft in length with a beam of 60ft and was built roughly similar in construction to *Aikoku Maru* with a central superstructure flanked by cavernous cargo holds.

Amagisan Maru had arrived at Truk and anchored in the 6th Fleet anchorage, south west of Uman Island, three days before the

The stern section of *Aikoku Maru* today rests upright in Truk lagoon in 65m of water. The forward section of this large ship has been totally destroyed by the massive secondary munitions explosion. (Author)

The stern of the 10,500grt IJN auxiliary transport *Aikoku Maru* with docking bridge and auxiliary steering position with the defensive High Angle aft 5.5in gun above. (Ewan Rowell)

HAILSTONE raid. Strike 3D aircraft from *Bunker Hill* had been tasked to attack shipping found in the anchorage between Fefan and Uman Islands and at 1250, they attacked the largest ship present, *Amagisan Maru*, which was still at anchor at the southern end of the anchorage. She was armed with a 3.7in gun on a circular platform at her bow and a similar 3.7in at her stern along with lighter AA weaponry – but her defences were of little use against the US aircraft.

Five Curtis SB2C Helldivers and four TBF Avenger torpedo-bombers attacked – the Helldivers scoring a direct hit with a 1,000lb bomb. This hit was followed by an aerial torpedo attack from her starboard quarter. An action photograph taken by a US aircraft shows the torpedo porpoising after hitting the water before running straight for the starboard side just forward of the bridge superstructure. The torpedo hit and detonated, sending an expanding pillar of smoke and debris more than 100ft into the air. The *Amagisan Maru* was carrying a cargo of fuel in drums in her holds – and fuel in the foredeck Hold No. 2 ignited. As the plume of white smoke from the torpedo explosion dissipated, a large column of dense black smoke from the burning fuel started to billow up from the ship. Meanwhile, a second torpedo sped towards her stern. Within 15 minutes of the attack, she was burning fiercely and sinking by the bow.

The 367ft-long, 4,776grt naval auxiliary *Sankisan Maru* was anchored near to *Amagisan Maru* – she was attacked next. Unbeknown to the US pilots, her aft holds were filled with munitions – and when she took a direct hit aft, a massive secondary explosion almost vaporised the aft section from the bridge to the stern. Sections of ship were flung over the lagoon and her now severed prop, rudder and sternpost fell to the seabed below, the rest of the aft portion of the ship was gone.

The 9,527grt tanker *Fujisan Maru* had arrived at Truk on 14 February and anchored just off the fuel pier on the south shore of Dublon Island whilst she offloaded her precious cargo of heavy oil. For AA protection, she was fitted with two 120mm (4.7in) high-angle (HA) guns – one at the bow, one at the stern – and two 25mm AA autocannon.

A Mark XIII aerial torpedo hits the starboard side of the 7,624grt auxiliary transport ship *Amagisan Maru* just forward of the bridge, 17 February 1944, the first day of Operation HAILSTONE. An erratic torpedo run (left) ends with the torpedo broaching whilst a third torpedo runs straight and true towards the stern (bottom right). (National Archives 80-G-217624)

Once off-loading of her oil cargo was complete, she upped anchor and got under way – just as the Strike 2B aircraft from *Intrepid* swept in to attack the Dublon seaplane base and Eten Island airfield installations. Working up speed, she made for North Pass – almost 20 miles distant – to escape the lagoon. At her top unladen speed of 19 knots she would be there in just over an hour.

Once there, as *Fujisan Maru* started to move through North Pass towards open sea, Strike 3B *Bunker Hill* SB2C dive-bombers attacked her. She was struck by a single 1,000lb bomb, which caused a fire to break out. Despite the vulnerability of her predicament, luck was with her – as the tasking for the US strike groups was to attack the valuable Japanese warships grouped north west of North Pass. The US aircraft did not press home their attack on the tanker, turning their attention to the warships.

Seeing this concentration of US aircraft attacking the IJN warships ahead, and damaged and on fire, *Fujisan Maru* came about and headed back towards the perceived safety of the land-based AA gun batteries on the main islands in the centre of the lagoon. These would offer her some protection in addition to her own meagre AA defences.

Fujisan Maru survived DOG-DAY-MINUS-ONE, but she would be sunk the following day, DOG-DAY, after she was spotted under way heading east through the channel between Moen and Dublon Islands. She was attacked early in the day by dive-bombers; two 1,000lb armour-piercing bombs were near misses – but a third was a direct hit beside her aft engine room. A section of her hull, some 20m long, was ripped open and her bunker fuel was ignited. She slewed to a stop and began to sink by the stern – by 1100 she had to be abandoned.

The 6,938grt transport vessel *Fujikawa Maru* had been built as a passenger cargo vessel in 1938. She was 437ft long with a beam of 58ft, and after being requisitioned for war service, she was armed with light AA guns and two old British-made 6in Breach Loading (BL) guns, one set at her bow and one at her stern. These guns dated from 1899 and were most likely salvaged from obsolete decommissioned cruisers of the Russo-Japanese War of 1904–5. By the Second World War, they were antiques.

Fujikawa Maru had arrived at Truk a few weeks earlier with a cargo of thirty disassembled B6N Jill bombers and spare parts in her holds. She anchored in the 4th Fleet anchorage, south of Eten Island and a few days before DOG-DAY-MINUS-ONE, crew started carefully unloading her disassembled B6N Jill torpedo-bombers to Eten airfield, where technicians would assemble them.

By the morning of 17 February, the *Fujikawa Maru* had offloaded a large number of the disassembled aircraft from her holds – but many others still remained stowed aboard waiting their turn. Complete aircraft fuselages, detached wings and engines crowded her cavernous holds – all ready for delivery ashore and assembly.

Task Force 58 planners had identified the aircraft-carrier-shaped Eten Island airfield as one of the primary targets for attack. Anchored close by, *Fujikawa Maru* was thus right in the thick of the action on the first day of the raid as the initial waves of TF 58 aircraft bombed and strafed the airfield just after dawn. Her AA gunners had a busy day throwing up what resistance they could.

Strike 3E aircraft launched from *Bunker Hill* between 1310 and 1330, sweeping in towards Eten Island airfield and starting their attack. At 1430, *Fujikawa Maru* herself was targeted – she was virtually defenceless. One torpedo struck her just aft of the midships superstructure on the starboard side, blasting a triangular shaped hole through her thin shell plating into her innards. She started to flood and, still at anchor, began to settle slowly by the stern – allowing her crew sufficient time to abandon ship. *Fujikawa Maru* would remain afloat through the night and into the next morning when she would be targeted again and sunk.

In the run up to war, the 11,616grt passenger cargo liner *Heian Maru* was requisitioned by the IJN to operate as an armed submarine tender – she was dazzle painted and fitted with four 4.7in (12cm) single-mount deck guns and two dual mount Type 93 13mm AA machine guns. At 0435 on 17 February 1944, *Heian Maru* was anchored off Dublon Island opposite the Naval Station and the submarine-servicing base – aboard was Vice Admiral Takagi and his 6th Fleet staff. When an air raid alarm was declared, *Heian Maru* weighed anchor and got under way, steering a zigzag course north of Dublon.

Later that day, at about 1300, a Strike 3A *Bunker Hill* Curtis Helldiver bomber attacked her with two 1,000lb bombs. Although they missed astern, one of her propeller shafts was damaged and she started to take on water into Hold No. 6. Her crew pumped fuel to her bow tanks and managed to correct her trim – and after sunset, she was able to return to Dublon where Admiral Takagi and his staff disembarked along with some of the ship's cargo of Type 95 oxygen propelled torpedoes, which were now threatened by fires.

Heian Maru had survived DOG-DAY-MINUS-ONE – but she faced renewed attacks that night. Just after 0300, she was hit by two bombs that exploded above her engine room on the port side, starting fires that were soon out of control and threatening her remaining cargo of torpedoes in her forward holds. Her bridge was ablaze, the fires consuming the entire topmost wooden navigation bridge whilst at the lower levels, the glass in portholes started to melt and bubble. About 10 minutes later, the ship was again rocked by two more bombs – and her rate of sinking started to accelerate. By 0500 she had to be abandoned. At 0930, *Heian Maru*, still ravaged by fierce fires, was attacked again by *Bunker Hill* torpedo-bombers and hit on her port side amidships. She capsized to port and disappeared beneath the waters of the lagoon.

The 7,113-grt passenger cargo motor vessel MV *Hauraki*, built in Scotland during 1921 by William Denny & Brothers in Dumbarton, was the only Japanese war prize sunk during HAILSTONE. Following her seizure in 1942 in the Indian Ocean by the two Japanese merchant cruisers *Aikoku Maru* and *Hokoku Maru*, her name had been changed to *Hoki Maru*.

At dawn on 17 February, *Hoki Maru* was anchored south east of Eten Island. She was spotted by the first waves of aircraft and attacked by *Essex* Strike 2B TBF Avengers. She was damaged by bomb hits that started fires amidships. Around midday, she was attacked by *Yorktown* and *Bunker Hill* aircraft – and left ablaze and smoking heavily. After a difficult night fighting the fires, she was still afloat as dawn broke. She was soon attacked again – by three *Bunker Hill* aircraft with 1,000lb bombs. One caused a massive secondary explosion in the forward section of the ship as her cargo of bombs, ammunition and aviation fuel in 55-gallon drums in her foredeck holds ignited. Both sides of her hull in front of the bridge superstructure were blown out – the ship disappeared in a plume of smoke, sinking so quickly that by the time the smoke cleared, she was on the bottom of the lagoon.

And so the carnage went on throughout the day. TF 58 had achieved complete air superiority, the dive-bombers and TBFs receiving only limited AA fire from the Japanese ships as they attacked, whilst Hellcats suppressed shore-based AA fire. The waves of US aircraft could strike at Japanese shipping with little opposition.

At 0927, Task Unit 50.9.1, consisting of the two battleships *New Jersey* and *Iowa*, along with the cruisers *Minneapolis* and *New Orleans* and the destroyers *Burns* and *Bradford*, detached from Task Group 58.3 and proceeded to make a counter-clockwise sweep around the lagoon to intercept any Japanese vessels trying to escape their lagoon prison. The Unit was under the direct command of Spruance himself in *New Jersey* – he had spent the early years of his naval career in the big-gun era.

During this sweep, some 40 miles outside the lagoon, the 5,890-ton Japanese light cruiser *Katori*, was spotted, on fire and listing from earlier air attacks – but still under way with her two escort destroyers and a minesweeping trawler. In Spruance's last hurrah as a battleship commander, Task Unit 50.9.1 engaged the Japanese squadron.

The US destroyers fired six salvoes of torpedoes at *Katori* but missed. *Katori* replied with her own torpedoes – which also missed.

The battleship *Iowa* then closed with *Katori* and fired 59 16in shells and 129 5in shells at the stricken light cruiser – quickly straddling her. After being under attack by *Iowa* for just 13 minutes, *Katori* sank stern first. The destroyer *Maikaze* was also sunk – the action had been commanded by Spruance with deadly precision. Task Unit 50.9.1 rendezvoused with Task Group 58.3 at 0750 the following morning.

The last strike of DOG-DAY-MINUS-ONE, Strike 1F from *Enterprise*, launched between 1510 and 1520 against aircraft and installations at Moen airfield. The last strike 3F from *Bunker Hill*, operating with *Cowpens*, was launched at about 1520 tasked with degrading Eten Island airfield to render it unserviceable during the night – when the task force was potentially vulnerable to a night torpedo attack. Quarter-ton bombs with time delay fuzes of 2–6 hours were dropped on the airfield. (Days later, as other time-delay bombs dropped on Param Island airfield were collected by Japanese ground staff, they started to explode – the huge explosions being heard and felt on the neighbouring islands of Dublon and Moen.)

The major elements of the Combined Fleet were no longer present – and Task Force 58 had achieved total air superiority. Nevertheless, due to suspected minefields, shore batteries and the threat of kamikaze suicide units, the Task Force 58 ships remained well away from Truk during the night – in open water, protected by their own night CAP from the carriers *Belleau Wood*, *Cabot* and *Monterey*.

The reports of aircraft losses vary depending on which side you were. The Japanese reported seventy aircraft shot down and ninety-six destroyed on the ground during the first day of the raid with many more damaged.[20] The heavily bombed airfields had been rendered useless to the extent that not one Japanese plane would rise to meet the US attackers the following day. Twelve large Japanese ships were believed sunk with eight others reported as heavily damaged.

That night, a six-plane strike of Nakajima B5N Kate torpedo-bombers closed on Task Group 58.2. One of the torpedo-bombers eluded a *Yorktown* night-fighter and successfully torpedoed *Intrepid*, which had to retire towards Pearl for many months of repairs.

Seven US aviators, who had been shot down over Truk and plucked from the water by Japanese vessels, were taken ashore on Dublon Island, where other captured US service personnel transferred from other Pacific theatres were being held.

Most of the US personnel would subsequently be shipped to Japan for internment in prison or forced labour camps – but those unfortunate

Americans who were left on Truk would not leave alive. Four captured US aviators were brutally treated. Two were heavily beaten in attempts to force them to reveal the whereabouts of their aircraft carriers. Resisting interrogation, the two shirtless and blindfolded US aviators were led out from where they had been held at the hospital, surrounded by armed Japanese guards. A local Trukese, Rombert Rayphand, witnessed what happened next and later narrated that the two aviators, bound and gagged, were led towards the hill behind the hospital – being struck and clubbed with rifle butts.

A short distance up the hill the two aviators were knocked to the ground and beaten up. They were then tied to stakes in the ground. One guard placed a stick of dynamite between the two aviators as the rest of the Japanese guards ran away. The Japanese guard then lit the fuse on the dynamite and fled. The subsequent explosion blew the legs off both Americans. Lieutenant Shinji Sakagami returned to the scene and finding the two US aviators mortally wounded but still alive, he strangled them to death with his bare hands. (At the subsequent war crimes trials, he would be found guilty of their murder. He was executed by hanging in 1947.)

About a week later, Rayphand witnessed the two remaining US aviators being brought out of their confinement. Again, they were shirtless, gagged and blindfolded with their hands tied behind their backs. They were marched up the hill to the same area where the previous week's murders had been committed. This time a spot was chosen between two large coconut trees and a long metal bar was wedged across the gap between the branches of the two trees. The two Americans were tied by their hands to the bar – hanging suspended above the ground with their feet unable to reach the ground to support them.

The Japanese officer in charge of the party then ordered his men to line up in two columns of six men and to fix bayonets. On command, the first Japanese soldier of each column ran forward and bayoneted one of the US airmen. The second soldier in the respective lines then rushed forward to repeat the brutal assault – followed by each subsequent soldier in the line in turn. It took until the fourth soldier in each column for the aviators' screams to die away.

Once all twelve had practised their bayonet drill, the dead aviators were cut down and beheaded. Two holes were dug, and the two dead men were rolled into their shallow graves.[21]

(b) DOG-DAY, 18 February 1944
Just after 0200, during the darkness of the early hours of DOG-DAY, 18 February, the first radar-guided night attack against Japanese shipping

in Truk lagoon by the TBFs of Torpedo 10 was launched from *Enterprise*, which was steaming 100 nautical miles north east of Truk. Twelve TBFs armed with 500lb bombs roared off the flight-deck catapults into the blackness, lit only by a quarter moon. The TBFs vectored to Truk at an altitude of 500ft on a compass bearing – until Truk was detected on the radar screens when the group was 20 miles away. This night raid would be extremely successful.

The twelve TBFs split into two groups and despite being detected as they crossed the reef, and despite AA fire opening up, eight Japanese ships would be destroyed and five damaged. Some 60,000 tons of Japanese shipping went to the bottom of the lagoon for the loss of one TBF Avenger and several others damaged. As the TBFs returned towards their carriers they saw the planes of the initial fighter sweep inbound – the TBFs arrived over their carriers at 0555, just as the sun was coming up.

Just over an hour earlier, as on DOG-DAY-MINUS-ONE, an initial fighter sweep of fifty-seven Hellcats launched from *Enterprise*, *Yorktown*, *Essex* and *Bunker Hill* – timed to arrive over the lagoon just before dawn. Their mission was to seek out and destroy any remaining Japanese airborne opposition and destroy any enemy aircraft found on the ground.

Following the previous day's strikes, the few remaining serviceable Japanese fighters were unable to use runways, which were pockmarked with bomb craters from the last attacks of the previous evening. Not one Japanese fighter rose to meet the US air groups – although as the Hellcats swept over the lagoon, intense and accurate shore-based AA fire was encountered. The sky however belonged almost exclusively to the Hellcats.

Enterprise Hellcats made further strafing runs against Moen, Eten and Param Island airfields before turning to strafe shipping targets. *Yorktown* Hellcats strafed Moen No. 1 airfield, shooting up parked up planes without encountering any Japanese fighters over the target.

Strikes 1A, 2A and 3A then followed. *Enterprise* aircraft attacked the *Shotan Maru* and the oiler *Fujisan Maru*, underway between Moen and Dublon – sending it to the bottom. *Yorktown* planes hit Eten airfield, making ten strafing runs and destroying aircraft on the ground. The Hellcats then attacked other targets of opportunity – merchant shipping, pillboxes, destroyers and minesweepers along with the Moen seaplane base. *Cabot* and *Essex* planes attacked shipping at the Eten anchorage whilst *Bunker Hill* planes attacked targets around Uman Island.

As with the attacks of the previous day, successive flights of dive-bombers and torpedo-bombers, escorted by Hellcats, rose into the sky from the carriers throughout the day, ready to attack the beleaguered shipping in the lagoon.

Two Japanese ships south of Dublon Island, Truk, are bombed during Operation HAILSTONE. (National Archives 80-G-221244)

The submarine tender *Heian Maru*, damaged the day before, was attacked again and sunk. The 10,020grt oiler *Shinkoku Maru*, anchored in the Combined Fleet Anchorage north of Fefan Island, to the west of Moen Island, took a bomb hit on her port side aft during the night radar attack that opened a large hole into her cavernous engine room. Flooding of her vast, cathedral-like engine room spaces dragged her down by the stern.

The 6,438grt auxiliary transport *Yamagiri Maru* was attacked in the Repair Anchorage, north of Fefan Island by *Bunker Hill* SB2C Helldivers with 500lb and 1,000lb bombs. One bomb went straight into Hold No. 3 – whilst another hit the top of the bridge superstructure just forward of the smokestack. Fires took hold – and a plume of smoke rose up for thousands of feet, followed by a series of secondary explosions as munitions and fuel ignited and blew out the bottom of the hull.

The 370ft-long, 4,739grt Type 1B Standard passenger cargo vessel *Hanagawa Maru*, was spotted way out west, at anchor near the fuelling dock about 500yd off the south-eastern shore of Tol Island. The US aircrews mistakenly identified it as a large 12,000-ton oiler.

Torpedo-bombers from *Bunker Hill* and *Cowpens* combined for the Strike 3A, and four torpedo-bombers, flying in column, started their attack runs from the south on her starboard beam.

The first torpedo was a direct hit on the stationary *Hanagawa Maru*, between her bow and bridge superstructure – the explosion causing a large burst of flame as her cargo of aviation fuel in her foredeck holds ignited. Black fuel oil smoke billowed upwards – she had been dealt a mortal blow.

The stricken ship started to go quickly down by the head – and within 3–4 minutes, *Hanagawa Maru* had sunk from sight leaving only a burning slick on the surface. Burning debris floated ashore and reportedly started a fire in a mangrove swamp, which spread to some local buildings and a church.

One of the few IJN warships sunk was the Kamikaze-class destroyer *Oite*. On 15 February 1944, *Oite* had left Truk with subchaser *No. 28*, escorting the light cruiser *Agano* for Japan via Saipan. The US submarine *Skate* detected the naval vessels en route approximately 160 nautical miles north west of Truk and at sundown fired four torpedoes at *Agano* from a distance of 2,400yd – scoring three hits out of the four. The damage to the lightly armoured cruiser from the three torpedo hits was substantial – she caught fire and started slowly to sink. *Oite* searched for the submarine fruitlessly and *Skate* was able to escape undetected.

Oite stayed with the stricken *Agano* throughout the night, receiving the transfer of *Agano*'s fuel and more than 500 of her officers and men. *Oite* was then ordered to return to Truk with the survivors – ignorant of the imminent HAILSTONE raid.

During the fighter sweep early on 18 February, *Bunker Hill* Hellcats spotted *Oite* entering the lagoon through North Pass. During Strike 3B, she was attacked and strafed by Hellcats from *Bunker Hill* and *Monterey* – her captain was killed in his bridge and fires broke out aft of the smokestack. Captain Matsuda Takatomo of the *Agano* assumed command of the ship.

Five *Bunker Hill* torpedo-bombers then joined the attack. The new skipper of *Oite* threw his charge about in a desperate attempt to avoid the bombs and torpedoes of the US aircraft – but whilst making a high-speed evasive turn to starboard, *Oite* was hit by a single torpedo abaft the bridge. The effect of the torpedo on such a relatively small, lightly protected ship was catastrophic. Travelling at flank speed, she broke her back, the bow section slewing round to starboard as the aft section, her engines still turning, drove onwards. Both sections sank almost immediately. A total of 172 of the *Oite*'s crew and 522 crew of the *Agano* aboard her were killed, most of the *Agano* survivors being trapped below decks as she went down. There were only some twenty survivors in total.

The 5,831grt IJA transport *San Francisco Maru* was packed full of a war cargo comprising anti-invasion beach mines, munitions, army trucks, bulldozers, petrol-tanker fuel, ammunition, aircraft bombs, aircraft engines, Long Lance torpedoes as well as general cargo. She carried a deck cargo of Type 95 Ha-Go light tanks that would be deadly against lightly armed amphibious Marine landing troops. *San Francisco Maru* was hit by a number of 500lb bombs, one destroying Hold No. 5 and another blowing out the side of Hold No. 4. She was dragged under by the stern into deep water with all her valuable war supplies.

By the time US aircraft from these last strikes of the day were returning to their carriers, a further twenty-seven Japanese ships had been damaged. In all, over the two days of the assault, according to US figures, between 250 and 275 Japanese aircraft had been destroyed, the seaplane base at Moen had been put out of action, 90 per cent of the atoll's fuel supply had been set on fire and all the other airfields and installations were damaged to differing extents. In addition, forty-five Japanese ships had been sunk – over 220,000 tons of shipping – a two-day record for the entire war.

Task Force 58 now retired from the area, leaving behind only the lifeguard submarines to rescue downed US aviators. The US had lost seventeen aircraft to enemy action and twenty-six crewmen – and the carrier *Intrepid* had been put out of action for several months.[22]

Rear Admiral Michio Sumikawa, Chief of Staff of the 4th Fleet, reported that there had been 365 aircraft on Truk at the time of the attack and that 235 aircraft had been destroyed. In addition to the huge amount of valuable shipping sent to the bottom of the lagoon, military bases, infrastructure and airfields had all been extensively damaged.

The two days of the Operation HAILSTONE raids had achieved all their objectives. Japanese air power had been virtually obliterated, airstrips had been left unusable and land fortifications were largely smashed. Truk was left as an impotent, demolished enemy base, which the US forces were then able to simply bypass.

The Japanese still believed that an amphibious assault might take place and so, despite the hammering Truk had taken, the reinforcing and fortification of Truk would continue – and by the end of March 1944, over 30,000 troops had been stationed there. By mid-April 1944, all construction work on the land defences was complete and those

The 3,764grt auxiliary transport ship *Nippo Maru* was hit by three 500lb bombs from USS *Essex* TBF Avengers early on 17 February 1944. She sunk within a few hours and now rests in Truk lagoon in 50m of water. She still has her deck cargo of howitzers adjacent to her aft holds and a Type 95 Ha-Go tank forward of the bridge superstructure on the port side. (Author)

radar units that had been inoperative during HAILSTONE were now in service. For future Allied raids, advance warning was given, and valuable equipment could be got under cover and fighters scrambled into the air.

As with Rabaul, Truk would be bypassed – and the defenders left isolated and cut off. Truk began to starve – however any possible resurgence of Japanese air strength at Truk would still require to be neutralised. The Allies had to ensure that the Japanese in Truk were prevented from getting aircraft airborne to bomb Allied shipping and attack the Allied forces massing in the increasing number of US-held territories such as Eniwetok (north east of Truk), and the Solomon Islands to the south for the drive north west across the Pacific towards the ultimate goal, Japan itself.

★ ★ ★

The 10,020grt oiler *Shinkoku Maru* took a hit on her port side aft on 18 February 1944 that opened up her machinery spaces and sent her to the bottom of Truk lagoon, where she now rests upright in 40m of water. Note her replenishment at sea tripod abreast the smokestack, the engine room skylights forward and the elevated flying bridge walkway on the port side connecting all three islands. (Author)

A Type 95 Ha-Go light tank sits on the foredeck in front of the bridge superstructure of the 5,831grt IJA transport *San Francisco Maru*, bombed and sunk at Truk by TF 58 aircraft on 17 February 1944 during Operation HAILSTONE. (Ewan Rowell)

Anti-invasion Japanese beach mines stored in the foredeck holds of the IJA transport *San Francisco Maru*, bombed and sunk at Truk on 17 February 1944. (Ewan Rowell)

Overall, in the Marshall Islands operations, the Americans had lost 611 men, suffered 2,341 wounded and 260 missing, whilst the Japanese lost over 11,000 men and 358 captured. The relatively light casualties incurred during the seizure of Kwajalein, Majuro and Eniwetok atolls was in stark comparison with the heavy losses sustained in the Gilberts at Tarawa and Makin – and showed that changes in training and tactics after Tarawa had been effective.

In the invasion of the Gilbert Islands, although the Americans had emerged victorious, they had been taught a bloody lesson at Tarawa where the new amphibious assault concept had been trialled – and found wanting in many ways. There they suffered more than 3,000 dead and wounded on the tiny Tarawa atoll island of Betio alone.

The heavy casualties and gruesome fighting conditions for both sides convinced General Holland M. Smith, Commanding General of V Amphibious Corps, that Tarawa should have been bypassed, although other US admirals disagreed.

The Operation FLINTLOCK invasion of the Marshall Islands by contrast went much better – in no small measure due to the harsh lessons learned at Tarawa. In the Marshalls, after nearly one month of a heavy air and naval bombardment that decimated Japanese garrison

Above: Looking forward inside the bridge of the IJN auxiliary transport vessel *Nippo Maru*, sunk at Truk on 17 February 1944 by TF 58 aircraft during Operation HAILSTONE. The telemotor is still present, although the spokes of the helm have rotted or been burnt away to leave only the circular brass band to which they were screwed. The engine order telegraph is to right of the telemotor. Looking out through the bridge windows the foredeck goalpost kingposts still stand, braced by a bridge at their top. (Ewan Rowell)

Left: The engine room of the IJN auxiliary transport *Kensho Maru*, sunk at Truk on 18 February 1944 during Operation HAILSTONE. The six-cylinder Burmeister & Wain diesel engine sits fore and aft below the diver – whilst the engine-room skylights above are open and allow light to bathe this vast space. (Ewan Rowell)

The wreck of a Mitsubishi G4M Type 1 long-range attack bomber (Allied reporting name Betty) rests not far from Eten Island, Truk. (Ewan Rowell)

troop numbers, the Americans outnumbered the enemy defenders nearly 6 to 1 and brought heavier firepower to the battlefield.

Once the Gilberts and Marshalls had been taken, the Allies had secured valuable safe fleet anchorages and were able to construct strategic naval bases, fortifications and airfields for land-based air to prepare for an assault on the Mariana Islands. The new base at Majuro, 2,000 miles west of Pearl Harbor, was of the utmost importance – as well as the airfield on Kwajalein, which was suitable for long-range strategic bombers. The clear progress and the general refining of tactics and strategy through battle experience allowed Nimitz to accelerate his programme of operations.

Service Squadron 10 arrived at Majuro and ServRon 4 was merged into it. Commercial tankers could now bypass Hawaii and be routed directly to Majuro. To make up operational losses of aircraft on the TF 58 carriers, ComAirPac established a carrier-aircraft replacement pool at Majuro for 150–300 aircraft. These could be ferried as required to the distant Task Force 58 by the escort carriers now assigned to ServRon 10.

But the Japanese had also learned brutal lessons from their bloody experiences at Tarawa and Kwajalein. They realised that beach-line defences were too vulnerable to the Allied pre-invasion softening up naval and aerial bombardment. They would change their tactics in the subsequent campaign for the Mariana and Palau Islands where *defence in depth*, on Guam and Peleliu, would be much harder to overcome than the beach defence at Kwajalein.

Although the Japanese would deploy troops in prepared defensive positions on subsequent landing beaches to resist the initial landings, where possible the main bulk of their forces on craggy, hilly islands such as Guam and Peleliu would be held inland in prepared deep caves that were immune to the deadly pre-invasion 'Spruance Haircut' bombardment. The majority of the Japanese troops on these islands would survive the pre-invasion bombardment and be able to counter-attack at chosen times, when tactical conditions suited them best.

The loss of the Gilbert and Marshall Islands forced the Japanese to draw back to a new defensive perimeter, the *Absolute National Defence Zone*, which included the Marianas and Palau. Urgent heavy fortifications were set in place for an anticipated US assault – the Japanese knew that if captured, the airfields on these islands would put US land-based heavy bombers within range of Tokyo itself.

On 1 March 1944, shortly after the Truk raid, the IJN Combined Fleet was reorganised as the 1st Mobile Fleet.

Chapter 12

Preparations for the Mariana and Palau Islands Campaign

(i) Scouting the Marianas

After the Truk raid, Task Force 58 split up – but most of the carriers remained deep inside Japanese waters. *Enterprise* along with the light cruiser *San Diego* (CL-53) and four destroyers headed east to Majuro, bombing bypassed Jaluit on the way on 21 February. *Cabot* and the damaged *Intrepid* had already departed.

Keen to keep up the pressure on the Japanese, Nimitz ordered Spruance to conduct a raid on the Mariana Islands to destroy enemy planes, shipping and shore-based facilities and provide fresh aerial reconnaissance photographs. Military planners back in Pearl could analyse the photography as they prepared Operation FORAGER, the invasion of the Northern Mariana Islands of Saipan, Tinian and Rota, and the US territory of Guam that Japan had invaded and seized on 8 December 1941.

Spruance accordingly released Mitscher to head further north west to carry out these Mariana air strikes. For the first time, Mitscher, aboard his flag ship *Yorktown*, now had independent command over the twenty-nine ships of a slimmed down task force that was centred on three heavy carriers and three light carriers. These formed two task groups of three flattops each – Montgomery's TG 58.2, *Yorktown*, *Essex* and *Belleau Wood*, and Sherman's TG 58.3, *Bunker Hill*, *Monterey* and *Cowpens*.

On 21 February, as Mitscher's two task groups penetrated deeper into Japanese waters than ever before, the force was spotted by a Japanese long-range reconnaissance Betty bomber. Fighters from the CAP were vectored towards the fast twin-engine bomber – but were unable to catch it. Mitscher now had to assume that his two task groups had been spotted – he knew that Japanese land-based air and its powerful naval units holed up in the Marianas would be on the alert and waiting. But even as he received a despatch of a Japanese radio transmission confirming that his force HAD been spotted, flushed with the success of the stunning smashing of Truk, he instructed a signal to be sent out to his ships: 'WE HAVE BEEN SIGHTED BY THE ENEMY. WE WILL FIGHT OUR WAY IN.'[1]

Mitscher expected an attack would be made that evening shortly after sunset and aboard his ships, as night approached, his crews made their preparations – AA gunners checked the operation of their weapons and magazines. Mitscher decided to let his AA gunners deal with any enemy aircraft that approached during the night, feeling that his pilots were still not experienced enough in specialist night operations. Although he had night-fighters available, the faulty night-fighter direction that had led to a Japanese torpedo-bomber scoring a hit on *Intrepid* on the night of 17/18 February during Operation HAILSTONE kept his planes on the deck.

As dusk came and darkness fell that evening, Mitscher stood on the wing of his flag bridge on *Yorktown* with Elmont Waite, a journalist with the *Saturday Evening Post*. As the task force sped north west, deep into enemy territory, Mitscher remarked almost casually, 'It's the first time we've done this, you know.'[2]

The twenty-nine US ships of the task force churned up the sea as they closed the Marianas – their wakes, green phosphorescent trails swirling astern. Japanese pilots found the tracks – and these led them straight through the darkness to the task force.

At 2200, the Japanese attack began – in pitch blackness. Eight bogeys closed TG 58.2, two of them approaching *Yorktown* and *Essex* but being successfully fought off by AA gunners. Repeated attacks went on through the night – but AA fire from the screen, and skilful manoeuvring of the ships, resulted in not a single ship being hit, whilst accurate AA fire splashed some ten enemy planes.

As the nautical dawn half-light of 22 February began weakly to illuminate the seas, Mitscher's carriers were about 100 miles west of the Marianas, positioned there so that they could turn into the wind for aircraft launch and recovery. An initial Hellcat fighter sweep was launched and soon TF 58 aircraft were roaring over Guam, Saipan, Tinian and Rota. In response, seventy-four Japanese fighters rose into the air to intercept the Hellcats – and some fifty-one were promptly shot down. As airfields on Saipan, Guam and Tinian were strafed and bombed, more than seventy enemy aircraft were reported destroyed on the ground.

From 0800 to 1500, the bombers sank several Japanese transport ships – whilst others fled for the open sea, where unknowingly US submarines awaited them. Approximately 45,000 tons of Japanese shipping would be sunk in the following days.

In all, a final tally of some 168 Japanese aircraft were destroyed in the Mariana raids – whilst Mitscher lost 6 aircraft, 6 pilots and 2 aircrew. But many photographs had been successfully captured of the beaches where the future invasion landings would take place.

Shortly after 1500, on 22 February, Mitscher gave the order to reverse course – and the task force retired south eastwards towards Majuro. En route, Mitscher addressed his crews: 'After the Nips' loss of face at Truk, we expected a fight, we had a fight, we won a fight. I am proud to state that I firmly believe that this force can knock hell out of the Japs anywhere, anytime. Your standard is high. I can only congratulate all hands on an outstanding performance and give you a stupendous "well done".'[3]

With such a fighting spirit and such an experienced command of his task force, it is little wonder that Mitscher was so highly respected by both his superiors and by his men. His record stood for itself. In the 6 weeks he had been in command, a total of 5,456 sorties had been flown from the fast carriers with an estimated 484 Japanese aircraft destroyed, and 32 Japanese ships had been sunk and another 18 damaged. Mitscher's men admired him – he had made the grade in their eyes with three wins from three separate fights.

Mitscher later told Captain Luis de Florez:

There are just so many Jap planes on any island. We'll go in and take it on the chin. We'll swap punches with them. I know I'll have losses, but I'm stronger than they are. If it takes two task forces, we'll get two task forces. I don't give a damn now if they do spot me. I can go anywhere and nobody can stop me. If I go in and destroy all their aircraft, their damned island is no good to them anyway.[4]

The role of the fast carriers in the Pacific War had now morphed from sporadic raiding to steady offensive action, from *hit and run* to *hit and stay*. The Task Force 58 raids on Truk and the Marianas were in fact, almost unknowingly at the time, a revolution in naval warfare. By giving the fast carriers 'extreme mobility' they could roam almost at will, destroy the enemy air power and prevent their fleet from interfering in amphibious operations. Their mission was now clearly strategic – no longer confined to tactical guarding of invasion beaches as in the early days.

Mitscher's brilliant command aside, a number of other factors had led to these successes. There had been an overwhelming increase in the number of fast combat ships joining the fleet since September 1943. By February 1944, Mitscher, and these new ships had together altered the course of the war in the Pacific. The Gilberts had been taken, the Marshalls had been taken, Truk had been neutralised and the Marianas had been scouted and degraded – leaving them open to attack and invasion. US aircraft and pilots had been proven to be superior to their Japanese counterparts, Truk's fearsome reputation and strength had proved an illusion.

Just six weeks after Operation HAILSTONE, Task Force 58 would assault the Palauan chain of islands on 30 and 31 March 1944 in Operation DESECRATE 1, part of the preparations for the Allied invasion of western New Guinea.

With the conclusion of the Mariana raids and the South Pacific campaign, a series of high-ranking personnel changes took place. Admiral Halsey, Commander South Pacific (COMSOPAC), was now effectively out of a job – he would report to Nimitz as Commander Third Fleet in May 1944.

Perhaps the most major change concerned Rear Admiral Pete Mitscher, who had in a short period of time so effectively demonstrated his capabilities to Nimitz, King, Spruance and to the rank and file of his men. On 16 March, he was promoted from senior carrier division commander to be Commander Fast-Carrier Forces Pacific Fleet.

Five days later he was promoted to vice admiral – as simultaneously Spruance was elevated from vice admiral to full admiral. The battleship commander Rear Admiral W.A. 'Ching' Lee was promoted to vice admiral, as was one of Nimitz's most trusted but today little-known officers, Rear Admiral John Hoover. Rear Admiral A.E. Montgomery, who had commanded Task Group 58.2, relieved Mitscher as ComCarDiv 3.

(ii) The First Air Assault on Palau – Operation DESECRATE 1, 30 and 31 March 1944

From an Allied perspective, the relative ease with which Task Force 58 had attacked Truk and the Marianas had revealed the simple flaw in the Japanese concept of regarding their island air bases as unsinkable carriers – they could not move. Once neutralised by mobile air from the carriers, the islands could simply be bypassed and raided again from time to time to prevent their threat being restored.

The rapidity with which Kwajalein and Eniwetok had been cleared for airfields and the successful neutralisation of Mili, Jaluit, Maloelap, Wotje and Truk along with the development of Majuro as a fleet anchorage now allowed an acceleration of the Pacific timetable of operations. The Joint Chiefs of Staff ordered Nimitz to continue with the neutralisation by air of Truk – and to land at Saipan, the largest of the Northern Mariana Islands, on 15 June. Saipan was a key bastion of Japan's *Absolute National Defence Zone* and Japan had strongly committed to its defence. Nimitz was to plan for an assault on Formosa in February 1945.

In a simultaneous second drive, MacArthur was to press ahead and secure New Guinea, then assault the southern Philippines, notably Mindanao, in late 1944. He was to plan for landings on Luzon in February 1945 as Nimitz assaulted Formosa. US strategists felt that the Japanese would not have sufficient resources to be able to stop two such simultaneous powerful drives.

The decision to make these two deep advances took away the importance of Rabaul, which had already been left far behind the front by the incursions of Task Force 58 far into Japanese-held waters – and by MacArthur's occupation of the Admiralty Islands. The invasion of Rabaul was unnecessary and was never discussed again – it was simply bypassed. With Truk neutralised as an airbase, the Japanese withdrew the last aircraft of CarDiv 2 from Rabaul on 20 February 1944, just a few days after Operation HAILSTONE ended.

In February and March 1944, the Allies seized Manus Island (north west of Rabaul), Green Island (east of Rabaul) and Amirau Island in the Bismarck archipelago (north of Rabaul). With airfields now established on Bougainville (to the south), the encirclement of the once-mighty Japanese base at Rabaul was complete. Routine bombing raids would be made on Rabaul by land-based planes beginning in early March. Cut off from re-supply and under continual air attack, the Rabaul base and its many thousands of Japanese defenders became useless to Japan's war effort, being reduced to simply trying to survive and hold out.

Continuing the thrust west, the next major Allied operations would take place in April 1944. They were RECKLESS, the seizure of Hollandia, a large port on the north coast of New Guinea (today called Jayapura), and PERSECUTION, the invasion of the coastal town of Aitape, on the north coast of Papua New Guinea.

New Guinea is the world's second largest island, after Greenland, and the largest island in the southern hemisphere. The eastern half of the island today is the independent state of Papua New Guinea, in the Second World War it was an Australian mandated territory. New Guinea sits to the north of Australia and has Indonesia to its west, the Philippines to its north west and the open expanses of the Philippine Sea to its north. Both Hollandia and Aitape had been occupied since 1942 by the Japanese, who had developed facilities and infrastructure to support their originally planned expansion east towards the Solomons and south towards Australia. These two Allied operations, RECKLESS and PERSECUTION, would bring the Central and Southwest Pacific Forces together, something that would not be repeated again until both reached the Luzon bottleneck separately.

Nimitz was to deploy Task Force 58 for close air support during the Hollandia landings by MacArthur's Southwest Pacific Forces. But Nimitz feared that his fast carriers would be brought within range of the 200–300 Japanese planes believed to be based at Hollandia and New Guinea airfields. The Hollandia landings were set for 15 April and Nimitz requested that Japanese aircraft based at Hollandia be knocked out by 5 April. He simultaneously despatched *Saratoga* west into the Indian Ocean to join British forces in tying down Japanese planes in South and South-East Asia.

Land-based Japanese aircraft from the airfields scattered throughout the Palauan chain of islands, which lie some 700 miles north west of Hollandia, would be able to subject the fast carriers to day and night attacks during the operations. Allied strategic planners therefore determined that if the use of Palau as a Japanese air and naval base could be denied for a minimum of one month, Japan's ability to retaliate against the planned Hollandia operation would be greatly reduced.

Admiral Spruance would be in over-all command of naval operations aboard his flagship, the heavy cruiser *Indianapolis* – but as usual, he left tactical command of the carriers to Vice Admiral Mitscher, now Commander Fast-Carrier Forces Pacific Fleet. Vice Admiral 'Ching' Lee, in command of the battleships, would assume tactical command of the task force should the Japanese offer battle with their own heavy units. For the first time two of the TF 58 task groups held four carriers.

The islands of Palau and the Marianas formed the principal strong points in a chain of islands that were Japan's last eastern line of defence, the *Absolute National Defence Zone*. After the accelerating reverses suffered by the Japanese since the disaster of the Battle of Midway in June 1942, instead of expanding into the Pacific, Japan would attempt to hold this Defence Zone until she could rebuild her strength for a final decisive battle in mid-1944. The *Absolute National Defence Zone* perimeter ran from Western New Guinea to the Mariana Islands via the Carolines – preparations for the Defence Zone were to be completed by spring 1944.

Unfortunately for the Japanese, the *Absolute National Defence Zone* was overrun before it was ever completed. Admiral Halsey's South Pacific Forces, operating from Guadalcanal, had advanced up the Solomon Islands chain as far as Bougainville by November 1943. Two months later, in January 1944, Allied forces reached Cape Gloucester on the western end of New Britain Island. US and Australian forces would press to the western end of New Guinea by mid-1944. (The Japanese would be forced to retreat to the Dutch East Indies and the *Absolute National Defence Zone* would be demolished by October 1944. General Douglas MacArthur's forces would be able to invade the Japanese-held Philippines, beginning with landings on the eastern island of Leyte on 20 October 1944.)

For the Allies, the Palau and Mariana Islands groups represented important targets for several reasons – Palau was a barrier to an assault on the Philippines. The Marianas allowed the Japanese land-based air cover for naval operations, and conversely, if taken, the Marianas would give the Americans a base from which to deploy long-range heavy bombers that could strike directly against the Japanese home islands. In the summer and latter part of 1944, Allied forces would assault these targets sequentially, securing first the Marianas and then the Palauan islands on their way to the Philippines.

After the US overflight of Truk on 4 February, Admiral Koga, Commander-in-Chief of the Combined Fleet, aware that his warships stationed there were now vulnerable, gave up Truk as a major naval base. As elements of the IJN headed to Palau from Truk after the overflight, Japanese commanders focused their attention on the Palauan chain of islands. From being essentially a staging area well behind the front line, the Palauan islands would very shortly be in the thick of the action. Significant shipments of supplies, bunker oil and coal were sent to Palau – ammunition dumps were fully provisioned, and fuel and water stockpiled.

Koga liked to base himself at a forward position so that he could directly command whenever a fleet operation developed – hence his presence at Truk. With Truk now in range of US long-range bombers, he decided to withdraw to the comparative safety of Palau, more than a thousand nautical miles to the west – where he would still be

241

relatively close to the action. On 10 February 1944, he departed Truk in the battleship *Musashi*, escorted by the light cruiser *Ōyodo* and the destroyers *Hatsuharu*, *Michishio*, *Shiratsuyu* and *Tamanami*, bound for Yokosuka in Japan. *Musashi* was the last IJN battleship to leave Truk before the HAILSTONE raid. All other major IJN vessels left shortly afterwards, bound for Palau, Japan or Singapore.

Musashi arrived at Yokosuka on 15 February and began embarking ammunition, provisions and fuel for the Palau garrison, along with a cargo of 3,800 mines and some 40 Isuzu and Nissan trucks that were loaded as deck cargo on her after deck. On her foredeck, crated 60kg and 250kg aerial bombs and torpedoes as well as boxes of 12.7mm AA ammunition were secured.

After a brief few days in Japan discussing the strategic situation with his superiors, Koga departed Yokosuka for Palau aboard *Musashi*, escorted by the destroyers *Michishio* and *Shiratsuyu*. *Musashi* and the squadron arrived at Palau on 27 February.

The two battleships *Yamato* and *Nagato* came and went from Palau towards the end of February and early March. The Japanese warships based in Palau maintained a high state of readiness in preparation for the anticipated US advance, carrying out training exercises inside the Palauan lagoon.

Peleliu, the small island to the south of the main Palauan island of Babeldaob, was the base for the Japanese Air Flotilla 26, one of two flotillas of its Air Fleet 14 which had suffered heavy losses of aircraft and crew in the defence of Rabaul. It was still in the process of regrouping and a programme had been started to train new pilots to make up for those lost at Rabaul.

Until early 1944, the Palaus had been well to the rear of any front-line combat areas. Palau had only been used as a staging point and training area for troops and supplies being sent to reinforce forward positions in the South-West and Central Pacific. Defence of the Palauan islands had until this point been the responsibility of the Combined Fleet and the naval units based there.

With the fall of the Gilbert and Marshall Islands outposts such as the Kwajalein, Majuro and Eniwetok to the east, the need to reinforce strategically important island garrisons in the *Absolute National Defence Zone* became more urgent. Palau was a key component of the defence zone and was to be held at all costs – as part of its overall responsibility for defence of the Central Pacific islands, the IJA took over responsibility for the defence of Palau. In March 1944, Lieutenant General Hideyoshi Obata of the newly created IJA 31st Army, headquartered in Guam, was given command of the inner line of national defence with some 80,000 men under his control.

The main Palauan Islands are surrounded by a barrier reef through which there were only three principal channels leading to its harbours and anchorages. Allied planners began to work out the details of the TF 58 strikes on Palau, which would destroy any Japanese naval units, aircraft and merchant shipping located. The use of the Palauan lagoon as a natural harbour would also be denied to the Japanese for thirty days by carrier aircraft, which would air drop mines in and around the three entrance channels, as well as in the approaches to Palau. The depth of the water and the narrow entrances to the Palauan lagoon were ideal for air-dropped mines.

The aerial mines would be laid in two distinct phases. Initially, *moored magnetic mines*, with short delay arming periods of less than an hour, would be dropped by parachute from TBF Avenger aircraft in the three main channels through the reef. This operation would be concurrent with the first strike on the islands and would prevent enemy shipping escaping from attack in the lagoon.

In the second phase, further minefields of hard to detect *ground mines* (with arming delay periods of two to thirty-five days) would be laid in the most important anchorages and channels inside the Palauan lagoon and also in the approaches to the archipelago. These delayed arming ground mines would close off the islands to the Japanese for one to two months after the air strikes. The Japanese would be prevented from clearing the channels completely for thirty-five days and would be uncertain of clearance for some considerable time thereafter.

Twelve US submarines would be deployed around the Palauan archipelago to intercept any Japanese Fleet units or merchant ships that might try to escape during the approach of the Fifth Fleet towards the western Carolines – and any that tried to escape as the strikes went in. The date for the Task Force 58 air strike against Palau was set as 1 April 1944.

Admiral Spruance produced an operation plan whereby three of the four carrier groups of Task Force 58 would be used to attack Palau and the less important bases of Woleai, Yap and Ulithi.

Fleet Organisation
Commander Fifth Fleet – Admiral Raymond A. Spruance
Chief of Staff – Captain C.J. Moore
Commander Task Force 58 – Vice Admiral M.A. Mitscher (ComFastCarForPac)
Chief of Staff – Captain A.A. Burke

1. Task Group 58.1 – Rear Admiral J.W. Reeves, Jr (ComCarDiv 4):
   Enterprise (CV-6), Air Group 10
   Belleau Wood (CVL-24) (light carrier), Air Group 24
   Cowpens (CVL-25) (light carrier), Air Group 25

   Screen: Cruiser Division 13: *Santa Fe, Mobile, Beloxi* and *Oakland* and twenty-five destroyers of DesRon 46, DesRon 50 and DesRon 1.

2. Task Group 58.2 – Rear Admiral A.E. Montgomery (ComCarDiv 3):
   Bunker Hill (CV-17), Air Group 8
   Hornet (CV-12), Air Group 2
   Cabot (CVL-28) (light carrier), Air Group 31
   Monterey (CVL-26) light carrier), Air Group 30

   Screen: Battle Division 7 battleships *Iowa* and *New Jersey*, Cruiser Division 6, *Wichita, San Francisco, Minneapolis, New Orleans, Boston* and *Baltimore* and eight destroyers of DesRon 52.

3. Task Group 58.3 – Rear Admiral S.P. Ginder (ComCarDiv 11):
   Yorktown (CV-10), Air Group 5
   Lexington (CV-16), Air Group 16
   Princeton (CVL-23) (light carrier), Air Group 23
   Langley (CVL-27) (light carrier), Air Group 32

   Screen: Battle Division 8 battleships *Massachusetts* and *North Carolina*. Battle Division 9 battleships *South Dakota* and *Alabama*. Cruiser Division 4 cruisers *Louisville, Portland, Indianapolis, Canberra* and *San Juan* and sixteen destroyers of DesRon 6, DesRon 23 and DesRon 28.

With the operation plan settled, the powerful task force of carriers, battleships, cruisers, support vessels and destroyers began to assemble from Fifth Fleet ships at the eastern Majuro atoll anchorage and at Espiritu Santo to the south.

Lexington (CV-16) had been undergoing repairs at the naval shipyard at Bremerton, Washington, to fix her rudder that had been damaged at Kwajalein in December. She arrived in Majuro in early March and Mitscher hoisted his flag aboard her. Mitscher gave her a warmup with live battle-practice air strikes against bypassed Mili atoll, to the south east, on 18 March, escorted by two battleships. The new Essex-class ninety-plane carrier *Hornet* (CV-12) reported to Majuro on 20 March. The light carrier *Cowpens* had put into Pearl on 4 March after the raids on Truk and the Marianas, before returning to Majuro. She would sail from there to rejoin TG 58.1 in time for forthcoming raids, scheduled to commence on 1 April 1944.

Those Task Force 58 units staging at Majuro sortied on 23 March 1944, swinging south to avoid Japanese search planes based at Truk. The task force would be refuelled by oilers en route and protected by routine Combat Air Patrols and Anti-Submarine Patrols.

Following the Truk raid, with *Cowpens* returning to Pearl, the battle-hardened TG 58.1 units, *Enterprise*, *Belleau Wood* and escorts had initially patrolled the New Hebrides island chain. On 20 March, under cover of carrier air from *Enterprise*, *Belleau Wood* and two escort carriers, 4,000 Marines landed on the small island of Emirau, in the Bismarck archipelago, north east of New Guinea. The operation was the finale of General MacArthur's Operation CARTWHEEL for the encirclement of Rabaul.

On 26 March, as the ships that had sortied southwards from Majuro and those that had sortied from Espiritu Santo now headed north west towards Palau, a PBY Catalina flying boat dropped a container with new orders onto *Enterprise*'s flight deck. *Enterprise* immediately turned northwards and moved to rendezvous with Task Force 58. *Cowpens*, sailing from Majuro, joined *Enterprise* and *Belleau Wood* the following day, 27 March, and would provide CAP and antisubmarine patrols.

On 25 March, when TF 58 was approximately 700 miles from Truk, it was believed that a distant Japanese search plane had spotted the task force. Another Japanese search plane was spotted the following day, 26 March, as the task force was being refuelled after rendezvous with fleet oilers. But despite being in range of air bases on Truk, Woleai, Palau and Papua New Guinea, no attack was made by the Japanese until 29 March.

As Japanese command struggled to interpret the reconnaissance sightings, now that the task force had definitely been detected, Admiral Spruance determined to strike immediately against Palau. The element of surprise had been lost and there was little point in the planned clandestine approach. He brought forward the attack by two days from 1 April to 30 March to allow the Japanese as little time as possible to prepare and reinforce. Task Force 58 would make a straight push directly towards Palau, at an increased speed of 22 knots – so as to reach their planned launching position by 30 March 1944. Each of the carriers maintained an eight-plane Combat Air Patrol and a four-plane Anti-Submarine Patrol from just before sunrise at 0515 local time to sunset at 1806 local time.

Initially unaware of the gathering of the massive task force and its clandestine approach to Palau, the Japanese Combined Fleet HQ was in the process of transferring from Truk to Koror, Palau. (It would officially be installed there on 29 March 1944 – just one day before DESECRATE 1.) But once the task force had been detected by reconnaissance aircraft on 25 March, Admiral Koga despatched his main naval units away from Palau, moving them northwards to be ready for a larger naval surface engagement. The 3rd Fleet carriers reassembled at Tawi Tawi, an anchorage between Mindanao and Borneo in the Celebes Sea.

On 28 March, the Combined Fleet's flag on *Musashi*, anchored in the Palauan lagoon, was lowered and temporarily moved ashore in anticipation of the US air raid. Koga intended to return to *Musashi* once the air raid was over – but he would later decide to move his HQ to Davao in the Philippines.

At 1530 on 29 March, *Musashi*, along with the 2nd Fleet cruisers *Atago*, *Chōkai* and *Takao*, escorted by the destroyers *Fujinami*, *Harusame*, *Michishio* and *Shiratsuyu* and a convoy of merchant ships, began to retire from Palau, moving northwards up the west coast of Babelthuap, inside the lagoon and rendezvousing with DesDiv 17's *Hamakaze*, *Isokaze*, *Tanikaze* and *Urakaze*. At 1745, *Musashi* was torpedoed by the US submarine *Tunny* as she was clearing Toachel Mlengui, the West Pass through the barrier reef of the Palauan lagoon. Despite the hole punched in her port bow and subsequent flooding of her some of her forward compartments, the underwater protection system of the great battleship had been designed to withstand a number of such torpedo hits. She was still able to make 24 knots and clear the area and head for Kure in Japan.

Many Army transport ships and merchantmen thronged the harbours and anchorages inside the Palauan lagoon at this time. But difficulties with communications meant that some vessels were not in a position to react in time to the approach of the US task force. Many ships' captains felt that their ships would be more vulnerable to attack in the open sea by US aircraft, submarines and surface vessels. They chose to keep their ships dotted throughout Palau's scattered jungle-covered islands, some nosing their vessels close to rocky cliffs in the hope that the islands and terrain would give them some protection from raiding aircraft. Some captains had their ships move parallel to the cliffs and then camouflaged them with branches and foliage to try and avoid detection from the skies above. As no orders came from the IJA HQ, the IJA transport vessels remained anchored in Palau. Most of the precious naval tankers and oilers present were vessels that had been damaged elsewhere by torpedoes or bombing attacks and were not in any condition to make good an escape. Few orders were issued to the Japanese air forces in Palau – notably those in the large airfield on the southern island of Peleliu. No orders for withdrawal or reinforcement came – just a simple order to fight as hard as possible.

On 29 March, when Task Force 58 was still 300 miles from Palau and well within range of Japanese aircraft, enemy planes began approaching from the Palau direction. In the early hours, four Hellcats from *Hornet*'s CAP were radar-vectored almost 70 miles out at an altitude of 14,000ft to a large radar echo approaching rapidly. As the CAP approached what appeared to be six single-engine fighters, when they were spotted, the Japanese pilots climbed and disappeared into the clouds. But 20 minutes later a Betty was detected making a low-flying approach just above the waves towards TG 58.2. The CAP Hellcats swooped, and after a 10-minute tail-end chase, hit the Betty and sent it crashing into the water ablaze.[5]

The *Enterprise* CAP spotted a long-range reconnaissance Betty bomber visually, at a distance of about 7 miles as it flew towards the carriers – almost skimming the waves at 100ft, too low to have been detected by shipboard radar. The eight CAP F6F Hellcats split into two divisions of four and swooped down on the Betty from 6,000ft – clocking 385mph and reaching shooting distance after a chase of about 3 minutes. The first Hellcat division bracketed the Betty – with two approaching from the left and two from the right – whilst the Betty's only evasive manoeuvre was to weave from right to left.

As the fighters began their second run at the Betty, a ball of fire from unprotected fuel tanks appeared on the starboard wing root and grew until the wing and part of the fuselage were ablaze. The plane then crashed into the water in a fireball – its fuselage and wings disintegrating. The forward part of the fuselage continued to float for about 15 minutes and the smoke could be seen from the distant *Enterprise*.[6] *Langley*'s CAP shot down a Betty and 2 hours later, the *Hornet* CAP shot down another.

At sundown, just as the Combat Air Patrols were being recovered for the night, a flight of six Japanese aircraft approaching from the south east was picked up by radar some 25 miles out. The Japanese formation split into two sections – with aircraft approaching the carriers from both port and starboard. The ships of the TG 58.3 screen commenced AA fire and within 1 minute of firing, one plane had caught fire and crashed starboard of the task group, and 3 minutes later, a second plane was shot down.

One carrier was forced to take evasive manoeuvres before the last Hellcat had landed. The pilot was ordered to ditch his Hellcat off the Fletcher-class destroyer *Dortch* (DD-670), which recovered the pilot. An unlucky fighter pilot on *Cowpens* was swept overboard when the retractable wing of a Hellcat suddenly swung open during a sharp turn on deck. He could not be found and was listed as Missing – Presumed Dead.

The Japanese aircraft had disappeared from US radars by 2000 local time. As the task force continued to close on Palau, intelligence reports were being received that Japanese warships were fleeing Palau. A night attack by Japanese torpedo-bombers was anticipated but although CAP night-fighters and picket planes were launched, no contact developed.

On 29 March, a large convoy, PATA-07, was formed up in Palau's western lagoon to try to escape before the anticipated imminent US strike and head to Takao, Formosa. The convoy included the fleet oiler *Akebono Maru*, the auxiliary transport *Goshu Maru*, the IJN requisitioned standard Type 1C steamers *Raizan Maru* and *Ryuko Maru* and the IJA transports *Kibi Maru*, *Teshio Maru* and *Hokutai Maru*. The convoy was to be escorted by *Patrol Boat 31*, the IJN Second-class destroyer *Wakatake*, the auxiliary subchaser *Cha-26* and several picket boats. At the far southern end of the convoy, several other freighters were congregating in the lagoon, waiting their turn to form up.

Although the convoy had been scheduled to leave the western lagoon that evening, logistical problems resulted in departure being delayed until first light at 0500 the next morning, 30 March.

However, 2 hours earlier, 0300 local time, the task groups of Task Force 58 had arrived at their designated holding points south of Palau and were turning into the wind in readiness to begin launchings. Task Group 58.1 was the closest to Palau at 65 nautical miles, TG 58.2 at about 75 nautical miles, whilst TG 58.3 was the most distant at 119 nautical miles.

(a) K-DAY, 30 March 1944
Dawn

Following the template used during Operation HAILSTONE six weeks previously at Truk, with CAP night-fighters aloft, an initial fighter sweep of seventy-two Hellcats would be followed by a succession of group strikes of dive-bombers and torpedo-bombers escorted by Hellcats throughout the day designated A, B, C, D, E and F – with a gap between each launching. In a departure from the nomenclature for the HAILSTONE Truk raid, the strikes from TG 58.1 were given the prefix '2' and TG 58.2 strikes were prefixed by '1'. Thus, the TG 58.1 strikes were coded 2A, 2 B, 2C, 2D, 2E and 2F, whilst the TG 58.2 strikes were coded 1A, 1B and 1C–1F and the TG 58.3 strikes 3A–3 F.

Commencing at 0430 local time, the seventy-two Hellcats launched from the fast carriers, the launch being timed so that the Hellcats would be over the target just before sunrise at about 0600 local time.

Meanwhile, in the Palauan lagoon, as the first rays of nautical dawn were filtering over the eastern horizon, almost simultaneously with the launch of the initial fighter sweep of Hellcats 65–120 miles to the south, the Japanese ships and escorts of convoy PATA 07 began to leave the anchorages of the western lagoon and move north up the west side of the main Palauan island of Babelthuap. Led by picket boats and destroyers, the convoy was heading for Toachel Mlengui, the West Pass through the lagoon's barrier reef into open ocean. The convoy ships – and the inbound Hellcats – remained completely unaware of each other.

In line astern the Japanese ships processed north up the west side of Babelthuap in the main narrow deep-water channel that leads up towards Toachel Mlengui. The azure-blue waters of the deep shipping channel were bordered on either side by near vertical coral reef walls that were flanked by dangerous light-green/brown coral reef flats just a few metres deep. There is little room to manoeuvre for a large ship in the channel.

Fifty minutes after the convoy started to move north through Kosabang Harbor and Komebail Lagoon, after 70 minutes' flight time, the seventy-two Hellcats swept over the skies above the Palauan Islands, each group tasked to patrol at its allocated altitude. TG 58.1 air groups from the battle-hardened *Enterprise* and one CVL were again, as at Truk, tasked as the Low Attack Group – where the most enemy contact could be expected. Allocated for ground-attack assignments, they would be in the thick of the battle. TG 58.3 fighters would provide Intermediate Cover from 10,000–15,000ft whilst TG 58.2 would provide High Cover at 25,000ft.

The major Japanese airfield on the southern Palauan island of Peleliu was high on the list of targets. An airstrip had been cleared on each of Ngesebus and Babelthuap Islands, but the airfields were found not yet to be operational. There were submarine and seaplane bases on Arakabesan Island and a seaplane base on Koror.

As the Hellcats of one division of *Enterprise* Air Group 10 dived to strafe Peleliu airfield, they found a number of Betty bombers parked up on the airfield – but none of the anticipated Japanese fighters. It was assumed that alerted to the approach of the Hellcats, the Japanese fighters had already taken off. The Hellcats made several strafing runs and shot up the Bettys, which burst into flames when hit. They received limited AA fire from the ground.

After the attack runs, the division swung north over Urukthapel (just to the south of Koror Island) and spotted some 15 freighters, 1 oiler, 1 destroyer and a hospital ship in the anchorages. After continuing north, they located the unfinished airfield at the south of Babelthuap and then returned to Peleliu where they encountered some twenty of the missing Japanese fighters, which were believed to have been well dispersed and camouflaged to evade being spotted on the first sweep. The *Bunker Hill* division of Hellcats also strafed Peleliu airfield, and just as they were pulling up, the division was attacked by twelve Zekes at 3,000ft – a series of violent, uncontrolled dogfights developed. The US aviators reported that the Zekes were extremely manoeuvrable but that their tactics were to shy away from a pitched battle with the Hellcats. The Zekes seemed to prefer to attack single or damaged US aircraft, and a series of dogfights broke out.

At one point, a number of Zekes closed on the Commander of the *Enterprise* Air Group 10, Lieutenant Commander W.R. Kane, who had become separated from his division. He spent some 10 minutes trying to shake the Zekes off his tail but after damaging one Zeke, first one then the other of his 0.50 calibre Browning machine guns stopped firing. The Zeke continued to pursue him but when they arrived just 100ft short of the Peleliu runway, both Japanese pilots broke off the engagement, allowing Kane to rejoin his section. Kane's wingman got on the tail of one Zeke shooting it down; then another Zeke was shot down in flames.[7]

Meanwhile, the other division of *Enterprise* Air Group 10 was dogfighting with Zekes and strafing ground targets. Up north on Babelthuap, an oil storage facility near a barracks was set on fire; the phosphate plant in Angaur was strafed and began to smoke. AA fire from land-based batteries was poor and largely ineffective. A Japanese destroyer was attacked and sunk 38km out of the Toachel Mlengui passage. In total US aircrew reported that some thirty-five ships had been spotted in the various Palauan anchorages below them.

Enterprise lost two Hellcats shot down and three others damaged by AA fire and by Japanese aircraft. One Hellcat was bracketed by two Zekes from above after a strafing dive – and was hit in the engine. The Hellcat started to lose power and by the time it had laboured back to *Enterprise*, the engine was smoking and about to cut out. The engine was replaced, and the damaged engine thrown overboard – the other damage was all repairable. The Hellcats were back on their carrier by 0724. Despite the losses, some thirty-five Japanese aircraft were reported shot down.

For the first time in action, carrier-based aircraft would lay aerial mines – with two objectives:

1. To prevent the escape of ships from the Palau lagoon during the early phase of the raid by dropping moored Mark 10 Mod 6 magnetic mines by parachute. These mines would have a short arming delay of 45 minutes, so that they would be live in time to catch any Japanese ships that might try to escape the lagoon.

The Mark 10 mines consisted of an anchor, a release mechanism for the mine, a tether cable cut to the desired length – and a buoyant warhead with 425lb of TNT. Once the mine apparatus had been dropped and sank to the bottom, after the pre-set time, the release mechanism would activate and release the buoyant warhead to float up to the pre-set depth beneath the surface, held to the anchor by its pre-cut tether. The magnetic mines would be spaced at least at 200yd intervals to prevent sympathetic shockwave detonations should a mine adjacent be detonated. When a ship moved into the vicinity of the mine, its magnetic field would induce a current in the mine's search coil, actuating the magnetic influence trigger mechanism.

2. To deny the Japanese the use of the lagoon anchorages for at least thirty days to allow the Hollandia operation to proceed. Mark 25 induction-type ground mines with fuze delays of two to thirty-five days would be dropped by parachute in important channels and choke points amongst the islands and reefs within the lagoon. These mines were the same size and shape as the moored Mark 10 magnetic mines but as they were designed to lie on the seabed, they didn't have to accommodate the heavy anchor and release system. Their warhead could therefore be significantly heavier – with some 1,100lb of cast TNT or Torpex. Sitting on the seabed, these mines armed themselves after a pre-set time with a combination of magnetic, acoustic and pressure-sensitive mechanisms. They were extremely difficult to detect and were designed to sense a reduction in hydrostatic pressure when lifted off the seabed if detected – and detonate. Lying on the seabed, the Mark 25 mines would not be picked up during a standard sweep – the Japanese could never be sure if they had eliminated all the mines or not. Both types of mine were designed to let smaller vessels such as minesweepers pass by harmlessly – only detonating when a large vessel passed nearby.

The aerial mines would be parachute dropped by TBF Avengers from 200ft at a speed of 180 knots. Flying this slowly, and this low, during the mine drop, the TBFs were very vulnerable to AA fire. Hellcat escorts would strafe all land-based AA batteries and ships encountered in the vicinity of the airdrop to protect the low-flying Avengers from AA fire.

Launching at 0445 with the Hellcats of the initial fighter sweep, TBFs of Mining Group No. 1 from *Bunker Hill*, *Hornet* and *Lexington* would arrive over Palau shortly after the sweep, and lay a minefield of tethered Mark 10 magnetic mines just after sunrise in the southern arm of the channel that leads to Toachel Mlengui (West Passage) – to prevent ships in that anchorage escaping. Four other TBFs would lay Mark 10 mines off the seaward side of Malakal Pass, which leads from the east through dangerous reefs into Malakal Harbour itself. Nine more TBF Avengers of Mining Group 1X took off at 0900 – escorted by twelve Hellcats, they would lay mines between Arakabesan and Ngargol Islands. The Japanese ships present would be sealed inside their lagoon prison. Six TBFs of Mining Group 2 launched at 1315, escorted by eight Hellcats dropping Mark 25 mines in the Yoo Passage. The final mine-laying operation, by six TBFs of Mining Group No. 2X, would launch with Strikes 1E and 1F against shipping and land installations at 1500 local time. A total of thirty-three Mark 25 ground mines were detailed for the entrance channels with another fifteen around the approaches and anchorages of Arakabesan Island and its seaplane base.

During the initial fighter sweep, *Lexington*, *Bunker Hill* and *Monterey* Hellcats all spotted the large northbound convoy PATA-07 as they swept over the southern Palauan Islands. Such high-valuable targets were given priority and they were quickly attacked as up ahead, TG 58.2 TBF Avengers were air-dropping their mines in the shipping channel and in West Passage to block it and seal the convoy ships in the lagoon. The lead ships of the convoy were strafed – the fighters and TBFs meeting limited AA fire from the ships' own defences.

With the initial fighter sweep and mine-laying operation now underway, Strike 1A from TG 58.2 *Bunker Hill* and *Hornet* each launched 12 Hellcats escorting 12 dive-bombers and 9 TBFs armed with torpedoes whilst 6 TBFs launched from a light carrier armed with incendiary and fragmentation bombs. In total 38 planes roared off the flight decks.

At 0530, TG 58.1 *Enterprise* and one CVL launched Strike 2A to arrive over the target at 0645–0700. Twenty Hellcat fighters escorted 12 TBFs, of which 6 were armed with torpedoes set for depths of 8ft or 12ft, for use against warships and shipping, whilst the other 6 Avengers carried fragmentation clusters and incendiary bombs, all fuzed with no delay, for use against the seaplane bases. Strike 3A from *Yorktown*, *Lexington* and one CVL launched shortly after to arrive on target at 0715–0730 with 24 Hellcats escorting 24 dive-bombers and 12 TBFs armed with torpedoes. The CVL launched 6 TBFs armed with incendiary and fragmentation bombs. At 0645, TG 58.2 Strike 1B from *Bunker Hill* and *Hornet* launched 32 Hellcats, 30 dive-bombers and 9 torpedo-bombers and an Observer Group to arrive on target at 0815–0830.

Although the inbound flights found Palau and Koror partially obscured by cloud, many merchant ships were located and attacked by

View of the island and flight deck of USS *Enterprise* (CV-6), March 1944. This photograph was taken looking aft from one of her planes as it passes low over the ship. Crew cluster on the open bridge below the Mk37 gun director. There are 40mm guns to left of shot whilst a banged up F6F Hellcat is parked aft of the island. (National Archives 80-G-251016)

the dive-bombers amidst heavy AA fire. It was difficult to get clear IDs of ships attacked due to the difficult terrain of multiple scattered islands, the heavy AA fire and the part cloud cover – but hits were observed on a large freighter in the north of Urukthapel Bay, possibly the *Nagisan Maru* – and an oiler, possibly the *Iro*, and several other ships.

As at Truk six weeks before, group strikes A–F continued remorselessly throughout the day, aircraft from different carriers gathering at rendezvous points before proceeding in formation to their designated striking areas. Strike groups usually comprised both dive-bombers and torpedo-bombers, as by attacking simultaneously, dive-bombers from high altitude and torpedo-bombers near sea level, Japanese AA fire was split.

The beleaguered Japanese vessels, with no air cover, were protected by too few and too poor shipboard AA guns. Even their most advanced AA guns were inaccurate, the sights largely ineffective against the new fast US aircraft. The 25mm Type 96 auto cannon was one of Japan's most effective AA guns with a rate of fire of between 200 and 260 rounds per minute. But it was most effective only at close ranges of fewer than 1,000m with fire at aircraft at a height of 1,000m and beyond a range of 2,000m being completely ineffective.

The Japanese 25mm Type 96 was in fact a mediocre weapon hampered by slow training and slow elevation speeds, excessive vibration and muzzle flash. Worse, ammunition was fed from a fifteen-round fixed magazine so that the gun had to cease firing every time the magazine had to be changed. The Type 96 was much inferior to the 40mm Bofors used by US vessels which could put out a sustained rate of fire with a constant-fire top-fed ammunition-clip design. Many of the Japanese ships had larger 3in to 5.5in bow and stern guns – but these were often virtual antiques, salvaged from old decommissioned military vessels from the early part of the twentieth century. These guns were effective against submarines on the surface but of little use against fast, modern aircraft.

As US aircraft started to attack convoy PATA-07, which was moving up the west coast in the narrow shipping channel, the slow, large Japanese ships began to make such evasive manoeuvres as they could. After seeing the aerial mines being dropped ahead of them and West Passage effectively sealed off, the convoy was dissolved, and the ships scattered. But with little room to manoeuvre in the narrow channel, during the process *Kibi Maru* ran aground on the reef flat on the western side of the channel. Stranded on the reef, she was an easy target – and would be attacked by a number of different strike groups from different carriers throughout the day. *Yorktown* dive-bombers scored a hit on her with a 1,000lb bomb whilst *Princeton*, *Enterprise* and *Lexington* aircraft all attacked her – scoring hits and near misses with bombs, whilst Hellcats repeatedly strafed her. She was set on fire fore and aft, and was left a total loss. But despite all the damage and crew killed, as she lay holed, filled with water and stranded on the reef, she still managed to return light AA fire.

Of the other ships in the convoy, dive-bombers attacked *Raizan Maru* in Komebail Lagoon just after 0600 local time. One bomb hit her on the port side astern causing an explosion. She remained afloat initially but would eventually succumb.

Teshio Maru came about and started to head south back down the main channel through Komebail Lagoon towards Koror. As she did so she was strafed, torpedoed and bombed by aircraft from *Bunker Hill* and *Belleau Wood*. She took a bomb hit on her starboard side into Hold No. 1 and was crippled at her stern by a bomb that went right through the poop deck of her stern castle before exploding inside and damaging her steering gear. Unnavigable, she drifted with the current in the main channel until she beached on the Rael Edeng Reef in the western part of Komebail Lagoon.

Ryuko Maru was attacked by *Lexington* Helldivers and three bomb hits were reported. She started to smoke, took on a list but remained afloat. The following day, whilst seeking shelter close into the jungle-clad high cliffs of the north shore of Ngerchaol, the northern claw of Malakal Harbour, she was attacked and sunk by *Yorktown* TBFs.

Hokutai Maru successfully came about and headed back south towards Malakal Harbour – but to no avail. She, like all the ships of PATA-07, would be sunk over the two days of the air raid. The destroyer *Wakatake*, escorting the convoy, was sunk west of Babelthuap in Karamadoo Bay near West Passage. The escort destroyer *Patrol Boat 31*, on duty ahead of the convoy, had left the lagoon before the attack went in. She was quickly sunk, as was the auxiliary subchaser *Cha-26* and a number of other auxiliary subchasers and picket boats.

US aircraft were vectored to a point south east of the Kossol Passage, where it had been reported that several ships were on their way out of the lagoon, amongst them one to two light cruisers. The US pilots recognised the first speeding warship as an old destroyer and immediately began strafing runs to silence her AA fire. SBD Dauntless dive-bombers then split into two divisions and pushed over for their first dive-bomb run. One 1,000lb bomb was a near miss at the bow – lifting the destroyer's bow up in the water – the others were further off. One of the Dauntlesses made a perfect dive on the ship but didn't pull out of the dive as expected and continued until it impacted into the water and disintegrated – the pilot must surely have been hit by AA fire. Another Dauntless took small-calibre AA fire hits to its engine, which started to smoke. The aircraft developed an instability and the pilot had to turn to nurse it back toward the carrier. On the way, the plane started to lose altitude and had to be ditched 20 miles south west of Angaur. The crew safely got off and were picked up 3 hours later by a destroyer.

Other dive-bombers continued the attack on the destroyer after the first division's bombs were used up. One was a hit at the stern and the ship immediately slowed drastically from its high speed to about 8 knots –

desperately making for a rain squall in the distance, which might cloak its position. After further attacks the destroyer was seen to be moving in circles – a classic indication of a jammed rudder. Six TBF Avengers started their attack with a hit amidships that caused a huge plume of white water to erupt some 20–30m high. They were followed in by *Yorktown* aircraft. The destroyer finally succumbed, broke in two and sunk.

Two smaller ships were spotted steaming west of Kossol Passage, attempting to escape the carnage. They were heavily strafed, and one blew up from an apparent secondary explosion of ammunition, whilst the other ship was set on fire.

Enemy air bases at Koror and Arakabesan were attacked, whilst bombs were dropped on warehouses and other buildings – although no planes were spotted other than two anchored seaplanes. The seaplane base on the western side of Arakabesan, the site of the present Palau Pacific Resort, was peppered with bombs and direct hits were scored on repair and shore facilities which caused fires to break out. Two Type 95 Nakajima E8N Dave reconnaissance seaplanes were sunk along with two Nakajima A6M Rufe (Zero variant) seaplane fighters. US aircraft encountered heavy 20mm and 40mm AA fire over Koror, with heavy concentrations over nearby Arakabesan where the seaplane base was situated.

Two large, fast Shiretoko-class fleet oilers, IJN *Iro* and IJN *Sata*, were anchored in the lagoon undergoing repairs. Each was 470ft 8in long with a beam of 58ft – the oilers displaced 15,450 tons and could carry 8,000 tonnes of fuel oil. Damaged by a torpedo strike by the US submarine *Tunny* a few days earlier, *Iro* had entered Palau's lagoon on 23 March and been anchored up for repair in the sheltered Urukthapel anchorage to the south of Ngeruktabel, the southern claw of Malakal Harbour. She had arrived carrying her very volatile and dangerous flammable cargo and for safety reasons she had been kept well clear of the other vessels anchored within Malakal Harbour itself. *Sata* was already at anchor undergoing repairs ½ nautical mile away to her north east.

Tankers and oilers were priority targets – and during the initial fighter sweep the valuable *Iro* and *Sata* were quickly spotted and identified. Three *Bunker Hill* dive-bombers attacked *Iro* dropping six 1,000lb bombs on the ship at about 0730 (local) and reporting one hit. The following day, 31 March, she was found to be still afloat – and was attacked by *Yorktown* dive-bombers. One 1,000lb bomb hit the ship on the starboard aft quarter and was a direct hit in the cavernous engine room. A large explosion resulted – followed by a fire breaking out. Despite this, 200 of her crew were able to escape the ship – but 50 had perished.

Mortally wounded, she settled by the stern – fuel flooding out of breached cargo compartments and causing a large slick. Hundreds of 55-gallon fuel drums floated out from her dry cargo spaces. As her stern sank and grounded on the bottom, her bow rose in the air – straining at her starboard anchor chain and revealing the damage to the bottom of her stem caused by the earlier torpedo strike by USS *Tunny*. The metal of her bow was so hot from the fires that white steam billowed up from it.

Although she had settled by the stern, *Iro's* bow and forward tanks retained their buoyancy and remained sticking up out of the water. Her cargo of fuel on fire, she burned for several days after the strike, finally succumbing and sinking nearly three weeks later on 17 April 1944.

Half a mile away, *Sata* was attacked by *Hornet* TBFs. She too was hit in the stern at the engine-room area, this time by an aerial torpedo. She settled by the stern – her stern hitting the seabed and deforming slightly, but as with *Iro*, the buoyancy of her bow tanks kept her bow proud of the water. The following day, at about 0700, *Sata* was bombed

Operation DESECRATE 1, Palau 30/31 March 1944. The 15,450-ton oiler IJN *Iro* is ablaze and billowing clouds of black fuel smoke. (National Archives 80-G-45307)

257

The oiler IJN *Iro* sinks by the stern amidst a slick of fuel oil. Her bow section is hot from the intense fires that swept her, and steam billows from her metal work. She strains at her anchor chain and the torpedo damage to her forefoot sustained a week earlier on 22 March by the submarine USS *Tunny* is visible, whilst 55-gallon fuel drums from her dry cargo spaces bob in the water. (National Archives 80-G-45321)

The wreck of the fleet oiler IJN *Iro* sits on her keel today in Palau's western lagoon. (Author)

at mast-head level by two *Lexington* TBFs and took two to three further hits. One bomb was a near miss between the torpedo damage and her rudder – whilst a large 2,000lb bomb with a delayed fuze was dropped from 150ft and was a near miss forward of the bridge superstructure along the waterline on the port side. Coming into the water at an angle, the bomb travelled directly under the keel of the tanker before exploding and blasting a large hole some 10m across directly up into one of her oil cargo tanks. The loss of much of her remaining buoyancy in her forward tanks was too much – she succumbed, rolled over to port, capsized and sank.

Strike 1D from TG 58.2 carriers launched 32 Hellcats, 30 VB dive-bombers and 9 Avenger torpedo-bombers, timed to be on target at 1115–1130. The strike groups strafed Peleliu hitting a Betty and a Val, before moving north and strafing the ships in the western anchorages and knocking out a lighthouse at Toachel Mlengui (West Pass), a radio station and hitting a freighter grounded on a reef south of West Pass, near to Karamado Bay. Two Nakajima A6M2-N Rufes were set on fire

A F6F Hellcat fighter swings in for another attack (left). The oiler IJN *Iro* is already ablaze and billowing clouds of black smoke from her stern at bottom centre of shot and has just taken a near miss on her starboard beam. Her sister oiler IJN *Sata* is already down by the stern and taking near misses in the centre right of shot. To the top of the shot inside Malakal Harbour, the tanker IJN *Amatsu Maru* is ablaze at the stern. (National Archives 80-G-45323)

at Koror along with a hangar. The large transport *Nagisan Maru* was attacked and three hits scored, one in the bridge and two at the stern. As the flight broke off the attacks about 20 minutes later, she was seen to be smouldering and going down by the stern. Hits were also scored on a medium tanker outside the claws of the Malakal Harbour, believed to be the *Asashio* or *Akebono Maru*, and another medium freighter believed to be the *Kamikaze Maru* or *Gozan Maru*.

Strike 1D aircraft also targeted the 10,567-ton Type 1TL Standard Merchant Tanker *Amatsu Maru* – a big ship at 526ft long overall with a beam of 65ft 7in. She was bombed by *Enterprise* dive-bombers with hits by 1,000lb bombs reported around the fantail and at the bow. One bomb struck her, or was a near miss, at the stern on the starboard side that caused a fire to take hold in the engine room.

About an hour later, another section of dive-bombers attacked her and she took a direct hit amidships which caused a large explosion that killed ten of her crew. Hit now by at least three 1,000lb bombs she sank slowly by the stern – and aerial reconnaissance photographs taken early the

The 10,567-ton Type 1TL standard merchant tanker IJN *Amatsu Maru*, at anchor in Malakal Harbour, Palau, takes a near miss whilst another freighter also has a near miss. (National Archives Series 80-G-45000)

following day, 31 March, show her down by the stern with only her bow, foremast and the top of her bridge superstructure showing above the water. She would remain in this half-sunken attitude for some months.

The requisitioned 4,916grt passenger cargo vessel *Kamikaze Maru* was anchored in the Urukthapel Island area of the Western Lagoon, her foredeck Hold No. 2 filled with a deadly cargo of 30ft-long Type 93 surface-launched Long Lance torpedoes.

As the raid started, *Kamikaze Maru* worked up a head of steam to get underway and she was manoeuvring in amongst Palau's jungle-clad small islands to the south west of Malakal Harbour at 3 knots when six Curtis Helldivers from *Bunker Hill* attacked her with 1,000lb and 500lb bombs. She was hit forward of the bridge and amidships – and three near misses sent plumes of white water skyward, the force of the explosion transmitting through the incompressible water buckling her plating. The hit forward of the bridge triggered a significant secondary explosion, which caused fires to break out. White smoke billowed high into the air – and *Kamikaze Maru* slewed to a stop as her crew fought to control the fire and repair the damage. Later the same day, just after midday, she was attacked by TBF Avenger torpedo-bombers from

The wreck of the Type 1TL tanker *Amatsu Maru* today sits upright in 41m of water in Malakal Harbour. (Author)

Bunker Hill and also hit by rockets. She succumbed and sank shortly thereafter, settling on the seabed upright in about 35m of water with the tips of her masts showing above the surface.

The earlier Type 91 torpedoes had used compressed air as the oxidizer with an 11ft long internal air cylinder charged to about 2,500–3000psi – the same pressure as today's conventional scuba cylinders. Compressed air however left a noticeable bubble trail. The Type 93 torpedo carried on *Kamikaze Maru* ingeniously used compressed oxygen as the fuel oxidizer in place of compressed air. Compressed oxygen is dangerous to handle – but IJN engineers found that by starting the torpedo's engine with compressed air, then gradually switching to oxygen they were able to overcome the explosions, which had hampered it before. To conceal the use of very dangerous pure oxygen from the ship's crew, the Japanese called the oxygen tank the *secondary air tank*.

Since air is only 21 per cent oxygen and 78 per cent nitrogen, pure 100 per cent oxygen provides five times as much oxidizer in the same tank volume and this greatly increased torpedo range. The absence of inert nitrogen also resulted in significantly fewer exhaust bubbles as the combustion product was only carbon dioxide and water vapour. With CO_2 being significantly soluble in water, the resulting exhaust gas mixture greatly reduced tell-tale bubbles in its track.

The Japanese Type 93 torpedo had a maximum range of about 25 miles at 38 knots and it carried a large 1,080lb high-explosive warhead. Its long range, high speed and heavy warhead marked it as a quantum leap forward in torpedo development – and it was far ahead of any Allied torpedo of the time. The US Navy's standard surface-launched torpedo of the Second World War, the Mark 15, had a maximum range of just 7.4 nautical miles at 26 knots or just 3 nautical miles at 45 knots and it carried a smaller 827lb warhead.

Enterprise and *Belleau Wood* launched 16 Hellcats, 12 VB dive-bombers and 9 TBF Avengers for Strike 2E, the fifth group strike of the day – intended to arrive over Palau at 1414–1430. Several of the Hellcats were loaded with 1,000lb bombs fuzed with delays of several hours to be dropped on Peleliu airfield and deny the Japanese the opportunity of repairing it overnight. The remaining Hellcats and Avengers carried four 500lb GP bombs each. The strike group was joined by eight Hellcats from *Cowpens* for subsequent attacks on shipping in the Malakal anchorage where a freighter and an oiler were hit along with smaller vessels. Two large ships anchored either side of the northern tip of Urukthapel were also attacked. By this time, five ships were observed burning in the Malakal anchorage with four damaged.

Arriving over Palau between 1445 and 1500, Strike 2E also included a Photo Mission Avenger launched from *Enterprise*. Two of the escort Hellcats had a 45-minute duel with a Nakajima Ki-27 Nate – a small old monoplane which ducked in and out of the clouds as it frantically tried to outmanoeuvre the two far faster and more heavily armed US fighters. Eventually it was hit – but as the pilot made to bail out, his parachute caught the tail assembly of the Nate and he was taken down with his plane to crash below.

This was the last flight from TG 58.1 carriers *Enterprise*, *Cowpens* and *Belleau Wood*. As soon as their aircraft were recovered, the Group started to move northwards in preparation for strikes against Yap and Ulithi to the north east. *Enterprise* herself had flown 221 sorties claiming 5 enemy aircraft shot down, more than 30 planes destroyed or damaged on the ground, 1 oiler, 1 large transport and 3 medium freighters sunk – and 9 freighters, 3 destroyers and 1 minelayer damaged.

In all, a total of 454 sorties were flown during the 6 group strikes, A–F, on K-DAY, 30 March, against shipping and ground installations. More than thirty Japanese aircraft had been damaged or destroyed on the ground on Peleliu airfield and Arakabesan Island seaplane base during the Initial Fighter Sweep with an additional twenty-eight aircraft reported destroyed throughout the day by the strike groups. Few serviceable Japanese aircraft remained.

As a result, Japanese aircraft were scrambled from other island airfields and rushed to Palau. Twelve Betty bombers from Saipan arrived in the late afternoon – immediately taking off to attack Task Force 58. They scored little success however due to the intense AA fire thrown at them from the screen of battleships, cruisers, destroyers – and from the carriers themselves. None of the task-force ships were damaged.

The US Combat Air Patrols of eight Hellcats had flown routinely throughout the day to protect the carriers: four planes circling the carriers at 5,000ft and four more at 10,000ft. At about 1700, they were ordered to intercept an unidentified incoming contact about 50 miles away from the carriers.

As they closed the contact, they spotted ten to twelve Japanese aircraft, which they identified as Nakajima B6N Jill torpedo-bombers or Yokosuka D4Y Judy dive-bombers. All but one of the aircraft were quickly shot down – the one surviving aircraft, a Judy, continued to head towards the task force at speed.

Two of the Hellcats, capable of a top speed of 380mph, turned to chase after the Judy – which had a fast top speed for a dive-bomber of 342mph. The Judy had closed to within 10 nautical miles of the task force by the time the two Hellcats were close enough to engage. The Judy was hit – and exploded. As with most Japanese aircraft, the Judy had sacrificed armour and fuel protection for speed.

As the two Hellcats turned to head back to their carrier, they spotted two more Judy dive-bombers hugging the waves and closing on the task force. Two more Hellcats soon joined the chase and one was able to open fire at extreme range of 1,000m. The Judys dropped their bomb loads and escaped unscathed.

That night, some sixty fighters arrived at Peleliu from Saipan in the evening. The scene was set for a fighter duel the following morning.

The first day of Operation DESECRATE 1, 30 March 1944, seemed to have completely degraded Japanese air cover and given total air superiority to US aircraft. But the Americans were unaware of the Japanese reinforcements of aircraft that had arrived overnight. Action reports throughout the day and the results of photo-reconnaissance missions revealed that most of the shipping found in the lagoon had been sunk or badly damaged.

As Task Group 58.1 detached to sortie against Yap and Ulithi, Task Groups 58.2 and 58.3 readied to attack the Palaus again the following day, K-DAY PLUS ONE.

(b) K-DAY PLUS ONE, 31 March 1944

Following TG 58.1's departure the night before, there would be a reduced number of sixty Hellcats from the remaining Task Groups 58.2 and 58 for the Initial Fighter Sweep. The Hellcats launched at around 0530 (local), the twelve Hellcats from each carrier being split into three divisions of four that rendezvoused at 7,000ft en route to the target. A Target Observer Group of Hellcats launched shortly thereafter. The planes of the first Mining Mission of the day began to lift off 10 minutes after the Hellcats had launched. They were escorted by Hellcats, each TBF Avenger carried a single Mark 25 ground mine with delayed arming.

On the way to Palau, a Betty bomber approached. The Hellcats immediately attacked it – the Betty taking a hit that caused the starboard engine and unprotected fuel tank to burst into flame. The Betty streaked through the sky ablaze before falling from the sky to disintegrate in the water. As the sixty Hellcats approached Palau, they moved up to their assigned patrol altitudes, *Princeton* planes at 10,000ft, *Yorktown* planes at 15,000ft and *Bunker Hill* planes at 20,000ft.

Hellcats were soon strafing Peleliu airfield covered by the divisions above them. Five Zekes were found on Combat Air Patrol – two were shot down and three escaped into cloud cover, allowing the attacks to proceed on the airfield. From there the Hellcats moved to attack the airfield under construction on the main island of Babelthuap.

The high-altitude patrol of Hellcats at 20,000ft spotted two four-plane Japanese groups at the same altitude, one group being identified as Mitsubishi A6M3 Zero variant *Hamp* fighters. As the Japanese planes tried to evade the attacking Hellcats, the US fighters' speed advantage allowed them to follow the climb and shoot down two of them. The other group of four planes was identified as Zekes, about 4,000ft below them. With a significant speed advantage from their 4,000ft dive, the Hellcats were each able to pick one Zeke and fire from a full overhead run at full deflection. All four Zekes were shot down in this one pass.

Many other groups of bogies were present, and a series of vicious dogfights erupted into a general melee. US pilots reported a total of sixty Japanese planes airborne during the initial fighter sweep – these were the fighters that had arrived from Saipan the evening before, along with the few serviceable aircraft that had survived the previous day's attacks. The sky turned into a swirling mass of individual dogfights with aircraft harrying or being chased in every direction. The Japanese aircraft were no match for the modern Hellcats and appeared to give up the offensive, scattering to save themselves and dipping into cloud cover where they could.

As the TF 58 aircraft assaulted Palau, Combat Air Patrols of eight Hellcats patrolled the air space around the carriers throughout the day: four planes circling the carriers at 5,000ft and four more at 10,000ft.

As the Hellcats occupied the Zekes, Air Target Observer planes worked to identify targets for subsequent attack by the dive- and torpedo-bombers. The Observers found few ships left in seaworthy shape in the anchorages below – most of the shipping was already damaged or disabled in some way with just two ships in Malakal Harbour that appeared undamaged. Those ships would be attacked again – before bomb runs on land installations. The TF 58 planes would then fly south again to attack Peleliu airfield en route back to the carriers in their southern holding position. As Avengers bombed the airfield, Hellcats strafed Japanese aircraft spotted inside protective revetments.

As the Hellcats won air superiority, the dive- and torpedo-bombers following on behind began their work. Strike 1A-2 from TG 58.2 carrier *Hornet* launched at 0535 with twelve Hellcats and four Avengers loaded with one 1,000lb bomb and two smaller bombs on the wing racks fuzed for immediate detonation – assigned to attack shipping and land installations. The nine Strike 1A-2 Avengers from TG 58.2 *Monterey* carried a selection of 100lb fragmentation bombs, incendiary bombs and

100lb general purpose (GP) bombs. This was the last strike by *Monterey* aircraft against Palau.

Strike 3A-2 from Task Group 58.3 carriers *Yorktown* and *Lexington* launched just after 0600 and comprised a total of 46 aircraft – 20 Hellcats, 14 VB dive-bombers and 12 Avengers.

With the Japanese AA fire now largely suppressed, it was decided to arm the Hellcats with 500lb or 1,000lb bombs – the powerful aircraft could easily carrier launch with such a pay load and it gave the strike groups more hitting power. The Hellcats would carry a 500lb GP bomb with a short 4–5 second delay fuze to allow a mast-head attack. The dive-bombers each carried a more powerful 1,000lb bomb.

The second strike of the day, Strike B, launched so that the TBF torpedo-bombers, and SBD Dauntless and SB2C Helldiver dive-bombers, escorted by Hellcats would arrive over their targets at 0815–0900 tasked with attacking shipping and land targets.

TBFs of Mining Group 4 carrying Mark 25 mines arrived over Palau, some dropping their mines in the Malakal Pass, the main eastern entrance to Malakal Harbour, whilst others were laid in Toachel ra Ngel, the more minor eastern channel into the harbour. More were dropped in the channel between the islands of Babelthuap and Koror. The escort fighters went in ahead of the Avengers and strafed AA batteries on Arakabesan and Koror to suppress AA fire and allow the vulnerable Avengers to drop their mines from 400ft at 200 knots.

Strike 3C-2 was launched as DESCECRATE 1 was drawing to a finale – this was the penultimate strike from *Lexington*. There were 39 aircraft comprising 9 Hellcats again carrying 500lb bombs, the dive-bombers carrying 1,000lb bombs and 11 Avengers each carrying a Mark 25 magnetic ground mine with arming delays of between 14 and 35 days, whilst two TBFs carried Mark 10 tethered mines. These would be laid in the main channel leading north up the west side of Babelthuap Island to Toachel Mlengui, the West Passage through the lagoon's barrier reef to open ocean. On this strike, no AA fire was encountered, and few strafing targets were found. In the early afternoon, Strike 3D was *Lexington*'s final strike of the day and was again directed at damaging airfields and island installations. On their return south to the carriers they again hit Peleliu airfield with long-delay fuzed bombs to deny the airstrip to the Japanese. Landing of returning aircraft began at 1532 and finished by 1554 whilst the carrier was already speeding on its way away from Palau towards Woleai to deliver its next strike.

Task Force 58 air operations against Palau had ceased after some 1,426 sorties. The Americans had lost twenty-five aircraft in combat and another nineteen operationally.[8] Of the forty-four US airmen who ditched at sea, lifeguard submarines, destroyers and seaplanes successfully recovered twenty-six.

Task Force 58 had neutralised Palau, relieving Nimitz and MacArthur of their worries about their northern flank being attacked during the Hollandia operation.

All three task groups attacked Woleai, beginning at 0646 ship's time (+2 hours local) on 1 April with a few planes hitting Ulithi. The raid on this small Japanese island would be called off after the third strike for lack of targets and TF 58 retired towards Majuro.

(c) Aftermath

During DESECRATE 1, Admiral Koga, operating from his newly installed Combined Fleet HQ at Koror, Palau, survived the two days of gruelling air attacks on 30 and 31 March. His HQ had only been officially installed there days before on 29 March 1944. When a seeming lull in the attacks came in the afternoon on 31 March, he decided to leave Palau by Kawanishi H8K Emily flying boat. He perhaps believed that the two-day air raid was a softening up operation and that a naval bombardment would follow, presaging an amphibious landing by US Marines.

With Palau's air ability now totally degraded and with a consequent lack of reconnaissance intelligence, he was no doubt unaware that the lull in the air attacks was in fact the end of the US operation. Unbeknownst to him, Task Force 58 was already withdrawing at high speed northwards to strike at Yap, Ulithi and Woleai. The huge US task force was moving north as fast as possible to get out of range of any Japanese torpedo aircraft which might mount a night torpedo attack.

As Admiral Koga boarded his Kawanishi H8K Emily flying boat that evening, 31 March 1944, his staff boarded a second Emily whilst a third aircraft would act as escort. The Emilys took off from Palau's battered landscape and turned due west in the direction of Davao, some 625 miles away in the Philippines, where Koga intended to set up his new HQ. But on the way there, the aircraft ran into a severe tropical depression and became separated.

Commander-in-Chief of the Combined Fleet, Admiral Koga, died that night when his plane crashed in a heavy storm near Davao. His whereabouts remained a mystery for a time – his plane appearing to have simply disappeared. Koga himself was never seen again.

The second Emily, with several staff officers, had become separated from the other two aircraft and water landed at about 0200 on 1 April, about 450 miles north of Davao, off Cebu in the Philippines. Locals heard an aircraft engine spluttering for some time before it faltered and then stopped as the giant flying boat plunged into the sea and exploded.

Locals got into canoes and paddled out to the site where a group of twelve survivors was found about 3km offshore, swimming for shore and towing the dead body of one of their colleagues. The majority of the Emily's occupants had survived and recounted how their Emily had been shot down by AA fire from a submarine. The survivors were subsequently captured by Filipino guerrillas, led by an American.

A blackened wooden box was washed ashore which held a quantity of military papers, including two Japanese operational maps detailing bases, landing fields and other facilities in Indochina, Hainan, the Philippines and southern China. The Japanese mounted a massive effort to attempt to find and recover the prisoners and the intelligence documents before they fell into US hands.

The US-led guerrillas took their Japanese prisoners into the interior of Cebu and held them for ten days until intense Japanese rescue efforts located the group and forced them to surrender. The crash survivors turned out to be high-ranking Japanese officials led by Vice Admiral Shigeru Fukodome, Chief of Staff of the Combined Fleet. Before surrendering, the guerrillas placed the captured papers inside two empty mortar shell containers and sent them to a rendezvous with a US submarine for onward transmission to US intelligence.

Once delivered to US intelligence in Australia, the documents revealed important information about Japanese defences in the Philippines and other areas. They also disclosed a strategic weakness in Japan's central Philippine defence; Leyte stood out as the soft underbelly of the Japanese position and was poorly defended. Once this was confirmed by other US intelligence operations, this precious intelligence led to the acceleration of the US return to the Philippines from December to October 1944 and to a change of landing site from Mindanao to Leyte.

During DESECRATE 1, more than forty Japanese ships were sunk or damaged – some 130,000 tons of shipping. The ex-Momi-class destroyer *Patrol Boat No. 31*, the destroyer *Wakatake*, the IJN subchasers, *Ch 6*, *Ch 10* and *Ch 12*, four smaller auxiliary subchasers *Cha-22*, *Cha-26*, *Cha-52* and *Cha-53*, the converted auxiliary subchaser *Showa Maru No. 5* and several picket boats had all been sent to the bottom. The valuable fleet oilers *Iro*, *Sata* and *Ose*, the auxiliary oiler *Akebono Maru*, the tankers

Amatsu Maru, Asashio Maru and *Unyu Maru No. 2* had all been sunk and the tanker *Hishi Maru No. 2* damaged. The loss of so many oilers and tankers at Palau was a crippling blow to the Combined Fleet and to Japan's ability to sustain her distant war effort. The shortage of tankers after DESECRATE 1, coming so soon after the loss of the tankers *Fujisan Maru, Hoyo Maru* and *Shinkoku Maru* at Truk six weeks earlier, severely limited the range of the fleet and degraded Japan's ability to transport oil from the Netherlands East Indies to the Empire.

The Fleet Repair Ship *Akashi* had been sunk along with the fleet aircraft transport *Goshu Maru*, the Torpedo Boat tender *Kamikaze Maru*, the net layer *Nissho Maru No. 5* and the Submarine Tender *Urakami Maru* along with many requisitioned freighters such as *Akita Maru No. 3, Bichu Maru, Chuyo Maru, Gozan Maru, Hokutai Maru* and the two ships named *Kibi Maru* and the *Nagisan Maru*.

A claimed 110 Japanese aircraft were shot down over Palau and the seas around, with no air opposition encountered on the other islands. A further fifteen Japanese aircraft were also claimed as severely damaged, probably downed. The US ships AA fire shot down four Japanese aircraft. Including aircraft destroyed or severely damaged on the ground in Peleliu airfield, Arakabesan Seaplane base, Koror, Woleai and elsewhere, US pilots claimed a total of 214 aircraft rendered unusable to the Japanese – although the total claimed has been challenged and never finally agreed.[9]

The sea approaches and exit routes for shipping to Palau had been successfully mined and Palau harbour was blocked until it could be swept, whilst sweeping operations were made difficult by the extensive use of the hard-to-detect ground mines, which self-activated at irregular intervals. The underwater terrain made it impossible to sweep for the ground mines successfully.

The task groups' anti-aircraft screen had proved to be very effective against Japanese air attacks, in particular the feared night torpedo attack. The principle of the Initial Fighter Sweep had again been proved sound, successfully eliminating air opposition over the target as at Truk.

The fighter escort for the vulnerable minelaying Avengers was crucial to the successful mine drop. Japanese AA fire was intense but had been successfully suppressed by repeated strafing by Hellcats as the Avengers made their low-speed, low-altitude drops.

Some Japanese aircrew and aircraft were withdrawn to Davao in April and May where rebuilding of the decimated air groups began. Other surviving pilots were evacuated to Saipan where more aircraft were sent to allow the reconstitution of Japanese air strength to begin.

After the end of the fighting in the South Pacific theatre in March 1944, there was no longer any need for Nimitz to split his operations into South and Central Pacific, all were now Central. On 14 April 1944, he abolished the title Central Pacific Force and on 26 April the Fifth Fleet was formally established, the title by which the force had been known administratively. Simultaneously, all forces under Admiral Halsey became known as the Third Fleet. The same day, Spruance shifted his flag to Pearl Harbor to begin planning the Marianas campaign, leaving Mitscher on his own until June.

The war moved onwards – towards Japan.

Above: The bow of the 2,840grt IJA cargo ship *Teshio Maru* with 3in-gun, sunk by TF 58 aircraft at Palau during Operation DESECRATE 1 on 30/31 March 1944. (Author)

Opposite above: An Aichi E13A IJN twin-float seaplane, Allied reporting name Jake, sunk by TF 58 aircraft during Operation DESECRATE 1 at Palau on 30/31 March 1944. The aircraft appears to have been sunk whilst stationary or taxiing as the propeller tips are not bent backwards. (Author)

Opposite below: This Vought F4U Corsair lies in shallow water north of Toachel Mlengui, the West Pass through Palau's surrounding barrier reef. The fate of the pilot is unknown. (Author)

270

(iii) The Hollandia and Aitape Landings – Operations RECKLESS and PERSECUTION, 22–7 April 1944

On 22 April 1944, the Allied landings at Hollandia on New Guinea (Operation RECKLESS) and Aitape on the north coast of New Guinea (Operation PERSECUTION) began the Allied Western New Guinea campaign.

In the run up to these landings, the Task Force 58 fast carriers sortied from Majuro on 13 April under Mitscher's direct command – three task groups of four carriers each commanded by Clark, Montgomery and Reeves. They made a dummy move towards Palau – then commenced air attacks along the New Guinea coast on 21 April, encountering only sporadic attacks by Japanese snooper aircraft. Mitscher routinely launched night-fighter CAP to guard enemy night torpedo attacks.

Fifth Fleet participation in the Hollandia and Aitape operations was not however required, it was a Seventh Fleet operation under MacArthur's Southwest Pacific command. Hollandia was served by several large airfields from which land-based bombers could operate and by April, all Japanese air in New Guinea had been smashed. Task Force 58 had already destroyed Palau as an air base for staging aircraft.

On 24 April, Task Force 58 withdrew to the new anchorage at Manus, the largest of the Admiralty Islands in Papua New Guinea, where its ServRon oilers were waiting.

(iv) Fast-Carrier Strikes Against Truk, 29–30 April 1944

Along with the neutralisation of Palau, MacArthur's Hollandia landing forces had to be protected by the continued neutralisation of Truk. When B-24 Liberator bombers based in the South Pacific carried out the first land-based daylight raid on Truk on 29 March, five weeks after Operation HAILSTONE, they were surprised when ninety Japanese fighters attacked them. The heavily armed B-24 bombers shot down thirty-one planes and shot up more on the ground, losing two of their own number. Further B-24 bombing runs also encountered stiff resistance. It was plain that Truk had been restored as an operative air base – it would have to be attacked again in force. Nimitz passed the word to Mitscher at the Manus Island fleet anchorage.

Task Force 58 sortied twelve carriers for a raid intended to once again reduce Truk – scheduled for 29–30 April 1944. The objective of this raid was to destroy enemy shore installations, stores, fuel dumps, ammunition stores and shipping – with the emphasis on destruction of shore installations and aircraft that could threaten Allied operations.

The twelve carriers under Vice Admiral Mitscher's command were subdivided into three task groups of four carriers each:

1. Task Group 58.1 – Rear Admiral J.J. Clark:
   Hornet (CV-12), Air Group 2
   Belleau Wood (CVL-24), Air Group 24
   Cowpens (CVL-25), Air Group 25
   Bataan (CVL-29), Air Group 50
2. Task Group 58.2 – Rear Admiral A.E. Montgomery:
   Yorktown (CV-10), Air Group 5
   Bunker Hill (CV-17), Air Group 8
   Monterey (CVL-26), Air Group 30
   Cabot (CVL-28), Air Group 31
3. Task Group 58.3 – Rear Admiral J.W. Reeves Jr:
   Enterprise (CV-6), Air Group 10
   Lexington (CV-16), Air Group 16
   Princeton (CVL-23), Air Group 23
   Langley (CVL-27), Air Group 32

The raid would take the same format as Operation HAILSTONE two months earlier. The task force would stand well off Truk and launch an initial fighter sweep of Hellcats timed to arrive over Truk at dawn. The Hellcats would clear the skies of enemy aircraft and suppress AA fire. Once the fighter sweep had achieved air supremacy, successive composite group strikes of dive-bombers and torpedo-bombers, escorted by Hellcats, would pummel Truk for the two days of the raid. But unlike HAILSTONE, this time the Japanese would not be surprised, they would be ready and waiting.

On 29 April, as CAP and ASP patrols from the Independence-class light carriers *Bataan*, *Monterey*, *Langley* and *Princeton* covered the task force, the initial fighter sweep by TF 58 Hellcats began launching at 0440, timed to arrive over Truk at sunrise 0600. TG 58.3 Hellcats from *Enterprise*, *Langley* and *Lexington* had been assigned the low-altitude patrol. TG 58.1 Hellcats from *Hornet*, *Belleau Wood*, *Bataan* and *Cowpens* were assigned to the vicinity of Param Island. TG 58.2 Hellcats from *Yorktown* and *Bunker Hill* were assigned the 13,000–16,000ft altitude.

As the Hellcats approached Truk, they rose up to their designated patrol altitudes and as they swept over the lagoon, they encountered heavy AA fire. It was clear the Japanese had been alerted as more than fifty Zekes rose into the air from Moen No. 1, Eten and Param airfields to join five that were already on Combat Air Patrol. Almost sixty Zeros now engaged the Hellcats, concealing themselves where they could in cloud layers before suddenly emerging to attack the Hellcats.

A complicated dogfight took place over Dublon Island at about 8,000ft, with some 8–10 Zekes duelling with about 16 Hellcats in a swirl of individual contests – but the Japanese pilots were by now showing the results of the harsh attrition of their best pilots and the poor quality of their replacements. They now displayed less combat ability in each successive engagement – it being noted in subsequent US action reports that although they handled their planes more smartly, they appeared weak on gunnery.

The 16 Hellcats from *Yorktown* shot down 5 Zekes and 1 Kawasaki Ki-61 Tony fighter, strafed 1 Betty and 2 single-engine planes on Eten Island – and a small cargo vessel between Dublon and Fefan Islands, leaving it ablaze. *Cabot* Hellcats shot down 17 enemy planes and *Lexington*'s 20 more, but both VF squadrons lost 4 planes each. The 8 Hellcats from *Langley* destroyed 20 Japanese fighters. Mitscher's aviators had established air supremacy in the skies above Truk within a few hours.

Meanwhile, back out at sea, Japanese aircraft sighted Mitscher's task force just before 0700 and launched an immediate torpedo attack. Between 20 and 45 Japanese fighters, escorting 6–8 Nakajima B6N Jill torpedo-bombers, attacked. The Japanese planes penetrated the US fighter defence and headed for the carriers, initially concentrating on *Yorktown* and *Monterey*. The attack was however ultimately driven off by CAP Hellcats and shipborne AA fire. A Japanese submarine then attacked, unsuccessfully, before being sunk by a destroyer in the screen. The task-force flagship *Lexington*, making ready to launch a strike, and vulnerable with rows of spotted, gassed and armed dive- and torpedo-bombers, was then targeted by two Yokosuka D4Y Judy dive-bombers. One Judy was knocked down, splashing into the sea less than 100ft from the ship. The other Judy dropped its bomb but missed, before turning to flee back towards Truk chased by a number of CAP fighters.

On *Hornet*, the first composite strike of Dog Day, Strike 2A, began with launching at about 0500 of 12 Hellcats, 14 SB2 Helldivers and 8 TBF torpedo-bombers, which along with similar groups from *Belleau Wood* and *Cowpens* were tasked with targeting Param Island with its important airfield. The Helldivers targeted medium and heavy AA emplacements and barracks with 1,000lb bombs whilst the TBFs, loaded with twelve 100lb GP bombs each, targeted the runway and aircraft dispersal areas north of the runway. The Hellcats carried out strafing runs on AA positions and shot up parked up fighters and buildings.

Strike 2B launched at 0645 from *Hornet* – their mission, to bomb and strike installations on Fefan Island, with their primary targets being the AA positions, ammunition magazines and a power station. All Helldivers were armed with one 1,000lb bomb and two 100lb GP bombs each whilst all the TBF torpedo-bombers carried twelve 100lb bombs, some with four 5in rockets in addition.

Strike 2C launched at 0900, with four of the *Hornet* Hellcats carrying 500lb bombs, whilst the *Belleau Wood* Hellcats carried single 500lb bombs and the TBFs four 500lb GP bombs – their targets were the Tarik and Faleu Islands and Param airfield. Strike 2D launched at 1100 to hit the Nomoi Islands, a group of three large atolls located about 160 nautical miles south east of Truk. There they would bomb and strafe the airfield on the southern atoll of Satawan – where an oil dump was set on fire. Strike 2E launched at 1315, to bomb and strafe Param Island. Strike 2F launched at 1505, again to strafe and bomb Param Island.

Yorktown Strike 3A aircraft launched at 0521, targeting the man-made carrier-shaped Eten Island, tasked with destroying Takeshima air base aircraft and facilities there with 100lb GP bombs and 130lb fragmentation clusters. Strike 3B launched at 0720, targeting the hangar area section of Eten Island airstrip – no airborne enemy were encountered.

Once the attack was completed, the strike aircraft moved to attack AA positions on the south-east part of Dublon Island nearby and on Moen Island, from where intense AA fire was being thrown up. Parked up aircraft and two small barges in the lagoon were also strafed.

Yorktown Strike 3C aircraft launched at 0905, targeting ground installations on Dublon Island – and successive strikes continued until its last strike, 3F, launched at 1500. The Strike 3F aircraft were tasked with attacking Eten Island installations, the TBF torpedo-bombers carrying 2,000lb GP bombs intended to crater the island's runway and prevent enemy planes from being flown in and landed during the night.

Bunker Hill Strike 3A had launched at 0522 to strike the Dublon seaplane base, encountering heavy AA fire from positions on Moen and Dublon, which were strafed. There were thirty to forty aircraft observed on the seaplane ramp, mostly Aichi E13A Jake seaplanes. The US aircraft strafed AA positions on Fefan Island as they withdrew. Strike 3B launched against targets in Dublon town whilst Strike 3C was against targets of opportunity. Strikes 3D, 3E and the last strike of the day, 3F, were against various targets in Dublon Town and the seaplane base.

As the aircraft of the last strikes returned to their carriers and drew the first day of strikes to a close, it was clear that not much of value remained to be hit the next day.

On 30 April, DOG-DAY-PLUS-ONE, the Hellcat fighter sweep launched at 0627, this time, given the air superiority, it was combined with the first composite striking group. When no airborne enemy aircraft were encountered, the Hellcats swooped to strafe AA positions ahead of the dive- and torpedo-bombers. The last strikes of the day launched just after noon against Dublon, the Moen seaplane base and the Moen Radar Station. By the end of the operation, US planes from the three carrier task groups had flown 2,200 sorties.

But by this time however, late April 1944, larger Japanese vessels had virtually abandoned Truk – and the only ships of any size found during

USS *Enterprise* (CV-6) TBM Avenger torpedo-bombers warming up on the after-flight deck, c. May 1944. An F6F Hellcat fighter is on the midships elevator, in the foreground. (National Archives 80-G-K-1590)

the raid were one medium freighter and a Wakatake-class destroyer. A small freighter, two subchasers and a number of other smaller craft were also sunk or damaged.

The Japanese estimated the total number of their aircraft destroyed in the air and on the ground as being just over 90, whilst US pilots claimed about 123. There were 20 US carrier aircraft shot down by the heaviest AA fire faced to date, while 6 US aircraft had been lost in combat and 9 more operationally. Although 46 US aircrew had been shot down or ditched, over half were subsequently picked up, 22 alone by the US lifeguard submarine *Tang*.

This devastating attack finally ended Japanese attempts to continue the use of Truk as an airfield. The air facilities at Dublon, Eten Island, Fefan and Param Islands had been destroyed and nearly half of the 4th Fleet HQ damaged, with its communications capability severely disrupted.

With Mitscher's carrier air having won control of the skies, he was able to detach his heavy surface ships for other taskings. Mitscher's cruisers bombarded Satawan atoll in the outer Nomoi Islands group on 30 April, whilst Vice Admiral 'Ching' Lee formed the battle line of battleships to shell Ponape on 1 May. Mitscher felt secure enough to despatch TG 58.2 and TG 58.3 towards Majuro for replenishment whilst TG 58.1 was retained in theatre to provide air support for 'Ching' Lee's battleships.

To protect the Hollandia landing forces from a build-up of Japanese forces at Palau, as had happened at Truk, TGs 58.1, 58.2 and 58.3 also carried out a follow-up raid on Palau between 29 April and 1 May, code name Operation DESECRATE 2, designed to enforce the continued neutralisation of Palau and to prevent the Japanese from rebuilding their air potential.

In January 1944, ComAirPac had established a rotation schedule for air groups on a basis of nine months' combat operations – but this was now shortened to six months due to the intense nature of the Central Pacific campaign. Thus, after the Hollandia operation, six air groups were rotated home in the one month from the carriers and breathing space was given for regrouping, reequipping and reassignment.

More carriers were also now reporting for duty. *Essex* had been overhauled and was ready once again for action. The brand-new Essex-class 27,100-ton (standard) *Wasp* (CV-18) joined the fleet, as did the last of the new Independence-class 11,000-ton light carriers *San Jacinto* (CVL-30).

Mitscher already had four carriers per task group, but with so many new carriers now available, a new task group of three flattops was created. To blood the new carriers, and their new air groups and new officers, Mitscher decided on a live battle practice operation against Marcus and Wake Islands. He formed TG 58.6 under Rear Admiral Montgomery comprising *Essex*, *Wasp* and *San Jacinto*.

Montgomery's TG 58.6 departed Majuro on 14 May and divided into two as it approached Marcus. *San Jacinto* steamed to the north and west – searching for enemy picket boats, whilst *Essex* and *Wasp* attacked the island on the 20th. The aircraft encountered heavy AA fire that made bombing accuracy difficult and prevented the effective use of aircraft rockets, which needed the aircraft to make a long steady glide in towards the target.

All air groups from the three TG 58.6 carriers attacked installations on Wake on 24 May and the resulting damage to both Marcus and Wake was sufficient to isolate them from the subsequent Marianas operation. A new tactic was trialled, where each pilot was pre-briefed on his assigned target before take-off – it failed. Admiral Pownall, as ComAirPAc, concluded that each island target was unique, and selection would be left to tactical air commanders.

Towards the end of May 1944, the greatest battle of the Pacific since Midway was looming – the invasion of the largest island of the Northern Mariana Islands, Saipan, which Japan considered part of the last line of defence of the Japanese homeland.

With overwhelming numbers of carriers, planes, pilots and ships, TF 58 was capable of covering the landing at Saipan Island – as well as fighting the Japanese carrier-battleship fleet. Seven months of overwhelming aerial victories had welded it into the most powerful naval fighting force of its time.

Chapter 13

The Mariana and Palau Islands Campaign – Operation FORAGER, June–November 1944

In the campaigns of 1943 and those of the first half of 1944, the Allies had successfully captured the Solomon Islands, the Gilbert Islands, the Marshall Islands and the Papuan peninsula of New Guinea. The Japanese however still held the Philippines, the Caroline Islands, the Palau Islands and the Mariana Islands – and the islands of the Palau and Mariana archipelagos formed the principal strong points in a chain of islands that Japan's military regarded as its last line of defence to the east.

From an Allied perspective, the Palaus and Marianas represented important targets for several reasons:

1. Palau was a strategic Japanese barrier to deployment to the Philippines.
2. The Marianas afforded the Japanese land-based air cover and an air capability to strike at Allied operations.
3. Conversely, if the Marianas could be taken then they would give the Allies airfields from which the new US ultra-long-range Boeing B-29 Superfortress strategic heavy bomber could be deployed directly against the Japanese home islands.
4. Allied air assets and supplies could also be staged directly westwards from the Marianas as the Allied forces advanced.

Given the rate of strategic progress to date, the Joint Chiefs thought it now possible to speed up the original *Rainbow 5* timetable of pending operations. On 13 June 1944, the Joint Chiefs asked General Douglas MacArthur and Admiral Chester Nimitz for their opinions on:

1. Advancing scheduled target dates for operations against the Japanese stronghold of Formosa (known today as Taiwan).
2. Bypassing presently selected objectives prior to those operations against Formosa.
3. Bypassing other pre-selected objectives and choosing new ones – including striking at the Japanese home islands.

The two commanders subsequently produced two radically different strategies:

1. General Douglas MacArthur proposed the recapture of the Philippines, followed by the capture of Okinawa – thus allowing an attack on the Japanese homeland islands.
2. Admiral Chester Nimitz proposed a more direct strategy of bypassing the Philippines, but seizing Okinawa and Formosa as staging areas for direct attacks on the Japanese homeland islands. These would be followed by the future invasion of Japan's southernmost home islands.

Both strategies, for different reasons, called for the direct invasion of the small Palauan island of Peleliu, the powerful Japanese airfield and base that had been attacked earlier in March 1944 during Operation DESECRATE 1 and again on 29 April–1 May in the follow-up Operation DESECRATE 2.

In July 1944, President Franklin D. Roosevelt would travel to Pearl Harbor to meet both commanders personally. After hearing their competing proposals, he would elect to go with General MacArthur's strategy. But before General MacArthur could retake the Philippines, the Palau Islands, specifically the southern islands of Peleliu and Angaur and the potent air threat they posed, would be neutralised and the islands taken. The Japanese airfield on Peleliu could be turned into a powerful US airfield that could protect General MacArthur's right flank.

However, before Roosevelt travelled to Hawaii in July 1944 to decide which commander's plan to adopt, the existing pre-planned Mariana and Palau Islands campaign, code name Operation FORAGER, would continue. This operation, following the Gilbert and Marshall Islands campaign, was intended to neutralise Japanese bases in the Central

Pacific, support the Allied drive to retake the Philippines and provide bases for a strategic bombing campaign against the Japanese home islands. In Operation FORAGER, the Americans planned to assault the Marianas, island by island – and then take Palau, which lies some 800 miles distant from Guam and just over halfway between Guam and the Philippines, which are some 1,500 miles apart.

In June 1944, a month before General MacArthur's strategy to retake the Philippines would be approved, Operation FORAGER began – with Saipan being assaulted first, followed by Guam and then Tinian. Saipan was some 1,000 miles from the US forward base at Eniwetok atoll.

The Mariana Islands, also called the Marianas, are a crescent-shaped north–south archipelago of the summits of fifteen mostly dormant volcanic mountains rising out of the abyssal depths of the western North Pacific. They lie to the south south east of Japan, north of New Guinea and east of the Philippines. Saipan is the largest and most northerly of the Northern Mariana Islands with Tinian and Rota to its south and the US territory island of Guam furthest south.

The Northern Marianas had been administered by Japan under her League of Nations South Pacific Mandate of 1919, which granted her control of the Pacific Ocean islands that had been part of German New Guinea.

Guam, the large island near the very south of the Marianas, was separate from the Northern Marianas – it had been a US territory since the conclusion of the Spanish-American War in 1898. Japanese troops had invaded and seized Guam on 8 December 1941, shortly after the attack on Pearl Harbor – and during the Japanese occupation the indigenous people had been subjected to forced labour, separation of families, imprisonment, execution and internment in concentration camps. It was a brutal occupation.

Saipan is the largest island of the Northern Mariana Islands, and the second largest in the Mariana archipelago after Guam. Saipan's location, 120 miles north east of Guam at the north of the chain, made it a logical and crucial first target for the Allied operation. With Saipan in US hands, Guam and Tinian to its south would be cut off from support from the north, and from Japan itself.

Saipan was the Japanese Command Post for the Western Pacific and the centre of its island network of unsinkable aircraft carriers. With many airfields strung throughout the Marianas, Japan staged aircraft from the home islands, and the Bonin-Volcano islands to the north, through Saipan to all of its southern outposts such as Wake, Truk, New Guinea and the Palaus. IJN Fleet units used Saipan as a safe anchorage.

As part of the last line of defence of the Japanese homeland, it had been strongly fortified with coastal artillery batteries, shore defences, underground fortifications and an airstrip. Some 30,000 troops were stationed there by mid-1944.

Japanese air defence of the Western Pacific Area was the responsibility of their 1st Air Fleet, whose HQ was based in the Mariana island of Tinian. There were four major bases in the Marianas, at Guam, Tinian, Saipan and Rota. Two were located in the Carolines at Babelthuap in the Palaus and Yap, and one base at Iwo Jima in the Volcano Islands. In February 1944, all land-based aircraft had been withdrawn from the isolated outpost of Rabaul and there were by mid-1944 more than 1,600 aircraft based on these 7 islands, which could concentrate on any one point to repulse an Allied assault.[1]

If Japanese land-based air from this network of island airfields failed to beat off an Allied approach, then Japanese aircraft carriers would engage with their aircraft. US intelligence estimated that some 400 Japanese land-based aircraft were scattered throughout the Marianas and Palaus alone.[2]

Following the death of Commander-in-Chief of the Combined Fleet Admiral Koga on 31 March 1944, Admiral Soemu Toyoda was appointed in his place. The Japanese had created their 1st Mobile Fleet on 1 March 1944 – and by June 1944 it was formed from the long established 2nd Fleet and the more recent incarnation of the 3rd Fleet, which had been re-formed as an aircraft carrier task force in July 1942, immediately after the disastrous Battle of Midway. The 2nd Fleet was commanded by Vice Admiral Takeo Kurita and comprised mainly cruisers and destroyers. Vice Admiral Jisaburō Ozawa commanded the more powerful 3rd Fleet and had operational control of the combined 1st Mobile Fleet.

The 3rd Fleet now comprised 4 individual carrier divisions (CarDivs 1, 2, 3 and 4) that were modelled on the US task-group formation of 3 carriers. In total, there were 9 aircraft carriers that carried 450 planes in all and 2 old battleships converted to be half carriers.[3] The 3rd Fleet was escorted by a screen of 3rd BatDiv battleships, cruisers and destroyers. By this time, in June 1944, Japan lagged behind the USA in carrier production – they had only one new fleet carrier ready for combat, the 29,300-ton *Taihō*, which sailed with CarDiv 1 as Ozawa's flagship.

CarDiv 1 was commanded by Vice Admiral Jisaburō Ozawa and comprised the three carriers *Taihō*, *Shōkaku* and *Zuikaku*. *Taihō* had an armoured flight deck like British carriers and carried seventy-five aircraft. She bristled with modern AA weaponry aircraft.

Shōkaku and *Zuikaku* were veterans of the Battle of the Coral Sea, each carrying seventy-five aircraft. In total, the three carriers of CarDiv 1, *Taihō*, *Shōkaku* and *Zuikaku*, could launch 81 Zekes, 81 Yokosuka D4Y Judy dive-bombers and 54 Nakajima B6N Jill torpedo-bombers and 9 Judy reconnaissance aircraft.[4]

CarDiv 2 was commanded by Rear Admiral Takaji Jojima and comprised the three carriers *Jun'yō*, *Hiyō* and *Ryūhō*. *Jun'yō* and *Hiyō* were converted 24,150-ton Hiyō-class carriers: *Jun'yō* had originally been laid down as the passenger liner *Kashiwara Maru* whilst *Hiyō* had originally been laid down as the passenger liner *Izumo Maru*. The two Hiyō-class carriers were 720ft long and powered by six Kampon boilers and two shafts that gave them a speed of 25.5 knots. They each carried fifty-four planes. Joining them was the 700ft-long 13,360-ton light carrier *Ryūhō*, converted from the submarine tender *Taigei*, which could carry thirty-six planes. The three carriers of CarDiv 2 could field a combined striking force of 81 Zekes, 27 Aichi D3A Val dive-bombers, 27 B6N Jill attack-bombers and 9 D4Y Judy dive-bombers as scout planes.[5]

CarDiv 3 was commanded by Rear Admiral Sueo Obayashi and comprised three smaller flattops of the light carrier (CVL) type: the 674ft-long, 11,413-ton former sub-tender *Zuihō*, which carried thirty-six planes and could make 28 knots, and the new 28.9 knots, 11,190-ton, 632ft-long converted seaplane tenders *Chitose* and *Chiyoda*, each of which carried thirty planes. CarDiv 3 was intended to have fielded ninety aircraft for bombing operations only – but it was found that launching of heavily laden bombers was not possible from the short flight decks of these converted light carriers. The bombers were removed in favour of 63 lighter-armed Zeke fighter-bombers, 12 Nakajima B5N Kate torpedo-bombers and 6 Nakajima B6N Jill torpedo-bombers.[6]

CarDiv 4 comprised the converted First-World-War dreadnought-era Ise-class battleships *Ise* and *Hyūga*. Both these 29,980-ton battleships originally carried twelve 14in Type 41 guns in three pairs of dual-mount superfiring turrets. The first superfiring pair of turrets was situated forward of the superstructure, the second superfiring pair of turrets was amidships and the last pair of superfiring turrets was situated aft of the rear superstructure. These two battleships had been reconstructed and modernised in the 1920s and 1930s with their forward superstructure enlarged with multiple platforms added to their tripod foremast to create a pagoda mast. After the loss of the IJN large carriers during the Battle of Midway in mid-1942, both battleships were reconstructed with the two rear pairs of main after battery turrets being removed and a short flight deck constructed in their place. The flight deck provided the ability to operate an air group of twenty-two to twenty-four catapult-launched aircraft. The air group was intended to comprise twelve Yokosuka D4Y Judy dive-bombers and twelve Aichi E16A Paul reconnaissance aircraft. The flight deck however was so short that although the aircraft could be launched, they could not be recovered and had to land on a conventional carrier or land ashore. All these carriers had radar, although Japanese command doubted if the operators were proficient in its use as yet.

In May 1944, General MacArthur's forces moved north west up the New Guinea coast from Hollandia to assault the island of Wakde on 18 May. The island was declared captured on 20 May and Wakde airfield, which covered the whole island, was operational on 21 May. MacArthur could then assault Biak Island, 225 miles further west from Wakde, off West Papua, on 27 May. There 11,400 IJA troops were heavily dug in in a honeycomb fortress of caves and a fierce prolonged battle would develop.

Japan responded to MacArthur's advances west across New Guinea by sending aircraft and warships to strengthen their defences. Ozawa's 1st Mobile Fleet (comprising the 2nd and 3rd Fleet units) arrived at the Japanese Fleet anchorage of Tawi Tawi off Borneo on 13/14 May.

Japanese command had anticipated that the next main US attack would come from somewhere near the western Carolines or Palau and they had distributed 500 land-based aircraft between the Marianas and New Guinea on their unsinkable carriers. Admiral Kakuji Kakuda's 1st Air Fleet (land-based air) was however suffering heavy losses against Allied fighters during the Battle of Biak. With reinforcements of aircraft from Japan grounded by bad weather, the burden of repulsing the Allied New Guinea advance fell to Vice Admiral Jisaburō Ozawa and the 1st Mobile Fleet, which at this time comprised:

1. The 2nd Fleet units of 4th CruDiv, 5th CruDiv, 7th CruDiv, 2nd CruDesron.
2. The 3rd Fleet units of CarDivs 1, 2, 3 and 4 along with 3rd BatDiv, 10th CruDesron, the converted heavy aircraft cruiser *Mogami* and the 601st Naval Air Group.

Ozawa structured his battle line of four 3rd BatDiv battleships under the command of Vice Admiral Kurita, of the 2nd Fleet, deploying with the CarDiv 3 light carriers *Zuihō*, *Chitose* and *Chiyoda*. A fifth battleship accompanied the CarDiv 2 carriers *Jun'yō*, *Hiyō* and *Ryūhō*. In addition,

7 cruisers and 28 destroyers were spread across CarDivs 1, 2 and 3 – whose combined 9 carriers could field 450 aircraft.

Japanese carrier air capability had by mid-1944 been largely decimated. CarDiv 1 had lost most of its veteran pilots at Rabaul and in the Marshalls – and by May 1944, its replacement pilots had had less than five months' training. CarDiv 2 had some veterans who had escaped from Rabaul to Singapore in February. CarDiv 3 had only been organised after the Truk raid and had pilots with less than three months in the cockpit.

The land-based Japanese pilots, largely all trainees after the Truk raid in February 1944, were still on the whole raw and new to the cockpit. The average new Japanese pilot by now had about one-half of the training his predecessor had had just a year previously – whilst US pilots had at least 525 hours flying time before being assigned to a carrier. In terms of

USS *Essex* (CV-9), with a deck load of Curtiss SB2C-1C Helldiver bombers and Grumman TBF Avenger torpedo planes, turns in formation with other Task Force 58 ships, 27 May 1944, prior to the Marianas operation. Turning astern are USS *San Jacinto* (CVL-30) and USS *Wasp* (CV-18). (National Archives 80-G-373623)

fighter aircraft, the Mitsubishi A6M Zero was inferior in speed, armour and armament to the F6F Hellcat, introduced in 1943.

Aboard the 1st Mobile Fleet carriers at Tawi Tawi, pilots had resumed training in March, although their training was impeded as the airstrip had not been fully completed.

The overall lack of experience and training meant that Japanese 3rd Fleet carrier air groups lacked cohesion – and night and combat experience. The pilots were mostly green and not ready for battle. The 3rd Fleet carriers and their 2nd Fleet battleship escorts may have formed the largest Japanese naval fighting force of the war – but it was also the most undertrained and inexperienced.

Facing this Japanese threat was the US Fifth Fleet, which included the fifteen carriers of Task Force 58. For any surface action that required the battle line of battleships to be formed, the Fifth Fleet now had seven new state-of-the-art fast battleships.

(i) Battle of Saipan, 15 June–9 July 1944

With the landings on Saipan slated to begin on 15 June, the great question faced by the Americans was whether Japan would commit her fleet to defend the Marianas. US analysts believed that a major naval battle would develop – but planning for such an engagement would require a different strategy from that formulated for the Gilbert and Marshall Islands campaigns, where contact with the Japanese Fleet had been planned for – but was not really expected. Knowing that the Marianas formed a bastion of Japan's last line of defence, Admiral Nimitz expected that the Japanese would use every asset and tactic available. He was right, Japan would attempt to defend its precious Saipan base at all costs.

For the Mariana operation, Task Force 58 grew to comprise more than 600 vessels including 7 heavy fast carriers, 8 light fast carriers, 7 fast battleships, 3 heavy cruisers, 7 light cruisers and some 60 destroyers. The fleet organisation for the Mariana and Palau campaign was finalised as follows:

Commander-in-Chief US Fleet – Admiral E.J. King, CNO.
Commander-in-Chief Pacific Fleet – Admiral C.W. Nimitz, CINCPOA.
Commander Fifth Fleet – Admiral R.A. Spruance.
Commander Task Force 51 (CTF 51) (Amphibious Force) – Vice Admiral R.K. Turner.
Commander Task Force 58 – Vice Admiral M.A. Mitscher.
Chief of Staff – Captain A.A. Burke.

1. Task Group 58.1 – Commander Task Group (CTG 58.1) – Rear Admiral J.J. Clark:
   Hornet (CV-12) – Captain W.D. Sample, Air Group 2
   Yorktown (CV-10) – Captain R.E. Jennings, Air Group 1
   Belleau Wood (CVL-24) – Captain J. Perry, Air Group 24
   Bataan (CVL-29) – Captain V.H. Schaeffer, Air Group 50
2. Task Group 58.2 – Rear Admiral A.E. Montgomery (CTG 58.2):
   Bunker Hill (CV-17) – Captain T.P. Jeter, Air Group 8
   Wasp (CV-18) – Captain C.A.F. Sprague, Air Group 14
   Monterey (CVL-26) – Captain S.H. Ingersol, Air Group 28
   Cabot (CVL-28) – Captain S.J. Michael, Air Group 31
3. Task Group 58.3 – Rear Admiral J.W. Reeves Jr (CTG 58.3):
   Enterprise (CV-6) – Captain M.B. Gardner, Air Group 10
   Lexington (CV-16) – Captain E.W. Litch, Air Group 16
   San Jacinto (CVL-30) – Captain H.M. Martin, Air Group 51
   Princeton (CVL-23) – Captain W.H. Buraker, Air Group 27
4. Task Group 58.4 – Rear Admiral W.K. Harrill (CTG 58.4):
   Essex (CV-9) – Captain R.A. Ofstie, Air Group 15
   Langley (CVL-27) – Captain W.M. Dillon, Air Group 32
   Cowpens (CVL-25) – Captain H.W. Taylor, Air Group 25
5. Task Group 58.7 (Battle Line) – Vice Admiral W.W. Lee (ComBat-Pac) (CTG 58.7)

Before any landings in the Marianas, a heavy naval and air bombardment would soften up the enemy – delivered by a bombardment force comprising 8 escort carriers, 7 pre-war older battleships, 6 heavy cruisers, 5 light cruisers and a screen of destroyers. Two escort carriers attached to the service squadrons would carry replacement aircraft for those that would be lost. More than twenty-four submarines would screen the naval units and provide search and recovery of downed pilots.

Combat Air Patrols (CAP) would protect the surface ships during the operation – and also protect the invasion landing craft. CAP aircraft could be vectored to counter any threat by new ship radars that had recently been installed on the TF 58 carriers. These new radars scanned the vertical plane and were able to detect incoming enemy aircraft at ranges of up to 150 nautical miles. Task Force 58 fighter direction was coordinated from *Lexington* – assisted by a fighter director officer on each of the four task-group flagships. The amphibious command ships also carried fighter directors to protect the transports and landing craft.

Anti-submarine and search patrols by carrier aircraft guarded against Japanese submarines and surface ships. The destroyers of the screen also carried the latest sonar submarine-detection equipment. Thirty-seven Avenger torpedo-bombers were equipped with airborne radar that could see enemy ships up to 32 miles ahead.

Whilst CAP aircraft could and should detect enemy surface ships closing, if enemy naval units eluded them, search radars on most other US ships could scan as far as their antennae could see – to the horizon. This gave coverage out to about 30 miles for the old battleships of the amphibious force with their high top-hamper. This distance was just outside the range of enemy naval guns – the largest, the 18.1in (46cm) main battery guns of the super battleship *Yamato* had a maximum range of about 25 miles. The possibility therefore existed that enemy capital ships, having eluded the CAP aircraft, could suddenly appear over the horizon, close quickly and start shelling US naval units.

To protect the Saipan landings, long-range detection of enemy fleet movements would rest with the far-ranging US submarines. They however could only safely observe whilst submerged at periscope depth - and so their range of visibility to the horizon was short, just a few miles. At periscope depth, with such limited visibility, they could not ascertain the size and composition of an enemy naval force that could be spread out over a vast area. Shore-installed high-frequency radio direction finders (HF/DF) could pinpoint enemy transmissions – but they also could not determine the size and composition of the enemy.

Whilst the 'S' in the Douglas SBD Dauntless dive-bomber and Curtiss SB2C Helldiver stood for 'Scout', the SBDs and SB2Cs were being used by this time of the war more often for bombing missions than for scouting. These long-range patrol bombers, along with seaplanes and radar equipped carrier search planes, would be deployed to protect the fleet and the landings – but Navy patrol planes suffered from serious radio transmission difficulties and army bombers were poor for patrol duties because of the inexperience of their pilots in locating and accurately reporting enemy naval units in open water.

In the run-up to the Mariana and Palau campaign, ComAirPac equipped a number of the single-seat F6F Hellcat fighters for search duties – they had a combat radius of 340 nautical miles and a ferry range, the total range between take-off and landing, of some 1330 nautical miles.

By June 1944, Mitscher had only twenty-four night F6F-3N Hellcats and three night F4U-2 Corsairs to protect the task force. These were equipped with airborne radars, which used a rotating beam of radio waves that searched a conical area of 120 degrees dead ahead. These could detect aircraft up to 65 miles ahead – but they were not dependable.

All airborne radar could detect aircraft ahead, and generally were able to detect a single plane up to 5 miles ahead. Shipboard radar thus performed all the fleet's aircraft detection in mid-1944 and effective airborne early warning radar still lay some way away in the future.

Task Force 58 carried a total of 448 Hellcat day-fighters, 27 Hellcat and Corsair night-fighters, 174 Curtiss SB2C Helldiver bombers, 59 Dauntless SBD dive-bombers and 193 TBF and TBM Avenger torpedo-bombers. (Whilst Avengers made by Grumman were designated TBF, the Avengers made by General Motors were designated TBM.) In addition, the escort carriers carried some 80 TBM Avengers and 110 FM Wildcat fighters, improved versions of the earlier F4F Wildcat.

As the opening moves of the invasion of Saipan began, the ninety-three ships of Task Force 58 departed Majuro on 6 June 1944 bound for the Marianas – refuelling from ServRon 10 oilers two days later, on 8 June. The task force steamed generally north west with the individual task groups holding position 12–15 miles from each other.

A pre-dawn air strike had been scheduled for 12 June – but progress of the task force was so good that Mitscher felt he could get in a strike on the afternoon of 11 June, one day early, to avoid a certain all-out attack during the night by Japanese air as the task force approached and was likely spotted. By carrying out an afternoon strike, this would break the pattern established at Truk and Palau of attacks beginning at dawn. Admiral Spruance, commanding the fleet aboard the cruiser *Indianapolis*, accepted Mitscher's reasoning and gave the go-ahead.

As Task Force 58 closed on the Marianas, Mitscher hastily reconfigured his forces for the early strike. The fighters were readied for the afternoon strike whilst bombing strikes were rescheduled for early the following morning, 12 June.

Meanwhile, on 10 June, Admiral Soemu Toyoda, Commander-in-Chief of the IJN Combined Fleet initiated Operation KON, the third attempt to relieve Biak far to the south on the northern coast of Papua, just to the north west of New Guinea. The BatDiv 1 super battleships *Yamato* and *Musashi*, alongside DesRon 2's light cruiser *Noshiro* and the destroyers *Okinami* and *Shimakaze* under the command of Vice Admiral Matome Ugaki, were detached from the Mobile Fleet and moved east from their Tawi Tawi anchorage in the southern Philippines, across the Celebes Sea to the Moluccas, the famous Spice Islands that lie to the west of Papua New Guinea. From here an attack to relieve Japanese forces at Biak would be made against MacArthur's lighter naval units and shipping.

At 1300 on 11 June, some 190 miles east of Guam, more than 200 Hellcat fighters were launched from the US carriers to fly fighter sweeps over Guam, Saipan, Rota and Tinian Islands – with 10 aircraft carrying spare life rafts for any downed aviators. The Japanese were taken completely by surprise, and the US fighters quickly gained air supremacy.

Rear Admiral Jocko Clark's TG 58.1 Hellcats strafed Guam and Rota, encountering heavy land-based AA fire before they were then engaged by some thirty Japanese fighters. But such was the supremacy of the Hellcats, and their battle-hardened pilots, that all thirty Japanese fighters were shot down.

Above Tinian, TG 58.2 Hellcats from *Monterey* pounced on a landing circle of Betty bombers, which they quickly shot up.

On Saipan, clouds of smoke billowed from fires deliberately lit by the Japanese to obscure ground installations. However, by dropping to 500ft, camera-equipped Hellcats still got good photographs of Japanese fortifications and installations. Hellcats cratered and strafed the Saipan airfields – although the fighter sweep met continued heavy AA fire, the heaviest to date.

US fighters claimed 150 enemy aircraft destroyed for the day across the islands, most of them caught on the ground, parked up on airfield tarmac. In return, eleven Hellcats were shot down, with eight pilots lost and three pilots rescued. For these losses, the Task Force 58 fast carriers had swept the Marianas clear of Japanese aircraft – there would be no enemy night attack on the carrier task force.

Meanwhile, aboard Task Force 58, with the ground assault on Saipan set for 15 June, Mitscher's carrier aircraft continued to pound the Marianas on the three days following the fighter sweep on the afternoon of 11 June. Mitscher wanted to conserve his bombs for the expected naval battle and so the Avengers used rockets against land targets. The heavy AA fire encountered was particularly daunting for the rocket-carrying Avengers, which required a slow and low approach to aim and launch their rockets, making them more susceptible to ground AA fire. On 13 June, the popular skipper of *Lexington*'s Torpedo 16, Commander Robert H. Isely, was shot down during such a rocket attack. This led to objections from Avenger pilots to the rocket attacks and led to the rockets subsequently being moved to fighters. The VT-16 Action Report stated: 'the rocket is a weapon of dubious merits penalising an airplane already vulnerable to the attacks demanded of it'.

Marianas Operation, 13 June 1944. An F6F Hellcat is ready for launch aboard USS *Lexington* (CV-16). USS *North Carolina* and two other TG 58.7 battleships are in the distance. (National Archives 80-G-236892)

On 12 and 13 June, a Japanese convoy was attacked – with ten transports vessels and four small escort vessels sunk. Another convoy was located by a *Yorktown* SBD scout-bomber, well to the east of Guam, on the 12th. Jocko Clark (CTG 58.1) despatched twenty Hellcats carrying bombs, guided by two radar-equipped night-fighters, to hit the convoy. Although the convoy was located, little damage was inflicted, the Hellcat fighter pilots having little experience in bombing shipping. Meanwhile, TG 58.1 aircraft from *Hornet* dropped warning leaflets to the Chamorro natives on Guam.

The naval bombardment of Saipan began on 13 June 1944 to soften up land targets. Vice Admiral 'Ching' Lee's seven TG 58.7 fast battleships opened fire with their main battery big guns from a distance of 10,000yd (more than 5 miles), staying well offshore to avoid near shore minefields. The 16in guns of the famous battleships *Washington* (BB-56), *North Carolina* (BB-55), *Iowa* (BB-61), *New Jersey* (BB-62), *South Dakota* (BB-57), *Alabama* (BB-60) and *Indiana* (BB-58) all went into action, along with the 8in guns of the heavy cruisers *Wichita*, *Minneapolis*, *New Orleans* and

San Francisco and the smaller batteries of some thirteen destroyers of the screen.

The main landing support bombardment force, under the command of Rear Admiral Jesse B. Oldendorf, in his flagship, the Northampton-class cruiser *Louisville* (CA-28), arrived the following day, 14 June. His 7 older battleships, 6 heavy cruisers, 5 light cruisers and 26 destroyers commenced a naval bombardment that continued throughout the landings on 15 June – with devastating accuracy. Their gunners had trained with Marine Corps fire-control experts at the shore bombardment range in Hawaii and had more experience and training in shore bombardment than the fast battleships, which were more suited to naval engagements. In all, the combined 14 battleships fired some 165,000 shells, destroying land targets, conducting counter-battery missions, destroying AA gun emplacements and burning all unburnt cane fields that would offer the enemy cover. The bombardment however failed to degrade the entrenched enemy fortifications significantly. TF 58 aircraft would fly continuous fighter sweep and CAP and anti-submarine patrols from DOG-DAY-MINUS-ONE.

Admiral Kakuda's 1st Air Fleet (land-based planes) had already taken heavy losses at the Battle of Biak – and after some 150 Japanese land-based aircraft were destroyed during the TF 58 fighter sweeps of Saipan, Tinian and Guam on 11 June, there were very few Japanese planes left to defend the Marianas. When the US invasion of the Marianas began, Operation KON was postponed on 12 June and *Yamato*, *Musashi* and escorts were joined by the heavy cruisers *Haguro* and *Myōkō* and the destroyer *Asagumo*. The powerful force departed Batjan on 13 June to rendezvous with the Mobile Fleet in the Philippine Sea. The battle for the Marianas was beginning to develop.

Meanwhile, intercepted Japanese radio signals, decoded from an aviation code book seized during the Hollandia operation, had revealed to Spruance that the Japanese were staging aircraft from the Japanese home islands into the Bonin and Volcano Islands to the north (particularly Iwo Jima and Chichi Jima), for an imminent attack on the US Saipan invasion forces. Spruance tasked Mitscher (CTF 58) to send two fast-carrier task groups north to eliminate that threat of air attack. The carrier air strikes were to take place on 16–17 June and the detached task groups were then to re-join Task Force 58 immediately, before any possible naval battle could take place. As yet completely unaware of any Japanese sortie from Tawi Tawi, if any such sortie were to materialise, Spruance would recall the two detached task groups – in time to have his whole task force united to face the enemy. Mitscher selected Rear Admirals J.J. (Jocko) Clark CTG 58.1 and W.K. Harrill CTG 58.4 to go north.

Task Groups 58.1 and 58.4 rendezvoused north of the Marianas on 14 June. That night however Admiral Spruance received his first intelligence of the movement of the Japanese Mobile Fleet from Tawi Tawi. He shrewdly calculated that battle could not be joined before 17 June – and subsequent intelligence updates put the possibility of battle back to the morning of 18 June. He accordingly ordered Clark and Harrill to trim their air strikes to one day, 16 June – and then move to rendezvous off the Marianas with the remainder of Task Force 58 on the morning of 18 June, in time for the anticipated battle.

With characteristic aggression, on receiving these orders, Clark charged north at full speed to get in the attack on the 15th – giving him the two days, not one, for the strikes he felt he needed. When his TG 58.1 arrived on station 135 miles off Iwo Jima on the afternoon of the 15th, he launched his strike aircraft in heavy weather – the fighters quickly sweeping the skies above Iwo Jima, Chichi Jima and Haha Jima of some twenty-four Zekes before bombing shipping and land installations to great effect. Intending to continue the raid for a second day on 16 June, that night Clark put up two night-fighters over Chichi Jima to keep Japanese night planes from taking off and to keep them grounded at dawn so that a dawn fighter sweep would not be required.

The weather continued to worsen overnight and by the morning of 16 June, it became impossible to launch or retrieve aircraft from the pitching decks of the US carriers. The weather however improved sufficiently in the afternoon to allow three more strikes to take place. The seven fast carriers of the two task groups then turned to speed south through the night to re-join Mitscher and Task Force 58. Spruance's northern flank was secure for the time being.

The US invasion fleet transport vessels moved into place off Saipan just after 0500 on 15 June – and the pre-invasion naval bombardment commenced at 0530. As the invasion troops and their assets afloat readied to begin the attack, a diversionary force of Marines carried out a dummy landing at the large village of Garapan, on Saipan's west coast – moving to within 5,000yd of the shore.

For the initial main landing, more than 300 amphibious LVTs carrying some 8,000 Marines moved forward from their mother ships at 0700. As this was happening, the naval big-gun bombardment of Saipan paused briefly between 0700 and 0730 to allow for an air strike. Once completed, the big guns began firing again. By 0900 the Marines were ashore and engaging the enemy on the west coast of Saipan.

Careful Japanese artillery preparation of the battlefield offshore, by placing range flags in the lagoon, allowed the Japanese to hit and destroy twenty inbound amphibious tanks. On the shore, strategically placed barbed wire, artillery and machine-gun emplacements and trenches inflicted a heavy toll on the Marines. But despite this, by nightfall, the 2nd and 4th Marines had a 6-mile-wide beachhead established that stretched inshore for half a mile. The Japanese counter-attacked at night – but were fought back with heavy losses

Close air support for the assault troops was provided by the Commander Support Aircraft who had a team of fifteen officers and forty-six men afloat – and a smaller air support unit ashore after 15 June. They coordinated requests for air support missions from forty-one air liaison parties, each of which comprised one officer and five men per battalion and regiment.

There was only one radio circuit available for radio transmissions back to the amphibious command ship *Rocky Mount* (AGC-3), the 'support air request net'. Nevertheless, despite difficulties with liaison and control, close air support combined excellently with the precision shore-bombardment gunnery of Oldendorf's older battleships to lay down an excellent barrage. The three-and-a-half days of pre-invasion bombardment was an unprecedented amount of heavy support for the Marines. Japanese records narrate that all the main body of Japanese defenders could do was watch helplessly as they were pummelled.

That night, 15 June, a Japanese torpedo-plane attack from Yap on the task force was successfully fought off by carrier night-fighters and shipborne AA fire.

Ashore, after repelling Japanese night counter-attacks, the Marines pushed inland the next day, 16 June. Japanese resistance to the ground troops was tenacious, forcing General Holland Smith to commit his reserve that had been held offshore, the 27th Infantry Division, to join the two assault Marine divisions and begin pushing towards Aslito airfield. This reserve had been intended to assault Guam on the 18th. In light of these developments, Admiral Nimitz now postponed that operation.

The Japanese continued their tactic of counter-attacking after dark on the two following nights, pushing the US Army troops back and forcing them to abandon the airfield. The Japanese would however finally give up Aslito airfield on 18 June.

In all, some 71,000 US troops of V Amphibious Corps, comprising the 2nd and 4th Marine Divisions and the 27th Infantry Division landed on Saipan, meeting opposition from more than 30,000 well-dug-in Japanese troops. The presence of the Fifth Fleet off the Marianas prevented Japanese re-enforcement troop convoys from arriving after 15 June.

From the Japanese perspective, the Mariana Islands group, including Guam, Tinian and Saipan, formed part of their inner circle of defence and was of critical importance. Japanese land-based fighters and bomber aircraft on these islands controlled the sea lanes to Japan and protected the Japanese home islands. The Japanese knew that if the Marianas came under Allied control, US strategic bombers would be in range of the Japanese home islands. The Pacific War had reached another crucial juncture – of such importance that the IJN decided that the time had finally come for the much sought after *Kantai Kessen* – the *decisive battle*. If successful, the battle would at a stroke vindicate Japan's pre-war naval doctrine derived from Alfred Thayer Mahan's pivotal book, *Influence of Sea Power Upon History, 1660–1783*. It would change the course of the war.

As furious bitter fighting raged ashore on Saipan, Admiral Soemu Toyoda, Commander-in-Chief of the IJN Combined Fleet, commenced Operation A-GO, the Japanese tactical plan to deal with a US attack on the Marianas. More than 1,700 planes had been gathered at shore bases in Singapore, the Dutch East Indies, the Philippines and New Guinea.

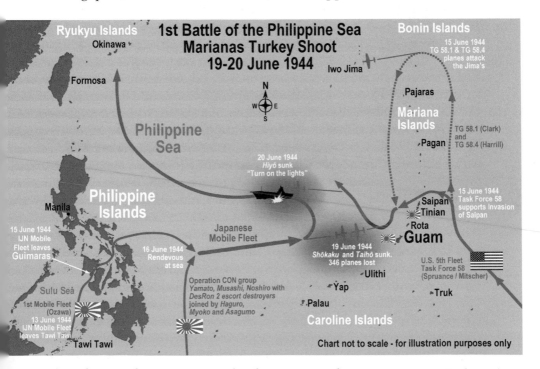

Chart showing the First Battle of the Philippine Sea, the 'Great Marianas Turkey Shoot'. (Author)

There were 500 land-based aircraft already available based on Tinian, Guam and Saipan. Toyoda planned to concentrate large numbers of these aircraft with the carriers, battleships, cruisers and destroyers of the 1st Mobile Fleet.

In the opening phase of the hoped-for decisive battle, land-based air would attack the US naval force and degrade it so badly that in the second phase, the decisive naval battle, the Japanese Mobile Fleet would be victorious.

Operation A-GO involved launching a large-scale fleet attack on US naval forces in the Marianas to change the course of the war. Toyoda was committing nearly all of the IJN's serviceable warships of the 1st Mobile Fleet.

The First Battle of the Philippine Sea, involving 24 aircraft carriers and a combined 1,350 carrier aircraft, was only days away. It would be the last of five great carrier versus carrier battles – and the greatest carrier battle in history. It would be an epic confrontation and indeed would be a decisive battle, but not the decisive battle Japan hoped for. Japan's ability to fight large-scale carrier operations would be virtually eliminated.

(ii) First Battle of the Philippine Sea, 19–20 June 1944

'Great Marianas Turkey Shoot'
Japan had a number of possible advantages for the coming battle. Though outnumbered in ships and carrier-based aircraft, in Operation A-GO, Vice Admiral Jisaburō Ozawa, Commander-in-Chief of the IJN 1st Mobile Fleet, could supplement his carrier air power with land-based aircraft from airbases such as Guam and Saipan. The Japanese aircraft had superior range, which allowed them to engage the US carriers whilst their own carriers remained beyond the range of US aircraft. With island airbases scattered through their Pacific holdings, Ozawa hoped to launch his carrier planes from great range. They would attack the US naval units and then would land on nearby airfields, from where they could shuttle back towards the carriers and attack US ships on the return flight. The Japanese Fleet might be able to hit the US Fleet – without US aircraft being able to strike back at the Japanese ships.

Operation A-GO had been planned some time previously and had originally envisaged luring the US naval forces to a location favourable to the Japanese, where land-based air would be available, such as the Palaus or the western Carolines, where battle would be joined.

Little attempt would be made to conceal the movement of a naval force commanded by Ozawa himself, which would act as the bait – it had to be spotted if the Americans were to bite. It seems however that the original intention of luring the US Fleet to a specific spot was now abandoned and that a simple full-scale naval battle was now envisaged.

The Japanese 1st Mobile Fleet at this point comprised 5 fleet carriers, 4 light carriers, 5 battleships, 11 heavy cruisers, 2 light cruisers, 31 destroyers, 24 submarines and 6 oilers. Some 450 carrier aircraft and 300 land-based aircraft were immediately available. Ozawa would command the 1st Mobile Fleet from his newly commissioned flagship, the carrier *Taihō*, which had extensive command facilities, reinforced torpedo blisters, a large air group and was the first Japanese carrier to be fitted with an armoured flight deck like the British carriers that could withstand bomb hits with minimal damage.

The US Fifth Fleet fielded 7 fleet carriers, 8 light carriers, 7 battleships, 8 heavy cruisers, 13 light cruisers, 68 destroyers and 28 submarines. The Task Force 58 carriers carried some 900 aircraft.

On the morning of 13 June, Ozawa's 1st Mobile Fleet sortied from Tawi Tawi (in the southern Philippines) for passage north to a stop over at Guimaras, a small island adjacent to the much larger Panay Island at the north east of the Sulu Sea, the sea that is encircled by the Philippine Islands. The Mobile Fleet arrived at Guimaras on 14 June and refuelling from oilers began. That afternoon, the alert for Operation A-GO was issued. The US landings on Saipan began on 15 June – whilst Clark's TG 58.1 and Harrill's TG 58.4 were far to the north, closing on the Jimas.

At 0800 on 15 June, the Mobile Fleet began to depart Guimaras, heading east towards the Visayan Sea. From there, the Mobile Fleet would rendezvous on 16 June in the open expanses of the western part of the Philippine Sea, with the *Yamato* group, which was en route from the Moluccas after their aborted sortie towards Biak off New Guinea. At 1000, elements of Ozawa's force were spotted by the US submarine *Redfin* (SS-272) and reported back.

By 1730, the CarDiv 1 carriers *Taihō*, *Shōkaku* and *Zuikaku* with their screen of battleships, cruisers and destroyers had crossed the Visayan Sea eastwards and were passing through the San Bernardino Strait between the large Philippine islands of Luzon to the north and Samar to the south. The strait opens eastwards into the Philippine Sea – Saipan lay almost 1,500 nautical miles further east across the Philippine Sea.

Just after 1800, the US submarine *Flying Fish* (SS-229) sighted the Japanese carrier and battleship force steaming out of the San Bernardino Strait into the Philippine Sea. US submarines were under instructions to report sightings of enemy ships before attacking, so *Flying Fish* waited until nightfall before surfacing to radio its report.

An hour after *Flying Fish* sighted the Japanese carrier and battleship force at the San Bernardino Strait, and several hundred miles to the south, the US submarine *Seahorse* (SS-304) sighted a Japanese battleship and cruiser (the *Yamato* group) to the south, 200 miles east of Mindanao.

Armed with the two submarine sightings, of the Mobile Fleet to the north and the *Yamato* group to the south, Spruance at first believed that the Japanese were laying a trap using divided forces – as had been their naval tradition from the Battle of Tsushima in 1905 until the Battle of Midway in 1942.[7] He was unaware that the two Japanese naval forces were in fact converging for a rendezvous in the Philippine Sea – and a combined action against the US forces. Task Force 58 was ordered to move west of Saipan into the Philippine Sea to intercept. The much-anticipated battle was now imminent.

The next day, 16 June, Spruance boarded the amphibious command ship *Rocky Mount* for a conference with his amphibious commander Kelly Turner and aides to work out how best to protect the fleet and the beachhead on Saipan from any attack by Japanese Fleet units. They determined to implement three changes:

1. Task Force 58 would be reinforced by 5 heavy cruisers, 3 light cruisers and 21 destroyers from Kelly Turner's fire-support force. Once this had been completed, the strengthened Task Force 58 would steam westwards in search of the enemy.
2. To guard against a possible flank attack by the southern *Yamato* force of battleships, the seven fire-support old battleships and three cruisers would form their own battle line 25 miles west of Saipan.
3. In the darkness of the night of 17 June, all transport vessels would retire 200 miles to the east of Saipan, well beyond the range of air or surface attack. They would remain there until after the battle. The eight escort carriers and a screen of destroyers would remain off Saipan until after the battle – in support of the forces already ashore.

Spruance by now believed that a carrier battle similar to Midway was developing and he designated the Japanese carriers as the primary target for his own carrier bombers.[8] He was advised that the Japanese carriers could possibly remain at a distance of 600 miles, outwith the range of Mitscher's planes – and shuttle their aircraft to Guam. This would allow them to attack Task Force 58 both inbound and outbound.

On the afternoon of 16 June, Vice Admiral Ugaki's returning Operation KON task force of *Yamato, Musashi* and escorts successfully rendezvoused with the Mobile Fleet in the Philippine Sea. The Mobile Fleet units commenced refuelling from the 1st Supply Force oilers *Hayusui Maru, Nichiei Maru, Kokuyo Maru* and *Seiyo Maru.* Refuelling of the main units was completed by 2000 on 17 June. The oilers then departed the area for a designated standby point at 14-40N, 134-20E.

On the night of 16/17 June, Mitscher ordered the two task groups, 58.1 and 58.4, returning south towards Saipan after hitting the Jimas, to alter course and search to the south west, towards the Philippines. If there was no contact, they were then to move to their designated rendezvous point with the rest of TF 58 as arranged, on the morning of the 18th.[9]

After consulting with Nimitz at Pacific Fleet HQ in Hawaii, Spruance ordered Task Force 58 to reform and move west of Saipan into the Philippine Sea – with orders that when the carriers rendezvoused to reform TF 58, Vice Admiral 'Ching' Lee, in command of the fast battleships of TG 58.7 would form his battle line 15 miles ahead of the carrier task groups with orders to 'destroy enemy fleet either by fleet action if the enemy elects to fight or by sinking slowed or crippled ships if enemy retreats'. Lee would be in formation and ready to fight when battle was joined. Spruance, true to form in allowing his subordinates control, said: 'I shall issue general directives (only) when necessary . . .'.[10] Lee would have tactical command of his battlewagons just as Mitscher would have command of his carriers. The older battleships, cruisers and escort CVE carrier groups of Task Force 52 were ordered to remain near Saipan to protect the land invasion fleet and provide air support for the beachhead and troops ashore.

In the US task force, on the morning of 17 June, as the Task Groups 58.2 and 58.3 off Saipan turned all air support at Saipan to the 'jeep' CVE escort carriers, Clark and Harrill's distant south-west-bound Task Groups 58.1 and 58.4 were launching search planes to the extreme range of 350 miles out – seeking Ozawa's ships. Nothing was spotted and the two task groups moved back south eastwards towards their rendezvous with the rest of Task Force 58. By midday on 17 June, when Spruance issued his battle plan, he left no doubt about his intentions: 'Actions against the enemy must be pushed vigorously by all hands to ensure complete destruction of his fleet.' Mitscher advised Reeves and Montgomery, commanders of TG 58.2 and 58.3, off Saipan that the attack was likely coming from the west.

During the night of 17/18 June, the US submarine *Cavalla* (SS-244), on her maiden patrol and en route to her station in the eastern Philippines, identified a radar contact as a large enemy carrier task force coming in from the west and advancing in the Philippine Sea. *Cavalla* surfaced at 2245 on 17 June and transmitted the contact report to Commander Submarines Pacific and COMINCH (Nimitz) before tracking the force for several hours, relaying reports to TF 58.

At daybreak on 18 June, Admiral Spruance informed Mitscher and Lee: 'In my opinion the main attack will come from the west but might be diverted to come from the southwest.'[11] He was unconcerned about the northern flank now as this was well covered by Clark and Harrill's returning Task Groups 58.1 and 58.4 and reported to be quiet.

Clark and Harrill's task groups rendezvoused with Mitscher on the morning of the 18th and the reformed Task Force 58 began to move west, launching search aircraft to probe the perimeter. Most believed that the task force would press westward during the day, to locate the main body of the Japanese Fleet and Ozawa's fleet carriers before sunset – thus allowing 'Ching' Lee's battleships to close for a radar-guided night gunnery duel. During the morning Mitscher asked Lee: 'Do you desire night engagement? . . . Otherwise we should retire to the eastward tonight.' Lee to almost universal surprise replied: 'Do not, repeat not, believe we should seek night engagement.' He told Mitscher: 'Possible advantages of radar more than offset by difficulties of communications and lack of training in fleet tactics at night.' Lee strongly opposed a night surface action – he had personally experienced the confused night action off Guadalcanal in November 1942 and believed his crews were not adequately trained for it. He would however 'press pursuit of damaged or fleeing enemy . . . at any time'.[12]

Spruance accepted Lee's decision and agreed to a night retirement towards Saipan, much to the bewilderment of the aviators in the task force who felt that Spruance was throwing away the tremendous advantages of surprise and aggressiveness.[13] Spruance however was guarding against a two-prong attack from different directions by the two Japanese naval groups.

Between noon and nightfall that day, 18 June, as a result of constant changes in the general south west heading to launch and retrieve search aircraft, TF 58 had only made 115 miles to westward. When no further intelligence reports on the whereabouts of either of the Japanese naval forces was received, at 2030 Spruance turned TF 58 to head eastward, retiring back towards Saipan.

Saipan operation, June 1944. A Japanese twin-engine plane is shot down while attacking TG 52.11 escort carriers off Saipan, 18 June 1944. Seen from USS *Kitkun Bay*. TBM-1C planes are on deck. (National Archives 80-G-239462)

At about 2200, a radio direction report was received pinpointing a Japanese radio transmission from a point some 350 miles to the west. The intercepted radio transmission was an apparent despatch from Ozawa to his land-based air forces on Guam. Although apparently corroborating the fact that the Japanese force was approaching from the west, the Japanese were known to send a single vessel to break radio silence as a deception and mislead their enemy as to the location of their forces. Was it a ruse?

Mitscher enthusiastically received this 2200 report, which apparently gave the enemy's position. If TF 58 reversed course to the west at 0130, in the early hours of 19 June, it would arrive just 200 miles from the enemy force at 0500, the optimum distance and time for launching a maximum carrier strike against the Japanese units. At 2325, he had Spruance's flagship *Indianapolis* called by voice radio: 'propose coming to course 270° at 0130 in order to commence treatment at 0500. Advise.'[14] Aboard *Indianapolis*, Spruance conferred with his subordinates and advisors, poring over a large chart of the Philippine Sea. He balanced the position as he knew it, pondering the various permutations of how the battle could develop, assessing the intelligence reports including a concerning message from Admiral Lockwood to the submarine *Stingray* (SS-186) asking for amplification of a radio message that had apparently been jammed by the Japanese. *Stingray* was 175 miles east south east of the radio direction contact and this suggested to Spruance that *Stingray* had perhaps located a Japanese southern force and was having difficulty transmitting its report. He feared an end run around the Saipan shipping by a Japanese naval force.

Just after midnight, at 0038 on 19 June, Spruance replied to Mitscher: 'Change proposed in your . . . message does not appear advisable. Believe indication given by *Stingray* more accurate than that contained in [CINCPAC radio bearing]. If that is so, continuation as at present seems preferable. End run by other fast ones [carriers, battleships] remains a possibility and must not be overlooked.'[15] At 0105, Spruance was advised that the submarine *Finback* (SS-230) had seen searchlights 5 hours before at a point north east of the recent radio bearing report. This perhaps indicated a third possible enemy force and strengthened Spruance's resolve to head eastward.

Spruance, a non-aviator admiral, had adopted formalist tactics of caution and no risk – particularly in the absence of reliable intelligence. He was under orders from Nimitz that protection of the Saipan invasion fleet was the primary mission of Task Force 58. Spruance was concerned that the Japanese might attempt to lure his main force away from the Marianas with a diversionary force as they then sent in an attack force to destroy the landing fleet. Locating and destroying the Japanese Fleet was not his primary mission – he was unwilling to allow the main Pacific Fleet strike force of Task Force 58 to be drawn westward, away from Saipan, and the vulnerable amphibious forces there ashore.

The aviators such as Mitscher and his staff were surprised by the decision, but Mitscher accepted the decision without comment. They believed that their airmen and aircraft were much superior to the Japanese by this point of the war and that it was not a case of winning or losing a battle, more of how well they could win. For Spruance however there were no doubt echoes of the First World War – when Churchill had stated that Admiral Jellicoe, in charge of the British Grand Fleet, was the only man who could lose the war in an afternoon, by making such a severe mistake that the British Fleet could be annihilated in battle and lose control of the seas.

Far to the west, aboard his flagship *Taihō*, Vice Admiral Ozawa had anticipated Spruance's likely caution – rightly concluding that Spruance would keep his forces within 100 miles of Saipan. Accurate scouting reports from his long-range reconnaissance aircraft had confirmed the general position of TF 58. At 1520, a search plane from *Shōkaku* had reported an enemy task force 380 miles from Yap Island. More contact reports were received at 1600 – but it was too late in the day for Ozawa to launch a strike. He would wait until the following morning to launch CarDiv 1's striking force, pending further clarification of the tactical position. The intelligence reports he was receiving were superior to the intelligence Spruance was getting at this point.

At 2023 on 18 June, making preparations for the expected contact the next day, he radioed Admiral Kakuda on Guam, commanding the 1st Air Fleet, which included all land-based naval aircraft located in the Philippines, to be ready to commence the decisive battle just after dawn. This was the radio transmission pinpointed by CINCPAC radio direction finders and passed to Spruance at about 2200.

At 2100, Ozawa divided the Mobile Fleet into two forces, A and B. He ordered the three small light carriers of Rear Admiral Obayashi (ComCarDiv 3) and Vice Admiral Kurita's battle force of battleships, cruisers and destroyers to form a vanguard Force C – under Kurita's command from the heavy cruiser *Atago*.

Force C comprised:

1. The three light carriers of CarDiv 3, *Chitose*, *Chiyoda* and *Zuihō*.
2. The two super battleships of the 1st Battle Squadron (BatDiv 1), *Yamato* and *Musashi*.
3. The two older battleships of BatDiv3, *Kongō* and *Haruna*.
4. The CruDiv 4 heavy cruisers *Chōkai*, *Maya* and *Takao*.
5. The CruDiv 7 heavy cruisers *Kumano*, *Suzuya*, *Tone* and *Chikuma*.
6. The DesRon 2 light cruiser *Noshiro*.
7. DesDiv 31 destroyers *Asashimo*, *Kishinami* and *Okinami*.
8. DesDiv 32 destroyers *Fujinami*, the super destroyer *Shimakaze* (41 knots and 15 torpedo tubes) and *Hamakaze*.

The CarDiv 3 three light carriers *Chitose*, *Chiyoda* and *Zuihō* each carried an air unit of 21 A6M Zekes, 3 Nakajima B6N Jill torpedo-bombers and 6 Nakajima B5N Kate torpedo-bombers. In total CarDiv 3 could field

63 Zeke fighters, 9 B6N Jill torpedo-bombers and 18 B5N Kate torpedo-bombers.

The vanguard Force C would steam 100 miles ahead of the large Mobile Fleet carriers in the two forces A and B.

Force A, under Ozawa's command, comprised:

1. CarDiv 1 fleet carriers:
   Taihō
   Shōkaku
   Zuikaku
   With their air units comprising in total:
   79 Mitsubishi A6M Zeke fighters
   70 Yokosuka D4Y Judy dive-bombers
   7 Aichi D3A Val dive-bombers
   51 Nakajima B6N Jill torpedo-bombers
2. The two heavy cruisers of CruDiv 5 under Rear Admiral Shintaro Hashimoto: *Myōkō* (10 x 8in guns)
   Haguro (10 x 7.9in guns)
3. The light cruiser *Yahagi*
4. The nine destroyers:
   Asagumo
   Isokaze
   Tanikaze
   Urakaze
   Akizuki
   Hatsuzuki
   Wakatsuki
   Shimotsuki
   Minazuki

Force B – Rear Admiral Takaji Joshima, comprised:

1. CarDiv 2 converted carriers:
   Jun'yō
   Hiyō
   and the light carrier *Ryūhō*
   With their air units comprising:
   81 A6M Zeke fighters
   27 Yokosuka D4Y Judy dive-bombers
   9 Aichi D3A Val dive-bombers
   18 Nakajima B6N Jill torpedo-bombers

2. The battleship *Nagato* (8 x 16in main battery guns).
3. The heavy cruiser *Mogami* (15 x 6in guns)
4. The nine destroyers:
   Michishio
   Yamagumo
   Nowaki
   Hamakaze
   Hayashimo
   Akishimo
   Shiratsuyu
   Shigure
   Samidare
   Harusame

The Mobile Fleet forces included 24 submarines and refuelling was provided by the1st Supply Force of 4 oilers and 4 destroyers and the 2nd Supply Force of 2 oilers and 2 destroyers.

Ozawa hoped that Kurita's vanguard Force C, containing four battleships and five cruisers, would divert the Americans from the carriers of his A and B Forces. Force C steamed out about 100 miles ahead of the rest of the Mobile Fleet – due east into the Philippine Sea, headed for Saipan. Ozawa was gambling that Spruance's caution would keep his fast-carrier task force within 100 miles of Saipan.

The Japanese plan of battle envisaged that at dawn on 19 June, the vanguard Force C would be 280 miles distant from Task Force 58, and the main Mobile Fleet body of Forces A and B, following on behind, would be 400 miles distant. Ozawa would then launch his planes from beyond the range of Mitscher's planes, attack TF 58 and then shuttle them to Guam. Should Mitscher's aircraft find Kurita's vanguard Force C before this and attack, the AA guns of Kurita's warships, allied to Rear Admiral Obayashi's sixty-three fighters from the three Force C, CarDiv 3 light carriers would delay the US attackers long enough to allow Ozawa to launch or recall his fighters from Forces A and B.

Throughout the night of 18/19 June, snoopers from both sides sighted the opposing fleets. US flying boats and long-range land-based search aircraft operating from Manus Island in the Admiralties and from tenders off Saipan scoured the seas whilst Japanese scouts from island airfields did likewise. But Spruance continued to receive conflicting intelligence reports and, ironically, a US seaplane picked up all forty of Ozawa's ships on its search radar at 0115 but could not transmit the report because of atmospheric conditions. Spruance got the report 7 hours too late. In the absence of firm intelligence as to the whereabouts of the Japanese Mobile Fleet, Spruance chose to remain where he was, covering the Saipan landing areas. Ozawa on the other hand had good scouting reports from his long-range planes and knew the general position of TF 58.

Throughout the early hours of 19 June, as dawn approached, Mitscher had his carrier aircraft gassed and his pilots readied for the imminent air battle and for the possibility that the Japanese Fleet might come within range. At dawn, Task Force 58 would be relatively close to the Marianas, from where Japanese aircraft could attack. It was a defensive role, the element of surprise of a night move westward had been lost. Everyone waited anxiously for daylight to arrive.

The Battle of the Philippine Sea would take place on 19 and 20 June 1944 – and was subsequently nicknamed the 'Great Marianas Turkey Shoot' by US aviators for the severely disproportional loss ratio of US to Japanese aircraft.

19 June 1944
At 0530 on 19 June, ironically the exact time when, had the task force steamed west the night before, Mitscher had hoped to have been aggressively launching a dawn strike on the Japanese Fleet, Task Force 58 was manoeuvring about 150 miles west south west of Saipan and 100 miles north west of Guam. The huge force comprised four carrier task groups and 'Ching' Lee's Task Force 58.7 battle line of battleships. The three stronger carrier groups steamed in a north–south line abreast, with the centres of the groups 12–15 miles apart. Due west of the middle group, Lee's battle line steamed with the weakest carrier group, Harrill's Task Group 58.4. Each task group was deployed in a circle 4 miles in diameter with the carriers in the centre of the circle of their respective groups and surrounded by a screen of battleships, cruisers and destroyers. The whole task force occupied an area of sea some 35 miles by 25 miles – it was massive.

The sea area was dominated by roughly easterly trade winds, and so the day began with the TF 58 carriers turning north east into the wind to begin launching dawn search, antisubmarine and Combat Air Patrols (CAP). Spruance suggested that if the daybreak searches revealed no targets, that the scout-bombers could be sent to crater airfields on Rota and Guam. Mitscher had to advise Spruance that this was not possible as his bombers' contact-fuzed bombs had largely been used up in the earlier strikes – and he was left with only the armour-piercing bombs needed to attack shipping. AP bombs were unsuitable for land targets.

The US Fleet air control system radars would be able to vector CAP fighters to intercept any enemy planes well in advance of them approaching and threatening the fleet. If any enemy aircraft did get past the CAP fighters then they would face a gunline of the battleships, cruisers and destroyers of the screen – that could now fire barrages of VT-proximity fuzed shells.

The sun rose at 0545 – it was a clear bright day with unlimited ceiling and visibility. As the first rays of sunlight broke over the horizon, the Japanese had already launched their morning land-based search patrols of some fifty aircraft stationed on Guam. Far to the west, in the Kurita's vanguard Force C, steaming east some 100 miles ahead of the main body of the Mobile Fleet, reconnaissance aircraft had launched at 0430 from the battleships and cruisers to scout ahead. Further to the west, the Mobile Fleet carriers launched their CAP and scout aircraft.

On the US ships, two or three inbound bogeys were spotted on radar screens and CAP fighters from *Monterey* charged after them. The squawk box connecting Flag Plot to the Combat Information Center announced: 'Tally-hoed two Judys; splash one.'[16] The other long-range Japanese search bomber had escaped to inform Ozawa of the latest position of Task Force 58.

At 0550, a Japanese A6M Zeke scout plane flying from Guam, located Task Force 58, 160 miles west of Saipan. After radioing in his sighting to Kurita's staff in the vanguard, the Zeke, which was carrying bombs, attacked the picket destroyer *Stockham* (DD-683) in Lee's battle line. It was shot down by AA fire from the destroyer *Yarnall* (DD-541). Now that the Japanese were alerted, they began launching their Guam-based aircraft for an attack. These launchings on Guam were detected on US ship radars and a group of about thirty F6F Hellcats was launched from *Belleau Wood* to intercept.

At 0619, with his search patrols and CAP airborne, Spruance changed course again, this time to run west south west towards the advancing enemy fleet. He had been previously advised that Japanese aircraft could land and refuel at Guam to press their attacks against TF 58 – so he instructed Mitscher to launch a fighter force to attack Guam. To launch his aircraft, Mitscher had to turn his carriers back into the easterly wind each time, such that by 1000 the task force would be back in virtually the same position it had been at dawn. Such was the versatility and capability of carrier air however that even from a distance of 200–300 miles, whilst the fast carriers were steaming to attack in one direction, Mitscher's fighters could disrupt Japanese land-based air at Guam and prevent enemy aircraft coming in from this southern flank.

At 0720, as the inbound Hellcats from *Belleau Wood* arrived in Guam airspace, they reported that Japanese aircraft were in the process of taking off from the Orote Field air base on Guam – and requested assistance. Minutes later, radar contacts of more land-based Japanese aircraft coming up from the south west from other islands were detected. Jocko Clark (CTG 58.1) despatched additional Hellcat fighters for Guam and between 0800 and 0900, a series of fierce dogfights developed near Guam, which resulted in thirty-five Japanese fighters being downed for the loss of a single Hellcat. *Hornet* launched a strike of Helldivers and Avengers escorted by Hellcats to bomb and crater Orote Field.

At about 0830, Rear Admiral Obayashi, in command of the three small vanguard force CarDiv 3 carriers *Chitose*, *Chiyoda* and *Zuihō*, armed with good intelligence as to the whereabouts of TF 58, began launching a strike of 69 aircraft made up of 16 fighters, 45 fighter-bombers and 8 torpedo-bombers – target, the US carriers.

A hundred miles to the west, in the main body of the Mobile Fleet carrier force, following after the Force C vanguard, Admiral Ozawa in Force A began launching a second strike of 120 planes at 0856 from the large fleet carriers *Taihō*, *Shōkaku* and *Zuikaku* of CarDiv 1. A total of 48 fighters, 53 bombers and 27 torpedo-bombers roared off from the carrier flight decks.

At 0910, as Warrant Officer Sakio Komatsu was taking off from the flagship *Taihō*, he spotted a torpedo from the US submarine *Albacore* heading straight towards the flagship. He turned his aircraft towards it, then crash dived into the water, detonating the torpedo and protecting the ship at the expense of his own life. A second torpedo from *Albacore* was not however spotted – and it struck *Taihō*'s starboard side. Initially it seemed that only minor damage had been caused – the flooding was contained, and the carrier's propulsion and navigation systems were unaffected. But the explosion had ruptured two aviation fuel tanks and as *Taihō* resumed her flight operations, gasoline vapour from the ruptured fuel tanks began to fill the hangar decks, creating a very dangerous situation aboard.

At 0900, Spruance finally received the delayed 0115 seaplane contact report placing forty Japanese naval units 360 miles to the west – but it was too late now to be of use, the carriers could be anywhere. An hour later, at 0950, the first inbound Japanese carrier aircraft began to register on Lee's battle line radar, 130 miles out. This was Obayashi's Force C vanguard CarDiv 3 strike of 16 fighters, 45 fighter-bombers and 8 torpedo-bombers.

At 1000, Rear Admiral Takaji Joshima, in Force B, launched a third strike of 15 fighters, 25 fighter-bombers and 7 torpedo-bombers from the CarDiv 2 carriers *Jun'yō* and *Hiyō* and the light carrier *Ryūhō*. Shortly after, Ozawa (Force A) launched a fourth strike from the CarDiv 1 fleet carriers *Taihō*, *Shōkaku* and *Zuikaku*, of 30 fighters, 36 dive-bombers, 10 fighter-bombers and 6 torpedo planes.[17] In all there would be 4 waves of the Japanese attack.

The individual fighter directors in each of the five US task groups began operations, using the two radio channels common to all ships to direct fighters to the contacts. As Mitscher got the radar contact reports of inbound strike planes he immediately recalled his Hellcat fighters which had been dogfighting over Guam – the skies there now being relatively clear of enemy land-based aircraft. Mitscher said to Burke: 'Get those fighters back from Guam.' A radio transmission with the simple words 'Hey, Rube!' was sent out. This was an old circus cry used to call for help in a fight, that had been borrowed by the Navy and would be incomprehensible to any Japanese ears listening.

Aboard the carriers, ship's buglers sounded general quarters, and as the *bong-bong-bong* of the warning bell resonated throughout the ship, sailors raced throughout passageways to their action stations, watertight doors slamming shut behind them. The ships readied for battle. Ready rooms were scrambled.

Mitscher, sitting in his swivel chair on the wing of his flag bridge aboard *Lexington*, held his force steady until 1023, when he turned Task Force 58 into the wind on an east south east course. He then ordered all of his 450 fighter aircraft aloft, deploying them in several layers, ready for the arrival of the Japanese aircraft.

Once his fighters were aloft, Mitscher then launched all 192 Avenger torpedo-bombers, 174 Helldivers and 59 Douglas Dauntless dive-bombers on his carriers – to clear the area of the anticipated battle by orbiting in a holding pattern to the east of Guam. The slower, less agile bombers could not dogfight with nimble Japanese fighters. With their departure, the carrier flight decks would be left clear to handle the Hellcats, which would soon be in the thick of the action and would need to land, refuel, rearm and take off again. Getting the bombers off the carriers would also avoid these precious strike aircraft being stowed in hangar decks throughout the battle – with unarmoured flight decks above, they and consequently the carriers would be vulnerable to Japanese bombs.

Mitscher gained a valuable 15 minutes to complete the launching of his fighter and departing bomber aircraft when the incoming Japanese strike aircraft began circling at 20,000ft, 100 miles out, and 200 miles from Guam as they regrouped into formation for the attack on the

US carriers.[18] As the US dive-bombers and torpedo-bombers cleared the area for Guam, the 450 Hellcat fighters could now operate unhindered from the carriers, filling the sky above TF 58 and out to 60 miles to the west of the task force.

At 1015, the fighter director officer on *Yorktown* reported: 'Large bogey at 265–105 miles on course 090 at estimated angels 24 [24,000ft].'

Then at 1037: 'Friendly planes have tally-hoed bogey at angels 15 to 25.'[19]

The first group of eleven Hellcats from *Essex* contacted the inbound Japanese first strike planes of the three Force C vanguard carriers, *Chitose*, *Chiyoda* and *Zuihō*, 90 miles out. Very quickly, other groups of Hellcats from *Bunker Hill*, *Cowpens* and *Princeton* were joining the developing battle, and such was the supremacy of US aircraft and pilots that within minutes of the contact, twenty-five Japanese aircraft had been shot down for the loss of one Hellcat. Those Japanese aircraft of this first wave that had survived the initial contact with the Hellcats were soon met by other Hellcats and sixteen more were shot down.

The surviving Japanese aircraft of the first wave came on relentlessly towards the task force, making unsuccessful attacks that caused no damage on the destroyers *Yarnall* and *Stockham*, on picket duty for the battle line. One bogey scored a direct 500lb bomb hit on the battleship *South Dakota*, which killed or injured more than fifty crew. But the battleship was designed to take this sort of strike – and her fighting capability was unaffected. She was the only US ship damaged in this attack and no attacks were pressed to the US carriers. At 1048, one Japanese dive-bomber made a suicide attack on the sister South Dakota-class battleship *Indiana*. Shipboard AA gunners opened up, quickly shooting down the bogey. However, despite the success of the initial contacts, it was not lost on the Americans that the Japanese naval aircraft were coming in from aircraft carriers that at the moment were completely immune to US attack.

As the two great carrier aircraft forces began to engage, the battle would quickly develop into the worst decimation of Japanese aircraft in the Pacific War – with Japanese planes 'falling like leaves,' as Commander McCampbell reported it.

At 1103, TG 58.3 commander Rear Admiral J.W. Reeves requested that a search and attack group be sent out 250 miles from the task force to try and locate the Japanese carriers. Mitscher signalled back: 'APPROVED X APPROVED X WISH WE COULD GO WITH YOU.'[20] But because of jamming on the limited radio channels caused by the large number of US aircraft aloft, Reeves could not get his message through to the torpedo and dive-bombers orbiting east of Guam. Shortly afterwards, Mitscher recalled the bombers – and so as to pit the airstrips and make it difficult for the Japanese to shuttle their aircraft, he instructed his Chief of Staff, Captain Arleigh Burke: 'Tell 'em to drop their bombs on Guam and Rota on the way back.'[21] Throughout the whole battle, Mitscher would stay on the wing of his bridge on *Lexington*, whilst officers emerged from Flag Plot to brief him on developments

At 1109, the second wave of incoming Japanese aircraft from the Ozawa's Force A carriers *Taihō*, *Shōkaku* and *Zuikaku* was detected on TF 58 radar screens at high altitude, 130 miles out. Initially estimated at 65 bogeys, this wave in fact comprised 48 fighters, 53 dive-bombers and 27 torpedo-bombers. F6F Hellcats had now filled the sky above the task force, and out to 60 miles to its west. The US fighter director vectored a sufficient number of them out to meet the inbound threat. The Japanese force of 128 aircraft was contacted 60 miles out – and decimated, with some 70 enemy aircraft shot down. The number and ease with which Japanese planes were being downed led one US pilot in *Lexington*'s Fighting Sixteen ready room to yell: 'Hell, this is like an old-time turkey shoot.'[22] And so the legendary nickname for the battle, the 'Great Marianas Turkey Shoot' was born. From 1130 to 1430, sporadic numbers of surviving bogeys were met by Hellcats as they tried to press home the attack.

A handful of Japanese bombers successfully broke through the AA screen and were able to attack the TF 58 carriers. Six attacked Montgomery's TG 58.2, *Bunker Hill*, *Wasp*, *Monterey* and *Cabot*, scoring two near misses that caused casualties on two carriers. Four of the six bogeys were shot down.

A number of enemy aircraft made an ineffective attack on Reeves' TG 58.3. Four Yokosuka D4Y Judy dive-bombers attacked *Lexington*, *Enterprise* and the light carrier *Princeton* and were met with dense AA fire. A group of torpedo aircraft attacked *Enterprise* – no hits were scored but one torpedo exploded in the wake of the ship. Three torpedo aircraft attacked *Princeton* – but were shot down. Two torpedoes were launched at *Lexington* – but missed.

The battleship *Indiana* was forced to make evasive manoeuvres at about 1150 when attacked by a torpedo-bomber, the torpedo exploding harmlessly in her wake. Then, at about 1213, a Japanese fighter made a strafing run on *Indiana*, but the battleship's AA gunners shot away its tail and the bogey crashed into the sea. Shortly afterwards, a burning Nakajima B5N torpedo-bomber crashed into her starboard side – but as with the earlier bomb hit on her sister *South Dakota*, the hit was of little effect on a modern battleship and the BB was able to remain on station.

The action in this heavy attack by Ozawa's second wave was certainly intense – but little real damage had been done. In all, almost 100 Japanese planes were downed.

The third wave of 47 aircraft comprised 15 fighters, 25 fighter-bombers and 7 torpedo-bombers from the Force B carriers *Jun'yō*, *Hiyō* and *Ryūhō*. These planes came in from the north and were intercepted by forty Hellcats, some 50 miles out from the task force. Seven bogeys were downed – but a few broke through and made an ineffective attack on Harrill's TG 58.4 carriers, *Essex*, *Langley* and *Cowpens*. Four Judys attacked TG 58.3, *Lexington*, *Enterprise* and *Princeton*, and as a mass of AA fire targeted them, two torpedoes were dropped towards Mitscher's flagship *Lexington* – but they missed by a fair margin.

The fourth wave of 30 fighters, 36 dive-bombers, 10 fighter-bombers and 6 torpedo planes had launched between 1100 and 1130 from the Force A carriers *Taihō*, *Shōkaku* and *Zuikaku*. But these pilots had been given an incorrect position for Task Force 58 and failed to locate it. The Japanese aircraft broke up into loose groups that turned to head towards Guam and Rota to refuel. One group of eighteen bogeys from *Zuikaku* heading for Rota, by chance came across Montgomery's Task Group 58.2, comprising *Bunker Hill*, *Wasp*, *Monterey* and *Cabot*. The Japanese attacked – but half of them were shot down by Hellcats. Another small group of nine dive-bombers attacked *Wasp* and *Bunker Hill*, but scored no hits, with eight being shot down.

A large group of forty-nine aircraft from the fourth wave had flown for Guam – and were intercepted over Orote Field as they landed, by twenty-seven Hellcats from *Cowpens*, *Essex* and *Hornet*. Of these forty-nine, thirty were shot down and the nineteen that successfully landed were damaged beyond repair on the ground.

The overwhelming US air superiority came as little surprise to the veteran US pilots who had confronted the Japanese A6M Zeke at Rabaul, in the Gilberts, the Marshalls and at Truk, where the Hellcat had simply outclassed the Zeke. The new US pilot recruits who had joined the carriers after the Truk raid were stunned at how relatively easy it was to down an unarmoured Zeke, whose fuel tanks caught fire when hit – in stark contrast to the armoured Hellcat with its self-sealing fuel tanks.

By 1430 that afternoon, the heaviest strikes were over, and Mitscher began requesting reports from the task-group commanders. The results seemed almost impossible to believe, despite the combat kill reports made by the pilots. In total, on the first day of the battle, the 4 Japanese carrier air strikes had launched 373 carrier aircraft and some 50 aircraft had launched from Guam.[23]

Battle of the Philippine Sea, June 1944. Planes of TG 58.2 produce high condensation trails on Combat Air Patrol just before the Japanese air attack on 19 June 1944. (National Archives 80-G-238157)

It seemed by early afternoon that, in all, more than 300 Japanese planes had already been destroyed, a stunning US air victory at a cost of 18 US fighters and 12 bombers lost – although some of the downed flight crews were rescued. For all the huge loss of Japanese aircraft, little damage had been suffered by the US ships.

But the ever tight-lipped Mitscher made little comment on the combat reports, even though 15–20 miles to the south east off *Lexington*'s beam, smoke from the punishing attacks on Guam could be seen rising high into the air. He was concerned that despite the slaughter of enemy aircraft, the enemy carriers remained afloat – somewhere far out to the west, undetected. They had escaped damage completely – and Mitscher estimated that Ozawa could still have some 200 planes afloat. Neither Ozawa's nine carriers nor his battle line of capital ships had been contacted – and they still posed a formidable threat. Not a single Task Force 58 aircraft had sighted the enemy carrier force so far, all day.

During the battle, the distance between Mitscher's TF 58 carriers and Ozawa's carriers, far out to the west, had been opening all day. The battle had naturally drifted east towards Guam due to Japanese planes attempting to land there – and the US carriers having to manoeuvre into the east wind to launch their aircraft. The tactical situation had not changed all day – Task Force 58 was positioned between the enemy fleet and Japanese land bases on Guam and Rota. The Japanese carriers were somewhere down-wind of Mitscher to the west.

By 1500, as combat action reports were fed back, Spruance knew that the Japanese force had lost the bulk of its main weapon of attack, their aircraft. As TF 58 was still recovering its aircraft and unable yet to move westward, Spruance turned tactical command of the carriers over to Mitscher.

The individual totals of enemy kills were simply staggering. Commander McCampbell's VF-15 from *Essex* alone had accounted

An F6F-3 Hellcat fighter lands aboard USS *Lexington* (CV-16) during the 'Great Marianas Turkey Shoot', 19 June 1944, covered by 40mm guns in the foreground and 20mm guns in the gun gallery along the starboard side of the flight deck. (National Archives 80-G-236955)

for seventy enemy aircraft. On *Lexington*, after landing, Lieutenant Alexander Vraciu, USNR, crawled out of his Hellcat's cockpit and held up six fingers, as Mitscher waved from the bridge. His Hellcat's guns had downed six 'turkeys' in less than 18 minutes – bringing the ace's total number of kills for the war to eighteen. Mitscher left the flag bridge and made his way down to the flight deck to congratulate Vraciu personally, shaking his hand as onboard photographers snapped iconic images. Mitscher then said: 'I'd like to pose with him. Not for publication. To keep for myself.'[24]

At 1630, Admiral Spruance signalled: 'DESIRE TO ATTACK ENEMY TOMORROW IF WE KNOW HIS POSITION WITH SUFFICIENT ACCURACY. . . IF NOT, WE MUST CONTINUE SEARCHES TOMORROW TO ENSURE ADEQUATE PROTECTION OF SAIPAN.'[25]

As night fell and it was clear that the Japanese attack was for the time being over, Spruance notified Vice Admiral Richmond Kelly Turner, in command of the Amphibious Force landings on Saipan, that he could recall his shipping to Saipan from its safe point 200 miles to the east

Aboard USS *Lexington*, Lieutenant Junior Grade Alexander Vraciu, USNR, of Fighting Squadron 16, holds up six fingers to signify 'kills' during the 'Great Marianas Turkey Shoot', 19 June 1944. (National Archives 80-G-23684166)

315

of Guam. He allowed Mitscher to detach one task group to remain off Guam – as the destroyers of Task Group 58.4 required to refuel.

At about 2000, once his aircraft were recovered, Mitscher put the task force on a westerly heading, pushing westwards to get into a position to attack the Japanese Fleet. He and his staff were not optimistic about finding the enemy – and many thought the best opportunity of destroying the fleet had been lost by the cautious approach adopted in the last few days. The four *Essex* night-fighters hit Guam and Rota overnight, shooting down three bogeys and destroying more Japanese aircraft on the ground at dawn.

Meanwhile, on the Japanese 1st Mobile Fleet, in the darkness of night far to the west, Ozawa was making his preparations for the next day. He had originally planned to resume his attacks the following day – but such was the magnitude of his aircraft losses that he abandoned that plan and at 2000 began to withdraw from the area. He was still getting accurate reports of Mitscher's TF 58 position – whilst Mitscher had poorer reporting, having to rely mainly on long-range flying boats operating from Saipan.

Unknown to Spruance and Mitscher however, in addition to the huge loss of planes, the Japanese carriers themselves had also suffered terrible damage. At 1220, three torpedoes from a spread of six fired from the submarine *Cavalla* had hit the fleet carrier *Shōkaku* on her starboard side, starting fires and causing this veteran of the Pearl Harbor raid and the Battle of the Coral Sea to fall out of formation and slew to a halt. One torpedo had hit the forward aviation fuel tanks near the main hangar – where aircraft that had just landed were being refuelled and re-armed. At such a vulnerable time, the fuel caught fire and set off refuelling aircraft and munitions – fuel from shattered fuel pipes caused fires to take hold.

Shōkaku began to settle by the bow, and as the flooding and fires quickly got out of control, the order to Abandon Ship was given. Before this could be completed however, the carrier sunk by the bow at just after 1400, some 140 miles north of the island of Yap. A total of 1,272 officers and men were lost, including 376 members of Air Group 601.

Meanwhile the new carrier *Taihō*, Ozawa's flagship, which had been torpedoed by *Albacore* just after 0900 that morning, was falling victim to poor damage control. Although her flight and navigation systems had remained undamaged, explosive fumes and gasoline vapours had been building up in her hangar deck all morning. To try and clear these vapours, a damage-control officer ordered her ventilation system to be run at full blast. This had the effect of spreading the dangerous gasoline vapours throughout the entire carrier – and at approximately 1430, a spark from an electric generator on the hangar deck ignited the fumes, triggering a series of catastrophic explosions.

It was immediately clear that *Taihō* had been mortally wounded – and as she struggled to remain afloat, Ozawa transferred his flag and staff to the nearby destroyer *Wakatsuki*. Soon afterwards, a second series of explosions ripped through *Taihō* at 1530 – and shortly after, Japan's newest carrier, commissioned only 3 months earlier, sank quickly with the loss of 1,650 officers and men from a crew of 2,150.

A further twenty-two aircraft had been lost with the sinkings of *Shōkaku* and *Taihō*. It was a bitter blow to the Japanese. For with no significant damage being done to the US ships, Japanese naval air power had been decimated and they had lost two of their finest carriers. Ozawa had committed 373 carrier aircraft and some 50 land-based planes to his attacks and searches. More than 300 had been lost in the great air battle. Adding those aircraft lost operationally and those land-based planes shot down or destroyed over Guam, some 346 aircraft had been lost.[26]

20 June 1944

As dawn broke, Mitscher's carriers were steaming on a north-westerly course and beginning to launch search aircraft to patrol further to the north west. Vice Admiral Lee's battle line of battleships had formed up with their supporting cruisers and destroyers as the vanguard of Task Force 58. But despite US aircraft continuing their long-range searches throughout the morning, the Japanese Fleet was not spotted – the whereabouts of the Japanese 1st Mobile Fleet still eluded Mitscher.

By noon, as everyone afloat still waited expectantly for an anticipated contact, from his flag bridge on *Lexington* Mitscher placed his task-force strike crews on standby and sent a long-range search group 475 miles out into the ocean. It was a very long way out – and Mitscher told Commander Ernest Snowden of *Lexington*'s Air Group 16: 'I want you to go back and tell those boys that if you make contact and anybody gets shot down, I'll come and pick them up even if I have to steam the whole damn fleet up after them.'[27] After 3 hours on patrol, the search planes turned to head back to the carriers – there had still been no sight of the enemy.

Likewise, Spruance too had received no further contact reports of the whereabouts of the Japanese Fleet since the submarine *Cavalla* had torpedoed *Shōkaku* at noon the previous day, now a full 24 hours ago. He had no idea that in fact, by now, both *Shōkaku* and *Taihō* were sitting at the bottom of the Pacific.

Although for the best part of the day there had been no sign of the Mobile Fleet, just after 1500, with just a few hours of daylight left, Lieutenant R.S. Nelson of *Enterprise*, flying an Avenger from Torpedo 10 was approaching the end of his 325-mile search area. Before he turned back, in the distance he spotted the telltale tracks of the wakes of big ships. After closing for a better look and fixing his position, at 1542 Nelson sent his historic voice radio report: 'Enemy fleet sighted. Latitude 15-02, longitude 135-25. Course 270, speed 20.' He repeated his report three times.

Aboard *Lexington*, Mitscher slid down from his chair on the flag-bridge wing and went into Flag Plot. There, seconds later, Mitscher's Chief of Staff Arleigh Burke announced: 'Indications are our birds have sighted something big.'[28] Mitscher waited for confirmation of the sighting and verification of the enemy distance, course and speed. That confirmation came very quickly when just a few minutes later, the tracks and ships were spotted by another scout plane, which sent a report via Morse code on continuous wave: 'Many ships, one carrier 134-12E, 14-44N.' The two dead reckoning sighting reports were about 70 nautical miles apart – but it was good enough to mount an attack. Nelson took his Avenger closer for a better look – whilst the other scout plane turned to head back for the carriers to deliver the report in person.[29]

The two contact reports placed the Japanese Mobile Fleet some 275 miles west north west of the US task force, moving away to the west at 20 knots. The Japanese naval units were reported to be oiling – re-fuelling at sea from the oilers of the 1st and 2nd Supply Forces.

Mitscher knew that if an immediate strike was launched, by the time his aircraft arrived over the enemy they would have just 30 minutes of daylight for the attack. They would be in complete darkness as they returned to their carriers and landed. His pilots were trained for daytime operations and were not trained in night-time operations, which were the reserve of specialist night-fighters at the time. Operating at such extreme range, it was likely that many aircraft would run out of fuel on the return leg as they searched in darkness for their carriers. Out of gas, many would be forced to ditch in the sea. He could expect heavy losses of aircraft – but this was perhaps his last chance to strike a fatal blow against the enemy fleet before it moved out of range. Ozawa's carriers could not be allowed to survive to wreak havoc another day.

It was a terrible dilemma to be placed in – involving huge risk to his pilots. He mulled over the options with his senior staff members, conferring with his task-force air operations officer Commander Gus Widhelm who advised a strike was possible: 'We can make it, but's going to be tight.'[30] Conscious that every second he delayed launching a strike brought the darkness of night closer and reduced the chances of success and the safe return of his pilots, Mitscher made his decision within just 5 minutes of the confirmation. At 1553, he instructed Widhelm: 'Launch 'em'. He advised Spruance that he was going to launch a full attack, with everything he had, and his subsequent Action Report sets out his reasoning:

> The decision to launch strikes was based on so damaging and slowing enemy carriers and her ships that our battle line could close during the night and at daylight sink all the ships that our battle line could reach. It was believed that this was the last time that the Japanese could be brought to grips and their enemy fleet destroyed once and for all. Taking advantage of this opportunity was going to cost us a great deal in planes and pilots because we were launching at maximum range of our aircraft at such time as it would be necessary to recover them after dark. It was realised also that this single shot venture for planes which were sent out in the afternoon would probably be not all operational for a morning strike. Consequently, Fifth Fleet was informed that the carriers were firing their bolt.[31]

At 1610, ship's squawk boxes announced: 'Pilots, man your planes.' Pilots leapt into action, scrambling from their ready rooms to their aircraft – engines were fired up and turned over. Just 11 minutes later, the eleven carriers turned east south east into the wind and within a few more minutes, flight-deck officers were waving the planes in quick succession down the flight decks into the air.

By 1630 the first deckloads of 240 planes were off the carrier – although 14 had to abort and return to their carriers. In the event, 226 strike aircraft would press home the attack – 95 Hellcat fighters (some carrying 500lb bombs), 77 dive-bombers and 54 Avenger torpedo planes setting off on a bearing of 290° True. The 77 dive-bombers in the strike comprised 51 Curtiss SB2C Helldivers and 26 Douglas SBD Dauntless dive-bombers – it would be the last carrier action the rugged old warrior, the SBD Dauntless, would take part in. Aerial torpedoes would put a bigger hole in a ship under the waterline than bombs – but as the Avenger torpedo-bombers had been used mainly for strikes against island land targets since late 1943, they now mostly carried 500lb bombs instead of torpedoes.[32]

With the first deckloads of strike aircraft airborne, at 1636 the carriers swung back around from an east-south-east heading to a north-west heading, to close the Japanese Fleet once again. The enemy fleet lay 275 nautical miles distant – and local sunset was just 90 minutes or so away.

Meanwhile, on the Japanese ships, Ozawa was alerted at 1615 to intercepted US contact reports. He ceased his refuelling operations, and at 1645 altered course from west to north west – and increased speed to 24 knots. With about 2 hour's daylight and nautical twilight left, he no doubt hoped to escape, disappearing into the darkness of night.

The prospect of a night water landing was a frightening thought for the US pilots to contemplate as they roared off flight decks. Lieutenant Commander J.D. Arnold of *Hornet*'s Air Group 2 commented: 'decided . . . it would be best to . . . attack, retire as far as possible before darkness set in, notify the ship . . . then have all planes in the group land in the same vicinity so that rafts could be lashed together and mutual rescues could be affected'.[33]

Shortly after the 226 strike aircraft had formed up aloft and begun to disappear to the north west, another message came in to Flag Plot from the search aircraft shadowing the Mobile Fleet. This placed the enemy fleet now a further 60 miles to the west – more than 330 miles away. It was a devastating blow. For whilst the original position had given the strike aircraft a sporting chance of returning safely to the task force, both Mitscher and the strike pilots quickly worked out that the new distance and bearing would consume every last ounce of fuel. It was now almost inevitable that many aircraft would not make it back to the carriers, running out of fuel and being forced to ditch in the sea in darkness.

Mitscher now again faced a terrible dilemma in the light of this third message. Should he recall the first deckload of strike planes – or let them go and possibly strike a great blow against the seemingly intact Japanese carriers? It would be a blow that could possibly shorten the war and save countless lives – but at the expense of the lives of many of his pilots and planes. After poring over his charts, he made the fateful and heavy decision not to recall the planes of the first wave. He however cancelled the planned second strike and informed Spruance that the remainder of the aircraft would be held until the morning.

At 1840, shortly before sunset and after 2 hours flying more than 250 miles, the lead US aircraft spotted the Japanese Fleet. Six oilers appeared to have just broken off refuelling six destroyers of the screen. Then, 30 miles further off in the distance spanning the horizon from west to north west, the great prize began to appear. The Force C vanguard light carriers *Chitose*, *Chiyoda* and *Zuihō* of CarDiv3 slowly hove into view, screened by the battleship line of the BatDiv 1 super battleships *Yamato* and *Musashi* and the BatDiv3 battleships *Kongō* and *Haruna*. The CruDiv 4 heavy cruisers *Chōkai*, *Maya* and *Takao*, the CruDiv 7 heavy cruisers *Kumano*, *Suzuya*, *Tone* and *Chikuma* were present along with the DesRon 2 light cruiser *Noshiro*, the DesDiv 31 destroyers *Asashimo*, *Kishinami* and *Okinami* and the DesDiv 32 destroyers *Fujinami*, *Hamakaze* and the super destroyer *Shimakaze*. The CarDiv 2 carriers *Jun'yō* and *Hiyō* and the light carrier *Ryūhō* were steaming 10 miles to starboard with their screen. The one remaining CarDiv 1 fleet carrier *Zuikaku*, with Ozawa himself now aboard, steamed 20 miles north east of CarDiv2, with its screen of cruisers and destroyers. Ozawa had only seventy-five planes left to protect his fleet.

The sun was low towards the horizon with only about 30 minutes of nautical twilight left. With time so short, and low on fuel, the strike group from *Wasp* immediately attacked – each aircraft acting independently, diving at the oilers to prevent them refuelling the carriers for a fast run home. Two of the six oilers were so badly damaged that they subsequently had to be abandoned and scuttled. A third was set ablaze but managed to subsequently get under way. At least six Zekes attacked the *Wasp* group, downing one SB2C Helldiver and one Hellcat.

The remainder of the US strike force planes swept past the engaged group of oilers and screening destroyers – towards the Mobile Fleet itself. The Japanese screen opened its AA fire with a large burst of flack at 24,000ft followed by AA fire at 10,000ft and smaller calibre AA weapons below that. The Japanese battleships and cruisers even opened up with their main batteries.

Ozawa's seventy-five remaining Zekes and fighter-bombers lifted off from the carriers and engaged the US aircraft, knocking down twenty US planes before they were engulfed by the strength of US numbers. The majority of the Japanese CAP were shot down.

As they approached the carriers, the US pilots anxiously watched their fuel gauges – seeing them drop below the halfway mark. Throwing caution to the wind, to use every second of daylight and preserve every ounce of fuel, they attacked the carriers independently without waiting to form up into sections as they normally would. As US bombs began to

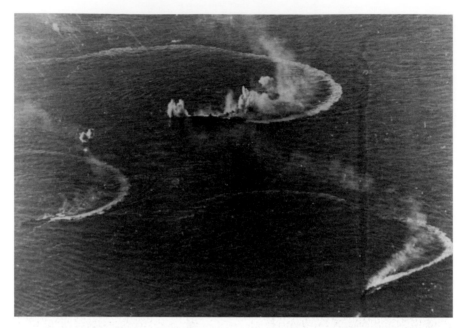

Battle of the Philippine Sea, June 1944. The Japanese aircraft carrier *Zuikaku* (centre) and two destroyers manoeuvring whilst under attack by US Navy aircraft in the late afternoon of 20 June 1944. *Zuikaku* was hit by several bombs but survived. (National Archives 80-G-238025)

strike their targets, the success of the Battle Midway, where the refuelling aircraft had caught fire on flight decks, would not be repeated.

Five Japanese carriers were hit – four would ultimately survive. Bombs from *Enterprise* Torpedo 10 hit *Ryūhō* but caused little damage. Some *Enterprise* dive-bombers joined *Yorktown*'s Bombing 1 and *Hornet*'s Torpedo 2, hitting *Zuikaku* aft of her bridge and setting her on fire to such an extent that she was prematurely abandoned as attempts were made to bring the fires under control. Torpedo 28 from *Monterey*, Torpedo 31 from *Cabot* and Torpedo 8 from *Bunker Hill* bombed the light carrier *Chiyoda* putting the flight deck out of action and starting fires. *Jun'yō* was also hit, crushing her smokestack and bringing down her mast. She had to abandon flight operations but remained afloat.

Torpedo 24 from *Belleau Wood* were the only Avengers equipped with torpedoes, instead of bombs – and four attacked CarDiv 2 *Hiyō*. Intense Japanese AA fire successfully knocked out the lead US plane – forcing the rear gunner and radioman to bail out. But the pilot, now alone, pressed home a diversionary attack that distracted the Japanese AA gunners enough to allow the next two Avengers to attack her starboard

Battle of the Philippine Sea, June 1944. A Japanese light carrier, a battleship, a cruiser and other ships of CarDiv 3 under attack by TF 58 planes, 20 June 1944. (National Archives 80-G-238159)

beam and quarter. Their Mark 13 torpedoes hit *Hiyō*, one breaching her hull at her engine room, whilst the other damaged her steering gear. *Hiyō* was set on fire – the flames spreading and setting off explosions throughout her hull. Some 2 hours after the torpedoes hit, she sank with the loss of 247 crew. The two aircrew who had bailed out of their Avenger were recovered the next day but the pilot himself ran out of fuel on the return journey to the task force and ditched in the darkness. He was never found.

Running low on fuel and with nautical twilight now gone, at 1900, Mitscher's pilots disengaged and turned back onto a course of 090° towards their own carriers, now some 250 miles away in the darkness. As they did so, the final tally for the battle seemed to be one Japanese carrier, *Hiyō*, sunk, along with three other carriers, *Zuikaku*, *Jun'yō* and *Chiyoda*, damaged by bombs. The Kongō-class battleship *Haruna* had been hit by two bombs, one directly on a main battery turret – forcing the flooding of her turret magazine to avoid a secondary magazine explosion. The cruiser *Maya* had been bombed and two Japanese oilers had been damaged and scuttled. Some sixty-five Japanese aircraft had been shot down for the loss of twenty US aircraft destroyed by Japanese shipborne AA fire and by fighters.

Whilst *Hiyō*'s fate was plainly apparent to US forces, no US eyes had seen *Shōkaku* or *Taihō* sink the day before – from a US perspective, they could still be operational. Aboard TF 58, the action was seen as a victory, but not the crushing blow that had been hoped for.

There was no moon that night, the night sky was black, filled with stars and the occasional lightning flash. The 200 or so surviving US planes, low on fuel now, had to fly for 2 hours almost 300 miles back towards their carriers. Although they flew essentially independently, some grouped together for mutual support – but as a result of battle damage, several aircraft had to ditch in the sea along the way.

Mitscher had been out on the flag-bridge wing since he launched his pilots. He anxiously awaited their return, checking his watch. At 2015, when the pilots were about 70 miles out and starting to pick up homing beacon signals, US shipboard radars began to pick them up on their screens, inbound from the west. Mitscher changed the axis of his fleet, spreading the task groups out to a distance of 15 miles apart, and having the carriers increase speed to 22 knots as they steamed west towards the returning aircraft to allow a possible pick-up of those aviators who had already gone into the water. In the returning US aircraft, cocooned in darkness, pilots anxiously checked their fuel tanks, which were by now almost empty.

Just a few miles short of the carriers, ditchings in large numbers began as planes started to run out of fuel, their engines stuttering and misfiring before going silent. Some groups of aircrews agreed to ditch together to increase the possibility of being spotted and rescued.

The initial visual contact by TF 58 of those planes whose fuel had held out was made at 2030 – scattered aircraft appearing without pattern in the western sky. Mitscher reversed course from a westward heading to an easterly heading to bring the carriers into the wind at 22 knots for aircraft landings to begin.

At 2045, a few aircraft began to orbit the task force in apparent confusion in the darkness, and the sky began to fill up over the task groups as more aircraft arrived. The pilots could easily see the iridescent wakes of the carriers in the darkness. But the planes had no fuel to search, locate their own carrier and perhaps make several attempts at landing.

Jocko Clark, commander of Task Group 58.1, turned on his group's lights – and then Mitscher slipped down from his swivel chair on the bridge wing, walked into Flag Plot and ordered the whole task force to do the same, saying to his Chief of Staff Captain Burke: 'Turn on the lights.'[34] Going further, he had each group's flagship display a searchlight beam that was visible for tens of miles whilst cruisers and destroyers far out in the screen fired star shells to help the aircraft locate the task force and to illuminate the carriers.

It would have been an astonishing sight for any Japanese night-fighters or submarines lurking unseen in the darkness – but with mass ditchings of so many aircraft, Mitscher was facing the worst disaster in naval-aviation history, the risk was justified. The pilots were ordered to land on any available carrier deck and not waste time and fuel searching for their own carrier. The scramble to land began at 2050 and would go on for 2 hours.

Despite this, as they started to near the task force, more aircraft ran out of fuel and were forced to ditch in the ocean. In all, some eighty of the returning aircraft were lost, some crashing on flight decks as their fuel gave out just as they made to land. Many planes, so damaged, were pushed overboard to allow others to land. Some carrier flight decks were so overcrowded that operational aircraft were pushed overboard to make space for others to land. Some planes were able to ditch alongside ships - whilst others mistakenly attempted to land on cruisers or destroyers. Once in the water, airmen were able to train their small waterproof flashlights on the ships – allowing destroyers to weave between them and pick them up.

Of the 226 US aircraft that had pressed the attack, 100 planes with 100 pilots and 109 aircrew had been lost – 20 to enemy action in the battle and a further estimated 80 as they ran out of fuel on the return flight or as they attempted to land.

At 2252, when the last of the returning aircraft had landed, Mitscher once again turned the task force west to pursue the enemy – but with more than 100 US aircraft lost on Day 2 of the battle, either downed, ditched or pushed overboard, he only had a hundred of the aircraft that had taken part in the strike left. Over the coming days search and rescue missions recovered approximately three-quarters of the downed aircrews from the sea. There were fifty-one pilots and fifty aircrew picked from the sea near the task force and during the subsequent pursuit of the fleeing enemy fleet. Another thirty-five pilots and twenty-six aircrew were picked up by PBMs, float planes and destroyers. By dusk on 21 June, all but sixteen pilots and twenty-two aircrew were still missing.[35] On the carriers, two ship's officers and four crew had been killed during the night landings and deck crashes.

At 0130 that night, 21 June, a PBM report was received giving the location of the Japanese Mobile Fleet. A classic stern chase of the fleeing Mobile Fleet was now on. But fuel shortages on the smaller destroyers, which had a shorter range, were now looming. Spruance however wanted to press home the attack and catch any damaged Japanese stragglers and possibly get a further air strike off at dawn. He wanted to hit the Japanese Mobile Fleet before it reached the cover of land-based air from enemy air bases in the Ryukyu Islands or from Japan.

Spruance ordered Rear Admiral Harrill, in command of Task Group 58.4, on station to the east at Guam, to advance – and bring the oilers. He also instructed Mitscher to send out searches by long-range radar-equipped Avengers. At 0450, Mitscher informed Spruance that as a result of fuel shortages, he thought it not possible to close the enemy at a speed greater than 15 knots. Worse, recovery of the returning aircraft had forced an easterly heading and taken TF 58 60 miles farther away from the Mobile Fleet.

A classic stern chase of the fleeing Imperial Fleet was now developing – and at 1050, Spruance detached 'Ching' Lee and the battle line of the seven fast battleships *Washington*, *North Carolina*, *Iowa*, *New Jersey*, *South Dakota*, *Alabama* and *Indiana*, with the cruisers *Wichita*, *Minneapolis*, *New Orleans* and *San Francisco* and a screen of fourteen destroyers, along with *Bunker Hill* and *Wasp*, to pursue Ozawa and the retreating Mobile Fleet. But both the air searches and the battle-line warships failed to make contact with the enemy, although they did locate many of the downed US aviators.

Later that morning, Avenger search planes finally located Ozawa's Mobile Fleet – but the distance was opening. A strike by Hellcats carrying bombs was launched – but failed to make contact with the fleeing Japanese Fleet.

As 21 June wore on, and other searches were launched that failed to contact the Mobile Fleet, it became increasingly apparent that the enemy would make good their escape. That night at 1920, Admiral Spruance cancelled the search – Task Force 58 came about and headed back towards Saipan. Ozawa and the Mobile Fleet had escaped to Okinawa. The First Battle of the Philippine Sea had ended.

The Japanese had lost a total of some 475 carrier aircraft, float planes and land-based aircraft – including most pilots and crews.[36] Clark's Task Group 58.1 was detached to hit the Jimas again on 24 June as Task Force 58 retired towards their naval base at Eniwetok. Another 66 Japanese planes were destroyed. In contrast with this combined tally of more than 500 aircraft destroyed, Mitscher had lost 100 planes – but only 16 pilots and 33 crew. But the victory was actually greater than was known at the time. For the Americans were still unaware that two enemy fleet carriers, a light carrier and two oilers were all now at the bottom of the Pacific. Japan had lost nearly 3,000 pilots and sailors.

Aboard USS *Lexington* (CV-16), officers and crew in front of Japanese flags painted on the carrier's island to signify 143 'kills' claimed by her Air Group 16 during the Battle of the Philippine Sea, photographed 21 June 1944. (National Archives 80-G-23642)

But although the aircraft tally was stunning and the invasion beaches at Saipan had been protected, to US eyes the Japanese Mobile Fleet had escaped. One carrier was known to have been sunk for sure, *Hiyō* – but whilst it was known that possibly one or two other flattops had been damaged, no US eyes had seen *Shōkaku* or *Taihō* go down on 19 June. There was no reason to suspect that in fact three Japanese carriers had been sent to the bottom. There was thus a palpable sense of gloom on the flag bridge of *Lexington* – the Japanese were left with a force of at least six, but possibly seven or eight carriers that could still inflict much damage to the Allied cause. Mitscher's Action Report summed it up: 'The enemy had escaped. He had been badly hurt by one aggressive carrier strike at the one time he was within range. His fleet was not sunk.'[37]

Japan had mounted the operation in an attempt to win a decisive battle. There had indeed been a decisive battle – the largest carrier versus carrier battle in history had taken place. But it was not the decisive battle the Japanese had hoped for – Imperial naval forces had been decisively defeated and forced to flee without a major big-gun surface action. Japan had suffered heavy and irreplaceable losses of carrier-borne and land-based aircraft, and of pilots and aircrew. Ozawa had only 47 aircraft in fighting shape – 25 Zekes, 6 torpedo-bombers, 2 dive-bombers and 12 miscellaneous aircraft.[38] *Zuikaku* was now the last remaining fleet carrier of the six which had attacked Pearl Harbor. Four had been sunk at Midway and *Shōkaku* had been sunk here.

On 23 June, Spruance ordered Task Force 58 to head to their Eniwetok base – but detached Harrill's Task Group 58.4 to keep station off Guam. Rear Admiral Jocko Clark received orders for his Task Group 58.1 to bomb Pagan Island, some 200 miles north of Saipan en route to Eniwetok – but as he headed north, his Japanese-language radio listener reported that more than 100 Japanese aircraft had been staged into Iwo Jima and Chichi Jima for an attack on US shipping off Saipan once the weather cleared.

Consequently, the next day, 24 June, Clark's TG 58.1 aircraft were launched for a strike on the 'Jimas'. The Japanese retaliated with three strikes against his task group, but these were intercepted by his CAP aircraft — and those enemy aircraft that got past the CAP fighters were beaten off by shipboard AA fire. As a result, sixty-six Japanese aircraft were destroyed, and these losses were sufficient to thwart Japanese attempts at the relief of Saipan and the raiding of shipping off Guam. Nevertheless, the air threat from the Jimas remained ever present and would have to be kept neutralised.

Task Force 58 had now destroyed an estimated 90 per cent of the Japanese carrier air groups and the Japanese only had enough pilots left to form a new air group on one of their light carriers. As a direct result, at the Battle of Leyte Gulf a few months later, their largely impotent remaining carriers would be used solely as decoys.

The fact that in the early hours of 19 June, before the battle, Spruance had elected not to turn west towards the enemy to get in position for an attack at 0500 on the morning of 20 June has caused much debate and controversy over the years. The Japanese Fleet and six, possibly eight, carriers had escaped annihilation. Had Spruance's cautious actions allowed the escape of the Japanese Mobile Fleet – in much the same way Jellicoe's prudence had allowed the Imperial German Navy High Seas Fleet to escape the British Grand Fleet at the Battle of Jutland, in

1916? Commander-in-Chief of the US Fleet, Ernest J. King, COMINCH, backed Spruance's decision: 'In his plans for what developed into the Battle of the Philippine Sea, Spruance was rightly guided by this basic obligation' to protect and secure the invasion forces on and off Saipan.[39]

But during the summer of 1944, as Allied strategists made their plans for the Philippines campaign, the threat posed by the Japanese Mobile Fleet, and the six, possibly eight carriers weighed heavily on every Allied move and thrust. Those six carriers would soon almost cause a US military disaster at Leyte Gulf.

The Japanese garrison on Saipan however had received no relief despite the huge Japanese losses at sea – and organised Japanese resistance ended on 9 July.

The First Battle of the Philippine Sea paved the way for successful Allied landings on Guam and Tinian a few weeks later in July 1944. In the meantime, TF 58 aircraft kept up the pressure, hitting the Visayas on 14 July, and Manila and the Visayas again on the 21, 22 and 24 July.

Chapter 14

Prelude to the Philippines Campaign

(i) Guam and Tinian, July 1944

Following the defeat of the Japanese Mobile Fleet in the Philippine Sea in June 1944, Japanese resistance in Saipan still had to be mopped up. The Mariana island of Tinian, just south of Saipan, had to be seized along with the US island territory of Guam at the south of the Mariana chain.

(a) 2nd Battle of Guam, 21 July–10 August 1944

Guam is a large island of some 210 square miles, with jungle-covered mountains in its central and northern areas. Its shore is ringed by reefs, where heavy surf breaks – and high cliffs. A high ridge of mountains dominates the south west of the island.

The Japanese had seized Guam at the outset of the war almost three years earlier on 8 December 1941 – shortly after the attack on Pearl Harbor. It was now heavily fortified and harboured airfields and a garrison of more than 18,000 troops. Tinian had 1 main airfield, 3 small fighter strips and a garrison of 8,500 troops.

The fast carriers of Task Force 58 had a number of vital roles to fulfil in the remaining operations of the Mariana campaign. With regards to Saipan, where US troops now held a beachhead, they would require to isolate the beachhead from any possible attack by enemy carrier and land-based aircraft – and prevent any enemy fleet attack on Allied shipping offshore. TF 58 would also require to interdict the Japanese from reinforcing their existing forces on Guam, Saipan and the other Mariana Islands. Task Force 58 aircraft would also provide close air support for the US amphibious ground troops as they made their landings on Guam and Tinian. Most of the close air support for the Saipan beachhead was provided by escort carriers and land-based Seventh Air Force fighters. With the Japanese Fleet not presenting any immediate threat after their crushing defeat at the 'Great Marianas Turkey Shoot', the TF 58 carriers had to deal with only isolated snoopers from several distant Japanese land bases.

On the morning of 22 June, two escort carriers launched the first Army P-47 Thunderbolts to Aslito Field on Saipan and escort carrier planes would continue to provide air support for the troops on Saipan until the island fell on 9 July. With this development, allied to the absence of the enemy fleet, the bulk of Task Force 58 retired from the Saipan area towards their forward base at Eniwetok on 23 June. There they would regroup and replenish before their deployment for the forthcoming Guam and Tinian landings, which had now been put back to the end of July as a result of the main reserve force for the landings having been committed on Saipan. Whilst three TF 58 task groups rested and revictualled at Eniwetok, Harrill's TG 58.4 (*Essex*, *Langley* and *Cowpens*) continued to strike Guam and Rota from 23 June–3 July. Task-group composition would change repeatedly during this period as commanders, air groups and new carriers arrived, whilst others went back to Pearl Harbor and yards on the West Coast for overhaul or refit.

Mitscher wanted to destroy the enemy planes and installations Jocko Clark had left behind at Iwo Jima and Chichi Jima during his raid on 24 June. Thus, on 30 June, he despatched Clark's TG 58.1, *Hornet*, *Yorktown* and *Bataan*, and Dave Davison's TG 58.2, *Wasp*, *Franklin*, *Monterey* and *Cabot*, to hit those islands.

On 3–4 July, Clark and Davison's two Task Groups 58.1 and 58.2 arrived on station off the Jimas and launched their attack – destroying more than seventy-five enemy aircraft, mostly in the air. The operation concluded with a 2½-hour cruiser bombardment of Iwo Jima. Fifty-four Japanese aircraft survived the US operation at Iwo Jima and Chichi Jima, but to avoid further losses they were recalled to Japan.

Simultaneously, on 4 July, TG 58.3 aircraft from *Enterprise*, *Lexington*, *San Jacinto* and *Princeton* struck Guam during the day. This was followed by a night naval bombardment of the island by destroyers before TG 58.3 retired towards Eniwetok, following after TG 58.4, which had departed the previous day.

On 5 July, Clark and Davison's Task Groups 58.1 and 58.2, coming south from the 3–4 July raid on Iwo Jima and Chichi Jima, hit Guam and Rota. These carrier raids thus began the reduction of Guam's defences in preparation for the amphibious assault slated for 21 July.

Tinian would be assaulted three days later on 24 July. On 6 July, the pre-invasion bombardment of Guam began, with Task Groups 58.1 and 58.2 rotating their attention between Guam and Rota for a full week.

With several carriers having retired to Pearl and yards on the West Coast for overhaul, Task Force 58 had been reorganised by the time the carriers of Montgomery's TG 58.3 and Bogan's 58.4, returning from their strikes at Guam and Rota, arrived at Eniwetok on 13 and 14 July. The reorganised Task Force 58 now comprised:

1. TG 58.1:
   Hornet
   Yorktown
   Cabot
2. TG 58.2:
   Wasp
   Franklin
3. TG 58.3:
   Lexington
   Bunker Hill
   San Jacinto
4. TG 58.4:
   Essex
   Langley
   Princeton

The Navy's Underwater Demolition Teams 3, 4 and 6 (UDT) were assigned to Guam, with UDTs 5, 6 and 7 being involved at Tinian (and Saipan). The UDT was an elite special-purpose force of specialists in combat swimming, closed circuit diving on oxygen rebreathers and underwater demolition. They were first in, operational from 14 July and continuing until 17 July. In preparation for the landings, UDT swimmers reconnoitred the invasion beaches and waters just offshore – in daylight and under direct enemy observation from the shore. They located reefs, rocks and shoals that would interfere with landing craft and demolished Japanese underwater obstacles with explosives.

The development of the UDT followed on from the Battle of Tarawa in November 1943 when aerial reconnaissance had incorrectly led planners to believe that dangerous coral reefs and flats were submerged deep enough to allow assault landing craft to safely pass right over. As history records, the landing craft foundered on the shallow reefs – and heavily laden US Marines were forced to abandon their landing craft in chest-deep water, some 1,000yd from shore and wade to shore, terribly exposed to Japanese fire. They suffered heavy casualties.

UDT combat swimmers just wore dark-blue navy swim trunks, canvas shoes, knee pads and gloves and carried only a large knife. To accurately measure water depths off the invasion beaches, the UDT swimmers turned themselves into human measuring sticks by painting black rings and dashes every 6in around their legs and torsos – from their feet right up to the full height of their upstretched arms. To create a seabed grid of accurate water depth across the reefs and beaches, they laid a grid of lines across the seabed that had knots every 25yd, where the water depth would be sounded. (Such was their bravery that when the Mariana operations were over, Admiral Turner recommended over 60 Silver Stars and over 300 Bronze Stars with Vs for UDT 3-7, an accolade that is unprecedented in US Navy/Marine Corps history.)

The day after the UDTs began their dangerous work, on 15 July, P-47s, joined by other escort carrier planes, began to drop napalm bombs to ignite the undergrowth and clear the jungle at the beach landing sites.

The TF 58 fast carriers continued to strike at targets in the Mariana Islands for another week – being joined on 18 July and the following days by naval bombardment ships. Guam and Tinian were bombarded heavily for several days prior to the amphibious assaults.

As a result of the invasion operation being delayed, the target Mariana Islands sustained the heaviest and most thorough pre-invasion bombardment of the Pacific War to date. In the hour preceding the landings on Guam on 21 July, three of Mitscher's task groups launched full deckload strikes – a total of 312 planes that dropped 124 tons of bombs on the assault beaches. The US Marines and Army 77th Infantry Division then stormed ashore, landing on both sides of the Orote Peninsula on the western side of Guam, intent on securing Apra Harbour. The 3rd Marine Division landed to the north of the peninsula whilst the 77th Infantry Division landed to the south along with the 1st Provisional Marine Brigade.

The planes of the TF 58 fast carriers and five escort carriers provided close support for the landings – but despite this, Japanese artillery sank twenty US landing craft and inflicted heavy casualties on the landing troops. By nightfall however US Marines and 77th Infantry Division troops had successfully established two beachheads, 2,000m deep.

Japanese troops counter-attacked throughout the early days of the Second Battle of Guam, as the US forces established their position and landed more troops. The Japanese attacks were mostly at night using infiltration tactics – but they were successfully driven back with heavy losses. Further landings were made by the 77th Infantry Division on 23–4 July but lacking amphibious vehicles, the Army troops were dropped off at the edge of the reef and had to wade ashore. The two beachheads were linked on 28 July and by 29 July the Orote Peninsula had been secured. The Japanese were now driven from the southern portion of Guam, withdrawing to the mountainous central and northern parts of the island. It would take until 10 August before organised Japanese resistance on Guam ended. More than 18,000 Japanese had been killed defending Guam with only 485 surrendering.

(b) Battle of Tinian, 24 July–1 August 1944

The invasion of Tinian by the 4th Marine Division began on 24 July, three days after the Guam landings. There were 9,000 Japanese troops stationed on the island, which had a working airfield and several airstrips completed or under construction. Tinian was well protected by natural barriers, most of the island had cliffs close to the waterline, some of which were more than 100ft high. The main part of the island was a limestone plateau that did not have the inland mountains of Saipan and Guam. Tinian was within the range of artillery firing across the strait from Saipan – as well as P-47s now based on the airfield on Guam. Organised Japanese resistance on Tinian ended on 1 August. Of the garrison of 8,500 Japanese troops, 313 survived.

(c) Aftermath

The conquest of the Mariana Island chain was a major stepping stone in the Pacific War. With its island bases to the west and south now flanked, Japan fell back to its inner defence line, extending along the islands that border South-East Asia, excepting the Palau Islands, which now projected as a vulnerable lone salient in the western Carolines.

Immediately following the occupation of the Mariana Islands, the US Navy construction battalions and Army engineers began to lay down huge aerodromes for the new very long-range B-29 Superfortress strategic bombers, which would go on to operate from these airfields until the end of the war. On 24 November 1944, the first B-29 strike on Japan itself would lift off from Saipan and in 1945, the nuclear attacks on Hiroshima and Nagasaki would be launched from Tinian.

Several key islands held by the Japanese still had to be captured for the drive north west towards Japan to continue. The Japanese surface fleet had escaped destruction at the First Battle of the Philippines, and its heavy ships and carriers allied to the remaining Japanese land-based air power were a constant and unpredictable threat. The road to the

Luzon bottleneck was still in the future – but when it was reached, the liberation of the Philippines and the blockade of Japan could begin.

But there were millions of battle-hardened Japanese veteran troops in China – and in Japan itself. Whilst the D-Day invasion of Normandy had successfully taken place a few weeks earlier in Europe on 6 June 1944, Allied planners envisaged that a similar invasion of the Japanese homeland still lay some two years in the future, in 1946. The Allies knew that future campaigns would come up against the inner bulwarks of Japan – and that air, sea and ground attacks by the Japanese would be remorseless and never ending, all the way from the Philippines to Tokyo.

(ii) Aerial Photo-reconnaissance and the 2nd Palau Air Assault – Operation SNAPSHOT, 23–30 July 1944

The area of sea between Luzon, at the north of the Philippines islands, Taiwan (then called Formosa) and China allowed Japanese shipping access to the South China Sea and to the rich natural resources of South-East Asia that she relied upon for her war effort. It also allowed shipping from Japan to ferry the munitions and materiel of war to her island territories. To enable an air and sea blockade of these vital Japanese shipping lanes and to ultimately cork the Luzon bottleneck, a better fleet anchorage was needed than Saipan or Guam – such as offered by Palau, Yap, Ulithi and several other islands. The Palauan island chain had a fine large harbour and an expansive lagoon that offered a fine anchorage that had been used by Japan as a major shipping and naval hub since the 1930s. Admiral Nimitz intended to seize the islands of the Palau archipelago in September – and to prepare for that operation, initial reconnaissance photographs of the Palaus and other possible island anchorages were required. The photo-reconnaissance operation was designated SNAPSHOT and formed part of the larger Operation FORAGER, the Mariana and Palau Islands campaign.

Leaving Task Group 58.4 to screen the concurrent Guam and Tinian landings, on 22 July, Vice Admiral Mitscher despatched Clark's Task Group 58.1, Davison's TG 58.2 and Montgomery's TG 58.3 towards Palau, Ulithi and Yap for an air attack and photo-reconnaissance mission slated for 25 July and the three following days.

The primary objective of the raid would be to obtain complete photographic coverage of the islands in preparation for the planned land invasion of Palau – it was still envisaged at this time that all the major Palauan Islands would be assaulted and taken. The proposed invasion beaches at Babelthuap, Arakabesan, Koror, Angaur and other islands were to be photographed in detail. The secondary objective of the raid would be to destroy enemy aircraft, shipping and ground installations.

Task Group 58.1 would raid Ulithi atoll, which lies midway between Guam and Palau – and also hit Yap atoll, immediately to the west of Ulithi, and north east of Palau. The Japanese had established a radio and weather station on Ulithi and occasionally used the lagoon as an anchorage. Yap had an airfield and a garrison of more than 4,000 IJA troops and some 1,500 IJN service personnel.

Task Group 58.2 and Task Group 58.3, commanded by Vice Admiral Mitscher aboard *Lexington*, would raid the Palauan chain of islands. The Task Force 58 carriers would fly their own Combat Air Patrols and Anti-Submarine Patrols and also be protected by the battleships *New Jersey*, *Washington*, *Indiana*, *Alabama* and *Iowa* and a screen of cruisers, destroyers and submarines.

On 25 July, the three task groups arrived at their holding station, some 120 miles north east of Palau and roughly midway between Palau and Yap. At about 1200 local time initial fighter sweeps of forty Hellcats from each task group launched against Palauan airfields on Peleliu, Ngesebus Island (just to the north of Peleliu) and Babelthuap, the northern and largest island of the Palaus, on which there were several airfields. The Arakabesan seaplane and submarine base, just north of Koror Island, would also be targeted.

As the fighter sweep went in, *Wasp* Hellcats caught and destroyed eight single-engine seaplanes and an Emily flying boat at the Arakabesan seaplane base. AA fire was intense and knocked down two US aircraft. Three single-engine aircraft were strafed at Babelthuap airfield. Following the fighter sweep, composite strikes of Hellcats, dive- and torpedo-bombers went in against shipping, AA positions and ground installations.

During the three days of strikes, fuel installations on Malakal were bombed and set afire again – as they had been in March during DESECRATE 1. An ammunition dump in Malakal was blown up and a radio station was destroyed on Koror, along with buildings and storage facilities. A fuel dump on Ngesebus was set ablaze and the phosphate plant and bauxite open mine in Babelthuap was destroyed and rendered useless. The carrier *Franklin* launched sixteen Hellcat fighters armed with rockets, and these were used in limited dogfights against Zekes on the first day of the strikes – and against land targets and shipping.

At Peleliu airfield, thirteen single-engine and eight twin-engine aircraft were destroyed – whilst at Ngesebus, eight aircraft were bombed and destroyed. Those Japanese fighters encountered aloft were shot down. After the first day, no further airborne enemy fighters were encountered.

Divisions of four Hellcats and three Avengers each were sent out in a three-sector search of an area stretching 50 miles in all directions from Palau. Search planes from *San Jacinto* discovered the IJN minelayer *Sokuten*, on her way to lay mines at Ulithi atoll, 30 nautical miles north east of the largest Palauan island of Babelthuap. The minelayer was escorted by a long-range Aichi E13A1 Jake seaplane. The four *San Jacinto* Hellcats engaged *Sokuten* and shot down the Jake. During strafing by the Hellcats, the minelayer's cargo of mines detonated, and she sank quickly.

On 27 July, the 1,500-ton, No. 1-class armed fast transport *T.1* was sunk, along with several other smaller vessels. *T.1* had been spotted moored close to and parallel with high cliffs – she was camouflaged with nets and a dense matting of branches and foliage in an attempt to make her undetectable from the air. Other vessels were moored in small bays and similarly camouflaged. When the initial US aerial reconnaissance photos were studied back afloat on the task-force vessels, it became clear that the cliffs had man-made artificial straight lines where none should be; funnel openings and outlines of hulls were spotted amongst the foliage. Once targets were identified, strikes were sent in. Ships still beached or disabled from the DESECRATE 1 raid in March, such as *Teshio Maru* and *Hokutai Maru*, were hit again.

During the raid, Task Group 58.2 lost 2 Hellcats and 2 Helldivers to ground-based AA fire – whilst Task Group 58.3 lost 2 Hellcats, 1 Helldiver and 2 Avengers. But by the late afternoon of day three of the raid, 27 July, the Palau objectives had been accomplished and the two task groups were ordered to retire to the Saipan area. Task Group 58.1 joined them as it returned from the Ulithi and Yap raid on 29 July 1944.

The fast carriers of Task Force 58 were able to use Saipan as an anchorage from July until November 1944 – and the tankers of ServRon 10 used the anchorage from August 1944 to February 1945. Guam became a ServRon 10 base in September 1944 and a fast-carrier anchorage in November that same year.

(iii) Raiding the Jimas and the Bonins, August 1944

With Operation SNAPSHOT complete, in early August, as Task Force 58 retired from the western Carolines, Rear Admiral Clark, CTG 58.1, and Rear Admiral Montgomery, CTG 58.3, received orders from Mitscher to head back north to the Bonin and Volcano Islands to knock out a new concentration of Japanese planes and a reported light carrier. It would be Clark's fourth raid on the Jimas since 16 June. Rear Admiral Davison withdrew TG 58.2, *Wasp, Yorktown* and *Princeton*, to Eniwetok to rest, replenish and plan for operations against the Philippines.

As Clark, CTG 58.1 (*Hornet, Franklin* and *Cabot*), and Montgomery, CTG 58.3 (*Bunker Hill, Lexington* and *San Jacinto*), closed on the Jimas, they launched aircraft against Chichi Jima, Haha Jima, Muko Jima and the Bonins on 4–5 August. No light carrier was spotted – but a fleeing convoy of eight freighters and three escorts was detected. Clark's TG 58.1 planes sunk nine of the ships whilst his cruisers sunk the remaining two – 20,000 tons of Japanese shipping had just gone to the bottom of the Pacific.

During these raids, some twenty-four Japanese planes were shot up on the ground whilst land installations were bombed and shelled by cruisers on 6 August. Unknown to the Americans, Iwo Jima was open to occupation after these raids – but with the time gained after the raids ended, Japan immediately began to reinforce Iwo Jima into a virtually unassailable fortress.

With the raids complete, Task Force 58 headed for Eniwetok, anchoring there on 9 August for a two-week rest – its last before the final push towards Japan.

(iv) Task Force 38 is Formed

The Navy's operational planner, the Commander Fifth Fleet, needed time at Pearl Harbor to plan the details of each successive major amphibious operation – before taking command of the forces at sea to execute the operation. After the successes of the first half of 1944, it was clear that the enemy had to be driven back relentlessly without quarter. There could be no operational inactivity between campaigns whilst campaign planning took place.

To allow a continuous aggressive thrust forward, the Navy's solution, adopted on 5–6 May 1944 in a meeting in San Francisco between Admirals King (COMINCH, CNO) and Nimitz (CINPOA) to which Admiral Halsey was invited, was a two-platoon system of fleet commanders. One commander and staff would be engaged on the beach at Pearl planning forthcoming operations, whilst the other commander would be in charge of Task Force 58 as it fought at sea. When one operation ended, the commanders and staff would rotate.

Halsey was informed in June that with the end of the Solomons campaign, he would be relieved as Commander of the South Pacific

Area (COMSOPAC) and would go back to sea as Commander of the Third Fleet, although the Third Fleet at this point consisted only of three destroyers and one battleship. Halsey would however rotate with Admiral Spruance, Commander Fifth Fleet, and would be in tactical command of the Fifth Fleet, which consisted at this time of over 500 warships. When Spruance had command, Nimitz's forces would be known as Fifth Fleet, whilst under Halsey they would be known as Third Fleet. Task-force designations would be similarly altered with Task Force 58 under Spruance becoming Task Force 38 under Halsey. The ships would stay the same – and it was hoped that the enemy might be confused into thinking that two separate fleets were at sea. The subterfuge worked for a while.

When Admiral Spruance rotated home, Halsey as Commander Third Fleet would have King's appointment of the aviator Vice Admiral John Sidney 'Slew' McCain exercising tactical command of the fast carriers. McCain would rotate posts with Mitscher. On 15 June, the day Spruance put his Marines and Army ashore at Saipan, Halsey handed over the South Pacific to his deputy and flew to Pearl Harbor where he set up his HQ on 17 June and began planning operations to follow on from the invasion of Saipan, Tinian and Guam. King was putting an emphasis on naval aviation, insisting that all non-aviator fleet and task-force commanders should have naval aviators as chiefs of staff.

On 10 August, the day after Task Force 58 anchored at Eniwetok, Admiral Nimitz arrived in the Marshalls for final conferences with his commanders before the forthcoming Philippines campaign, presenting a Gold Star to Mitscher, in lieu of a third Distinguished Service Medal.

Admiral Halsey, with his flag on the battleship *New Jersey*, relieved Admiral Spruance on 26 August in the scheduled rotation of command. As Admiral Spruance left the fighting area, the Fifth Fleet morphed into the Third Fleet – Task Force 58 became a paper force, whilst the same ships and the same service personnel were redesignated as Task Force 38.

Vice Admiral John Sidney 'Slew' McCain, Mitscher's rotation successor, had however little experience in fast-carrier task-force operations. Tactical command of TF 38 would therefore remain with Mitscher aboard *Lexington* for three more months whilst 'Slew' McCain relieved Jocko Clark (CTG 58.1) as Commander of TG 38.1, by way of an interim learning assignment.

When Halsey took command of the Third Fleet, he saw himself as the fast-carrier commander, above Mitscher and McCain, who were the tactical carrier commanders. Halsey however lacked Mitscher's knowledge and experience of carrier combat. As he took command, he visited Mitscher's flagship: 'I hadn't been with the fleet for more than two years; I wanted to see what the new carriers and planes looked like.'[1] Carrier warfare had evolved and developed since Halsey, as Commander of Carrier Division 2, had led his series of hit-and-run raids from *Enterprise* against Japanese positions in the Gilberts, Marshalls and Wake Island, more than three years earlier in February and March 1942 before delivering Doolittle's bombers for their raid on Tokyo in April 1942. Halsey would need the advice and guidance of seasoned veterans, as neither he nor any of his staff, or indeed 'Slew' McCain, had taken part in any of the Task Force 58 operations to date. Mitscher, on the other hand, had unparalleled battle experience, as did his Chief of Staff, Arleigh A. Burke and the remaining veteran Task Group 58 commanders.

Halsey was however an aviator – and was not expected to shy away from risks nor be reluctant to seek battle, as the non-aviator Spruance had appeared to be at times. Halsey's style of command was very different to Spruance. Rather than issuing detailed operational plans as Spruance had done, Halsey operated by despatch, sending communications, which were perhaps often not as clear as they could have been. But having missed the great carrier battles of the Coral Sea, Midway and the Philippine Sea, true to his nickname, 'Bull' Halsey wanted to seek out and destroy the Japanese carriers at the earliest opportunity.

MacArthur, the Allied Supreme Commander in the Southwest Pacific Area, had made the liberation of the Philippines his primary aim – something he had promised when he withdrew his forces from there in 1941 in the face of the initial Japanese onslaught. The Philippines comprise more than 7,600 islands with 3 principal geographical divisions:

1. Luzon (the largest island) situated in the northern portion of the archipelago.
2. The central Visayas Islands.
3. Mindanao (the second largest island) to the south.

Back in June 1944, MacArthur had set out that the operational stepping stones to retaking the capital, Manila, as being:

1. Mindanao Island in the southern Philippines – 25 October.
2. Leyte Island in the central Philippines – 15 November.
3. Aparri on the northern tip of Luzon – 15 January 1945.
4. Mindoro Island, south of Luzon – February 1945.
5. Lingayen Gulf, on the west coast of Luzon, north of Manila – 1 April 1945.

All these operations except the last would depend on land-based air. Admiral Nimitz, backed by Admiral King, agreed to land at Leyte, on the east coast of the Philippines, where air bases could be established. Nimitz however proposed bypassing Luzon, in favour of simultaneous landings in March 1945 in south-west Formosa (modern-day Taiwan) and the adjacent Chinese coast at Amoy (modern-day Xiamen) – and quickly to plug the bottleneck of Japanese supply lines to and from South-East Asia, the Indonesian and Philippines archipelagos, and thus hasten the defeat of Japan.

By mid-August 1944, the operational timetable laid out by the Joint Chiefs of Staff back on 12 March 1944 still remained in place. Palau was scheduled to be taken by Nimitz by 15 September, the southern Philippines by MacArthur commencing in October. To cork the bottleneck, Nimitz was to plan for an invasion of Formosa, and MacArthur for an invasion of Luzon, in February 1945.

But such was the rapid progress made to date that many Allied planners advocated bypassing all of these places. Halsey had proposed bypassing the Palaus and western Carolines in May, but Nimitz and indeed Halsey's influential Chief of Staff, Rear Admiral Robert Bostwick Carney, had disagreed.

The Joint Chiefs of Staff had asked Nimitz and MacArthur on 13 June if they felt the Philippines and Formosa could be bypassed in favour of a direct landing on Kyushu, the third largest and most southern of the five main islands of Japan. Both said no – and stressed that air and naval bases were needed in the Palaus or Morotai, then in the southern or central Philippines before moving to Luzon or Formosa to cork the Luzon bottleneck and begin the air and sea blockade to strangle Japan. A direct thrust at Japan was considered too dangerous at this point – given Japan's interior air and shipping defences.

Early in July 1944, MacArthur and Nimitz agreed that the land and sea advance towards Japan should be supported by land-based air all the way. They agreed that Mindanao, the second largest island in the Philippines, in the south, would have to be taken after Palau – the date for the seizure was set for 15 November.

Allied strategists still greatly feared the potential of Japanese land-based air power spread across their multitude of island airfields, their so-called 'unsinkable carriers'. Augmented by carrier air, these planes could cause significant Allied losses. An intermediate base was therefore required that could provide sustained land-based air support – the task of supporting the planned major invasion operations could not be left to the fast carriers alone.

The possible ways forward towards a final attack on Japan itself were hotly debated – but MacArthur decided, with JCS approval, to assault Morotai Island in the Halmahera group of eastern Indonesian Maluku Islands, then known as the Moluccas. The Halmahera group of islands lie roughly midway between New Guinea and modern-day Sulawesi, one of the four Greater Sunda Islands of Indonesia. The invasion of Morotai would take place on 15 September, the same day that Nimitz's forces would land in the Palaus.

By the time Task Force 38 sortied from Eniwetok on 28 August, with Admiral Halsey exercising tactical command, the firm dates for the Pacific campaign to move north west from New Guinea had been set as:

1. Morotai Island and Peleliu Island (Palau archipelago) – invasion on 15 September 1944.
2. Mindanao, the second largest Philippine island, in the south of the archipelago – invasion on 15 November.
3. Leyte Island, in the central Visayas group of the Philippines – invasion on 20 December.

Halsey was tasked with supporting the landings at Morotai and Peleliu on 15 September and reducing the 650 Japanese aircraft believed to be based in some 63 Japanese airfields in or near the Philippines. He had 10 weeks to accomplish this before the invasion of the large island of Mindanao on 15 November.

For the thrust north west, Halsey and Mitscher now had sixteen fast carriers. This would be the first time the fast-carrier task force had operated at full strength since the attack on the Japanese Mobile Fleet at the First Battle of the Philippines in June.

Fleet Organisation
Commander Third Fleet – Admiral W.F. Halsey
CTF 38 – Vice Admiral M.A. Mitscher
1. CTG 38.1 – Vice Admiral J.S. McCain:
   Hornet (CV-12) – Captain A.K. Doyle, Air Group 2
   Wasp (CV-18) – Captain O.A. Weller, Air Group 14
   Belleau Wood (CVL-24) – Captain J. Perry, Air Group 21
   Cowpens (CVL-25) – Captain J.W. Taylor, Air Group 22
   Monterey (CVL-26) – Captain S.I. Ingersoll, Air Group 28
2. CTG 38.2 – Rear Admiral G.F. Bogan:
   Intrepid (CV-11) – Captain J.F. Bolger, Air Group 18
   Bunker Hill (CV-17) – Captain M.R. Greer, Air Group 8

Cabot (CVL-28) – Captain S.J. Michael, Air Group 31
Independence (CVL-22) – Captain E.C. Ewen, Night Air Group 41
3. CTG 38.3 – Rear Admiral F.C. Sherman:
   Essex (CV-9) – Captain C.W. Wieber, Air Group 15
   Lexington (CV-16) – Captain E.W. Litch, Air Group 19
   Princeton (CVL-23) – Captain W.H. Buraker, Air Group 27
   Langley (CVL-27) – Captain W.M. Dillon, Air Group 32
4. CTG 38.4 – Rear Admiral R.E. Davison:
   Franklin (CV-13) – Captain J.M. Shoemaker, Air Group 13
   Enterprise (CV-6) – Captain C.D. Glover, Air Group 20
   San Jacinto (CVL-30) – Captain M.H. Kernodle, Air Group 51

Departing Eniwetok on 28 August, TG 38.4 launched strikes against Iwo Jima and Chichi Jima once again from 31 August–2 September – before moving on to Yap on 6 September. The light carrier *Monterey* raided Wake Island on 5 September. From 6–8 September, Task Groups 38.1, 38.2 and 38.3 bombed the Palauan Islands – refuelling off Palau on 9 September and assuming a supporting role whilst the other carriers attacked airfields on Mindanao on 9 and 10 September.

Admiral Halsey opened his attack on the central Philippines on 12 September, flying 1,200 sorties – followed by another 1,200 sorties on the 13th. He was surprised by the lack of land-based Japanese aircraft encountered, which crystallised his thoughts about the weakness of enemy air power. In the strikes against the Visayan Islands, his planes shot down 173 enemy planes and destroyed 305 more on the ground, sunk 59 ships, damaged many more and destroyed shore installations. TF 38 lost eight planes in combat and one operationally.[2] The Japanese had been dealt another crippling blow.

On 12 September 1944, Ensign Thomas C. Tillar from *Hornet*'s Air Group 2 was engaged by three Japanese fighters during a bombing mission against an island off Cebu. During the dogfight, his F6F Hellcat was hit and disabled, he had to ditch his F6F about 600yd off the small island of Apit, some 4 miles west of Leyte. Once safely down on the water, he broke out his life raft and clambered into it, as his aircraft settled into the water and sank.

Friendly local Filipinos in outriggers came out and picked him up from his life raft. Once ashore, he was surrounded by a crowd of some 200 locals, one of whom was a Philippine Army soldier – who himself had been captured by the Japanese, imprisoned in Luzon for eighteen months before escaping to Apit and hiding out. He was able to interpret between Tillar and the locals – who revealed just how weak Japanese defences were. For whilst there were some 15,000 Japanese troops stationed on Cebu, there were none on Leyte Island itself.

Later the same day, after signalling to patrolling US aircraft with his survival kit mirror, Tillar was picked up by a PBY Catalina flying boat. He was returned to the cruiser *Wichita* (CA-45) where he was interviewed by the CruDiv commander Rear Admiral Charles Turner Joy, who passed on the local intelligence of the surprisingly weak Japanese troop strength in the Central Philippines to Halsey. This first-hand information confirmed Halsey's suspicions that Japanese defences in the Philippines were nothing but a hollow shell.[3]

On 14 September TF 38 hit Mindanao and the Visayas and then hit enemy installations around Manila and the Visayas on the 21st, 22nd and 24th. By the end of September 1944, in the last 3 weeks of Task Force 38 operations, 893 Japanese planes airborne and parked had been destroyed whilst 67 ships totalling 224,000 tons of shipping had been sunk.[4] The fast carriers had now secured several forward bases, the major one being Ulithi, which was occupied on 23 September. Ulithi is the westernmost atoll in the Caroline Islands – lying 850 miles east

Murderers' Row. Third Fleet carriers anchored in Ulithi Atoll, Carolines. The ships, left to right, are: *Wasp* (CV-18), *Yorktown* (CV-10), *Hornet* (CV-12) and *Hancock* (CV-19). A destroyer escort passes by, giving scale to the image. The F6F Hellcat fighters in the foreground are on board USS *Ticonderoga* (CV-14). (National Archives 80-G-294150)

of the Philippines and 1,300 miles south of Tokyo, and was perfectly positioned to act as a staging area for West Pacific operations.

With the September raids a clear success that drew little enemy resistance, and armed with reliable intelligence, Halsey cut short the other planned strikes and headed his carriers north. He now knew that the ten weeks provisionally allocated to reduce Japanese air power for the Mindanao invasion were no longer required – and that with the fast carriers already in command of the air in the Western Pacific, there would be no need for a landing on Mindanao at all. Supported by Task Force 38, MacArthur's Sixth Army could go directly to Leyte, in the central Philippines, which was much closer to Manila – and Tokyo. Leyte offered many deep-water approaches and sandy beaches for amphibious assaults and fast resupply.

Halsey made this recommendation to Nimitz – and trusting Halsey's judgement, Nimitz and MacArthur endorsed it. Halsey's recommendation was passed to President Franklin D. Roosevelt, who was then meeting with the other Allied heads of state and combined planners at Quebec. They took just 90 minutes of deliberation to agree to the cancellation of the planned landing on Mindanao. US troops would as a result wade ashore at Leyte on 20 October 1944, two months earlier than the original date of 20 December.

Halsey had also, after the early September raids, wanted to cancel the operation to seize Morotai Island, and Peleliu Island in the Palaus, which was to begin on 15 September - but it was too late in the day to stop it. The landings on Morotai took place smoothly – McCain's TG 38.1 holding station 50 miles offshore for air strikes along with six escort carriers. The landings on Peleliu would be a terrible ordeal.

The subsequent landings on Leyte and Luzon would be under MacArthur's command – and the new Allied strategy fundamentally changed the campaign. Allied troops who were then gathering for three landings, at Yap in the Caroline Islands, the Talaud Islands (north west of Sulawesi in Indonesia) and Mindanao, were re-tasked to the accelerated Leyte operation on 20 October. The plan for the capture of Formosa and Amoy was also cancelled as Japanese forces were overrunning US 14th Air Force bomber bases in China. This would leave any Formosa operation without air support. If troops were committed to Formosa, the timetable for the leap forward and north to Okinawa in the Ryukyus would be slowed down.

The island of Leyte would be the first objective of the Philippines campaign and would be followed by landings on Mindoro Island, which lies to the south west of the largest Philippines island, Luzon.

Luzon itself, the northernmost large island in the Philippines, would be assaulted later – it lies directly south across the Bashi Channel from Taiwan (then Formosa) and has the open expanses of the South China Sea to its west and the Philippine Sea to its east.

With the Leyte operation imminent, the question of subsequent targets after the next targets, Mindoro and Luzon, was answered by a new timetable from Admiral Nimitz. Iwo Jima in the Volcano Islands would be assaulted and taken in late January 1945 – and Okinawa in the Ryukyu Islands would be assaulted on 1 March. Both Iwo Jima and Okinawa would be needed as air bases, Iwo as a base for fighters that would escort B-29 Superfortress bombers hitting the Japanese home islands. It would also provide an emergency landing airfield for disabled bombers returning from Japan. Okinawa would be used as a supply base and airfield for medium to heavy bombers.

The Joint Chiefs agreed Nimitz's plan on 3 October and brought forward the invasion of Luzon to about 20 December, the original date for the invasion of Leyte. The fast carriers would support MacArthur at Luzon from where the Army Air Force could then operate in support of the Okinawa operation. Formosa, bypassed under the new timetable, would be neutralised from the air.

After the invasions of Leyte, Luzon, Iwo Jima and Okinawa there was only one last objective left – Japan itself. But exactly how Japan would be finally defeated thereafter was hotly debated by Allied strategists:

1. The Army favoured an invasion, such as had taken place in Europe against Germany.
2. The Navy favoured an air-sea blockade to starve and pound Japan into submission.

The Joint Chiefs of Staff determined on 11 July 1944 that Japan would be invaded – believing that a blockade would be too prolonged.

(v) New Carriers and New Planes

The Americans knew that Japan had been dealt punishing body blows and was severely weakened. They also knew that Japanese planes and pilots were inferior to theirs. But nevertheless, ComAirPAc warned in late July 1944: 'An improvement of Japanese aircraft even halfway to German standards would cause our carrier forces considerable difficulty.' Admirals Towers and Pownall cautioned about 'the potential vulnerability of aircraft carriers to effectively coordinated torpedo and bombing attacks'. They believed that Japan might change its strategy as the US carriers closed on Japan. ComAirPac analysis in June 1944 cautioned: 'Losses will be heavier. Overconfidence is not justified.'[5]

Following the defeat of the Japanese Mobile Fleet in the First Battle of the Philippines and the subsequent capture of Saipan in early July 1944, carrier raids and smaller landings continued through the summer of 1944 without fear of enemy fleet action or significant air intervention.

Three new Essex-class carriers had reported for duty in the Pacific. *Franklin* (CV-13) had arrived at Eniwetok in June and become Rear Admiral Ralph E. Davison's flagship. *Hancock* (CV-19) arrived at Ulithi on 5 October 1944, followed by *Ticonderoga* (CV-14) on 29 October.

During the latter part of 1944, new Essex-class carrier commissionings took place at a rate of about one a month with *Bennington* (CV-20) in August, *Shangri-La* (CV-38) in September, *Randolph* (CV-15) in October and *Bon Homme Richard* (CV-31) in November. Late 1944 saw launchings for fitting out of the Essex-class carriers *Antietam* (CV-36), *Lake Champlain* (CV-39) and *Boxer* (CV-21). These carriers were almost identical to the earlier Essexes except for slightly longer flight decks on some – and, as night operations intensified, more powerful longer range 40mm Bofors AA guns were substituted for the less effective short-range 20mm Oerlikon. Mark 12 5in/38 calibre DP naval guns, common on surface warships, were added to the carriers. Its increasingly accurate proximity fuzed VT shells proved very effective with a horizontal range of 16,000m and able to knock down aircraft by shell fragments, not direct hits, up to a ceiling of 37,200ft.

The primary defence of the fast carriers remained the Combat Air Patrol (CAP) interceptor aircraft that were vectored towards the enemy by fighter director officers using ship-based radar. Early in the summer of 1944, the Navy began to install the new Mark 22 radar which, adapted to shipboard fire-control systems, operated with the older Mark 4 and Mark 12 radars to give an improved fix on enemy aircraft. The F6F-3 Hellcat now flew at speeds of up to 376mph at 17,000ft and had defeated the Zero and every other Japanese fighter then in the air. By autumn 1944, each fast carrier was better equipped to cope with enemy aircraft incursions than ever before.

Earlier that year, in spring 1944, Nimitz had called for 1.67 carrier air groups per fast carrier – meaning that 32 carrier air groups would be in commission by 30 June 1945 and 39 by December 1945.

Nimitz felt that as the fleet neared Japan, enemy shipping targets would decrease and consequently the need for torpedo bombing would decrease. But expecting determined resistance, more fighters would be required. Admiral King COMINCH had accepted Nimitz's proposal for more fighters at the expense of torpedo-bombers – and on 31 July 1944, had authorised the alteration of heavy carrier air groups from the existing 18 torpedo-bombers (VT), 36 dive-bombers (VB) and 36 fighters (VF) per air group to 18 torpedo VT bombers, 24 VB dive-bombers 'with VF to capacity'. This would give about 54 fighters per air group.[6]

The restructuring of air groups had begun in late August 1944, with each large air group exchanging twelve Curtiss SB2C Helldiver dive-bombers for twelve F6F-3 Hellcat fighters. The SB2C Helldiver pilots were checked out in fighters – and those pilots then assigned to Hellcats found the fighters now equipped with a single 500lb general purpose GP bomb. All heavy carriers had their fifty-four fighters by November 1944.

After correcting a pilot visibility weakness that had prevented the F4U Corsair being deployed to carriers, the 'Whistling Death' fighter-bomber had been deemed ready for assignment to carriers back in April 1944. But few had actually been deployed to carriers, as the Corsair was now the standard Marine Corps fighter and could not be spared for carrier operations. Although other fighters were being developed for introduction to the fleet in 1945 and 1946, by the end of the summer of 1944, the Navy still depended on the F6F-5 Hellcat for its main carrier fighter strength – with the F4U-1 and F4U-4 Corsairs being deployed as and when the Marines could afford to release them. All fighters, starting with the F6F-3 Hellcat, would be capable of service as fighter-bombers and fighters were going to be further improved with four new additions, the 20mm cannon, napalm bombs and 5in and 11.75in rockets. The 20mm cannon carried much more punch than the previous 50-calibre machine gun.

Napalm was essentially liquid gas in a bomb casing that started fires when dropped and in mid-1944 this was dramatically improved by the addition of a gelatine thickener to the gas that allowed the mixture to cling to a surface and burn with great intensity. Dropped in jettisonable used fuel tanks these firebombs could spread a sheet of flame over 25,000 sq. ft for a full minute, which then continued to smoulder for 5–10 more minutes. Napalm bombs made their first combat deployment in the Marianas during the summer of 1944 and would go on to be used as an incendiary in fire-bombing campaigns for the rest of the war. Napalm has also fuelled most tank, ship and infantry flamethrowers and has seen use in more recent theatres such as Vietnam. Today, many nations maintain large stockpiles of napalm-based weapons of various types.

The aircraft-launched rocket was perhaps the most significant improvement to the carrier aircraft offensive capability. An improved 5in rocket was introduced during spring 1944, the HVAR (High Velocity

Aircraft Rocket), nicknamed the 'Holy Moses' – with eight launchers mounted per fighter. It went into combat in August 1944 and became extremely popular with pilots. With these rockets, one aircraft now packed as much punch as a salvo from a destroyer.

The 11.75in Tiny Tim air to ground rocket, under design for carrier planes, incorporated free-drop release and ignition away from the plane. Once perfected, this would give one plane the same effect as a 12in battleship gun and a thirty-six-plane squadron the firepower of one volley from a division of three heavy cruisers.

During the summer, the fighters and fighter-bombers were moving away from bombs to 5in rockets whilst dive-bombers and torpedo planes shifted to bombs only. Fighters were now multi-role versatile aircraft that could deploy napalm, 50-calibre guns, rockets and 20mm cannon against land targets.

In July 1944, as a result of the increase in fighter numbers, the Navy now had too many bombers. The last Douglas SBD Dauntless dive-bomber left the carriers – whilst improved SB2C-3 Helldiver and later SB2C-4 aircraft arrived. No new scout-bombers were planned – the requirement for the visual search of the old scout-bomber had now been superseded by other aircraft that carried radar.

The Navy realised it needed a single plane type that could perform all types of attack, to dive bomb, to carry out a mast-head horizontal bomb run, drop napalm, fire rockets, launch an aerial torpedo, strafe and dogfight with enemy fighters. A plane with a powerful fast engine, sufficient armour and range, that was capable of carrier operations and all this by a single pilot. Thus, the old VSB (scout-bomber), VB (dive-bomber) and VT (torpedo plane) designations were dropped in favour of one all-purpose attack aircraft, the bomber-torpedo plane, designation VBT. Although several VBTs were under development for deployment in 1945 and 1946, by June 1944 a makeshift VBT, the Douglas BTD Destroyer, was produced – but only thirty were ever built. They did however provide the groundwork for a much superior plane, the BT2D, which could fly to 344mph at 15,600ft with a range of 1,250 miles giving a combat radius of over 500 miles. It required a shorter carrier flight deck, could carry a 3-ton payload of rockets, bombs and/or torpedoes and mounted two 20mm wing guns and an APS-4 radar. Although the Navy initially ordered fifteen of these new aircraft on 6 July 1944, Douglas and BuAer engineers laboured over the prototype for the rest of 1944 and it did not become operational. The Grumman TBF-1C Avenger was modified for higher cruising altitudes, better speed and range and improved bomb capability.

Night-fighting capability was improved, largely as a result of the obvious paralysis that had come with the darkness of night during the Battle of the Philippine Sea – a paralysis that had prevented the Japanese Fleet being attacked. Lack of night-search training and skills had restricted Spruance's ability to gather intelligence – and the lack of night training had led to the near disastrous night recovery and water landings of 20 June on day two of the battle.

ComAirPac now required all carrier pilots to qualify in night landings before going into combat. On 5 July, the recently repaired light carrier *Independence* was designated as a night carrier – and several night-fighter and torpedo detachments were shaped at Pearl into Night Air Group 41, which comprised nineteen F6F-5N Hellcats and eight TBM-1D Avengers. *Independence* and her Night Air Group sailed for Eniwetok on 17 August 1944.

The air admirals wanted to go further than the night carrier *Independence* and create a *night carrier task group*. It was generally agreed that this should be centred on *Enterprise*, which had initiated night defensive air operations in the Gilberts and whose Torpedo 10 had originated offensive night air operations at Truk during Operation HAILSTONE on 18 February 1944 – with the first radar-guided night attack on Japanese shipping at 0200. Eight Japanese ships were sunk in darkness in this one attack, including the valuable 10,020grt oiler *Shinkoku Maru* – whilst five other ships were damaged, all for the loss of one of the twelve TBF Avengers. *Enterprise* night-fighters had acquitted themselves well during the Saipan landings – and so, *Enterprise* was earmarked for future conversion to a night carrier.

Admiral King CNO, although originally envisioning a night-carrier task group of *Enterprise* and four escorts, had agreed in late July to have the light carriers *Independence* and *Bataan* assigned to the night task group, to operate along with *Enterprise*. But it was early days, and the fleet wouldn't have a two-carrier night group until the end of the year.

All night aircraft would be equipped with radar – the APS-6 being fitted into the new F6F-5N Hellcat night-fighter could pinpoint a carrier up to 22 miles away. The TBM Avengers carried the ASD-1 radars which could see a flattop 40 miles distant. Night pilots trained and qualified in night procedures and tactics off Hawaii. With these new carriers, weapons and aircraft, for the first time in the Pacific War the Navy felt that with 38,000 planes it had enough planes and pilots to carry on the offensive.

In June 1944, Task Force 58 had abandoned its bases at Majuro and Kwajalein for new bases closer to the fighting – at Eniwetok in the western Marshalls, Manus in the Admiralties and, once pacified, Saipan. On 23 September, Ulithi atoll in the Carolines was occupied. Ulithi atoll islands surround one of the largest lagoons in the world which was an ideal natural harbour – and lay just 1,300 miles south of Tokyo on the same meridian of longitude. Service Squadron 10 arrived soon afterwards to convert Ulithi into a major forward Pacific base that would be used during the major naval operations towards the end of the war, including Leyte Gulf and Okinawa.

As Ulithi was being prepared as a naval anchorage, the fast carriers of TG 38.1 entered Seeadler Harbour on Manus Island in the Admiralties on 29 September. TG 38.2 went to Saipan on the 28 September and TG 38.3 anchored in Kossol Passage at the north end of the Palau archipelago on the 27th. Both Task Groups 38.2 and 38.3 were able to move to Ulithi lagoon on 1–2 October, whilst TG 38.4 remained off the Palaus until later in October.

The forty or so ships of Service Squadron 10 moved 1,400 miles west across the Pacific from Eniwetok to Ulithi in October – when a whole floating base was established within a month. ServRon 4 operated as a complete floating naval base with a complement of tenders, repair ships and concrete barges. A 'floating tank farm' of obsolete tankers provided a reserve fuel supply of 400,000 barrels of fuel oil and aviation gasoline. Floating dry docks that could lift a battleship were towed to Ulithi. ServRon 2 also served the Pacific Fleet operating all repair, salvage and hospital ships in the combat zone.

In the vast expanses of the Pacific the fast carriers would now be operating at extreme range for long periods of time and it was not practical for them to have to return to Ulithi for fuel and replacement aircraft on a regular basis. Thus, the At Sea Logistics Service Group was created, comprising 34 oilers that were protected by 11 escort carriers, 19 destroyers and 26 destroyer escorts. These ships were grouped into replenishment task units of nine to twelve oilers that would sortie for a rendezvous with the fast carriers just a short distance from combat areas.

The creation of replenishment task units allowed continuous at-sea rotation. Fuelling from merchant tankers at Ulithi, after oiling fleet units, each replenishment task unit would be relieved every few days during active operations by another replenishment task unit. The relieved unit then returned to Ulithi to replenish once again from merchant tankers.

Each replenishment task unit also had one escort CVE carrier, a 'jeep carrier' that would provide Combat Air Patrols and carry replacement aircraft and pilots for the fast carriers along with a destroyer screen.

Halsey set each replenishment rendezvous at the extreme range of Japanese land-based aircraft, which were never able to disrupt replenishment at sea operations successfully. The At Sea Logistics Service Group gave the fast-carrier task force great mobility and range – and enabled fast-carrier aircraft to now attack Japan's inner defences. Such was the rapid progress of the Pacific War that Manus was abandoned in October and Saipan was abandoned in November, in favour of Eniwetok, Ulithi and other anchorages closer to the enemy.

By summer 1944, the so-called Gun Club, non-aviator admirals who still clung to the cherished but now outdated belief of the primacy of the battleship in the fleet, had lost control of the Navy. The flood of young admirals with aviator's wings was too great and all new aviator chiefs of staff were directed to be upgraded from captain to commodore or rear admiral. As 1944 wore on, the US Navy was morphing into an air navy. The importance of air power at sea was undoubted – and now determined the very character of the US Fleet itself. Naval planners could begin to consider what the future post-war period would look like – what form and what composition would be required for the Navy to police the peace that would follow after the war. A carrier fleet of vast proportions was envisaged – with twenty-one fast carriers and twenty-two escort carriers. With the era of the primacy of the battleship now clearly ended, the post-war Navy would hold only nine battleships.

The success of the carrier operations against Rabaul, the Gilberts, the Marshalls, Truk and Palau was clear. Even before the display of carrier power at the 'Great Marianas Turkey Shoot', the naval aviators in Washington had succeeded in getting a naval construction programme commissioned that would produce a vast carrier fleet – before any post-war scaling down took place. By 1 July 1944, with it looking likely that the war would last at least until the end of 1945, the Navy already had in commission ten Essex-class heavy carriers, the venerable pre-war carriers *Saratoga* and *Enterprise* – and nine Independence-class light carriers. In addition, keels had already been laid down in 1943 for eight more Essex-class carriers and two of the new Midway-class battle carriers. Four more Essex-class keels had been laid down in the first six months of 1944 and Nimitz was pressing for rapid completion of carriers under construction.

The thirty-five carriers in commission, or under construction, at the beginning of summer 1944 however seemed insufficient to ensure final victory against Japan. Thus, during summer 1944, three more Essex-class carriers, another Midway-class battle carrier and two light carriers of a new Saipan-class were laid down, with one more Essex-class being laid down as late as January 1945.

Mitscher, as a result of his unparalled combat experience, had determined that the four-carrier task group was the optimal size – and so it would be. With the current carrier construction programme, by summer 1945, the Pacific Fleet would have 17 heavy carriers and 9 light carriers and so could be organised into 2 separate fast-carrier task forces of 13 carriers each that could operate independently and provide the fleet with great flexibility. Mitscher and McCain could then command at sea simultaneously and there would be no need to rotate carrier task-force commanders. By the end of 1945, barring any sinkings to enemy action, with these new additions, the Pacific Fleet would have 20 heavy carriers, 9 light carriers and 2 large Midway-class battle carriers. The men and the weapons for the final campaigns against Japan were firmly set during summer 1944 and would not change to any significant degree until Japan was nearing the end of her war.

By 1 July 1944, with the defeat of Japan's Mobile Fleet at the First Battle of the Philippine Sea, naval air had won control of the Central Pacific skies. But would a fleet of carriers more than double the size of Task Force 58 really be necessary by 1946? The Navy air admirals would eventually have forty-one carriers (excluding the antiquated *Ranger*) from which they could scale down post war to a realistic peacetime fleet.

(vi) Japan

During summer 1944, when the USA was already beginning to consider post-war naval planning, in stark contrast to the planned forty-one US carriers, the numbers of Japanese carriers and their aircraft had been decimated. The IJN was fighting for its very survival.

The loss of Saipan early in July was admitted to the Japanese people by the government, an unusual step at the time when the reality of the war's progress was shielded from the population. This shook the nation's confidence – and led directly to the downfall of General Hideki Tojo and his military cabinet. Realising that the catastrophic losses of fleet and air forces meant that no effective defence of Japan could be mounted, Japanese naval leaders came to believe that defeat was now inevitable and began to press for peace. The Emperor's Supreme Naval Adviser declared: 'Hell is on us.' To Japanese eyes, 'the loss of Saipan was the turning point in the trend of the Pacific war'.[7]

The Japanese carrier fleet had been seriously weakened by the loss of three carriers and many hundreds of planes in the First Battle of the

Philippine Sea and in the subsequent September carrier raids – *Shōkaku*, *Hiyō* and the new *Taihō* all now lay at the bottom of the Pacific. But the IJN still boasted many fine warships that remained a potent threat and that could, in the right circumstances, still strike a significant blow.

Japan by this stage however had already lost the industrial output contest against the USA. She could never, even at the best of times, match US industrial might once the great juggernaut was mobilised. But with such high attrition of her shipping, her shipbuilding industry was now under strain, not least as a result of submarine attacks on supply ships.

After Midway in 1942, the IJN had planned for 20 new fast carriers to be built from the keel up, 6 Taihō-class, 8 17,000-ton Unryū-class and 7 modified Unryūs. But only *Taihō* and 6 of the Unryūs had actually been laid down to date – and even then, the newly commissioned *Taihō* had joined the fleet in March 1944, just in time to be sunk in the Philippine Sea three months later. Ships under conversion to carriers included the 64,800-ton *Shinano* and the 12,500-ton light carrier *Ibuki*, both due for commissioning in early 1945 along with the remainder of the Unryūs.[8]

Japanese military planners anticipated that the Allies would land in the Philippines in November 1944 – and so by late summer 1944, they believed they had just four months to train new aircrews to replace those lost in the 'Great Marianas Turkey Shoot' in June, and to bring possibly three new carriers of the Unryū-class to full readiness.

Pressing the construction programme as hard as possible, the lead ship of the class, the 17,150-ton *Unryū*, was commissioned on 6 August 1944. This was followed four days later by her 17,460-ton sister ship *Amagi*. Each of these two new carriers carried fifty-four aircraft and could make 34 knots. Vice Admiral Ozawa moved his flag to the newly commissioned *Amagi* as Commander 3rd Fleet and ComCarDiv 1, which then consisted of *Amagi, Unryū* and *Zuikaku*. They were joined on 15 October by the 17,260-ton sister ship *Katsuragi*. CarDiv 2 was dissolved and its ships *Jun'yō* and *Ryūhō* were transferred to CarDiv 4 under the command of Rear Admiral Chiaki Matsuda, whose other carriers were the half-battleships *Ise* and *Hyūga*. CarDiv 3 comprised the light carriers *Zuihō, Chitose* and *Chiyoda*.

The Japanese naval fighter the Mitsubishi A6M Zero had by now long been considered inferior to the new US naval fighters such as the F6F Hellcat. It was hoped that the new 408mph Kawanishi N1K2-J *Shiden-Kai* fighter would soon be ready for deployment to the carriers. The planned successor to the Zero, the 390mph Mitsubishi A7M *Reppū* fighter, which had been under development since 1942, had been lagging behind schedule in development and a prototype with an improved engine only flew in October 1944 – but mass production would never begin.

The Navy would however soon receive the first of 400 of the new Kawanishi N1K2-J *Shiden-Kai* fighters, the finest land-based Japanese fighter of the Second World War. It carried four heavy 20mm wing-mounted cannon and was fitted with bullet-proof cockpit glass. With a top speed of 408mph at 20,000ft and exceptional manoeuvrability, due to a mercury switch that automatically extended combat flaps during turns, creating more lift and allowing tighter turns, the *Shiden-Kai* could compete against the best of the new US fighters, the Hellcat, F4U Corsair and P-51 Mustang.

By mid-November, if all these developments came to pass, Admiral Toyoda would once again have a powerful fleet, one that included Ozawa's fast-carrier force of 5 heavy carriers, 4 light carriers and the 2 half-battleships *Ise* and *Hyūga*. But, with such high attrition of Japan's pilots and aircrew, Japan's weakness lay in the untrained replacement pilots who needed time they didn't have to train ashore before going for carrier training. Sinkings of tankers and oilers at Truk, Palau and elsewhere in the Pacific had created a fuel shortage which hampered large-scale training operations and carrier practice. Those carrier operations which had been undertaken in the Inland Sea of Japan had resulted in carrier deck crashes – and the deaths of inexperienced pilots.

The IJN 2nd Fleet battleships and cruisers had all survived the Marianas campaign and had redeployed to the Lingga Roads anchorage, south of Singapore, under Vice Admiral Kurita. But in reality, faced with the air power of the numerically superior US carriers, they were now vulnerable in combat. Realising this, Captain Eiichiro Jyo of the light carrier *Chiyoda* recommended to Admiral Ozawa 'the immediate organisation of special attack units to carry out crash-dive tactics' against the US fast carriers. He was advocating the use of suicide attacks – a strategy endorsed by the veteran carrier commander Admiral Obayashi.[9] This still seemed extreme to most Japanese high-command leaders and Ozawa rejected the idea – but Vice Admiral Takijirō Ōnishi, scheduled to take command of land-based air forces in the Philippines in October, knew that Japanese naval and air forces could not defeat the US Navy with conventional tactics. He began developing plans for his kamikaze corps of suicide planes.

Chapter 15

The Battles of Peleliu and Angaur – Operation STALEMATE II, September–November 1944

By October 1944, the Philippines protected the eastern flank of Japan's crumbling South-East Asia Empire. The Philippines were crucial to Japan remaining in the war, albeit that the hope of victory was now very slim. The Philippines would be defended vigorously by the Japanese Fleet based in Singapore and in Japan, and by more than 400,000 ground troops based throughout its thousands of islands. Land-based air forces would stage to the Philippines from Japan, China and other areas.

Allied planners had determined as far back as 2 December 1943 that an air and sea blockade of Japan would be the main objective of operations in the Pacific. MacArthur's Southwest and Nimitz's Central Pacific Forces had since then been moving separately towards a common objective, the area of Formosa-Luzon-China, where a major assault was to take place in spring 1945.

The success or failure of the imminent Allied operations at Leyte and Luzon had become crucial to Japan's very survival. If the Allies secured Leyte, in the central Philippines, they could stage aircraft, warships and amphibious forces from there west to the East Indies and north to Formosa (Taiwan) and the east coast of China. Japan's vital lines of communications to her raw materials in her South-East Asia territories could be cut and resupply and reinforcement of her island garrisons would be interdicted. The Mobile Fleet's fuel came north from the East Indies whilst munitions and ordnance went south from Japan to her scattered island garrisons. The great Japanese north–south supply of war materiel and resources could be choked at the Luzon-Formosa-China bottleneck. The Allies would attempt to cork the Luzon bottleneck.

There were several other strategic possibilities arising from Japan's tenure of the Philippines. If US forces could gain control, they could coordinate with British forces in India to overrun the East Indies and cut off vital supplies and resources. From the Philippines, the Allies could land in China and link up with Chiang Kai-shek, the leader of the Republic of China, who Japan had been fighting in the bitter Second Sino-Japanese War since invading in 1937.

The Allies knew the proposed campaign would be brutal and bloody and last many months – but if the Philippines could be taken, Japan would ultimately be defeated.

As Allied plans were formulated for November landings in the Philippines, Admiral Toyoda, Commander-in-Chief of the Combined Fleet, still had a significant number of carriers available, under the tactical command of Vice Admiral Jisaburō Ozawa. Although CarDiv 2 had been dissolved in July after the Battle of Philippine Sea, his carrier forces comprised:

1. CarDiv 1 – Vice Admiral Jisaburō Ozawa (ComCarDiv 1):
   Amagi
   Unryū
   Zuikaku
   Katsuragi
2. CarDiv 3 – Rear Admiral Sueo Obayashi (ComCarDiv 3):
   Zuihō
   Chitose
   Chiyoda
3. CarDiv 4 – Rear Admiral Chiaki Matsuda (ComCarDiv 4):
   Ise (half-battleship),
   Hyūga (half-battleship)
   Jun'yō
   Ryūhō

Those carriers damaged at the Philippine Sea in June were still undergoing repairs – whilst the new Unryūs were completing shake-down trials. As soon as the damaged and new carriers were seaworthy and operational, Ozawa intended to take his carrier force to Singapore to join with the battleships and cruisers of Vice Admiral Takeo Kurita's 2nd Fleet. Together, this would be a powerful naval force that was once again able to sortie and challenge Allied forces.

Admiral Toyoda had little option other than committing the Mobile Fleet to meet the Allies at Leyte and Luzon. With the fleet's fuel coming from the East Indies and its munitions from Japan, the Luzon bottleneck simply had to be kept open. (Interrogated at war's end in the *United States Strategic Bombing Survey (Pacific), Interrogations of Japanese Officials*, Toyoda commented, 'There would be no sense in saving the fleet at the expense of the loss of the Philippines.')

(i) Operation STALEMATE II, 15 September– 27 November 1944

On 15 September 1944, the same day as Allied troops were landing on Morotai Island, in the Halmahera group of eastern Indonesian islands, US Marines and, later, the US Army's 81st Infantry Division landed on the Palauan Islands of Peleliu and Angaur – mission, to capture the important airstrip and secure the eastern flank for US forces preparing to attack Japanese forces in the Philippines. Peleliu had been closely photographed during Operation SNAPSHOT at the end of July – but this small island alone was occupied by about 11,000 Japanese 14th Infantry Division troops.

The commander of the US 1st Marine Division predicted that the small island of Peleliu, which covers just some 5 square miles in total, would be secured within four days. However, Japanese defenders were well dug into pre-prepared and heavily fortified cave defences and would offer stiff resistance. The Battle of Peleliu would be a brutal, bloody and drawn-out battle, which raged for more than two months from 15 September until November. It was called the toughest battle of the war by some Marines.

After their earlier heavy losses in the US invasions of the Solomons, Gilberts, Marshalls and Marianas, the IJA assembled a research team to develop new tactics for the defence of their islands. The devastating softening up pre-invasion naval and air bombardment of earlier amphibious assaults, nicknamed the 'Spruance Haircut', had decimated the Japanese defenders and their defensive redoubts – before US troops even attempted to land. Bloodied from the brutal pre-invasion naval bombardments, Japan determined to abandon this old and failed tactic of trying to stop the invaders on the beach – and a new strategy of *defence in depth* was developed. In place of the beach defence strategy, there would only be light Japanese resistance on the landing beaches – simply as a delaying tactic. The bulk of the Japanese defensive force would be held inland in pre-prepared deep-cave and fortified shelter positions, where naval and air bombardment would do limited damage. Once Allied troops were ashore, Japanese troops could choose their time to counter-attack, emerging from their hidden positions to destroy the Allied beachhead.

The Japanese strategic aim was to obstruct and delay the Allied thrust in the Western Pacific, tying up Allied troops by prolonging the defence of the islands. This cave-defence strategy would culminate in the 73-day long Battle of Peleliu, which would leave 6,500 US Marines killed in action. To this day, there are still some 2,900 IJA troops Missing in Action on Peleliu, most still inside cave complexes that were sealed up or collapsed and destroyed by the Americans. The old tactic of the 'banzai charge' was also discontinued – now seen as wasteful of men and ineffective. The new tactic of defence in depth would force the Americans into a war of attrition requiring them to deploy increasing numbers of men and machines.

When it appeared that the Palauan Islands would become the focus of possible US amphibious landings, the IJA 14th Division was ordered to Palau and to the atolls of Yap and Ulithi. The 14th Division was a battle-hardened major army unit that had previously been deployed in Manchuria to defend Japan's frontier against Chinese and Soviet forces. The 14th Division troops were ordered to defend Palau and Yap to the last man – but no effort was to be expended defending Ulithi atoll, which lay almost 350 nautical miles to the north east in the direction of Guam. US troops landed there unopposed on 23 September 1944.

The 14th Division had arrived on Palau on 24 April 1944 and together with the 1st Amphibious Brigade and other IJA and IJN service personnel already on the islands, a total of nearly 35,000 troops were stationed in the Palaus with an additional 8–10,000 on Yap atoll, which lies almost 250 nautical miles north east of Palau, again in the direction of Guam.

The Japanese expected the large Palauan island of Babelthuap to be the primary objective for any Allied assault and stationed nearly 25,000 troops there. There were 10,500 IJA troops, under the command of Colonel Kunio Nakagawa, stationed on Peleliu, towards the south of the Palauan archipelago, whilst 14,000 troops were stationed on the southernmost island of Angaur. The IJA troops displaced locals from their land, seized buildings deemed necessary for defence and started work to strengthen the island defences.

The many natural cave formations on the Palauan Islands were perfect for use as defensive positions. Japanese construction crews got to work, improving existing caves by digging them out and enlarging them, as well as creating new tunnel complexes. Multiple small tunnel entrances were created that could be used as covering, or supporting, firing positions. Gun emplacements, ammunition dumps and communication centres were all constructed.

The honeycomb cave system made maximum use of observation points and interlocking fields of fire – and communication tunnels ran between firing positions, and deeper into a large underground system where troops could quickly withdraw and redeploy as necessary. Many caves were interconnected with larger tunnels so that heavy weapons and artillery could be moved from position to position.

The cave systems featured hidden escape routes, camouflaged entrances, multiple levels, built-in obstacles and sharp turns designed to protect Japanese troops from rifle fire, artillery fire and the feared flamethrowers. Large quantities of water, food and ammunition were stockpiled in these underground positions to sustain a prolonged period of defence.

Japanese engineers added sliding armoured steel doors with multiple openings to accommodate both artillery and machine guns. Slanted cave entrances were constructed to thwart grenade and flamethrower attacks. The caves and bunkers were connected to an extensive subterranean system throughout central Peleliu, which allowed the Japanese to evacuate or reoccupy positions as needed.

The Japanese were well armed with Type 97 81mm and Type 96 150mm mortars. These were portable, easily concealed and had a rapid rate of fire. They could be fired out of caves or slit trenches and the 81mm had a range of 2,800m. The Type 96 150mm mortar was the largest mortar in the IJA and had a range of 3,900m. In addition, the Japanese also deployed 20mm AA cannon and were supported by a light tank unit and AA detachments.

The Japanese also used the natural terrain of the likely Palauan invasion beaches to their advantage. The northern end of the possible landing beaches on the west side of the island had a 30ft coral promontory that overlooked the beaches – a spot later known to the US Marines who assaulted it simply as 'The Point'. Here, the Japanese blasted holes into the coral ridge to accommodate 47mm anti-tank guns and six 20mm cannon. The positions were then sealed shut with reinforced concrete, leaving just a small slit that gave a field of fire towards the assault beaches. Similar near invisible reinforced concrete firing positions were created at the tree line along the 2-mile stretch of potential landing beaches.

The beaches were also filled with thousands of obstacles for landing craft. Beach mines were buried in large numbers along with heavy artillery shells buried with their fuzes exposed – and ready to explode when they were run over. A sacrificial battalion of IJA infantry was deployed along the beach to delay the initial landings as long as possible before the inevitable advance inland.

The US invasion plan would follow the same pattern as with previous amphibious landings, despite suffering some 3,000 casualties and 2 months of delaying tactics against entrenched Japanese defenders at the Battle of Biak in the New Guinea campaign.

On Peleliu, the 1st Marine Division, commanded by Major General William H. Rupertus, would land on the south-west beaches, due to their proximity to the airfield situated at the very south of the island. The 1st Marine Regiment would land at the northern end of the beaches, designated White 1 and 2. The 5th Marine Regiment would land in the centre: Orange 1 and 2. The 7th Marine Regiment would land at the southern end: Orange 3. The Division's artillery regiment – the 11th Marine Regiment – would land after the initial troop landings.

The assault plan called for the 1st and 7th Regiments to push inland to the east, guarding the central 5th Regiment's left and right flank. The 5th would capture the airfield, which was located directly east and to the centre of the landing beaches.

The 5th Marines were to push right across the island to the eastern shore, cutting the island in half. The 1st Marine Regiment would push north towards Umurbrogol, whilst the 7th Marine Regiment would clear the southern end of the island. Only one battalion was left behind in reserve, with the Army's 81st Infantry Division available for support from Angaur, the island just south of Peleliu.

On 4 September, the 1st Marine Division shipped off for the planned assault on 15 September, from their Solomon Islands station on Pavuvu, just north of Guadalcanal, a 2,100-mile trip across the Pacific to Peleliu. The Navy's Underwater Demolition Teams, UDTs 6 and 7, went in first – reconnoitring the beaches and waters just offshore, locating reefs, rocks and shoals that would interfere with landing craft and using explosives to demolish Japanese underwater obstacles.

On 6–8 September, the Palaus were pounded by McCain's TG 38.1, Bogan's TG 38.2 and Sherman's TG 38.3. Davison's TG 38.4 then took over the attack along with aircraft from ten escort carriers.

On 12 September, the three-day-long pre-invasion naval bombardment of Peleliu began as the battleships *Pennsylvania*, *Maryland*, *Mississippi*, *Tennessee* and *Idaho*, the heavy cruisers *Columbus*, *Indianapolis*, *Louisville*, *Minneapolis* and *Portland* and light cruisers *Cleveland*, *Denver* and *Honolulu*, led by the command ship

Mount McKinley, opened up with their big guns on the tiny island of 5 square miles. The punishing three-day-long pre-invasion bombardment paused only to allow air strikes from the carriers to take place.

The US assessment was that the naval bombardment had been a success – Rear Admiral Jesse Oldendorf commenting that the Navy had run out of targets. The bombardment had destroyed Japan's aircraft based on the island, as well as the buildings surrounding the airfield, but although there may not have been any obvious land targets left, unknown to the Americans, the majority of the deeply buried Japanese cave positions were completely unharmed and even the battalion left to defend the beaches was virtually unscathed. The Japanese remained hidden in their fortified positions, exercising strict firing discipline in holding their fire to avoid giving away their positions. They would attack the US troops that would soon begin their landings.

The Japanese had deployed mines around Angaur, Peleliu and the Kossol Passage, where US forces were likely to congregate during the expected invasion. Underwater Demolitions Team frogmen detected Japanese mines during their clandestine operations and mines were detected during reconnaissance by US submarines.

On 13 September, a US minesweeper unit swept the Kossol Passage to the north of Palau and other passages around Angaur and Peleliu in the south. A large number of mines were detected in the northern Kossol Passage, which the Japanese believed would be used as a US Fleet staging area and replenishment anchorage. The destroyer *Wadleigh* (DD-689) struck a mine and suffered extensive damage near the eastern entrance with the loss of four of her crew and fifteen injured. The minesweeper *YMS-19* also struck a mine and sank with the loss of nine of her crew. The destroyer *Perry* (DD-340) was sunk whilst sweeping along the south-east coast of Angaur after striking a mine.

On the morning of 15 September, just after 0800, the Marines began their amphibious assault, moving towards the designated invasion beaches from their mother ships in landing craft – a combination of Tracked Landing Vehicles (LVTs) and amphibious trucks (DUKWs or 'Ducks').

As the vulnerable landing craft, packed full of Marines, approached White and Orange beaches, the Japanese opened the steel doors guarding their dug-in gun positions on the 30ft-high coral promontory that projected out at the north, 'The Point'. They then opened up with their 47mm anti-tank guns and 20mm cannon, whilst positions to the south also opened fire. The exposed Marines were caught in a vicious artillery crossfire and by 0930, accurate Japanese fire had destroyed sixty LVTs and DUKW amphibious trucks.

The 1st Marines landed at 0832 but were quickly bogged down on the beaches by heavy fire whilst the 7th Marines to the south faced a cluttered Orange Beach 3, with natural and man-made obstacles that forced the LVTs to approach in column.

The 5th Marines in the centre made the most progress – using cover provided by coconut groves as they pushed toward the airfield, which was only a mile or so inland. As they reached the outskirts of the airfield, they were met with the first Japanese counter-attack as a company of Japanese light anti-infantry tanks raced across the airfield towards the Marines. The Marines engaged the Japanese counter-offensive with their own tanks and howitzers and called in fire support from naval guns offshore and dive-bombers. The Japanese tanks and escorting infantrymen were quickly decimated.

At the end of the first day, the Americans successfully controlled their 2-mile stretch of landing beaches. Their biggest push in the centre had moved just 1 mile inland to the outskirts of the airfield. The 1st Marines to the north encountered heavy resistance and made little progress; 200 Marines were already dead – and 900 wounded.

On the second day, the 5th Marines in the centre moved to capture the airfield and then push towards the eastern shore. They overran the airfield – taking heavy casualties from Japanese infantry and from heavy artillery fire from the Umurbrogol hills and ridges to the north.

After capturing 'The Point', the 1st Marines moved north into the Umurbrogol pocket, soon to be nick named 'Bloody Nose Ridge'. The Marines mounted several assaults on the series of ridges that were honeycombed with interconnecting caves and firing positions. But each assault resulted in heavy casualties to accurate Japanese fire. The 1st Marines became trapped in the narrow paths between the ridges, with each Japanese ridge fortification supporting the other with deadly crossfire.

The Marines took increasingly high casualties as they slowly advanced through the ridges. Japanese snipers began to target stretcher-bearers, knowing that if stretcher-bearers were injured or killed, more would have to return to replace them. The snipers could then pick them off.

Once night fell, Japanese troops stealthily infiltrated the US lines to attack the Marines in their foxholes as they slept. The Marines began digging out two-man foxholes, so one could sleep whilst the other kept watch. When the 1st Battalion of the 1st Marines attacked Hill 100, the battalion suffered 71 per cent casualties in six days of fighting.

By 17 September, all Marine Corps artillery was ashore and carrier air support was shifted to deep targets that artillery could not reach. The fast carriers of TG 38.4 retired on 18 September, the air support commanders moved ashore, and the Marines flew their F4U Corsairs into the captured airfield. Using 1,000lb and napalm bombs, dropped from just above tree height, these aircraft provided ideal close air support. Most of the island was secured by 22 September but Japanese resistance from Umurbrogol continued.

The 5th Marines were tasked to capture the tiny island of Ngesebus, just a few hundred metres to the north of Peleliu, to which it was connected by a small causeway. Ngesebus harboured many Japanese artillery positions and was the site of an airfield that was still under construction. The 5th Marines commander opted to make a shore-to-shore amphibious landing believing the causeway to be an obvious target for the island's defenders.

A coordinated pre-landing bombardment of Ngesebus began on 28 September – carried out by Army 155mm (6.1in) guns, naval guns from the ships offshore, howitzers from the 11th Marines and strafing runs from VMF-114 Corsairs. The assault LVTs opened up with their own 75mm (2.95in) weapons as they approached. Most of the Japanese defenders were killed in the bombardment, although the Marines still faced opposition in the ridges and caves. The island fell quickly, with relatively light casualties for the 5th Marines of 15 killed and 33 wounded – but 470 Japanese lay dead.

The stalemate at the mountainous Umurbrogol Pocket continued and by October 1944, the 7th Marines had suffered 46 per cent casualties by the time they were relieved by the 5th Marines under the command of Colonel Harold D. Harris. Pushing from the north, he adopted siege tactics, using bulldozers and flamethrower tanks to seal IJA troops in their caves or burn them out of their defensive positions.

Some of the caves had been hewn downwards so that any attackers would be silhouetted as they approached – however this feature was used by the Americans to their advantage. US bulldozers rolled 55-gallon drums of aviation fuel into the caves and then set the fuel on fire. On 30 October, the US Army 81st Infantry Division took over command of Peleliu operations from the battered Marines. Using the same tactics, they took another six weeks to reduce the Umurbrogol Pocket and secure 'Bloody Nose Ridge'.

After two months of the most brutal defence, on 24 November, Colonel Nakagawa, commander of the Japanese forces on Peleliu, proclaimed, 'Our sword is broken and we have run out of spears.'

He solemnly burnt his regimental colours and then performed ritual suicide – his remains were discovered in a cave complex in 1993.

The US Army declared the island secure on 27 November, ending the seventy-three-day-long battle. The 1st Marine Division had been severely mauled – suffering more than 6,500 casualties during their month on Peleliu, over a third of their entire division. It would remain out of action until the invasion of Okinawa on 1 April 1945. The 81st Infantry Division suffered nearly 3,300 casualties during their tenure on the island. IJA losses are estimated at 10,000 killed in action.

The battle was controversial due to the island's lack of strategic value and the high casualty rate. With Palau's airfields and anchorages neutralised by Operation DESECRATE 1 in March and by subsequent operations and the most recent naval bombardment, the defenders lacked the means to interfere with potential US operations in the Philippines. The Peleliu airfield, so cruelly fought over and so costly in casualties, never played a key role in subsequent Allied operations. Instead, Ulithi atoll was used as a staging base for the invasion of Okinawa. The high casualty rate exceeded all other amphibious operations during the Pacific War. On the recommendation of Admiral Halsey, the planned amphibious assault of Yap was cancelled. The battles for Peleliu and Angaur had highlighted the new Japanese tactic of defence in depth – which would be seen again at Iwo Jima and Okinawa.

There would be no invasion and battle with the substantial Japanese garrison on the largest Palauan island of Babelthuap – it was hit and bypassed. With most of the towns and villages there reduced to rubble, many of the remaining Japanese and civilians took to the jungle and hills. In the coming weeks and months, only a few Japanese submarines and fishing vessels were able to take food and supplies to the beleaguered inhabitants. With the shipping passages and harbours mined and US air power completely dominant, no Japanese ships could reach Palau. The Japanese troops were almost completely cut off from resupply and food shortage became an immediate problem. Palau began to starve, and martial law was declared.

The Japanese confiscated much of Palau's existing food supplies along with houses and gardens that could be used to produce food – causing much misery to the local inhabitants. Both troops and locals alike did what they could to produce enough food to survive. Sweet potatoes, the root vegetable taro, grown for its edible corn and leaves, and other vegetables were all cultivated where they could be grown. The lagoon held bountiful supplies of fish – but fishing by boat was dangerous due to repeated US air attack. Any livestock on the islands was soon eaten.

Local tropical fruits such as coconuts, bananas, breadfruit and mangoes were eaten, and they too became scarce.

Despite all the attempts at cultivation, there simply was not enough food to go around, and starvation and disease set in. Leaves, roots, lizards and rats were soon being eaten. By the end of the war, more than 2,000 of the stranded Japanese garrison on Babelthuap had died from starvation along with more than 500 civilians.

With Palau neutralised, Admiral Nimitz's strategy of island hopping along strategic islands on a path to bring US bombers within range of the Japanese home islands and pave the way for a possible invasion of Japan continued. The difficulties and losses incurred in taking such a small island as Peleliu provided a stark portent of what could be expected as the advance towards the Japanese home islands continued.

Task Force 38 McCain's TG 38.1 departed Palauan waters after the initial pre-invasion bombardment on 6–8 September, heading south west towards Morotai Island in the Halmaheras and taking station 50 miles offshore for air strikes on Morotai with six escort carriers. US and Australian forces carried out near perfectly organised landings on the south-west corner of Morotai on 15 September. The island was secured in two weeks and turned into an Allied base and two major airfields were ready by October. These would play an important role in the liberation of the Philippines during 1944 and 1945.

Chapter 16

The Philippine Campaign – Second Battle of the Philippine Sea, Leyte Gulf

To initiate the corking of the Luzon bottleneck, the Allies would land in strength at Leyte, an island directly west from the Marianas, situated towards the eastern side of the Visayas group of the central Philippines. This operation would trigger the Second Battle of the Philippine Sea, more commonly known today as the Battle of Leyte Gulf. Taking place over four days from 23–6 October 1944, and involving more than 200,000 military personnel, it is widely considered to have been the largest naval battle of the Second World War.

The invasion of Leyte by combined US and Australian forces would begin the isolation of Japan from the countries it had occupied in South-East Asia, which were a vital source of industrial materials such as rubber and the aluminium ore known as bauxite, essential in aircraft manufacture, and oil supplies. Japan's oil came primarily from the Dutch East Indies (modern-day Indonesia), then the fourth largest exporter of oil in the world – and seized in March 1942. (Japan obtained smaller amounts from Formosa, China and Burma.)

The Leyte operation would be followed by seizure of Mindoro Island in the west of the central Philippines and then by a landing at Lingayen Gulf, on the north-west side of the large northern island of Luzon, facing the South China Sea.

By autumn 1944, as the Leyte operation was being prepared, the Japanese had been driven from many of their island bases in the South and Central Pacific Ocean, whilst many others had been hit, neutralised and bypassed. Japanese troops on these beleaguered outposts were beginning to starve. Most of the Mariana Islands, east of the Philippines, had been invaded and seized by amphibious landings in June 1944. The US had now breached Japan's strategic inner defence ring and controlled strategic bases from which long-range Boeing B-29 Superfortress bombers could attack the Japanese home islands themselves. Allied intelligence reporting however highlighted that by November, Japanese land-based forces would be much strengthened.

Japan by this stage had fewer aircraft carriers and battleships combined than the Allies had carriers alone – it was already an uneven contest. Admiral Soemu Toyoda, Commander-in-Chief of the Combined Fleet, thus reorganised his forces as best he could, anticipating how to best meet the next Allied assault, which was felt likely to take place in November. The IJA and IJN agreed to cooperate in the defence of the Philippines –but Army pilots were not trained to fly over water. Thus, Japanese navy planes would be required to attack Task Force 38 – whilst Army land-based planes would attack Allied shipping off the beachhead at any invasion site.

Toyoda planned first to commit his navy land-based air to meet any Allied assault – just as he had done at the Marianas. Only if these planes failed to stop the landing would he then commit his carrier planes. But Toyoda knew that his air power would be understrength and undertrained – even by November. If the more than 1,000 combined land- and carrier-based aircraft available failed, then there was only one course of action left to him – the suicide planes of 1st Air Fleet Vice Admiral Takijirō Ōnishi.

But Toyoda's careful planning was about to be disrupted. Unbeknownst to the Japanese, the planned Allied landing at Leyte had been moved forward to 20 October following intelligence reports of Japanese strength – provided not least by Ensign Tillar of *Hornet*'s Air Group 2, once he was picked up after being shot down in his Hellcat off Cebu. The Leyte operation would be followed by landings at Mindoro Island, on 5 December, and then at Lingayen Gulf on Luzon, on 20 December. Japanese plans for a carrier battle in November had already been wrecked.

The heavy strikes in September by carrier aircraft against the Visayas and shipping in Manila Bay had resulted in many Japanese ships being sunk. The losses forced the Japanese to move their remaining ships to other anchorages, which they thought were outwith the range of US carrier aircraft and land-based bombers. One of these secure anchorages was Coron Bay at Busuanga Island in the Philippines, south west of Mindoro and just under 200 nautical miles south west of Manila, some

12–16 hours by sea. Many of the withdrawn Japanese ships arrived in Coron Bay on 23 September.

At 0550 on the morning of 24 September 1944, ninety-six Hellcat fighters (some in a fighter-escort role, others carrying bombs in a fighter-bomber role), and twenty-four SB2C Helldiver dive-bombers took off from Mitscher's Task Force 38 carriers *Intrepid*, *Cabot* and *Lexington*, east of Leyte, for a strike on shipping in Coron Bay. Some 350 miles distant, the carrier aircraft would only have a short time to operate over Coron Bay.

At 0855, the TF 38 strike aircraft reached Busuanga Island and found fifteen enemy ships anchored in Coron Bay and elsewhere around the island. The enemy shipping ranged from freighters and naval auxiliaries to destroyer escorts and 10,000-ton tankers. The US strike lasted just 15 minutes – but was deadly accurate.

At 0905, more than thirty US aircraft attacked the 118m long IJN seaplane tender *Akitsushima*, between Lajo and Manglet Island. Although *Akitsushima* opened up with her AA weapons, she had soon taken two direct bomb hits amidships – and within 15 minutes she had a heavy list to starboard. She was then hit by a large bomb on the stern catapult track on her port side, which triggered a large explosion – fuelled by aviation gasoline fires. The hull plating on her port quarter was blown out completely and her stern was almost severed, held only by her keel bar and starboard plating. She quickly capsized to port and sunk. Despite the rapidity of her sinking, most of the crew were able to swim to shore.

Air Group 31 from *Cabot* targeted the large 10,043-ton Type 1TL tanker *Okikawa Maru*, which was fully laden with fuel oil. The first groups of aircraft strafed her and then at 0910, SB2C Helldivers scored a hit on her portside aft. Less than 10 minutes later she was hit again in the boiler room and engine room. Her fuel oil and cargo of oil caught fire and as she began to drift to the north, the fires became so intense that she had to be abandoned. She finally settled by the stern, her burning fo'c'sle remaining projecting proud of the water. (The partially submerged hulk would be hit again in a follow-up raid on 9 October.)

Ten SB2C Helldivers attacked the 405ft-long 5,168grt Columbia-class transport vessel *Olympia Maru* – and left her sinking by the stern. The large auxiliary 6,353grt transport ship *Kogyo Maru* was attacked and took several bomb hits before sinking with the loss of thirty-five of her crew. The armed food transport ship IJN *Irako* opened up with her AA weapons – but she too was sunk. The 2,984grt transport vessel *Ekkai Maru* was sent to the bottom, with the loss of forty-four crew and fifteen passengers. The 9,929grt Type 2TL Standard Merchant Tanker *Taiei Maru* was also sunk.

The 446ft-long 6,492grt auxiliary transport IJA *Kyokuzan Maru* was the last ship to be attacked. She was so badly damaged that she had to be scuttled by her crew on the east side of Busuanga Island.

By the time the TF 38 strike aircraft broke off and headed back to their carriers, 350 miles distant, after just 15 minutes of action, they left a scene of carnage astern of them. Burning and sinking ships littered the waters around Busuanga Island. Black smoke billowed upwards, whilst down on the water, beleaguered crews abandoned ship to lifeboats and struck out for safety, leaving many of their comrades dead on soon to be submerged hulks.

(i) The Battle of Leyte Gulf, 23–6 October 1944

The Battle of Leyte Gulf is considered to have been the largest naval battle of the Second World War, involving more than 200,000 belligerents. It was also the first battle where Japanese aircraft carried out organised kamikaze suicide attacks. The battle in fact consisted of a number of distinct phases over a number of days, beginning with a submarine engagement in the Palawan Passage that was followed by four main engagements at different locations that came to be known as:

1. Battle of the Sibuyan Sea.
2. Battle of the Surigao Strait.
3. Battle off Samar.
4. Battle off Cape Engaño.

Leyte was the first battle in which Japan deployed organised kamikaze attacks and the last naval gunnery exchange between battleships in history. The IJN would suffer heavy losses – their Mobile Fleet would essentially be destroyed and would never sail in such strength again. Successfully cut off from their fuel supplies by the subsequent corking of the Luzon bottleneck, the surviving IJN Fleet units became stranded in their bases due to a lack of fuel.

US operations in the Philippine Islands fell within the Southwest Pacific theatre under General Douglas MacArthur. The original campaign plan had provided for the recapture of Mindanao Island in the southern Philippines on 15 November and for land-based aircraft to support the Leyte assault on 20 December. However, after the plan was changed on Halsey's recommendation with the landing on Mindanao

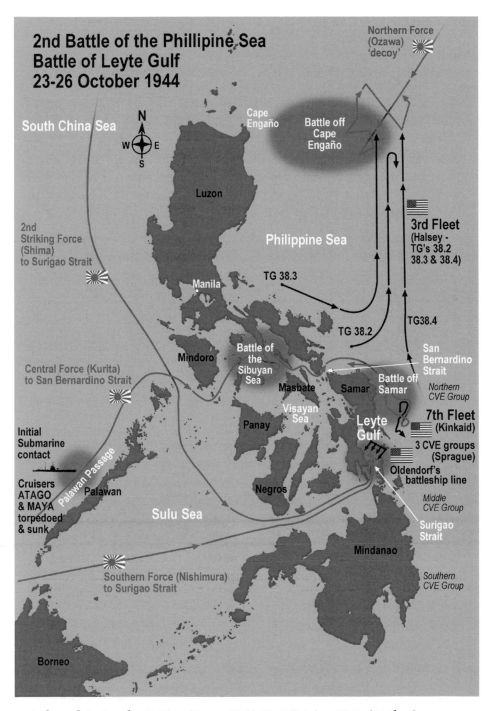

A chart showing the Battle of Leyte Gulf, 23–6 October 1944. (Author)

cancelled and the Leyte landings accelerated to 20 October, there would now be no land-based air support or ground troops from Mindanao available to support the Leyte operation – air support would have to come from the sea. The aircraft of Task Force 38, from Nimitz's Third Fleet, would support MacArthur's operation.

There would thus be two fleets in Philippine waters under separate commands for the Leyte operation. Halsey's Third Fleet, under Nimitz' command, would provide offensive power – whilst Vice Admiral Thomas C. Kinkaid's Seventh Fleet (which included units of the Royal Australian Navy), under the command of General MacArthur, would have a defensive role in providing close naval support. No unified command was established, and with Halsey reporting to Nimitz and Kinkaid reporting to MacArthur, this fundamental defect would produce a crisis – and near catastrophe. As at Saipan, the fast carriers of Halsey's Task Force 38 would join MacArthur's Seventh Fleet escort carriers to provide close air support – and engage the enemy fleet if it sought battle.

Although the Leyte operation was an army operation under MacArthur's command, Halsey would be free to use the Third Fleet to draw out and fight the Japanese Fleet. Nimitz made his fighting orders to Halsey clear, issued without reference to General MacArthur: 'In case opportunity for destruction of major portion of enemy fleet is offered or can be created, such destruction becomes the *primary task*.'[1] Halsey was thus authorised to seek out and destroy the Mobile Fleet, despite other mission commitments of search and support of the landings. This simple command would play a pivotal role as the battle developed. His orders were first to neutralise Japanese 2nd Air Fleet air power north of the Philippines, principally at Kyushu, Okinawa and Formosa. He was then to move southward towards the Japanese 1st Air Fleet bases under Vice Admiral Ōnishi on Luzon and the Visayas.

The operation that followed Leyte, to seize Mindoro Island off the south-west coast of Luzon, was scheduled for 5 December – and was a major concern for Halsey. If the Japanese carriers did not fight for Leyte, or survived a battle at Leyte, they would be free to strike at US shipping off Mindoro. Hundreds of Japanese aircraft could shuttle from airfields on China to carriers operating in the South China Sea to hit Mindoro. They could potentially trap MacArthur's amphibious forces and Task Force 38 on the west side of the Philippines. Halsey felt that the dangerous Japanese carriers needed to be eliminated at the earliest opportunity.

Task Force 38 was subdivided into 4 task groups, each comprising 2 large carriers, 2 light carriers, 2 new battleships and a screen of

3 cruisers and 14 destroyers – a total of 23 ships per task group. Halsey would command the Third Fleet from his flagship *New Jersey* in TG 38.2 with Mitscher in command of TF 38 aboard *Lexington* in TG 38.3. Task Force 38 was at its maximum unparalleled strength, able to field more than 1,000 aircraft.

Fleet Organisation
Commander-in-Chief Pacific Fleet – Admiral C.W. Nimitz
Commander Third Fleet – Admiral W.F. Halsey Jnr
Chief of Staff Rear – Admiral R.B. Carney
Commander Task Force 38 – Vice Admiral M.A. Mitscher
Chief of Staff – Commodore A.A. Burke
Commander Task Force 34 (Battle Line) – Vice Admiral W.A. 'Ching' Lee
Chief of Staff – Commodore T.P. Jeter
1. CTG 38.1 – Vice Admiral J.S. McCain:
   Wasp (CV-18)– Captain O.A. Weller, Air Group 14
   Hornet (CV-12) – Captain A.K. Doyle, Air Group 11
   Monterey (CVL-26) – Captain S.I. Ingersoll, Air Group 28
   Cowpens (CVL-25) – Captain H.W. Taylor, Air Group 22
   Hancock (CV-19) – Captain F.C. Dickey, Air Group 7
2. CTG 38.2 – Rear Admiral G.F. Bogan:
   Intrepid (CV-11) – Captain J.F. Bolger, Air Group 18
   Bunker Hill (CV-17) – Captain M.R. Greer, Air Group 8
   Cabot (CVL-28) – Captain S.J. Michael, Air Group 31
   Independence (CVL-22) – Captain E.C. Ewen, Night Air Group 41
3. CTG 38.3 – Rear Admiral F.C. Sherman:
   Essex (CV-9) – Captain C.W. Wieber, Air Group 15
   Lexington (CV-16) – Captain E.W. Litch, Air Group 19
   Princeton (CVL-23) – Captain W.H. Buraker, Air Group 27
   Langley (CVL-27) – Captain J.F. Wegforth, Air Group 44: Air Group 32
4. CTG 38.4 – Rear Admiral R.E. Davison:
   Franklin (CV-13) – Captain J.M. Shoemaker, Air Group 13
   Enterprise (CV-6) – Captain C.D. Glover Jr, Air Group 20
   Belleau Wood (CVL-24) – Captain J. Perry, Air Group 21
   San Jacinto (CVL-30) – Captain M.H. Kernodle, Air Group 51

After analysing the options open to the Allies, the IJN prepared four plans. *Shō-Gō 1* would be a major naval operation in the Philippines, whilst *Shō-Gō 2*, *Shō-Gō 3* and *Shō-Gō 4* were planned responses to attacks on Formosa, the Ryukyu Islands and the Kuril Islands respectively. These plans were complex and would commit much of the available Japanese naval forces towards a decisive battle – and would substantially deplete Japan's remaining thin reserves of fuel oil for her navy.

Task Force 38 sortied from Ulithi on 6 October and rendezvoused 375 miles west of the Marianas on 7 October 1944 to begin pre-landing attacks on Japanese airfields from where aircraft could threaten the planned Leyte landings on 20 October. Halsey's long-range Liberator scouts sunk the enemy picket boats and interdicted his search planes sufficiently that the task force closed unobserved on the night of the 9th, launching early on the morning of 10 October to strike in a 300-mile arc.

Task Force 38 aircraft attacked Okinawan airfields and shipping with great success – sinking 19 small warships and destroying over 100 Japanese aircraft at a loss of 21 US aircraft. Most of the downed US aircrew were picked up by lifeguard submarines. Halsey wrote later: 'The Japs were sound asleep . . . [we] spread havoc on the ground. . . . Ammunition and fuel storages . . . were left blazing and exploding . . . air facilities were demolished. Barracks were destroyed . . .'.[2]

The following day, 11 October, TF 38 aircraft launched for a fighter sweep over the airfields at Aparri, on the northern tip of Luzon. Then on 12 October, Halsey feinted his task force southwards towards Luzon, before at nightfall swinging 60° to starboard to head for a surprise attack on Formosa (Taiwan). But there, Japanese forces were on the alert and countered as Halsey began four days of heavy air attacks against Formosa – the carrier attacks triggered Japanese command into initiating *Shō-Gō 2*. Vice Admiral Kusaka, Chief of Staff to the Commander-in-Chief Admiral Toyoda, ordered Vice Admiral Shigeru Fukudome, the commander of the 2nd Air Fleet based in the Kyushu-Okinawa-Formosa district, to commit his land-based aircraft to the destruction of the US Fleet. A total of 200 Japanese Army aircraft, based in Formosa, were assigned to Vice Admiral Fukudome to strengthen his 100-strong 2nd Air Fleet. Admiral Toyoda flew to Formosa on 12 October to direct the air attacks against the Allied naval forces personally.

Japanese aircraft and AA fire successfully shot down forty-eight US carrier aircraft on 12 October – despite heavy losses of their own aircraft in the air, and on the ground. Swayed by reports of success by Japanese pilots, Admiral Toyoda changed his air defence plans. Late in the day, he ordered Rear Admirals Obayashi and Matsuda to send their 300 undertrained CarDivs 3 and 4 pilots and their aircraft to airfields on Formosa to join the attack. Instead of having his air power available to protect the Philippines, it would now be an all or nothing battle at Formosa.[3]

The aerial contest over Formosa gathered pace over the coming days. On 13 October, Japanese pilots flew 32 sorties against US forces. Then, the following day, the 14th, they flew 419 sorties – followed by another 199 sorties on 15 October.

But the Japanese pilots were largely green, undertrained and inexperienced – and despite the large numbers of aircraft committed, the battle developed into another turkey shoot – with Halsey's Hellcats shooting down most of the Japanese fighters and destroying many aircraft on the ground, along with land installations. In all, more than 500 Japanese planes were wiped out in the 4 days at Formosa. Toyoda had gambled – and lost. At Formosa, he had prematurely sacrificed his air strength – which had been earmarked for the defence of the Philippines.

Despite these huge losses, a number of Japanese torpedo planes manage to hit Allied shipping. The heavy cruiser *Canberra* (CA-70) was hit on 13 October and the light cruiser *Houston* (CL-81) on the 14th and again on 16 October. Both ships were seriously damaged and were taken under tow for Ulithi – escorted by cruisers, destroyers and the light carriers *Cabot* and *Cowpens*.

With the air battle over Formosa so convincingly won, the air threat from Formosa had been neutralised. Task Force 38 was now able to shift its focus to the Philippines and begin the isolation of the beachhead at Leyte for the beach assault on A-Day, 20 October. On 15 October, TG 38.4 began five days of air strikes against Luzon, concentrating on Manila and being joined by TG 38.1 and TG 38.2 on 18 October.

Such was progress, that many of the TF 38 fast-carrier aircraft duties could now be covered by the long-range planes of General George Kenney, Commander of the Army Air Forces, and the Fifth Air Force of General MacArthur's Southwest Pacific Area. These were now operating out of New Guinea and Morotai and could strike at enemy targets at Luzon and the East Indies. Given a breather, Halsey began to rotate his carrier task groups back to Ulithi for rest and replenishment.

Preliminary operations for the Leyte invasion landings began on 17 October with minesweeping and the landing of 6th Rangers on three small islands in Leyte Gulf, whilst the Navy's underwater demolition teams (UDT) revealed that the proposed main landing beaches for assault troops on Leyte were clear of obstacles. Following 4 hours of naval bombardment on A-Day, MacArthur's Sixth Army forces began landing at 1000 on the beaches of Dulag on the east shore of Leyte and at San Pedro Bay, on the north-west end of Leyte Gulf, the bay being bounded on the north and east by the large island of Samar, and on the west by Leyte.

Meanwhile, Halsey had no way of knowing that Toyoda had sacrificed his main land-based and carrier-based air strength in the disastrous Formosa air battle. Toyoda's strategy at Formosa, and the loss of the planes from the carriers, forced Vice Admiral Jisaburō Ozawa, commanding the carriers of the IJN 3rd Fleet, hastily to draw up an entirely new plan for the defence of the Philippines. On 17 October, as the initial Allied operations for the Leyte landings began, with no need for carriers that now carried no planes, and unable to unite the fleet at Singapore, Ozawa recommended to Toyoda that Vice Admiral Kurita's 2nd Fleet battleship and cruiser force at Singapore be placed directly under his command.

As it now seemed obvious to the Japanese that the Americans had chosen the Philippines as their next objective, Japan put into effect its *Shō-Gō 1* plan for the defence of the islands, where 432,000 troops were now stationed. It was a typically Japanese elaborate plan, in which success depended on the precise movements and coordination of four naval forces. The Japanese plan was daring and almost suicidal – but the twists and turns of the Pacific War had led to this moment where only a decisive Japanese victory in a large-scale fleet action would keep her Philippines supply lifeline open. Japan would commit its surface fleet in an all or nothing gamble with a coordinated attack on the Allied shipping and invasion forces at Leyte on the morning of 25 October.

Shō-Gō 1 would employ one decoy force, the Northern Force under the command of Vice Admiral Ozawa, which would sortie from the Inland Sea of Japan, which lies between the main home island of Honshu and the smaller eastern island of Shikoku. This Northern Force would deliberately attempt to be detected to the north in the open expanses of the Philippine Sea. The plan was then for the Northern Force to lure Halsey's Task Force 38 fast carriers away from Leyte Gulf where they were now standing by some 250 miles offshore, east of the Philippines in support of the US beachhead and invasion forces. The Northern Force would be centred around several carriers – but unknown to the Allies, these would have very few aircraft or trained aircrew.

As the Northern Force lured the US carriers away from Leyte, simultaneously, two other big-gun naval forces, the Central Force under Vice Admiral Takeo Kurita and the Southern Force commanded by Vice Admiral Shoji Nishimura, and supported by the Commander in Chief of the IJN 5th Fleet, Vice Admiral Kiyohide Shima's Second Striking Force, would approach the Philippines from the west.

Kurita's Central Force, based at the Lingga Roads anchorage, a group of islands south of Singapore, included the two super battleships *Yamato* and *Musashi*, each with nine 46cm (18.1in) guns in three triple turrets, the battleship *Nagato* with eight 41cm (16in) guns, two older battleships *Kongō* and *Haruna*, ten heavy cruisers, two light cruisers and fifteen destroyers. It was by far the strongest of the three forces. The Central Force would move to Brunei Bay, Borneo – and then pass through the central Philippines via the Sibuyan Sea and then the San Bernardino Strait, which lies between Luzon to the north and Samar Island to the south. Once safely though the San Bernardino Strait, the Central Force would pass south down the east coast of Samar to move on Leyte Gulf, south west of Samar, from the north.

The Southern Force, commanded by Vice Admiral Shoji Nishimura, would consist of the two old dreadnought-era battleships *Fūso* and *Yamashiro*, the heavy cruiser *Mogami* and escort destroyers. It would cross the Sulu and Mindanao Seas and pass through the Surigao Strait, which lies between the two southern islands of Leyte and Mindanao and hit Leyte Gulf from the south. This Southern Force would be supported by Vice Admiral Kiyohide Shima's force of the two heavy cruisers *Nachi* and *Ashigara*, the light cruiser *Abukuma* and seven destroyers, which would sortie from the Pescadores and head south through the Sulu Sea to rendezvous with the Southern Force for the final push through the Surigao Strait to Leyte.

Toyoda gave the order to initiate *Shō-Gō 1* on 18 October – and Kurita's Central Force and Nishimura's Southern Force sortied from Lingga the same day bound for Brunei Bay. Two days later, on 20 October, the US landings on Leyte began.

The daring Japanese plan was very much a last throw of the dice – for Ozawa's carriers of the decoy Northern Force were going to be sacrificed as bait, whilst Nishimura's Southern Force would face a strong line of US battleships at the Surigao Strait. But if Kurita's Central Force of the battleships *Yamato*, *Musashi*, *Nagato*, *Kongō* and *Haruna* along with their powerful cruisers and a destroyer escort managed to elude the US fast carriers, they could wreak havoc amongst the vulnerable Allied shipping at Leyte and devastate the landing beaches with a naval bombardment. But if Halsey however came down from the north, he could still cut off the Central Force's withdrawal back towards the San Bernardino Strait. If the Japanese Fleet was destroyed, as seemed entirely possible, Japan's main strength at sea after the engagement would be reduced to land-based air and submarines. It was clear to all that if it went wrong, the bold plan could turn out to be the end of the Japanese surface fleet.

In preparation for the operation, Ozawa had dissolved CarDiv 1. He left the three new and unbloodied Unryūs at their Inland Sea anchorage and moved his flag from *Amagi* to CarDiv 3's *Zuikaku*, assuming direct command of the task group, which now comprised *Zuikaku* and the light carriers *Zuihō*, *Chitose* and *Chiyoda*. As US troops were landing at Leyte on 20 October, the CarDiv 3 carriers loaded 116 aircraft, enough for a single strike on Luzon, in an attempt to trick Halsey into believing the Northern Force was also heading for the rendezvous at Leyte.

CarDiv 4, under the command of Rear Admiral Matsuda, with the half-battleships *Ise* and *Hyūga*, was no longer an operational carrier force – it had lost most of its aircraft at Formosa. The two Ise-class half-battleships were added to Ozawa's CarDiv 3 to give 14in big-gun support.

At 1700 on 20 October, just hours after General MacArthur finally stepped ashore at Leyte, Ozawa's decoy Northern Force of 4 carriers and 2 battleships escorted by 3 light cruisers and 8 destroyers sortied from the Inland Sea of Japan.

The famous IJA General Tomoyuki Yamashita had been assigned to command defence of the Philippines. He had earned the sobriquet the 'Tiger of Malaya' at the beginning of the Pacific War after he successfully led his troops down the Malayan peninsula, routed British and Commonwealth forces and won the surrender of Singapore in February 1942.

With 432,000 troops now stationed in the Philippines, Yamashita decided to make Leyte the main effort of Japanese defence. On 21 October, he ordered the 35th Army to coordinate with the IJN for the decisive battle. There would be troop landings at Ormoc Bay, a large bay on the west coast of Leyte Island, and the occupation of the central municipality of Jaro. Japanese battalions were ashore on Leyte by 25 October – with 34,000 troops successfully deployed to Leyte, along with 10,000 tons of materiel.

By 22 October, 200 available Japanese land-based aircraft had arrived in the Philippines. Hundreds more had been requested from China and Japan – and would begin arriving within days. Vice Admiral Ōnishi of the 1st Air Fleet, assigned with the 2nd Air Fleet to the defence of the Philippines, had little faith however in these largely green pilots. On 19 October he activated the Kamikaze Corps of suicide planes.[4]

Following 4 hours of heavy naval bombardment, the US Sixth Army had begun its landing on Leyte Island two days earlier on 20 October –

with good air cover and support coordinated from Kinkaid's Seventh Fleet amphibious HQ ship, *Wasatch* (AGC-9).

The eighteen escort carriers of Kinkaid's Escort Carrier Task Group 77.4, under the command of Rear Admiral Thomas L. Sprague, stationed east of Samar and Leyte were divided into three task units that were flying off Hellcats, Wildcats and Avengers for close support of landing troops. Meanwhile, the planes of Task Force 38 patrolled the skies, attacking enemy airfields and being joined by Fifth Air Force bombers. The Navy planes were soon able to use two captured airfields on Leyte for emergency landings.

Between 20 and 23 October, the aircraft from TG 77.4 CVE escort carriers, from the TF 38 fast carriers and the Army Air Force faced little opposition in the air – whilst destroying over 100 Japanese planes on the ground.

Now ashore, MacArthur's Sixth Army moved inland under this powerful air cover, aiming to gain as much ground as possible before a feared Japanese counter-attack on land, sea and in the air could develop. The waters offshore in the wide expanses of Leyte Gulf thronged with Allied shipping – whilst equipment piled up on the landing beaches as transport ships raced to unload their cargoes and clear Leyte Gulf before the expected Japanese counter-attack.

The apparent absence of Japanese Fleet units in the area allowed Halsey to concentrate his naval forces on guarding the San Bernardino Strait at the north of Samar and the Surigao Strait at the south of Samar, these being the only channels from the west that enemy warships could use to get close to Kinkaid's Seventh Fleet shipping supporting the Leyte landings.

With the landings having successfully begun on 20 October, movements of major Japanese Fleet units northward from the Singapore area were detected on 21 and 22 October. Kinkaid believed that if Japanese warships did appear off the landing beach, he could rely on the 16in and 14in big guns of Admiral Jesse B. Oldendorf's Task Group 77.2 battle line of the 6 older battleships, *West Virginia, Maryland, California, Tennessee, Mississippi* and *Pennsylvania*, escorted by the heavy cruisers *Louisville, Portland* and *Minneapolis* (all 8in main battery), 2 light cruisers and 9 destroyers. In addition, air support was available from the eighteen small TG 77.4 escort carriers – as well as the fast carriers of Task Force 38 and its screen of six fast battleships, cruisers and destroyers, 250 miles offshore to the east.

The Sixth Army made good progress ashore at Leyte. So, with an apparent absence of Japanese naval units, and with Oldendorf's

TG 77.2 battleships and cruisers, and the TG 77.4 escort carriers, in position, Halsey felt the situation safe enough to detach the five carriers of McCain's TG 38.1 carriers and Davison's TG 38.4 carriers and send them east to Ulithi for rest and replenishment.

(a) Prelude to Battle – Initial Submarine Action in the Palawan Passage, 23 October 1944

Kurita, the Central Force commander, and Nishimura, the Southern Force commander, now at Brunei Bay received their orders the same day – and both forces sortied separately for the Philippines on 22 October. The same day, Shima's Second Striking Force of cruisers and destroyers left Japanese waters, heading south to join and strengthen Nishimura's Southern Force of 2 battleships, 2 heavy cruisers and 7–8 destroyers.

Kurita's powerful Central Force, comprising the 5 battleships *Yamato*, *Musashi*, *Nagato*, *Kongō* and *Haruna*, 10 heavy cruisers *Atago*, *Maya*, *Takao*, *Chōkai*, *Myoko*, *Haguro*, *Kumano*, *Suzuya*, *Tone* and *Chikuma*, 2 light cruisers *Noshiro* and *Yahagi*, and 15 destroyers, headed north east from Brunei Bay for the Palawan Passage, which runs up the north-west side of Palawan Island. The east coast of Palawan forms the western boundary of the Sulu Sea.

Kurita intended to round the northern tip of Palawan Island, cross the Sibuyan Sea and then pass through the San Bernardino Strait between the southern tip of Luzon and Samar Island. Once through the Strait he would head south down the east coast of Samar to strike Allied shipping and the beachhead at Leyte Gulf, south west of Samar Island. By midnight on 22 October, the Central Force was passing in darkness north east along the Palawan Passage.

Palawan Island is 264 miles long but only 25 miles wide – and is the fifth largest island of the Philippines. The long, thin mountainous island runs north east–south west on the western periphery of the Philippines, essentially forming part of the archipelago's north-westernmost boundary. To its west are the Spratly Islands and then the open expanses of the South China Sea.

The Palawan Passage gives entry from the South China Sea to the Sulu Sea and to the Sibuyan Sea through a number of sounds to the north and south of Palawan Island. Two US submarines, *Darter* (SS-227) and *Dace* (SS-247), had been stationed on picket duty in the Passage, positioned in close proximity on the surface – in the darkness of the tropical night.

Just after midnight on 23 October, *Darter*'s radar detected Japanese naval units at a range of about 30,000yd – and soon afterwards visual contact was made by lookouts. The two submarines sent three contact reports back to Halsey, and then shadowed the Japanese force for several hours on the surface – as they manoeuvred to achieve a firing position ahead of Kurita's force for a submerged attack at first light.

Dace and *Darter* achieved their firing position just after 0500 – and attacked with devastating effect. *Darter* fired a salvo of six torpedoes at Kurita's flagship, the heavy cruiser *Atago* – at least four hit. *Darter* scored two hits on *Atago*'s sister ship, the heavy cruiser *Maya*, 10 minutes later. Both cruisers sank quickly, the *Atago* so quickly that Kurita himself ended up in the water, swimming for his life. He was picked up by the destroyer *Kishinami* before transferring to the battleship *Yamato*.

A third heavy cruiser, *Takao*, was so badly damaged that it had to turn to limp back south west to refuge in Borneo with two destroyer escorts: the two US submarines followed, looking to finish her off. *Darter* however ran aground on a shoal – and after all efforts to get her off failed, she had to be abandoned, her entire crew being safely transferred to *Dace*. *Takao* reached Singapore safely – but there the damage was assessed as being so bad that she could not be towed back to Japan for repair. She was effectively out of the war and would remain in Singapore harbour for the duration as a floating AA battery.

Armed with the submarine contact reports, Halsey could now assume that the Japanese Mobile Fleet was going to offer battle. He recalled Davison's TG 38.4 carriers from their 1,300-mile passage south east to Ulithi – but he would wait for further intelligence before recalling McCain's TG 38.1 carriers *Wasp, Hornet, Hancock, Monterey* and *Cowpens*, which were now some 600 miles away to the east, well on their way to Ulithi.

TG 38.2 *Bunker Hill* had also retired on 23 October for Ulithi to pick up more fighter aircraft, leaving Bogan's TG 38.2 now weakened and comprising only one heavy carrier, *Intrepid*, and the light carriers *Cabot* and *Independence*. From originally having seventeen fast carriers, Halsey was now left with eleven – he would need the remaining three groups of Task Force 38 at their best for the battle that now appeared to be imminent.

With McCain's TG 38.1 carriers now more than 600 miles to the east en route to Ulithi, to protect the beachhead and shipping at Leyte, Halsey ordered the three remaining task groups to close the eastern Philippine islands and launch search planes the next morning in a fan that would cover the western approaches for the entire length of the Philippines chain. The three task groups reached their stations that night, 23 October, and would cover the three possible approaches to

Leyte – via the Surigao Strait, the San Bernardino Strait and from the open expanses of the Philippine Sea to the north.

Ted Sherman's TG 38.3 comprising *Essex, Lexington, Princeton* and *Langley* would cover the northern area, taking station near Polillo Island, east of Luzon, and covering the open waters of the Philippine Sea, well to the north of the San Bernardino Strait. His planes would stop any attack coming down from the north.

Following *Bunker Hill*'s departure for Ulithi, Bogan's weakened TG 38.2, now only fielding *Intrepid* and two light carriers, would take station 140 nautical miles south east of Sherman's TG 38.3 and cover the San Bernardino Strait at the north end of Samar Island. The planes of TG 38.3 and 38.4 would be able to come to TG 38.2's aid if required.

Davison's TG 38.4, *Franklin, Enterprise, San Jacinto* and *Belleau Wood*, 120 nautical miles south east of Bogan's Task Group 38.2, would cover the Surigao Strait between Leyte Island to the north, and the large island of Mindanao and Dinagat Island to its south.

The scene was set for an historic battle the next day.

(b) Battle of the Sibuyan Sea, 24 October 1944

The search planes launched at daybreak and shortly after 0800 on 24 October, one of Bogan's planes reported contact with 5 battleships, 9 cruisers and 13 destroyers. This force was leaving the north of the Sulu Sea, south of Mindoro Island, bearing 050° and making 10–12 knots. This was Kurita's Central Force, which was heading roughly north east for the Sibuyan Sea, having already lost two of its heavy cruisers and had a third damaged in the submarine action off Palawan earlier.

The Sibuyan Sea, through which the Central Force was soon passing, is a small sea that separates the central Visayan Islands from the large northern island of Luzon. The Sea is ringed by the large islands of Mindoro to the north west, the southern coastline of Luzon to the north east and the islands of Masbate and Panay to its south. Moving eastwards between Masbate Island and Luzon, the San Bernardino Strait leads between the south coast of Luzon and the north coast of Samar Island into the Philippine Sea. If Kurita's force could get through the San Bernardino Strait, it could quickly sweep south along the east coast of Samar and pounce on the vulnerable Allied shipping and beachhead forces at Leyte.

In light of the contact reports, at 0827, Halsey ordered Sherman and Davison to close at their best speed on Bogan's weakened TG 38.2, which was missing *Bunker Hill* but was nearest the line of approach of the powerful enemy battleship force. At 0837, he ordered all task groups by TBS, 'Strike! Repeat: Strike!! Good luck!'[5]

At 0846, Halsey now recalled McCain's TG 38.1, perhaps the strongest of the carrier task groups – and now almost halfway along its 1,300-mile passage to Ulithi. An At-Sea Replenishment rendezvous was arranged for the following morning – but TG 38.1 might not be back in time to participate in any contact with Japanese naval forces.

At 0943, TF 38 search planes detected a second enemy force heading north eastward, south west of Negros Island, in the Sulu Sea, far to the south. This was Nishimura's weaker Southern Force of 2 old battleships, 3 heavy cruisers, 1 light cruiser and 8 destroyers. It was clearly heading for the Surigao Strait between Samar and Mindanao.

At 1000, up north in the Sibuyan Sea, Central Force lookouts on *Musashi* spotted the first wave of forty of Gerry Bogan's TG 38.2 inbound aircraft. At 1025, AA fire was opened and aircraft from all three US task groups were soon heavily engaged. As Bogan's TG 38.2 planes attacked Kurita's Central Force super battleships in the Sibuyan Sea, down south, Davison's TG 38.4 planes attacked the Southern Force with limited effect. Ted Sherman's TG 38.3 was the furthest north of the three task groups, on station off the Polillo Islands. His aircraft were raiding Japanese airfields on Luzon to prevent enemy land-based air attacks on Allied shipping and the beachhead at Leyte.

In response to Sherman's TG 38.3 raids, Vice Admiral Takijirō Ōnishi, in command of the 1st Air Group based on Luzon, launched three waves of fifty to sixty strike aircraft each to hit Sherman's carriers. These heavy Japanese air attacks forced Sherman to break off his Luzon strikes to concentrate on defending his own carriers.

Whilst most of the Japanese planes attacking Sherman's TG 38.3 were successfully downed or damaged – and US pilot reports led to an estimate of more than 150 enemy fighters shot down – a single Yokosuka D4Y3 Judy dive-bomber managed to get through the AA and CAP screen. At 0938, the Judy successfully hit the TG 38.3 light carrier *Princeton* (CVL-23) with a 550lb armour-piecing bomb, which easily penetrated the wooden flight deck and exploded on the hangar strength deck below. The carrier's sprinkler system was damaged, and fires took hold, and as they spread, a series of secondary explosions followed. Although the fires at first appeared to have been successfully brought under control, later in the day, at 1524, the wounded carrier was rocked by a large explosion as her magazine blew up, killing more than 100 crew and wounding many others. The light cruiser *Birmingham* (CL-62) had come alongside *Princeton* to provide firefighting support – and the explosion killed more than 200 of her crew and injured some 400 others whilst *Birmingham* was so badly damaged that she had to retire from the battle. (All subsequent efforts to save *Princeton* failed – her remaining crew had to be evacuated and she was scuttled at 1750 by torpedoes from the destroyer *Irwin* (DD-794) and the light cruiser *Reno* (CL-96). *Princeton* was the largest US ship sunk during the battle and the first fast carrier the Navy had lost since *Hornet* was torpedoed at the Battle of Santa Cruz two years earlier.)

As Ted Sherman's TG 38.3, up north off Polillo, fought off continued land-based enemy air attacks from Luzon, Kurita's powerful battleship Central Force continued to press east across the Sibuyan Sea. TF 38 scout planes were reporting that it was heading for the San Bernardino Strait.

Meanwhile, Nishimura's weaker Southern Force also pressed eastwards across the Sulu Sea – towards the Surigao Strait. Screened by destroyers, his two sister battleships *Fusō* and *Yamashiro* both carried twelve 36cm (14in) main battery guns in twin turrets, whilst his heavy cruiser *Mogami* carried fifteen 15.5cm (8in) main battery guns.

Battle of Leyte Gulf, October 1944. USS *Birmingham* (CL-62) comes alongside the burning USS *Princeton* (CVL-23) to assist with firefighting, 24 October 1944. (National Archives 80-G-281660-2)

Loss of USS *Princeton* (CVL-23), 24 October 1944. View of *Princeton*'s after port side and flight deck, seen from USS *Birmingham* as she came alongside to help fight fires on the afternoon of 24 October 1944. The aircraft elevator is blown out of position and turned upside down and the flight deck is buckled by the hangar deck explosions that followed the hit by a Japanese bomb. (National Archives 80-G-270359)

The Southern Force was to rendezvous with Shima's Second Striking Force of two heavy cruisers *Nachi* and *Ashigara*, the light cruiser *Abukuma* and seven destroyers for the final push through the Surigao Strait to Leyte. But Shima was still well to the north, heading south through the Sulu Sea for the rendezvous.

Halsey assessed that by midnight the combined Southern Force and Shima's Second Striking Force would be in range of the battleships of Vice Admiral Jesse Oldendorf's Seventh Fleet Task Group 77.2. The 6 older TG 77.2 battleships *West Virginia*, *Maryland*, *California*, *Tennessee*, *Mississippi* and *Pennsylvania* were on station off Leyte to cover the

Surigao Strait, along with 4 heavy cruisers, 4 light cruisers, 26 destroyers and 30 PT boats.

Satisfied that the weaker Southern Force could be dealt with by Oldendorf's big-gun battle line and the planes of Kinkaid's eighteen Seventh Fleet escort carriers, Halsey discontinued Task Force 38 air strikes against the Southern Force. He would concentrate his planes up north on the more powerful and more dangerous super battleship Central Force, which was clearly heading for the San Bernardino Strait for an attack on Leyte. Davison's TG 38.4 planes were the only ones able to reach the Southern Force – but they were more urgently needed to deal with the Central Force.

More than 250 TF 38 planes attacked the Central Force. 'Our planes hit the Central Force again and again throughout the day', wrote Halsey later.[6] The battleships *Nagato*, *Yamato*, *Musashi* and the cruiser *Tone* were all damaged whilst the heavy cruiser *Myōkō* was hit by a Mark 13 torpedo from an *Intrepid* Avenger at 1029 that put her starboard screws out of action. Her speed dropped to 15 knots and she had to retire to Borneo via Coron Bay, escorted by the destroyer *Kishinami*.

Japan's newest and largest battleship, the 71,659-ton (full load) *Musashi*, became a primary target for Task Force 38 aircraft. At 1027, eight Curtiss SB2C Helldiver dive-bombers from *Intrepid* made the first attack. *Musashi* took four near misses around the bow and amidships that blew in some of her plating allowing the two forward peak tanks to slowly flood. *Musashi* was also hit by a 1,000lb bomb on the roof of No. 1 turret, which bounced off and failed to penetrate. Eight VF-18 Hellcats then strafed the battleship to suppress her AA fire.

A few minutes later, as other aircraft joined the attack, *Musashi* was hit on her starboard side amidships, slightly abaft the bridge, by an aerial torpedo from an *Intrepid* Avenger torpedo-bomber. She had soon flooded in the vicinity of Boiler Room No. 11 with an estimated 3,000 tons of water, and taken on a 5.5° list to starboard. This was subsequently reduced to 1° by counter-flooding of compartments on the other side of the ship and the speed of the battleship was not affected. Her accurate AA fire shot down two Avengers in this attack.

Just after noon, another attack by a division of eight *Intrepid* Helldivers scored further bomb hits – one of which penetrated two decks before exploding on the horizontal armour deck above one of the engine rooms. Fragments from the explosion shattered a steam pipe in the engine room, forcing it and an adjacent boiler room to be abandoned. Despite, her AA fire knocking down two Helldivers, power to her port inboard propeller was lost, and the great ship's speed dropped to 22 knots on her three remaining shafts.

Nine Avengers attacked from both sides of the ship 3 minutes later, scoring three torpedo hits on the port side. *Musashi* fought on, but one torpedo explosion flooded another engine room. More counter-flooding reduced her list to 1° to port – but the combined level of flooding had now reduced her freeboard by 6ft.

At 1330, a third strike by a combined twenty-nine aircraft from *Essex* and *Lexington* resulted in four bomb hits and four more torpedo hits. As a fourth strike went in against the Central Force, *Musashi* was seen to be trailing astern of the battle line at 20 knots, her bow had settled by 13ft.

A fifth attack on the Central Force was made 2 hours later by sixty-nine planes from *Enterprise* and *Franklin*. Nine *Enterprise* Helldivers scored four hits with 1,000lb semi-armour-piercing bombs – the first hitting the command bridge and killing nearly everyone there. She was then hit by three more torpedoes from Avengers, which opened up her starboard bow. As she flooded further, her speed dropped to 16 knots and then to 13 knots, forcing Kurita to slow the rest of his fleet. She began to list further to port and her electrical power failed.

At 1525, the sixth attack on the Central Force was made by 75 aircraft from *Intrepid*, *Franklin* and *Cabot*, 37 of which targeted *Musashi* and scored 13 bomb hits and 11 more torpedo hits – for the loss of 3 Avengers and 3 Helldivers. *Musashi* had now been hit by an estimated 19 torpedoes and 17 bombs and her speed had dropped to 6 knots. Further counter-flooding succeeded in reducing her list to port from 10° to 6°.

At 1530, concerned about the danger to his fleet if he entered the San Bernardino Strait in daylight, Kurita ordered his Central Force to come to a new west north west course of 290°. Although in apparent retreat, Kurita was getting out of the range of US carrier aircraft. The battle in the Sibuyan Sea was over.

Shortly after beginning to withdraw, Kurita's Force approached the beleaguered *Musashi*, which was by now heading north to escape the Sibuyan Sea. Japan's largest battleship was listing to port, with her head now down by 26ft and her fo'c'sle deck awash. Kurita detailed her an escort of the heavy cruiser *Tone* and the two destroyers *Shimakaze* and *Kiyoshima*.

As the flooding continued, *Musashi*'s engines eventually had to be stopped – and by 1915 her list had increased to 12°. Her crew was ordered off – and by the time they had completed her abandonment, the list had increased dramatically to 30°.

Just 20 minutes later, at 1936, unseen by US eyes, *Musashi* finally succumbed and capsized on the surface. One of the heaviest and most powerfully armed battleships ever built by man then plunged down more than 3,000ft to the bottom of the Sibuyan Sea. Her captain, Toshihira Inoguchi, chose to go down with his ship – but more than 1,300 of her crew of 2,399 were saved.

The loss of *Musashi* was a spectacular Japanese naval loss – to add to the two cruisers *Atago* and *Maya* sunk and the cruiser *Takao* badly damaged by the US submarines *Darter* and *Dace* early the day before in the Palawan Passage. But Kurita still had four battleships and seven cruisers in his Central Force in the Sibuyan Sea that still posed a threat to the Leyte landing forces and shipping.

US pilot reports on 24 October of the damage to *Musashi* and other enemy units were passed to Halsey in his flagship, the battleship *New Jersey*, and these led him to believe that Kurita's Central Force was no longer as potent a threat as it had been. Mitscher however, aboard his flagship *Lexington*, had direct contact with the pilots as they returned from combat – and through long experience, he was inured to understandable over enthusiastic pilot reporting of mission results. His personal interviews of returning pilots aboard *Lexington* led him to doubt that the damage to the Central Force was as severe.[7]

When the Central Force turned to head west in an apparent withdrawal, Halsey did not discount the possibility that Kurita might yet turn his Central Force around towards the Strait. Halsey and his Third Fleet staff aboard *New Jersey* prepared a contingency plan to deal with the potential threat from Kurita's Central Force – the San Bernardino Strait would be covered by a powerful task force of fast battleships supported by two fast-carrier task groups.

At 1512, Halsey sent a preparatory battle plan despatch to his task-group commanders. If a surface engagement offered, he would detach 4 of the 6 fast battleships, 2 heavy cruisers, 3 light cruisers and 14 destroyers. A battle line 'WILL BE FORMED AS TF 34 UNDER V.ADM. LEE, COMMANDER BATTLE LINE. TF 34 WILL ENGAGE DECISIVELY AT LONG RANGES.'[8]

Halsey copied this despatch to Nimitz at Pacific Fleet HQ in Pearl and to Admiral King in Washington – but as there was no unified command structure, he did not copy it to Vice Admiral Kinkaid, of the Seventh Fleet at Leyte.

Halsey's despatch was however picked up by Seventh Fleet – but as the despatch didn't say *when* TF 34 would be formed, or under what circumstances, Kinkaid assumed that TF 34 *had* been formed – and would take station off the San Bernardino Strait. Nimitz at Pearl took the same understanding from the despatch.

To support the invasion forces at Leyte, Kinkaid had deployed his light carriers in three task units of six each, called 'Taffies', that were protected by destroyers and destroyer escorts. Each small CVE escort carrier carried an average of twenty-eight planes – and two of his eighteen CVEs had already departed for Morotai carrying defective aircraft for transfer ashore and repair.

The Northern CVE Group took station off the east coast of Samar Island. The Middle CVE Group took station broadly to the east of Leyte Gulf whilst the Southern Group took station south of the Surigao Strait. With Oldendorf's battleships to the west in the Surigao Strait, there were no battleships in Kinkaid's three escort-carrier task units that could deal with a direct attack by Japanese battleships. It was a potentially fatal situation – and as it transpired, Kurita's super battleship force would almost overwhelm Kinkaid's lighter, and now exposed, forces close to the Leyte beachhead the next day.

In numbers of big-gun warships, both opposing sides at the San Bernardino Strait appeared about even – each had 4 battleships, the Japanese had 6 cruisers to Lee's 5 – but crucially, Halsey, even with *Princeton* mortally wounded (but still afloat) at this point, still had 10 carriers – whilst the Japanese had almost no aircraft. At 1710, Halsey issued a further clarification by short-range TBS voice radio to his subordinate commanders of his position regarding TF 34. 'IF THE ENEMY SORTIES, TF 34 WILL BE FORMED WHEN DIRECTED BY ME.'

As this was a voice radio transmission, with the limitations of the day, it wasn't picked up by Seventh Fleet – nor was a telegraphic copy sent to Nimitz at Pearl or King at Washington. Kinkaid, Nimitz and King were therefore none the wiser about what Halsey was doing and still believed that TF 34 had already been formed.

To US eyes, both passages that allowed an approach and attack on Leyte, the San Bernardino Strait to the north of Samar and the Surigao Strait to the south of Leyte, now appeared to be well covered. But the critical question of concern to all US commanders was the whereabouts of the Japanese carriers. They hadn't been spotted yet – and Mitscher believed they were to the west in the South China Sea, whereas Halsey believed they were to the north. Ted Sherman in TG 38.3 up north off Polillo Island was 'strongly suspicious of the presence of Jap carriers to the northeast' and at 1405 he had obtained Mitscher's permission to launch an aerial search in that direction.[9]

After the war, Halsey learned that as Kurita's Central Force headed north west away from air attack, Kurita received a despatch from Admiral Toyoda, Commander in Chief of the Combined Fleet: 'WITH CONFIDENCE IN HEAVENLY GUIDANCE, THE ENTIRE FORCE WILL ATTACK.'[10]

At 1715, as dusk approached, Kurita turned the Central Force back eastwards towards the San Bernardino Strait, hoping to begin the passage of the Strait in darkness so that the following morning the Central Force could emerge from the Strait and head down the east coast of Samar to surprise the Americans and smash the landing forces at Leyte. The plan still depended on Ozawa's decoy Northern Force carriers luring the US carriers north and away from Samar. Ozawa's Northern Force however was still far to the north in the open expanses of the Philippine Sea – and had not yet been detected.

Earlier that morning, 24 October, far to the north Admiral Ozawa was implementing the deception battle plan and doing what he could to get his Northern Force detected. He had to lure the US fast carriers north.

Ozawa sent the half-battleships *Ise* and *Hyūga* south with a screen of the destroyers *Hatsutsuki*, *Akizuki*, *Wakatsuki* and *Shimotsuki*. This vanguard force was some 50 miles ahead of the main body of his force, seeking out contact. Ozawa put out bogus radio transmissions and sent out regular air searches.

At 1145, a seventy-six-plane strike launched from Ozawa's carriers – and at about 1330, the planes located and attacked the northernmost of the three TF 38 carrier groups, Ted Sherman's TG 38.3. The TG 38.3 Hellcats and the AA guns of the Sherman's screen wrought havoc with the Japanese strike – but rather than taking the bait that this was a carrier strike, the Americans concluded that this was yet another land-based air attack, like the one had had led to the serious damage to the *Princeton*.

Finally, at 1515, the vanguard of Ozawa's force was spotted by a land-based navy search plane. Then, at 1640, a *Lexington* Helldiver spotted the main body of Ozawa's Northern Force and reported the presence of the enemy carrier force heading south approximately 200 miles off Cape Engaño at the north-eastern tip of Luzon. At 1730, Sherman informed Halsey: '3 CARRIERS 2 LIGHT CRUISERS 3 DESTROYERS 18-32 N 125-28 E COURSE 270 SPEED 15.'[11]

As aircraft reports came in, it seemed that there was a 17-ship strong Japanese force to the north that included 1 heavy carrier of the Zuikaku-class, 3 light carriers of the Chitose and Zuihō-classes, 2 half-battleships with a flight deck aft, a heavy cruiser, a light cruiser of the Noshiro-class, 3 other anti-aircraft cruisers and a screen of 6 destroyers.[12] But the position, 200 miles north east of Cape Engaño, was too far for Halsey's planes to reach, even if dusk had not already fallen. No American could know that the Japanese carriers in fact only carried about 100 aircraft in total.

Despite having lost the carrier *Princeton*, in his subsequent Action Report 0900, Ted Sherman, CTG 38.3 explained:

> The carrier forces to the north were our meat; they were close enough so that they could not get away if we headed to the northward . . . As the sun went down the situation was entirely to my liking and I felt we had a chance to completely wipe out a major group of the enemy fleet including the precious carriers which he could ill afford to lose.[13]

At this time, off Polillo Island, east of Luzon, *Princeton* was still afloat – but now in her death throes. Mitscher calmly instructed: 'Tell Sherman to sink the *Princeton*.' He couldn't afford to have her remain afloat, but in sinking condition, as he pursued the Japanese carriers. The destroyer *Irwin* and cruiser *Reno* sunk her by torpedoes at dusk.

Halsey had a dilemma with a number of options before him. With the whereabouts of Ozawa's Northern Force now apparent, if Kurita and his still powerful Central Force did reverse course, coming about to head east toward the San Bernardino Strait, he would have two powerful Japanese naval forces to contend with, the Northern and Central Forces.

That evening, 'Ching' Lee, commander of the Task Force 34 battle line, advised Halsey that in his view, the Northern Force was playing decoy – and that he should form his line of battle off the San Bernardino Strait.[14] The US commanders discussed the possibility of leaving Lee's battle line and one carrier group to guard the San Bernardino Strait and sending the other two task groups north after the carriers of Ozawa's Northern Force. Halsey however, having already lost the *Princeton* to Luzon-based aircraft, determined that 'he would keep his fleet together because the entire operation would be under potential land-based air attack'.[15] By concentrating his forces, he would maximise AA fire protection. Kinkaid, down at Leyte, and Nimitz, at Pearl, believed that the Task Force 34 battle line had *already* been formed at San Bernardino.

If Task Force 38 remained concentrated and went north after the carriers of Ozawa's Northern Force, then it was obvious that Kurita's apparently retiring and damaged westward-bound Central Force might come about, pass through the San Bernardino Strait and attack the vulnerable Leyte landing forces and Seventh Fleet shipping. Whilst Halsey believed the Central Force might inflict damage, in his subsequent Action Report, he indicated that with the damage the Central Force had reportedly taken, he believed that 'its fighting power was too seriously impaired to win a decision'.[16]

Halsey felt that the three Japanese forces were clearly converging for a set rendezvous with the Northern Force carriers off Samar the next day for a combined attack on the transports at Leyte.[17] Weighing the pilot damage reports, he came to the view that the Central Force would only be capable of an indecisive hit-and-run-style operation, such as had been done at Guadalcanal – or a suicide effort. He felt the weaker Southern Force could safely be ignored and dealt with by Kinkaid's old battleships and Kinkaid's CVE escort carriers. The fresh and undamaged fleet carriers of the Northern Force had the potential to execute air strikes over hundreds of miles – they would be the paramount prize.

Halsey and his staff assessed that if the Central Force did turn around and head east through the San Bernardino Strait overnight, it would not enter Leyte Gulf until 1100 the next morning at the earliest. With no transports or supply ships, 'it could hope only to harry the landing operation (at Leyte). It could not consolidate any advantage . . . It could merely hit and run.'[18] By then, Oldendorf's battleships would have obliterated the weaker Southern Force at the Surigao Strait and would be able to move to meet Kurita's Central Force.

After listening to his officers after dinner, and mulling over the various options, with Ozawa's Northern Force now just 300 miles away, Halsey made his decision. He would keep his fleet together because the entire operation would be under potential land-based air attack. Addressing his Chief of Staff, Rear Admiral Robert Bostwick (Mick) Carney, he put his finger on the charted position for the Northern Force: 'Here's where we're going. Mick, start them north.'[19] Halsey later wrote: 'It preserved my fleet's integrity, it left the initiative with me, and it promised the greatest possibility of surprise.'[20]

At 1950, Halsey radioed Vice Admiral Kinkaid, aboard his command ship *Wasatch* at Leyte, and also Nimitz, at Pearl, with a brief despatch that was short of detail: 'CENTRAL FORCE HEAVILY DAMAGED ACCORDING TO STRIKE REPORTS x AM PROCEEDING NORTH WITH 3 GROUPS TO ATTACK CARRIER FORCE AT DAWN.'[21]

From the wording of this despatch, Kinkaid, King and Nimitz assumed that as Halsey was taking 'three groups' north after the enemy carriers, that the TF 34 battle line had now been formed as a separate entity and that those battleships, cruisers and destroyers were being left to guard the San Bernardino Strait and cover the Seventh Fleet flank. It appeared that Halsey was taking the two fast battleships not delegated to the battle line north with him to deal with the two Japanese half-battleships *Ise* and *Hyūga* in the Northern Force.

But in reality, unknown to Kinkaid, Nimitz and King, Task Force 34 had not been formed and *all* of Lee's TF 34 battleships and cruisers would shortly be on their way north with the TF 38 carriers. Shortly after the war, the US historian Comer Vann Woodward wrote: 'Everything was pulled out from San Bernardino Strait. Not so much as a picket destroyer was left.'[22]

Then, at 2006, a night Hellcat from *Independence* spotted Kurita's Central Force in the Sibuyan Sea – it had indeed come about and was now heading back east toward the San Bernardino Strait at 12 knots. But having already decided to head north in pursuit of the Japanese carriers, TF 38 continued on its mission to hit the enemy carriers the next day. Halsey had taken the bait.

At 2022, after passing on the contact report to Kinkaid at Leyte, Halsey ordered Bogan and Davison's Task Groups 38.2 and 38.4 to join Sherman's Task Group 38.3 up north off the east coast of Luzon, for the run to the north. He sent orders to McCain's distant TG 38.1 to break off refuelling and return for battle. He then went to bed, having been without sleep for two days.

The manner in which the battle now developed has been the subject of huge discussion, debate and criticism over the years. After the *Independence* night-fighter sighting of the Central Force was received by Kinkaid at 2024, he heard nothing more from Halsey. As there was no common chain of command, Halsey did not keep Kinkaid automatically informed of his plans. When he sent his despatch that he was proceeding north 'with three groups' he did not say how he was going to deal with the Kurita's Central Force or of his plans for the San Bernardino Strait.

Mitscher knew from Halsey's message to Kinkaid that the three TF 38 carrier groups were going north. He assumed that the preparatory battle plan Halsey had earlier issued at 1512 would now go into effect and that 4 of the 6 TF 38 battleships, 2 heavy and 3 light cruisers and 14 destroyers would form the battle line as Task Force 34 under Vice Admiral Lee, Commander Battle Line, to guard the San Bernardino Strait. Mitscher therefore believed that two remaining fast battleships would continue in support of the TF 38 carriers as it headed north to deal with the two half-battleships of the Northern Force.

The two half-battleships *Ise* and *Hyūga* and their screen, in the vanguard of Ozawa's Northern Force, had been spotted earlier that afternoon just after 1500. At 2230, now shrouded in darkness, they turned back towards the main body of Ozawa's Force to reform for the coming battle. Meantime, at 2300, far down south, Nishimura's Southern Force entered the western end of the Surigao Strait.

In Leyte Gulf, essentially sandwiched between Kurita's Central Force headed for the San Bernardo Strait to his north, and Nishimura's Southern Force entering the Surigao Strait to his south, Kinkaid was now unknowingly exposed and vulnerable. Believing that Lee's TF 34 battle line had already formed at San Bernardino, Kinkaid expected that two night big-gun duels were about to take place: 1. Lee's battle line of four fast battleships, cruisers and destroyers would take on the four battleships and escorts of Kurita's Central Force at the San Bernardino Strait; and 2. Oldendorf's battle line of six older battleships, cruisers, destroyers and PT boats would face off against Nishimura's two battleships and escorts of the Southern Force at the Surigao Strait.

Just after 2300, when it was clear from reports that Kurita was heading for the San Bernardino Strait to strike at Leyte, Halsey's Chief of Staff Commodore Arleigh Burke and Mitscher's operations officer Commander James H. Flatley were both sufficiently worried enough about the situation to go and wake Mitscher to suggest that he should urge Halsey to turn around and head back towards Leyte. But Mitscher had lost tactical command of TF 38 weeks earlier to Halsey – he replied: 'Does Admiral Halsey have that report?' When told he did, Mitscher famously replied: 'If he wants my advice he'll ask for it.' He went back to sleep.[23]

At midnight, Halsey turned over command to Mitscher as the three task groups rendezvoused off Luzon. The reformed Task Force 38 headed north at 16 knots as Halsey had earlier instructed, to achieve a good striking position the next day. It was only then that Mitscher learned, much to his surprise, that Lee's TF 34 battle line of four battleships had not been formed at San Bernardino – and that *all* six fast battleships were heading north with the TF 38 carriers. Mitscher increased speed to 20 knots – he wanted to get north, deal with the Japanese carriers and then head back south to attack Kurita's Central Force.

(c) Battle of the Surigao Strait, 24–5 October 1944

Meanwhile, south west of Leyte Gulf, the southernmost action in the complicated Battle of Leyte Gulf, the battle in the Surigao Strait had begun the evening before, 24 October. Although no one knew it at the time, the battle would prove to be the last big-gun clash between battleships in history – as Oldendorf's Seventh Fleet battleships, *Tennessee, California, West Virginia, Maryland, Pennsylvania* and *Mississippi*, along with his cruisers, destroyers and armed patrol boats (PT boats), decimated the Southern Force as it tried to break through the Surigao Strait into Leyte Gulf.

Nishimura's Southern Force of the two old dreadnought-era sister battleships *Fusō* and *Yamashiro*, the heavy cruiser *Mogami* and four destroyers had crossed the Sulu Sea eastwards and was approaching the Surigao Strait from the southwest. Shima's Second Striking Force of the two heavy cruisers *Nachi* and *Ashigara*, the light cruiser *Abukuma* and four destroyers was meantime far to the north in the Sulu Sea – heading south east to rendezvous with Nishimura to transit the Surigao Strait. But as a result of strict radio-silence procedures, the two forces failed to coordinate their activities correctly and would never link up. As the Southern Force approached the Strait, Shima's force was 25 miles astern. The Battle of the Surigao Strait would be fought entirely by Nishimura's Southern Force, which was running into a carefully and well-prepared trap.

In preparation for the coming battle, Oldendorf had positioned his six old battleships across the east exit from the Strait – to cap the enemy 'T' when Nishimura's Southern Force approached. The four heavy cruisers *Louisville, Portland, Minneapolis* and HMAS *Shropshire* flanked his battleships – whilst his four light cruisers and twenty-eight destroyers were ready to make torpedo attacks as the enemy warships advanced. Oldendorf also had thirty-nine fast and small PT motor torpedo boats that could make more than 40 knots and were armed with Mark 8 torpedoes that carried a 466lb warhead. Oldendorf sent his PT boats south west down the Strait to scout for the Japanese warships.

The Battle of the Surigao Strait began at 2236 when the first PT torpedo boats encountered and engaged Nishimura's oncoming Southern Force warships at the western entrance to Strait. Repeated torpedo attacks by the small PT boats would take place over the next 3½ hours – but no hits were scored. Nishimura's Southern Force passed through the PT boats and continued north east along the Strait.

At 0035, a Japanese scout plane from the heavy cruiser *Mogami* accurately reported the disposition of the Allied forces to Nishimura. But despite this, Nishimura pressed on north east up the Strait – he knew the success of the planned operation at Leyte Gulf the next day depended on his Force getting through.

In anticipation of breaking into Leyte Gulf, the Southern Force began to alter formation to line ahead with the destroyer *Michishio* in the lead, with the destroyers *Asagumo*, *Yamagumo* and *Shigure* following. The flag battleship *Yamashiro* followed behind the destroyers – with *Fusō* and then *Mogami* following. The Japanese ships would soon however be subjected to devastating torpedo attacks from large numbers of US destroyers deployed on both sides of their axis of advance. Five destroyers of DesRon 54 launched a torpedo attack, with a division of three destroyers coming in from the east whilst two destroyers attacked from the west, in a pincer movement from both sides.

The fog of war, and scant Japanese records, has clouded what actually took place. The battle has been the subject of great debate and competing theories, but most agree that at about 0300, the elderly battleship *Fusō* was hit by one to three torpedoes from the destroyer *Melvin* on her starboard side amidships. *Fusō* began to lose speed and list to starboard – and she then fell out of formation. Mortally wounded, at 0345 *Fusō* capsized, exploded and sank.

The flag battleship *Yamashiro* was also hit but was able to continue, however the destroyer *Yamagumo* was sunk with the destroyers *Michishio* and *Asagumo* both being badly damaged. Nishimura was now left only with the battleship *Yamashiro*, the heavy cruiser *Mogami* and the destroyer *Shigure*. By this time, Shima's Second Striking Force was still some 40 miles astern of Nishimura's force.

Nishimura's ships had been detected on US ship radars at 0302 at a range of 44,000yd – and in the darkness they were tracked on radar until the big guns of the flanking cruisers could open fire at 0350. The main battery guns of the US battleships then commenced firing just a few minutes later, the most modern battleship *West Virginia* opening up with her eight 16in guns at a distance of almost 23,000yd, just over 12 miles – and hitting *Yamashiro* with her first salvo. *Yamashiro* returned fire with the 14in guns of her No. 1 and No. 2 main battery. A few minutes later, *California* and *Tennessee* opened up with their big guns. A classic big-gun duel now developed – the US battleships had essentially *crossed the T* of the Japanese battle line. Japanese fire control proved less effective and little threatening fire was returned.

Operating under radar fire control, *Tennessee* went on to fire 69 14in shells during the battle, whilst *California* fired 63 14in shells and *West Virginia* fired 93 16in shells. The three other older US battleships had less advanced gunnery radar and struggled to hit the Japanese ships. *Maryland* visually ranged the Japanese ships from the splashes from the fall of shot and fired 48 16in shells. *Pennsylvania* was unable to find a target and her guns did not fire. *Mississippi* only fired once – with a full broadside salvo from her twelve 14in guns. Unknown at the time, this would be the last salvo ever to be fired by one battleship at another battleship – the era of these great steel titans was over. The Allied heavy cruisers, fitted with the latest radar equipment, fired over 2,000 rounds of armour-piercing 6in and 8in shells. *Yamashiro* and *Mogami* took a savage beating from this murderous hail of big shells – and from the torpedoes from US destroyers.

At 0409, Oldendorf gave the order to cease fire, having received reports that he was hitting his own ships in the darkness. *Yamashiro* and *Mogami*, both heavily damaged, took the opportunity to come about and retire south west down the Strait, along with the destroyer *Shigure*, which lost steering and slewed to a halt before being able to make way again.

Shortly after, at 0419, after being hit by two more torpedoes fired by the destroyer *Bennion*, Nishimura's flagship, the battleship *Yamashiro* rolled to port and capsized within 5 minutes before plunging to the seabed. Nishimura went down with his flagship, along with most of her 1,400 crew.

Mogami, although badly damaged, managed to limp away from the battle and eventually join Shima's Second Striking Force of the two heavy cruisers *Nachi* and *Ashigara*, the light cruiser *Abukuma* and eight destroyers, which by now was less than 10 miles away and heading north east up the Strait. *Abukuma* was hit by a torpedo and fell out of formation.

Shima's force then came across the floating debris of one to two sunken ships. Believing it was two separate sunken ships, one being the *Fusō*, he determined that there was little point in sacrificing his own force of lighter units. At 0506, he retired his cruisers from the Strait along with the damaged *Mogami* and the destroyers *Asagumo* and *Shigure*. His flagship, the heavy cruiser *Nachi*, collided with *Mogami* in the darkness, flooding *Mogami*'s steering room and causing her to fall behind.

After the big-gun duel, supported by fighters and torpedo planes, Oldendorf's battleship force headed south west down the Strait in a stern chase of any Southern Force surviving warships. The destroyer *Asagumo* was sunk at 0721 and *Mogami* was bombed in the Bohol Sea by Task Force 77.4.1 Avengers and subsequently had to be abandoned. She would be scuttled by torpedoes from a Japanese destroyer at 1307 the next day. Of Nishimura's seven ships, only the destroyer *Shigure* had escaped.

Nevertheless, despite the apparent overwhelming success of the contact, as dawn approached on 25 October, as a result of the stern chase, Oldendorf's battleships had been drawn 65 miles south west, and away from the Leyte beachhead. Leyte was now very exposed should an attack from the north develop.

Meanwhile, back off Leyte, Vice Admiral Kinkaid called a Seventh Fleet staff meeting at 0400 – to check for anything that had been omitted or could be actioned. Although no one could think of anything that was awry, Captain Richard H. Cruzen remarked to Kinkaid: 'Admiral, I can think of only one other thing. We have never directly asked Halsey if TF 34 is guarding San Bernardino.'

At 0412, Kinkaid sent a message to Halsey asking for confirmation: 'AM NOW ENGAGING ENEMY SURFACE FORCES SURIGAO STRAIT x QUESTION IS TF 34 GUARDING SAN BERNARDINO STRAIT.'[24] But it would take more than 2 hours for the message to reach Halsey in *New Jersey*.

At 0430, Kinkaid ordered ten search aircraft readied on the CVE escort carriers. One would be a flight of fighter torpedo-bombers to chase down and sink any ships crippled in Surigao Strait. The other would be a flight to search north up the east coast of Samar, north east of Leyte, to look for any ships that had perhaps evaded Lee's battle line, which he still believed was already positioned at the San Bernardino Strait at the north of Samar. PBY Catalina flying boats were also believed to be making searches to the north.[25]

No one knew that in fact Kurita's Central Force, after reversing course in darkness, had already successfully passed completely unopposed through the San Bernardino Strait and emerged into the Philippine Sea at 0300 that morning. The Central Force was now steaming south along the east coast of Samar, heading for Leyte.

The super battleship *Musashi* may well have been sunk in the Sibuyan Sea, but the Central Force still boasted 4 battleships, *Yamato*, *Nagato*, *Kongō* and *Haruna*, 6 heavy cruisers, 2 light cruisers, *Noshiro* and *Yahagi*, and 11 destroyers. The contest was still afoot.

Halsey and the Task Force 38 carriers, which could have dealt with the Central Force, were by now far away to the north – chasing Ozawa's decoy Northern Force.

The scene was set for an epic showdown off Samar.

(d) Battle off Samar, 25 October 1944

By dawn on 25 October, even as Kurita's Central Force battleships headed south down the east coast of Samar towards Leyte, Allied intelligence as to the whereabouts of the Japanese naval forces was still sketchy.

At 0648, Halsey was surprised to receive Kinkaid's despatch sent at 0412 seeking confirmation as to whether Lee's TF 34 battle line had in fact been formed at San Bernardino. Halsey replied at 0705: 'NEGATIVE x IT IS WITH OUR CARRIERS NOW ENGAGING ENEMY CARRIERS.'[26] It was too late for Kinkaid to do anything. San Bernardino had been ignored until too late – and at this point, no one knew the exact location of the Central Force or the Northern Force.

Halsey had taken the bait – and his entire Third Fleet was now steaming up north chasing after the decoy Northern Force. With Halsey's entire force now far away, the only remaining US forces near San Bernardino Strait were the three Seventh Fleet CVE escort carrier task units, totalling sixteen escort carriers, under the command of Rear Admiral Thomas L. Sprague. The CVE escort carriers were slow and small, only carrying twenty-eight planes apiece. The CVEs relied on their own CAP and a screen of destroyers and smaller destroyer escorts for protection – and those were virtually impotent against the modern Japanese battleships heading their way.

The CVEs and their destroyer escorts were in fact more used to screening convoys from submarine attack. They had few anti-ship aerial torpedoes aboard – as they normally relied on protection from enemy surface warships by the Third Fleet. Many of the planes were armed for Combat Air Patrol, anti-submarine work and close infantry support. With no torpedoes and bombs, they would be largely ineffectual against the enemy heavy warships, reduced to making dummy runs to draw fire away from the beleaguered escort carriers.

Rear Admiral Clifton Sprague was in command of the Northern CVE Group (of the three escort carrier groups), Task Unit 77.4.3 (Taffy 3), which was patrolling north east of Samar. Sprague believed that Lee's battle line was positioned to his north at San Bernardino and was providing protection from an attack from that direction. He wasn't aware that just how exposed he was with Halsey's Third Fleet now far away to the north chasing Ozawa's carriers.

With no warning, at 0645, the twenty-three southbound warships of Kurita's Central Force were sighted visually to the north by the Taffy 3 escort carriers off Samar. Being unaware that Halsey had bitten Ozawa's bait, Kurita assumed he had found a Task Force 38 carrier group. He ordered a 'General Attack', his fleet splitting into divisions to attack independently.

Kinkaid's escort carrier planes, which were pursuing the fleeing surviving Southern Force warships westwards down at the Surigao Strait, were recalled and vectored to attack Kurita's Central Force.

Oldendorf's battleships were still 65 miles away in Surigao Strait on their stern chase of the fleeing Southern Force – even at full speed towards Leyte Gulf they would not arrive for 3 hours.

As Kurita's force closed Sprague's exposed six-carrier task unit Taffy 3 for the kill, Sprague ordered his carriers to launch their planes and then retire – he ordered his three destroyers and four destroyer escorts to make smoke to cover their retreat. At 0706, as a rain squall briefly shielded the carriers, Sprague then ordered his destroyers to launch a torpedo attack on the Japanese units to disrupt the Japanese advance.

The super battleship *Yamato* had now closed sufficiently to open up with her main battery – the fearsome 18.1in shells falling in amongst the six unarmoured Taffy 3 escort carriers. Sprague's destroyers and destroyer escorts attacked, opening up with their 5in guns once in range. But their guns had a shorter range and were not heavy enough to have much effect on the much bigger and heavily armoured Japanese warships – nor had they armour to defend against enemy big-gun hits. Wildcat and Hellcat fighters and TBM Avengers from Sprague's carriers attacked, strafing, bombing, dropping torpedoes and firing rockets at the Japanese warships until they ran out of ammunition.

At 0707, Kinkaid radioed Halsey to advise that his ships were being attacked by heavy Japanese warships – but the message like all others would take more than an hour to be transmitted, received and delivered. US radio communications at the time required at least 1 hour in plain language and up to 5 hours or more in code. No help would come from Halsey – and the battle off Samar was an unequal competition.

Closest to the approaching Japanese units, the destroyer *Johnston* (DD-557) charged into the Japanese formation at flank speed, firing her main 5in battery and launching ten torpedoes at the heavy cruiser *Kumano*. One torpedo struck *Kumano* and blew her bow off, forcing her out of line to withdraw.

Two Taffy 3 destroyers, *Hoel* (DD-533) and *Heermann* (DD-532), and the destroyer escort *Samuel B. Roberts* (DE-413) then attacked. *Hoel* began an attack from 18,000yd on the nearest enemy battleship, *Kongō*. When she had closed to 14,000yd, she was able to commence firing with her 5in battery – *Kongō* replied with her own 14in main battery. At 9,000yd *Hoel* launched a salvo of torpedoes that forced *Kongō* to turn sharply to comb the tracks and lose ground on the fleeing escort carriers. *Hoel* was hit minutes afterwards and three of her guns were knocked out along with the port engine.

Notwithstanding the damage she had taken, *Hoel* turned to engage the battleships *Haruna* and Kurita's flagship *Yamato*, firing a half salvo of torpedoes and hitting *Yamato*, which was forced to turn to evade her torpedoes. *Hoel* however was by now crippled and surrounded by a number of Japanese destroyers who fired at her remorselessly, even as her crew abandoned ship. After the small ship had taken more than 40 hits, she capsized and sank at 0855 with the loss of 253 officers and men. There were only 86 survivors.

The destroyer *Heermann* began a torpedo run at the heavy cruiser *Haguro*. As she launched her torpedoes, her guns came in range of the heavy cruiser *Chikuma* and she opened up with her 5in battery. She then altered course to fire three torpedoes at the battleship *Kongō* before switching her targeting again and launching three torpedoes at the battleship *Haruna* from 4,400yd. She then withdrew.

Heermann laid another smoke screen to cover the carriers before re-entering the fray to engage four enemy heavy cruisers and begin a gunnery duel again with the better armed and armoured *Chikuma*. *Heermann* was struck by a number of 8in shells from the heavy cruiser and was holed in the bow. Flooding caused her bow to settle until her anchors were awash – but her actions, allied to hits from aircraft, forced *Chikuma* to withdraw. The heavy cruiser would subsequently sink during the Japanese retreat. The heavy cruiser *Tone* now attacked *Heermann*, which withdrew to lay more smoke. Taffy 2 units now began to arrive to assist their Taffy 3 comrades. *Tone* was attacked and hit by aircraft – and she too was forced to withdraw.

The Taffy 3 destroyer escort *Samuel B. Roberts* charged towards the heavy cruiser *Chōkai* on a torpedo run. Her commanding officer Copeland announced to his crew that they were making a torpedo run. 'The outcome is doubtful, but we will do our duty.'

Roberts got in so close to the Japanese ship that its guns could not be depressed sufficiently to hit her. Once within torpedo range, three Mark 15 torpedoes were launched, one blowing *Chōkai*'s stern off. *Roberts* fought on for another hour, setting the bridge of the heavy cruiser *Chikuma* on fire with hits from its 5in gun – before she was hit by a 14in shell from the battleship *Kongō*. The effect of the hit on such a small unarmoured ship was devastating. A hole 40ft long by 10ft wide was opened up on her port side at her engine room aft. The order to abandon ship was given at 0935 and she sank 30 minutes later, taking ninety of her crew with her.

As the Japanese forces dealt with the daring destroyer attacks and attempted to close Kinkaid's carriers, the planes of the escort carriers attacked with whatever weapons they had. But crucially, Kurita's Central Force had no air cover – and the US aircraft could attack unopposed other than by shipborne AA fire.

As the fast Japanese warships, capable of almost 30 knots, continued to close the range, the escort carriers could not outrun them. They opened up with their meagre armament of a single 5in DP gun mounted on the stern. With the Avenger's bombs and torpedoes expended, they made dummy runs to distract the enemy battleships.

Just after 0800, the heavy cruiser *Chikuma* opened up with her 5in guns on the escort carrier *Gambier Bay* (CVE-73) at a range of 5 miles. Shells struck *Gambier Bay*'s flight deck – and after further hits, she slewed to a stop. Three Japanese cruisers closed the disabled carrier to point-blank range and shelled her until she capsized and sank just after 0900. She was the only US carrier sunk by direct gun fire during the Second World War.

That morning, as Kurita's Central Force was attacking Sprague's escort carrier groups off Samar, Admiral Ōnishi sent in the first organised flight of kamikaze suicide planes – kamikazes crashing into several of the escort carriers. At about 1050, the jeep carrier *St Lo* (CVE-63) took a hit from a A6M Zero kamikaze on her flight deck, which set off secondary explosions and set her ablaze. She had to be quickly abandoned at 1100 and sank shortly afterwards at 1125 with the loss of 114 crew.

In the action, Sprague had lost five of his ships: the two escort carriers *Gambier Bay* and *St Lo*, two destroyers and a destroyer escort. TG 77.4 had lost 105 planes.[27] But despite the US losses in shipping and men, such was the damage and confusion caused by the US defensive actions, that Kurita still believed that the Japanese force was engaging major US Fleet units, rather than small CVE escort carriers and destroyers.

At about noon, having sunk 1 US escort carrier, damaged others and having sunk 2 destroyers and 1 destroyer escort, Kurita received an inaccurate contact report by radio that US carriers were closing in from the north. With US land-based aircraft operating out of Leyte, he feared being trapped in Leyte Gulf. He had already lost three of his heavy cruisers – and he decided that he must now head out to sea to engage what he believed were the remainder of the US fast carriers. Interviewed after the war, he remarked: 'The destruction of enemy aircraft carriers was a kind of obsession with me, and I fell victim to it.'[28] He made his decision to clear Leyte Gulf at 1230.

At 1310 McCain's planes arrived from extreme range – such that after striking Kurita's Central Force they had to land and rearm on airfields

Battle of Leyte Gulf, October 1944. Explosion on USS *St Lo* (CVE-63) after being hit by a kamikaze off Samar, 25 October 1944. (National Archives 80-G-270516)

on Leyte. Together with planes from TG 77.4 they sank a light cruiser and a destroyer and damaged most of the other ships.

No US Fleet carriers however presented themselves to Kurita's force – and by 1730 his units were running low on fuel. Kurita turned the Central Force for home, in full retreat north towards the San Bernardino Strait.[29] He had chosen to go after the illusory US carriers with his big guns – but the US carriers were in fact much further north. By not pressing on with his powerful battleships against the escort carriers to hit Leyte, Kurita had lost the opportunity of hitting the beachhead and destroying vulnerable shipping there. A golden opportunity had been squandered.

In the battle, more than 1,000 US service personnel had been killed in action – more than had been killed at the Coral Sea and Midway combined. But the light US forces acquitted themselves with great valour – and had prevented a serious attack on the Allied forces at Leyte.

Halsey later wrote: 'I opened my hand and let the bird fly away off Luzon. So did the enemy off Samar.'[30]

(e) Battle off Cape Engaño, 25 October 1944

After the carriers of the Northern Force were spotted in the late afternoon of 24 October, far to the north and east of Cape Engaño on the north-east tip of Luzon, some 300 nautical miles distant, Halsey had taken the bait. That evening, he had steamed all three task groups north at an increased speed of 25 knots. Halsey had fallen for the ruse by the decoy Northern Force. The 5 heavy carriers of Task Force 38 *Intrepid, Franklin, Lexington, Enterprise* and *Essex*, with the 5 light carriers *Independence, Belleau Wood, Langley, Cabot* and *San Jacinto*, the 6 fast battleships *Alabama, Iowa, Massachusetts, New Jersey, South Dakota* and *Washington*, 8 cruisers and more than 40 destroyers surged through the darkness of a tropical night into the early hours of 25 October – chasing the enemy carriers. The Task Force 38 air groups together could field more than 600 combat aircraft – and was overwhelmingly more powerful than Ozawa's Northern Force, which comprised the heavy carrier *Zuikaku*, the 3 light carriers *Chitose, Zuihō* and *Chiyoda*, the 2 half-battleships *Ise* and *Hyūga*, 3 light cruisers and 9 destroyers. Crucially, the Japanese carriers had few planes.

At 0100 on 25 October, radar-equipped night Hellcats were launched from *Independence* to search 350 miles out from the carriers. Just over an hour later, at 0208, a series of reports came in – five enemy warships had been detected just 80 miles to the north of TF 38. At 0214, 5 minutes later, another report came in correcting the number of ships and giving their course as 110°, they were running roughly east south east. These were Rear Admiral Matsuda's detached vanguard force of the half-battleships *Ise, Hyūga* and escorts, which were still deliberately trying to get themselves spotted and trigger a night engagement – and lure Halsey further north. At 0220, one plane reported another group of ships 40 miles astern of the first force – it was the main body of the Northern Force. Another report at 0235 confirmed the sighting. Halsey wrote later: 'We had them!'[31]

At 0255, Halsey ordered Lee to form his line of battle 10 miles ahead of the carriers – it was a complicated manoeuvre to pull his six battleships out of the three task groups in the dead of night. Lee ordered his battleships to alter course and slow to 15 knots to draw them carefully out of the formation of carriers, cruisers and destroyers. The *Iowa, New Jersey, Massachusetts, South Dakota, Washington* and *Alabama* then increased speed and moved ahead to take up their position as the task force pressed north.

Halsey ordered his task-group commanders to arm their first deckload strike at once and to launch at earliest dawn with a second strike to follow afterward as soon as possible. He then learned that

Oldendorf's six older battleships were now engaging Nishimura's two battleships and lighter units of the Southern Force in the Surigao Strait, which the Japanese force had entered at 2300. The radar on the night Hellcat that had been shadowing the Northern Force however unfortunately chose that time to break down – and radar contact with the enemy ships was lost.

In Ozawa's decoy Northern Force, when lightning strikes were misidentified as Task Force 38 being attacked by land-based aircraft, Ozawa recalled Matsuda's vanguard force of the two half-battleships *Ise* and *Hyūga*, and their destroyer escorts *Hatsutsuki*, *Akizuki*, *Wakatsuki* and *Shimotsuki* to rendezvous with his nearly empty carriers. Thus, when the time of the battle expected by the Americans came, with nautical daylight at 0430, the Japanese warships spotted in the early hours by the *Independence* night Hellcat were nowhere to be seen. As no Japanese surface contact was initially detected, Mitscher concluded incorrectly that his search planes had scared Ozawa's Northern Force into turning around.

However, as daylight approached, although there was no surface contact for Lee's battlewagons to engage, aboard the US carriers preparations were made for a daybreak launch. The CAP was cleared off the deck – followed by the search planes.

At 0630, as search planes fanned out in their search pattern, Mitscher launched 10 deckload strikes of a total 180 strike aircraft. The strike divisions headed north east to await contact flashes from the search planes once a sighting of the enemy was made. A total of 60 Hellcats, 65 Curtiss SB2C Helldiver dive-bombers and 55 Avenger torpedo-bombers roared down the flight decks to orbit ahead of the task force. Meantime, on the Japanese carriers, Ozawa was launching seventy-five of his own meagre aircraft to attack the US task force.

Meantime, at 0648, Halsey received Kinkaid's despatch from Leyte Gulf: 'AM NOW ENGAGING ENEMY SURFACE FORCES SURIGAO STRAIT x QUESTION IS TF 34 GUARDING SAN BERNARDINO STRAIT.' Halsey replied: 'NEGATIVE x IT IS WITH OUR CARRIERS NOW ENGAGING ENEMY CARRIERS.'[32]

The four Japanese carriers of the Northern Force had steamed south to a position some 100 miles north east of Task Force 38 before Mitscher's search aircraft registered on their radar screens. Once detected, Ozawa immediately turned his four carriers and their escorts around to draw Halsey north – successfully opening the distance by 40 miles before Mitscher's aircraft were visually sighted at 0710. At 0735, US aviators reported sightings of the enemy fleet 140 miles north east of TF 38.

The half-battleship *Ise* escorted *Zuikaku* whilst the cruiser *Ōyodo* escorted the light carrier *Zuihō*. The destroyers *Hatsutsuki*, *Akizuki*, *Wakatsuki* and *Shimotsuki* formed a protective ring around the carriers to provide AA cover and the half-battleship *Hyūga* and the light cruiser *Tama* screened the two light carriers *Chitose* and *Chiyoda*. Ozawa began launching his last twenty-nine planes. Lee's battlewagons sprinted forward to the fight. It seemed that Halsey had succeeded in catching the enemy carrier fleet and would deliver a crushing blow off Cape Engaño that might change the course of the war.

At 0802, Halsey received another despatch from Kinkaid: 'ENEMY VESSELS RETIRING SURIGAO STRAIT x OUR LIGHT FORCES IN PURSUIT.'[33]

Meanwhile, far to the north, the attack by Mitscher's aircraft on Ozawa's Northern Force began just after 0800 as Hellcats pounced and quickly destroyed Ozawa's CAP of about thirty aircraft. At 0820, Air Group 15 of *Essex* was the first to engage the four Japanese carriers. By the intensity of the air attack, Ozawa knew that his decoy mission had succeeded – he had lured the entire Task Force 38 north, away from Leyte.

At 0822, aboard his flagship, the battleship *New Jersey*, Halsey received a further despatch from Kinkaid: 'ENEMY BBS AND CRUISER REPORTED FIRING ON TU 77.4.3 FROM 15 MILES ASTERN.' This was the beginning of the Battle off Samar as Kurita's Central Force, having penetrated the San Bernardino Strait during the night, with the element of surprise attacked Kinkaid's escort carriers. But Halsey was confident of Kinkaid's ability to look after himself: 'I figured that the eighteen little carriers [in actuality sixteen as two had departed the day before for Morotai] had enough planes to protect themselves until Oldendorf could bring up his heavy ships.'[34]

Unbeknownst to Halsey, Ozawa's carriers had few aircraft left able to provide CAP air cover – the Japanese decoy carriers were now sitting ducks. Those remaining Japanese aircraft that were found aloft were quickly shot down by the sixty Hellcats. With the CAP destroyed, the Japanese carriers were then attacked, with most TF 38 planes initially attacking the light carrier *Chitose*.

Japanese AA fire opened but at 0835 in the first bombing strike by *Essex* aircraft, *Chitose* was hit by bombs and by three aerial torpedoes. Her boiler rooms were flooded, her rudder damaged and she quickly took on a 27° list. Counter-flooding successfully reduced the list to 15° – but after the flooding had put both engine rooms out of action, she slewed to a stop, dead in the water. (Shortly afterwards, as the flooding continued unabated and her list increased, she would roll over to port and sink stern first with the loss of more than 900 of her crew.)

The light carrier *Zuihō* was attacked in close succession to *Chitose* just after 0830. *Zuihō* took three near misses at her stern and one direct hit by a single 550lb bomb on the aft section of her flight deck that started several fires, bulged her flight deck and knocked out her steering – she took on a small list to port.

Zuikaku was hit by three bombs on her flight deck on her port side amidships that started fires in her upper and lower hangars. She was then hit just minutes later by a torpedo on her port side aft of amidships that damaged her port-side forward shaft and caused severe flooding that brought on a sharp port list, that was soon brought under control to 6°. She was left with two operational shafts and could still make 23 knots.

As the attacks went in against the Japanese carriers 140 miles north east of TF 38, at 0830 Halsey received a fourth despatch from Kinkaid, whose escort carriers, destroyers and destroyer escorts had now been surprised by the sudden appearance of Kurita's southbound Central Force off Samar: 'URGENTLY NEED FAST BBS LEYTE GULF AT ONCE.'[35] The despatch surprised Halsey – who felt that his primary task was not to protect the Seventh Fleet but to strike with his Third Fleet against the prize, the Japanese carriers.

At 0850, a flash report of the progress TF 38 planes were making with their attack on the Northern Force carriers reached Halsey aboard *New Jersey*: 'ONE CARRIER SUNK AFTER TREMENDOUS EXPLOSION x 2 CARRIERS 1CL HIT BADLY OTHER CARRIER UNTOUCHED x FORCE COURSE 150 SPEED 17.'[36]

Although Halsey believed his attack on the Japanese carriers was going well, he needed more time to finish off the three remaining carriers of Ozawa's Northern Force. But nevertheless, with Kinkaid appealing for assistance, he ordered McCain's TG 38.1, which was refuelling to the east, to head south towards Samar at best possible speed, and notified Kinkaid. But the fast carriers and Lee's fast battleships, so desperately needed off Samar, were still with Halsey far to the north – more than 300 miles from Leyte.

At 0900, Halsey received a fifth despatch from Kinkaid: 'OUR CVES BEING ATTACKED BY 4 BBS 8 CRUISERS PLUS OTHERS x REQUEST LEE COVER LEYTE AT TOP SPEED x REQUEST FAST CARRIERS MAKE IMMEDIATE STRIKE.'

Then at 0922, a sixth despatch: 'CTU 77.4.3 UNDER ATTACK BY CRUISERS AND BBS 0700 . . . REQUEST IMMEDIATE AIR STRIKE x

ALSO REQUEST SUPPORT BY HEAVY SHIPS x MY OBBS [Oldendorf's old battleships] LOW IN AMMUNITION.'[37]

Kinkaid's Seventh Fleet escort carriers, destroyers and destroyer escorts were at this point fighting for their very survival down off Samar. Oldendorf's old battleships were still far away, leaving Kinkaid's destroyers and destroyer escorts to make heroic but almost suicidal attacks on the heavy Japanese warships as his escort carriers were pummelled.

Halsey responded within 5 minutes: 'I AM STILL ENGAGING ENEMY CARRIERS x MCCAIN WITH 5 CARRIERS 4 HEAVY CRUISERS HAS BEEN ORDERED TO ASSIST YOU IMMEDIATELY.' Halsey later wrote that he gave his position so Kinkaid would know there was no possibility of the fast battleships reaching him.[38]

At 1000 Halsey received another clear, uncoded, despatch from Kinkaid: 'WHERE IS LEE x SEND LEE.'

Admiral King in Washington, and Nimitz at Pearl Harbor, also had no idea of the whereabouts of Lee and his battleships. Nimitz sent a terse coded message to Halsey: 'TURKEY TROTS TO WATER x FROM CINCPAC x WHERE IS, REPEAT, WHERE IS TASK FORCE 34 x THE WORLD WONDERS.'[39]

The first four words and the last three words of the message were padding used to confuse enemy crypto analysts. The communications staff on Halsey's flagship *New Jersey* deleted the first four words correctly – but left in the last three words. When Halsey read the message at 1000, he took the message as a stinging rebuke. Infuriated, he lost his temper – grabbing his cap and throwing it to the deck. But the meaning of Nimitz's message was clear – the fast battleships were not where Nimitz thought they should be.

Almost simultaneously with the confusion reigning on the flag bridge aboard *New Jersey*, the second wave of TF 38 strike aircraft arrived above the beleaguered Japanese Northern Force – this time concentrating mainly on the light carrier *Chiyoda*. Aircraft from *Franklin* and *Lexington* closed *Chiyoda*, scored four hits, leaving her crippled and ablaze.

Second wave TF 38 planes also attacked *Zuihō* but were driven off with rocket batteries and Dual Purpose AA guns. Several torpedo attacks were made on *Zuikaku*, but these were driven off by AA fire or avoided. Three Japanese carriers remained afloat – along with the two undamaged half-battleships *Ise* and *Hyūga*.

Faced with the developing situation for Kinkaid off Samar, Halsey ordered Lee's TF 34 battle line and Bogan's Task Group 38.2 to proceed south towards San Bernardino. Sherman's TG 38.3 and Davison's

TG 38.4 would continue their attacks against the Northern Force carriers. Between 1000 and 1115, Halsey reshuffled his forces whilst Bogan's nearly empty destroyers were refuelled for their high-speed run south to relieve Kinkaid. Ted Sherman shared Halsey's frustration, writing in his subsequent Action Report: 'We ruled the sea in our vicinity, there were no enemy aircraft in the air to bother us, the enemy was in full retreat, and the only remaining objective was to prevent his cripples from getting away.'[40]

Halsey notified Kinkaid: 'TG 38.2 PLUS 6 FAST BBS PROCEEDING LEYTE BUT UNABLE ARRIVE BEFORE 0800 TOMORROW.'[41] Halsey then informed Nimitz: 'TASK FORCE 34 WITH ME ENGAGING CARRIER FORCE. AM NOW PROCEEDING WITH TASK GROUP 38.2 AND ALL FAST BB TO REINFORCE KINKAID . . .'[42]

At 1115, a frustrated and conflicted Halsey changed course from 000° to 180° – from due north to due south. The Japanese Northern Force lay just 42 miles from the muzzles of his 16in battleship guns in an exposed position. *Chitose* had been sunk, *Chiyoda* was dead in the water, *Zuihō* was crippled and *Zuikaku* could only make 18 knots and had a damaged flight deck. The enemy carriers had few planes left to defend them.

Halsey had in the meantime been receiving another set of despatches from Kinkaid that included: 'ENEMY RETIRING TO NORTHEASTWARD.' Then finally at 1145: 'ENEMY FORCE OF 3 BB 2 CA 9 DD 11-43N 126-12 E COURSE 225 SPEED 20.'[43] This position put Kurita's Central Force 55 miles north east of Leyte Gulf – but although the course was not towards the entrance, that was likely where they were heading. Although all six fast battleships were heading south, Halsey's best chance of intercepting Kurita was to send his fastest ships in advance – the only two battleships that could sustain high speeds were his flagship *New Jersey* and *Iowa*. Throwing a screen of light cruisers and destroyers around them as TG 34.5, the two-battleship vanguard force raced ahead at 28 knots, preparing for 30 knots. With his destroyers now refuelled, Bogan's three TG 38.2 carriers were also heading south to San Bernardino.

Halsey was sending all six fast battleships south, choosing not to split his force and leave two battleships behind to finish off Ozawa's half-battleships *Ise* and *Hyūga*. He wanted to have overwhelming force when Lee's battleships met Kurita's. The two Ise-class half-battleships would escape to fight again – and down south off Samar Kurita's four fast battleships in the Central Force would also escape through the San Bernardino Strait.

Despite having turned his battleships and TG 38.2 to head south at 1115, aircraft flying from the remaining two Task Groups 38.3 and 38.4 could still pummel the Northern Force carriers. Sherman and Davison's planes struck the Northern Force again and again. Ozawa's flagship *Zuikaku* was hit by seven torpedoes and nine bombs and began to list – forcing him to transfer his flag to the light cruiser *Ōyodo*. *Zuikaku* eventually rolled over and sank stern first just after 1400, taking Rear Admiral Kaizuka Takeo and 842 of her crew to their deaths with her.

The damaged light carrier *Zuihō* was repeatedly attacked and hit by a torpedo and two bombs. Both engine rooms and one boiler room flooded, and her speed slowed to 12 knots. At 1445, she slewed to a stop and lay dead in the water. She was attacked again, and her list increased to 23°. She was eventually abandoned at 1510, and finally succumbed and sank shortly afterwards at 1526 with the loss of 215 officers and men.

Earlier, the battleship *Hyūga* and support ships had attempted to take the crippled *Chiyoda* in tow. But the tow had to be broken off at about 1230 when the third US attack came in. Despite further attempts to tow, at about 1630, *Chiyoda* was closed by the four US cruisers *Santa Fe*, *Mobile*, *Wichita* and *New Orleans* and their support destroyers and shortly afterwards sunk by gunfire.

The more heavily armoured half-battleships *Ise* and *Hyūga* fared better. Throwing up intense AA fire, they and several destroyers managed to avoid destruction. The surviving units of the Northern Force retired in disarray late in the afternoon – with four US fast light cruisers in pursuit and two wolf packs of US submarines waiting across its course. That night just after 2100 the light cruiser IJN *Tama* was torpedoed by the US submarine *Jallao* (SS-358) north east of Luzon – she sank with all hands.

The final losses in the Battle off Cape Engaño for the Northern Force were: sunk: 4 carriers, 1 light cruiser, 2 destroyers; damaged: 2 battleships, 2 light cruisers, 4 destroyers.

Japan's last great naval battle, her last attempt to win a decisive battle, had failed. Her carriers had been intentionally sacrificed – and were gone. Kurita with his powerful battleship Central Force had worried about refuelling, picking up survivors and then been lured north by false reports of enemy carriers to the north. He had not pushed on for the Leyte beachhead, where he could have attacked Allied shipping – and bombarded the Allied beachhead.

Had Kurita pressed into Leyte Gulf, then by 1400 his Central Force, comprising not least the super battleship *Yamato*, would have engaged Oldendorf's battle line of six old battleships and the planes of McCain's five TG 38.1 carriers coming in at speed from the east after their aborted passage to Ulithi. But after the strike at Leyte, Kurita would then have had to face Lee's TF 34 battle line of six fast battleships and their escorts racing down from the north and Halsey's three other Task Groups 38.2, 38.3 and 38.4. In all, Kurita would then have faced the full strength of Task Force 38 and Lee's line of fast battlewagons. Kurita decided to save what he could of the Central Force – much to the relief of Kinkaid and his battered Seventh Fleet escort carrier force.

Shortly after 1300, as Kurita's Central Force retired north towards the San Bernardino Strait, aircraft from McCain's five distant TG 38.1 carriers, returning from Ulithi far to the east, attacked – but did little damage. Halsey's vanguard force was still far away to the north – charging down at speed.

At about 2000, Halsey sent up six night-Avengers from *Independence* and at 2200, the Avengers reported fifteen enemy ships passing along the east coast of Samar into the San Bernardino Strait. Kurita's Central Force was in full retreat re-entering San Bernardino Strait – but the two fast battleships of Halsey's southbound Task Group 34.5 were still 2 hours away to the north.

Shortly after midnight, one of TG 34.5's scouting destroyers made contact with a Japanese Central Force straggler. Halsey watched from the bridge of his flagship *New Jersey* as his cruisers devastated the unfortunate vessel with 6in shells – before a destroyer delivered the *coup de grâce* with torpedoes. This set off a secondary explosion so violent that on his flag bridge Halsey felt the shock arrive from 15 miles away.[44]

At 0300 the next morning, just as a severe tropical thunderstorm had caused the shadowing Avenger to lose contact with Kurita's Central Force, Halsey launched a strike of four Avengers and five Hellcats, each armed with one 500lb bomb – but the strike failed to locate Kurita.

At dawn, McCain (TG 38.1) and Bogan (TG 38.2) launched strikes over the Sibuyan Sea that sank one light cruiser and damaged a heavy cruiser. Kurita would eventually reach Manila safely.

The complicated and confusing Battle of Leyte Gulf was over. Leyte Gulf and the beachhead was safe for the Allies – it was a striking victory. They had lost the light carrier *Princeton*, the 2 escort carriers *Gambier Bay* and *St Lo*, 2 destroyers *Hoel* and *Johnston* and 1 destroyer escort *Samuel B. Roberts* – some 36,000 tons of shipping in all.

But the IJN had lost 45 per cent of the ships engaged. Three Japanese battleships, *Musashi*, *Yamashiro* and *Fusō*, had been sunk along with the heavy carrier *Zuikaku* and the three light carriers *Zuihō*, *Chiyoda* and *Chitose*. Six heavy cruisers had gone to the bottom, Kurita's flagship *Atago* along with *Maya*, *Suzuya*, *Chōkai*, *Chikuma* and *Mogami*. The four light cruisers *Noshiro*, *Abukuma*, *Tama* and *Kinu* had been sunk along with nine destroyers – a total of some 305,710 tons of shipping.[45]

The Japanese forces had been beset by poor communications, a lack of carrier planes and pilots, an untrained land-based naval air force that was wiped out over Formosa – and inferior equipment and aircraft. The Japanese Fleet had been sacrificed in a last-ditch battle to save the Philippines. Kurita had withdrawn, not sharing the spirit of supreme sacrifice of the kamikaze. He had failed in his mission – and the battle had been lost.

The Battle of Leyte Gulf has long been debated – and caused much controversy. Some have argued that prime responsibility for letting Kurita's Central Force penetrate the San Bernardino Strait undetected and attack Kinkaid's vulnerable Seventh Fleet escort carriers rested with Halsey. 'Bull' Halsey, true to his nickname, took Ozawa's bait and was lured north – thus denuding the San Bernardino Strait of Lee's battle line and the air power of Task Force 38. But there is much to be said in Halsey's defence, the primacy of the Japanese carriers was his priority in terms of his orders. For his part, Kinkaid failed to send air searches north during the night and failed to guard MacArthur's right flank and rear. As they say, no plan survives contact with the enemy.

Halsey was subsequently able to write in his official report to Admirals King and Nimitz of 'the elimination of serious naval threat to our operations for many months, if not forever'.[46] He never admitted any error in leaving the San Bernardino Strait open and unprotected, advising King in January when he returned to Washington that instead of running south with Lee and Bogan to relieve Kinkaid's Seventh Fleet, he should have stayed north to finish off Ozawa's Northern Force with his big guns when they were so close. King replied: 'No. It wasn't a mistake. You couldn't have done otherwise.'[47] In a statement to Theodore Taylor, author of *The Magnificent Mitscher*, on 9 April 1953, Halsey commented: 'I wish that Spruance had been with Mitscher at Leyte Gulf and I had been with Mitscher in the Battle of the Philippine Sea.'[48]

Chapter 17

The Liberation of the Philippines – Corking the Luzon Bottleneck

The Allied invasion of Leyte was intended to begin the isolation of Japan from its territories in South-East Asia, a vital source of Japan's industrial and oil supplies. So important were the Philippines that following the First Battle of the Philippine Sea on 19 and 20 June 1944 the Japanese had been heavily reinforcing their forces there – there were by now 432,000 Japanese troops stationed in the Philippines. The Japanese Fleet may have been defeated at the Battle of Leyte Gulf – but that did not alter Japan's plans to hold Leyte and the Philippines. They would be bitterly fought over.

The liberation of the Philippines was a MacArthur Sixth Army operation that called for the Navy to pass control of air operations at Leyte to the Sixth Army on 27 October. General MacArthur directed that the fast carriers make no more strikes against land targets unless requested to do so by Army commanders. Intensive Japanese air raids however quickly caused MacArthur to revise his plans and request that both the fast and escort carriers remain on station to support the Sixth Army and attack Japanese convoys and airfields.

Bogan's TG 38.2 and Davison's TG 38.4 were sent to strike targets in the Visayas and on Luzon between 28 and 30 October, facing severe enemy counter-attacks. The TF 38 carriers interdicted a Japanese submarine attack – but were then subjected to a sustained kamikaze attack in which *Franklin* (CV-13) and *Belleau Wood* (CVL-24) were both hit, killing 158 men in total and destroying 45 planes. Both were forced to withdraw for repairs. *Intrepid* took a glancing blow from a kamikaze

USS *Belleau Wood* (CVL-24) burns aft after being hit by a kamikaze off the Philippines, 30 October 1944. Flight-deck crew are moving undamaged TBM torpedo planes away from the flames as others fight the fires. USS *Franklin* (CV-13), also hit by a kamikaze, is on fire in the distance. (National Archives 80-G-342020)

in a gun gallery that killed six men but did not diminish her fighting ability.

With the fast carriers nearing the end of their ammunition, food and supplies, Davison's TG 38.4 was released on 29–30 October to head for Ulithi, along with the by now exhausted escort carrier groups. Bogan's three carriers of TG 38.2 were left to cover Leyte on 31 October, along with a few P-38s and P-61 Black Widow night-fighters.

At Ulithi, the long-awaited change of command of the fast carriers took place on 30 October 1944. A physically drained Vice Admiral Mitscher turned Task Force 38 over to Vice Admiral McCain, issuing a letter as he went, on 30 October 1944, 'To the Officers and Men of Task Force THIRTY-EIGHT', in which he stated:

> The outer defense system of Japan has been destroyed, exposing their vital inner lines to continuing attack. The enemy fleet has been greatly depleted by your efforts; the enemy naval air force which has been our most persistent opponent for ten months has been eliminated. For the enemy, the hand-writing is on the wall. The final phase has begun. . . . I wish you great success in the future, and give to all hands a heartfelt 'Well Done' for the past.[1]

Mitscher was then to disembark *Lexington* at 0400 on 1 November to return by seaplane to Pearl on shore leave and planning duty. As he made his way through the dimly lit hangar deck, more than 100 of his pilots and officers had assembled, some in uniform, others in pyjamas and robes, to see him off. He would return with Spruance, when they relieved Halsey and McCain at the completion of the Philippines operation. On 31 October Rear Admiral Alfred Montgomery took over Task Group 38.1.

The apparently weak Allied air defence at Leyte Gulf and off Samar tempted the Japanese into counter-attacking. Leyte was out of range of General George Kenney's land-based AAF aircraft – and so MacArthur was dependant on carrier air, which could never provide the same blanket support. The paucity of air cover allowed Japanese troops to pour into Leyte – with some 34,000 troops arriving to begin fierce sustained fighting.

Reports received of a possible movement of the surviving Japanese Mobile Fleet units under Kurita and Shima toward the Surigao Strait gave the Allies cause for concern. Ted Sherman and TG 38.3 sped back to join Bogan's three TG 38.2 carriers and reinforced protection of the Allied shipping off Leyte – Montgomery's TG 38.1 arrived shortly thereafter.

The three powerful task groups hit Japanese airfields on Luzon on 5 and 6 November, catching the Japanese off guard and destroying more than 400 aircraft, most of them on the ground. The operation cost twenty-five US aircraft destroyed. On 5 November, a kamikaze hit *Lexington*'s signal bridge, killing forty-seven men. Vice Admiral McCain moved his flag from *Lexington* to *Wasp* and then returned to Ulithi with *Wasp* to allow a change of air groups to take place. Command of Task Force 38 was passed to his senior CarDiv commander, Ted Sherman, until 13 November.

Less than a week later, on 11 November, several hundred carrier planes sank a convoy of 5 Japanese transports carrying some 10,000 Japanese troops to Leyte – the 4 escort destroyers were also sunk.

Halsey was keen for his fast carriers to attack surviving heavy Japanese ships at the important enemy anchorage of Brunei Bay in north west Borneo – before heading north for a strike at Tokyo itself. But Generals MacArthur and Kenney (AAF) and Sherman (CTF 38) met at Leyte on 10 November however and assessed that fast-carrier support was still essential to Sixth Army operations at Leyte. Task Force 38 aircraft would continue to attack Luzon airfields and shipping throughout November.

On 13 and 14 November, TF 38 aircraft sank a Japanese light cruiser and 5 destroyers along with 7 merchant ships – destroying more than 75 enemy aircraft. Five days later a follow-up carrier strike destroyed a similar number of aircraft on the ground. Sherman's TG 38.3 then returned to Ulithi with Davison's TG 38.4 after unsuccessfully testing napalm on 22 November in a strike against Yap Island in the western Carolines.

On 25 November, Montgomery's TG 38.1 and Bogan's TG 38.2 carried out a final strike on Luzon, as fast-carrier operations in support of Leyte came to an end. TF 38 torpedo and dive-bombers sunk a heavy cruiser, several Japanese naval transports and destroyed many aircraft. But this raid triggered a violent Japanese retaliation in which kamikazes hit *Intrepid*, *Essex* and *Cabot* and a near miss damaged *Hancock*. The damage to the carriers was significant enough to trigger the cancellation of the strike against the Visayas planned for 26 November. Admiral Halsey insisted that his fast carriers should not again be exposed in such a way for routine operations, until a better way of handling the kamikaze threat had been conceived.

Leyte now had two operational airfields from which land-based P-38s and P-40 Warhawks could operate. As General Kenney's Army Air Force assumed responsibility for Leyte's defence, the remaining Task Force 38 carrier groups were released to return to Ulithi.

With the loss of four carriers at the Battle of Leyte Gulf, the IJN's CarDiv 3 had been decimated. But Japan still had five carriers remaining, which were gathered together into CarDiv 1: *Unryū*, *Amagi*, *Katsuragi*, *Jun'yō* and the light carrier *Ryūhō*. But these carriers had few planes and few pilots – as well as little fuel for operations. Other than the serious threat posed by *Yamato*, the Japanese Fleet for all practical purposes was now at the bottom of the Pacific.

A Yokosuka D4Y Judy kamikaze plane explodes of the flight deck of USS *Essex* (CV-9), off Luzon, 25 November 1944. (National Archives 80-G-270736)

The construction of the third Yamato-class battleship at Yokosuka had been suspended in June 1942, following the losses of the fleet carriers *Akagi*, *Kaga*, *Sōryū* and *Hiryū* at the Battle of Midway. Reconstruction began to convert the partially completed hull to be the huge 68,059-ton carrier *Shinano*, which would be protected by the 17,700 tons of battleship horizontal deck armour and vertical side armour already installed around the magazines. Her forward main battery barbettes had also already been installed – and this advanced state of construction prevented her being converted into a fleet carrier. She would become an 872ft-long heavily armoured support carrier that would carry reserve aircraft, fuel and ordnance in support of other fleet carriers. It was hoped that if she were completed in late 1944 and was able to operate in the South China Sea, she might be able to shuttle planes, even kamikazes, to hit Allied shipping off Mindoro in December.

Shinano was Japan's last great carrier throw of the dice. She was launched on 5 October 1944 and carried out sea trials in Tokyo Bay on 11 November 1944. She was then commissioned one week later on 19 November and Captain Abe Toshio was assigned as her commanding officer. But the carrier was in reality not yet fully completed, most of her watertight doors had still to be installed and internal bulkheads were still peppered with holes for electrical cables, ventilation ducts and pipes that had yet to be sealed.

Despite her unfinished condition, the demands of war meant that on 28 November 1944, just over one week after her commission, *Shinano* took on six *Shinyo* suicide boats and 50 Yokosuka MXY-7 *Ohka* piloted bombs, later to be nicknamed by US sailors the *Baka*, which means *fool* or *idiot* in Japanese. These new *Ohka* kamikazes carried 2,400lb of explosives in the nose and were to be dropped from attack aircraft. *Shinano* was ordered to Kure to pick up an air group and train in the Inland Sea, then to proceed to the relief of the Philippines with her *Ohka*-piloted bombs. She departed Yokosuka for Kure the same day. On the offensive, US submarines were patrolling the waters close to Japan.

On 0309, the next day, 29 November, *Shinano* was attacked in darkness in Tokyo Bay by the US submarine *Archerfish* (SS-311) – and hit on her starboard side by four torpedoes. As *Archerfish* went deep, diving to 400ft to escape depth charging from the destroyer escorts, onboard the new carrier it initially seemed that the damage was controllable. But although *Shinano* was able to maintain her course and speed, deep inside her hull water was spreading remorselessly through the openings of her incomplete internal finishings and pipework. *Shinano* slowly took on a list to starboard that forced Captain Abe Toshio to counter-flood the three outboard port boiler rooms.

As the first light of dawn arrived, *Shinano* had managed to steam some 36 nautical miles from the position where she had been attacked a few hours earlier and was still able to make 11 knots. Her boiler feed water however now failed – and by 0745, *Shinano* had slewed to a stop and wallowed immobile in the water.

At 0850, the destroyers *Hamakaze* and *Isokaze* took her in tow – in an effort to drag her for beaching at Cape Ushio. The tow was a painfully slow 3 knots – and the massive weight of her water-logged hull was too much and the tow eventually had to be abandoned.

Dead in the water once again, the list to starboard slowly increased and at 1018 Captain Abe Toshio gave the order to abandon ship. The destroyer *Yukikaze* came alongside and took about half her crew off. Less than an hour later, the great carrier rolled over to starboard and like most sinking battleships, turned turtle on the surface – before going down by the stern. A total of 1,435 officers and men perished – including Captain Abe Toshio, who chose to go down with his ship. *Shinano* was gone – only seven weeks after being launched.

Just over a week later, on 9 December, the escort carrier *Jun'yō* was severely damaged and forced to withdraw after an attack by two US submarines off Nagasaki. Shortly after that, on 19 December, *Unryū*, en route through the East China Sea with supplies, was torpedoed and sunk 200 nautical miles south east of Shanghai by the US submarine *Redfish* (SS-395).

With this attrition of her remaining carriers, Japan now kept her flattops in port – along with most of her battleships, cruisers and destroyers. The two half-carriers *Ise* and *Hyūga* made one of the last runs from Singapore to Japan carrying gasoline in February 1945, before they too ended their sailing days.

Japanese carrier construction however did continue as late as March 1945 on the 18,300-ton Ikoma-class carrier *Ikoma* (laid down in July 1943), the 17,500-ton 745ft-long Unryū-class *Kasagi* (laid down in April 1943) and *Aso* (laid down in June 1943) as well as the 14,800-ton cruiser *Ibuki*, which was undergoing conversion to a light carrier at Sasebo Naval Arsenal. These carriers were almost three-quarters completed by the time Japan moved her construction focus to creating weapons for the defence of the Japanese home islands against invasion.[2]

Delays in the development of modern carrier planes, allied to a lack of trained pilots and lack of fuel, sealed the fate of Japan's carriers. Fighter factories had been severely damaged by B-29 bombing attacks that began in June 1944 from China, and from the Mariana Islands in November. Construction had slowed significantly on the improved variant of the Zeke 32 (Allied reporting name Hamp), a variant of the A6M Zero, and the new Kawanishi N1K *Shiden-Kai* (Rex). Only eight new Mitsubishi A7M *Reppū* fighters (Sam) came off the production line at Nagoya before an earthquake on 7 December combined with B-29 bombing raids had demolished the factory.

In 1945, all planes and pilots were designated for the defence of the homeland – the majority in a suicide capacity.

From the Allied perspective, the new and deadly kamikaze attacks had to be countered. Essentially this meant more fighters and pilots were needed – at the expense of dive-bombers and torpedo-bombers. But pilot training had been cut back since June 1944.

The Marines wanted their own escort carriers to support their infantry landings, so in October 1944, a special Marine Carrier Groups Command was established to begin training escort carrier pilots. On 2 December, Admiral King directed that ten Marine Corps fighter squadrons of eighteen planes each be given 'immediate carrier qualification' and temporarily assigned to the fast carriers. Each trainee Marine pilot would make just twelve landings in Corsairs aboard *Saratoga, Ranger* or one escort carrier to qualify. The first units to qualify were Marine Fighting Squadrons 124 and 213, reporting aboard *Essex* at the end of December and bringing their own mechanics to service the aircraft.

As these new aircraft became available, each carrier air group changed in composition from 54 fighters (VF), 24 bombers (VB) and 18 torpedo planes (VT) to 73 VF fighters, 15 VB bombers and 15 VT torpedo-bombers. King reversed pilot-training cutbacks, increasing numbers from 6,000 to 8,000 pilots per year and also provided an increased 2 air groups per carrier – to cover the pilot fatigue resulting from constant air operations and kamikaze attacks. The faster F4U Corsairs would now assume precedence as fighters, the F6F Hellcats would operate as fighter-bombers – with four Hellcats operating as night-fighters. In January 1945, as a temporary expedient, Ted Sherman got fighter-oriented air groups consisting of ninety-one VF fighters and fifteen VT torpedo planes aboard *Essex* and *Wasp*.

As a defensive strategy, McCain expanded his cruising formation by stationing radar picket ships, TOMCATs, 60 miles ahead of the carriers in the likely direction of Japanese attack. These radar picket ships were destroyers that had additional radars and fighter direction equipment fitted along with more AA weapons for self-defence, usually at the expense of removing deck-mounted five-tube torpedo swivel launchers. The TOMCATS were the nearest ships to Japanese airfields and usually the first vessels detected by incoming waves of kamikazes. They were often heavily attacked.

Vertically, in the air, McCain began dawn to dusk Combat Air Patrols (CAP) above the carriers at all altitudes, with 2–4 fighters flying at low altitude in each of the 4 quadrants with 5–6 such units outside the screen. DADCAP was a dawn to dusk combat patrol launched at dawn and relieved at sunset by BATCAP for dusk patrol. RAPCAP radar picket planes and SCOCAP scouting line planes were positioned over the TOMCAT picket destroyers. When returning strike aircraft reached the picket ships, they would circle them. Any snooping kamikazes that failed to circle would be picked off by the defensive fighters.

The Three Strike system was introduced. Whilst one fighter patrol operated over an enemy airfield, a second patrol was prepared for take-off and a third patrol was en route either to or from the target or being rearmed. During darkness, night-fighters would be over enemy airfields harassing air operations below and preventing Japanese aircraft from taking off. It was hoped that the combination of more fighters and these new tactics would diminish the threat to the carriers of kamikaze attacks.

The heavy damage inflicted on Task Force 38 during November restricted Halsey to having three task groups of four day carriers each. *Enterprise* would spend December at Pearl Harbor converting into a night flattop with Night Air Group 90 – whilst the night carrier *Independence* continued with Task Force 38. On 19 December, Night Carrier Division 7 was finally formed comprising *Enterprise* and *Independence*, with Rear Admiral Matt Gardner in command. *Enterprise*, the 'Big E', sailed for combat on 24 December with the fliers training en route.

Before US forces could begin the second half of the Philippines campaign, and launch the invasion of the large northern island of Luzon, a base of operation had to be established close to Luzon to provide advancing ground troops with air support. Japanese aircraft and kamikazes had been pounding the Allied positions on Leyte, to the south east, to such an extent that it was clear that enemy air in the central Philippines could not be eliminated by the Army Air Force. The invasion of the large island of Mindoro, south west of Luzon, was scheduled for 5 December. Once taken, airfields on Mindoro would provide land-based air support for the ground troops assaulting Luzon to the north.

In advance of the invasion on 5 December, on 1 December, Halsey sortied three TF 38 task groups from the forward fleet anchorage at Ulithi – for Mindoro. However, General MacArthur was persuaded on 30 November by the US admirals to postpone the Mindoro operation for ten days. When Task Force 38, en route for Mindoro, received word on the afternoon of 1 December, the carriers came about and returned to Ulithi.

The invasion of Luzon was put back from 20 December to 9 January – allowing the TF 38 admirals a few more weeks to train their crews and practise handling task groups.

Fleet Organisation
Commander Third Fleet – Admiral W.F. Halsey Jr
Chief of Staff – Rear Admiral R.B. Carney
Commander Task Force 38 – Vice Admiral J.S. McCain
Chief of Staff – Rear Admiral W.D. Baker
1. CTG 38.1 – Rear Admiral A.E. Montgomery (ComCarDiv 3):
   Yorktown (CV-10) – Captain T.S. Combs, Air Group 3
   Wasp (CV-18) – Captain O.A. Weller, Air Group 81
   Cowpens (CVL-25) – Captain G.H. DeBaun, Air Group 22
   Monterey (CVL-26) – Captain S.H. Ingersoll, Air Group 28

Dazzle-painted US Third Fleet carriers at anchor at Ulithi Atoll, 8 December 1944. *Wasp* (CV-18), *Yorktown* (CV-10), *Hornet* (CV-19), *Hancock* (CV-19) and *Ticonderoga* (CV-14). *Lexington* (CV-16) is in the left background. (National Archives 80-G-294129)

    2. CTG 38.2 – Rear Admiral G.F. Bogan (ComCarDiv4):
       Lexington (CV-16) – Captain E.W. Litch, Air Group 20
       Hancock (CV-19) – Captain R.F. Hickey, Air Group 7
       Hornet (CV-12) – Captain A.K. Doyle, Air Group 11
       Cabot (CVL-28) – Captain S.J. Michael, Air Group 29
       Independence (CVL-22) – Captain E.C. Ewen, Night Air group 41
    3. CTG 38.3 – Rear Admiral F.C. Sherman (ComCarDiv 1):
       Essex (CV-9) – Captain C.W. Wieber, Air Group 4
       Ticonderoga (CV-14) – Captain Dixie Kiefer, Air Group 80
       Langley (CVL-27) – Captain J.F. Wegforth, Air Group 44
       San Jacinto (CVL-30) – Captain M.H. Kernodle, Air Group 45

Because of the continued kamikaze threat, the fast carriers would remain mobile in the second half of the Philippines campaign, striking at strategic targets and leaving close support at Mindoro to the six escort carriers of the newly created Escort Carrier Force Pacific Fleet under the command of Rear Admiral Calvin T. Durgin.

Task Force 38 sortied from Ulithi on 10–11 December heading for Luzon targets whilst General Kenney's Army Air Forces (AAF) covered all targets south of Manila. Tasked with keeping enemy fighters grounded during the landings on Mindoro, the TF 38 fast carriers blanketed Luzon continuously day and night from 14–16 December, keeping Japanese aircraft in Luzon grounded and shooting up more than 200 enemy aircraft, mostly on the ground, for the loss of 27 US aircraft. Task Force 38 then withdrew to refuel before being assigned to support the Seventh Fleet landing on Mindoro, which took place on 15 December.

On the night of 17/18 December, TF 38 ran into trouble whilst searching in heavy weather for a refuelling rendezvous with their service squadron. Despite a number of reports of an imminent severe storm, Halsey continued with the attempt to refuel – until the Force was beset by what had developed into a tight typhoon. Halsey eventually was forced to give up the attempt to refuel at noon on 18 December – as well as his Luzon strikes.

Task Force 38 headed south in heavy seas – the strong winds blowing roughly east to west. On the smaller light carriers, planes broke their lashings – and as they moved about suffered damage. Fires broke out on *Monterey* and *Cowpens* – and some planes fell overboard. As the wind and seas intensified, three destroyers, low on fuel and without ballast to stabilise them, capsized and sank with the loss of nearly 800 men. The damage caused to Task Force 38 by the typhoon took the fast carriers out of action temporarily – although by now, Kenney's land-based AAF had begun to cover Mindoro from Leyte.

TF 38 returned to Ulithi on 24 December and Admiral Nimitz arrived to spend Christmas Day with Halsey aboard *New Jersey*. Admiral Gardner and *Enterprise* arrived to form Night Task Group 38.5 with *Independence* on 5 January 1945. The first Marines also flew aboard – although during January they would lose seven pilots killed and thirteen F4U Corsairs written off to deck crashes.

Damage repaired, fast-carrier operations restarted on 30 December 1944 for strikes in support of MacArthur's planned landing at Lingayen Gulf, Luzon on 9 January 1945. For six days beginning on 3 January, Task Force 38 aircraft pounded Japanese airfields on Luzon, Formosa, the Pescadores Islands, the Sakishima Gunto Islands and on Okinawa. More than 150 enemy planes were destroyed. In heavy weather, several kamikazes got through gaps in the continuous TOMCAT picket and CAP patrols of McCain's 'Big Blue Blanket' to sink or damage Seventh Fleet shipping.

On 4 January, the escort carrier *Ommaney Bay* (CVE-79) was hit by a kamikaze whilst transiting the Sulu Sea, west of Mindoro. One of two bombs carried by the kamikaze penetrated the flight deck and exploded in the hangar deck amongst fully gassed up planes, setting off a series of explosions and creating intense fires that cooked off ammunition and prevented assistance by destroyer escorts. She eventually had to be scuttled by torpedo. On 6 January, during the pre-invasion bombardment the light cruiser *Columbia* (CL-56) was hit by a kamikaze in Lingayen Gulf but survived.

On 9 January, code named S-Day, the invasion of Luzon began as more than seventy Allied warships entered Lingayen Gulf and commenced a pre-invasion bombardment of Japanese shore positions at 0700. Task Force 38 hit Formosa with all available planes to cover the landing forces. The 10,519grt oiler *Kuroshio Maru* was sunk along with the small 1,091grt Type 2TL standard merchant tanker *Kaiho Maru*, which was carrying 680 troops (of which almost half lost their lives) and the 3,580grt cargo ship *Fukuyama Maru*.

The landing forces faced a strong kamikaze attack, in which the damaged destroyer *Columbia*, lying close inshore and surrounded by landing craft, was again hit by a kamikaze – and again survived.

The Sixth Army began going ashore at Lingayen an hour later at 0800, covered by Oldendorf's six old battleships and Rear Admiral Durgin's seventeen escort carriers. Jeep carrier losses were unusually high at eighty-six aircraft, forty of them operationally as many Marine pilots were still inexperienced in carrier landings. TF 38 aircraft provided close air support for the landings, strafing and bombing Japanese positions. However, no enemy carriers challenged the Seventh Fleet operations off Mindoro – the destruction of Japan's carriers and other warships in the Battle of Leyte Gulf had paid dividends.

With TF 38 operations in the Philippines now paused, Nimitz released the fast carriers from supporting the Lingayen beachhead to strike westwards into the South China Sea in an operation codenamed PLAN GRATITUDE. It was hoped Japanese merchant shipping would be plentiful as reports had been received on 7 January of a large Japanese convoy of more than 100 ships moving up the coast of China towards the Formosa Straits and Japan.

After refuelling, Task Force 38 slipped into the South China Sea, passing through the Bashi Channel, between Luzon and Formosa, so close that the fast carriers were just 80 miles south of the enemy airfields on Formosa. Nimitz and MacArthur both wanted to eliminate the surviving Japanese battleships and cruisers near Singapore, which could still appear to bombard the Lingayen beachhead or attempt to cut off MacArthur's supply route to Mindoro. Halsey was after the half-battleships *Ise* and *Hyūga*, which had narrowly escaped his big guns in October at Leyte Gulf, and which were now believed by naval intelligence to be at Cam Ranh Bay, north of Saigon in French Indochina, modern-day Vietnam.

Halsey hoped to approach Cam Ranh Bay undetected and, with the element of surprise, isolate *Ise* and *Hyūga* so that they could not run south to the safety of Singapore. But when, on 11 January, the task force approached Cam Ranh Bay it was found the two Ises were long gone. They had left almost two weeks earlier on 1 January for the Lingga Roads anchorage near Singapore – from where they would return to Japan in mid-February.

Nevertheless, TF 38 aircraft sank 44 enemy ships, totalling 132,700 tons, and destroyed more than 100 Japanese aircraft. The operation cost twenty-three US carrier planes downed – but most of the pilots were rescued. Halsey wrote: 'The Jap supply route from Singapore, Burma, Borneo and the Dutch East Indies was shattered. We left the pieces to be picked up by our submarines and land-based planes.'[3]

Halsey then ran north for strikes against Formosa and the nearby Chinese coast on 15 January. On 16 January, TF 38 aircraft attacked Hong Kong, Hainan Island, Canton, Swatow and Macao with Japanese AA fire knocking down twenty-two US aircraft. After a break due to bad weather, TF 38 bombed Formosa, the Pescadores and the Sakashima Islands on 21 January.

Now operating close to the Japanese home islands, these attacks provoked a fierce kamikaze response: 2 kamikazes hit the Essex-class carrier *Ticonderoga* (CV-14) killing 143 and wounding 202, including Captain Dixie Kiefer, severely damaging the island superstructure and forcing her to retire to Ulithi for repair. Another kamikaze hit the TOMCAT destroyer *Borie* (DD-704) and a Japanese bomber hit *Langley* – whilst a loose bomb from a landing Avenger caused a serious fire and killed fifty-two crew on *Hancock*.

That night, 21 January, seven Avengers sank a Japanese tanker off Formosa and the following day Task Force 38 aircraft attacked and photographed the Sakishima and Ryukyu Islands, particularly Okinawa. These operations brought Task Force 38 fast-carrier actions in support of the Philippine operation to a close. Task Force 38 turned to head for Ulithi, arriving there on 25 January 1945.

Meanwhile MacArthur's Sixth Army moved inland at Lingayen, seizing the enemy airfields that would allow General Kenney's AAF planes a base from where they could support the drive overland to Manila.

The Allies finally liberated Manila on 3 February – and all major Japanese organised resistance on Luzon ceased on 14 April. By early

1945, the plugging of the Luzon bottleneck was nearly complete with Army Air Forces operating from Luzon airfields and the Navy using Manila and building a major base and anchorage at Leyte-Samar, which the fast carriers would eventually use.

With this strong Allied presence in the Philippines, Japanese vessels making the long run from the East Indies north to the home islands with precious cargoes were in great danger. Enemy shipping was open both to attack by Allied aircraft based in the Philippines as well as by the ever present and far-ranging US submarines. If Japanese ships survived that part of the voyage, then as they neared Japan, they would pass through waters and harbours that were now being aerially mined by long-range B-29 bombers flying from the Marianas and by medium bombers flying from Leyte. With the fall of Manila, the long-range naval and air blockade of Japan had begun.

The aircraft of the Fast-Carrier Task Force had destroyed thousands of Japanese aircraft during the Philippine campaign between September 1944 and January 1945 – and had sunk or disabled the major strength of the Japanese Fleet. They had supported MacArthur's Sixth Army alongside the escort carriers, fighting against super battleships and the might of the IJN – as well as fighting off the kamikaze threat of Japanese human guided missiles in planes, *Kaiten* one-man suicide submarines, *Shinyo* suicide boats and *Ohka* piloted bombs. One US task group, other than for a three-day stop at Ulithi, had been at sea for a record eighty-four days.

Japan had sacrificed her carriers, many major surface fleet units and her last effective naval air squadrons in attempting to retain the Philippines. Although back in 1942 with the Battles of the Coral Sea and Midway, Japan had essentially lost the ability to win the war, when she lost the Philippines and her vital supplies of oil, rubber and gasoline, Japan had lost the war.

With Japan's petroleum supply sealed off at Luzon, Admiral King looked to the final encirclement of Japan by the US Fleet. The conquest of the bypassed East Indies was assigned to the USA's ally, Great Britain – who had a steadily growing Eastern Fleet.

After five months as Commander Third Fleet, Admiral Halsey hauled down his flag on *New Jersey* on 26 January 1945. He and Vice Admiral McCain went on shore leave and planning duty – to begin focusing on plans for covering future amphibious landings on Japan itself. Admirals Spruance and Mitscher returned to their previous commands. The Third Fleet once again became the Fifth Fleet, and Task Force 38 once again became Task Force 58.

Chapter 18

Raiding Tokyo and the Invasions of Iwo Jima and Okinawa, February–April 1945

By mid-February 1945, the Japanese surface fleet was largely destroyed and with the corking of the Luzon bottleneck, Japan was cut off from her major fuel stores. As Japan retreated to defence of her homeland islands, and as the Allies closed in, the US fast carriers were now faced with operating on the periphery of the Asian continent – a stark change from the open ocean and scattered islands of their march westwards to date. In place of sudden strikes such as had neutralised Truk and Palau, or supporting landings as at Kwajalein or Saipan, the fast carriers now had to target large numbers of enemy land-based aircraft. At this time, land-based tactical air could not take part in the final attack on Japan until new air bases were seized and constructed at Iwo Jima and Okinawa that would allow land-based air operations at relatively close range to Japan.

The fast carriers now had three roles:

1. To carry out air strikes on Japanese merchant shipping in the East China Sea, south west of Japan.
2. To support Army and Marine Corps landing forces as they seized island bases surrounding the Japanese home islands – a task made difficult by the proximity of enemy kamikaze bases.
3. To strike directly against Japan itself and degrade her industry, airfields and coastal traffic – augmenting the large-scale strategic bombing campaign by Marianas-based B-29s.

To be close to the action on the periphery of Asia, beginning in mid-January, Nimitz moved his HQ forward from Pearl Harbor to Guam. Advanced Headquarters Guam was established on 29 January 1945.

When Admirals Spruance and Mitscher took over command from Halsey and McCain on 27 January 1945, the Pacific Fleet faced two more Central Pacific operations before the aptly codenamed Operation DOWNFALL, the final assault on Japan, could be made.

1. Operation DETACHMENT – beginning 19 February 1945, the island of Iwo Jima would be seized. Iwo Jima, one of the Volcano Islands south of Japan, is only 8 square miles and is dominated by Mount Suribachi at its south-west end. Three Japanese airfields were present – and lying 750 miles south of Tokyo, once taken, Iwo could be utilised as an air base for long-range P-51 Mustang fighters to escort the Boeing B-29 Superfortress four-engine heavy bomber on raids over Japan. Iwo could also serve as an emergency landing base for damaged B-29s returning from raids on Japan that were unable to reach their main bases at Guam and Saipan.
2. Operation ICEBERG – beginning 1 April 1945, the 66-mile-long island of Okinawa would be seized – followed by the seizure of other nearby Ryukyu Islands. Okinawa lies 400 miles south of the main Japanese island of Kyushu, a primary target for Operation DOWNFALL.

The question of how to progress the war after Okinawa became a hot topic. The Joint Chiefs of Staff had decided back in July 1944 on an invasion of the main Japanese home islands. Japan had an estimated 3,500,000 well-trained troops available to defend her home islands – and the almost fanatical commitment of these troops had been starkly demonstrated in campaigns such as the invasion of Saipan, where the US forces had suffered 3,426 killed in action and 13,099 wounded to account for 23,811 Japanese defenders. Less than 300 Japanese were taken prisoner, mainly those that were too badly wounded to fight or commit ritual *hara-kiri* suicide. In Europe, the Soviets had suffered more than 350,000 casualties in their final 23-day assault against German forces holding Berlin and central Germany. A land invasion was a daunting prospect.

Based on the Saipan experience, expected Allied battle casualties in the invasion of Japan were estimated at 1,700,000 to 2,000,000. The best-case scenario put casualties at 500,000. These figures made a deep impression on those having to grapple with planning Operation DOWNFALL.

The Navy admirals such as King, Nimitz, Spruance and Sherman championed a tight air-sea blockade of Japan that would neutralise its war industry and capability, just as they had done at Rabaul, Truk and other bypassed islands – and as Britain had done to Germany in the North Sea in the First World War. They believed that strategic bombing by B-29s and aerial mining of Japanese waters would then force Japan to surrender – saving a vast number of expected Allied ground troop casualties.

Admiral King CNO had determined in late September 1944 that a naval blockade would require an advance base along the coast of China and so, now on his rotation ashore, Halsey had been assigned to study post-Okinawa operations. He opposed the blockade, and virtually alone amongst the high-ranking admirals, believed that the 'gradual encirclement and strangulation' of Japan was 'a waste of time'. He championed a direct invasion of the southernmost main Japanese homeland island of Kyushu.[1] Like Halsey, US Army planners believed that the US public would not stand for a long drawn-out air-sea blockade of Japan. Their strategy for final victory was founded on invasion and occupation of the Japanese home islands.

Either way, the next major landing after Operation DETACHMENT would take place at Okinawa about six months after the surrender of Germany. This would allow time for Allied forces in Europe to be redeployed to the Pacific. On 17 January 1945, as they had done previously on 11 July 1944, the Joint Chiefs of Staff again opted to proceed towards the invasion of Kyushu – with the Army tentatively setting a date for landings there of 1 November 1945.

On 27 February 1945, the Navy presented an alternative operation plan for an earlier landing to take place, on 20 August 1945. Before then, fast-carrier forces would attack Japan until shortly before the planned land assault, when the carriers would switch for surprise strikes against the Shanghai–Ningpo area to the south of Shanghai and the mouth of the Yangtze River. There were existing Japanese airfields in the Chusan and Ningpo area and a deep-water anchorage at Nimrod, which if seized would allow land-based air attacks on occupied China and on Japan from the west.

The four-carrier British Pacific Fleet would carry out a diversionary attack on Hong Kong and Canton on 7–8 July and again on 17–18 July. The British Force would then return to Ulithi where the Allied carriers would be divided into two task forces. Beginning on 14 August, the Eastern Carrier Force, composed of one British carrier task group and two US day-carrier task groups, would attack targets on Kyushu and

Honshu from the south. The same day, the Western Carrier Force, composed of one night- and two day-carrier US task groups would enter the East China Sea for a week of strikes against Kyushu, south Korea and the Shanghai–Ningpo area. Land-based air from the Marianas, Luzon, China, Iwo Jima and Okinawa would also participate.

The Joint Chiefs of Staff studied the proposal and made its decision on 25 May 1945, the armies' proposal for landings on Kyushu was approved – D-Day would be 1 November 1945. The Navy plan for the seizure of the Chusan–Ningpo area would be indefinitely postponed. The plan for a naval blockade was dead, even though the admirals continued to fight on against any immediate invasion of Japan.

Four new heavy Essex-class fast carriers joined the Pacific Fleet towards the end of 1944 and would be deployed during the Iwo Jima-Okinawa operations – *Bennington* (CV-20) was commissioned on 6 August 1944, *Shangri-La* (CV-38) on 15 September 1944, *Randolph* (CV-15) on 9 October 1944 and *Bon Homme Richard* (CV-31) on 26 November 1944.

Several more Essex-class carriers were also nearing completion in naval dockyards, destined to take part in the final operations against Japan. *Antietam* (CV-36) was commissioned in January 1945, *Boxer* (CV-21) in April 1945 and *Lake Champlain* (CV-39) in June 1945. New launchings of Essex-class carriers for fitting out included *Kearsarge* (CV-33) on 5 May 1945 and *Tarawa* (CV-40) on 12 May 1945 – but the war would be over by the time these two new launchings were commissioned.

The first two of three Midway-class carriers were launched for fitting out, *Midway* (CV-41) on 20 March 1945 and *Franklin D. Roosevelt* (CV-42) on 29 April 1945, so named after the US president who had died that month. These were larger carriers than the Essex-class so that they could support deck armour like the British carriers – and a sufficiently large air group. The class retained the 'strength deck' at the hangar deck level but also had an armoured flight deck that was part of the superstructure. With other carriers also under construction the Navy in March cancelled the planned construction of six additional Essex-class carriers and two other Midways.

The Navy proposed changing over after August 1945 from the F6F-5 Hellcat fighter, which had a top speed of 386mph, to the new Grumman F8F-1 Bearcat, which had a top speed of 421mph. The F4U-4 Corsair with a top speed of 446mph had begun to reach the fleet in October 1944 and was gradually being assigned to the carriers, some equipped with 20mm cannon, others with the .50-calibre machine gun. The first navy Corsairs went into action in April 1945. For most of 1945, the fast carriers would deploy the latest versions of tried and tested naval aircraft, the F6F-5 Hellcat, TBM-3 Avenger, SB2C-5 Helldiver and the newly arrived F4U-4 Corsair. The F8F-1 Bearcat would appear late in the year – intended to completely replace the Hellcat in 1946.

The carrier pilots for the invasion of Iwo Jima in February 1945 were commanded by experienced veterans – and all pilots now averaged 525 hours of flying time in training before they received their combat assignment. By December 1944, the average Japanese pilot had 275 hours training in the air – and high pilot attrition would reduce this to 100 hours by July 1945. Task Force 58 could now launch more than 1,000 aircraft in experienced skilled hands.

The concept of at-sea supply of fuel and aircraft replenishment of the fast carriers by Service Squadrons had proved so successful that this was now expanded to cover food, ammunition, clothing, general stores, personnel and salvage services. The general logistics support group ServRon 6 had been created on 5 December 1944 and would be first utilised at Iwo Jima. ServRon 10 fuel storage and service ships remained at Ulithi whilst ships stores and repair base facilities were transferred to the new base being constructed at Leyte-Samar. ServRons 6 and 10 gave up using the bases at Saipan, Guam and Palau in February 1945 and concentrated at Ulithi. The fast carriers would continue to use Eniwetok, Guam and Ulithi until June, the latter of which the British would also use along with Manus Island. Task Force 58 now had the potential to remain at sea for months at a time – crew and pilot fatigue from constant operations and kamikaze attacks would be the limiting factor.

The Navy's command structure also had significant changes. Admiral William D. Leahy, Chief of Staff to the President and Chairman of the Joint Chiefs of Staff, along with Admiral King (COMINCH-CNO) and Admiral Nimitz (CINCPAC-CINCPOA) were promoted to the new rank of fleet admiral in December 1944.

Command in the Pacific was still divided between Southwest and Central Pacific theatres. It was envisaged that MacArthur would have completed the Luzon–Philippine mop-up operation by the summer of 1945 whilst Nimitz would direct the Iwo Jima, Okinawa and possible Chusan operations. Once completed, the Southwest and Central Pacific theatres would merge for the final campaign against Japan. In April 1945, the Joint Chiefs of Staff determined that Nimitz would command all naval forces and MacArthur all ground forces in the Pacific.

Spruance and the Fifth Fleet now had Rear Admiral Joseph James 'Jocko' Clark as Mitscher's right-hand man, Commander Task Group (CTG) 58.1, with Dave Davison as CTG 58.2, Frederick C. 'Ted' Sherman as CTG 58.3, Arthur Radford as CTG 58.4 and Matt Gardner leading the night carriers as CTG 58.5.

Tactically, the fast-carrier task force underwent no major changes for the Iwo Jima and Okinawa operations. Although the night-carrier groups changed slightly, with the light carrier *Independence* going back to Pearl to reconvert as a day carrier, the two pre-war heavy carriers *Saratoga* and *Enterprise* comprised Night CarDiv 7. *Saratoga* reported to Ulithi with 24 day fighters and her night planes, a total of 53 Hellcats and 17 Avengers ready to combat the perpetual kamikaze threat.

On 7 February 1945, Mitscher issued a memo to his admirals on fast-carrier tactics, concluding that the optimum size of each fast-carrier task group should be four carriers: three heavy carriers and one light carrier. Mobility and maximum defence of the carrier group would be essential for the next operation – where Task Force 58 would attack Formosa, the Ryukyus, the southern main home island of Kyushu – and Tokyo itself.

After excellent close support at Bougainville, Peleliu, Leyte and Luzon, the Marine aviators would take command of all tactical air (Navy, Marine and Army Air Force) after the beachheads at Iwo Jima, Okinawa and Chusan (if it went ahead) had been secured.

The small island of Iwo Jima is one of the Japanese Volcano Islands that lie south of the Bonin Islands and are part of the Ogasawara archipelago. Mount Suribachi, at its south-west end, is a dormant volcanic vent some 160m high, which is a resurgent dome or raised centre of a larger submerged volcanic caldera that surrounds the island. Situated only 750 miles south of Tokyo, it is only a little more than the length of mainland Britain away. But the IJN, with most of its fighting capability sunk or destroyed, could not prevent a US landing there.

Even though Japan had lost vast numbers of planes to date, Allied planners anticipated that its air strength would increase to 3,000 by March 1945. Japan however was giving priority to defending the home islands themselves. With Iwo outside the range of many Japanese aircraft from the mainland, there would only be light Japanese air attacks on the Allied landing troops, staged mainly through the Bonin Islands to the north.

Japan knew that it could not win a battle for Iwo Jima – but hoped to inflict huge casualties on the US forces, such that the Allies would reconsider the invasion of the home islands. As at Peleliu, rather than establishing defences on the beach to attempt to directly repel the landings, Lieutenant General Tadamichi Kuribayashi, in command of the defence of Iwo Jima, created strong, mutually supporting defences in depth with an extensive system of bunkers and tunnels that connected prepared positions.

Iwo Jima had been shelled by the Navy and hit by long-range medium bombers from time to time since June 1944 and more intensively for ten weeks prior to the land invasion. In addition, Major General Harry Schmidt, commander of the Marine landing force, had requested a ten-day heavy shelling of the island immediately preceding the invasion. However, Rear Admiral William P. Blandy, commander of the Amphibious Support Force (Task Force 52), felt that such a prolonged bombardment would not allow him time to replenish his ship's ordnance before the landings actually took place. In the end, Blandy agreed to a three-day naval bombardment.

(i) Raiding Tokyo and the Invasion of Iwo Jima – Operation DETACHMENT, February–March 1945

Admiral Spruance wanted the fast carriers to strike at Tokyo itself in raids that would tie up Japanese fighters over the home islands and prevent them interfering with the landings at Iwo Jima. At Ulithi, from 3–9 February 1945, air experts worked out the details of the Iwo Jima assault with ground commanders and briefed their pilots on close air support techniques, formulating a low-level strafing attack to take place as troops went ashore.

Task Force 58 sortied from Ulithi on 10 February 1945 – and after holding a rehearsal with the Marines at Tinian, the great carrier task force set course for Tokyo, with the intention of striking in advance of the Marine Corps landings on Iwo Jima. Spruance took all 8 of his battleships with him plus 1 new battlecruiser, 5 heavy cruisers and 11 light cruisers on the raid. Even though the Japanese Fleet was destroyed, and there were few Japanese naval units left to fight in a surface action, six of the eight battleships were armed with anti-ship armour-piercing shells. These six battlewagons would thus be unable to provide shore bombardment when they returned from Tokyo. Two battleships were left armed for shore bombardment. By now in fact, big-gun surface clashes were already a thing of the past – the AA guns and near invincible armour of battleships now seen as necessary to protect the carriers. The battleship now supported the fast carrier. The fleet was organised as follows:

Fleet Organisation
CINCPAC-CINCPOA – Fleet Admiral C.W. Nimitz
Commander Fifth Fleet – Admiral R.A. Spruance
Chief of Staff – Rear Admiral A.C. Davis

CTF 58 – Vice Admiral M. Mitscher
Chief of Staff – Commodore A.A. Burke
1. CTG 58.1 – Rear Admiral J.J. Clark:
   Hornet (CV-12) – Captain A.K. Doyle, Air Group 11
   Wasp (CV-18) – Captain O.A. Weller, Air Group 81
   Bennington (CV-20) – Captain J.B. Sykes, Air Group 82
   Belleau Wood (CVL-24) – Captain W.G. Tomlinson, Air Group 30
2. CTG 58.2 – Rear Admiral R.E. Davison:
   Lexington (CV-16) – Captain T.H. Robbins Jr, Air Group 9
   Hancock (CV-19) – Captain R.F. Hickey, Air Group 7
   San Jacinto (CVL-30) – Captain M.H. Kernodle, Air Group 45
3. CTG 58.3 – Rear Admiral F.C. Sherman:
   Essex (CV-9) – Captain C.W. Wieber, Air Group 4
   Bunker Hill (CV-17) – Captain G.A. Seitz, Air Group 84
   Cowpens (CVL-25) – Captain G.H. DeBaun, Air Group 46
4. CTG 58.4 – Rear Admiral A.W. Radford:
   Yorktown (CV-10) – Captain T.S. Combs, Air Group 3
   Randolph (CV-15) – Captain F.L. Baker, Air Group 12
   Langley (CVL-27) – Captain J.F. Wegforth, Air Group 23
   Cabot (CVL-28) – Captain W.W. Smith, Air Group 29
5. CTG 58.5 (night) – Rear Admiral M.B. Gardner:
   Enterprise (CV-6) – Captain G.B.H. Hall, Night Air Group 90
   Saratoga (CV-3) – Captain L.A. Moebus, Night Air Group 53

En route to Tokyo, heavy weather cloaked the task force and US submarines scouting far ahead of the task force ensured that the approach of the fast carriers to Japan was kept concealed. Arriving undetected 60 miles off the coast of Japan, and just 120 miles from Tokyo, at dawn on 16 February, Mitscher launched his planes. It was a symbolic moment, for almost three years earlier on 18 April 1942, when he was skipper of the earlier *Hornet* (CV-8), he had been the last carrier captain to send planes to attack Tokyo, launching sixteen B-25B medium bombers for the famous Doolittle Raid.

The initial TF 58 fighter sweep encountered Japanese fighters all the way from the coast to Tokyo – and five US pilots were lost dogfighting. The entanglement with Japanese fighters robbed the US pilots of the time needed to strafe ground targets – but the bombers that followed the fighter sweep were successfully able to deliver their weapons. US fighters and AA fire from the TOMCAT destroyer picket destroyed more than 300 Japanese planes in the air. But by the time the raid was over, sixty aircraft from the US task force had been lost – Air Group 9's skipper Phil Torrey, who had led the group in the attacks on Rabaul and Truk, being one of the casualties. The high loss rate, compared with similar raids in the Philippines, was prescient of the potential for similar high losses in future operations over Japan.

Task Group 58.5 night-fighters kept Japanese fighters grounded at Tokyo on the night of 16/17 February whilst attempts by radar guided Avengers to find any Japanese shipping targets were unsuccessful. Foul weather the next day allowed only one morning strike.

The fast carriers then swung south and headed for Iwo Jima to provide close support for the landings. En route, on 18 February, they bombed the naval base at Chichi Jima, which had a garrison of some 25,000 Japanese troops and was a major point for Japanese radio relay and communications surveillance in the Pacific. The 2 battleships not carrying armour-piercing shells, along with 3 cruisers, detached TF 58 to join the Iwo Jima bombardment force of 5 older battleships, 11 escort carriers, 4 cruisers and 10 destroyers.

Just after dawn on 19 February 1945, as the Marines prepared to land, the naval shore bombardment gunfire stopped from 0805 to 0815 to allow Marine Corsairs from Task Groups 58.2 and 58.3 to strafe and bomb the beach and Mount Suribachi. Each Hellcat carried six 5in rockets and one 500lb bomb – whilst the Helldivers and Avengers carried bombs and some napalm.

But as the Marines would soon find out, the intense bombardment of Iwo Jima had done little to degrade Japanese fortifications. As at Peleliu, the Japanese interlinked defensive positions with a honeycomb of caves, firing positions and bunkers had survived the naval bombardment and TF 58 softening up. The Japanese defenders came out of their protected positions as the Marines landed on the shifting black volcanic sand at the edge of the beach. Suffering terrible casualties, the Marines slowly pushed inland.

Task Force 58 remained on station for three days, providing effective air support for the operation and allowing Marine Corps artillery observers to fly off the escort carriers during the day, and from *Saratoga* at night, to direct fire and spot targets.

Japanese air attacks were light and dealt with quickly by day-fighters and by *Enterprise* night-fighters. On the morning of 21 February, Mitscher detached *Saratoga* to provide night defensive cover for the landing forces and she was assigned to the escort-carrier task group in the afternoon.

In the late afternoon of 21 February, taking advantage of low cloud cover and *Saratoga*'s weak escort, shortly after she had joined the escort carriers, fifty Japanese planes, staged through the Bonins, swooped at the Allied shipping. Within 3 minutes, six of the planes dived on *Saratoga* – scoring several bombs hits whilst two suicide planes also hit her. *Saratoga* got underway – but took another bomb hit 2 hours later. The flight deck on '*Sara*' had been wrecked and she was out of the war. As a result, 123 men had been killed with more than 100 wounded and 36 aircraft destroyed. In the same attack, the escort carrier *Bismarck Sea* (CVE-95) was sunk by two kamikazes with the loss of 318 men.[2] To date, she is the last US aircraft carrier in service to be sunk by enemy action.

The damaged *Saratoga* departed Iwo Jima late on 22 February, limping to Eniwetok for temporary repairs before heading back to Bremerton in the USA for major repairs. She arrived there on 16 March – and for the time being was now out of the war. This attack had wrecked the two-carrier night task group and meant that *Enterprise* had to keep aircraft aloft for 174 consecutive hours over Iwo Jima between 23 February and 2 March, straining pilots and ship's crew to the limit. The new Essex-class carrier *Bon Homme Richard* (CV-31) was designated as a night carrier to replace *Saratoga*, but she was still in the USA and would only be ready to

USS *Enterprise* (CV-6). Landing Signal Officer, Ensign R.J. Grant, guides in an F6F Hellcat fighter, March 1945. (National Archives 80-G-319008)

depart Norfolk, Virginia on 19 March 1945 to join the fleet. A two-carrier night task group would not be able to reform until late in 1945.

The Japanese launched no other large air attacks on Iwo Jima – and on 6 March the first P-51 Mustangs of the Seventh Air Force landed at the captured air strips. On 11 March the escort carriers were able to withdraw – to prepare for the invasion of Okinawa and three days later, the P-51s flew their last support missions. Organised Japanese resistance on Iwo Jima ended on 26 March 1945.[3]

The new air base at Iwo Jima was of major importance for the B-29 Superfortress bombers flying from their Mariana Island bases on Tinian, Saipan and Guam against the Japanese home islands and other bypassed Japanese bases such as at Truk, which still required to be kept neutralised. On 4 March, a crippled B-29 landed at Iwo and many more would follow until war's end.

The first of many raids on Tokyo, by 111 B-29s, had launched from the Marianas on 24 November 1944. A campaign of incendiary raids now started with the bombardment of Kobe on 4 February. The raids intensified as the Allies consolidated their position, with one of the most devastating

Pilots aboard a US Navy carrier receive last-minute instructions before taking off to attack industrial and military installations in Tokyo. (National Archives identifier 535789)

bombing raids in history taking place on the night of 9/10 March 1945 on Tokyo. On 7 April, 100 long-range P-51s, with a range of 1,650 miles with external tanks, arrived to begin escorting the B-29s to Japan.

The fast carriers returned for strikes against airfields in the Tokyo area on 25 February and against Nagoya, south west of Tokyo on the 26th. Bad weather led to the operation being less successful than hoped with less than fifty Japanese aircraft claimed destroyed. Heading back south towards Okinawa, TF 58 refuelled from ServRon 6 before Mitscher sent his carriers to bomb and carry out aerial reconnaissance photographs of the planned Okinawan invasion beaches. The task force then headed for Ulithi where the force anchored on 4 March, ending fast-carrier support of the Iwo Jima operation.

(ii) Invasion of Okinawa – Operation ICEBERG, 1 April–22 June 1945

Once back at Ulithi, Mitscher began to finalise preparations for the forthcoming campaign against Okinawa, trying to second guess what the Japanese might do – he wondered if they might employ poison gas. On 5 March, a long-distance Yokosuka P1Y1 kamikaze (Allied reporting name Frances) struck at Ulithi itself, crashing into *Randolph* (CV-15) on her starboard side just below the flight deck whilst she was taking on ammunition. The attack killed twenty-seven of her crew and the resulting damage was so severe that she was put out of action for a month whilst she underwent repairs. She would re-join the Okinawa Task Force on 7 April.

In addition to *Saratoga* heading stateside on 22 February for repairs, *Lexington* and *Cowpens* also returned to the USA for overhaul. Many air groups rotated out, and with the new air groups arrived the carriers *Franklin*, *Intrepid* and *Bataan* after overhaul.

On 14 March, the reshuffled TF 58 sortied from Ulithi for Japan. The plan was to neutralise airfields in the Japanese home islands that could be used to attack troops landing on Okinawa on and after 1 April. TF 58 aircraft would strike airfields on Kyushu as well as targeting any surviving Japanese naval units sheltering in ports such as at Kure.

The Japanese however detected the approach of TF 58. On 18 March, when TF 58 aircraft attacked more than forty airfields on Kyushu, they found few Japanese aircraft. And then as the TF 58 aircraft bombed and strafed Kyushu airfields, they were attacked themselves by large numbers of Japanese aircraft. At sea, Task Force 58 was also attacked – with kamikazes and bombers hitting or scoring near misses on *Enterprise* and *Intrepid* but causing only light damage. *Yorktown* however took heavier damage from a bomb hit that killed five of her crew and wounded twenty-six. Some 110 Japanese aircraft were reported destroyed.

On 18 March, US aerial photo-reconnaissance aircraft located concentrations of Japanese naval vessels at Kure and Kobe, including the battleships *Yamato* and *Haruna* and three light carriers. These ships would be priority targets for the next day's strikes along with Kure's oil storage tanks and naval infrastructure. TG 58.1, 58.3 and 58.4 would attack Kure whilst TG 58.2 would attack Kobe.

On 19 March, Mitscher launched more than 300 carrier aircraft at dawn, the fighters sweeping ahead of the dive-bombers and torpedo-bombers. As they approached Kure, the twenty Hellcats of VBF-17 were contacted by forty new, fast and well-armoured Kawanishi *Shiden-Kai* fighters. These 408mph Japanese aircraft were superior to the Hellcats – they were faster, and more manoeuvrable, being fitted with a mercury switch that automatically extended the flaps during turns, creating more lift. Ominously, they were flown not by green pilots, but by experienced veterans who shot down six Hellcats for the loss of four Japanese *Shiden-Kai*. The fighter-to-fighter loss ratio was perhaps a portent of the heavy losses that could be expected over the home islands in any subsequent invasion.

These *Shiden-Kai* were however outnumbered by the TF 58 carrier aircraft and Mitscher's bombers were able to successfully press home their first attack on Japanese carriers since Leyte five months previously. The light carrier *Ryūhō* was badly damaged whilst light damage was sustained by the heavy carrier *Amagi* and the battleship *Yamato*. Some 500 enemy planes were destroyed during these strikes on Japan.

Almost simultaneously, at dawn on the morning of 19 March, Japanese fighters, bombers and kamikazes launched for a counter-attack on Task Force 58. Japanese aircraft penetrated the AA screen undetected and hit *Wasp* (CV-18) with a single bomb that penetrated deep inside her – before exploding in the galley, killing cooks and mess attendants who were preparing breakfast. Fires were started but they were successfully brought under control within 15 minutes – but more than 200 crew had been killed.

The *Franklin* (CV-13) was operating some 50 miles from the Japanese mainland coast, closer than any other carrier during the war. Whilst launching her second strike of the day, she was hit by two SAP bombs just after 0700 from another Japanese aircraft that had avoided detection. One bomb hit the flight deck on the centreline and penetrated to the hangar deck before exploding. The second bomb hit aft, penetrating through two decks. More than thirty armed and fuelled planes were in the hangar and these caught fire, cooking off weapons loaded onto strike aircraft. *Franklin* was transformed into a blazing inferno of exploding ammunition and Tiny Tim rockets. She would have sunk had it not been for the heroic efforts of the skipper and crew – but although they saved the ship, 724 were killed and 265 wounded.[4]

A large force of 158 Helldivers and Avenger torpedo-bombers, escorted by 163 Hellcats and F4U Corsair fighters attacked Kure, where the 4 battleships *Hyūga, Ise, Haruna* and *Yamato* were found along with the 3 aircraft carriers *Katsuragi, Amagi* and the escort carrier *Kaiyō*. Ten other warships including the light cruiser *Ōyodo* were also spotted. *Hyūga* was hit by a single bomb that killed forty crew, whilst *Ise* was hit by two bombs. *Haruna* was hit by one bomb that caused little damage and *Yamato* was hit by a bomb on her bridge.

The escort carrier *Kaiyō* was hit and set on fire, causing flooding, that almost capsized the ship before she was towed into shallow water. *Katsuragi* took one bomb hit and a near miss that caused flooding and *Amagi* was hit by a single bomb on her flight deck. The US aircraft were subjected to heavy AA fire at Kure and eleven Helldivers and two Avengers were shot down.

After completing the raids on Kure and Kobe, TF 58 withdrew to the south, remaining under air attack whilst simultaneously flying further fighter sweeps over southern Kyushu. On 20 March, TG 58.2 was attacked – and the destroyer *Halsey Powell* (DD-686) in the screen was hit by a kamikaze. *Enterprise* was hit by friendly AA fire that damaged her flight deck and rendered it unusable.

Things were certainly hotting up over Japan – it was as though a wasp's nest had been shaken vigorously. The next day, 21 March, 48 enemy aircraft attempted to attack TF 58 and were intercepted by 150 US fighters. A flight of 18 Japanese Mitsubishi G4M Betty bombers carrying Yokosuka MXY-7 *Ohka* piloted rocket-powered kamikaze bombs was shot down 60 miles from the task force. These suicide-attack flying bombs could make 400mph in level flight and 620mph on a dive and were very hard to shoot down. (The first US ship to be sunk by *Ohka* would be the destroyer *Mannert L. Abele* on 12 April near Okinawa.)

Faced with this damage, TF 58 was reorganised on 22 March. The crippled TG 58.2 of *Franklin, Wasp* and *Enterprise* was detached and sent to Ulithi. The damage to *Franklin* was so bad that she never saw active duty again.

'Jocko' Clark now commanded four carriers, *Hornet, Belleau Wood, San Jacinto* and *Bennington*. Radford also had four carriers, *Yorktown, Intrepid, Langley* and *Independence*, recently arrived and now a day-carrier.

Ted Sherman had a five-carrier task group of *Essex*, *Bunker Hill*, *Hancock*, *Bataan* and *Cabot*. Sherman was eager to test his tactical theory that a task group, larger than the standard four carriers, would work. 'I have long advocated carriers and now have a chance to work with 5 to see how it works out. I believe 6–8 CVs can be efficiently operated in one task group and maybe more.'[5]

The invasion of Okinawa was scheduled for 1 April 1945, and the reshuffled TF 58 of thirteen carriers deployed to the east of Okinawa with a picket of six to eight destroyers. A minimum of fourteen to eighteen escort carriers also operated in the area at all times. A week of pre-invasion bombing and big-gun shelling of strategic targets on Okinawa would precede the landings.

As the three US fast carriers *Saratoga*, *Franklin* and *Wasp* had now been badly damaged and forced out of the war in just one month, on 25 March, Admirals Nimitz and Spruance warmly welcomed the arrival of the British Pacific Fleet group of four fleet carriers along with a screen of Australian, New Zealand and Canadian ships and six escort carriers. Designated Task Force 57 and under Vice Admiral Sir H.B. Rawlings RN, *Indomitable*, *Victorious*, *Illustrious* and *Indefatigable* each had a 3in-thick armoured flight deck that would prove particularly important against the kamikaze threat. Their mission was to neutralise Japanese airfields in the Sakashima Islands and provide air cover against the kamikaze attack. Although Allied landing forces would be entirely composed of US units, the British Pacific Fleet would provide some 450 planes, about 25 per cent of Allied naval air power.

As the pre-invasion softening up strikes took place, the Allied task groups maintained constant alerts as kamikazes and conventional bombers continually approached. The Japanese had discovered that US radar could not detect their aircraft coming in low singly – or in small groups at very high altitude.[6] With visual fighter direction taking precedence over radar there were no enemy hits on the carriers. Jocko Clark's planes sank a convoy of eight ships north of Okinawa on 24 March.[7] Four days later, a false report of an enemy fleet sortie got everyone's attention.

Combat air patrols continually fought off Japanese planes approaching the task force, and after poor results with the new 11.75in Tiny Tim rockets they were withdrawn from the carriers.

The British carriers of Task Force 57 had been assigned neutralisation of the Sakashima Gunto, a staging base of islands for Japanese planes south of Okinawa, as they shuttled between Kyushu and Formosa. On 26 and 27 March, British Seafires, the naval version of the Supermarine

Spitfire (the name abbreviated from the longer name Sea Spitfire), carried out Combat Air Patrols whilst Hellcats, Corsairs, Fireflies and Avengers bombed Miyako Island, 185 miles south of Okinawa. The Seafires were selected for CAP patrols due to their good high-altitude performance and, unlike the Hellcat and Corsair, their lack of ordnance carrying capability.

After withdrawing to refuel on 28 March, Task Force 57 resumed its Sakishima strikes on 31 March and came under its first kamikaze attack. Although British fighter direction was superb, it quickly became apparent that the light British 20mm and 2-pdr AA guns could not stop a kamikaze after it had begun its dive – but the armoured British flight decks would save the carriers. A kamikaze hit *Indefatigable* at the base of the island superstructure, killing several crew – but flight operations were unimpeded. Task Force 57 continued on station until relieved on 3 April by Task Group 58.1, to allow retiral for replenishment. Admiral Nimitz congratulated Vice Admiral Rawlings for the 'illustrious' performance of the task force, to which Rawlings replied with characteristic British sangfroid that the enemy would be pursued 'indomitably, indefatigably, and victoriously'.[8]

The US Tenth Army had over 102,000 soldiers for the assault on Okinawa and in addition there were 3 Marine divisions totalling over 88,000. The US troops began going ashore on 1 April in what was the largest amphibious assault in the Pacific theatre of the Second World War, moving ashore against light opposition under cover of more than 500 planes from escort and fast carriers that provided effective close support. As at Peleliu and Iwo Jima, some 67,000 Japanese 32nd Army troops and 9,000 IJN troops were dug in to the rear, waiting to strike at the US forces once they were established. In addition, some 39,000 local Ryukyuan people had been drafted.

To detect and intercept incoming Japanese air strikes, nineteen specially trained fighter director teams were stationed aboard radar picket destroyers around Okinawa for 'radar-defence-in-depth' and these ships became important Japanese targets.[9]

It took until 6 April before the Japanese struck at Task Force 58 in strength, deploying some 400 planes from Kyushu. Kamikazes attacking in small groups forced Mitscher to stow all his bombers below and scramble all his fighters. Jocko Clark's and Ted Sherman's task-group carriers came under sustained kamikaze attack. The Combat Air Patrol and good shipborne AA fire saved the force from significant damage, other than a near miss on *Belleau Wood*. Some 355 Japanese planes were destroyed. Between 6 April and 22 June, the Japanese flew

1,465 kamikaze aircraft in large-scale attacks from Kyushu. Land-based *Shinyo* suicide motorboats were also used.

At the peak of the air contest, Mitscher received intelligence via US submarines that the Japanese super battleship *Yamato* had sortied from the Inland Sea with a screen of one light cruiser and eight destroyers – and was likely to approach Okinawa on 7 April. The Japanese had launched Operation TEN-GO, an attempted attack by ten surface warships, which had been ordered to fight through the US screen then beach *Yamato* on Okinawa and fight from shore, using her guns as coastal artillery and her crew as naval infantry.

Mitscher launched search strikes on 7 April, arming his Curtiss SB2C Helldivers with 1,000lb and 250lb bombs and the fighters with 500lb bombs, whilst the TBM Avenger torpedo-bombers carried torpedoes. Early that afternoon, west south west of Kagoshima, Japan, in the East China Sea, long before *Yamato* could beach at Okinawa, some 386 US aircraft attacked the Japanese naval force in a 2-hour engagement. The pilots would focus on *Yamato*, torpedo-bomber pilots briefed to hit only one side of the great battleship to prevent effective counter-flooding – and to aim at the bow or stern, where, outwith the heavily armoured box of the 'citadel', the tapered armour belt was thinnest. The stern of a battleship with its exposed rudders and screws was its Achilles heel.

In the first wave, *Yamato* was hit by many bombs – but she was designed to withstand that type of punishment. But just after 1230, Jocko Clark's TG 58.1 Avengers scored four torpedo hits on her port side. *Yamato* developed a list to port of 7° but could still make 22 knots. An hour later, a second attack by Arthur Radford's TG 58.4 torpedo-bombers hit *Yamato* with several more torpedoes – the list to port increased to 15° and her speed dropped to 18 knots.

Counter-flooding had reduced the list to 10° before the third and most damaging attack began at about 1340. *Yamato* sustained more bomb hits that caused heavy casualties amongst her AA crew – and a number of near miss explosions stove in outer plating. Four more torpedoes hit her, and with her auxiliary steering room already underwater, the ship lost manoeuvrability and became stuck in a starboard turn – her speed had dropped to 10 knots and her list to port was again increasing. The rate of flooding increased and trapped many of her crew.

The order to abandon ship was given at 1401. Fires raged uncontrollably and alarms on the bridge warned of critical temperatures building up in her forward main battery magazines. Such was the danger of a catastrophic magazine explosion that when alarms on the bridge of *Yamato* warned of critical temperatures in one or more magazine, the magazine would normally be flooded to prevent a catastrophic propellant explosion – but the pumping stations had been put out of action.

Torpedoes from a final attack at 1405 on the starboard side hit the raised and now exposed hull beneath the armour belt. The rate of flooding increased remorselessly – as did the list to port. By 1420, all electrical power within the ship was dead. She had been hit by at least eleven torpedoes and many bombs.

The great ship continued to roll farther over to port – and as she reached a critical angle, her 25mm AA guns began to drop from their mounts into the sea followed by her main battery 18.1in gun turrets. The largest naval guns ever mounted on a battleship fell from their mounts to the seabed far below.

The suction created by her roll to port pulled crew trying to swim away from the ship back towards it. At 1423, as the roll had her on her beam ends, one of her two bow magazines exploded – creating a mushroom cloud nearly 4 miles high that was seen almost 100 miles away in Kyushu. The ship broke into two parts around No. 2 main battery turret, both sections sinking rapidly into 1,000ft (340m) of water with the loss of some 3,000 crew. The main section of the wreck landed upside down on the seabed – whilst the sleek contours of the bow righted the bow section as it planed down through the water column, such that it came to rest upright on the seabed.

Of *Yamato*'s screen, the light cruiser *Yahagi* was sunk along with four of the eight destroyers: *Asashimo, Hamakaze, Isokaze* and *Kasumi*. Some 3,700 Japanese sailors in total had died, including the admiral in charge. All this damage had been inflicted for the loss of ten US aircraft and twelve aircrew.

On the night of 7/8 April, Rear Admiral Davison returned from Ulithi with two repaired carriers – allowing Mitscher to reorganise TF 58 for a second time in the operation. Clark's TG 58.1 and Sherman's 58.3 remained the same – whilst TG 58.1 gave *Independence* to Davison's reformed TG 58.2, which now consisted of *Randolph, Enterprise* and *Independence*.

As the ground troops on Okinawa were now heavily engaged, Task Force 58 continued air support whilst being subjected to relentless kamikaze attack that caused more damage to the fast carriers. Kamikazes struck *Hancock* on 7 April and hit *Enterprise* on the 11th and *Intrepid* on the 16th, along with several picket destroyers. On 17 April, Mitscher again had to alter his task-force composition as he sent the damaged *Hancock* and *Enterprise* back to Ulithi for repair. Task Force 58 had again lost its night carrier. *Cabot* was detached for overhaul as was HMS *Illustrious*, relieved on 14 April by HMS *Formidable*.

The reorganised Task Force 58 would remain in the following shape from 17 April until 28 May 1945:

Fleet Organisation
CTF 58 – Vice Admiral M.A. Mitscher
1. CTG 58.1 – Rear Admiral J.J. Clark:
   Hornet
   Belleau Wood
   San Jacinto
   Bennington
2. CTG 58.3 – Rear Admiral F.C. Sherman:
   Essex
   Bunker Hill
   Bataan
   Randolph (with *Monterey* joining on 12 May)
3. CTG 58.4 – Rear Admiral A.W. Radford:
   Yorktown
   Intrepid
   Langley
   Independence (*Shangri-La* joined on 24 April, whilst *Langley* returned
      to base for overhaul on 18 May)
4. CTG 57.2 – Rear Admiral Sir Phillip Vian RN:
   Indomitable
   Victorious
   Formidable
   Indefatigable

TG 58.1 was sent back to Ulithi on 28 April for a ten-day R&R period.

On 30 April, with Berlin encircled, Adolph Hitler was believed to have shot himself in his bunker whilst Eva Braun, his wife of one day, also committed suicide. On 2 May, the Battle of Berlin ended and nearly 1,000,000 German troops in Italy and Austria surrendered unconditionally. In the coming days German forces in other theatres surrendered.

On 4 May, Field Marshall Bernard Montgomery took the unconditional surrender of all German forces in Holland, in north-west Germany and in Denmark. At sea, all German U-boats were ordered to cease operation. On 7 May, the Chief of Staff of the German Armed Forces High Command, General Alfred Jodl, signed an unconditional surrender document of all German Forces to the Allies with all active operations to cease on 8 May 1945. The war in Europe was over.

Japan was now left to fight on alone – but despite her clear predicament, she refused to end the war. Whilst the war in Europe may have been over, it was of little comfort to the hard-pressed US troops on Okinawa itself where the battle developed into one of the bloodiest in the Pacific, lasting eighty-two days from 1 April–22 June 1945 as the Army and Marines came up against fanatical Japanese troops.

Carriers flew air support missions until the second week of the assault when the Marine Corps air support unit got ashore and over 100 Marine Corps F4U Corsair fighter-bombers made the island's two operational airstrips their base. These aircraft were deployed to thwart the increasing number of kamikaze attacks whilst the carriers provided most of the close air support to the fighting troops below. The Marines had the use of only one airfield throughout April as the other was rained out, then shelled by Japanese artillery. Until more fighter strips were constructed by Army engineers, the fast carrier and picket destroyers had to support the Okinawa landing forces, placing them at great danger from kamikazes.

The Japanese positions particularly at Shuri Castle were almost impregnable and a massive air strike of 650 aircraft was set up against the Shuri defences – including 300 planes from Task Force 58. But even this number of planes was unable to neutralise the cave systems that protected Japanese ground troops. In June, progress with airfield construction on Okinawa had allowed 750 aircraft to arrive by 1 July, when the first bombing strike on the Japanese home island of Kyushu by aircraft flying from Okinawa took place.

The fast carriers continued to attack Japan, enemy positions on Okinawa and the Sakishima Gunto, fighting off Japanese rocket-powered, piloted *Ohka* kamikaze missiles. The British carriers returned to the fight in late April after replenishing at Leyte Gulf. They had no night-fighters and so were unable to stop the Japanese filling in at night their Sakishima airfields that had been cratered during daytime raids. On 4 May, kamikazes hit the British carriers *Formidable* and *Indomitable*. Whilst their 3in-thick armoured flight decks prevented serious damage to the ship's internals, several aircraft were destroyed and radar equipment badly damaged. On 9 May, two more kamikazes hit *Formidable* and *Victorious* – it had become clear that British AA weaponry and tactics were weak and being exploited and the British adopted the US tactic of picket destroyers on 14 May.

Whilst the British carriers had been built with armoured flight decks for operations in the Mediterranean where they would be attacked by bombers, the US carriers did not have armoured flight decks and were heavily damaged when hit. On 11 May, Mitscher's flagship *Bunker Hill* was hit by a kamikaze, with more than 350 men killed, including 13 of the admiral's staff and most of Fighting Group 84 asphyxiated in the ready room. Mitscher shifted his flag to the night carrier *Enterprise* whilst *Bunker Hill* limped home and out of the war.

USS *Bunker Hill* (CV-17) burning after being hit by two kamikazes in less than 1 minute, off Okinawa, 11 May 1945. (National Archives 80-G-323712)

USS *Bunker Hill* flight deck looking aft as crew fight the fires caused by two kamikaze hits, 11 May 1945. There were 372 crew killed and 264 wounded. (National Archives (80-G-274266)

On 14 May, three days after Mitscher had shifted his flag to *Enterprise,* a kamikaze hit her. Good damage control saved the old carrier, but she was also out of the war for many months. Mitscher shifted his flag again the next day, to *Randolph.*

On 18 May, with his ship's crews exhausted, Mitscher asked Spruance to detach Task Force 58 from its 60 square mile forward operating area, which lay less than 350 miles from Kyushu – and from where it had been on station for two months. *Bunker Hill* had been at sea for fifty-nine days solid when hit on 11 May. Ted Sherman recorded: 'Everybody is dead tired, we have been out of Ulithi 76 days now.' But in the circumstances, Spruance had no choice, he had to turn down Mitscher's request and keep Task Force 58 on station.[10]

But the worst was in fact over for Task Force 58 – and no more serious kamikaze attacks threatened the carriers themselves. On 20 May, Ted Sherman sent a strike of twelve TBMs with 500lb bombs to hit Shuri Castle, dropping their ordnance only 50yd ahead of advancing US troops and dislodging the enemy. Shuri was finally evacuated on 29 May and the kamikazes now focused on the US airfields on Okinawa and at shipping offshore. The carriers were no longer targets.

The British fast carriers of Task Force 57 made their last strikes against Sakishima airfields on 25 May, then withdrew to Sydney to replenish and prepare for the final campaign against Japan. The British carriers had proved themselves in the Pacific and they retired with a recommendation from Admiral Spruance that the British Pacific Force be integrated into the US Fast-Carrier Task Force, which was agreed by Admiral Nimitz.

Nimitz had wanted to implement a rotation of command of the fast carriers, with Halsey to relieve Spruance on about 1 May 1945 to allow Spruance to begin planning for the invasion of the Japanese home island of Kyushu. But Spruance had been needed at Okinawa and the rotation had been delayed. Now that the need for the fast carriers at Okinawa was finished, on 28 May, Mitscher handed over command of the fast carriers to John S. 'Slew' McCain who raised his flag on the new carrier *Shangri-La* (CV-38), which had been at Okinawa for the last month. With Halsey relieving Spruance, the Fifth Fleet once again became the Third Fleet and Task Force 58 became Task Force 38.

Much loved by his officers and men, the outgoing Mitscher was thoroughly exhausted by the long, arduous months in combat. The great champion of navy air had withdrawn into himself, sitting for long periods in silence and leaving his staff effectively to run the task force. He was ill, the strain of combat command had beaten him – and he would soon be sent to Washington to relieve Jake Fitch as Deputy Chief Naval Operation (DCNO) (Air), performing all strategy and resource policies and liaising with the Department of Defense and Department of the Navy.

With the rotation of command, the task-group commanders remained largely the same, with only minor changes in the set-up. Vice Admiral 'Ching' Lee, the battleship squadron commander with the fast carriers, returned home on 18 June – with Rear Admiral John F. Shafroth becoming acting battleship commander in his absence.

Halsey detached Sherman's TG 38.3 to Leyte for some R&R and took TF 38 north to strike Kyushu along with 'Jocko' Clark's TG 38.1 (*Hornet, Bennington, Belleau Wood* and *San Jacinto*) and Arthur Radford's TG 38.3 (*Yorktown, Shangri-La, Ticonderoga* and *Independence.*)

After getting off strikes against Kyushu airfields on 2–3 June, the approach of a tight typhoon from the south was spotted on the morning of 3 June. More information about the storm was provided from CINCPAC on the evening of 4 June – the storm was heading north, whilst the task force was heading eastward away from it. After listening to conflicting reports, at 1330 on 5 June, Halsey ordered the task force to come about and head west, in an attempt to cross ahead and in front of the typhoon.

As the two task groups headed west, the weather worsened after midnight – and became so severe that by 0535, 'Jocko' Clark had to order all ships to manoeuvre independently. Clark's TG 38.1 reached the eye of the typhoon at 0700, whilst Radford's TG38.3, manoeuvring some 20 miles away, missed the worst. In Clark's TG 38.1, such was the force of the sea hitting the carriers that the flight deck overhangs on *Hornet* and *Bennington* collapsed. The heavy cruiser *Pittsburgh* (CA-72) lost her bow, seventy-six planes were destroyed, and six men lost overboard. Many other ships suffered minor damage. TG 38.1 cleared the storm by the afternoon, 5 June.

On 6 June, Clark's damaged carriers and Radford's TG 38.3 carriers launched close air support strikes to Okinawa. The same day, TG 38.1 was reinforced by the new night carrier *Bon Homme Richard* (CV-31) with Night Air Group 91.

On 7 June, the fast carriers moved north to bomb the large Kanoya airfield on Kyushu the next day. On 8 June, the carriers dropped napalm on enemy fortifications on Okino Daito Island and the operation was concluded on 10 June with a bombardment of shore installations on Minami Daito Islands by Shafroth's three battleships.

Task Force 38 then headed for Leyte Gulf – where it arrived on 13 June, ninety-two days after the beginning of the Okinawa campaign. Plans for the seizure of additional islands near Okinawa such as Okino Daito and Kikai Jima were cancelled as unnecessary – as was the proposed Chusan operation to seize land and airfields near Shanghai late in May.

By 22 June, organised enemy resistance on Okinawa had ended, but at huge cost. There were approximately 160,000 casualties on both sides – at least 80,000 Allied, including 12,500 killed in action. Some 110,000 Japanese had been killed in action – including drafted

Okinawans wearing Japanese uniforms. Some 150,000 Okinawans had in total died, almost half the pre-war population of 300,000.

Both sides had lost many ships and aircraft, not least the battleship *Yamato*. The attacks by kamikazes had been ferocious – and it was thought that the defence of the Japanese homeland islands would see even more determined resistance. But Okinawa was now in Allied hands and could provide a fleet anchorage, troop staging areas and airfields close to Japan in preparation for the planned invasion of Japan itself – Operation DOWNFALL.

The southern Japanese home island of Kyushu was now in easy range of Allied land-based bombers and fighters – and regular air strikes to Kyushu began in July. Boeing B-29 Superfortress bombers would begin operating from Okinawa in August. With the fast carriers having served their purpose, they were now released from their close-support role.

The subsequent Court of Enquiry into why the Task Force 38 allowed itself to be beset by such a damaging typhoon sat in Guam on 15 June, and included two men who had sat in the December investigation into damage caused by the earlier typhoon encountered when the force was again under Halsey's command. The Court of Enquiry found against Halsey, McCain and Kosko and recommended that they be transferred to other duty. Fleet Admiral King agreed: 'The record shows conclusively that there was ineptness in obtaining, disseminating and acting upon meteorological data.' With the experience of the previous storm, he felt Halsey and McCain could have avoided the worst 'had they reacted to the situation as it developed with the weatherwise skill to be expected of professional seamen'. King concluded: 'the primary responsibility for the storm damage and losses in both cases attaches to Commander Third Fleet, Admiral William F. Halsey, Jr, US Navy'. No further action was however recommended – but Halsey would never get his fifth star during the war.[11]

Chapter 19

The Final Assault on Japan – Operation DOWNFALL, 1 November 1945–7 (Projected)

The question of how finally to defeat Japan and end the war divided Navy and Army top brass. The Army insisted on invading the southernmost island of Japan, Kyushu, and the largest island of Honshu, on which Tokyo is situated. The Navy admirals believed that Japan would surrender to an air and sea blockade, before Allied landings had to take place, with the feared huge loss of life.[1] Despite their misgivings over landings, the Navy made their preparations for the invasion of Japan.

On 25 May 1945, as the Okinawa campaign drew to a close, the Joint Chiefs of Staff (JCS) directed that the invasion of Japan should proceed, the campaign being given the codename Operation DOWNFALL. It would begin on 1 November 1945.

Operation DOWNFALL was divided into two parts:

1. The 6th Army landings at Kyushu were codenamed Operation OLYMPIC and would take place with a target date set for 1 November 1945.[2] (Early in August the code name OLYMPIC was leaked – and so the JCS renamed the operation as MAJESTIC.)
2. The 8th Army landings on the coast of Honshu near Tokyo were codenamed Operation CORONET. These landings would allow for a drive across the Kanto Plain to Tokyo. The operation was scheduled tentatively for 1 March 1946.

The Allied Combined Chiefs of Staff planners assessed that organised resistance in Japan would cease by 15 November 1946.[3]

By summer 1945, the US Navy had now largely become an air navy – the changing nature of the role of the naval aviation had seen the fast carriers sweep the enemy fleet from the Pacific. The fast carriers were now poised to go further and project naval power inland into Japan itself – thus moving from a maritime peripheral strategy to a continental strategy. But in the European war it was land-based air that had triumphed and led to the defeat of Germany.

At this time in 1945 there was no separate US Air Force – the Army had its own air force and the Navy had its own air. But there were growing calls for a unified US department of defence, with autonomy for the Army and Navy, and the creation of a new Air Force as an independent service equal to the Army and Navy. These calls raised fears amongst the admirals that a new separate Air Force would pull naval aviation away from the Navy. Naval airmen shuddered at the thought that navy air could come under the command of Army or Air Force generals. It would take until September 1947 for the US Air Force to be created, but in 1945 as these discussions took place, the war went on.

Japan's homeland air force was throwing up stiff resistance to Allied air raids. With the Kyushu landings scheduled to begin in just a few months on 1 November 1945, Japanese air capability had to be seriously degraded between the end of the Okinawa campaign in late June and November. This would become the primary role for the fast carriers.

Admiral Halsey believed the Kyushu invasion armada would require 'constant fighter cover for defense against violent and powerful kamikaze attack . . . The fast carrier force will be required to contribute heavily to the defense and for many weeks will be tied to the direct support of a major invasion . . .'. He continued: 'The glorious days of the carrier spearheading the Pacific offensive ended when the spear entered the heart of the Empire. Targets are scarce.'[4]

The fast carriers would blockade Japan, attack enemy airfields, shipping and industry, keep the kamikazes at bay and provide close air support for the landing forces, tasks it had refined to near perfection in the operations to date. Whatever the future of naval air power may have been at this stage, only the fast carriers could carry out these tasks.

Meanwhile, several carriers joined the Third Fleet for the November assault. The three new Essex-class carriers *Antietam* (CV-36), *Boxer* (CV-21) and *Lake Champlain* (CV-39) would be joined by their repaired and overhauled battle-hardened sister ships *Intrepid*, *Hornet* and *Wasp*. *Enterprise* and *Cabot* were also returning whilst *Saratoga* and *Langley* were reporting at Pearl Harbor after repairs.

With victory in Europe now secure with the unconditional surrender of Germany on 8 May 1945, the war in Europe was over. With naval units now freed up to strengthen the British Pacific Fleet, operating as Task Force 37, the Royal Navy despatched their new fleet carrier *Implacable* and the new light carriers *Colossus, Vengeance, Venerable* and *Glory*. The new British light carrier *Ocean* was also due to be commissioned in August. The eventual strength of the British Pacific Fleet was intended to be 4 battleships, 10 aircraft carriers, 16 cruisers, 40 destroyers and some 90 escort vessels.

Projections for the commissioning of new US carriers included the battle carriers *Midway* (CVB-41) due in September 1945, *Franklin D. Roosevelt* (CVB-42) due in October and the five Essex-class carriers, *Princeton* (CV-37) in October, *Kearsarge* (CV-33), *Tarawa* (CV-40) in November with *Leyte* (CV-32) and *Philippine Sea* (CV-47) to follow in December.

Such was the might of US wartime shipbuilding, that these projected commissionings were accelerated, with *Leyte* being launched for fitting out in August and *Philippine Sea* in September. The damaged *Bunker Hill* and *Franklin* were undergoing repairs, whilst the first of the two new Saipan-class light carriers, *Saipan* (CVL-48), was launched in July and was due to join the fleet in December after fitting out.

Other carriers were still in various stages of construction. In the USA *Valley Forge* (CV-45) and the second Saipan-class light carrier *Wright* (CVL-49) were due in February 1946, with *Oriskany* (CV-34) and the battle carrier *Coral Sea* (CVB-43) due in May 1946. The Royal Navy had two Colossus-class light carriers *Theseus* and *Triumph* launched in 1944 that were undergoing fitting out. The Royal Canadian Navy had the light carrier *Warrior* launched and fitting out.

On 12 August 1945, the US Navy felt able to cancel the construction of several new carriers – which would clearly only come into service after the war had ended. Two of its Essex-class, *Reprisal* (CV-35), scheduled for completion in July 1946, and *Iwo Jima* (CV-46), due in November 1946, were cancelled. The British did likewise. Nevertheless, for Operation DOWNFALL, Japan would be ringed by increasing numbers of fast carriers, island airfields and escort carriers.

The US Navy adopted the British concept of an armoured flight deck for their Midway-class battle carriers. On the more vulnerable Essex-class carriers, with their unarmoured flight deck, more 40mm Bofors AA guns were added that had the punch to knock a kamikaze out of the sky at longer range than the 20mm Oerlikon cannon. Due to its lack of stopping power against kamikazes, the Oerlikons were reduced in number.

Two new guns were also under development. The radar-controlled 5in/54-calibre had a greater range and altitude and began to join the fleet in April 1945, with first installations aboard *Midway* and *Franklin D. Roosevelt*. The new 3in/50-calibre rapid fire Dual Purpose (DP) gun had a longer range and was twice as effective as the Bofors 40mm gun, using proximity fuzed shells. It was first test fired on 1 September 1945.

Halsey advocated that 80 per cent of aircraft on the heavy carriers should be fighters – whilst Mitscher wanted all the F6F-5 Hellcats taken off the light carriers, as they were not fast enough to intercept high-altitude enemy snoopers. He recommended replacement with the F4U-4 Corsair until such time as the 455mph F8F-1 Bearcat was available. Hellcats and Corsairs would remain on the heavy carriers until likely the middle of 1946 when they would be replaced completely by F8F Bearcats. (The war would be over before the Bearcat saw combat service.)

Mitscher recommended the Curtiss SB2C Helldiver and TBM torpedo-plane be kept until a new VBT type torpedo-bomber joined the fleet, probably in 1946. Although the torpedo plane role was likely to vanish, the bulky TBM could house new airborne early warning radar which could spot enemy aircraft up to 75 miles away. Several TBMs were thus equipped – and plans were made to have corresponding equipment in four carriers. It was hoped that this might eliminate the need for destroyers to be used as radar pickets, which had proved a dangerously exposed role.

When Mitscher rotated and returned ashore on 28 May 1945, the Essex-class carrier air group comprised 73 fighters and fighter-bombers (VF and VBF Corsairs and Hellcats), 15 dive-bombers (SB2C Helldivers) and 15 torpedo-bombers (Avengers). The light carrier air group remained at 24 Hellcats (2 photographic) and 9 TBM Avengers.

Fighters were the key to combatting the deadly menace of the kamikaze, but bombers were still required to destroy enemy aircraft parked up on airfields as well as hitting shore installations. Back ashore, with the Japan operation very much in mind, Mitscher recommended that the light carriers should have their Avengers and Hellcats replaced by thirty-six F4U Corsair fighter-bombers and that these in turn be replaced as soon as practicable by forty-eight of the faster and smaller new F8F Bearcats, when they became available. The light carriers would then serve as all-fighter carriers to provide CAP.

Mitscher still championed fast-carrier task groups comprising three heavy carriers and one light carrier. Each heavy carrier should carry an air group of 48 fighters (F6F or F4U), 24 fighter-bombers (F4U eventually replacing SB2C), 18 torpedo planes, 2 photographic fighters –

along with a night squadron of 6 night Hellcats and 6 night Avengers. With this arrangement, the need for dedicated night carriers would be eliminated. Ultimately however, it was decided to retain the two night carriers *Bon Homme Richard* and *Enterprise* – but in separate day groups, and not as one night-carrier task group.[5]

Most of Mitscher's ideas were accepted in July and as new carrier air groups formed or came home, the new composition of their aircraft would be adopted. The heavy carriers would carry a 101-plane air group made up of 33 fighters, 24 fighter-bombers, 24 dive-bombers and 20 torpedo planes.

The light carriers would indeed change to carry only fighters, 36 in total. Some would change immediately to F6F Hellcats, the rest very soon to F4U Corsairs. The night carriers remained, carrying 37 night-fighters and 18 night torpedo planes. The new Midway-class battle carriers would carry air groups of 73 fighters (65 F4U Corsairs, 4 F6F photo Hellcats, 4 night F6F Hellcats) and 64 dive-bombers. The 2 new Saipan-class light carriers *Saipan* and *Wright* (improved versions of the Independence-class light carrier) were still under construction but would carry 48 Hellcats, divided into 24 fighters and 24 fighter-bombers, when they arrived.

Whilst it was a time of change for carrier air groups, it was also a time of change in the US Navy at the highest levels. President Roosevelt had been in declining health for some time. He died suddenly on 12 April 1945 and had been succeeded by Harry S. Truman – who knew little about naval aviation.

Fleet Admiral Nimitz (CINPAC-CINCPOA) wanted Admiral Spruance to command the Kyushu landings with Halsey to command Task Force 38 operations at sea. With Halsey meantime in command of TF 38 operations, Spruance began to gather his Fifth Fleet staff at Guam to begin planning the final great assault on Japan.

The plan was that during September and October 1945, all available carriers would join the fast-carrier task force, which would then on 24 October divide into two parts, Task Force 38 and Task Force 58. Task Force 38 would then be utilised for long-range operations against strategic targets up and down the Japanese coast – whilst Task Force 58 would be used solely for air defence and support at the beachheads. With two great fast-carrier task forces taking the fight to the enemy, this was the ultimate evolution of the fast-carrier concept.

Towards the end of the Okinawa campaign, Rear Admiral Frederick 'Ted' Sherman received word that he was to be promoted to vice admiral and appointed as Commander First Fast-Carrier Force Pacific and Commander Task Force 58. He was promoted to vice admiral on 13 July and told to be back by 15 August.

The other key carrier post was Commander Second Fast-Carrier Force Pacific, held since August 1944 by Vice Admiral John Sidney 'Slew' McCain – who had been criticised following the June and December typhoons. McCain had assumed command of Task Force 38 in October 1944 and fought in the Marianas campaign, at the Battle of the Philippine Sea and the Battle of Leyte Gulf – but like Mitscher, his health was also suffering from the constant demands of command. Vice Admiral John H. Towers would relieve Slew McCain in command of the Second Fast-Carrier Force and Task Force 38 on 14 August 1945 – but took a week longer as he gathered his staff.

The die was cast – the two Fast-Carrier Task Forces 38 and 58 would have the best men and best machines available – to destroy the Empire of Japan.

(i) Invasion of Kyushu – Operation OLYMPIC, 1 November 1945 (Projected)

To Allied eyes, the scale of the fight to come for Japan was immense, it was breathtaking. From the Japanese perspective however the fight would be virtually settled at the Kyushu beachhead.

The Japanese planned to abandon their defence-in-depth strategy such as used at Peleliu, Iwo Jima and Okinawa and send 3,000 kamikazes to hit Allied amphibious shipping off Kyushu – before the Allied assault troops could board their LVTs and DUKWs and head for shore, and before the lumbering naval transports and auxiliaries could offload their cargoes of tanks, heavy weapons, supplies and munitions. Only 350 kamikazes would attack the fast carriers, the priority for Japan was destruction of Allied troop and supply ships whilst they were still heavily laden. If it came off, the scale of the damage and loss to the Allies would be staggering.

There would be thousands of kamikaze aircraft, in every form that could fly – from simple trainer aircraft to the new jet-propelled *Ohka* piloted bombs with a 2,600lb warhead. These would be flown not by Japan's best pilots – but by poorly trained aviators, some with only 20 hours' flight time. If this initial kamikaze attack failed, another 3,500 conventional and suicide Army and Navy planes would move to the attack – supported by more than 5,000 suicide boats, 19 destroyers and 38 submarines. Kyushu in the south would be defended to the death. If these mass attacks failed to stop the Allied invasion armada at Kyushu, there would be only 3,000 planes left to defend the largest Japanese island of Honshu – and Tokyo itself.

Back in March, the Joint Chiefs of Staff had given Nimitz supreme command of the naval aspects of the operation, including the Seventh Fleet, which had been serving MacArthur's operations to date. Admiral Richmond Kelly Turner, who had held a number of senior Amphibious Force commands, including most recently that of more than 700,000 men at Okinawa, would command the amphibious landings. Nimitz would remain based at Guam and be served by four four-star admirals – Spruance, Halsey, Turner and Kinkaid. General MacArthur would command all operations ashore and would be based at Manila.

The Allied Kyushu landing forces would gather at Guam, Leyte-Samar and Okinawa, the fast carriers re-establishing their main base at Eniwetok in the Marshalls. The plan was not to conquer the whole island of Kyushu, but just the southernmost tip, which would then provide a staging ground and air-base facility for Operation CORONET.

For DOWNFALL, Halsey and Towers' carrier operations would be restricted to points east of the 135th meridian, effectively to Osaka Bay and most of Honshu. This would allow Allied carrier aircraft to strike at the major industrial cities, such as Tokyo, Nagoya and Yokohama as well as other large industrial targets and at Hokkaido Island to the north. The isolation of Kyushu, to the west of the 135th meridian, would be conducted by General Kenney's Far Eastern Air Forces who would strike at Kyushu, Shikoku Island, north east of Kyushu, and the west portion of Honshu Island, which held the ports of Hiroshima and Kure. B-29 Superfortress bombers from the Marianas and Okinawa would be coordinated into both areas.

Admiral Spruance, commanding Fifth Fleet, would arrive off Kyushu with Kelly Turner's amphibious landing forces and the embarked Sixth Army on 24 October. The combined Allied armada would be the greatest ever assembled with 42 aircraft carriers, 24 battleships and some 400 destroyers and escort vessels. Five days before the main invasion, on X-5, offshore islands would be taken to establish secure anchorages. From 24 October, the Navy would assume responsibility for the target area whilst General Kenney's Army Air Force planes would bomb enemy lines of communication from northern Kyushu to the assault area in the south. The admirals were very aware that large numbers of kamikazes would attack – and so set up an expanded anti-kamikaze force of thirteen shipboard and five landing force fighter director teams.

Air strikes would increase from 24 October and reach their peak on the day of the initial landings, X-Day, 1 November. Strike groups from Task Force 38, the escort carriers and Far Eastern Forces would be kept over the beachhead continually from 0700 to 1700. At night, twelve night-Hellcats and six P-61 AAF Black Widows would remain on station.

Halsey's Third Fleet would range north and east, keeping open Allied lines of communications to the beach and to Russia (which should be in the war against Japan by then) by attacking Japanese air, naval and ground forces in the northern island of Hokkaido and the southern Kuriles. The British Task Force 37 under Vice Admiral Rawlings would operate with the Third Fleet.

It was hoped that a sufficient beachhead on Kyushu would be secure by 4 November and allow land-based Army Air Force and Marine Corps planes to be brought in to help cover the beachhead and support Sixth Army operations as they moved inshore.

The fast carriers could then be released to join the Third Fleet for strikes in the north. By December 1945, the fast carriers would be ranging along the coast of Japan.

(ii) Invasion of Honshu – Operation CORONET, 1 March 1946 (Projected)

If after the fall of Kyushu, Japan did not surrender, then MacArthur and Nimitz would implement Operation CORONET – with landings on the Honshu coast 50 miles from Tokyo, tentatively set for 1 March 1946. The amphibious ships carrying the First, Eight and Tenth armies would face suicide glider bombs catapulted from caves 10 miles away.

(iii) Endgame

The great US and British carrier fleet for the Kyushu operation was largely already in place at Leyte-Samar and Sydney by mid-June 1945. OLYMPIC was scheduled to begin with the three TF 38 fast-carrier task groups that had completed the Okinawa operation – but more would be added as new, repaired and overhauled carriers joined the fleet. As was usual, for new air or ship crews, each would engage on battle practice on a live target. The British carrier *Implacable*, fresh from operations in the European theatre, was first for a live training run, hitting long-forgotten Truk on 14 June. US carriers of Task Group 12.4 hit Wake Island almost a week later – and on several occasions thereafter up to the first week of August.

The first phase of the Kyushu Operation OLYMPIC began on 1 July as Halsey's fast carriers sortied from Leyte, refuelling with ServRon 6 fast tankers east of Iwo Jima on 8 July. At the replenishment rendezvous, the Third Fleet was joined by the British Pacific Fleet units, which had departed Sydney on 28 June.

After re-fuelling was completed, Halsey launched his first strikes on 10 July. The fast-carrier strike planes headed for Tokyo and were surprised not to contact any Japanese fighters – they had been scattered in widely dispersed revetments at least 10 miles from any airfields. Nevertheless, although there was heavy AA fire from the ground, operating in relatively benign skies over Tokyo, the carrier fighter-bombers were able to destroy more than 100 grounded planes and obtained good aerial photo reconnaissance.[6] The Japanese had in fact abandoned any attempts to attack the fast carriers – and all their remaining aircraft had been harboured until October, when the Japanese anticipated the Allies would begin their landings. The aircraft could then be deployed against the invasion armada – when it appeared off Kyushu.

Moving north, on 15 July, Task Force 38 strikes went in against Honshu and worked over Hokkaido, the second largest and northmost island of Japan. Strike planes hit railways, shipping and air facilities, meeting light resistance. Some Allied commanders correctly believed that the enemy were hoarding their air power against an expected invasion – others believed Japan had little air power left.

A large amount of Honshu's coal and iron came from Hokkaido via train ferries – whose destruction was important. Six ferries were sunk in the first raids, his commander reporting back to Halsey: 'Pretty soon we'll have 'em moving their stuff by ox-carts and skiffs.'[7] Again, no enemy planes offered resistance and they were difficult to locate on the ground. But more than 50,000 tons of Japanese shipping and light naval craft had been sunk.

On 14 and 15 July, US Navy warships carried out an effective battleship-cruiser bombardment of the iron factory at Kamaishi on Honshu and the iron factory at Muroran, Hokkaido. They were then joined by a British force, that included the modern fast British battleship *King George V* and Royal New Zealand Navy heavy ships, in delivering a bombardment of industrial installations at Hitachi, 50 miles north of Tokyo. The British battleship *King George V* fired 267 14in main battery rounds – it was an historic occasion as it was the last time in history that a British battleship would fire in action.

On 18 July, the battleship *Nagato* was hit by Halsey's carrier planes at the Yokosuka Naval Base but remained afloat. The fast carriers also hit the engineering works and arms factory at Hitachi, encountering heavy AA fire but many enemy planes were shot down or damaged along with several ships sunk and locomotives, dumps and barracks destroyed.

Groups of cruisers and destroyers carried out bombardments of shore targets on the night of 24/25 July and on the night of 29 July US and British warships bombarded naval installations at Hamamatsu, in the Aichi Prefecture to the south of Tokyo. The final bombardment took place on 9 August, when Kamaishi was attacked again by US, British and New Zealand heavy units.

The last strikes of the war by the fast carriers were launched against the surviving Mobile Fleet units on 24 and 28 July 1945. Several capital ships were sunk at Kure, some settling on the bottom in shallow water with their upper works proud. On 24 July, Halsey at last hit the half-battleships *Ise* and *Hyūga*, which had escaped him at Leyte and the South China Sea sweep – along with the battleship *Haruna*. They would all be hit again on 28 July.

The heavy carriers *Amagi* and *Katsuragi* and the light carrier *Ryūhō* were severely damaged – along with the uncompleted carriers *Kasagi*, *Aso* and *Ibuki*. The light cruiser *Ōyodo* was sunk. Of Japan's twelve battleships in the war, only the crippled *Nagato* was afloat at Yokosuka. Of her twenty-five aircraft carriers, five were still afloat but damaged. Of her eighteen heavy cruisers, only two were now afloat – at Singapore. Of twenty-two light cruisers, only two were now afloat. Heavy Japanese AA fire was encountered in these operations, which took the toll of combat and operational losses of aircraft in the operation to 133 with 102 airmen lost. But no enemy interceptors had attacked the fleet.[8]

US submarines operating in the Sea of Japan had closed Japanese waters to supply shipping from China and Korea. By 1 August, aerial mining of Japanese coastal waters and harbours had virtually stopped all Japanese local coastal shipping. The devastating fire raids of Japanese cities brought the Japanese economy to a virtual standstill. Land-based bombing raids from Okinawa and the carrier air strikes and coastal bombardments by battleships, cruisers and destroyers had ravaged the east coast from Hokkaido to Kyushu.

On 26 July, the Allied forces, USA, Britain and China, issued the Potsdam Declaration calling for Japan's unconditional surrender – the alternative being 'prompt and utter destruction'. Japan rejected the demand two days later.

The end of July saw heavy weather beset the task force, although a shore bombardment of southern Honshu was delivered on 29 July and air strikes sent in against Kobe and Nagoya on 30 July. Typhoons and prolonged refuelling prevented further combat sorties – and then a special order from Admiral Nimitz arrived, instructing Halsey to take the Third Fleet well away from southern Japan.

On 6 August, the Boeing B-29 Superfortress *Enola Gay*, flying from North Field on Tinian in the Northern Mariana Islands, dropped the first atomic bomb, 'Little Boy', on Hiroshima – on the western end of the main island of Honshu. The possible effects of radiation fallout from the new weapon were unknown and so the Third Feet had been moved well clear. The bomb devastated Hiroshima with 70,000–80,000 people killed immediately – some 30 per cent of the population – and 19,700 injured and 170,000 rendered homeless. Over the next 2–4 months, the acute effects of the radiation would raise the number of dead to between 90,000 and 145,000 people.

Meanwhile, General MacArthur requested carrier strikes on the Misawa air base in northern Honshu, where US intelligence reports indicated a large enemy air fleet and airborne troop units were massing for a large-scale suicide landing on Okinawa. The Japanese were massing 200 medium bombers and 300 select troops for a suicide attack on B-29 bases in the Marianas. Halsey's heavy ships bombarded the Kamaishi factory on 8 August before his planes hit Misawa on the 9th, breaking up the Marianas suicide force and destroying more than 200 planes in revetments.

President Harry S. Truman called again for Japan's surrender 16 hours after the first bomb was dropped on Hiroshima. He warned Japan to 'expect a rain of ruin from the air, the like of which has never been seen on this earth'.

On the evening of 8 August, the Soviet Union declared war on Japan and soon after midnight on 9 August, invaded the Imperial Japanese puppet state of Manchuko. Hours later, on 9 August, the B-29 Superfortress *Bockscar* dropped the second atomic bomb on Nagasaki, this time a plutonium implosion bomb called 'Fat Man'. Between 39,000 and 80,000 people died immediately and in the coming months from the effects of the radiation. The original target had been the city of Kokura but on the day of the attack it was obscured by cloud. The target for a third bomb would probably have been Tokyo itself.

The Manhattan Project for the development of the atomic bomb had begun modestly in 1939 but grew to employ more than 130,000 people. The first nuclear device ever detonated was an implosion-type bomb test conducted in New Mexico on 16 July 1945. 'Little Boy' and 'Fat Man' were used a month later.

But despite the great size of the Manhattan Project as it reached its city destroying culmination, the work had been undertaken in strictest secrecy. Nimitz was made aware of the project in February 1945 whilst at Guam – and advised that the projected date when it would be available for use would be 1 August 1945. He asked: 'Don't those people realise we're fighting a war out here? This is February, and you're talking about the first of August.'

Halsey learned of the bomb drop on 22 July, but most of Nimitz's carrier admirals had no idea of the atomic project – and its use took them by complete surprise.[9] None had known that such a weapon could or did exist.

With no immediate surrender following the second atomic bomb on 9 August, the war continued. Halsey believed that the airfields in northern Honshu and Hokkaido were the only ones close enough to Russian forces for long-range Japanese air strikes against her new enemy. On 10 August, he launched more TF 38 strikes over north-east Honshu whilst coastal targets were subjected to a naval bombardment

Following the Nagasaki bombing, Emperor Hirohito intervened and ordered the Supreme Council for the Direction of the War to accept the Allies terms in the Potsdam Declaration for ending the war. Several days of behind the scenes negotiating began.

The OLYMPIC timetable provided that on the evening of 10 August, the British fast-carrier Task Force 37 was to retire to Manus Island to replenish whilst Task Force 38 was to withdraw to refuel, then retire to Eniwetok. But that night, Japan indicated she accepted Allied surrender terms in principle and was now discussing the details.

Vice Admiral Rawlings RN determined to hold off retiring his task force for another day to see what developed. During refuelling on 11 August, with a lack of fast fleet oilers, Rawlings accepted that he had to withdraw – but left *Indefatigable* and several escorts with the Third Fleet for the kill. Halsey also resolved not to retire as planned – but to press Japan until she surrendered, despite his fuel shortages limiting operations to short ranges. On 13 August, full deckload strikes claimed over 250 Japanese aircraft on the ground, whilst the CAP shot down 18 more.

Despite the dire position Japan found itself in and the Emperor's intervention to press for surrender, on 14–15 August, elements of the Staff Office of the Ministry of War of Japan, and members of the Imperial Guard, staged an attempted *coup d'état*, the Kyūjō Incident, in an attempt to prevent the announcement of Japan's surrender. Just before the announcement, after midnight on 15 August 1945, Major Kenji Hatanaka and Lieutenant Colonels Masataka Ida and Jiro Shiizaki visited Lieutenant General Takeshi Mori, commander of the First

Imperial Guards Division, who were responsible for the protection of the Imperial Family of Japan. They sought to secure his aid in a plot to isolate the Imperial Palace, place the Emperor under house arrest and prevent the announcement. At about 0130, after repeated refusals by Lieutenant General Mori, Hatanaka shot and killed him – but the plotters were not able to convince the Eastern District Army and the high command of the IJA to take part in the coup. When it was clear the coup had failed, Hatanaka shot himself in the head whilst Shiizaki stabbed himself with a dagger and then shot himself; Ida survived.

The last fast-carrier air operations against Japan took place that day, 15 August 1945, when a strike of 103 carrier aircraft launched at 0404 that hit Tokyo just after dawn, shooting down 30–40 airborne enemy planes.

Emperor Hirohito gave a recorded address across the Empire of Japan the same day, following on from the failed coup earlier that morning, in which he announced the surrender of Japan to the Allies. Halsey had another seventy-three carrier planes airborne and 5 minutes away from their target when he received a top-secret despatch from Nimitz: 'AIR ATTACK WILL BE SUSPENDED x ACKNOWLEDGE.'[10] A ceasefire came into effect that day.

A few uninformed Japanese pilots continued to attack, shooting down four *Yorktown* Hellcats over the coast, but no Japanese aircraft got through the defensive fighters to reach the task force. Off Wake Island, *Antietam*'s planned strikes for the next day were cancelled.

Although a ceasefire was now in effect, nothing could be taken for granted – and the fast carriers had to maintain a constant patrol against possible failure of disenfranchised elements of the Japanese military to abide by the terms of the ceasefire. Halsey ordered TF 38 to 'Area McCain', 100–200 miles south east of Tokyo, where the three task groups maintained their normal wartime patrols up to 23 August. The Japanese surrender was officially set for 2 September in Tokyo Bay.

Admiral Spruance ordered all Fifth Fleet units gathering at Guam for OLYMPIC to go to Okinawa, whilst he boarded a battleship for passage to Manila, conferring there for a week with MacArthur before proceeding to Okinawa on 30 August. The amphibious craft of his Fifth Fleet, which would have landed troops at Kyushu, was to occupy the Inland Sea as soon after the surrender as possible. The Third Fleet would carry out the emergency occupation of Tokyo Bay.

Late on 23 August, Halsey assigned his carriers to new operating areas. Some planes flew aerial surveillance over Japanese airfields whilst others dropped food and supplies to prisoners of war.

On 27 August, many ships of the Third Fleet entered Sagami Wan, although Task Force 38 was only represented by the light carrier *Cowpens* because Halsey felt that his carriers would be vulnerable there against any Japanese treachery.

A Fighting 88 pilot landed at Atsugi airfield later that same day with a banner that he ordered the Japanese to erect that bore the legend: 'WELCOME TO THE US ARMY FROM THE THIRD FLEET.' The next day Army paratroopers began to arrive – to find this tongue in cheek welcome sign by the Navy.[11] On 28 August, two staff officers from Admiral John H. Towers' Air Force, Pacific Fleet command arrived at Atsugi in a Torpedo 85 Avenger to begin preparatory talks.

The occupation of Japan by the Allies began formally on 28 August 1945. On 30 August, the ships in Sagami Wan moved into Tokyo Bay and Halsey shifted his flag ashore from the battleship *Missouri* to Tokosuka

Surrender of Japan, Tokyo Bay, 2 September 1945. Fleet Admiral Chester W. Nimitz, US Navy, signs the Instrument of Surrender as US Representative on board USS *Missouri* (BB-63). Standing directly behind him are, left to right: General of the Army Douglas MacArthur, Admiral William F. Halsey, US Navy and Rear Admiral Forrest Sherman, US Navy. (National Archives 80-G-701293)

Surrender of Japan, Tokyo Bay, 2 September 1945. Navy carrier planes fly in formation over the US and British fleets in Tokyo Bay during the surrender ceremonies. USS *Missouri* (BB-63), where the ceremony took place, is in the left foreground. (National Archives 80-G-421130)

naval base. When it became known that the Japanese surrender would be signed aboard the *Missouri* on 2 September, the carrier men looked on this choice with disdain. The fast carrier to them symbolised victory more than the battleship. The *Enterprise*, the 'Big E', had survived the whole Pacific War and fought in most of its battles – but she was still under repair in the USA and could not be present. There were however nine other heavy carriers to choose from – but the battleship *Missouri* was selected in honour of president Truman's home state.[12]

The Empire of Japan formally surrendered unconditionally to the Allies aboard *Missouri* on 2 September 1945 with General of the Army, MacArthur, representing the Allied powers as Supreme Commander. Fleet Admiral Nimitz signed the surrender agreement for the USA, flanked by two naval aviators, Admiral Halsey and Nimitz's Deputy Chief of Staff Vice Admiral Forrest Sherman. Standing in the front rank of witnesses alongside other Allied representatives and officers were fast-carrier commanders Jack Towers, Ted Sherman and Slew McCain – only Pete Mitscher was missing.

As the ceremony ended, 450 carrier planes from Task Force 38 roared in from the sea over Tokyo Bay in a final demonstration of carrier air power.

Britain used its fast carriers to facilitate the surrender and occupation of many Japanese holdings. Rear Admiral Harcourt assembled his 11th Aircraft Carrier Squadron at Sydney and despatched *Glory* to Rabaul. The bypassed South-Pacific garrisons surrendered to Allied representatives on her flight deck in Simpson Harbour on 6 September. Harcourt then hoisted his flag aboard *Indomitable* and departed for Hong Kong via the Philippines with the light carrier *Vengeance* and several escorts. Leaving his flagship outside Hong Kong harbour, for fear of lurking mines, he transferred to the cruiser *Swiftsure* to go ashore. Carrier planes sank a suicide boat trying to escape before Harcourt formally accepted the Japanese surrender of Hong Kong on 16 September.

Almost unbelievably, the world war was finally over without the need for a land invasion of Japan. How many countless thousands of Allied lives had been saved?

(iv) Aftermath

Some pockets of Japanese resistance on small Pacific islands refused to surrender. Some Japanese troops simply may never have heard of the surrender – others would not surrender until ordered to do so by their superior officers who had perhaps been killed, captured or disappeared.

A group of thirty-five IJA soldiers survived amongst the caves of Peleliu for eighteen months before surrendering in April 1947. Second Lieutenant Hiroo Onoda had taken to the hills on Lubang Island in the Philippines when the Allies landed, ordered never to surrender until told to do so. He continued a campaign as a Japanese holdout, initially living with three fellow soldiers and carrying out guerrilla activities, killing local Filipino inhabitants and being involved in several shoot-outs. One of the four left the group in 1949 and surrendered in 1950.

In 1952, letters and family pictures were air dropped urging the three remaining Japanese holdout soldiers to surrender – but they believed this was a trick. One Japanese soldier was shot and killed in 1954 and local police killed another in 1972 whilst he was burning rice collected by farmers as part of their guerrilla activities.

In 1974, Onoda met a young Japanese man, Norio Suzuki, who was travelling the world and, amongst other things, was searching for him.

They became friends, but although urged to surrender, Onoda said he would not surrender until he received orders from a superior officer. Suzuki returned to Japan with photographs of Onoda and himself.

Despite the passing of some thirty years, on learning of Onoda's position, the Japanese government managed to locate Onoda's former wartime officer and flew him to Lubang Island. Here he met Onoda, formally relieved him of his duties and ordered him to surrender – using commands he last used during the Second World War, thirty years earlier. Formally dressed in his wartime IJA uniform, Onoda ritually turned over his sword, his Second World War rifle, ammunition, hand grenades and a dagger.

Private Teruo Nakamura was the last known Japanese Second World War combatant to surrender – emerging from his hidden retreat on Morotai Island in Indonesia in December 1974. Reports of other holdouts circulated in newspapers in the 1980s. Two other Japanese soldiers, Shigeyuki Hashimoto and Kiyoaki Tanaka, joined the Malayan Communist Party guerrillas at the end of the war, fighting in southern Thailand until 1990 when a peace treaty was assigned, and they returned to Japan.

To this day there are still some 2,600 IJA troops Missing in Action in Palau – most still inside some of the 200 caves that have remained just as they were sealed in 1944 by US forces. Archaeologists are now carefully and painstakingly opening up and investigating these cave systems. Some are still booby-trapped – and most still hold dangerous ordnance. Every now and then, a cave sealed since 1944 is opened to be examined – and inevitably the remains of IJA soldiers missing in action are discovered.

The US Fleet underwent several changes immediately following war's end. Effective 1 January 1947, all numbered fleets were abolished, leaving only the Pacific Task Fleet and the Atlantic Task Fleet. General MacArthur controlled Japan, the Ryukyus and US forces in the Philippines and the Navy's CINCPAC controlled the rest.

In summer 1948, despite demobilisation and mothballing of all veteran wartime carriers, the numbered fleets reappeared as 'task fleets', the word 'task' being dropped early in 1950. The famous Third and Fifth Fleets were retired, the Seventh Fleet survived in the Far East and a new Sixth Fleet formed in the Mediterranean. Neither Japan nor any other nation which survived the Second World War could ever now challenge US supremacy at sea – and so the need for the fast-carrier task force disappeared immediately.

Appendix

Dramatis Personae

The list of pivotal characters in the Pacific War is enormous – but below are brief backgrounds of some of the main characters who are referenced heavily throughout this book.

(i) Fleet Admiral Ernest Joseph King (23 November 1878–25 June 1956)

As Commander in Chief, US Fleet (COMINCH) and Chief of Naval Operations (CNO), King directed the Navy's operations, planning and administration during the Second World War. A member of the Joint Chiefs of Staff, he was the US Navy's second most senior officer in the war after Fleet Admiral William D. Leahy.

Born in Lorain, Ohio, on 23 November 1878, whilst still a young man at the US Naval Academy, he served on the cruiser USS *San Francisco* during the Spanish-American War in 1898. After graduating from the academy in 1901, he served as a junior officer on the survey ship *Eagle* and the battleships *Illinois*, *Alabama* and *New Hampshire* and the cruiser *Cincinnati*.

He received his first command, the destroyer *Terry*, in 1914 and participated in the occupation of Veracruz, Mexico. After the war, he served as head of the Naval Postgraduate School, commanded a submarine squadron and served as Chief of the Bureau of Aeronautics.

King became Commander in Chief of the US Atlantic Fleet (CINCLANTFLT) in February 1941 and on 30 December 1941 was appointed Commander in Chief, US Fleet (COMINCH). Admiral Husband Kimmel was COMINCH at the time of the attack on Pearl Harbor on 7 December 1941 but was removed from command and reduced in rank from four-star to two-star rear admiral, before retiring from the Navy in early 1942.

On 18 March 1942, King (COMINCH) was appointed Chief of Naval Operations (CNO), the only officer to hold this combined command.

On 17 December 1944, King was appointed to the newly created rank of fleet admiral, the second of only four men to hold that rank in the US Navy during the war. At war's end, he stepped down from active duty on 15 December 1945. He died in 1956, aged 77 – having served fifty-five years on active duty in the US Navy.

(ii) Fleet Admiral Chester William Nimitz (24 February 1885–20 February 1966)

Fleet Admiral Nimitz was a colossus of the Pacific War, playing a major role as Commander in Chief, US Pacific Fleet (CINCPACFLT) and Commander-in-Chief Pacific Ocean Areas (CINCPOA).

Nimitz was born on 24 February 1885 in Fredericksburg, Texas. He originally applied to West Point for a career as an army officer, but no appointments were available. He turned to the Navy, graduating from the US Naval Academy in 1905. He joined the battleship *Ohio* and cruised to the Far East before transfer to the cruiser *Baltimore* on the Asiatic Station and billets on the gunboat *Panay*, the destroyer *Decatur* and cruiser *Denver*. In 1909 he was given command of the First Submarine Flotilla, commanding *Plunger*, *Snapper* and *Narwhal*. He went on to command the Atlantic Submarine Flotilla from May 1912 to March 1913.

After the US declaration of war on Germany in April 1917, Nimitz served on a refuelling ship for the first squadron of US Navy destroyers to cross the Atlantic to war in Europe, conducting the first-ever underway refuellings. He was appointed chief of staff to the Commander Submarine Force, US Atlantic Fleet (COMSUBLANT) on 6 February 1918.

Nimitz commanded destroyers and cruisers between the wars and on 15 June 1939 was appointed Chief of the Bureau of Navigation, conducting experiments in underway refuelling of large ships, a process that would become pivotal as the Pacific War unfolded.

Ten days after the Pearl Harbor raid of 7 December 1941, President Franklin D. Roosevelt appointed him as commander-in-chief US Pacific Fleet (CINCPACFLT), and he was promoted to admiral on 31 December 1941.

Nimitz's experience and expertise with submarines enabled him clinically to weigh the developing roles of battleship and carrier objectively. Naturally patient, he admitted his mistakes and made changes unhesitatingly. As overall fleet commander in the Pacific, he wisely selected the right people to advise him, such as Spruance and Forrest Sherman, whilst leaving air matters to John H. Towers. Peerless as a wartime strategist and theatre commander, he relieved Ernest King as CNO in December 1945 until 1947. He died at home in 1966 aged 80 and lies at Golden Gate National Cemetery in San Bruno alongside his wife and his dear friends Admiral Raymond A. Spruance, Admiral Richmond K. Turner and Admiral Charles A. Lockwood and their wives, an arrangement made by them all in life.

(iii) Fleet Admiral William Frederick Halsey Jr, KBE (30 October 1883–16 August 1959)

Fleet Admiral Halsey, known as 'Bill' or 'Bull' Halsey is, with Ernest King, William Leahy and Chester Nimitz, one of four US Navy fleet admirals of the Second World War. At the beginning of the Second World War, he commanded a naval task force centred on the carrier *Enterprise* in a series of raids against Japanese targets. He was subsequently appointed commander South Pacific Area and led Allied naval forces during the Guadalcanal campaign (1942–3) and the thrust up the Solomon Islands chain to the Philippines and on to Japan. He commanded the Third Fleet from 1943 and took part in the Battle for Leyte Gulf, the largest naval battle of the Second World War. He was promoted to fleet admiral in December 1945.

Born in Elizabeth, New Jersey on 30 October 1882, the son of US Navy Captain William F. Halsey Sr, he initially trained as a naval physician before graduating from the Naval Academy in 1904. His early naval career saw service in battleships such as *Kansas* and *Missouri*, before service aboard torpedo boats. He went on to command a number of torpedo boats and destroyers before being given command of the First Group of the Atlantic Fleet's Torpedo Flotilla in 1912–13. His First World War service saw him awarded the Navy Cross.

In 1934 he was given command of the carrier *Saratoga*, but with no naval aviation training, this command appointment was made subject to his completion of a Naval Aviation Air Observer course. Thinking that it was better to fly the aircraft personally than be a passenger at the mercy of the pilot, he boldly elected to enrol for the full twelve-week Naval Aviator course rather than the simpler Observer course, earning his Naval Aviator's Wings on 15 May 1935 at the age of 52, the oldest person to do so in the history of the US Navy. Captain Halsey was subsequently promoted to rear admiral in 1938, commanding carrier divisions and serving as overall commander of the Aircraft Battle Force.

At the outbreak of the Second World War, traditional naval thinking still saw the decisive battle as being a surface conflict between opposing battleships fleets – but Halsey envisioned naval air as vital for the future navy, believing the carrier, not the battleship, was the primary naval offensive weapon. Halsey was absent from Pearl Harbor when the surprise raid took place on 7 December 1941 – in November he had been ordered to take *Enterprise* to ferry aircraft to Wake Island and reinforce the detachment of US Marines stationed on the small coral island airfield. *Enterprise* was on her way back to Pearl, and was some 200 miles distant, when the surprise attack began.

Halsey was an aggressive commander by nature, energetic and demanding – bolstering morale and taking the fight to the enemy in the early months of the war when the USA had been rocked by the Pearl raid and the rapid, seemingly unstoppable, Japanese expansion. Halsey as commander of Carrier Division 2 on *Enterprise* led a series of hit and run raids through the Gilbert and Marshall Islands in February 1942, striking Wake Island in March and executing the famous Doolittle Raid in April 1942 against Tokyo itself. His slogan became famous through the Navy, 'Hit hard, hit fast, hit often'.

Returning to Pearl Harbor after the Doolittle Raid, he was hospitalised by severe shingles at the end of May 1942 and missed the Battle of Midway as Spruance took over his command, at his recommendation. Halsey was only fit enough to resume duties in autumn that year – when Nimitz appointed him commander of the South Pacific Area. He led the South Pacific naval forces through the Battle of the Santa Cruz Islands and the Naval Battle of Guadalcanal, before fighting up the Solomon Islands chain to Bougainville.

In May 1944 he was promoted to commanding officer of the newly formed Third Fleet and went on to command operations from the Philippines to Japan, leading the campaigns to take the Palaus, Leyte and Luzon and rotating command of the 'Big Blue Fleet' with Raymond Spruance. He was deeply criticised for his decisions during the Battle of Leyte Gulf in October 1944, when his aggressive nature led him to take the Third Fleet in a chase north after the Japanese decoy Northern Force of virtually planeless carriers. The Leyte beachhead was denuded of fast-carrier support and the Seventh Fleet escort carriers suffered a punishing attack from the battleships of the Japanese Central Force.

In January 1945, the Third Fleet attacked Formosa and Luzon and raided the South China Sea. Halsey led through the final stages of the war, striking targets on the Japanese homeland itself. He was present when Japan formally surrendered aboard his flagship, the battleship *Missouri*, on 2 September 1945.

Halsey retired from active service as a fleet admiral in March 1947 and died aged 76 on 16 August 1959. He is interred in Arlington National Cemetery.

(iv) Admiral Raymond Ames Spruance (3 July 1886–13 December 1969)

Admiral Spruance was a brilliant strategist and coordinator of the large Allied forces afloat in the Pacific during the Second World War. He commanded the amphibious operations of the Central Pacific campaign and commanded US naval forces during two of the most significant naval battles of the Pacific theatre, the Battle of Midway and the Battle of the Philippine Sea.

Spruance was born in Baltimore, Maryland, on 3 July 1886 and was raised in Indianapolis before graduating from the US Naval Academy in 1907. His first posting after graduating was aboard the battleship *Iowa* – before a transfer to the battleship *Minnesota*. He went on to command the destroyers *Bainbridge, Osborne* and three others – and served aboard the super-dreadnought *Pennsylvania* towards the end of the First World War.

Between the wars, he served as executive officer on the battleship *Mississippi* before being appointed commander of *Mississippi* in April 1938 and promoted to rear admiral.

At the outbreak of the Pacific War, Spruance commanded the four heavy cruisers and support ships of Cruiser Division 5 from his flagship, the heavy cruiser *Northampton*. His Cruiser Division 5 was part of the task force built around the carrier *Enterprise* that was commanded by Vice Admiral William F. Halsey.

When Halsey was hospitalised in late May 1942 with severe shingles, he recommended Spruance to Nimitz as his replacement. Appointing Spruance was something of a gamble as although he was a proven cruiser commander, he had no experience in handling carrier air – but Halsey assured Nimitz that Spruance was inheriting battle-hardened experienced staff.

Spruance went on to command at the pivotal Battle of Midway where his calm, collected and decisive nature led him to emerge from the battle as one of the greatest admirals in US naval history.

Shortly after Midway, Spruance became chief of staff to Nimitz and in September 1942 was appointed Deputy Commander in Chief of the

Pacific Fleet. In August 1943 he was placed in command of the Central Pacific Force, which was redesignated as the Fifth Fleet, command of the 'Big Blue Fleet' alternating between Spruance and Halsey.

Spruance directed Operation HAILSTONE against Truk in February 1944 and whilst screening the invasion of Saipan in June 1944, he defeated the Japanese Fleet in the Battle of the Philippine Sea, when 3 enemy carriers were sunk along with 2 oilers and some 700 enemy land-based and carrier planes downed.

Spruance was appointed Nimitz's successor as CINCPAC-CINCPOA on 24 November 1945, fading from the light post-war and retiring from the Navy in July 1948. He died on 13 December 1969 aged 83 and is interred at the Golden Gate National Cemetery near San Francisco.

(v) Admiral John Henry Towers (30 January 1885–30 April 1955)

John H. 'Jack' Towers was appointed Commander, Air Force, Pacific Fleet early in the war and directed the formation of the Pacific Fleet Air forces, its development, organisation and training – and this role included the fast-carrier task force in 1943. He became Nimitz's deputy in February 1944 and commander of the Second Fast-Carrier Force and Task Force 38 in August 1945, just before the war ended. On 31 October 1945 he left the fast carriers to become Commander Fifth Fleet. He relieved Spruance on 1 February 1946 as Commander in Chief Pacific Fleet (CINCPAC). He died on 30 April 1955 aged 70 and was buried at Arlington National Cemetery.

(vi) Admiral Marc Andrew Mitscher (26 January 1887–3 February 1947)

Marc A. 'Pete' Mitscher graduated from the Naval Academy in 1910 and moved to destroyers and cruisers, the latter being used for experimental launching of aircraft. He trained as a pilot and won his naval aviator's wings in 1916. After being part of an attempted first transatlantic crossing by air in 1919, he moved to spend two decades developing naval aviation – being given command of *Hornet* in 1941 and then the newly formed fast-carrier task force. He emerged from the Second World War as the acknowledged leader of carrier aviation – having led the fast-carrier task force in all its major operations, his first tour lasting an exhausting ten months from January to October 1944 followed by four more strenuous months under constant kamikaze attack. Of Mitscher,

Nimitz said: 'He is the most experienced and most able officer in the handling of fast carrier task forces who has yet been developed. It is doubtful if any officer has made more important contributions than he toward [the] extinction of the enemy fleet.'[1] After the war, he briefly commanded the new Eighth Fleet and then the Atlantic Fleet. But the strains of war had made him ill; no one knew how badly. He died on 3 February 1947 aged 60 and was buried at Arlington National Cemetery.

(vii) Admiral John Sidney McCain Sr (9 August 1884–6 September 1945)

John Sidney 'Slew' McCain graduated from the Naval Academy in 1906 and served aboard cruisers and battleships before graduating as a naval aviator in 1936 at the age of 52. He commanded the carrier *Ranger* from 1937–9 and then the Aircraft Scouting Force of the Atlantic Fleet.

After the Japanese attack on Pearl Harbor on 7 December 1941, Slew McCain was appointed Commander, Aircraft, South Pacific in May 1942, commanding all land-based Allied air operations during the Guadalcanal campaign. In October 1942 he was appointed head of the Bureau of Aeronautics and in August 1943 became Deputy Chief of Naval Operations for Air, based in Washington.

In August 1944, he returned to combat in the Pacific as commander of a carrier task group in Task Force 58, then under Mitscher's command – and went on to fight in the Marianas campaign, including the Battle of the Philippine Sea. He was present at the Battle of Leyte Gulf and shortly thereafter assumed command of Task Force 38 on 30 October 1944. He remained in command of the fast carriers through the Battle of Okinawa to the final raids on the Japanese home islands. He was present at the Japanese surrender ceremony in Tokyo Bay on 2 September 1945. As with Marc Mitscher, the strain of continued combat operations had taken its toll on his health and immediately after the surrender ceremony he was sent home to recuperate. He sadly died just four days later on 6 September 1945 at his home in California, aged 61, and was buried at Arlington National Cemetery.

(viii) Admiral Frederick Carl Sherman (27 May 1888–27 July 1957)

Frederick C. 'Ted' Sherman graduated from the Naval Academy in 1910 and served in submarines during the First World War. After qualifying as a naval aviator, he served as executive officer on the *Saratoga* in 1937 and then commanded *Lexington* from 1940 until her loss at the Battle of the Coral Sea in 1942. He commanded Carrier Division 2 in the Fast-Carrier Task Force in 1943 and then commanded Task Group 38.3 in 1944–5.

Ted Sherman was the only air admiral to lead fast-carriers forces from late 1942 to the end of the war and advanced the concept of the multi-carrier task formation. He distinguished himself at Rabaul, Leyte and Okinawa and relieved John Henry Towers as Commander Fifth Fleet at Tokyo on 18 January 1946. He retired in 1947 and died on 27 July 1957 aged 69.

Notes

Chapter 1: Naval Aviation – Genesis

1. Clark G. Reynolds, *The Fast Carriers – The Forging of an Air Navy* (Naval Institute Press, 1968), 2.
2. Captain S.W. Roskill, *Naval Policy Between the Wars: The Period of Anglo-American Antagonism, 1918–1928* (Collins, 1968), 310ff.
3. Lieutenant J. Grimes, USNR, *Aviation in the Fleet Exercises, 1923–1939* (Manuscript History, Navy Department, n.d.), 16–18.
4. Reynolds, *The Fast Carriers*, 17.
5. Quoted in Scot MacDonald, *Evolution of Aircraft Carriers* (Aviation History Unit, 1964), 22.
6. Quoted in Elting E. Morison, *Admiral Sims and the Modern American Navy* (Houghton Mifflin Co., 1942), 506.
7. Grimes, *Aviation in the Fleet Exercises*, 48.
8. Ibid., 62–3.
9. Ibid., 157–65.

Chapter 2: Prelude to War in the Pacific – A Little Bit of Background

1. James L. McCain, *Japan: A Modern History* (W.W. Norton & Co., 2002), 495.

Chapter 3: The Fast Carriers Begin to Appear

1. Captain Gumpei Sekine, IJN, 'Japan's Case for Sea Power', *Current History*, 41 (November 1934), 130.
2. Hector C. Bywater, 'The Coming Struggle for Sea Power', *Current History*, 41 (October 1934), 15.

3. Rear Admiral Toshiyuki Yokoi, IJN, 'Thoughts on Japan's Naval Defeat', *U.S. Naval Institute Proceedings*, 86 (October 1960), 72–4.

4. Lieutenant A.R. Buchanan, USNR (ed.) and the Aviation History Unit, *The Navy's Air War: A Mission Completed* (Harper & Bros, 1946), 16.

5. *Current Tactical Orders and Doctrine, U.S. Fleet Aircraft, Vol. One, Carrier Aircraft, USF-74 (Revised), March 1941*, prepared by Commander Aircraft Battle Force, 20 April 1941.

6. Grimes, *Aviation in the Fleet Exercises*, 216–17.

7. Henry Woodhouse, 'U.S. Naval Aeronautic Policies, 1904–42', *U.S. Naval Institute Proceedings*, 68 (February 1942), 164.

8. Bernard Brodie, *Sea Power in the Machine Age* (Princeton University Press, 1941), 433.

9. Louis Morton, *The War in the Pacific. Strategy and Command: The First Two Years*, Center of Military History, United States Army, 56.

10. Ibid.

11. Pearl Harbor Attack Hearings, Pt 15, 1903.

12. Norman Friedman, *The British Battleship 1906–1946* (Seaforth Publishing, 2015), 37.

13. Ronald H. Spector, *Eagle Against the Sun: The American War with Japan* (Random House, 1992).

Chapter 4: Let Loose the Dogs of War

1. Peter Wetzler, *Hirohito and War: Imperial Tradition and Military Decision Making in Prewar Japan* (University of Hawaii Press, 1998), 28–30, 39.

2. Masatake Okumiya and Jiro Horikoshi, *Zero! The Story of the Japanese Navy Air Force 1937–1945* (Cassell & Co. Ltd, 1957), 45. Jiro Horikoshi designed the Zero and Masatake Okumiya led many Zero squadrons during the war.

Chapter 5: 1942 – The US Navy Goes to War – The Coral Sea and Midway

1. Rear Admiral W.R. Sexton, Chairman, General Board, to Secretary of the Navy Frank Knox, Serial 174, 14 March 1942, and First Endorsement, 18 March 1942.

2. Robert E. Lester, *U.S. Navy Action and Operational Reports from World War II. Pacific Theater. Part 3. Fifth Fleet and Fifth Fleet Carrier Task Forces* (University Publications of America, 1990), v.
3. Vice Admiral Paul D. Stroop, quoted in *Carrier Warfare in the Pacific – An Oral History Collection*, ed. E.T. Wooldridge (Smithsonian Institution Press, 1993), 37.
4. Ibid., 38.
5. Ibid., 40.
6. Ibid, 44–5.
7. Okumiya and Horikoshi, *Zero!*, 113.
8. Ibid., 115.
9. J. Parshall and A. Tully, *Shattered Sword: The Untold Story of the Battle of Midway* (Potomac Books, 2005).
10. Okumiya and Horikoshi, *Zero!*, 341.
11. Theodore Taylor, *The Magnificent Mitscher* (Norton, 1954), 127.
12. H.P. Willmott, *The Barrier and the Javelin: Japanese and Allied Strategies, February to June 1942* (Naval Institute Press, 1983), 351.
13. Okumiya and Horikoshi, *Zero!*, 122.
14. Taylor, *The Magnificent Mitscher*, 130.
15. Okumiya and Horikoshi, *Zero!*, 123.
16. Ibid., 124.
17. Ibid., 124.
18. Ibid., 125.
19. Taylor, *The Magnificent Mitscher*, 135.

Chapter 6: From Defence to Offence – The Guadalcanal Campaign, 7 August 1942–9 February 1943

1. Jeter A. Isely and Philip A. Crowl, *U.S. Marines and Amphibious War: Its Theory and Its Practice in the Pacific* (Princeton University Press, 1951), 89–90.
2. Ibid., 96.
3. Ibid., 92–3.
4. William F. Halsey and Joseph Bryan, III, *Admiral Halsey's Story* (Whittlesey House, 1947), 97.
5. S.E. Morison, *History of US Naval Operations in World War II, Vol. V: The Struggle for Guadalcanal* (Little, Brown and Co., 1949), 137.
6. Halsey and Bryan, *Admiral Halsey's Story*, 94.
7. Ibid., 95.

8. Rear Admiral Francis D. Foley, quoted in *Carrier Warfare in the Pacific – An Oral History Collection*, ed. E.T. Wooldridge (Smithsonian Institution Press, 1993), 71.
9. Halsey and Bryan, *Admiral Halsey's Story*, 103.
10. Ibid., 104.
11. Ibid., 106.

Chapter 7: Summer of 1943 – The Allies Begin to Move West Across the Pacific

1. *Dictionary of American Naval Fighting Ships*, Vol. 1 (US Government Printing Office, 1959), Appendix 1, 'Battleships, 1886–1948', 198–9.
2. US Secretary, Office of the Combined Chiefs of Staff, 'Trident Conference, May 1943 Papers and Minutes of Meetings, 1943', declassified 29 October 1973.
3. Maurice Matloff, *Strategic Planning for Coalition Warfare, 1943–44*, official US Army history (US Government Printing Office, 1959), 91.
4. Ibid., 186–91.
5. Ibid., 207.
6. Ibid., 186–208.
7. Okumiya and Horikoshi, *Zero!*, 246.
8. Ibid., 249.
9. Weapons Systems Evaluation Group, WSEG Study No. 4, *Operational Experience of Fast Carrier Task Forces in World War II*, 15 August 1951, 21.
10. Masanori Ito with Roger Pineau, *The End of the Imperial Japanese Navy* (Weidenfeld & Nicolson, 1962), 84.

Chapter 8: US Fast Carriers and Naval Aircraft

1. Lieutenant William C. Bryant, USNR and Lieutenant H.I. Hermans, USNR, *History of Naval Fighter Direction, Carrier Warfare* (Vol I. of Essays in the History of Naval Air Operations) (Air History Unit, February 1946), 191–4.
2. Vice Admiral Truman J. Hedding, quoted in *Carrier Warfare in the Pacific – An Oral History Collection*, ed. E.T. Wooldridge (Smithsonian Institution Press, 1993), 117.
3. Robert E. Demme, 'Evolution of the Hellcat', repr. from *Skyways* magazine in *The Second Navy Reader* (Bobbs-Merrill, 1944), 193.
4. Transcript of interview with Lieutenant Colonel Edward A. Montgomery, USMC, *Night Fighter Operations in Great Britain* (Bureau of Aeronautics, 1943).

5. Okumiya and Horikoshi, *Zero!*, 125–6.
6. Ibid., 350.
7. Demme, 'Evolution of the Hellcat', 194, 198, 200–1. See also Captain Edward H. Eckelmeyer Jr, USN, 'The Story of the Self-Sealing Tank', *U.S. Naval Institute Proceedings*, 72 (February 1946), 205–19.
8. B. Rowland and W.B. Boyd, *US Navy Bureau of Ordnance in World War II* (US Government Printing Office, Washington, 1953), 303–4, 332–3.
9. Okumiya and Horikoshi, *Zero!*, 350.
10. Ibid., 351–2.

Chapter 9: Late 1943 – The Isolation of Rabaul – The Central Pacific Drive Begins

1. Halsey and Bryan, *Admiral Halsey's Story*, 125.
2. Ibid., 141.
3. Ibid., 146.
4. Ibid., 147.
5. Ibid., 148.
6. Reynolds, *The Fast Carriers*, 113.
7. US Marine Corps Historical Branch, G-3 Division, *History of US Marine Corps Operations in WWII. Central Pacific Drive* (US Government Printing Office, 1966), 53–71.

Chapter 10: Task Force 58 is Formed – The Gilbert and Marshall Islands Campaign Continues

1. Taylor, *The Magnificent Mitscher*, 202.
2. Ibid., 145.
3. Samuel E. Morison, *The Two Ocean War* (Little, Brown and Co., 1963), 107–8.
4. Taylor, *The Magnificent Mitscher*, 316.

Chapter 11: Central Pacific Drive, 1944 – The Gilbert and Marshall Islands Campaign Continues

1. Turner Action Report, 00165, 4 December 1943.
2. Reynolds, *The Fast Carriers*, 132–3.
3. Taylor, *The Magnificent Mitscher*, 178.
4. Samuel E. Morison, *History of US Naval Operations in World War I, Vol. VII: Aleutians, Gilberts and Marshalls* (Little, Brown and Co., 1949), 218–21.
5. Taylor, *The Magnificent Mitscher*, 179.

6. Commander-in-Chief, United States Pacific Fleet and Pacific Ocean Areas, *Command History, 7 December 1941–15 August 1945*, 137–8.
7. Isely and Crowl, *U.S. Marines and Amphibious War*, 292.
8. Holland M. Smith, General, U.S. Marine Corp, *Coral and Brass* (Fleet Marine Force Reference Publication, 1989), 149.
9. Isely and Crowl, *U.S. Marines and Amphibious War*, 291–2.
10. Elmont Waite, 'He Opened the Airway to Tokyo', *Saturday Evening Post*, 2 December 1944, 20.
11. Reynolds, *The Fast Carriers*, 136.
12. Lieutenant Oliver Jensen, USNR, *Carrier War* (Simon & Schuster, 1945), 97.
13. Battle Report TG 58.1.
14. Dan E. Bailey, *World War II Wrecks of the Truk Lagoon* (North River Diver Publications, 2000), 104.
15. Morison, *History of US Naval Operations, Vol. VII: Aleutians, Gilberts and Marshalls*, 320.
16. Reynolds, *The Fast Carriers*, 137.
17. 'Air Group Nine Comes Home', *Life*, 1 May 1944, 92–7.
18. *Yorktown* Aircraft Action Report.
19. *Enterprise* Aircraft Action Report.
20. Klaus Lindemann, *Hailstorm over Truk Lagoon* (Pacific Press Publications, 1989), 19.
21. William H. Stewart, *Ghost Fleet of the Truk Lagoon* (Pictorial Histories Publishing Co., 1986), 67–9.
22. Reynolds, *The Fast Carriers*, 139.

Chapter 12: Preparations for the Mariana and Palau Islands Campaign

1. Taylor, *The Magnificent Mitscher*, 186.
2. Ibid., 187.
3. *Carrier Air Group 9 (March 1942–March 1944)*, 23, ed. Lieutenant Robert Giroux, USNR (1945).
4. Taylor, *The Magnificent Mitscher*, 188.
5. *Hornet* Aircraft Action Report, Combat Air Patrol, 29 March 1944.
6. *Enterprise* Aircraft Action Report, Combat Air Patrol, 29 March 1944.
7. *Enterprise* Aircraft Action Report 1FS-1, Initial Fighter Sweep, 30 March 1944.
8. DESECRATE ONE Operation, Action Report of Commander Task Force 58, Vice Admiral Marc A. Mitscher, dated 12 April 1944.
9. Ibid.

Chapter 13: The Mariana and Palau Islands Campaign – Operation FORAGER, June–November 1944

1. Ito with Pineau, *End of the Imperial Japanese Navy*, 95.
2. Mitscher (CTF 58) Operations Plan No 7-44, Intelligence Annex, 24 May 1944.
3. Okumiya and Horikoshi, *Zero!*, 260.
4. Ibid., 259. Samuel E. Morison, *History of US Naval Operations in World War II, Vol. VIII: New Guinea and the Marianas* (Little, Brown and Co., 1957), 146, gives slightly different figures by Captain Toshikazu Ohmae, senior staff officer to Vice Admiral Ozawa in Appendix II.
5. Okumiya and Horikoshi, *Zero!*, 259.
6. Ibid., 260.
7. Vice Admiral E.P. Forrestal, USN, *Admiral Raymond A. Spruance, USN: A Study in Command* (US Government Printing Office, 1966), 138.
8. Fifth Fleet battle plan, 17 June, quoted in ibid., 243.
9. Admiral J.J. Clark, USN, with Clark G. Reynolds, *Carrier Admiral* (David McKay Company, 1967), 165.
10. Spruance to Mitscher, 17 June 1944, in Morison, *History of US Naval Operations, Vol. VIII: New Guinea and the Marianas*, 243.
11. Forrestal, *Admiral Raymond A. Spruance, USN*, 137.
12. Mitscher Action Report, 11 September 1944.
13. Spruance to Mitscher and Lee, 18 June 1944, in Forrestal, *Admiral Raymond A. Spruance*, 137.
14. Mitscher Action Report, 11 September 1944.
15. Ibid.
16. Taylor, *The Magnificent Mitscher*, 224.
17. Morison, *History of US Naval Operations, Vol. VIII: New Guinea and the Marianas*, 257–304.
18. Montgomery Action Report, 6 July 1944.
19. Taylor, *The Magnificent Mitscher*, 226.
20. Ibid., 227.
21. Ibid.
22. Overheard and quoted by Lieutenant Commander Paul D. Buie, skipper of *Lexington*'s VF-16 and quoted in Taylor, *The Magnificent Mitscher*, 227.
23. Reynolds, *The Fast Carriers*, 194.
24. Taylor, *The Magnificent Mitscher*, 229.
25. Spruance Action Report 00398, 14 July 1944.
26. Reynolds, *The Fast Carriers*, 194.
27. Taylor, *The Magnificent Mitscher*, 231.

28. Ibid.
29. David Lee Russell, *David McCampbell: Top Ace of US Naval Aviation in World War II* (McFarland, 2019), 102–3.
30. Lieutenant Commander Joseph Bryan III, USNR, and Phillip G. Reed, *Mission Beyond Darkness* (Duell, Sloan & Pearce, 1945), 15.
31. Mitscher Action Report.
32. Morison, *History of US Naval Operations, Vol. VIII: New Guinea and the Marianas*, 299.
33. *Hornet* Action Report, 0020, 1 July 1944, report of Commander Air Group 2.
34. Taylor, *The Magnificent Mitscher*, 234.
35. Ibid., 236.
36. Reynolds, *The Fast Carriers*, 204.
37. Mitscher Action Report, 11 September 1944.
38. Okumiya and Horikoshi, *Zero!*, 262.
39. Ernest J. King and Walter M. Whitehill, *Fleet Admiral King: A Naval King* (W.W. Norton & Co., 1952).

Chapter 14: Prelude to the Philippines Campaign

1. Halsey and Bryan, *Admiral Halsey's Story*, 159.
2. Ibid.
3. Ibid., 160. Clark and Reynolds, *Carrier Admiral*, 194–5.
4. ComAirPac Analysis, September 1944; Halsey and Bryan, *Admiral Halsey's Story*, 162, cites different figures of 1,005 enemy planes destroyed and 153 ships sunk.
5. ComAirPac Analysis, June 1944.
6. Reynolds, *The Fast Carriers*, 223.
7. Toshikazu Kase, *Journey to the Missouri* (Franklin Classics, 2018), 78.
8. Hajime Fukaya, 'Japan's Wartime Carrier Construction', *U.S. Naval Institute Proceedings*, 81 (September 1955), 1031–43.
9. Ito with Pineau, *End of the Imperial Japanese Navy*, 180–1. Also quoted in Captain Rikihei Inoguchi, Commander Tadashi Nakajima and Roger Pineau, *The Divine Wind: Japan's Kamikaze Force in World War II* (United States Naval Institute, 1958), 27.

Chapter 16: The Philippine Campaign – Second Battle of the Philippine Sea, Leyte Gulf

1. Samuel E. Morison, *History of US Naval Operations in World War II, Vol. XII: Leyte* (Little, Brown and Co., 1958), 58.

2. Halsey and Bryan, *Admiral Halsey's Story*, 164.
3. Ito with Pineau, *End of the Imperial Japanese Navy*, 209; Morison, *History of US Naval Operations, Vol. XII: Leyte*, 91; James A. Field, *The Japanese at Leyte Gulf* (Princeton University Press, 1947), 27
4. Morison, *History of US Naval Operations, Vol. XII: Leyte*, 165–9.
5. Halsey and Bryan, *Admiral Halsey's Story*, 169.
6. Ibid., 169.
7. Taylor, *The Magnificent Mitscher*, 260.
8. Reynolds, *The Fast Carriers*, 266.
9. Sherman Action Report, 0090, 2 December 1944.
10. Halsey and Bryan, *Admiral Halsey's Story*, 170.
11. Ibid., 171.
12. CINCPAC Nimitz, Communique No. 16G, 2.
13. Sherman Action Report, 0090, 2 December 1944.
14. Morison, *History of US Naval Operations, Vol. XII: Leyte*, 194. Taylor, *The Magnificent Mitscher*, 262.
15. Harold E. Stassen, Halsey's flag secretary to Clark G. Reynolds, 25 June 1964.
16. Halsey Action Report, 0088, 13 November 1944.
17. Halsey and Bryan, *Admiral Halsey's Story*, 171.
18. Ibid., 172.
19. Ibid.
20. Ibid.
21. Ibid. Hanson Baldwin, *The Battle of Leyte Gulf* (Doubleday Dolphin, 1955), 327.
22. C. Vann Woodward, *The Battle for Leyte Gulf* (Macmillan, 1947).
23. Morison, *History of US Naval Operations, Vol. XII: Leyte*, 194. Taylor, *The Magnificent Mitscher*, 262.
24. Halsey and Bryan, *Admiral Halsey's Story*, 174.
25. Morrison, *History of US Naval Operations, Vol. XII, Leyte*, 245.
26. Halsey and Bryan, *Admiral Halsey's Story*, 174.
27. Ibid., 179.
28. Kurita interviewed by Masanori Ito and quoted in Ito with Pineau, *End of the Imperial Japanese Navy*, 166.
29. Ibid., 166–7. Field, *Japanese at Leyte Gulf*, 125–8.
30. Halsey and Bryan, *Admiral Halsey's Story*, 179.
31. Ibid., 173.
32. Ibid., 174.
33. Ibid.
34. Ibid.
35. Ibid.

36. Ibid., 173.
37. Ibid., 175.
38. Ibid.
39. Captain Andrew Hamilton, USNR, 'Where is Task Force Thirty-Four?', *U.S. Naval Institute Proceedings*, 86 (October 1960), 76–80.
40. Sherman Action Report, 2 December 1944.
41. Halsey and Bryan, *Admiral Halsey's Story*, 176.
42. Halsey to Nimitz, 250215, from Messages, Halsey Action Report, 13 November 1944.
43. Halsey and Bryan, *Admiral Halsey's Story*, 177.
44. Ibid., 179.
45. Woodward, *Battle for Leyte Gulf*, 185.
46. Halsey Action Report, 13 November 1944.
47. Halsey and Bryan, *Admiral Halsey's Story*, 181.
48. Taylor, *The Magnificent Mitscher*, 265.

Chapter 17: The Liberation of the Philippines – Corking the Luzon Bottleneck

1. Letter by Vice Admiral M.A. Mitscher to Officers and Men of Task Force 38, dated 30 October 1944, Ulithi Atoll.
2. Fukaya, 'Japan's Wartime Carrier Construction', 1032–5.
3. Halsey and Bryan, *Admiral Halsey's Story*, 198.

Chapter 18: Raiding Tokyo and the Invasions of Iwo Jima and Okinawa, February–April 1945

1. Halsey and Bryan, *Admiral Halsey's Story*, 202.
2. Samuel E. Morison, *History of US Naval Operations in World War II, Vol. XIV: Victory in the Pacific* (Little, Brown and Co., 1960), 53–6.
3. W.S. Bartley, *Iwo Jima: Amphibious Epic* (US Marine Corps Historical Branch, G-3 Division, 1954), 116–18, 147, 187: Isley and Crowl, *The U.S. Marines and Amphibious War*, 509.
4. Father Joseph T. O'Callahan, SJ, *I was Chaplain on the Franklin* (Macmillan, 1956).
5. Mitscher Action Report, 0045, 13 March 1945.
6. Bryant and Hermans, *History of Naval Fighter Direction*, 216.
7. Clark and Reynolds, *Carrier Admiral*, 221.
8. Sydney D. Waters, *The Royal New Zealand Navy* (War History Branch, Department of Internal Affairs, 1956), 376.

9. Morison, *History of US Naval Operations, Vol. XIV: Victory in the Pacific*, 101.
10. Taylor, *The Magnificent Mitscher*, 299.
11. Colonel Hans C. Adamson, USAF and Captain George F. Kosko, USN, *Halsey's Typhoons* (Crown, 1967), 183.

Chapter 19: The Final Assault on Japan – Operation DOWNFALL, 1 November 1945–7 (Projected)

1. King and Whitehill, *Fleet Admiral King*, 598, 621.
2. Fleet Admiral William D. Leahy, USN, *I Was There* (Victor Gollancz Ltd, 1950), 383–5.
3. King and Whitehill, *Fleet Admiral King*, 611.
4. Halsey to Nimitz, 9 June 1945, quoted in Halsey Action Report, 00228, 14 July 1945.
5. ComCarDiv 7 War Diary, 1945.
6. Morison, *History of US Naval Operations, Vol. XIV: Victory in the Pacific*, 311; Halsey and Bryan, *Admiral Halsey's Story*, 259.
7. Halsey and Bryan, *Admiral Halsey's Story*, 209.
8. Ibid., 213.
9. Ibid., 215.
10. Ibid., 218.
11. Ibid., 224.
12. Robert G. Albion and Robert H. Connery, *Forrestal and the Navy* (Columbia University Press, 1962), 180.

Appendix: Dramatis Personae

1. Nimitz Fitness Report on Mitscher, quoted in Taylor, *The Magnificent Mitscher*, 304.

Select Bibliography

Adamson, Colonel Hans C., USAF and Kosko, Captain George F., USN, *Halsey's Typhoons*, Crown, 1967

Albion, Robert G. and Connery, Robert H, *Forrestal and the Navy*, Columbia University Press, 1962

Alden, Carroll Storrs and Westcott, Allan, *The United States Navy*, 2nd edn, rev., Lippincott, 1945

Alden, John D., *US Submarine Attacks during WWII*, Naval Institute Press, 1989

Bailey, Dan E., *WWII Wrecks of the Kwajalein and Truk Lagoons*, North River Diver Publication, 1989

Bailey, Dan E., *WWII Wrecks of Palau*, North River Diver Publications, 1991

Bailey, Dan E., *World War II Wrecks of the Truk Lagoon*, North River Diver Publications, 2000

Baldwin, Hanson, *The Battle for Leyte Gulf. Sea Fights and Shipwrecks*, Doubleday Dolphin, 1955

Blair, Clay Jr, *Silent Victory – the US Submarine War against Japan*, J.B. Lippincott Company, 1975

Boyd, Carl and Yoshida, Akihiko, *The Japanese Submarine Force and World War II*, Blue Jacket Books, Naval Institute Press, 1995

Broadwater, John D., *Kwajalein – Lagoon of Found Ships*, Three States Printing Company, 1971

Bryan, Joseph, III, *Aircraft Carrier*, Ballantine Books, 1954

Buchanan, Lieutenant A.R., USNR, *The United States and World War II*, Harper & Bros, 1964

Buchanan, Lieutenant A.R., USNR (ed.) and the Aviation History Unit, *The Navy's Air War: A Mission Completed*, Harper & Bros, 1946

Celander, Lars, *How Carriers Fought: Carrier Operations in WWII*, Casemate Publishers, 2018

Churchill, Winston, *The Second World War*, Houghton Mifflin Company, 1948–54

Clark, Admiral J.J., USN, with Reynolds, Clark G., *Carrier Admiral*, David McKay Company, 1967

Congress of the United States, *Report of the Joint Committee on the Investigation of the Pearl Harbor Attack*, Government Printing Office, Washington, 1946

Costello, John, *The Pacific War: 1941–1945*, William Morrow, 1982

Cressman, Robert J., *Official Chronology of the US Navy in World War II*, US Naval Institute Press, 1999

Crowl, Phillip A. and Love, Edmond F., *The United States Army in World War II – The War in the Pacific – Seizure of the Gilberts and Marshalls*, US Government Printing Office, 1955

Cutler, Thomas J., *The Battle of Leyte Gulf, 23–26 October 1944*, HarperCollins, 1994

Dictionary of American Naval Fighting Ships, Vol. 2, US Government Printing Office, Washington, 1963

Evans, David C. and Peattie, Mark R., *KAIGUN. Strategy, Tactics and Technology in the Imperial Japanese Navy 1887–1941*, Naval Institute Press, 1997

Falk, Stanley, *Bloodiest Victory – Palaus*, Ballantine Books, 1974

Field, James A., *The Japanese at Leyte Gulf*, Princeton University Press, 1947

Fletcher, Rear Admiral Frank Jack, 'THE BATTLE OF THE CORAL SEA. MAY 4–8 1942', Battle Report Serial 0010N, May 27, 1942

Forrestal, Vice Admiral E.P., USN, *Admiral Raymond A. Spruance, USN: A Study in Command*, US Government Printing Office, 1966

Francillon, R.J., *Japanese Aircraft of the Pacific War*, Funk & Wagnalls, 1970

Friedman, Norman, *The British Battleship 1906–1946*, Seaforth Publishing, 2015

Fukui, Shizuo, *Japanese Naval Vessels at the end of World War II*, Naval Institute Press, 1987

Green, William, *War Planes of the Second World War: Fighters, Vol. 4*, Garden City, 1961

Grimes, Lieutenant J., USNR, *Aviation in the Fleet Exercises, 1923–1939*, Manuscript History, Navy Department, n.d.

Grover, David H., *US Army Ships and Watercraft of World War II*, Naval Institute Press, 1987

Halsey, William F. and Bryan, Joseph, III, *Admiral Halsey's Story*, Whittlesey House, 1947

Hayashi, Hiroshi, *Senji Nippon Senmeiroku 1937–1950*, Senzen Senpaku Kenkyukai, 2006

Hocking, C., *Dictionary of Disasters at Sea during the Age of Steam*, Lloyd's Register of Shipping, 1969

Hornfischer, James D., *The Fleet at Flood Tide*, Bantam Books, 2016

Hough, Major Frank O., USMCR, *The Assault on Peleliu*, Historical Division HQ US Marine Corps, 1950

Inoguchi, Captain Rikihei, Nakajima, Commander Tadashi and Pineau, Roger, *The Divine Wind: Japan's Kamikaze Force in World War II*, United States Naval Institute, 1958

Isely, Jeter A. and Crowl, Philip A., *U.S. Marines and Amphibious War: Its Theory and Its Practice in the Pacific*, Princeton University Press, 1951

Isom, Dallas Woodbury, *Midway Inquest. Why the Japanese Lost the Battle of Midway*, Indiana University Press, 2007

Ito, Masanori with Roger Pineau, *The End of the Imperial Japanese Navy*, Weidenfeld & Nicolson, 1962

Jane, Fred T., *Jane's Fighting Ships 1944–45*, David & Charles Ltd, 1971

Jensen, Lieutenant Oliver, USNR, *Carrier War*, Simon & Schuster, 1945

Jentschura, Hansgeorg, *Warships of the Imperial Japanese Navy 1869–1945*, Naval Institute Press, 1976

King, Fleet Admiral Ernest J., *US Navy at War, 1941–1945*, United States Navy Department, 1945

King, Fleet Admiral Ernest J. and Whitehill, Walter M., *Fleet Admiral King: A Naval Record*, W.W. Norton, 1952

Koenig, William, *Epic Sea Battles*, Octopus Books Ltd, 1975

Leahy, Fleet Admiral William D., USN, *I Was There*, Victor Gollancz Ltd, 1950

Lester, Robert E. *US Navy Action and Operational Reports from World War II. Part 3. Fifth Fleet and Fifth Fleet Carrier Task Forces*, University Publications of America, 1990

Lindemann, Klaus, *Desecrate 1*, Pacific Press Publications, 1988

Lindemann, Klaus, *Hailstorm over Truk Lagoon*, Pacific Press Publications, 1989

Lloyd's of London, *Lloyd's Register of Shipping*, London

Macdonald, Rod, *Force Z Shipwrecks of the South China Sea – HMS Prince of Wales and HMS Repulse*, Whittles Publishing, 2013

Macdonald, Rod, *Dive Truk Lagoon – the Japanese Pacific WWII shipwrecks*, Whittles, 2014

Macdonald, Rod, *Dive Palau – the Shipwrecks*, Whittles, 2016

MacDonald, Scot, *Evolution of Aircraft Carriers*, Aviation History Unit, 1964

Mahan, Alfred Thayer, *Influence of Sea Power Upon History, 1660–1783*, Little, Brown & Co., 1890

Middlebrook, Martin, *The Sinking of the Prince of Wales & Repulse*, Allen Lane, 1977

Mitscher, Vice Admiral Marc A., USN, 'Desecrate One Operation, Action Report of 12 April 1944'

Morison, Elting E., *Admiral Sims and the Modern American Navy*, Houghton Mifflin Co., 1942

Morison, Samuel E., *History of US Naval Operations in World War II*, Little, Brown and Co.:
  Vol. IV, *Coral Sea, Midway and Submarine Actions*, 1949
  Vol. V, *The Struggle for Guadalcanal*, 1949
  Vol. VI, *Breaking the Bismarcks Barrier*, 1950
  Vol. VII, *Aleutians, Gilberts and Marshalls*, 1957
  Vol. VIII, *New Guinea and the Marianas*, 1957
  Vol. XII, *Leyte*, 1958
  Vol. XIII, *The Liberation of the Philippines*, 1959
  Vol. XIV, *Victory in the Pacific*, 1960

Morison, Samuel E., *The Two Ocean War*, Little, Brown and Co., 1963

Morton, Louis, *The War in the Pacific. Strategy and Command: The First Two Years*, Center of Military History, United States Army, 1962

Odgers, George, *Air War against Japan 1943–1945*, Advertiser Printing Co., 1957

Office of the Chief of Naval Operations – Division of Naval Intelligence. Government Printing Office:
  Japanese Merchant Ships Recognition Manual, ONI 208-J – Restricted, US, 1944
  Standard Classes of Japanese Merchant Ships, ONI 208-J (Revised), Supplement 3, 1945
  Far Eastern Small Craft, ONI 208-J, Supplement 2, 1945
  The Japanese Navy, ONI 222-J, 1945
  Aerial Views of Japanese Naval Vessels, ONI 41–42, 1945

Okumiya, Masatake and Horikoshi, Jiro, *Zero! The Story of the Japanese Navy Air Force 1937–1945*, Cassell & Co. Ltd, 1957

Peattie, Mark R., *Nanyo – The Rise and Fall of the Japanese in Micronesia 1885–1945*, University of Hawaii Press, 1988

Prados, John, *Combined Fleet Decoded*, Random House, 1995

Reynolds, Clark G., *The Fast Carriers – The Forging of an Air Navy*, Naval Institute Press, 1968

Reynolds, Quentin, *The Amazing Mr Doolittle*, Ayer Co. Publishing, 1971

Rosenberg, Phillip Alan, *Shipwrecks of Truk*, Philip Alan Rosenberg, 1981

Roskill, Captain S.W., *Naval Policy Between the Wars: The Period of Anglo-American Antagonism, 1918–1928*, Collins, 1968

Russell, David Lee, *David McCampbell: Top Ace of US Naval Aviation in World War II*, McFarland, 2019

Sherrod, Robert, *History of Marine Corps Aviation in WW II*, Combat Forces Press, 1952

Smallpage, Roy, *Truk: The Ultimate Wreck Site*, Underwater Publications, 1994

Spector, Ronald H., *Eagle Against the Sun: The American War with Japan*, Random House, 1992

Stewart, William H., *Ghost Fleet of the Truk Lagoon*, Pictorial Histories Publishing Co., 1986

Stille, Mark, *Imperial Japanese Navy Destroyers 1919–45 (1)*, Osprey Publishing, 2013

Stille, Mark, *Imperial Japanese Navy Destroyers 1919–45 (2)*, Osprey Publishing, 2013

Symonds, Craig L., *The Battle of Midway (Pivotal Moments in American History)*, Oxford University Press, 2013

Taylor, Theodore, *The Magnificent Mitscher*, Norton, 1954

Tillman, Barrett, 'Hellcats over Truk', *U.S. Naval Institute Proceedings*, 103 (1977)

Tillman, Barrett and Lawson, Robert, *US Navy Dive and Torpedo Bombers of World War II*, Motorbooks Int, 2001

Toll, Ian W., *Pacific Crucible: War at Sea in the Pacific, 1941–1943*, W.W. Norton & Co., 2012

Toll, Ian W., *The Conquering Tide: War in the Pacific Islands, 1942–1944*, W.W. Norton & Co., 2020

US Congressional Joint Committee Action Report on Pearl Harbor Attack Hearings, CINCPAC File No. A16-3, 1941

US Joint Army-Navy Assessment Committee, *Japanese Naval and Merchant Shipping Losses during World War II by All Causes*, US Government Printing Office, 1947

US Marine Corps Historical Branch, G-3 Division, *History of US Marine Corps Operations in WWII. Central Pacific Drive*, US Government Printing Office, 1966

US Navy Action and Operational Reports from World War II. Pacific Theater. Part 3. Fifth Fleet and Fifth Fleet Carrier Task Forces, University Publications of America, 1990

Wagner, Ray, *American Combat Planes*, Garden City, 1960

Warren, Alan, *Singapore 1942*, Talisman Publishing, 2002
Watts, A.J., *Japanese Warships of World War II*, Doubleday & Co. Inc., 1966
Woodward, C. Vann, *The Battle for Leyte Gulf*, Macmillan, 1947
Wooldridge, E.T. (ed.), *Carrier Warfare in the Pacific – An Oral History Collection*, Smithsonian Institution Press, 1993

Websites
Although too numerous to list, of particular note is the vast amount of original work and research contained in Nihon Kaigun: www. combinedfleet.com

Index

Page numbers in bold refer to significant areas of text.